My Boyfriend is a VAMPiRE

Book 13 & 14

Yu-Rang Han

My Boyfriend is a VAMPiRE

BOOKS 13 & 14

story & art by **Yu-Rang Han**

STAFF CREDITS

translation	ChanHee Grace Sung
adaptation	Bambi Eloriaga-Amago
lettering	Roland Amago
layout	Mheeya Wok
cover design	Nicky Lim
proofreader	Danielle King
editor	Adam Arnold
publisher	Jason DeAngelis
	Seven Seas Entertainment

MY BOYFRIEND IS A VAMPIRE BOOKS 13 & 14
Copyright © 2010 YU-RANG HAN. All rights reserved.
First published in Korea in 2010 by Samyang Publishing Co., Ltd.
English translation rights arranged by Samyang Publishing Co., Ltd. through
TOPAZ Agency Inc.

ISBN: 978-1-626920-10-1

Printed in Canada

First Printing: May 2014

10 9 8 7 6 5 4 3 2 1

FOLLOW US ONLINE: **www.gomanga.com**

BOOK 13

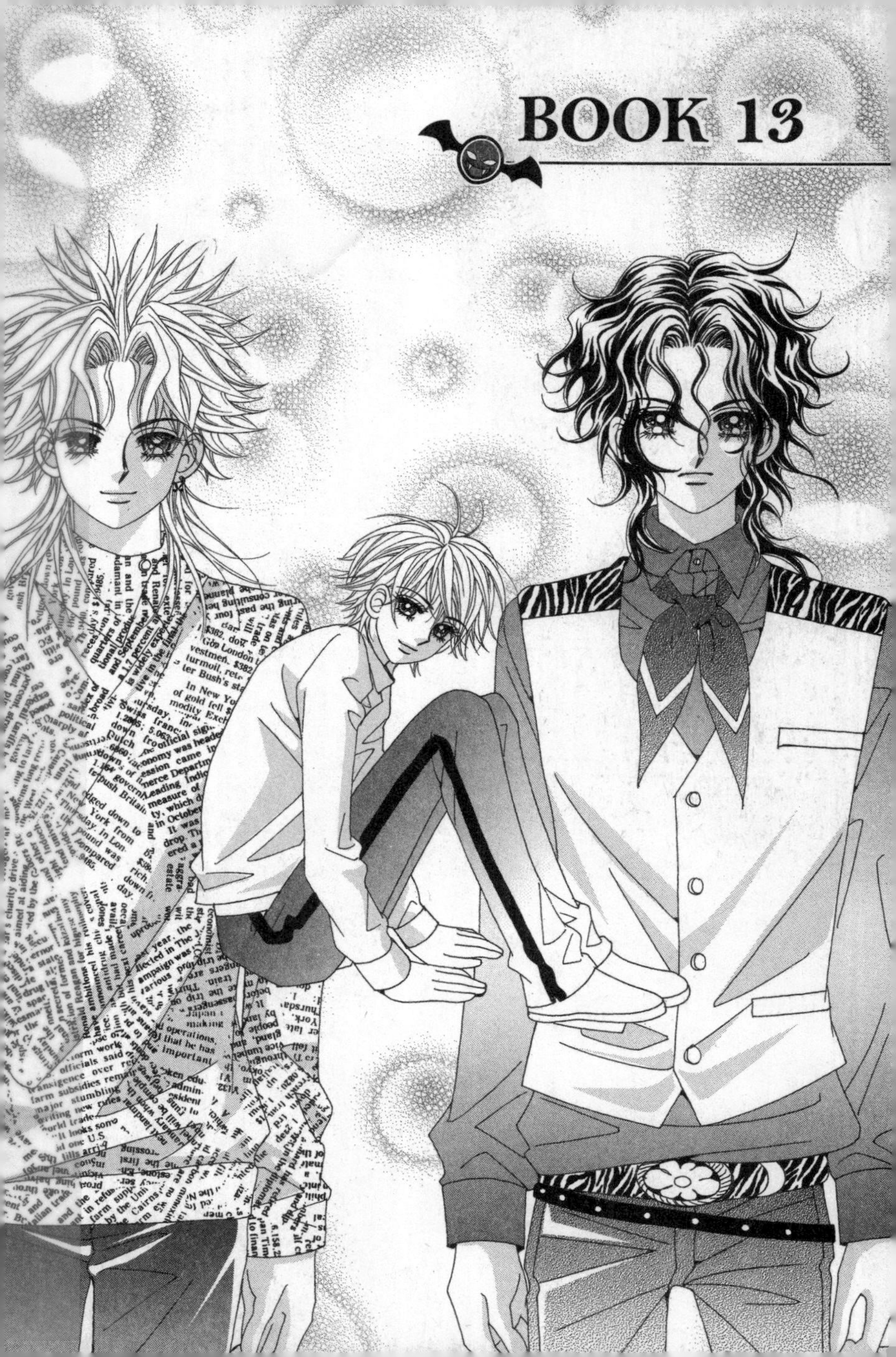

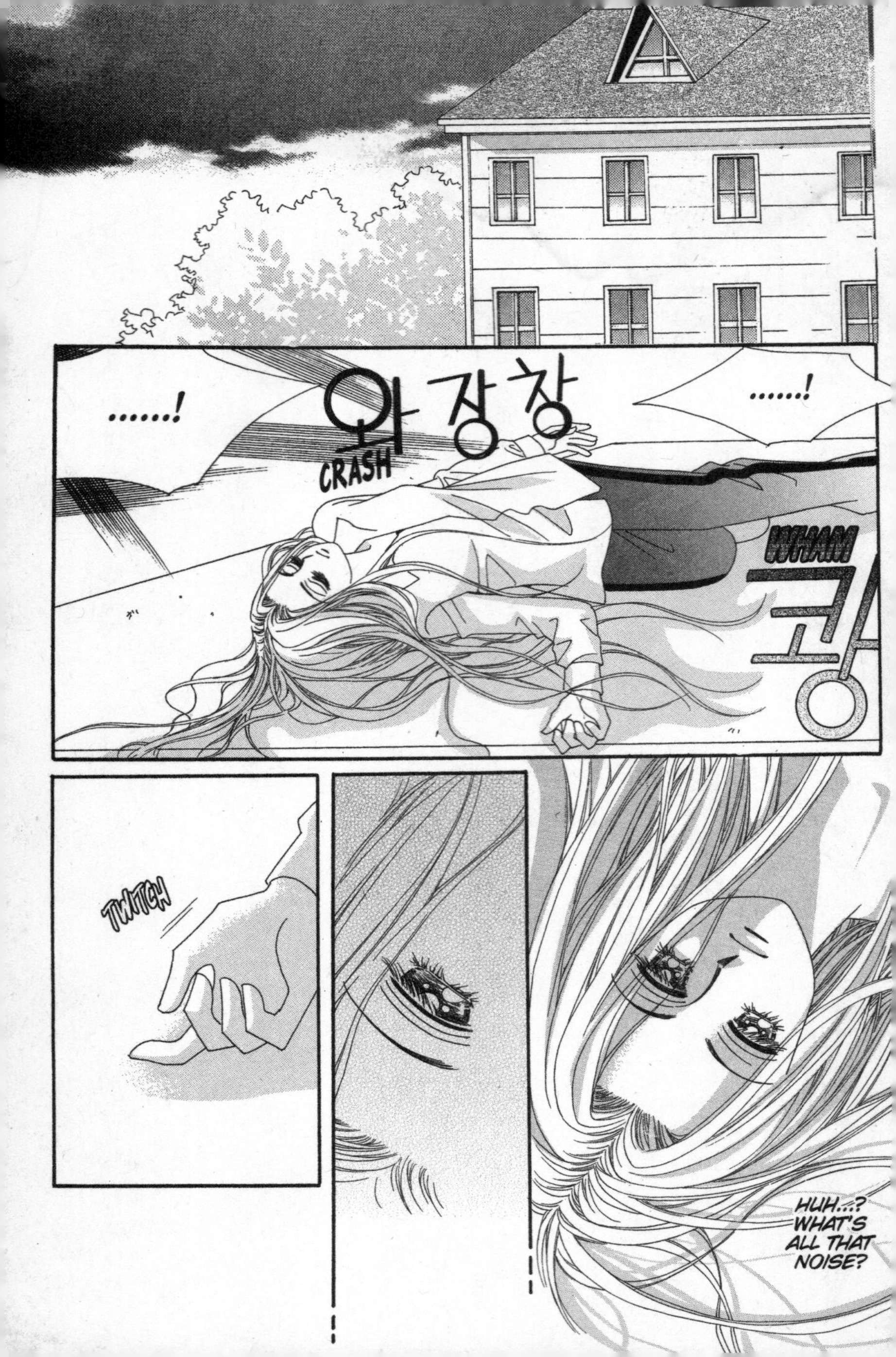

......!
와장창
CRASH
......!
WHAM
쿵
TWITCH
HUH...? WHAT'S ALL THAT NOISE?

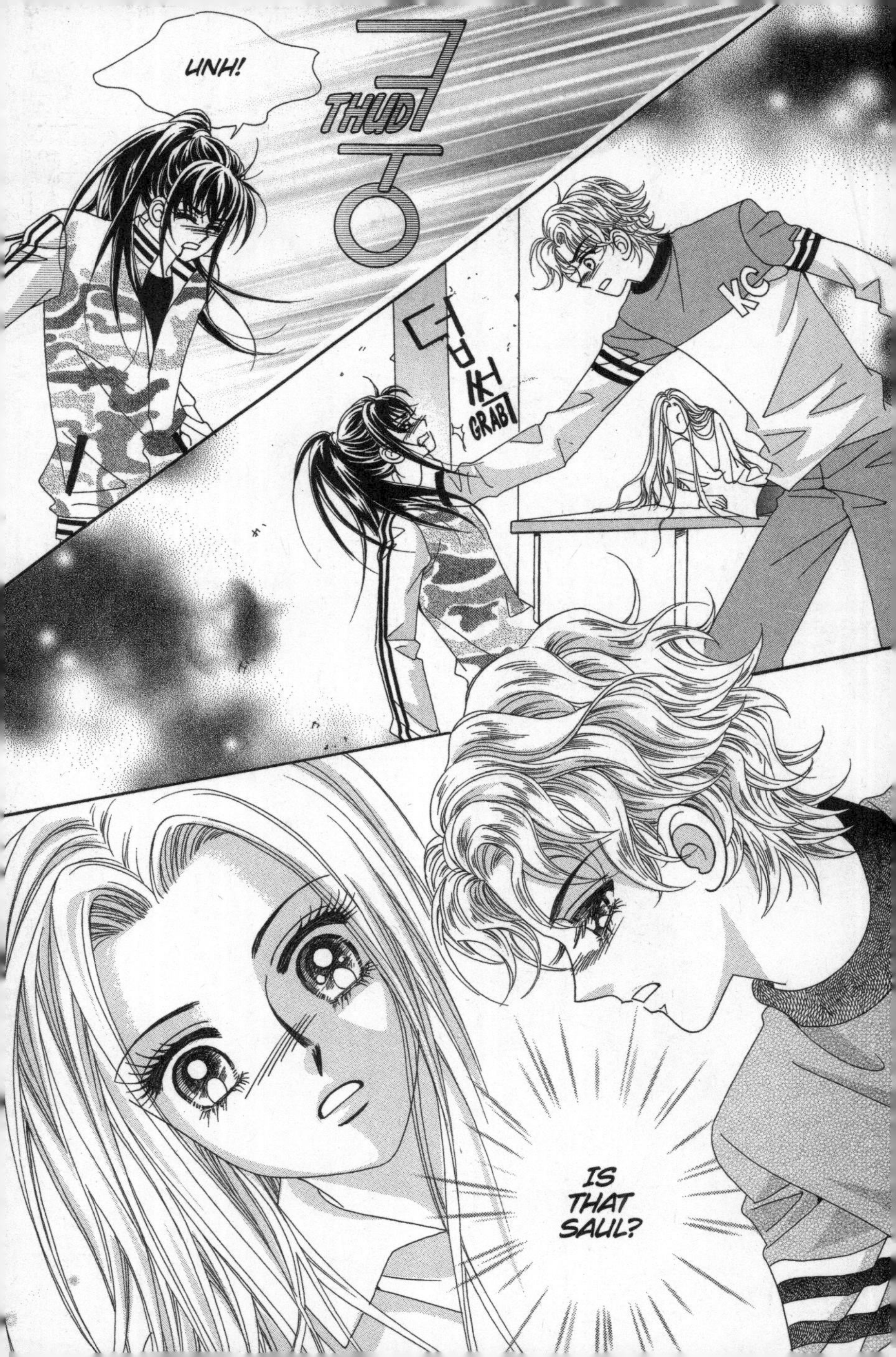
UNH!
쿵
THUD!
덥석
GRAB!
IS THAT SAUL?

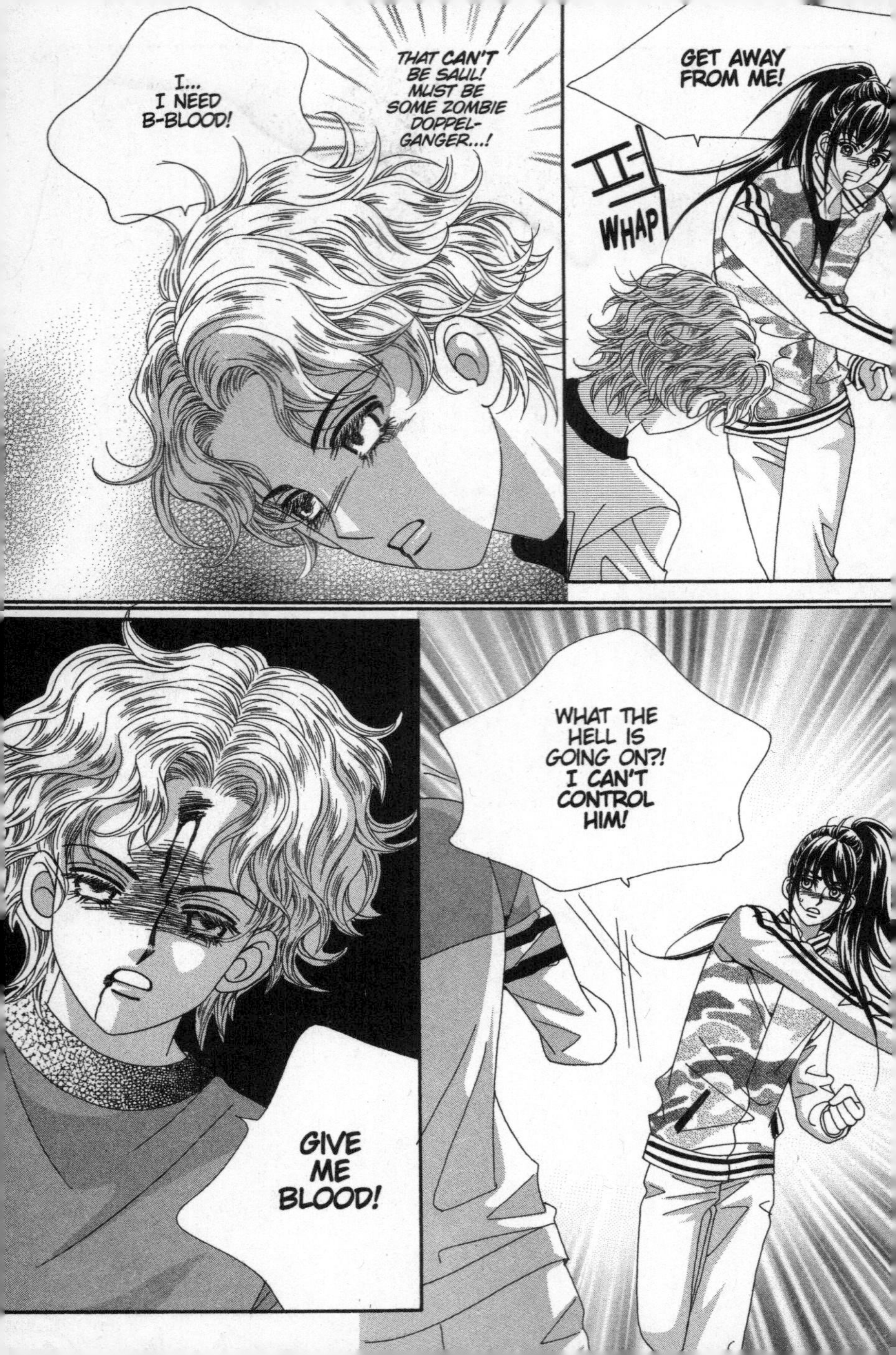
I... I NEED B-BLOOD!
THAT CAN'T BE SAUL! MUST BE SOME ZOMBIE DOPPEL-GANGER...!
GET AWAY FROM ME!
WHAP
GIVE ME BLOOD!
WHAT THE HELL IS GOING ON?! I CAN'T CONTROL HIM!

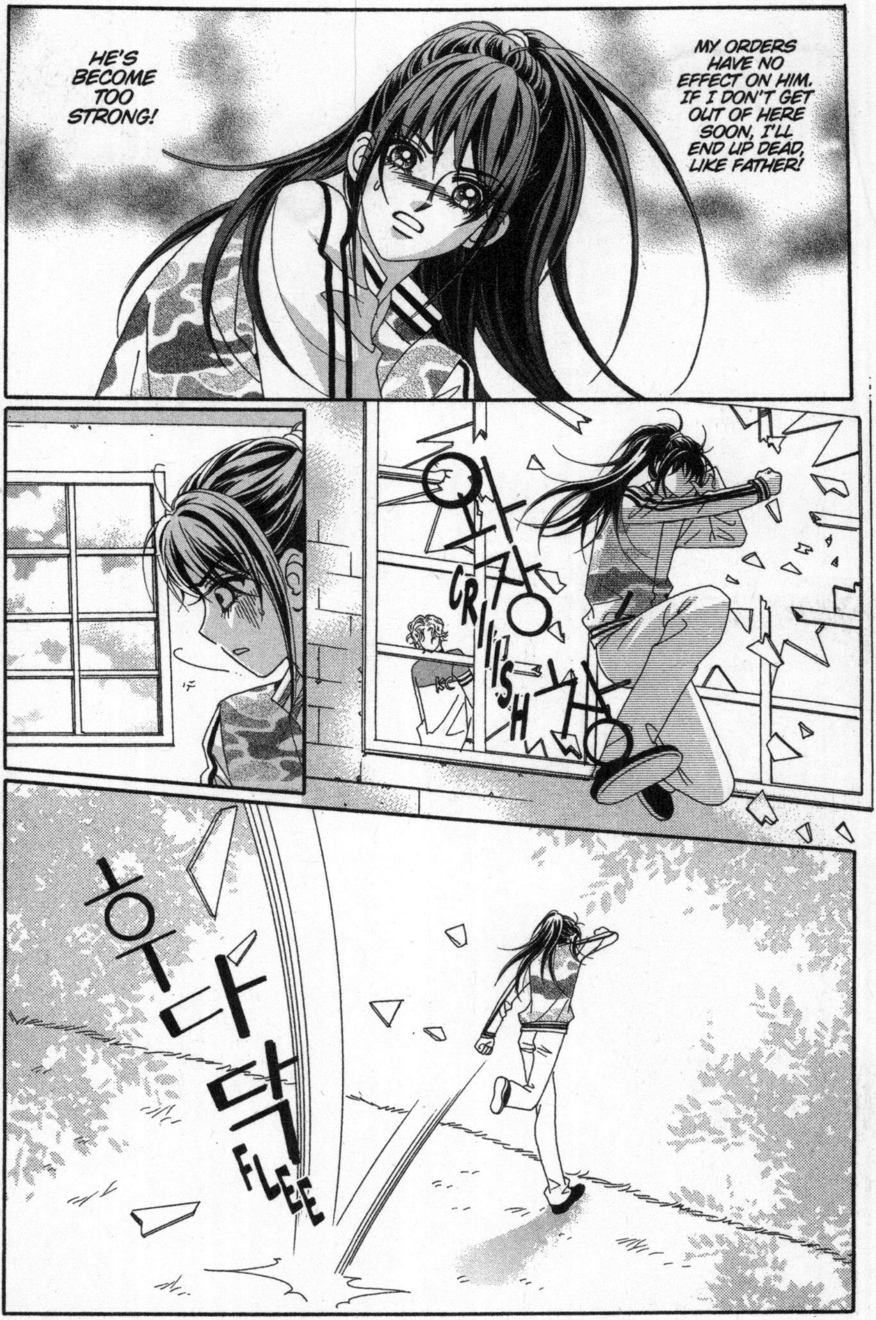
HE'S BECOME TOO STRONG!
MY ORDERS HAVE NO EFFECT ON HIM. IF I DON'T GET OUT OF HERE SOON, I'LL END UP DEAD, LIKE FATHER!
와장창
CRIIIISH
후다닥
FLEEE

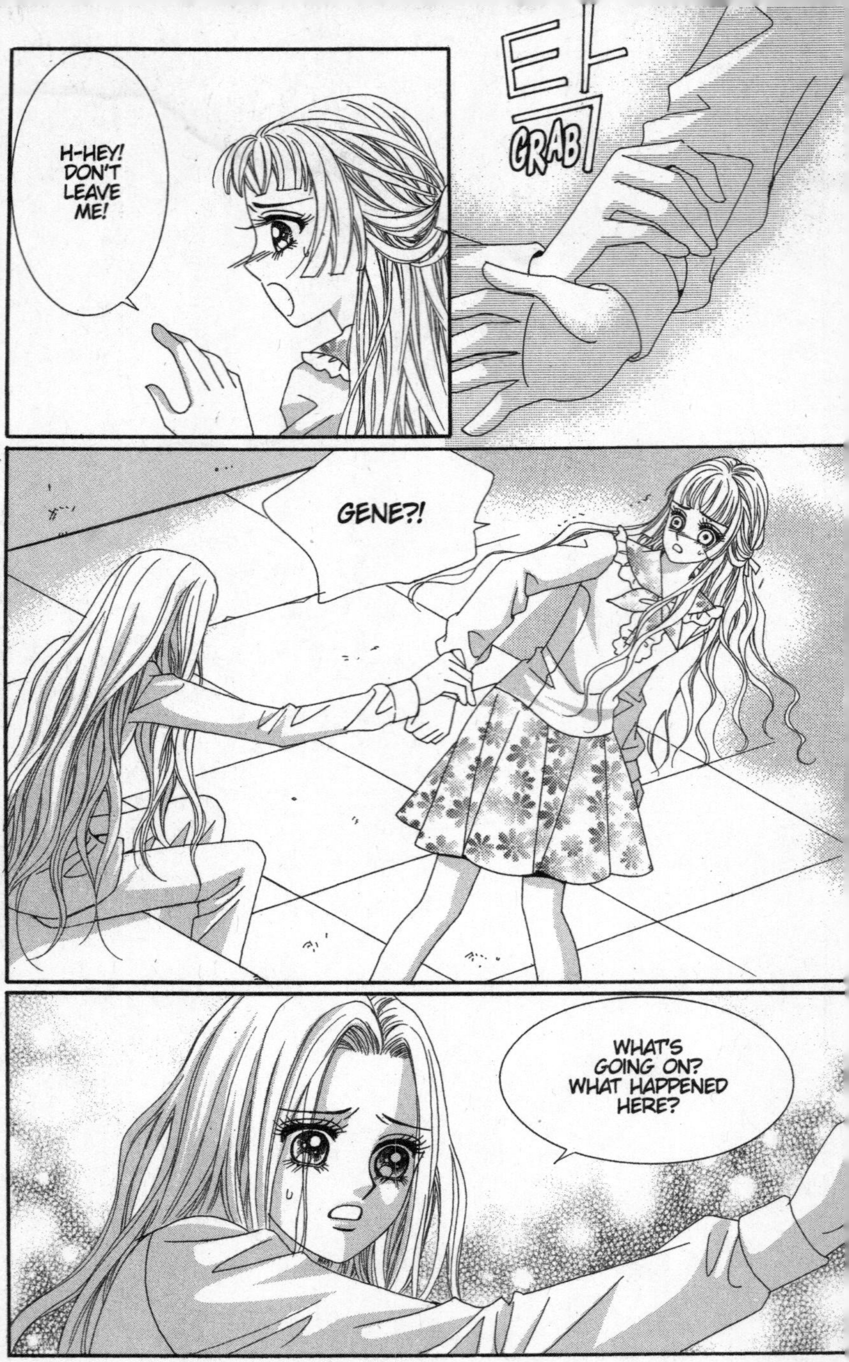
H-HEY! DON'T LEAVE ME!
탁
GRAB
GENE?!
WHAT'S GOING ON? WHAT HAPPENED HERE?

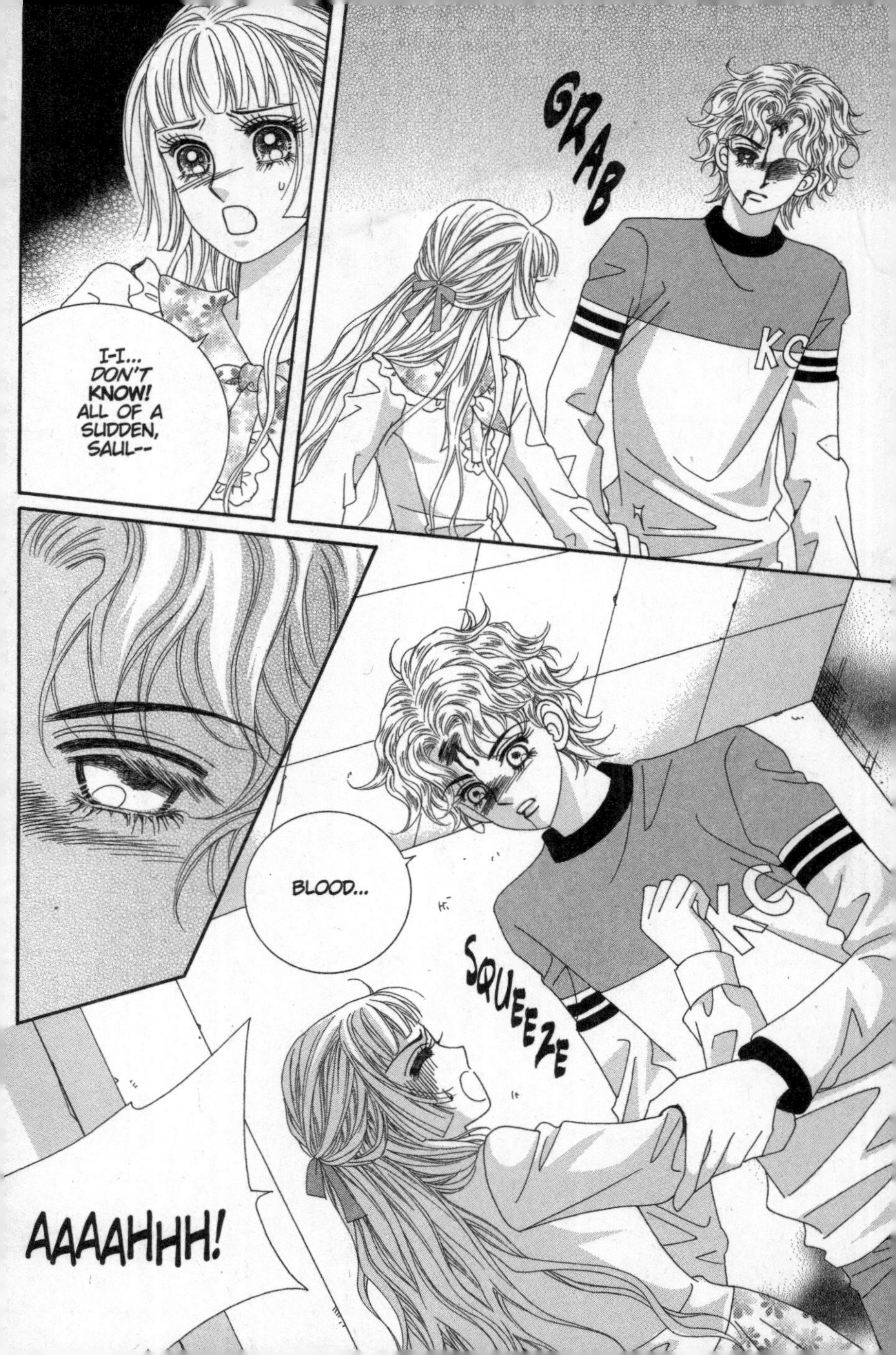
I-I... DON'T KNOW! ALL OF A SUDDEN, SAUL--
GRAB
BLOOD...
SQUEEZE
AAAAHHH!

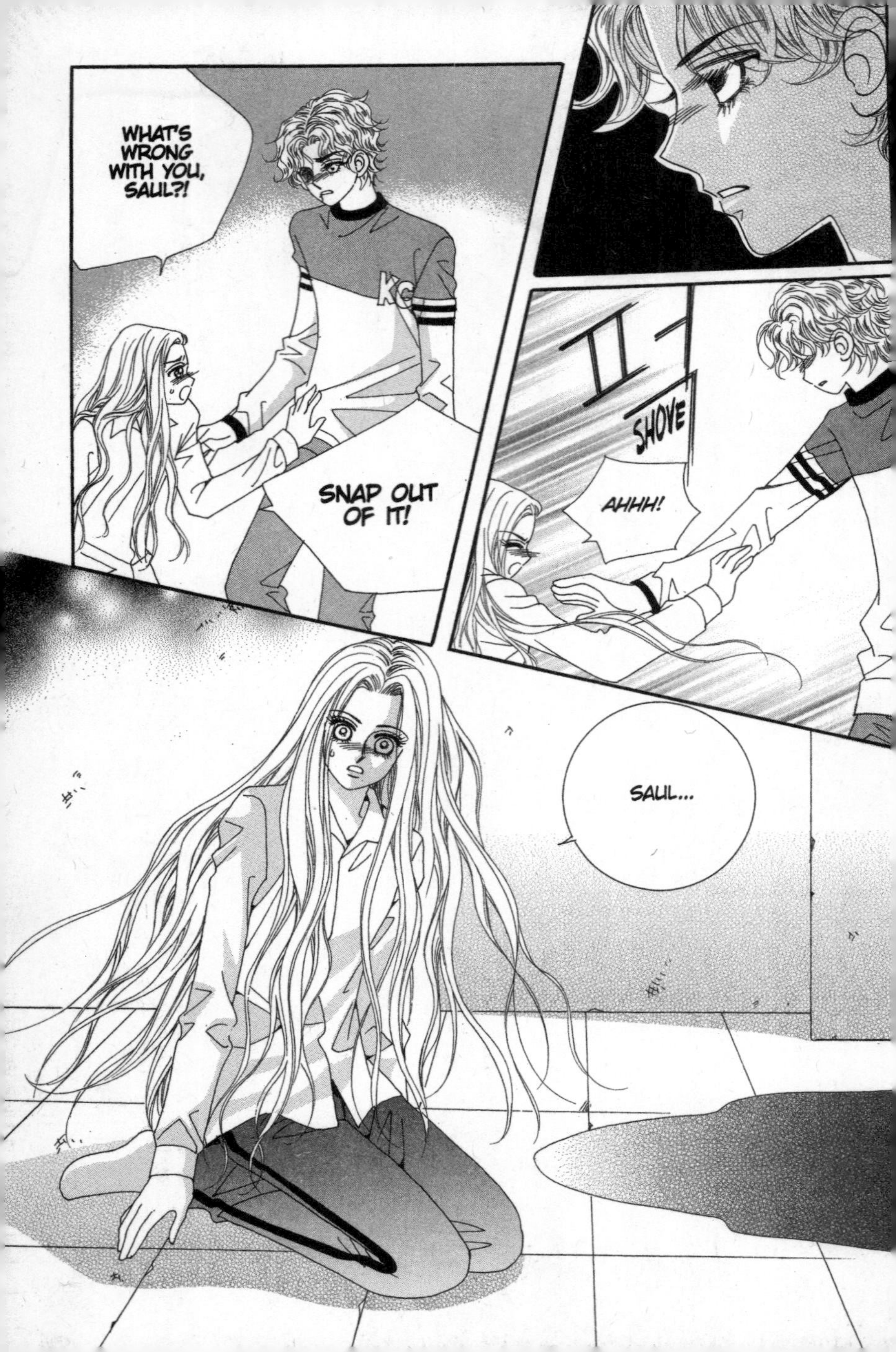
WHAT'S WRONG WITH YOU, SAUL?!
SNAP OUT OF IT!
SHOVE
AHHH!
SAUL...

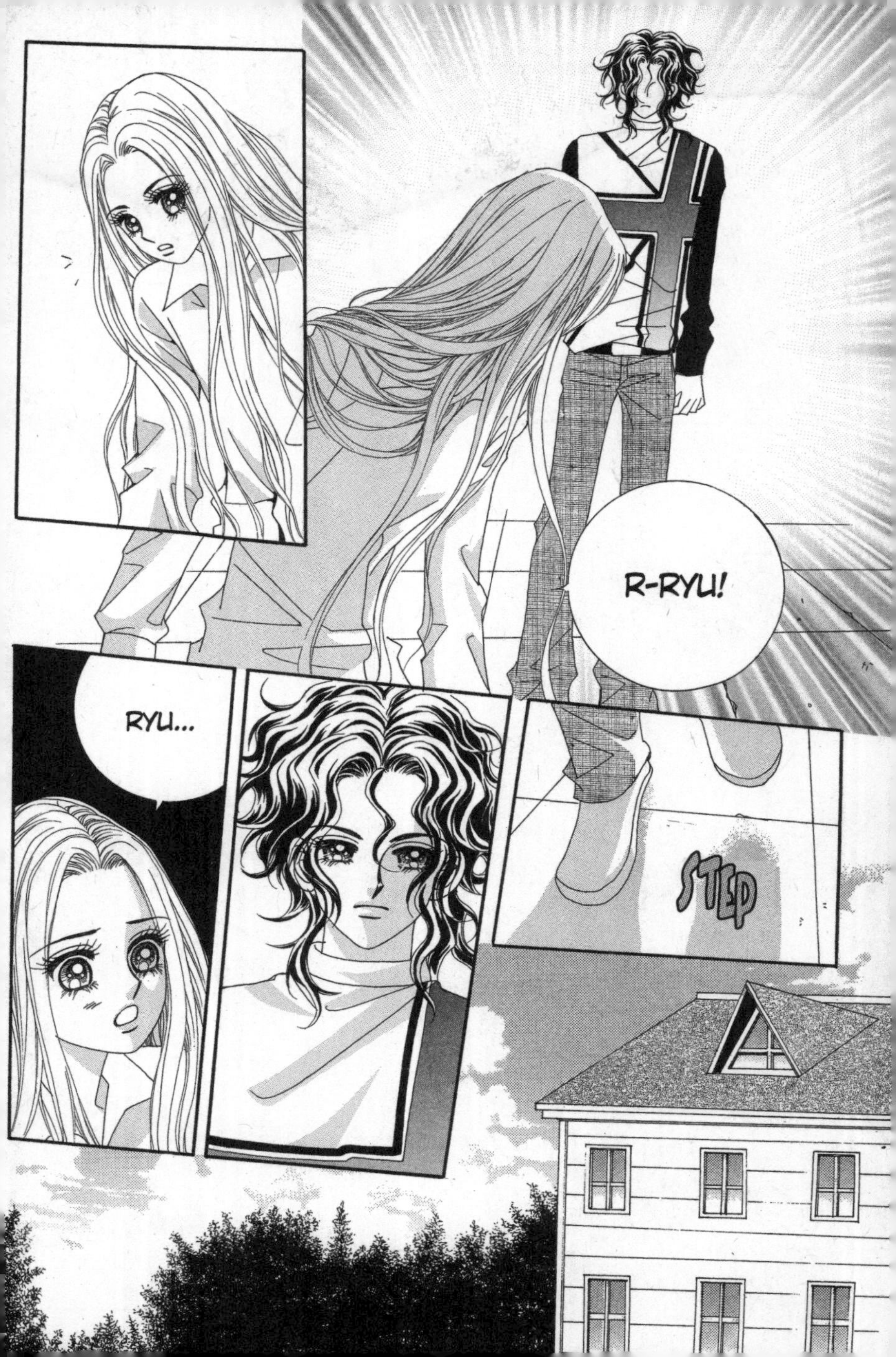
R-RYU!
RYU...
STEP

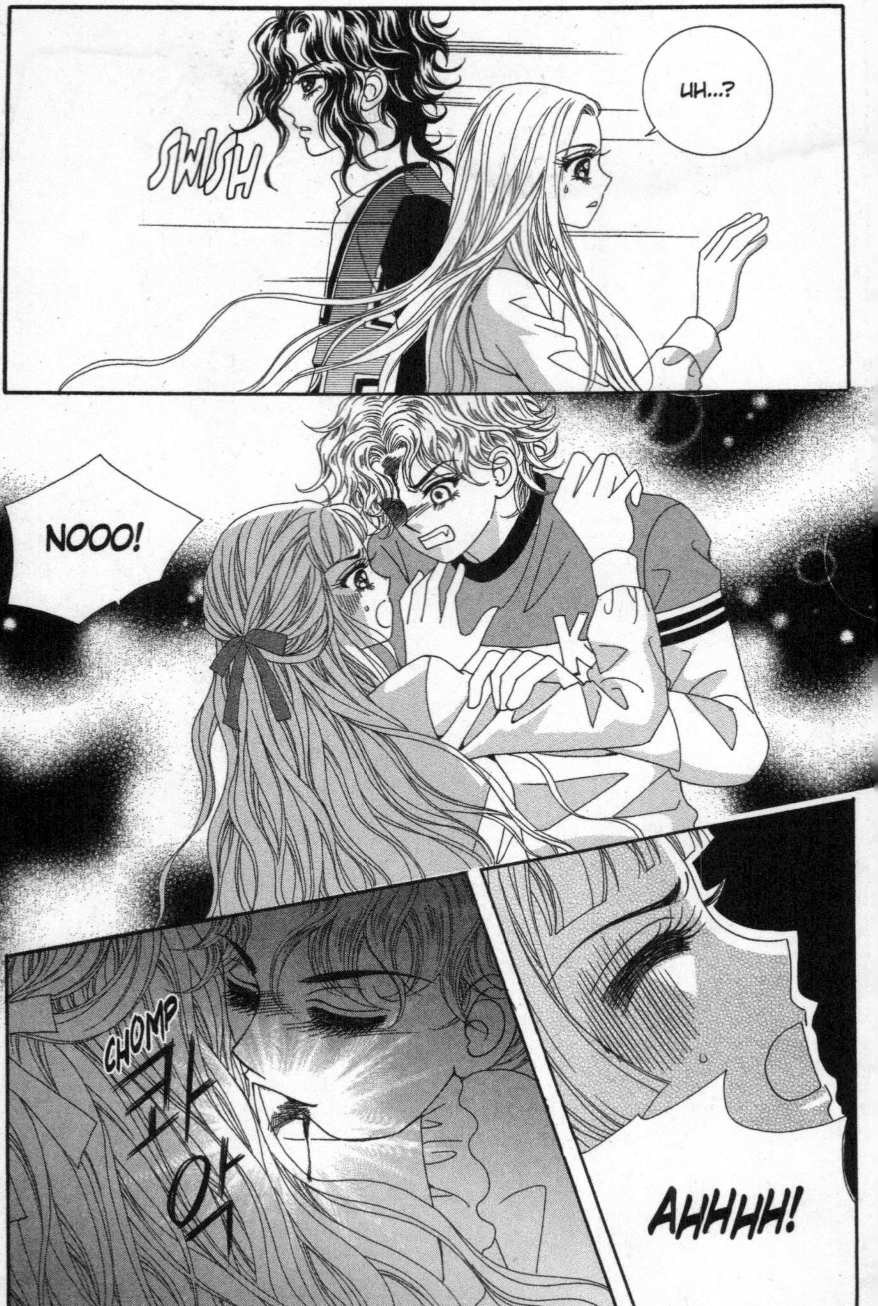
SWISH
UH...?
NOOO!
CHOMP
AHHHH!

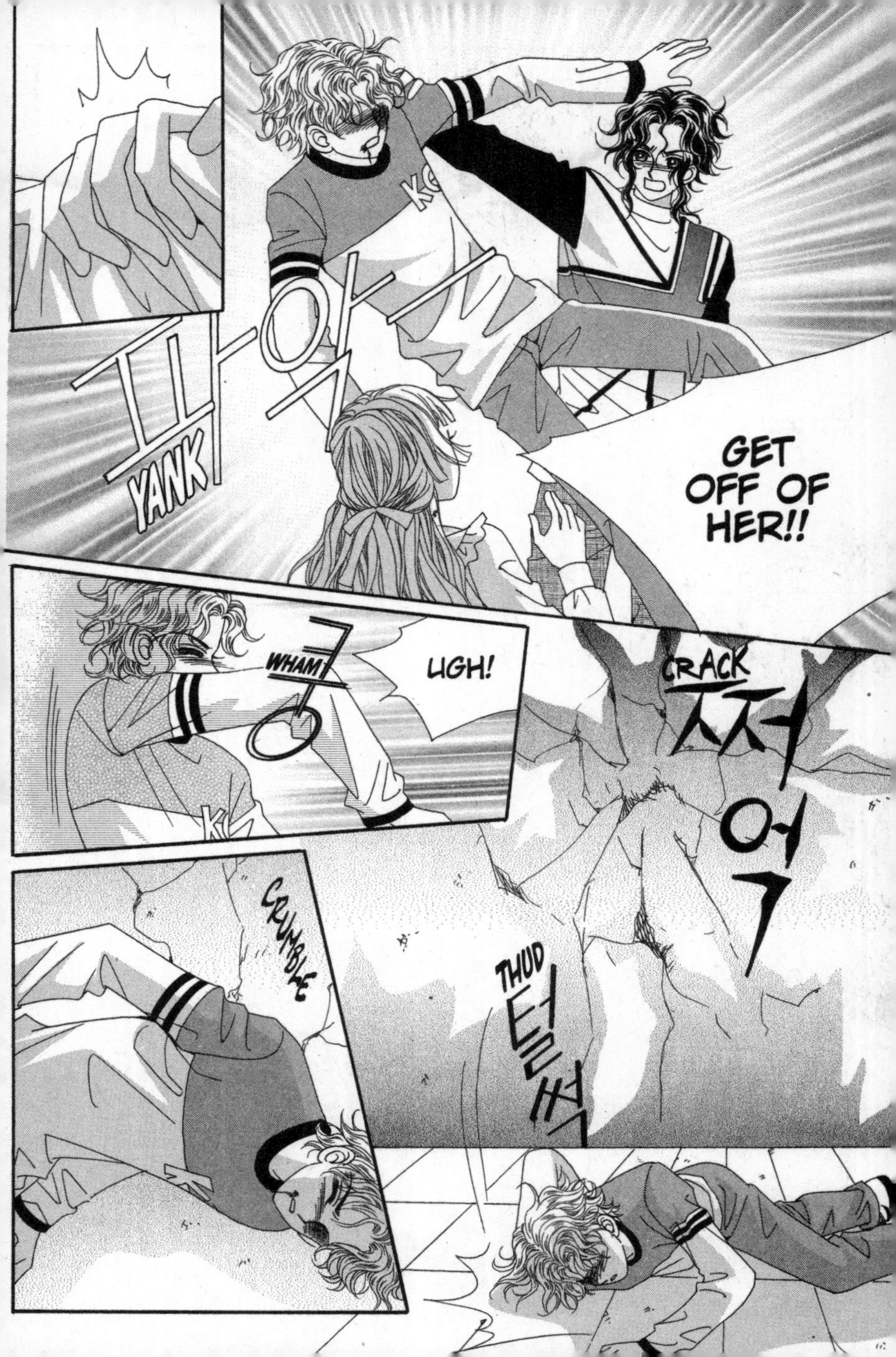
YANK
GET OFF OF HER!!
WHAM
쿵
UGH!
CRACK
쩌억
CRUMBLE
THUD
털썩

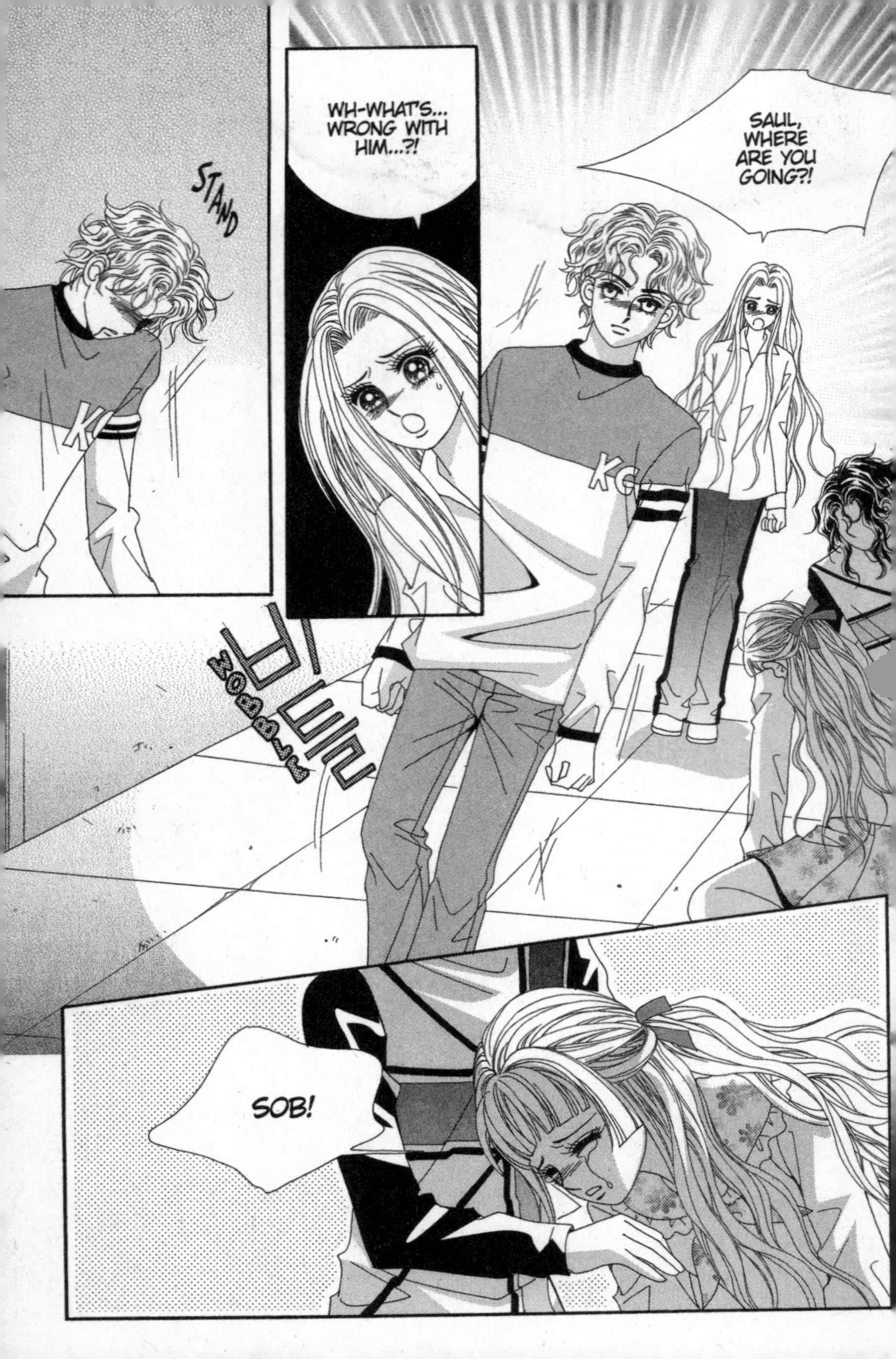
STAND
WH-WHAT'S... WRONG WITH HIM...?!
SAUL, WHERE ARE YOU GOING?!
WOBBLE
SOB!

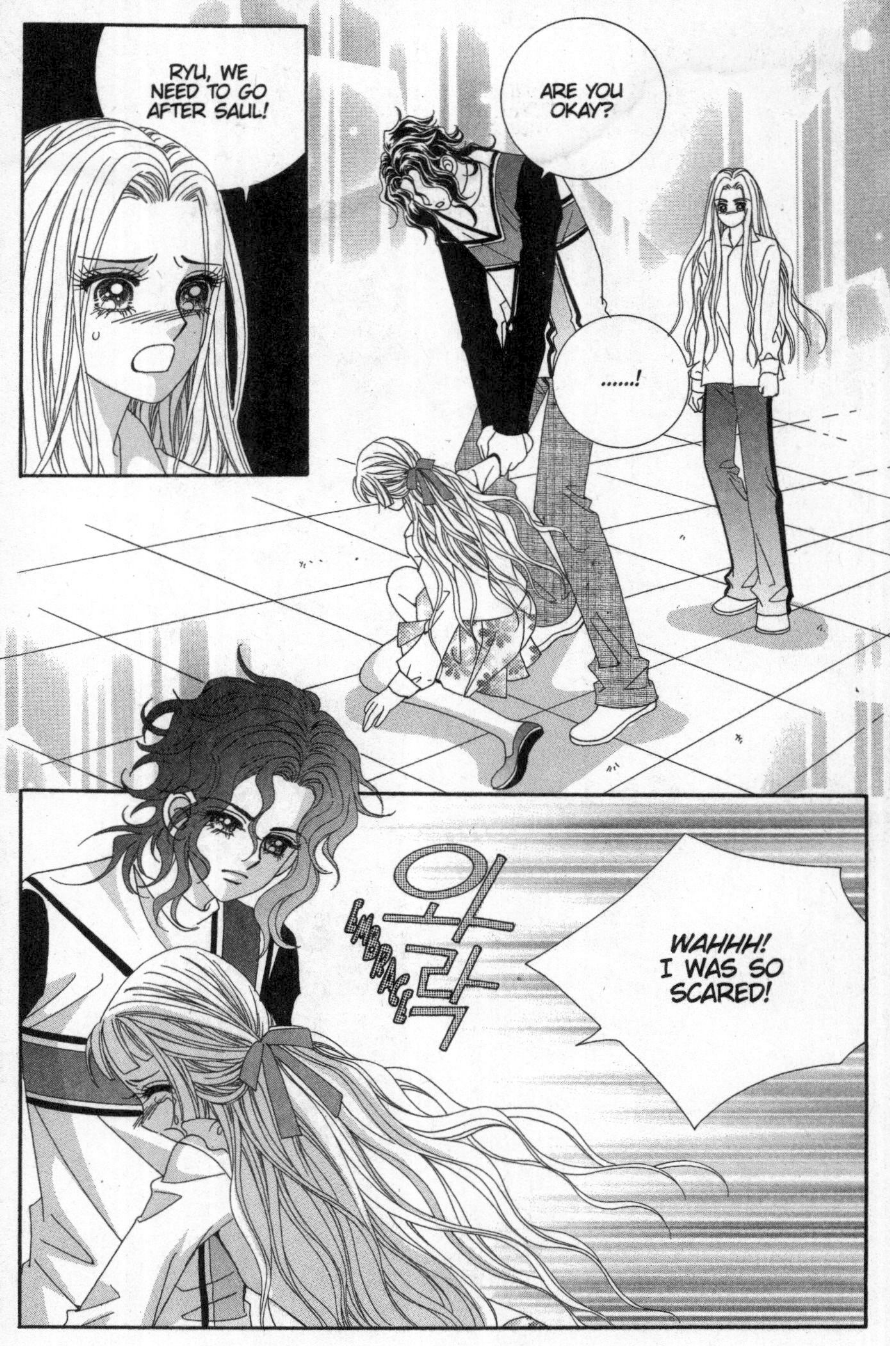
RYU, WE NEED TO GO AFTER SAUL!
ARE YOU OKAY?
......!
와락
EMBRACE
WAHHH! I WAS SO SCARED!

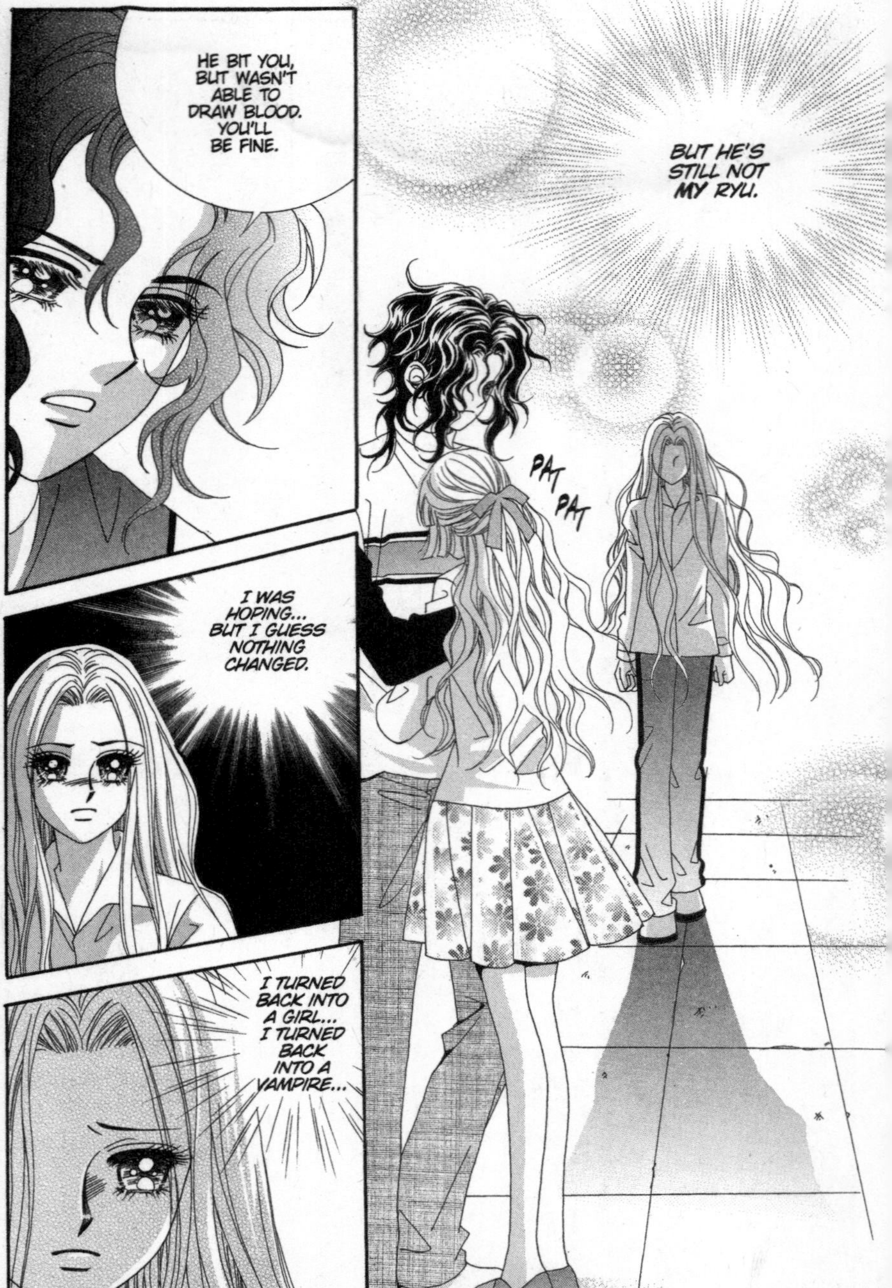
HE BIT YOU, BUT WASN'T ABLE TO DRAW BLOOD. YOU'LL BE FINE.
I WAS HOPING... BUT I GUESS NOTHING CHANGED.
I TURNED BACK INTO A GIRL... I TURNED BACK INTO A VAMPIRE...
BUT HE'S STILL NOT MY RYU.
PAT PAT

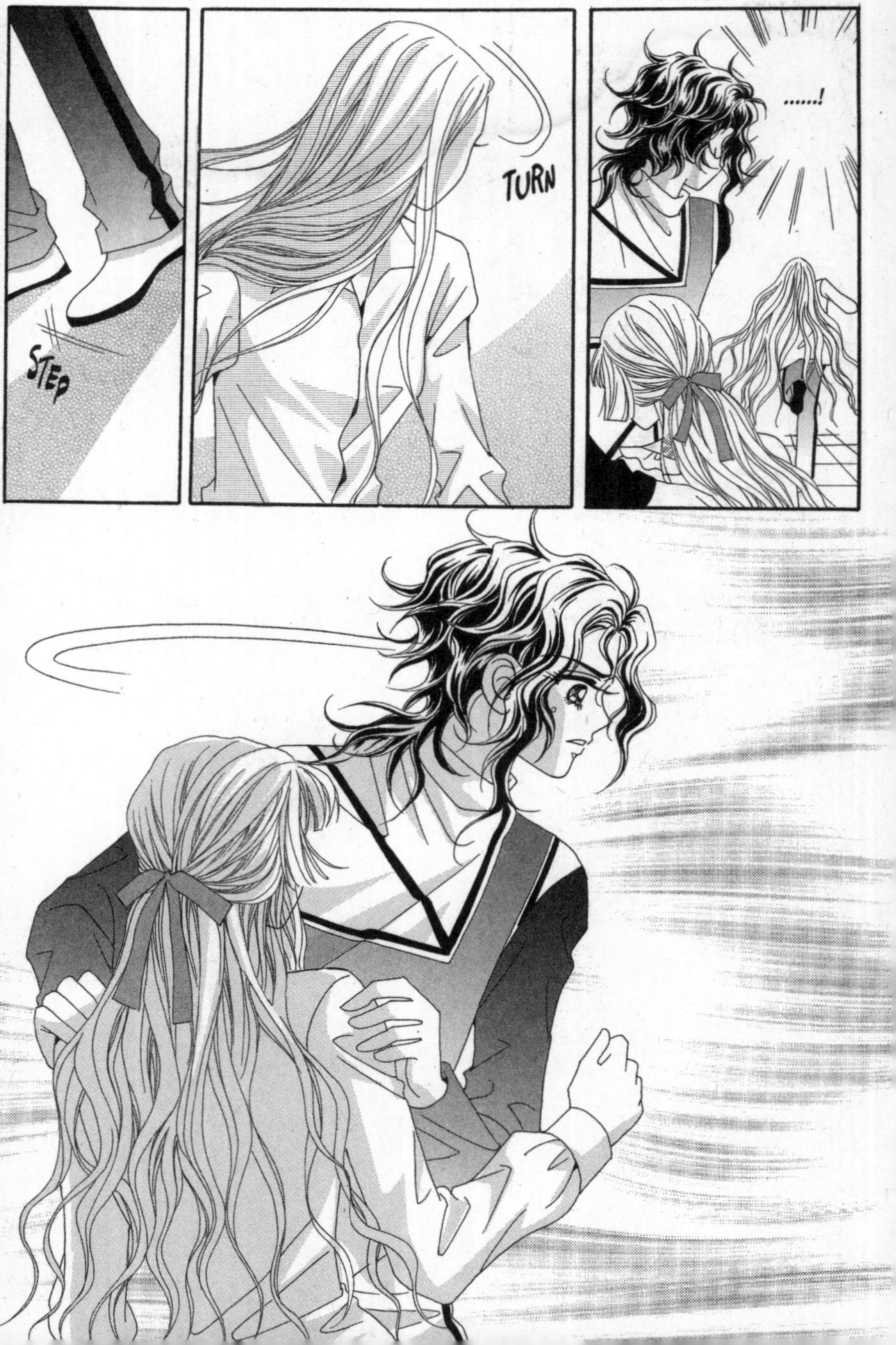
STEP
TURN
......!

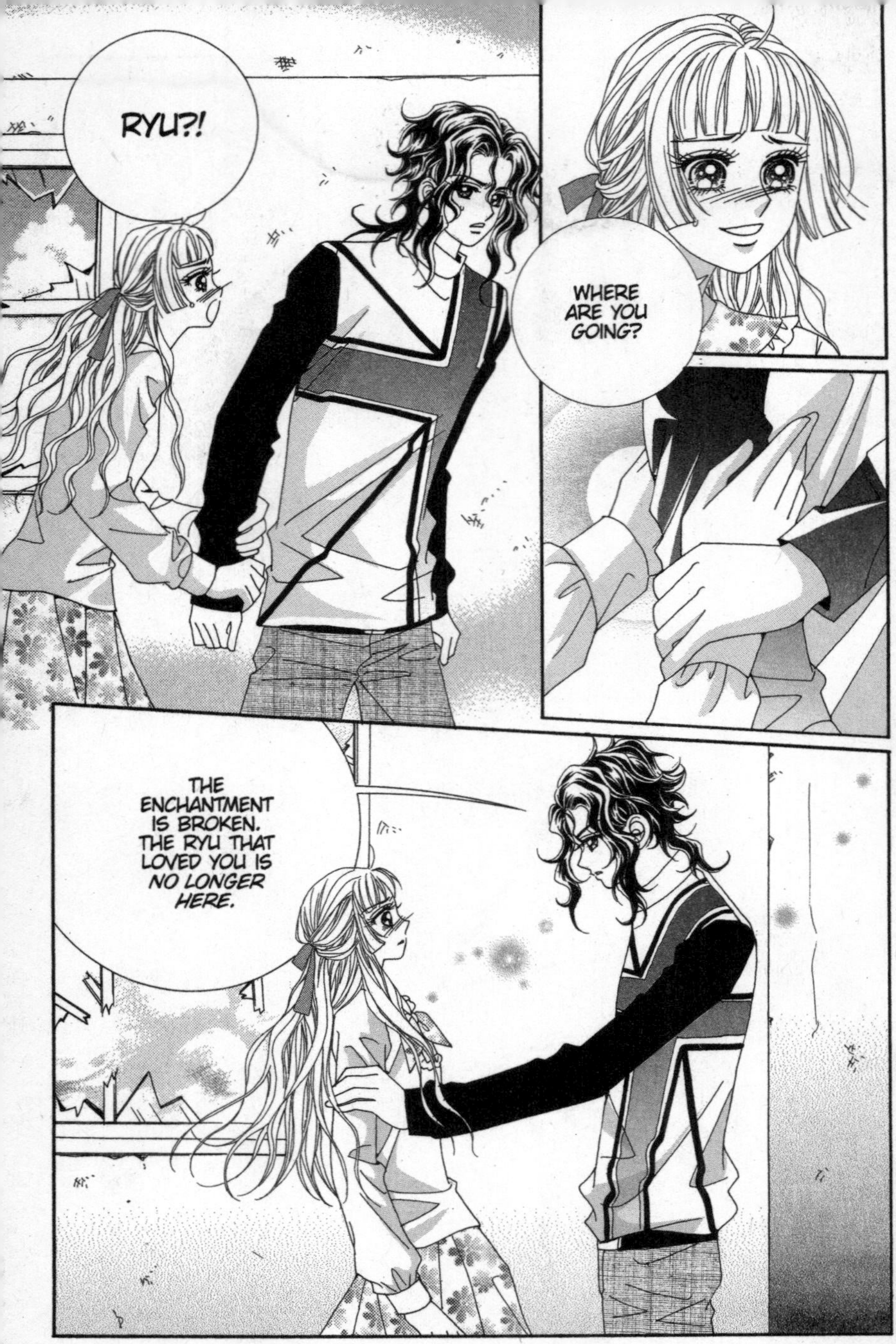
RYU?!
WHERE ARE YOU GOING?
THE ENCHANTMENT IS BROKEN. THE RYU THAT LOVED YOU IS *NO LONGER HERE.*

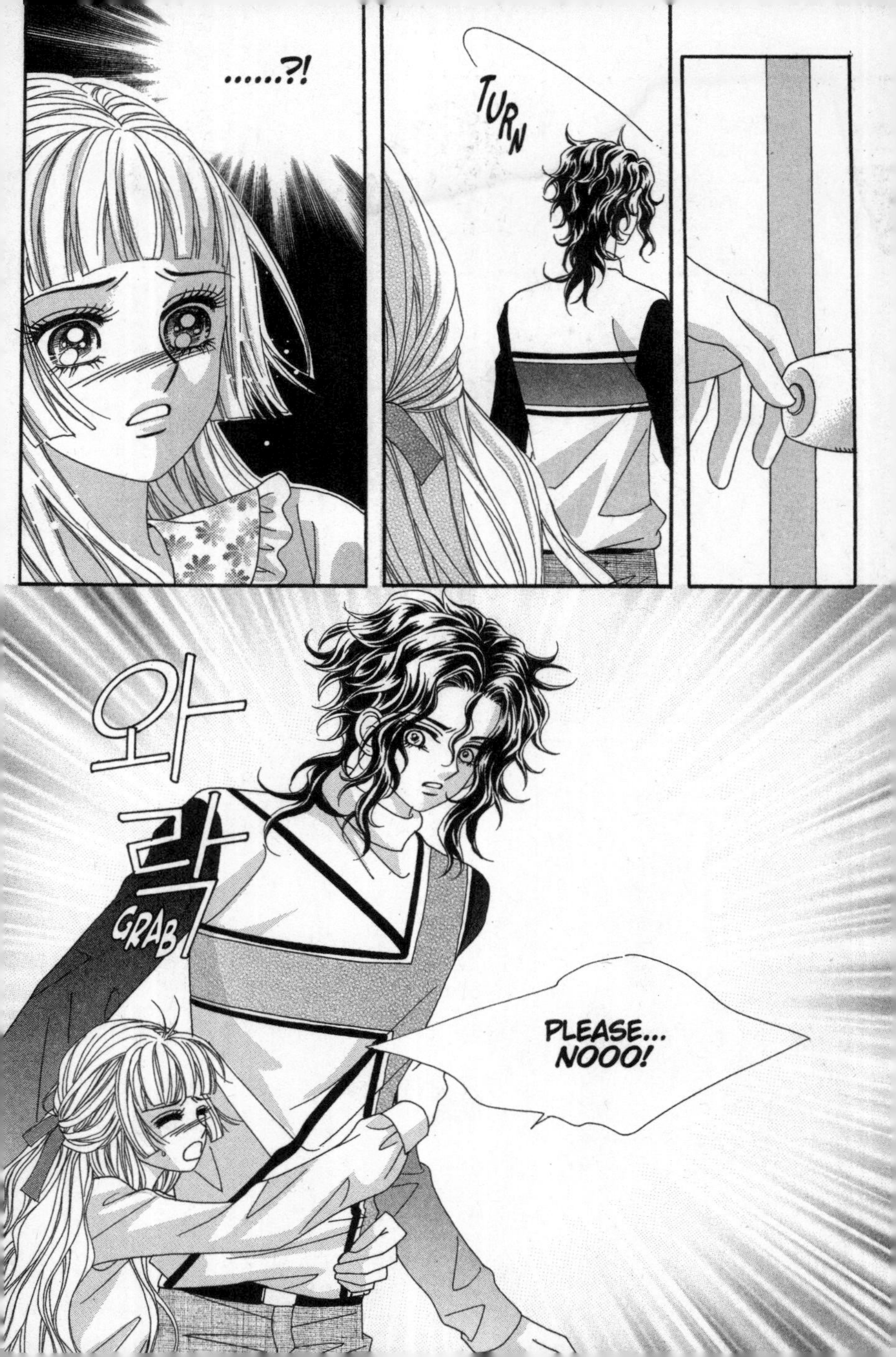
......?!
TURN
와락
GRAB
PLEASE...
NOOO!

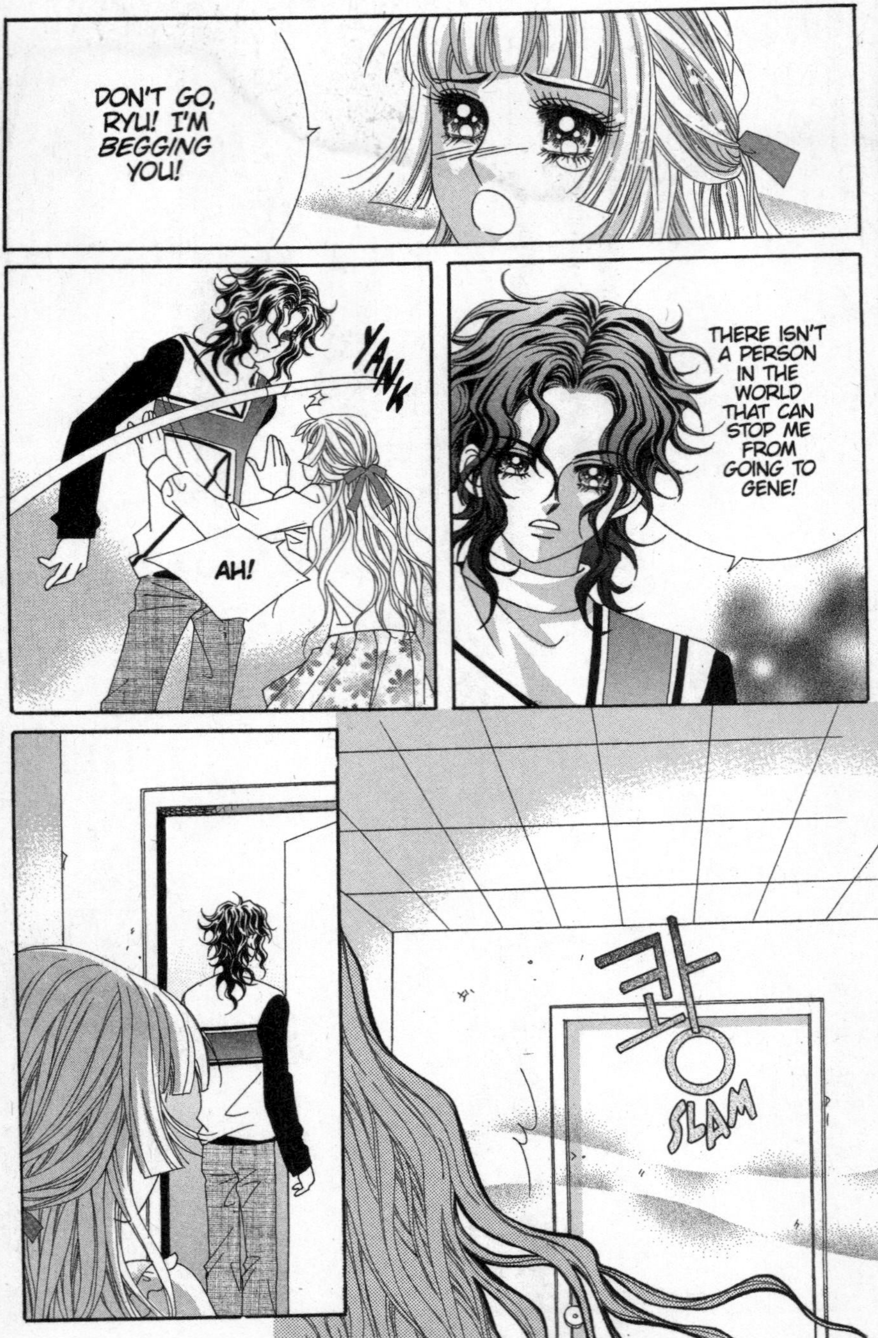
DON'T GO, RYU! I'M BEGGING YOU!
YANK
AH!
THERE ISN'T A PERSON IN THE WORLD THAT CAN STOP ME FROM GOING TO GENE!
SLAM

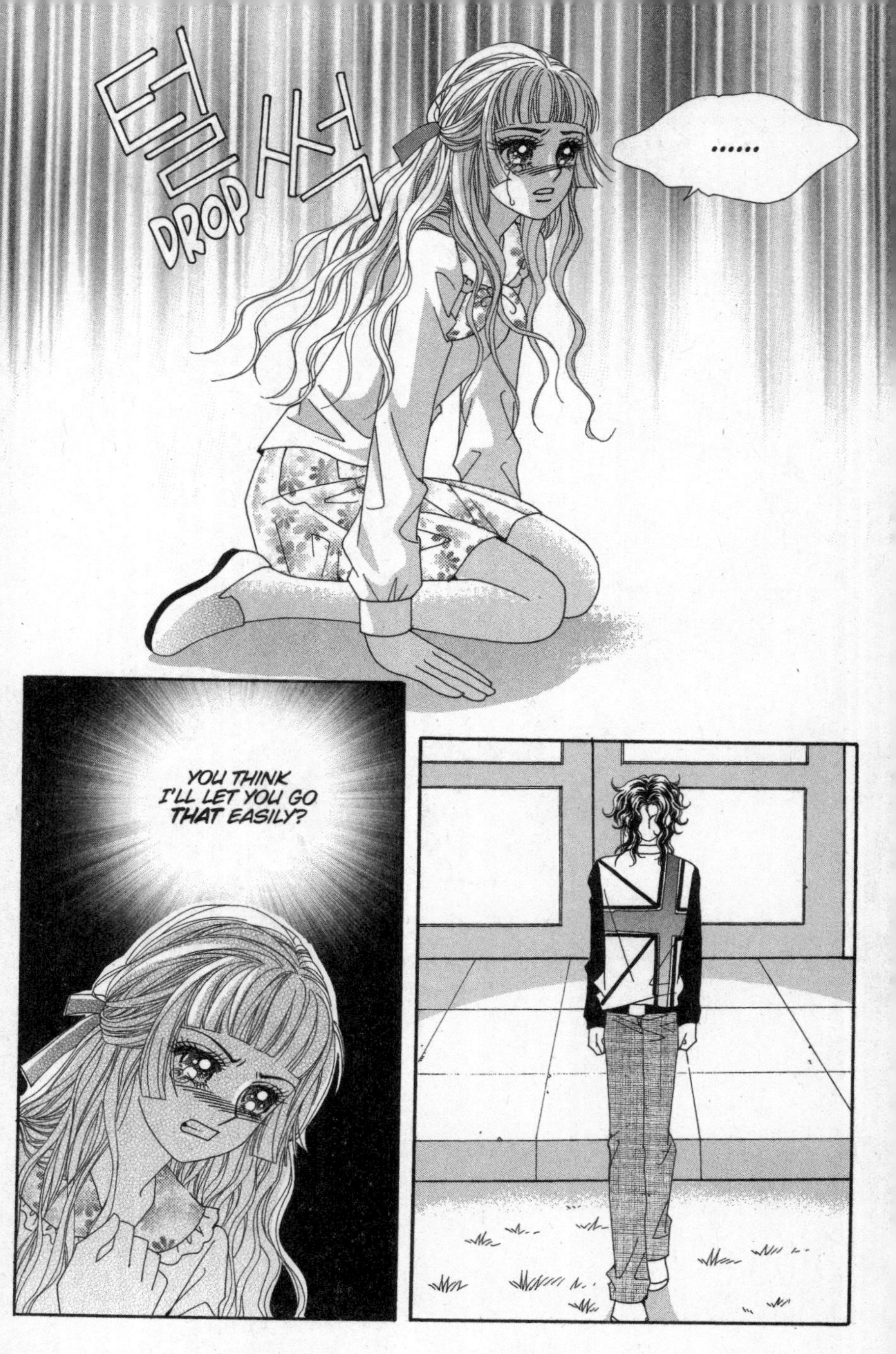
털썩
DROP
......
YOU THINK I'LL LET YOU GO THAT EASILY?

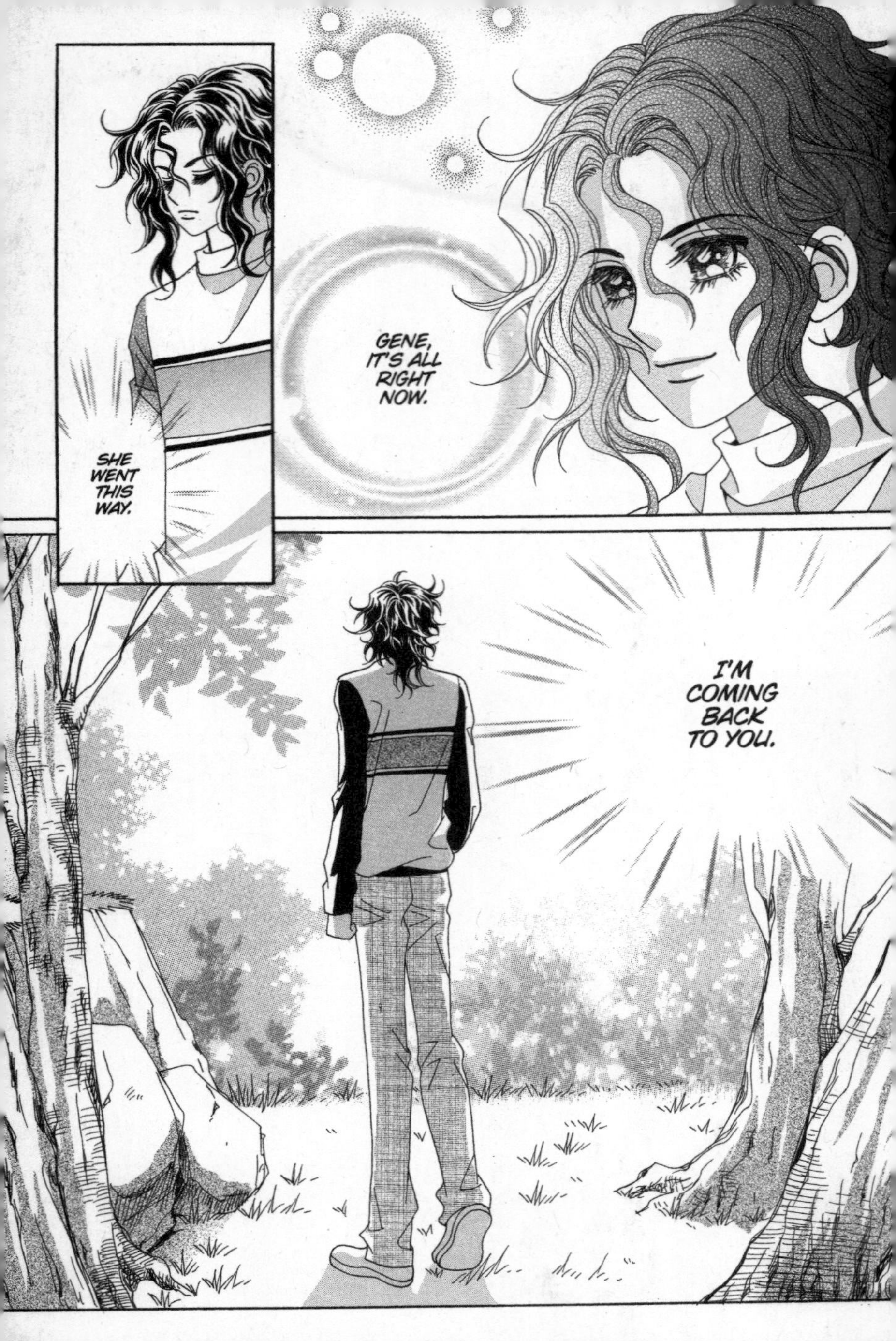
SHE WENT THIS WAY.
GENE, IT'S ALL RIGHT NOW.
I'M COMING BACK TO YOU.

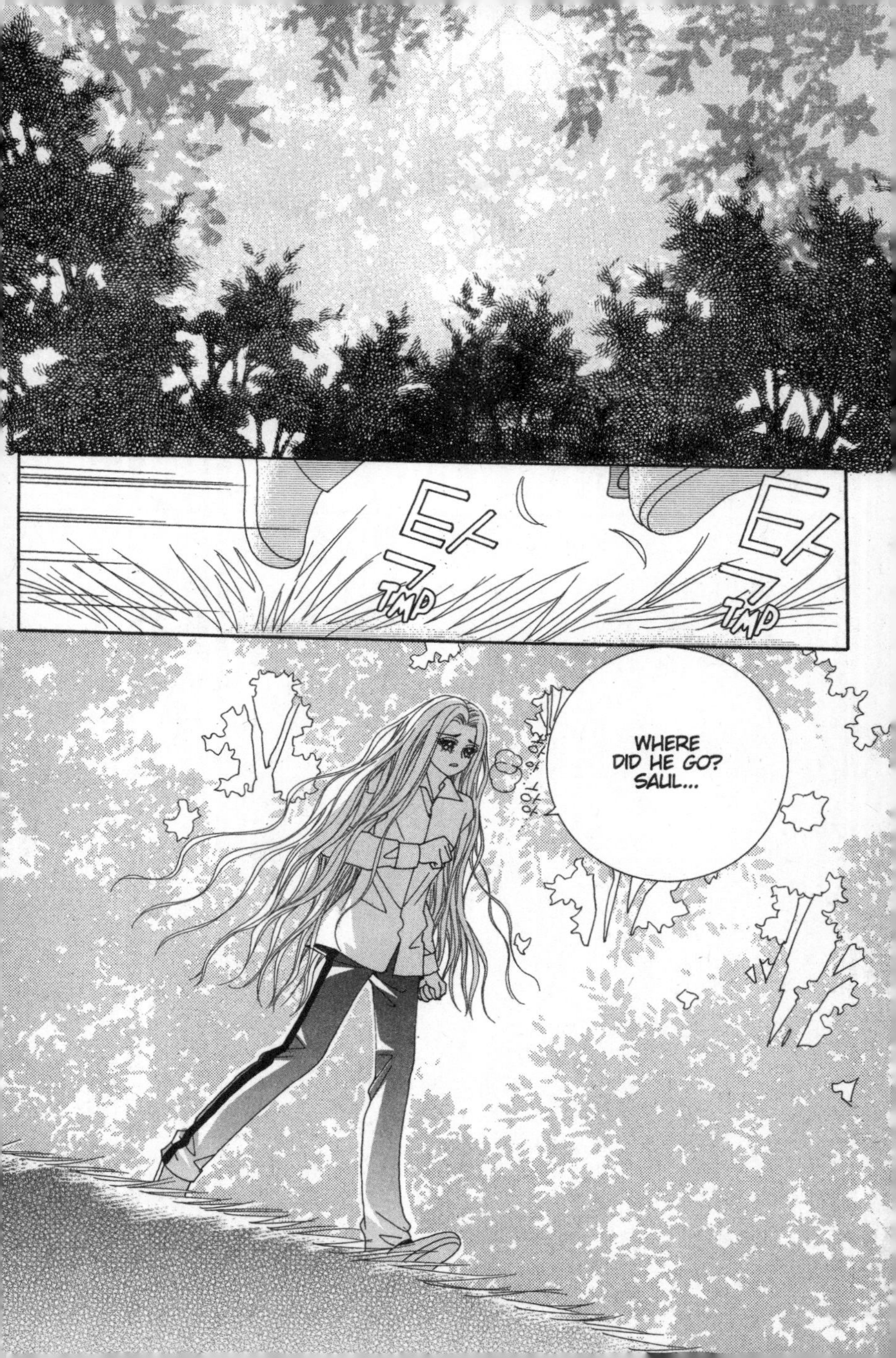
탁
TMP
탁
TMP
WHERE DID HE GO? SAUL...

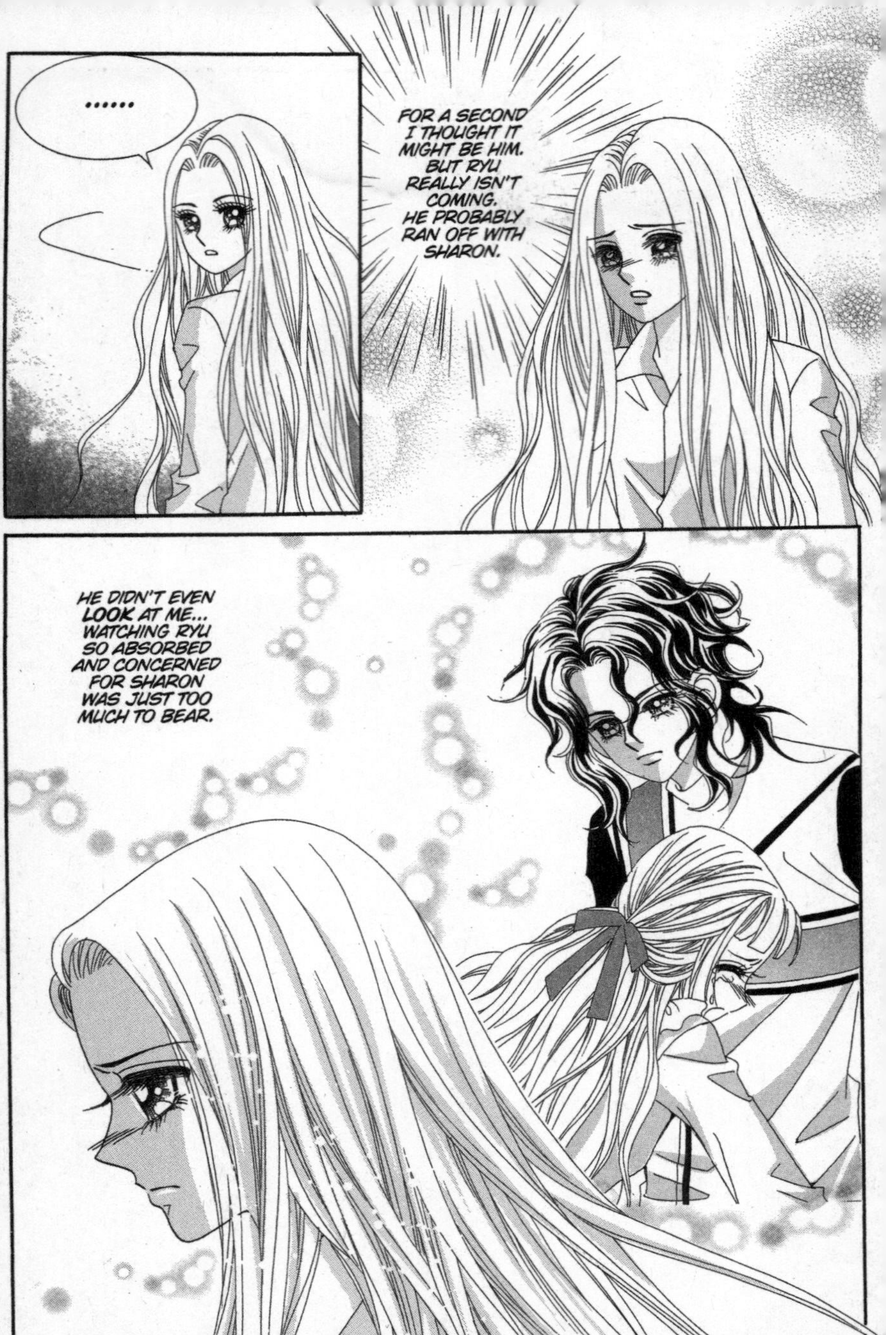
......
FOR A SECOND I THOUGHT IT MIGHT BE HIM. BUT RYU REALLY ISN'T COMING. HE PROBABLY RAN OFF WITH SHARON.
HE DIDN'T EVEN LOOK AT ME... WATCHING RYU SO ABSORBED AND CONCERNED FOR SHARON WAS JUST TOO MUCH TO BEAR.

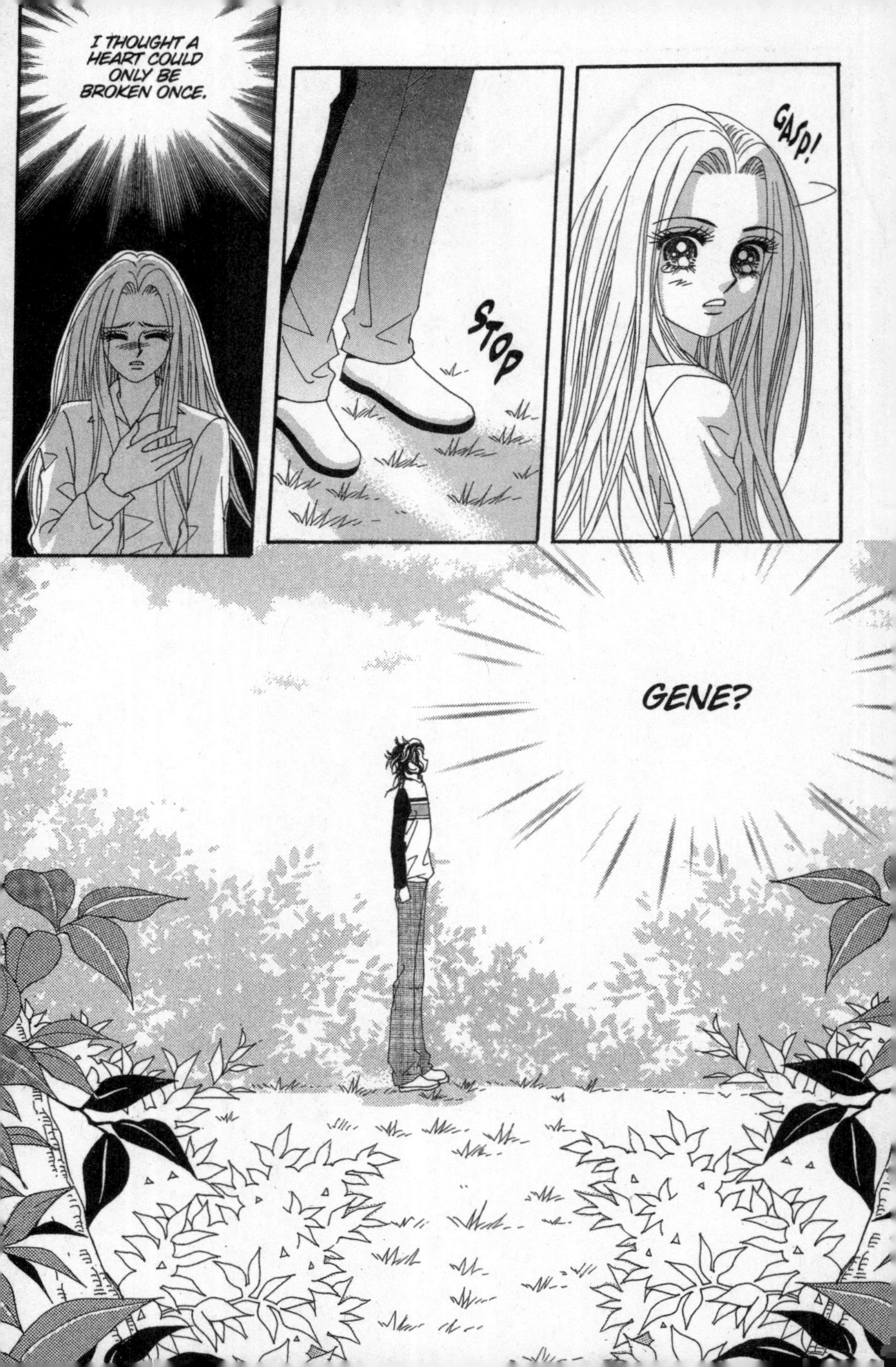
I THOUGHT A HEART COULD ONLY BE BROKEN ONCE.
STOP
GASP!
GENE?

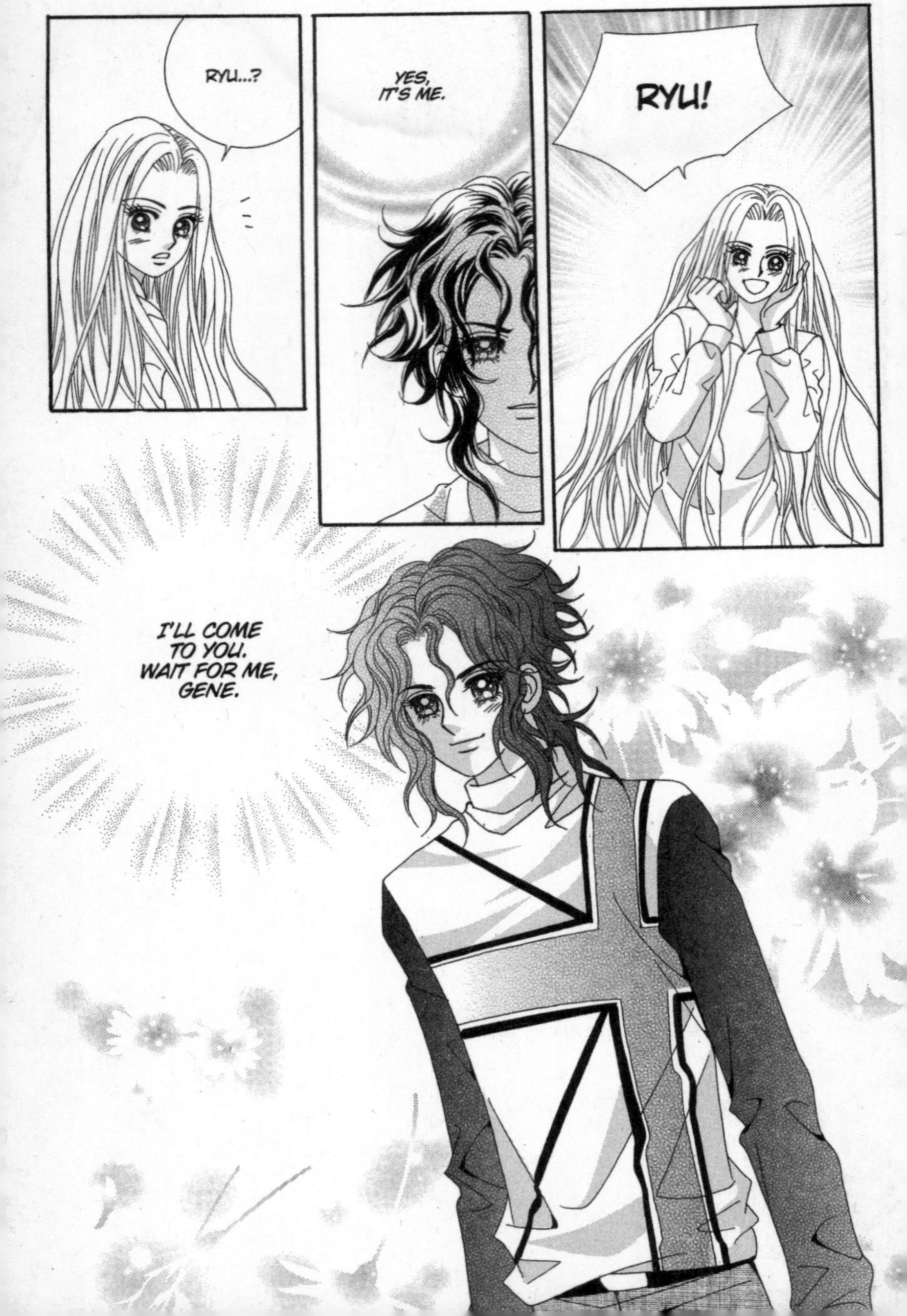
RYU...?
YES, IT'S ME.
RYU!
I'LL COME TO YOU. WAIT FOR ME, GENE.

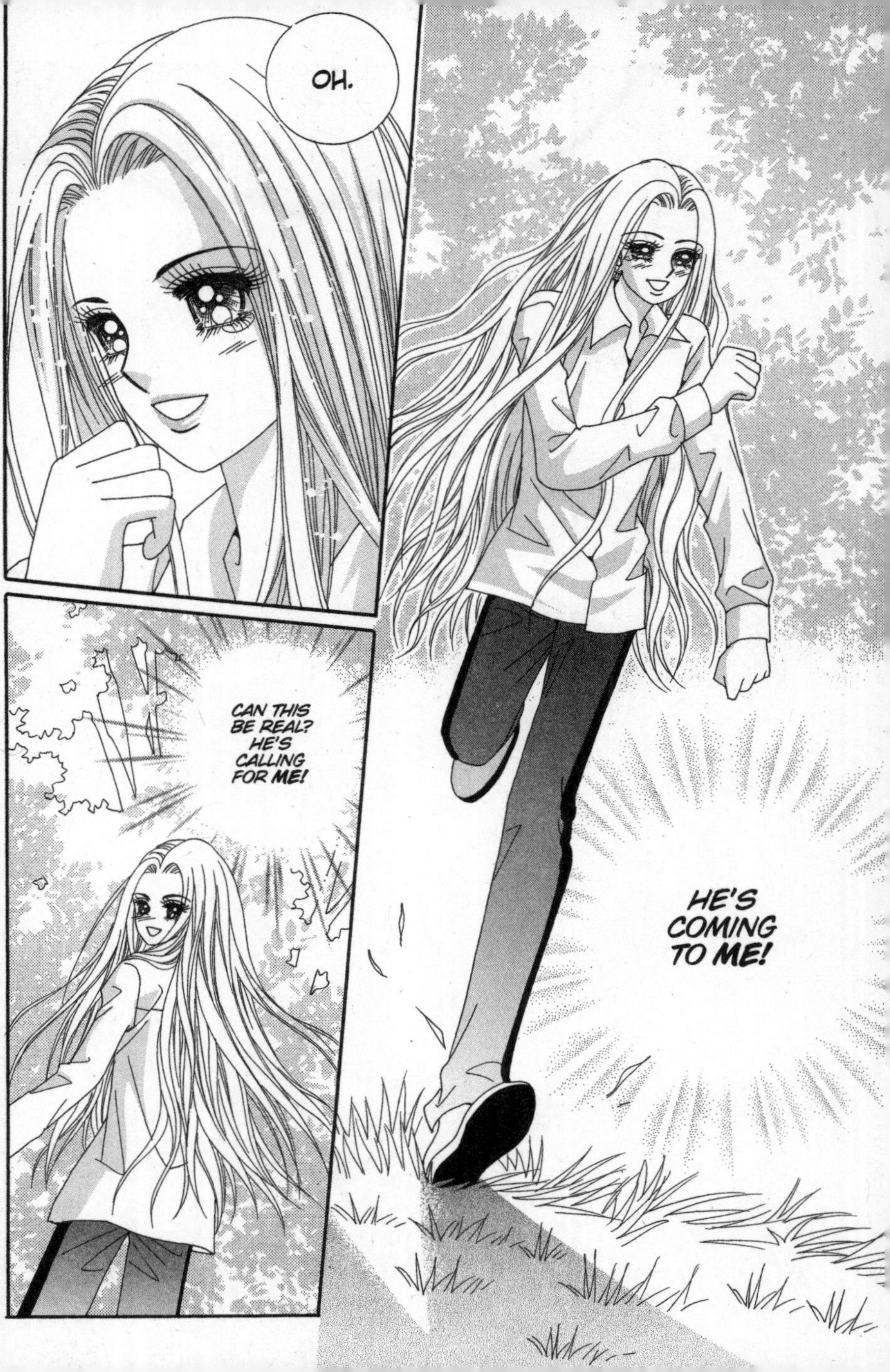
OH.
CAN THIS BE REAL? HE'S CALLING FOR ME!
HE'S COMING TO ME!

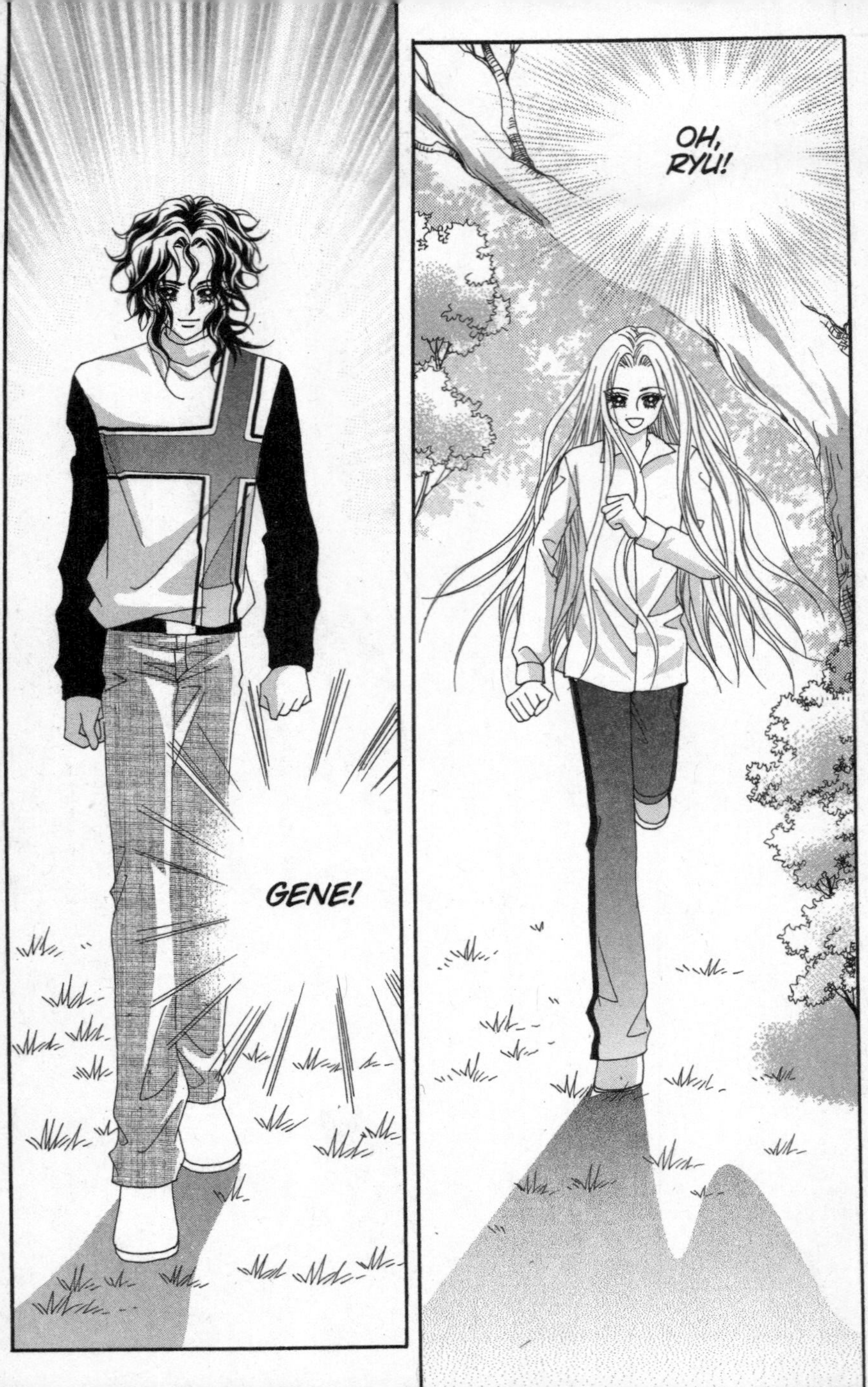
GENE!
OH, RYU!

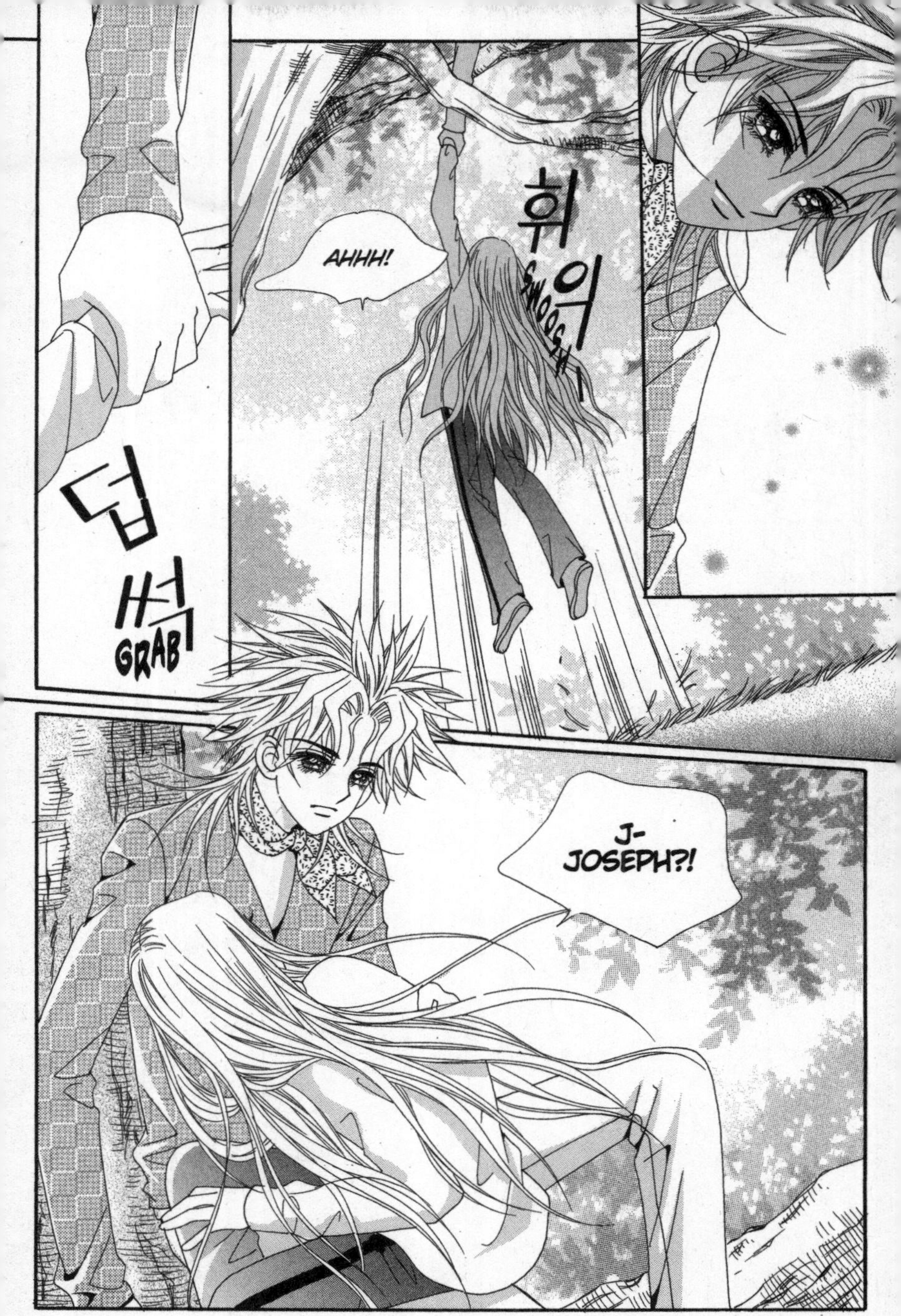

덥썩
GRAB!
AHHH!
휘익
SWOOSH
J-JOSEPH?!

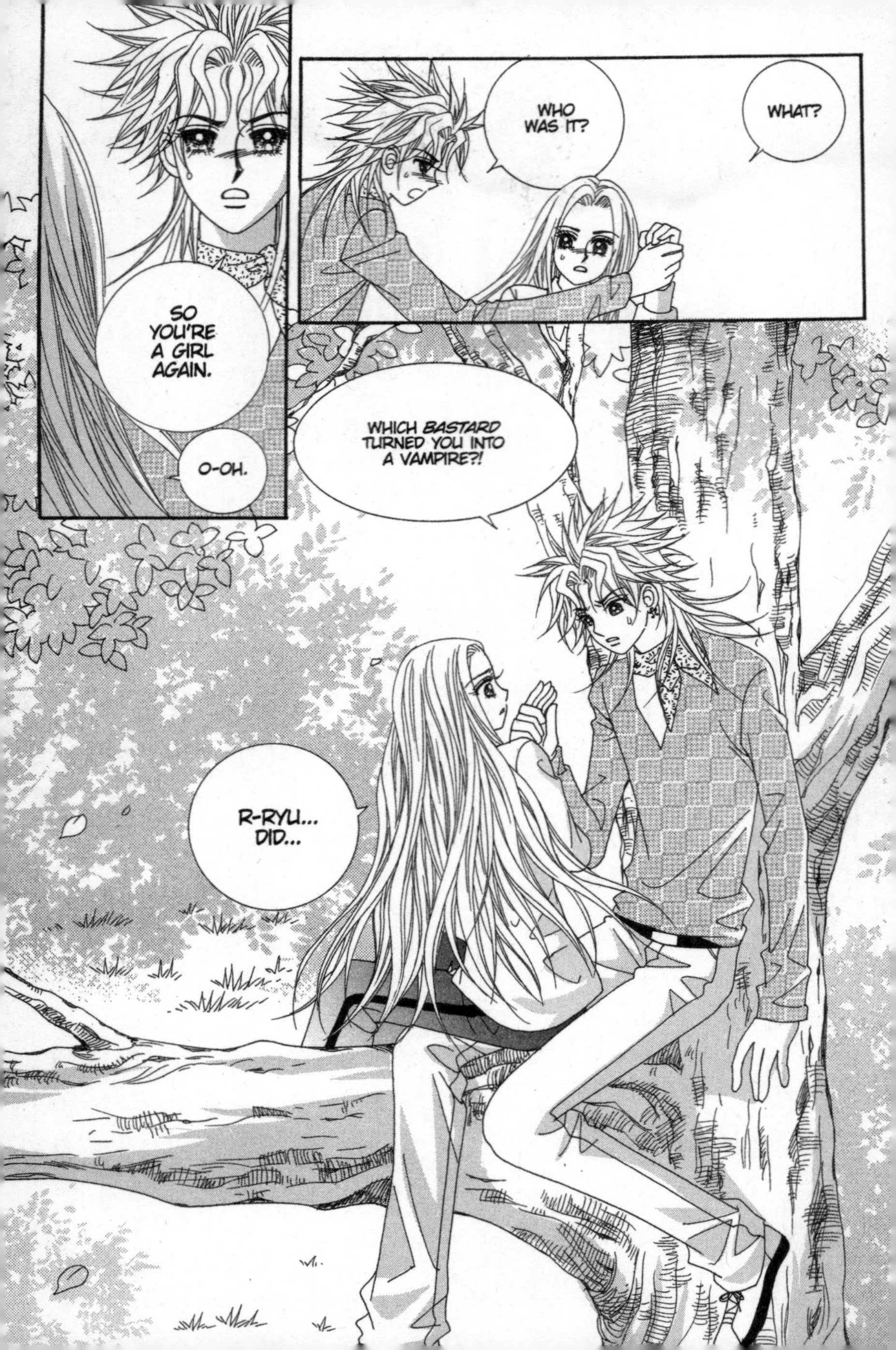
SO YOU'RE A GIRL AGAIN.
O-OH.
WHO WAS IT?
WHAT?
WHICH *BASTARD* TURNED YOU INTO A VAMPIRE?!
R-RYU... DID...

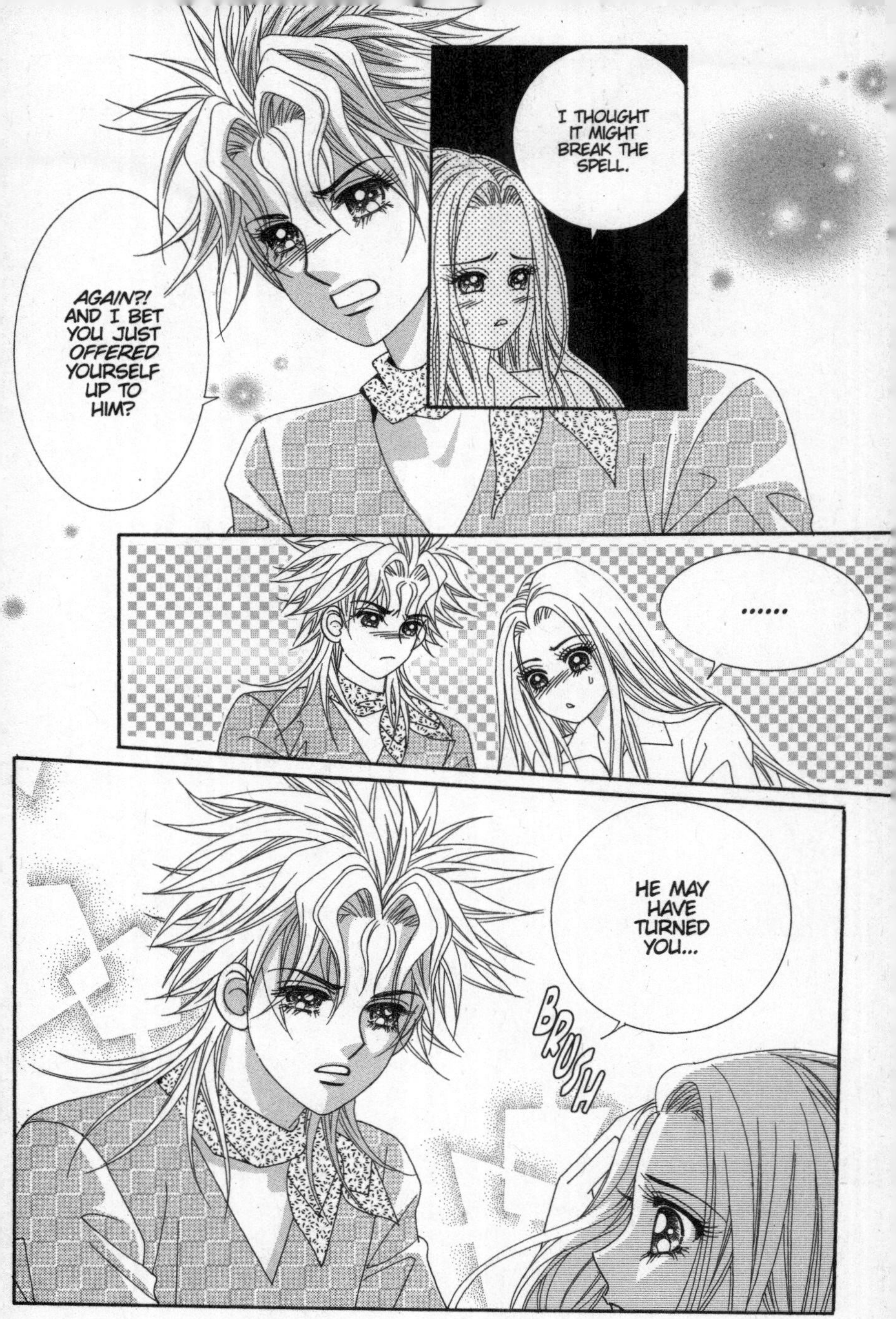
AGAIN?! AND I BET YOU JUST OFFERED YOURSELF UP TO HIM?
I THOUGHT IT MIGHT BREAK THE SPELL.
......
HE MAY HAVE TURNED YOU...
BRUSH

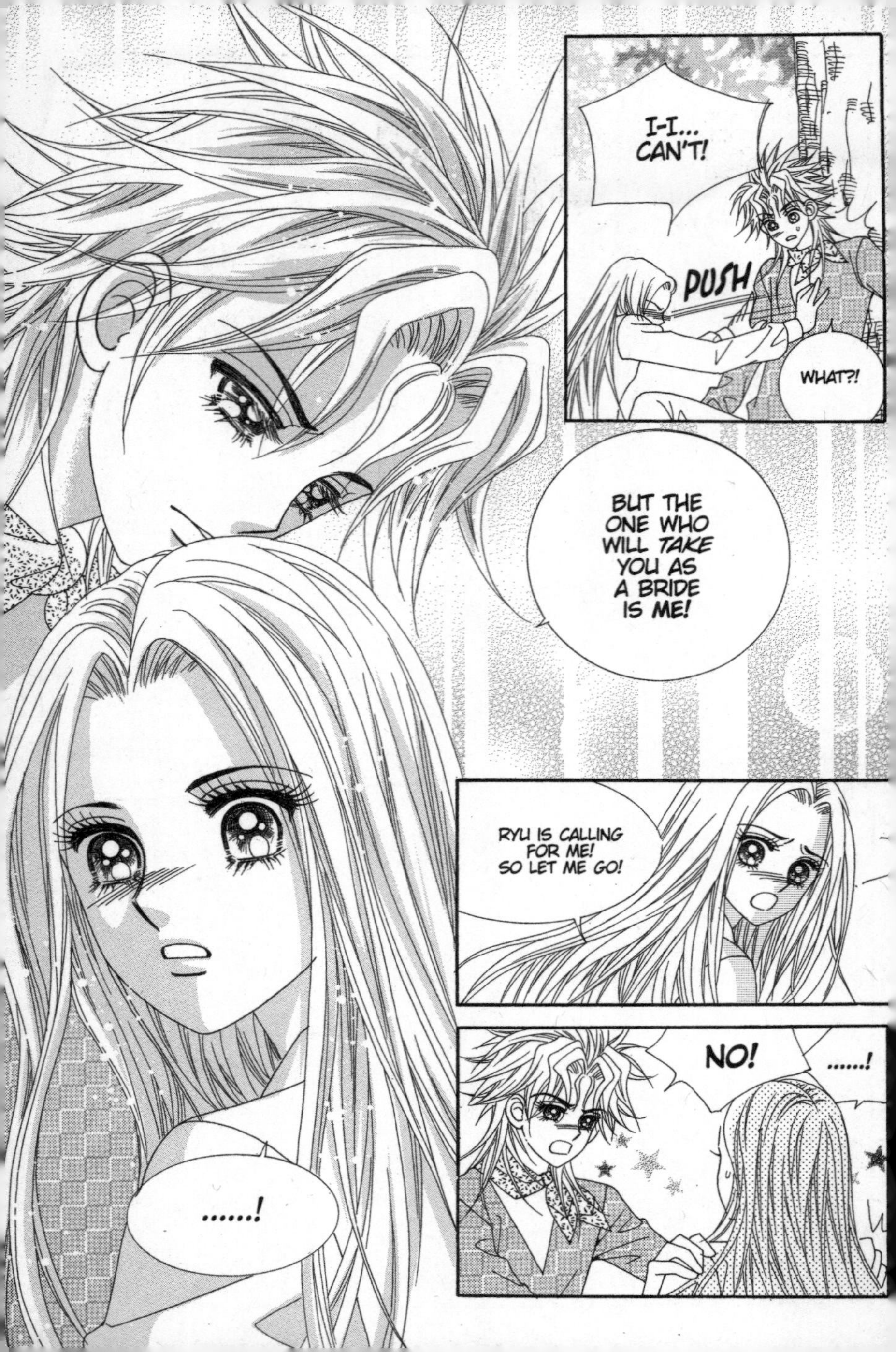
BUT THE ONE WHO WILL *TAKE* YOU AS A BRIDE IS ME!
......!
I-I... CAN'T!
PUSH
WHAT?!
RYU IS CALLING FOR ME! SO LET ME GO!
NO!
......!

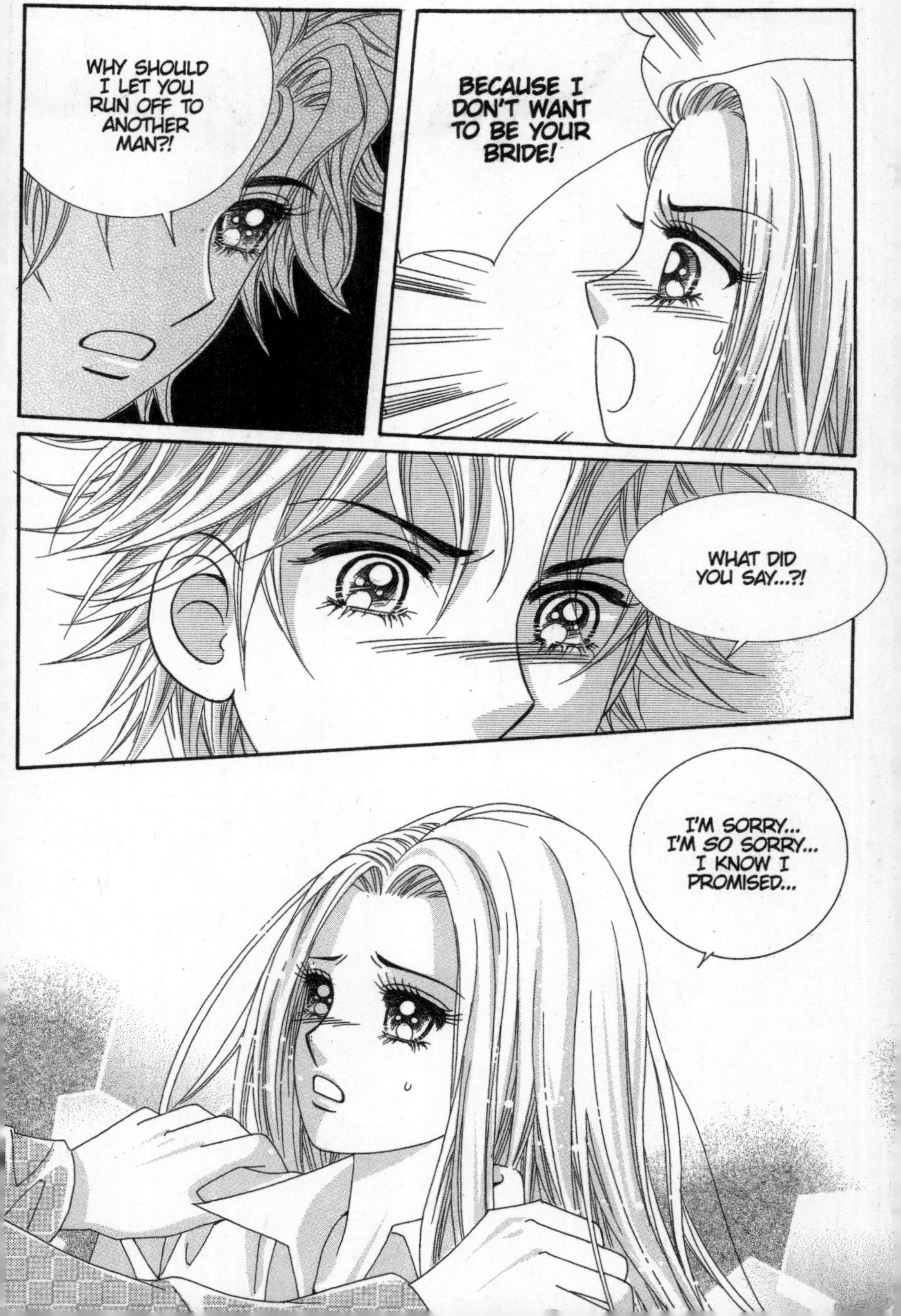
WHY SHOULD I LET YOU RUN OFF TO ANOTHER MAN?!
BECAUSE I DON'T WANT TO BE YOUR BRIDE!
WHAT DID YOU SAY...?!
I'M SORRY... I'M SO SORRY... I KNOW I PROMISED...

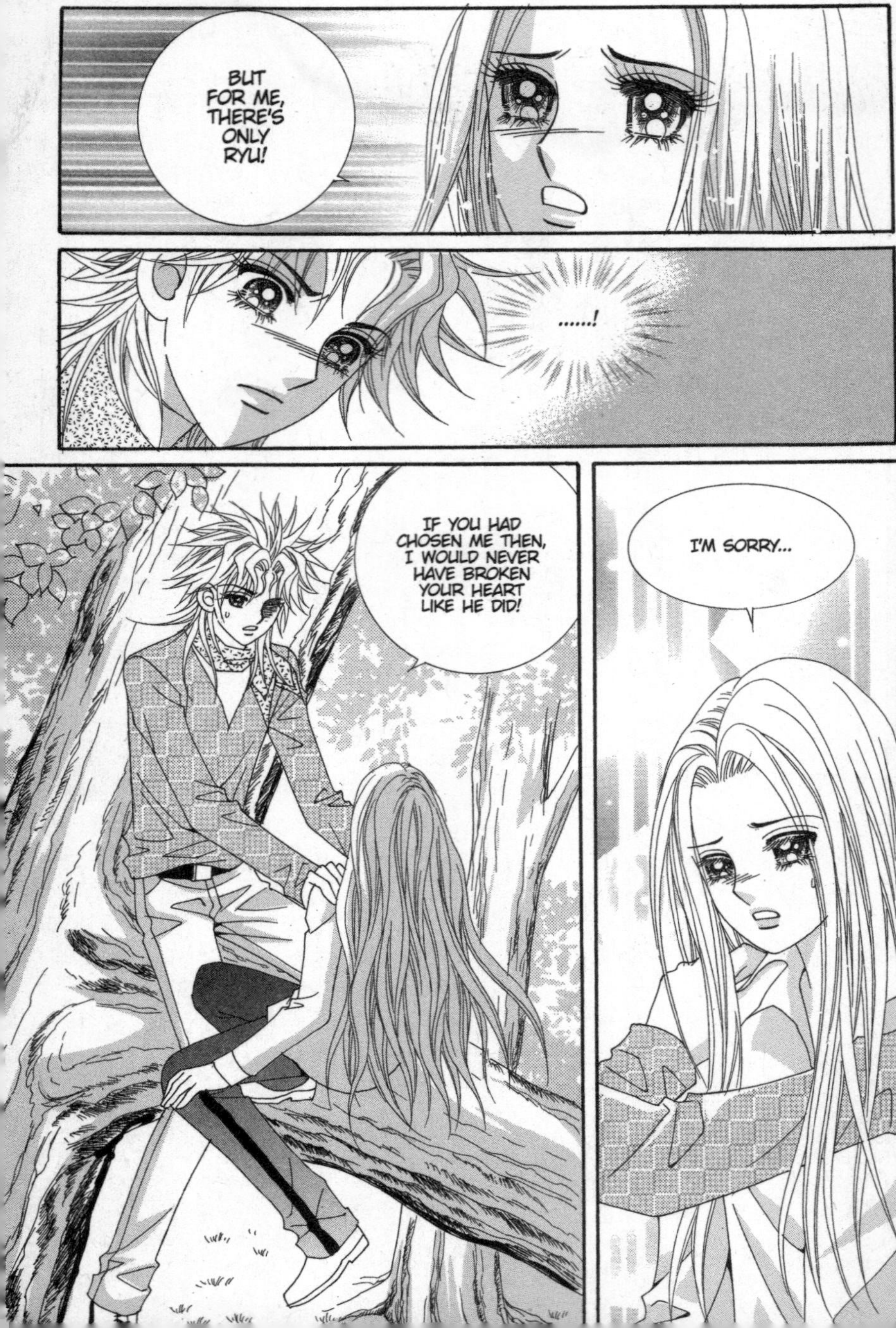
BUT FOR ME, THERE'S ONLY RYU!
......!
IF YOU HAD CHOSEN ME THEN, I WOULD NEVER HAVE BROKEN YOUR HEART LIKE HE DID!
I'M SORRY...

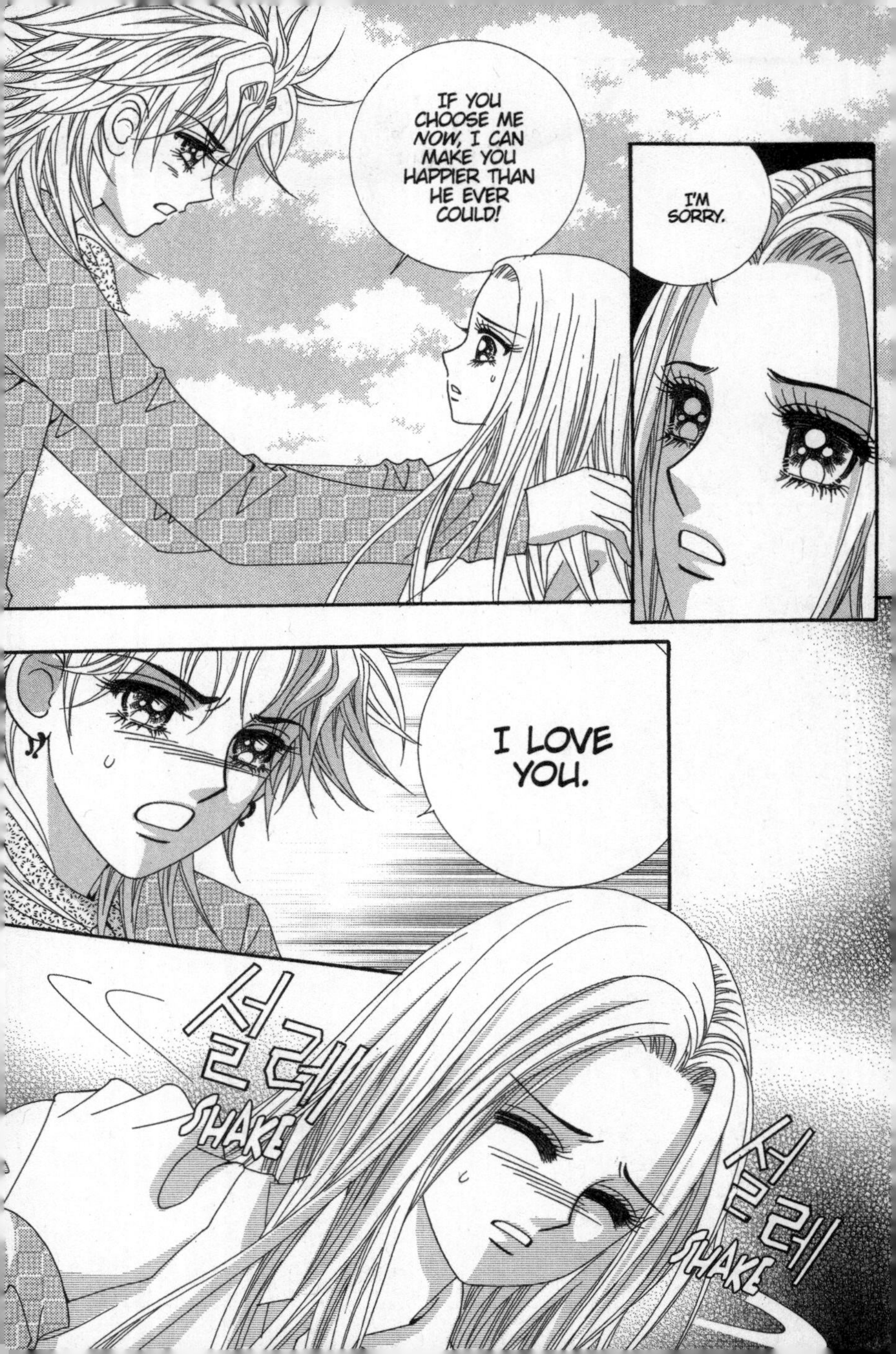
IF YOU CHOOSE ME NOW, I CAN MAKE YOU HAPPIER THAN HE EVER COULD!
I'M SORRY.
I LOVE YOU.
설레
SHAKE
설레
SHAKE

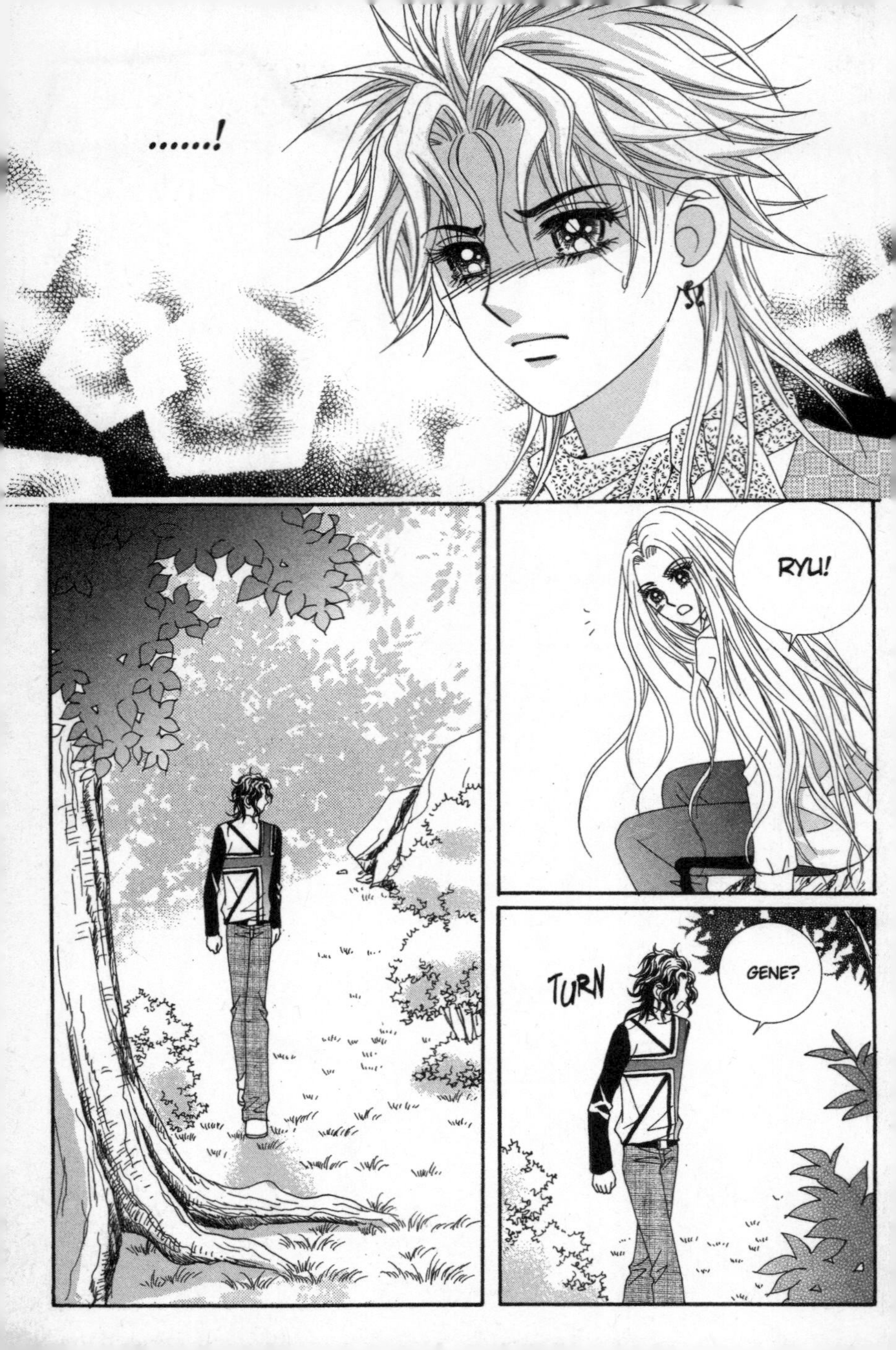
......!
RYU!
TURN
GENE?

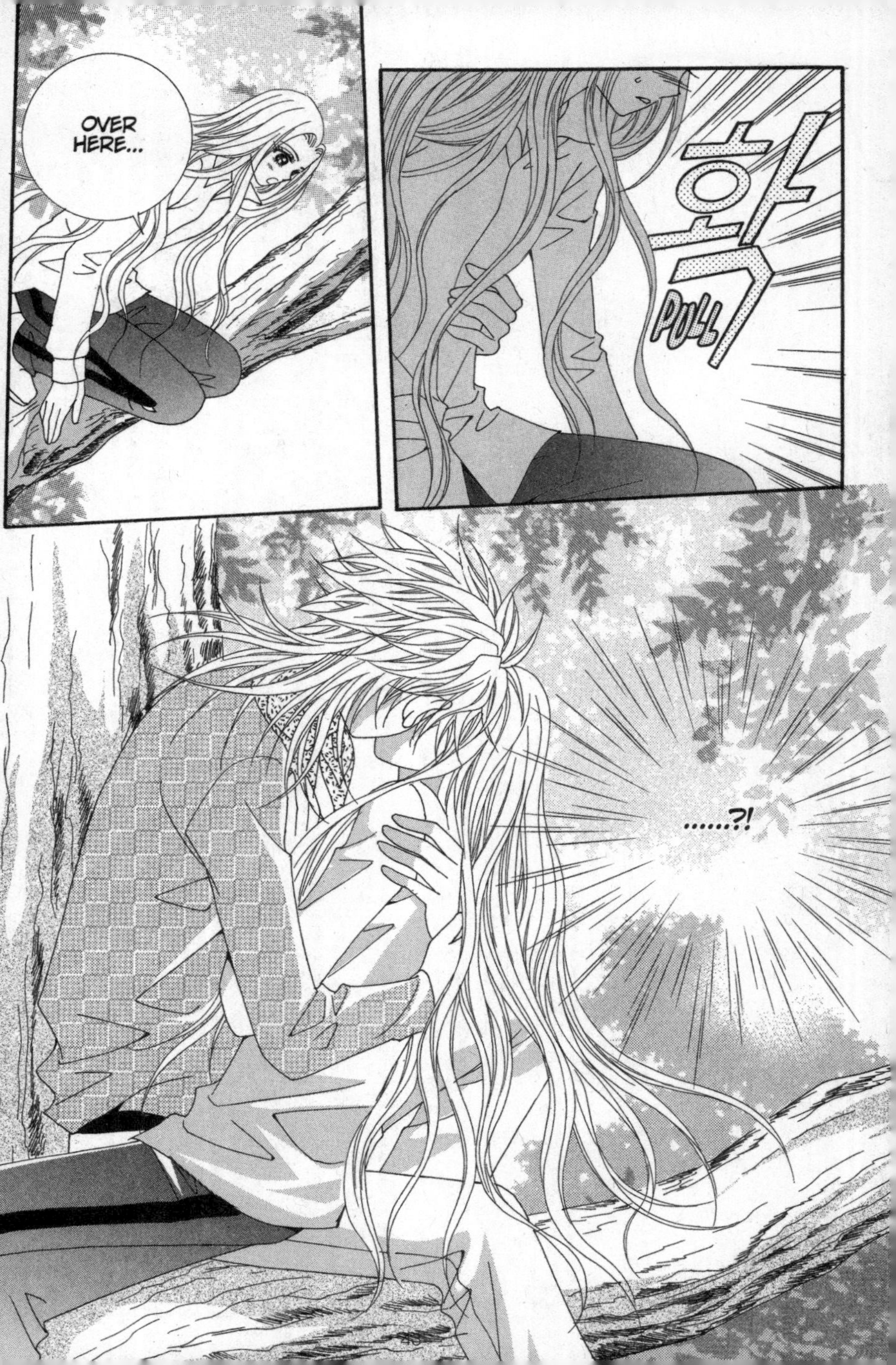
OVER HERE...
학
PULL
......?!

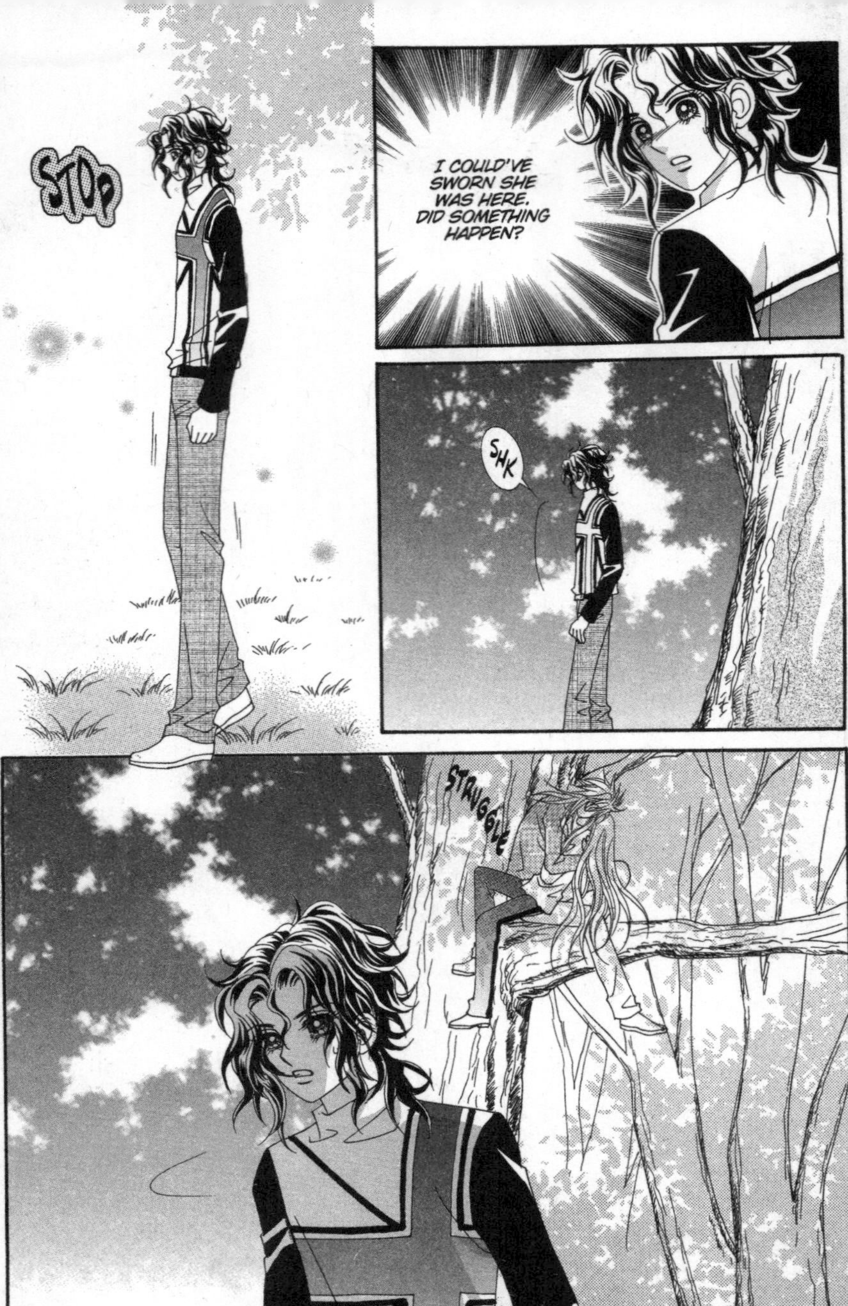
STOP
I COULD'VE SWORN SHE WAS HERE. DID SOMETHING HAPPEN?
SHK
STRUGGLE

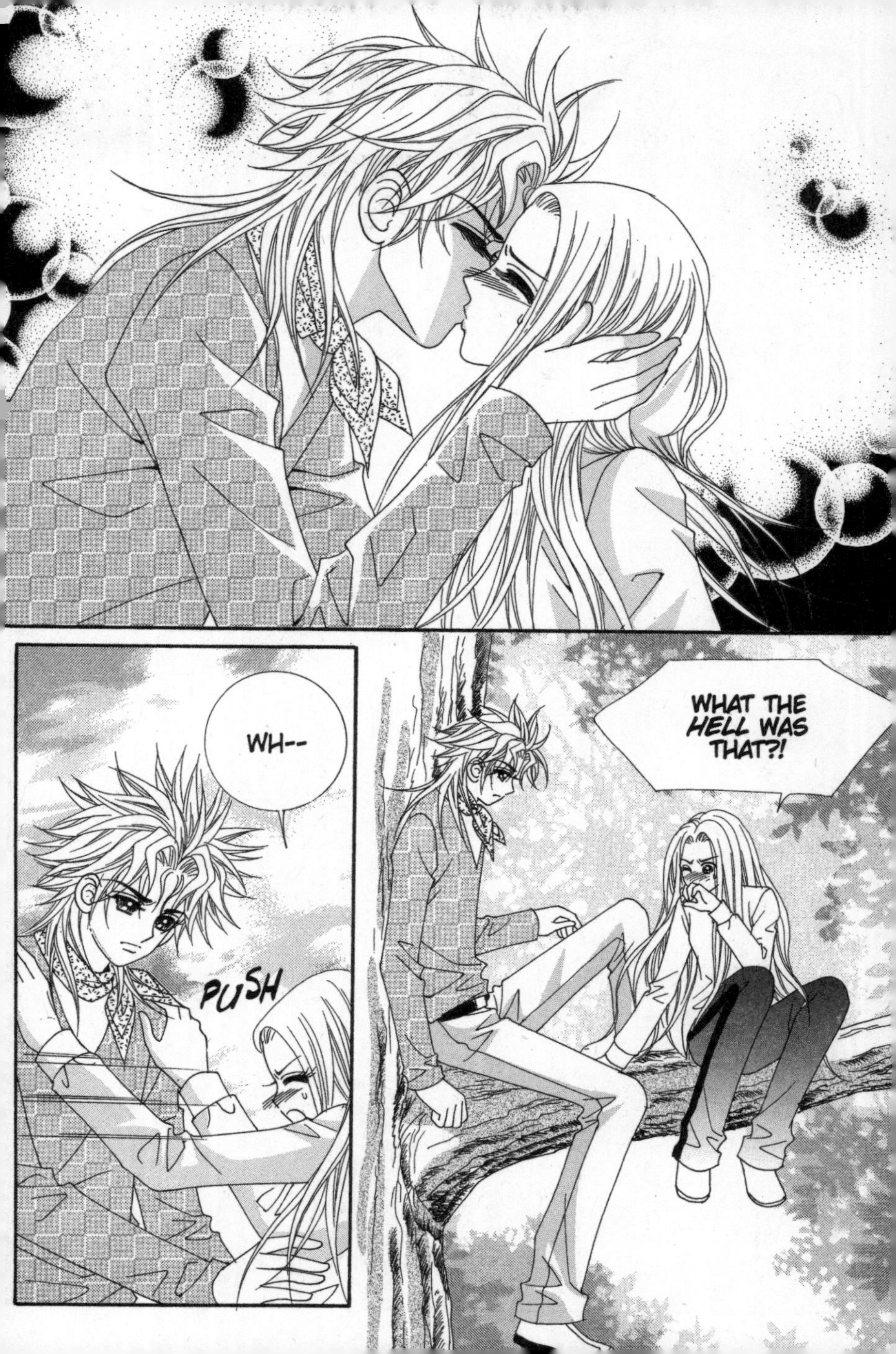
WH--
PUSH
WHAT THE HELL WAS THAT?!

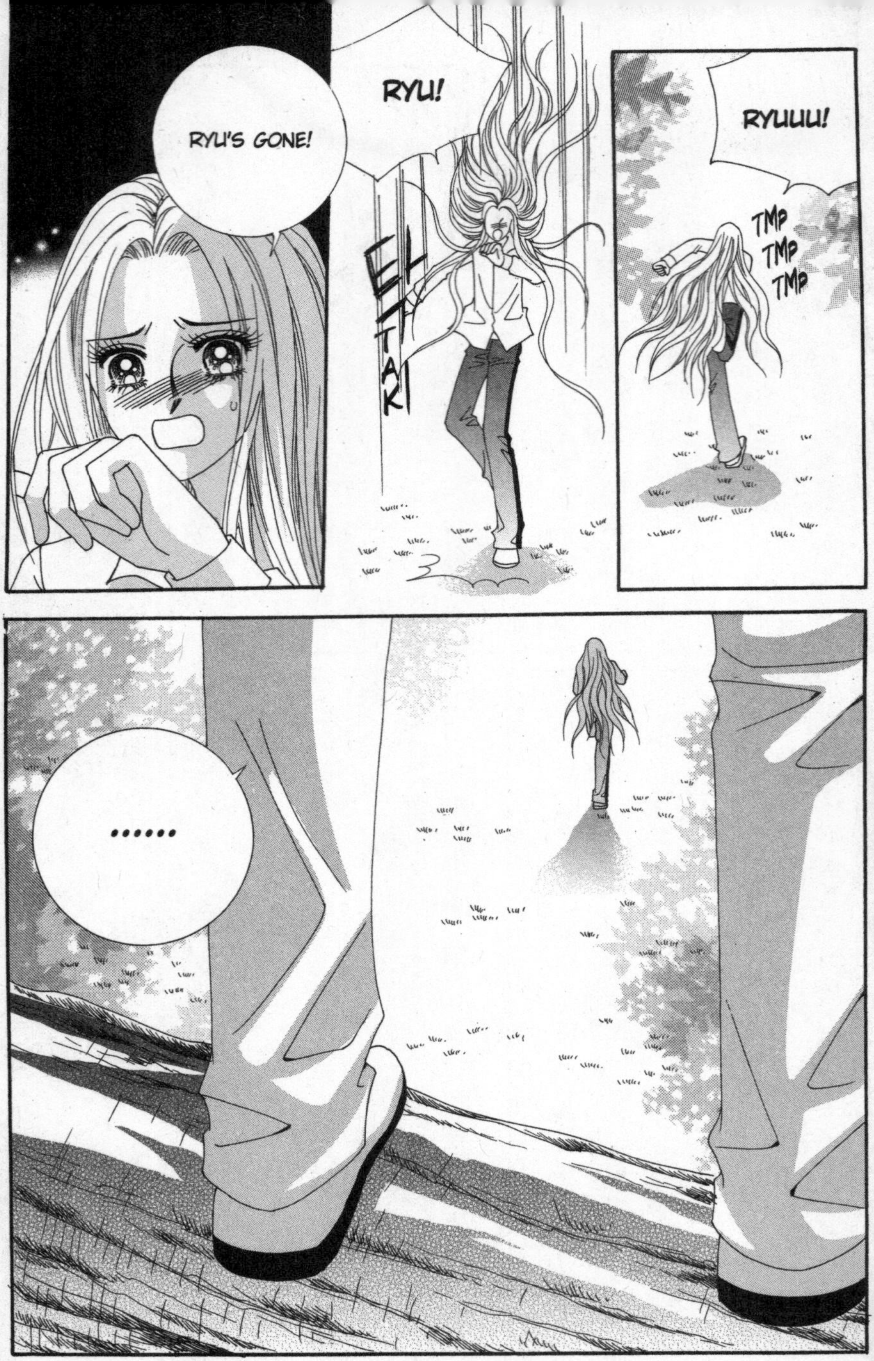
RYU'S GONE!
RYU!
TAK
RYUUU!
TMP
TMP
TMP
......

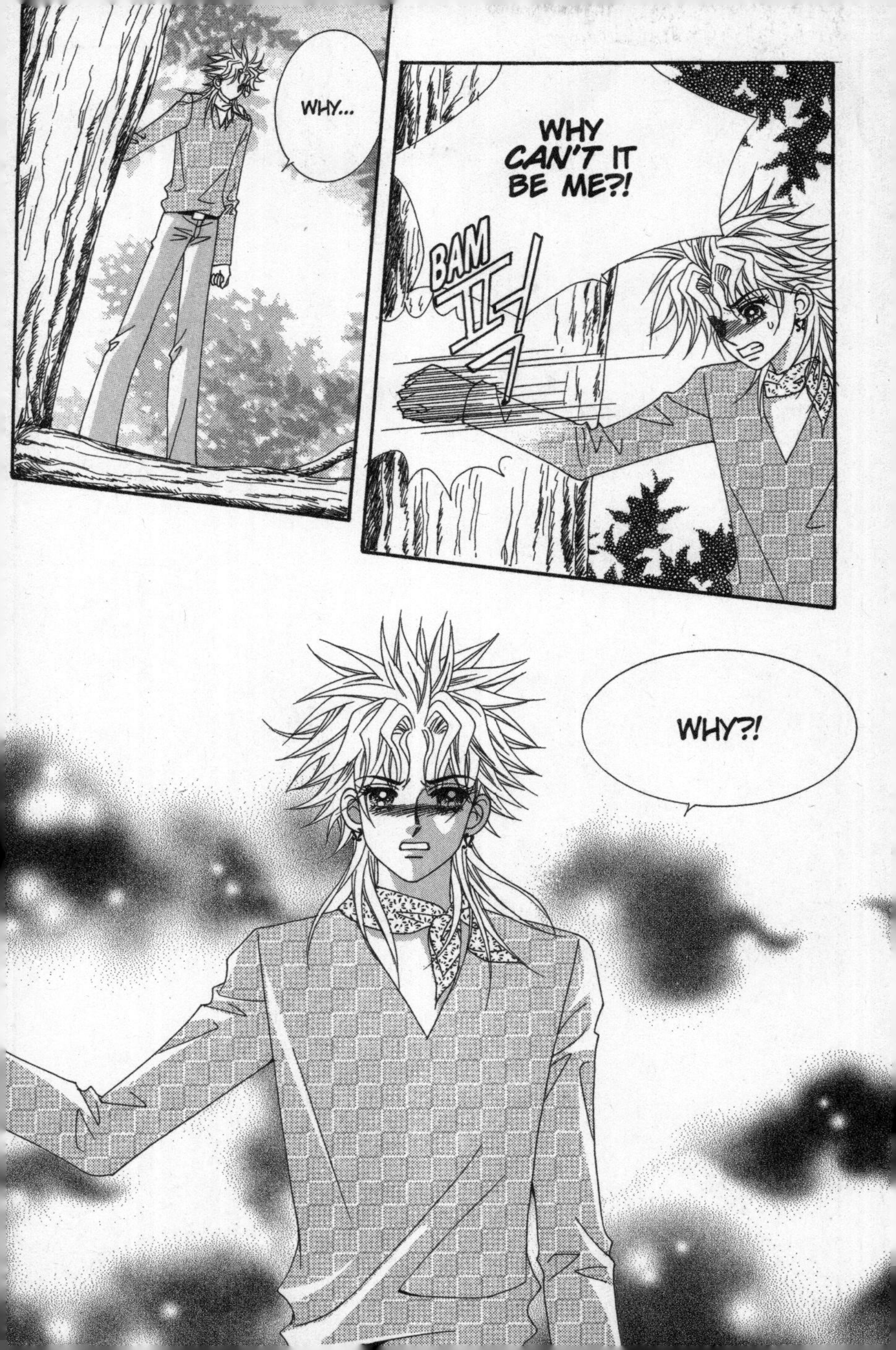
WHY...
WHY CAN'T IT BE ME?!
BAM
WHY?!

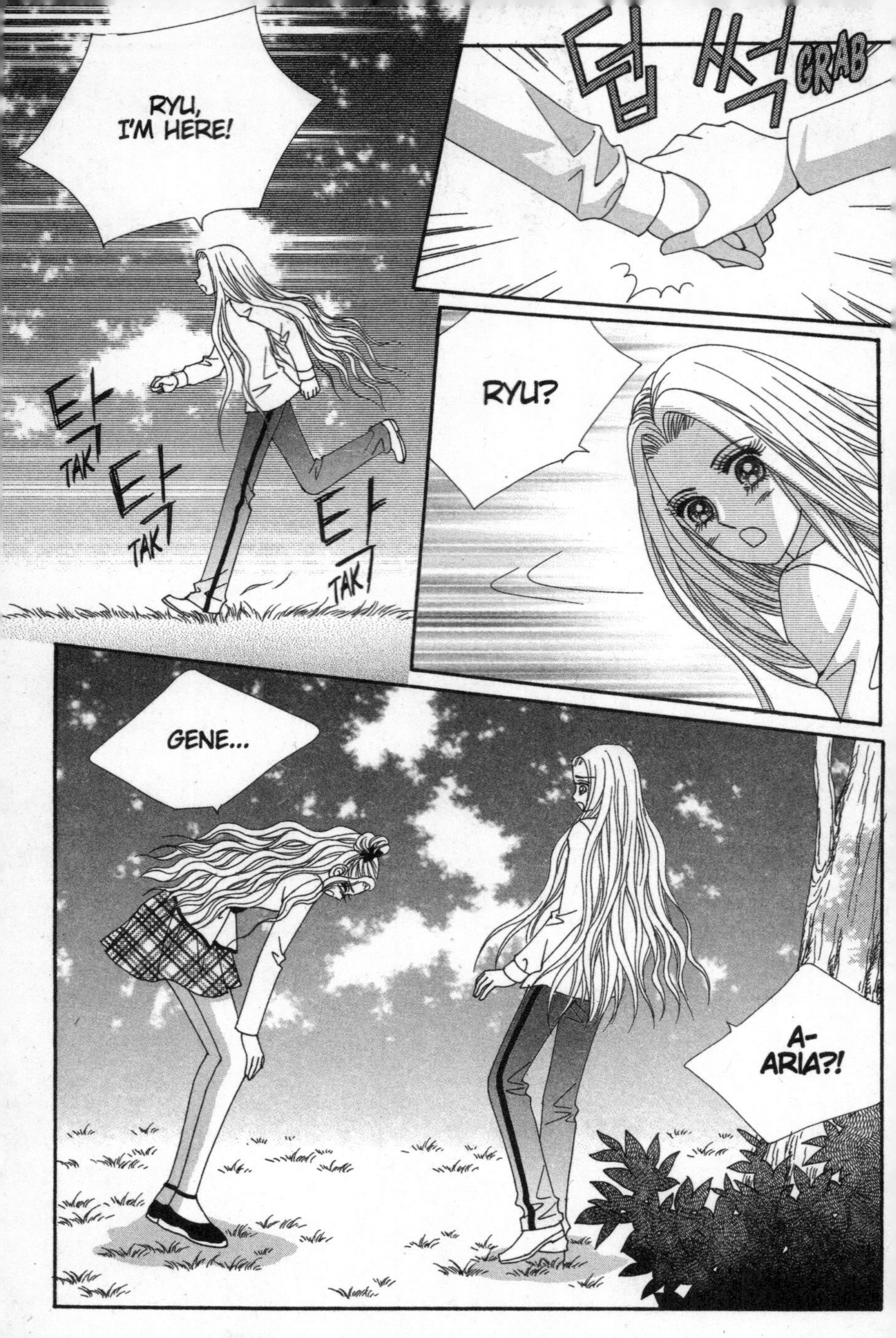
RYU, I'M HERE!
탁 TAK
탁 TAK
탁 TAK
덥석 GRAB
RYU?
GENE...
A- ARIA?!

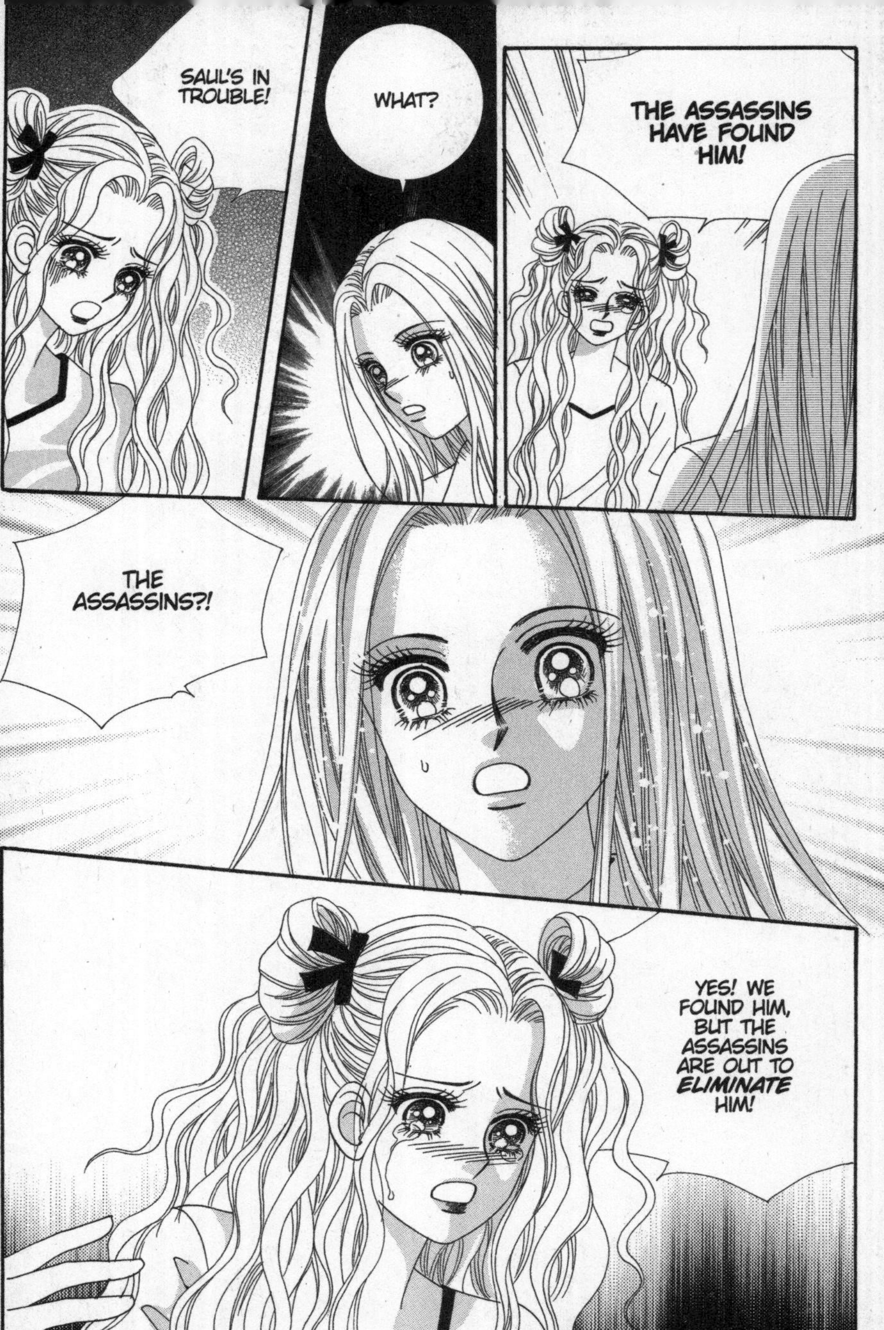
SAUL'S IN TROUBLE!
WHAT?
THE ASSASSINS HAVE FOUND HIM!
THE ASSASSINS?!
YES! WE FOUND HIM, BUT THE ASSASSINS ARE OUT TO *ELIMINATE* HIM!

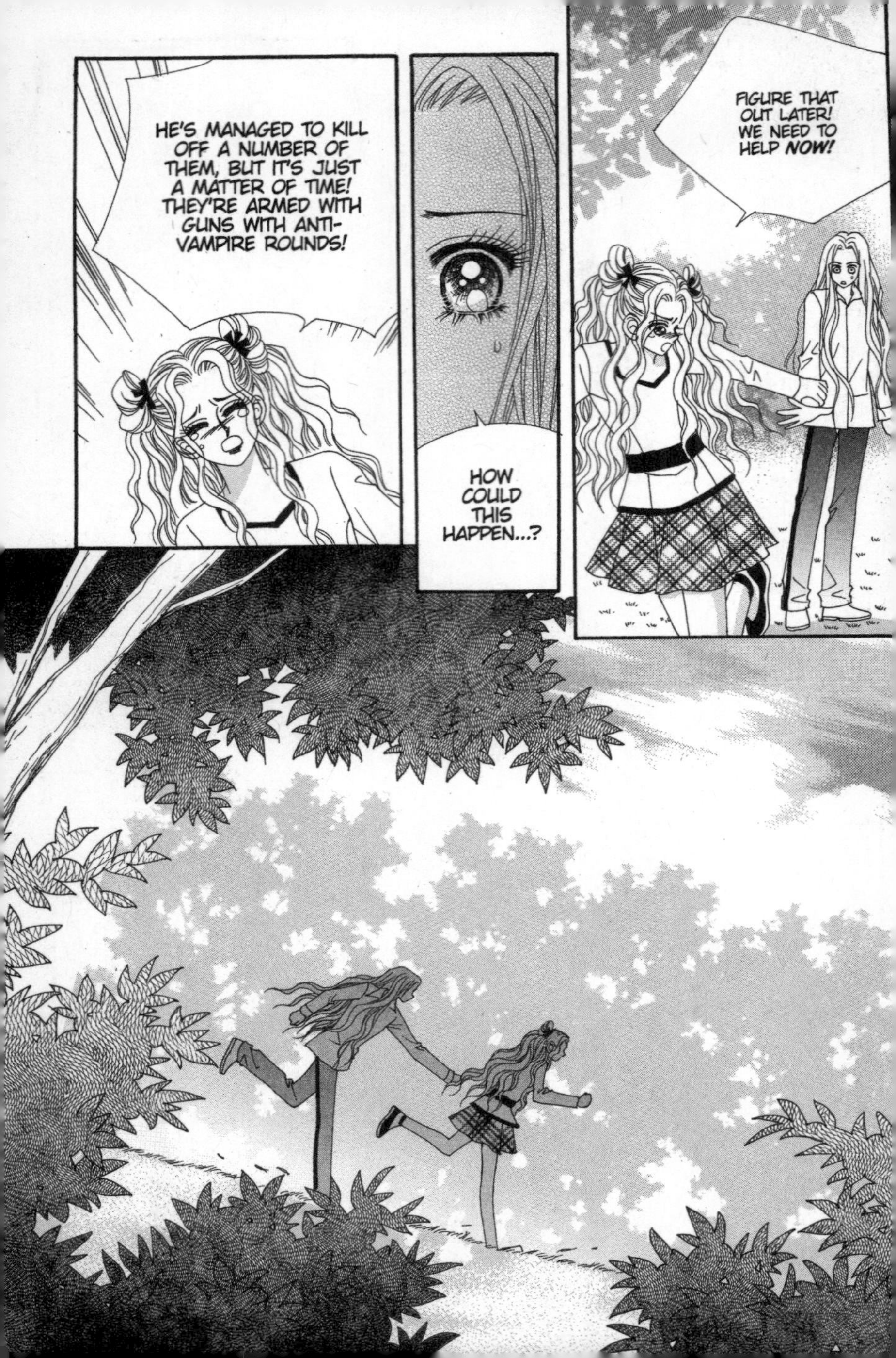
HE'S MANAGED TO KILL OFF A NUMBER OF THEM, BUT IT'S JUST A MATTER OF TIME! THEY'RE ARMED WITH GUNS WITH ANTI-VAMPIRE ROUNDS!
HOW COULD THIS HAPPEN...?
FIGURE THAT OUT LATER! WE NEED TO HELP NOW!

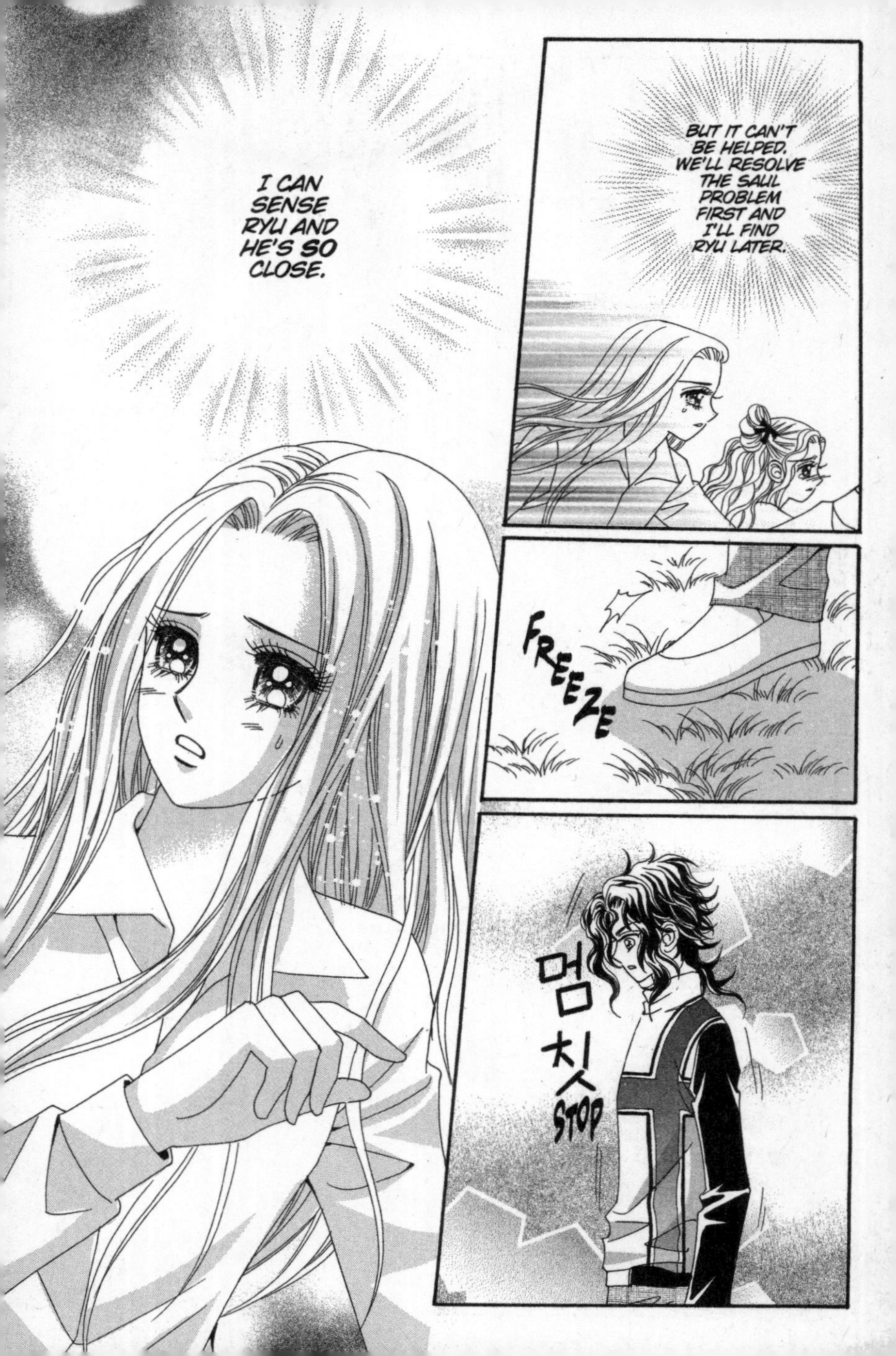
I CAN SENSE RYU AND HE'S SO CLOSE.
BUT IT CAN'T BE HELPED. WE'LL RESOLVE THE SAUL PROBLEM FIRST AND I'LL FIND RYU LATER.
FREEZE
멈칫
STOP

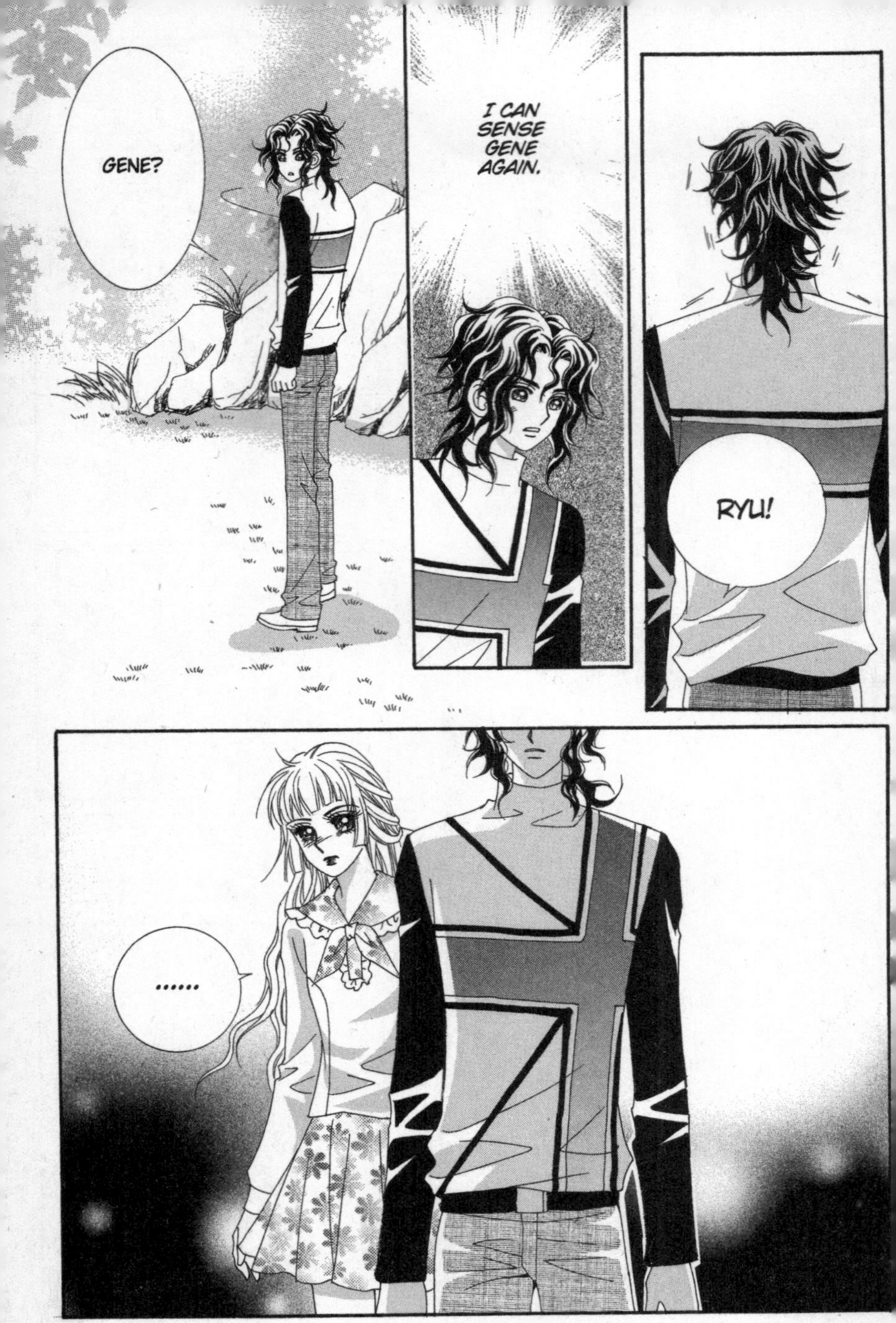

GENE?
I CAN SENSE GENE AGAIN.
RYU!
......

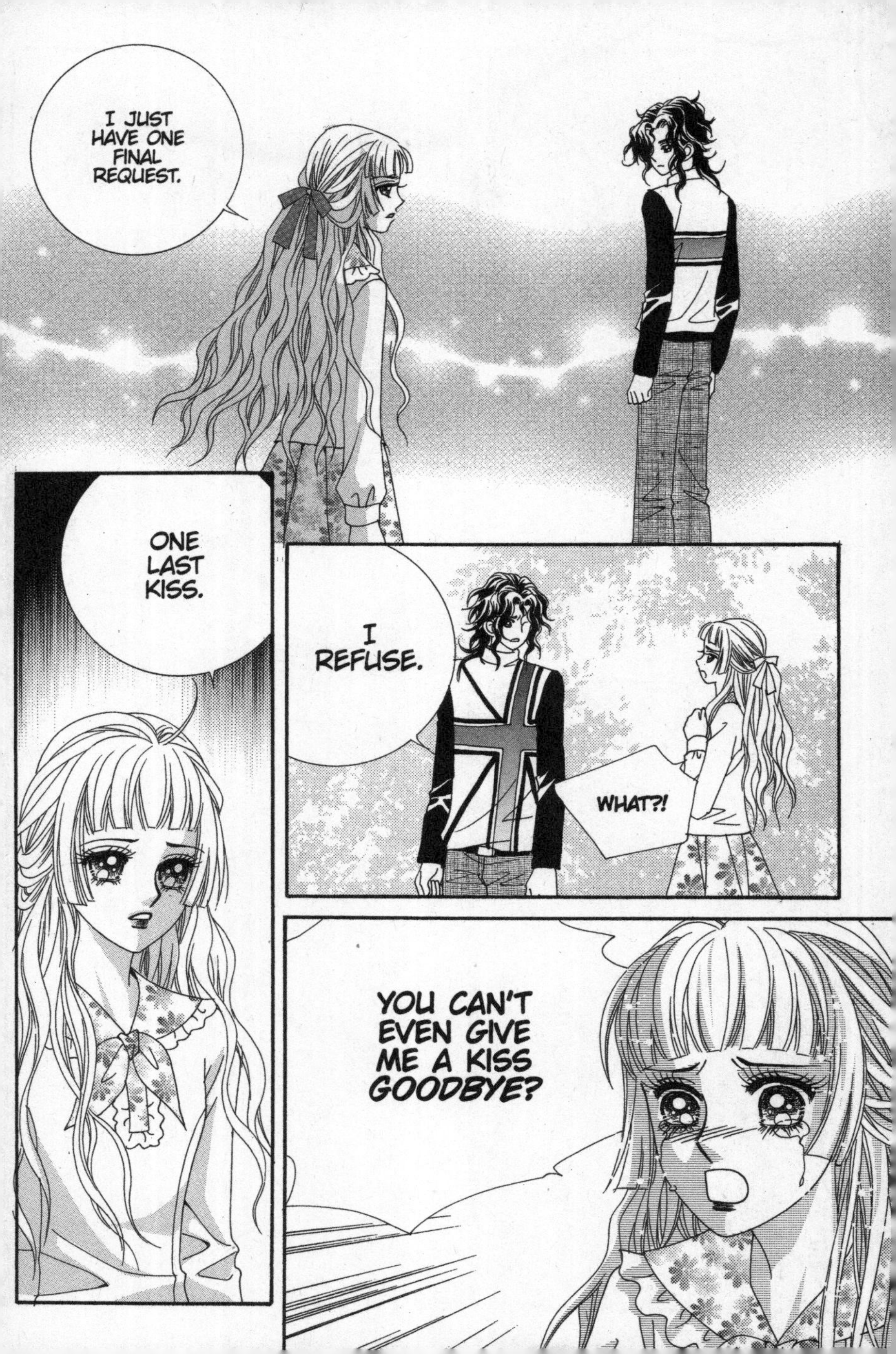
I JUST HAVE ONE FINAL REQUEST.
ONE LAST KISS.
I REFUSE.
WHAT?!
YOU CAN'T EVEN GIVE ME A KISS GOODBYE?

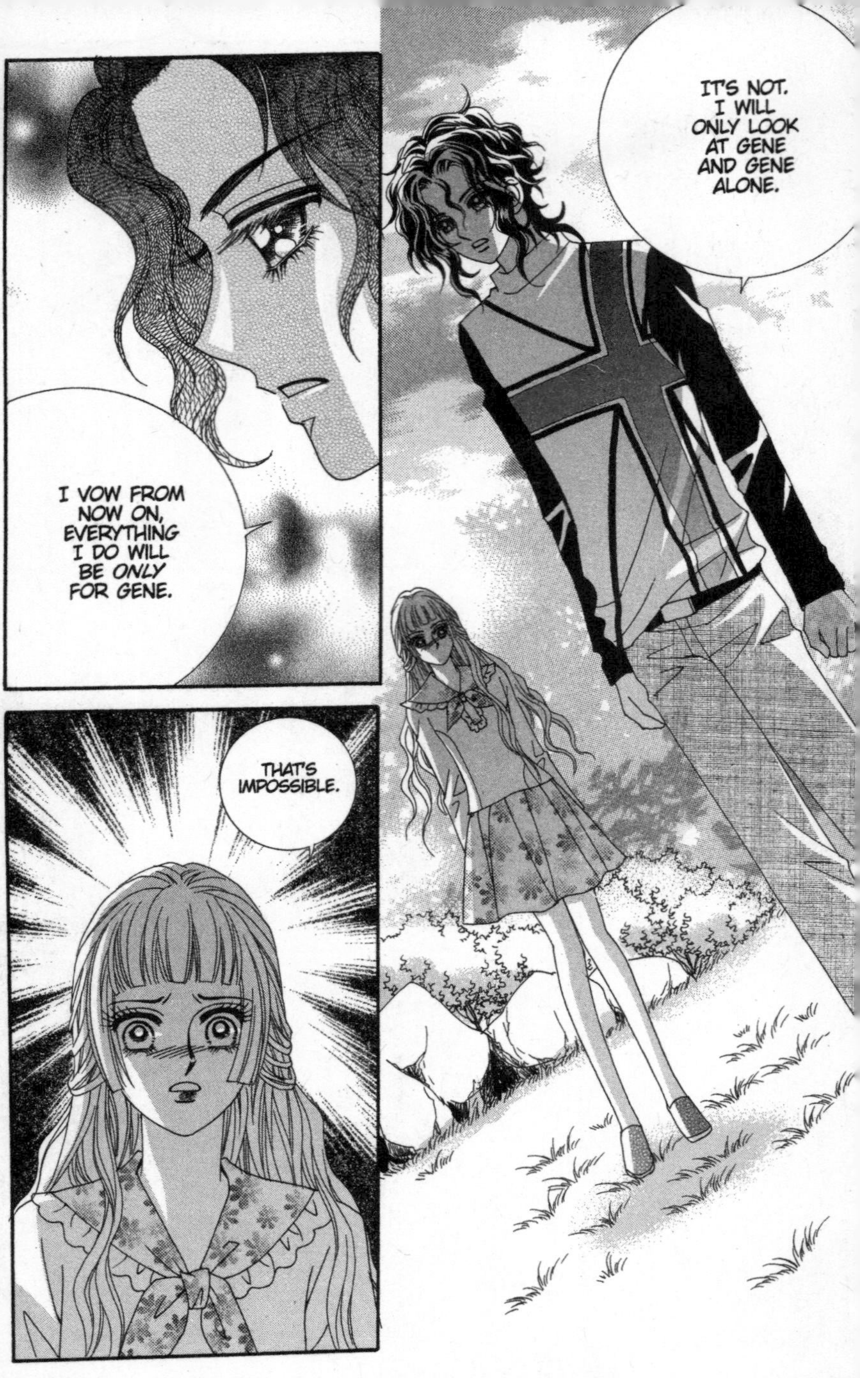
I VOW FROM NOW ON, EVERYTHING I DO WILL BE *ONLY* FOR GENE.
THAT'S IMPOSSIBLE.
IT'S NOT. I WILL ONLY LOOK AT GENE AND GENE ALONE.

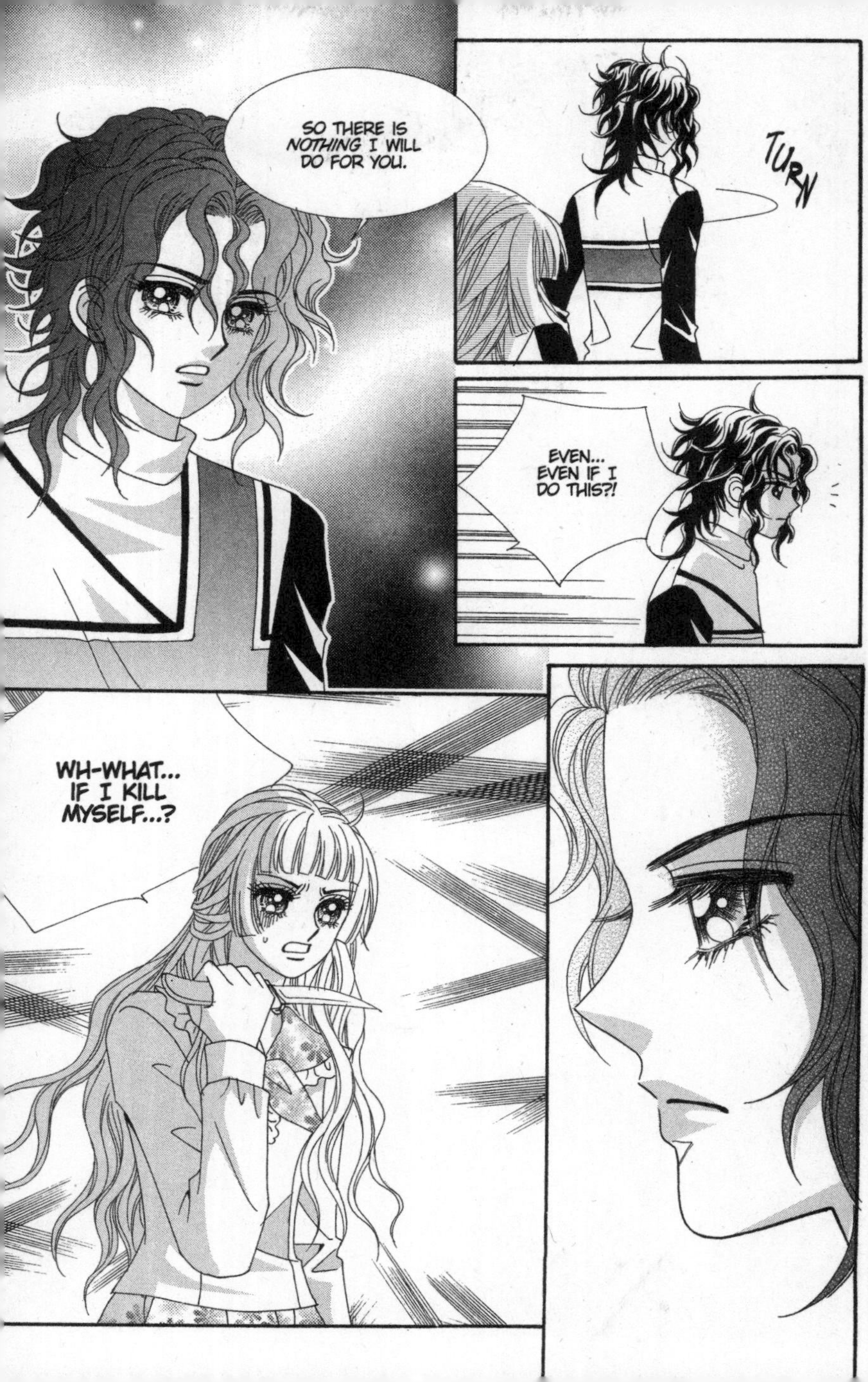
SO THERE IS *NOTHING* I WILL DO FOR YOU.
TURN
EVEN... EVEN IF I DO THIS?!
WH-WHAT... IF I KILL MYSELF...?

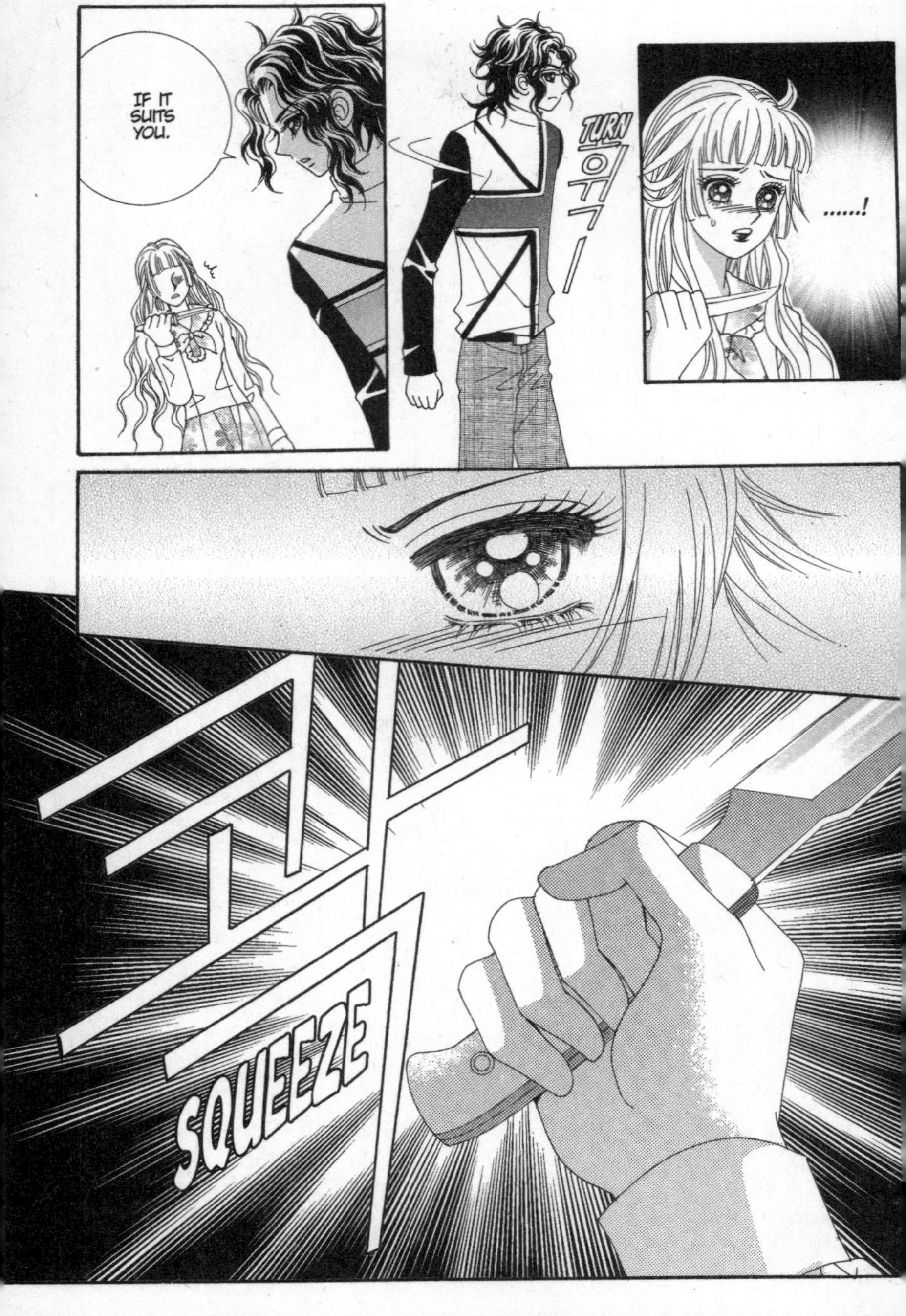
IF IT SUITS YOU.
TURN
......!
SQUEEZE

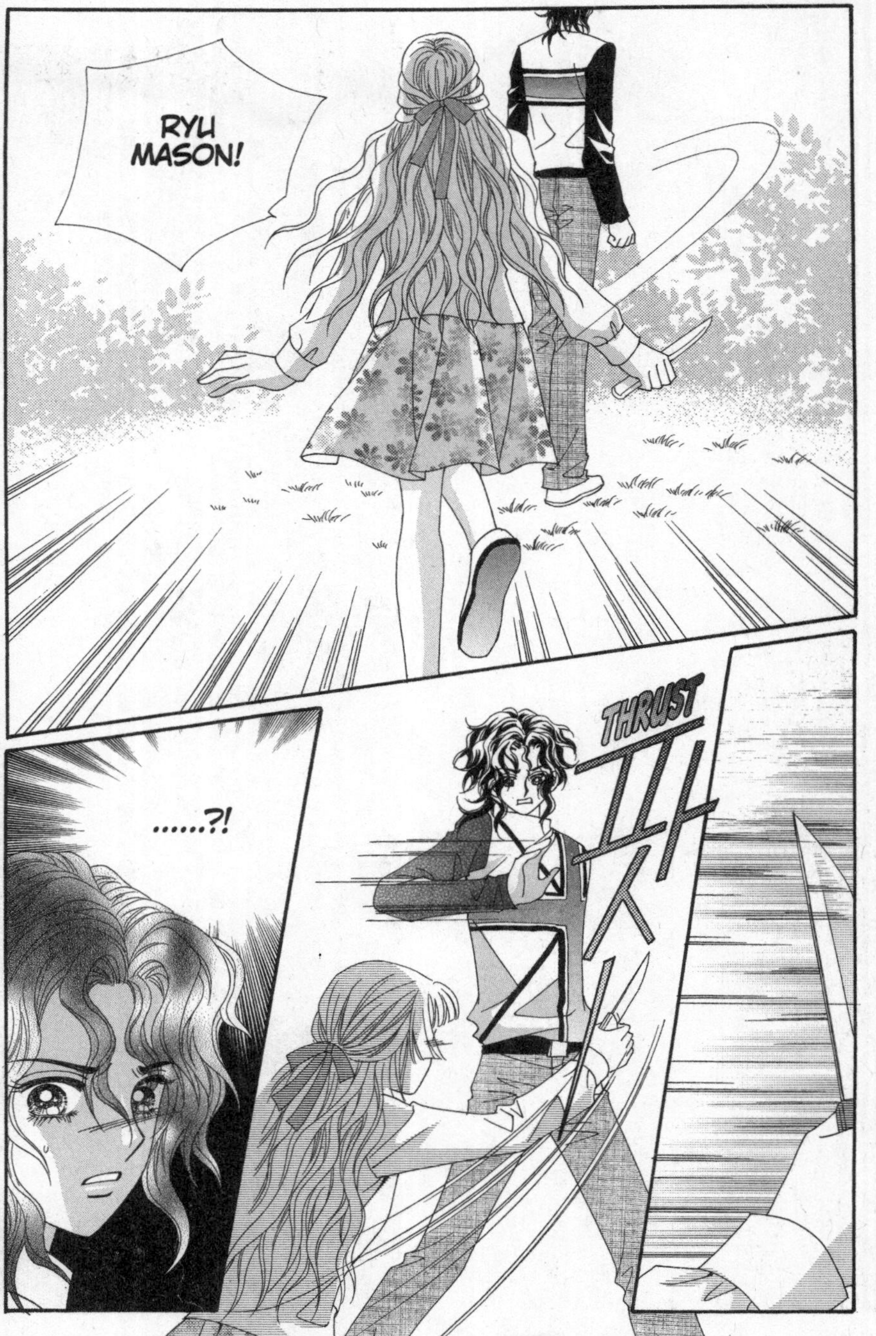
RYU MASON!
......?!
THRUST

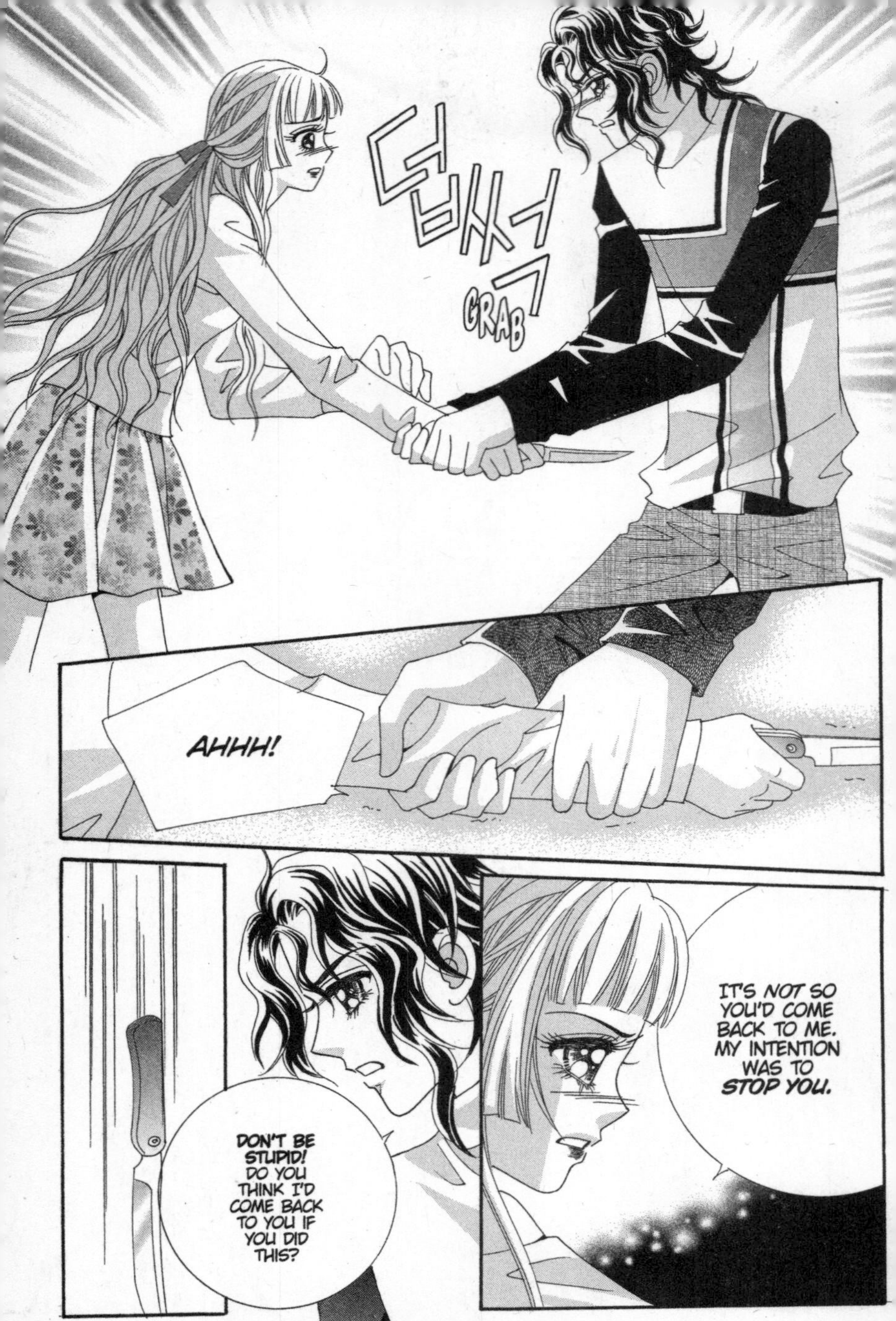
GRAB
AHHH!
DON'T BE STUPID! DO YOU THINK I'D COME BACK TO YOU IF YOU DID THIS?
IT'S *NOT* SO YOU'D COME BACK TO ME. MY INTENTION WAS TO **STOP YOU.**

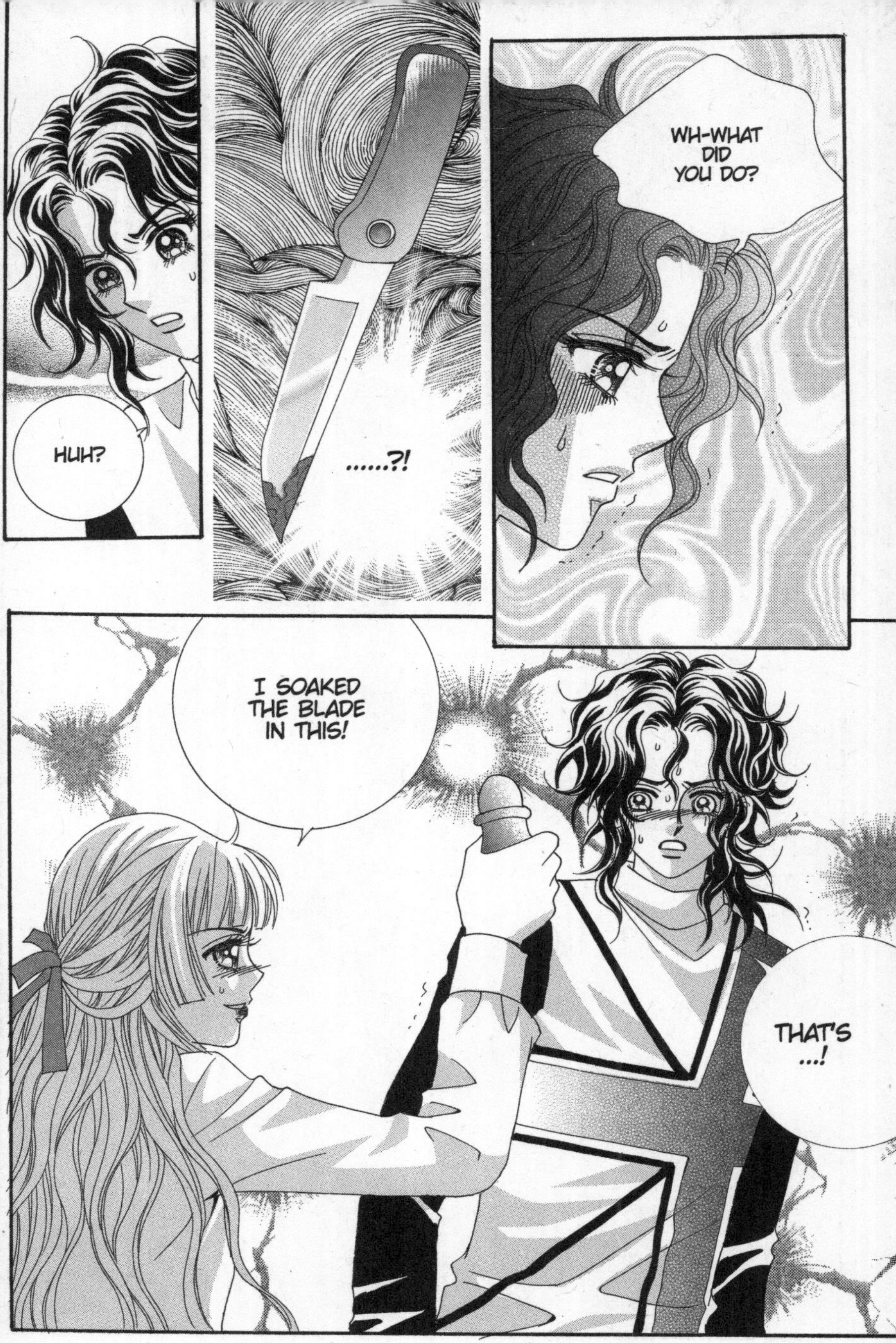
HUH?
......?!
WH-WHAT DID YOU DO?
I SOAKED THE BLADE IN THIS!
THAT'S ...!

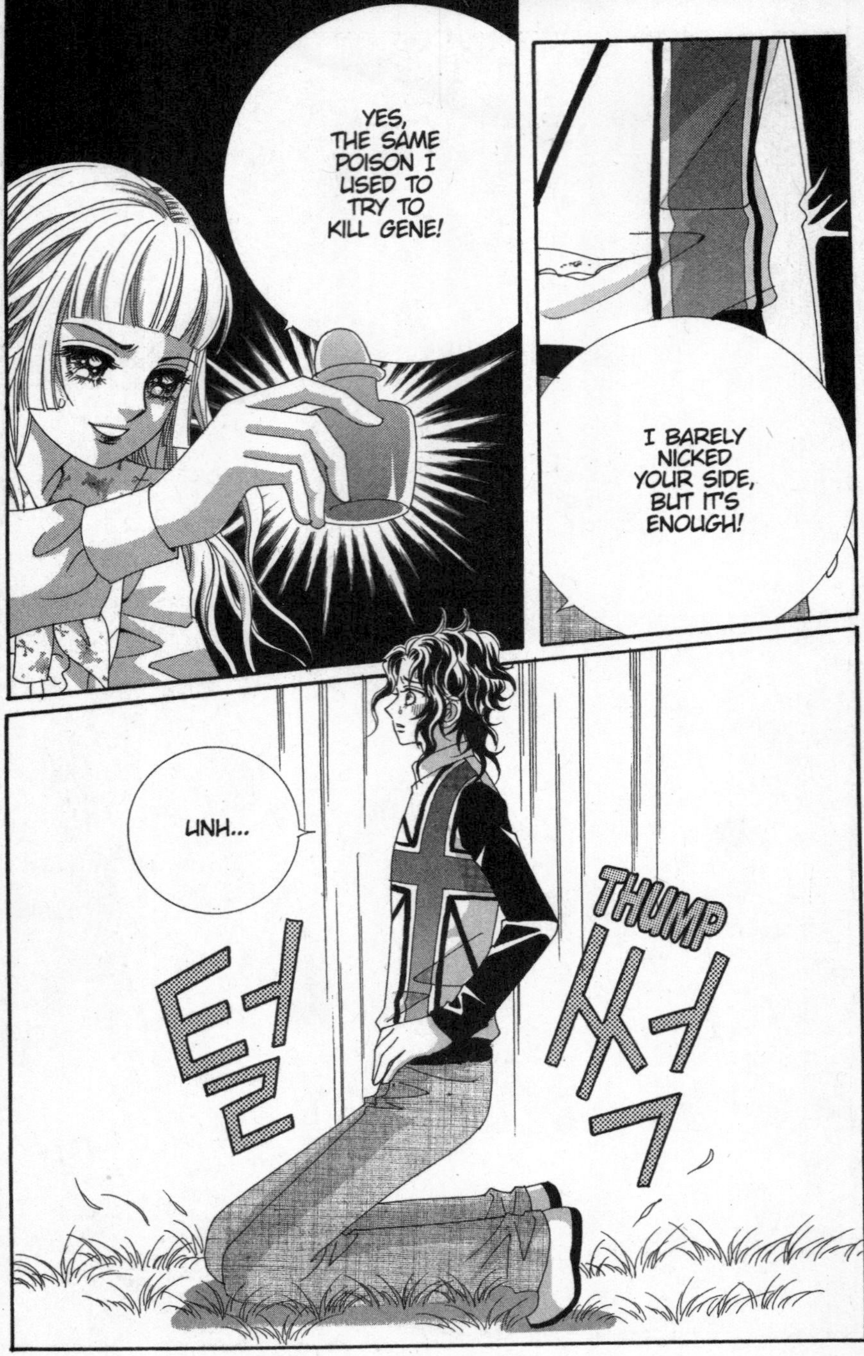
YES, THE SAME POISON I USED TO TRY TO KILL GENE!
I BARELY NICKED YOUR SIDE, BUT IT'S ENOUGH!
UNH...
THUMP
털썩

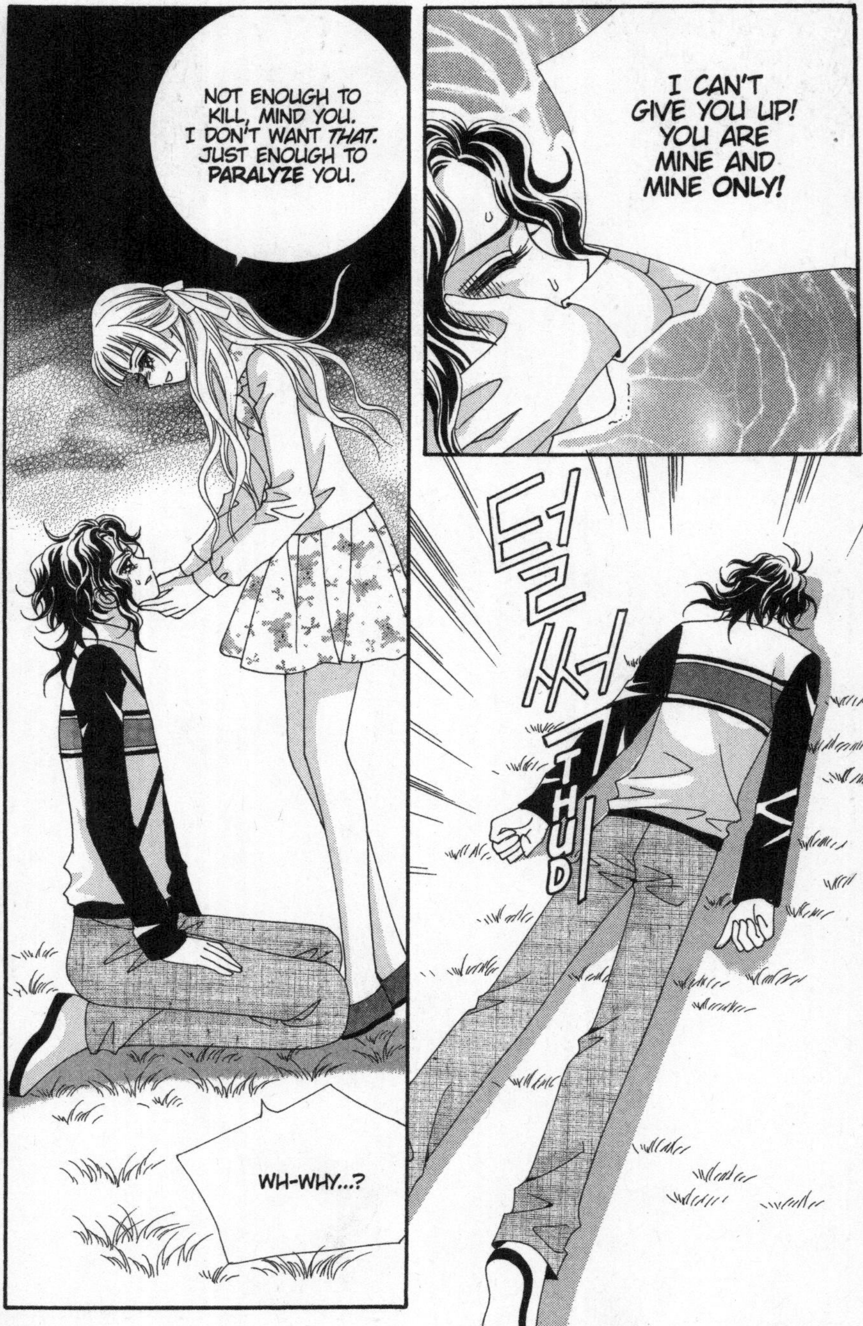
NOT ENOUGH TO KILL, MIND YOU. I DON'T WANT *THAT.* JUST ENOUGH TO PARALYZE YOU.
WH-WHY...?
I CAN'T GIVE YOU UP! YOU ARE MINE AND MINE ONLY!
털썩
THUD

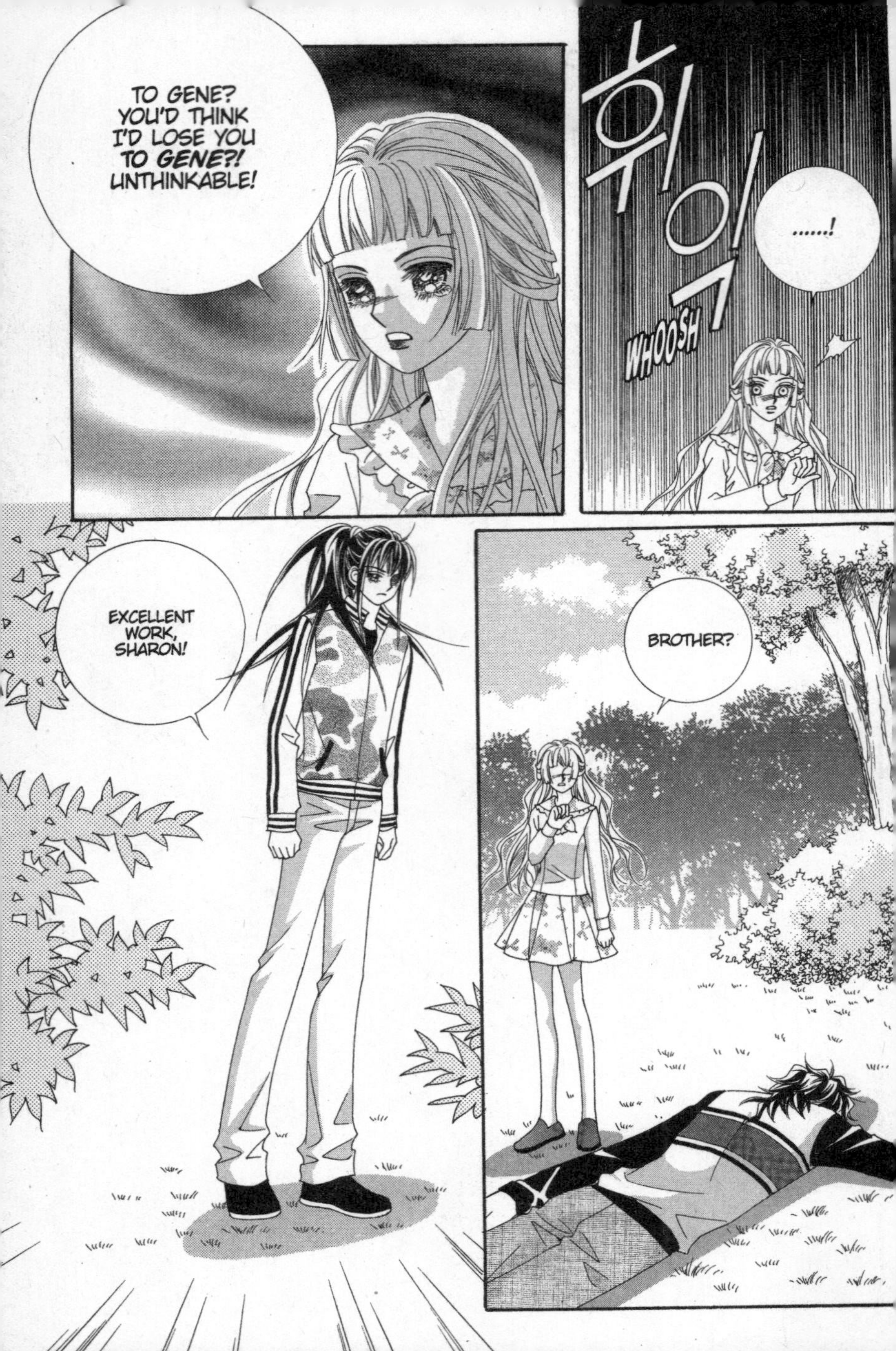
TO GENE? YOU'D THINK I'D LOSE YOU TO *GENE?!* UNTHINKABLE!
WHOOSH
......!
EXCELLENT WORK, SHARON!
BROTHER?

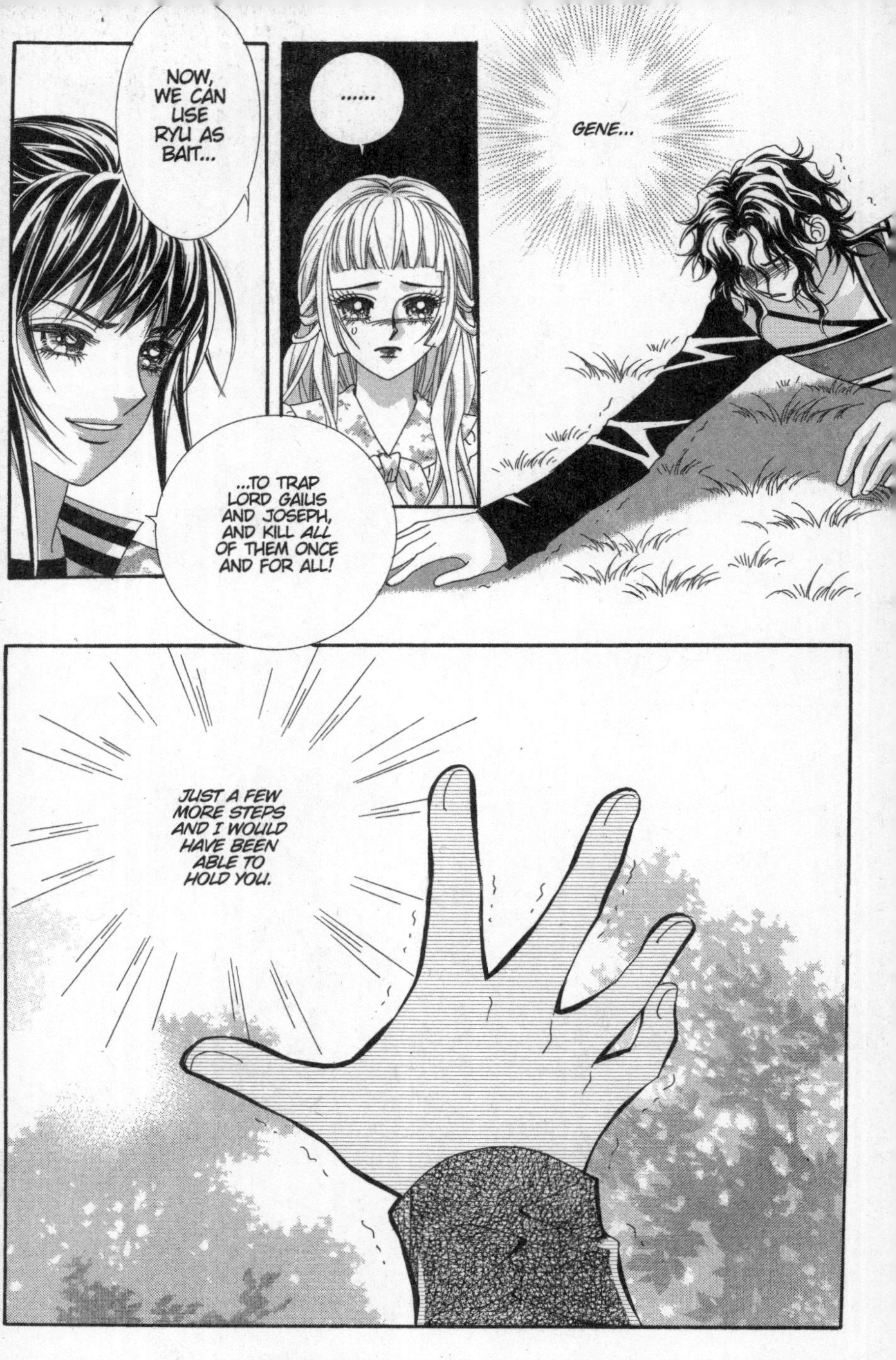
NOW, WE CAN USE RYU AS BAIT...
......
GENE...
...TO TRAP LORD GAIUS AND JOSEPH, AND KILL ALL OF THEM ONCE AND FOR ALL!
JUST A FEW MORE STEPS AND I WOULD HAVE BEEN ABLE TO HOLD YOU.

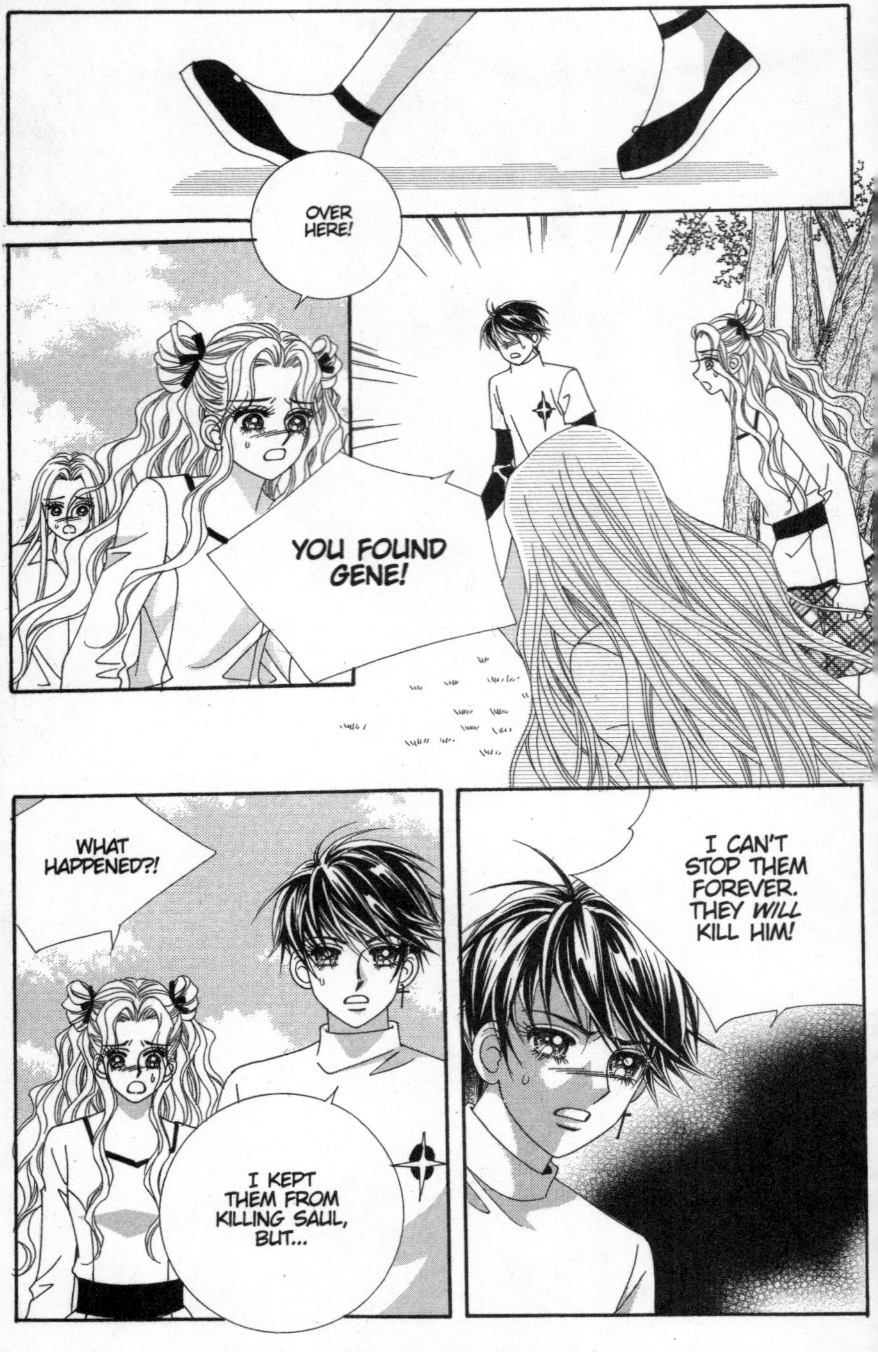
OVER HERE!
YOU FOUND GENE!
WHAT HAPPENED?!
I KEPT THEM FROM KILLING SAUL, BUT...
I CAN'T STOP THEM FOREVER. THEY WILL KILL HIM!

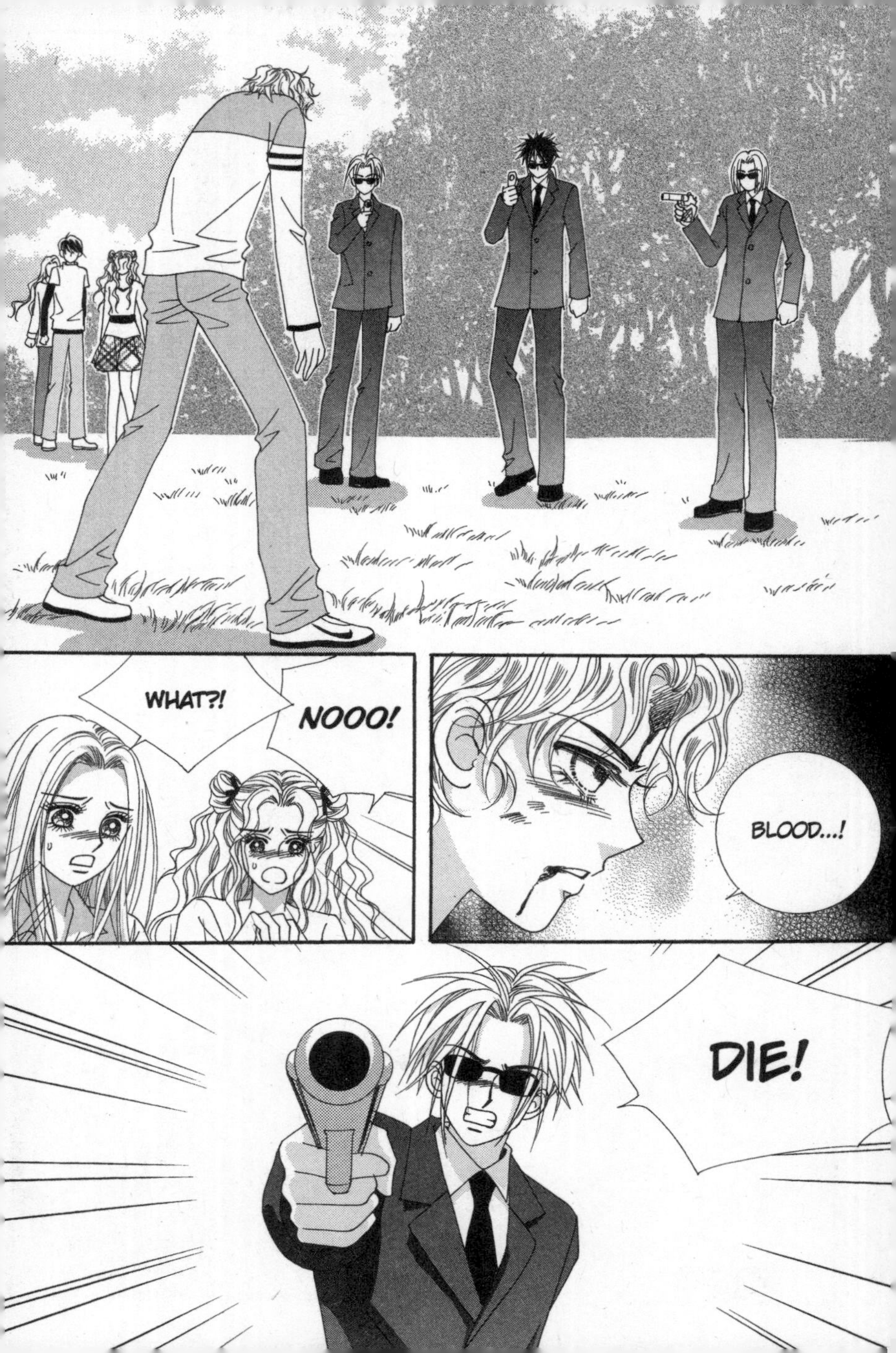

WHAT?!
NOOO!
BLOOD...!
DIE!

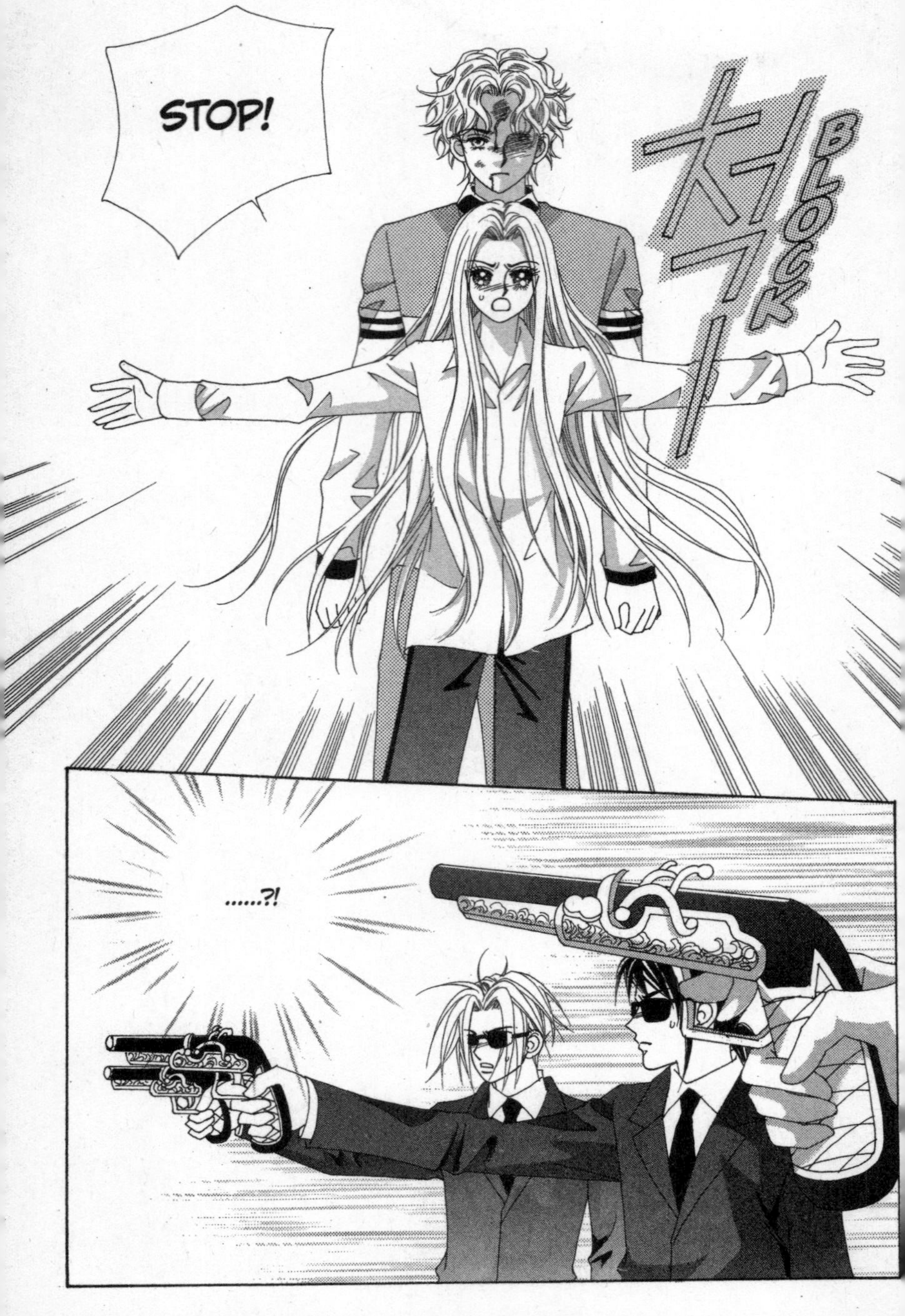
STOP!
BLOCK
......?!

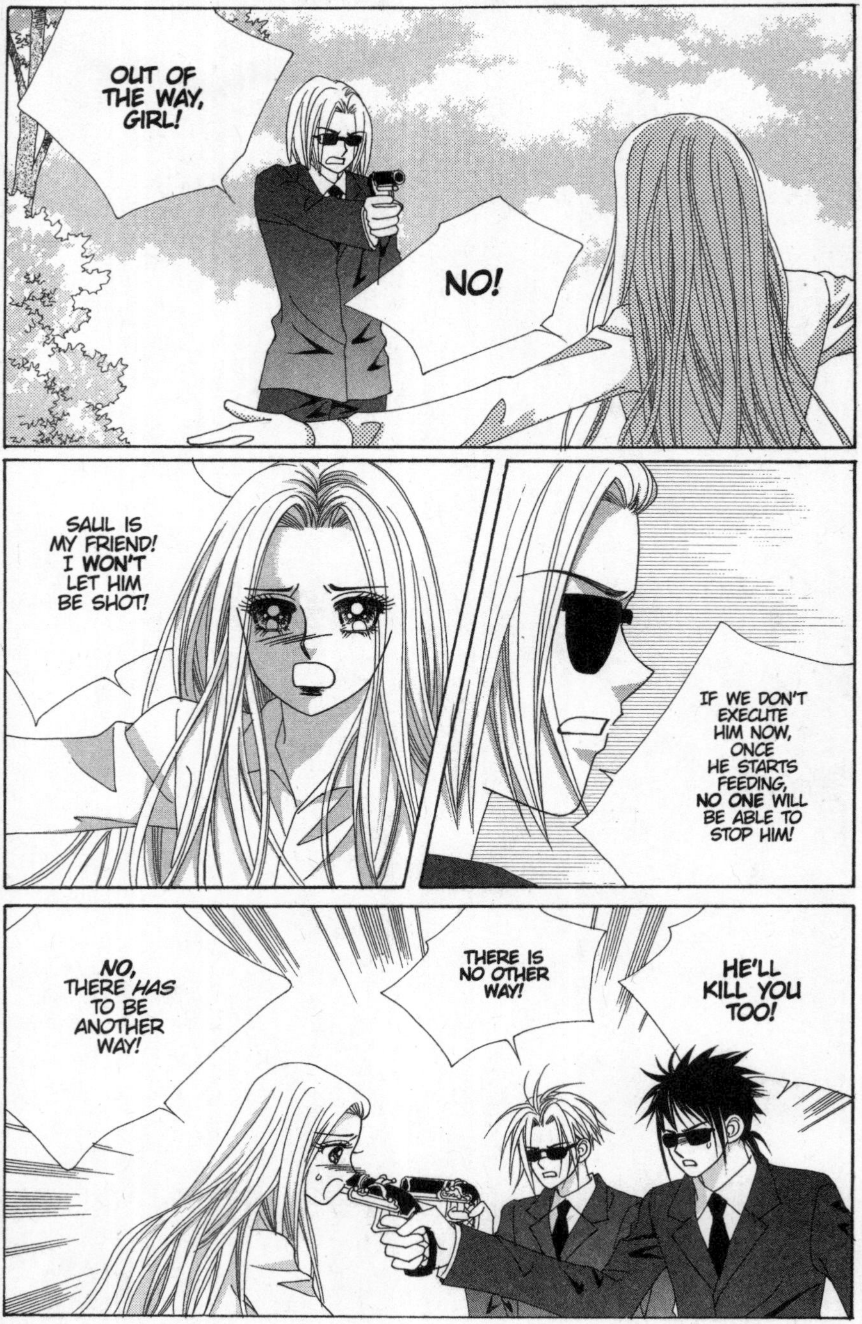
OUT OF THE WAY, GIRL!
NO!
SAUL IS MY FRIEND! I WON'T LET HIM BE SHOT!
IF WE DON'T EXECUTE HIM NOW, ONCE HE STARTS FEEDING, NO ONE WILL BE ABLE TO STOP HIM!
NO, THERE *HAS* TO BE ANOTHER WAY!
THERE IS NO OTHER WAY!
HE'LL KILL YOU TOO!

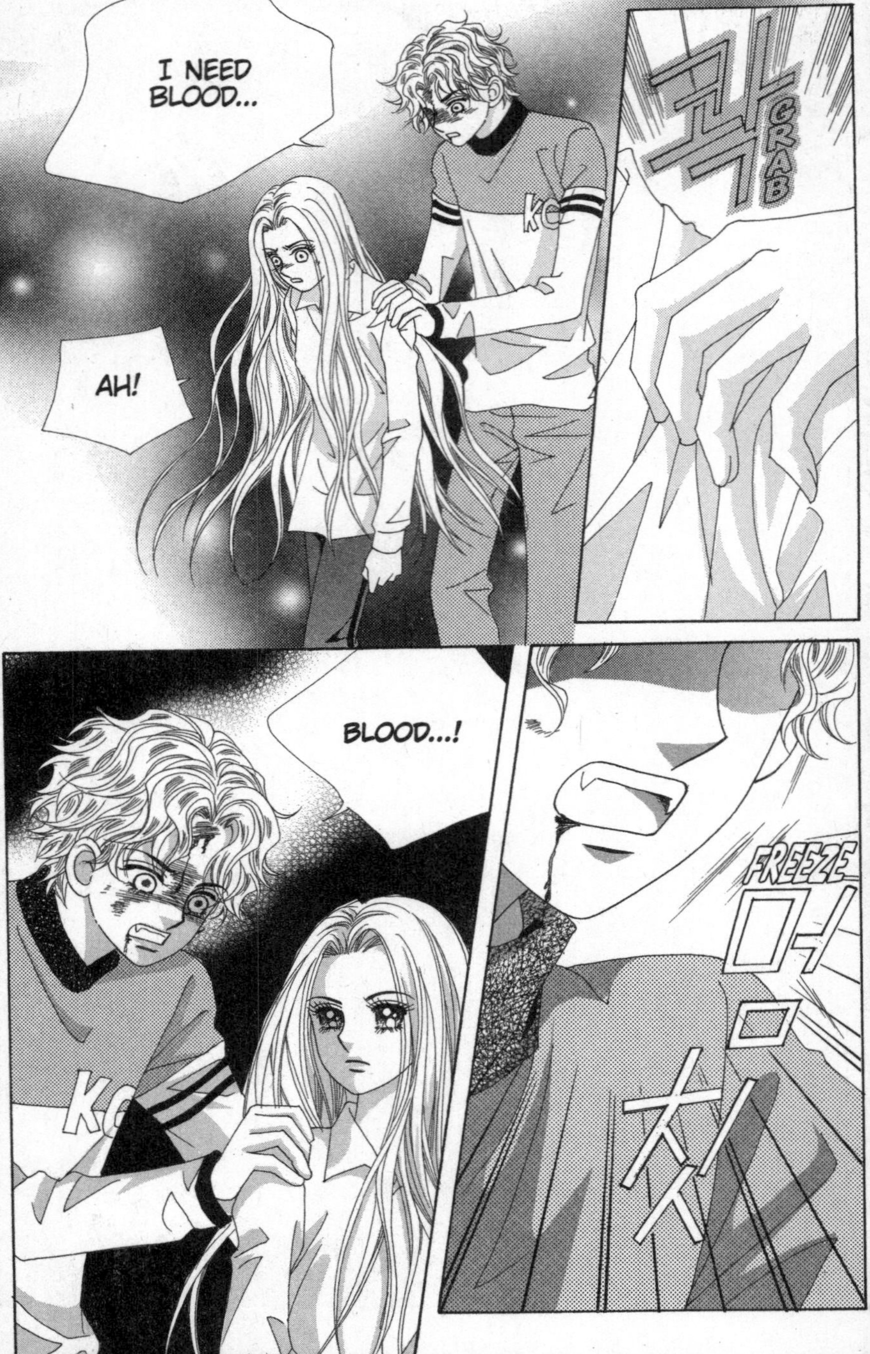
I NEED BLOOD...
AH!
GRAB
BLOOD...!
FREEZE
멈칫

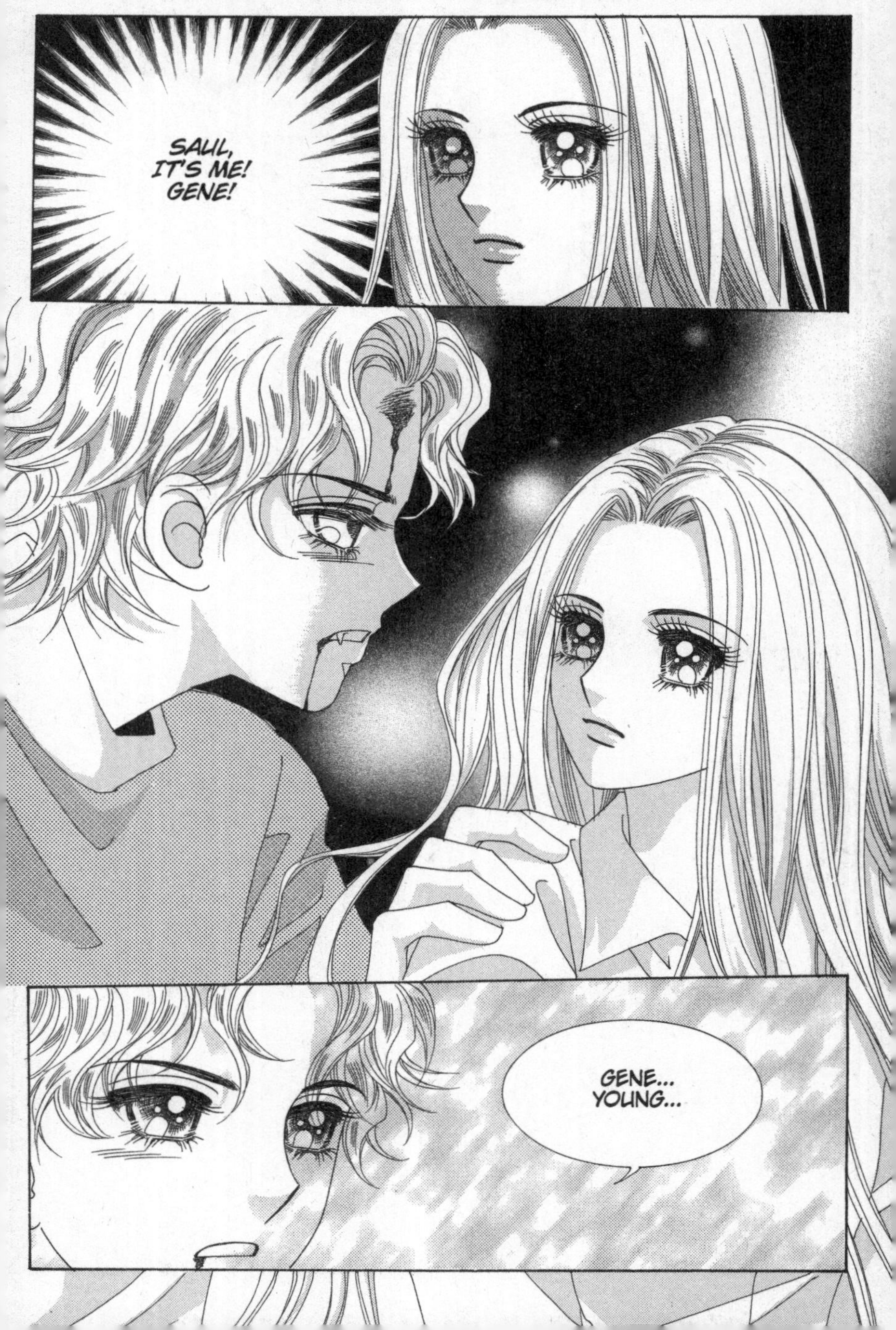
SAUL, IT'S ME! GENE!
GENE... YOUNG...

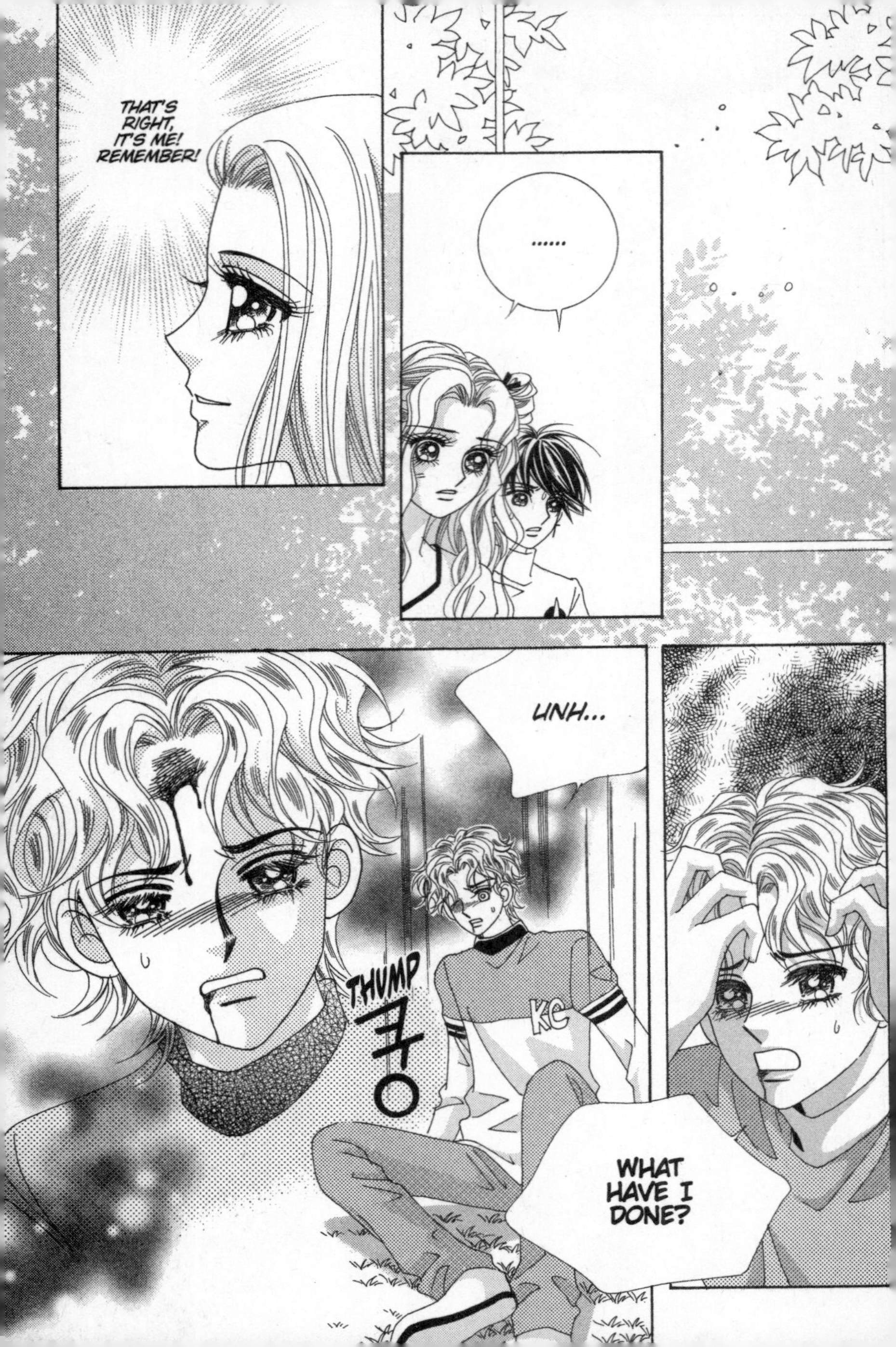
THAT'S RIGHT, IT'S ME! REMEMBER!
......
THUMP
쿵
UNH...
WHAT HAVE I DONE?

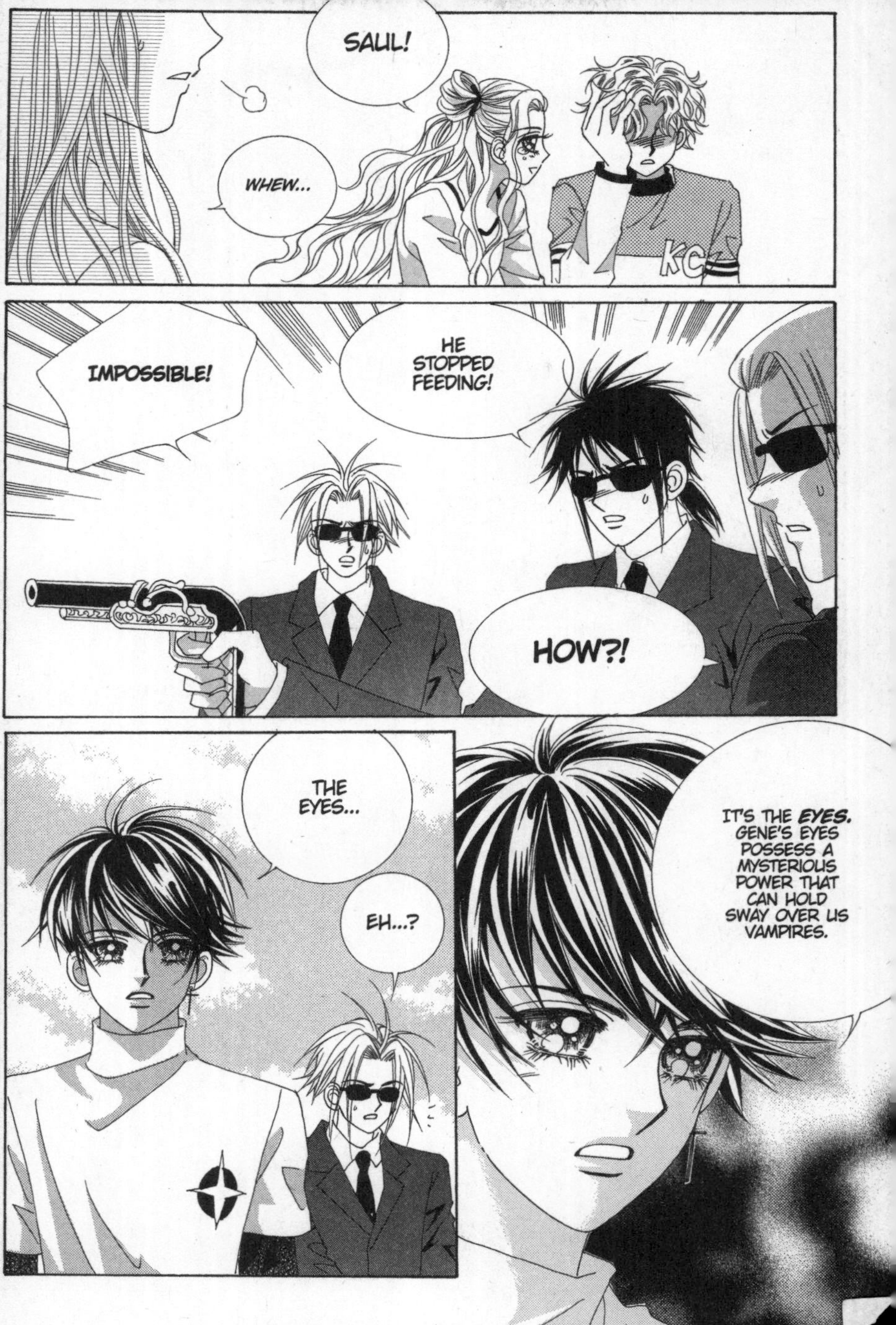
SAUL!
WHEW...
IMPOSSIBLE!
HE STOPPED FEEDING!
HOW?!
THE EYES...
EH...?
IT'S THE ***EYES.*** GENE'S EYES POSSESS A MYSTERIOUS POWER THAT CAN HOLD SWAY OVER US VAMPIRES.

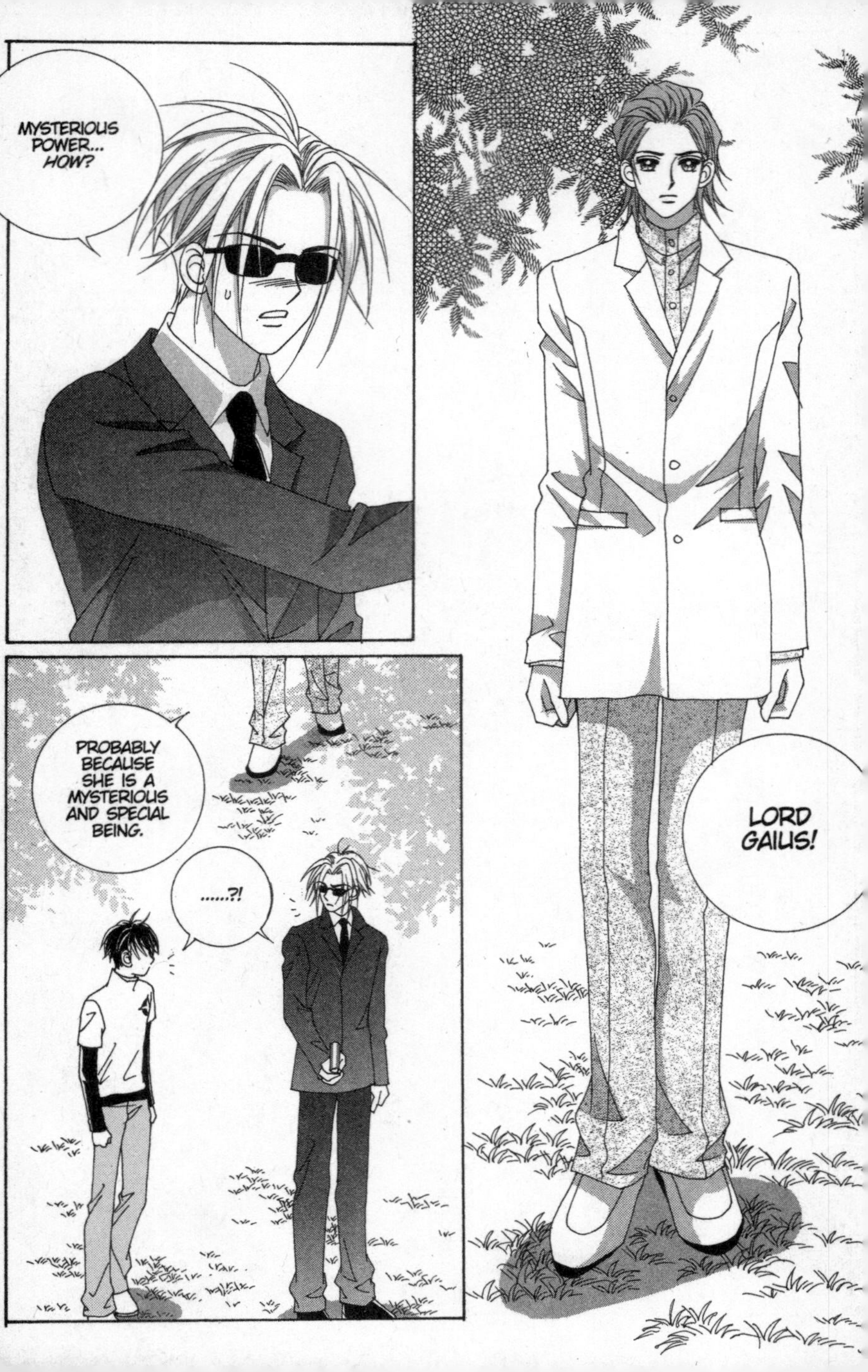
MYSTERIOUS POWER... HOW?
PROBABLY BECAUSE SHE IS A MYSTERIOUS AND SPECIAL BEING.
......?!
LORD GAIUS!

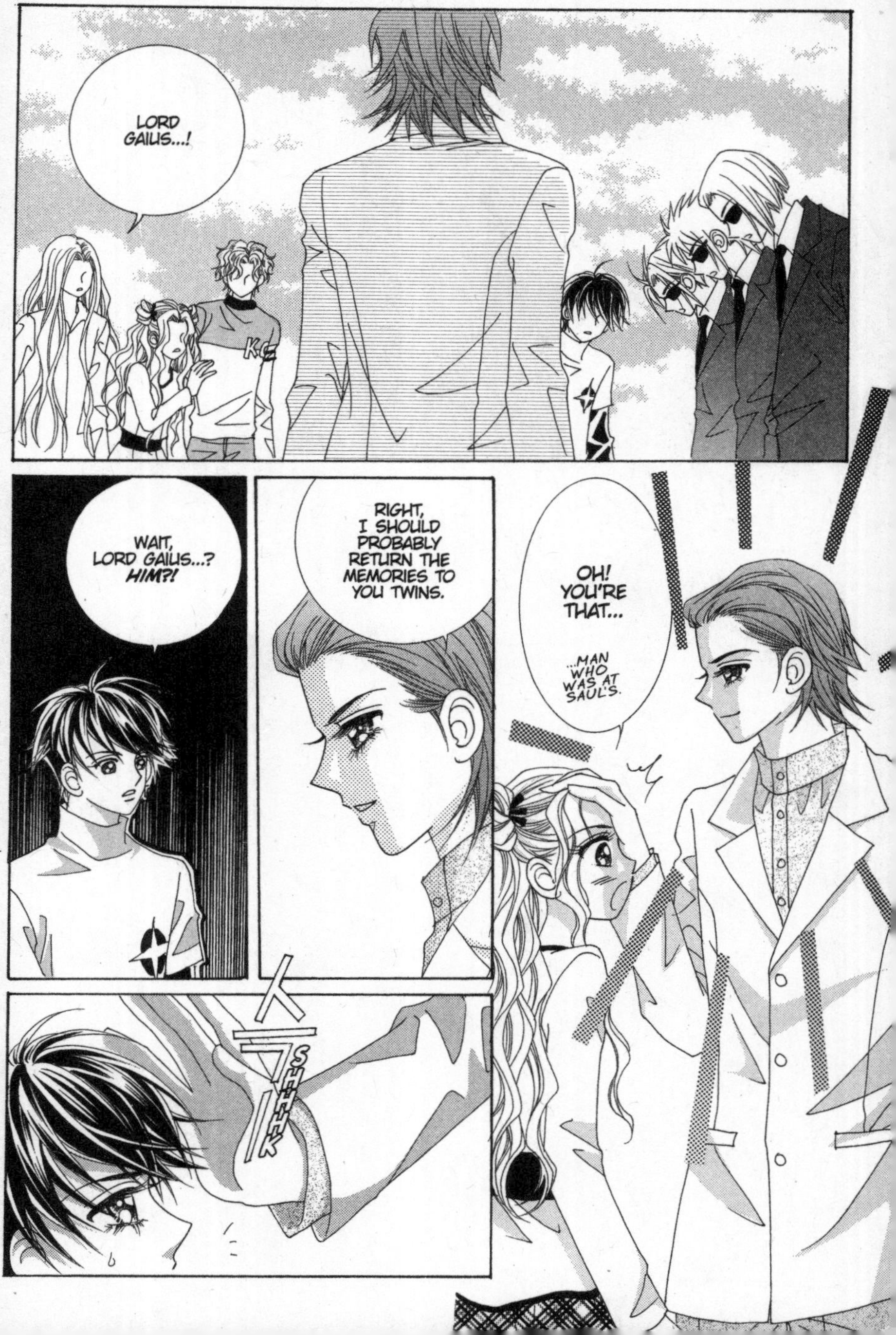
LORD GAIUS...!
WAIT, LORD GAIUS...? HIM?!
RIGHT, I SHOULD PROBABLY RETURN THE MEMORIES TO YOU TWINS.
OH! YOU'RE THAT...
...MAN WHO WAS AT SAUL'S.
SHHHHK

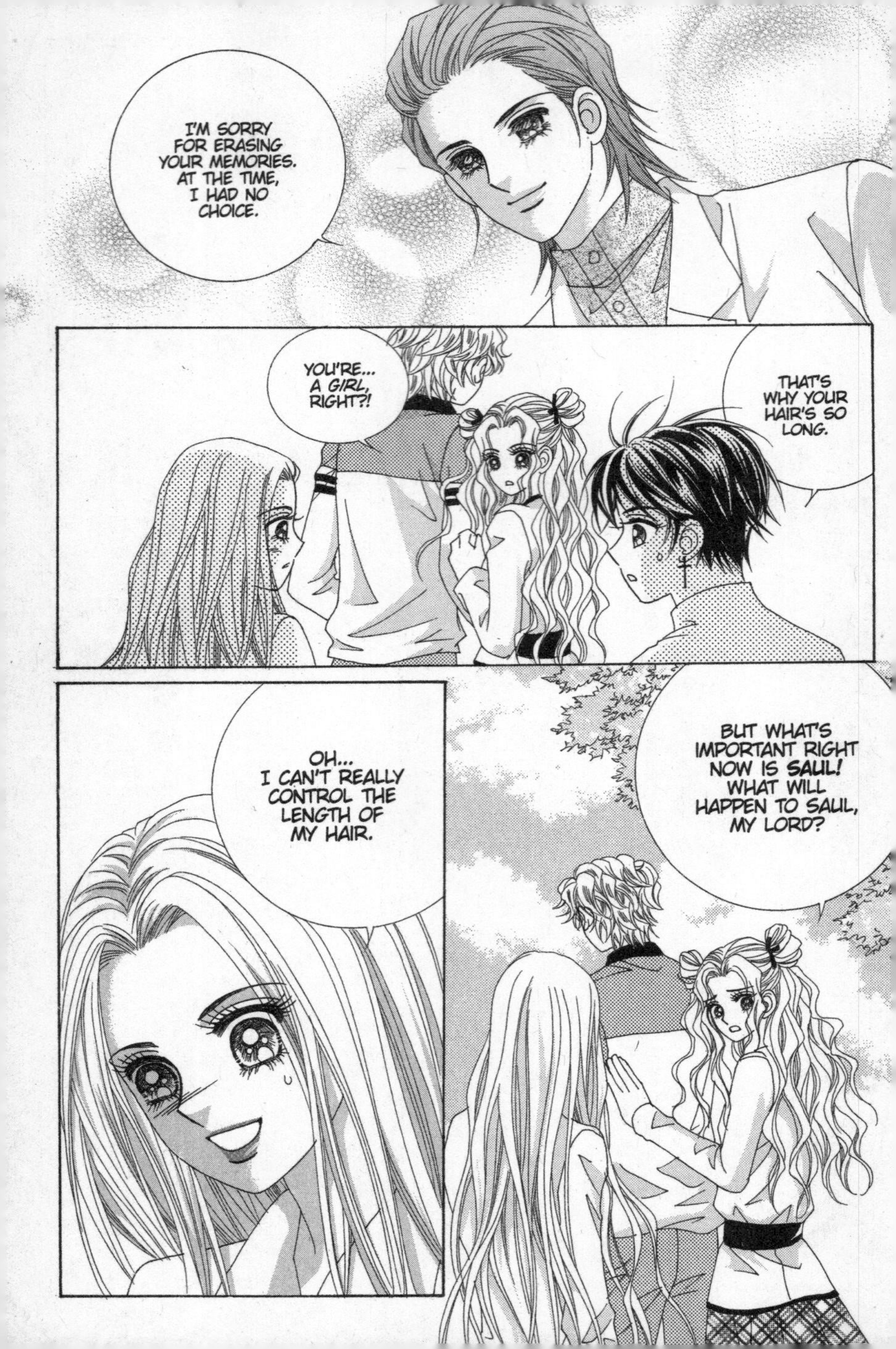
I'M SORRY FOR ERASING YOUR MEMORIES. AT THE TIME, I HAD NO CHOICE.
YOU'RE... A GIRL, RIGHT?!
THAT'S WHY YOUR HAIR'S SO LONG.
OH... I CAN'T REALLY CONTROL THE LENGTH OF MY HAIR.
BUT WHAT'S IMPORTANT RIGHT NOW IS SAUL! WHAT WILL HAPPEN TO SAUL, MY LORD?

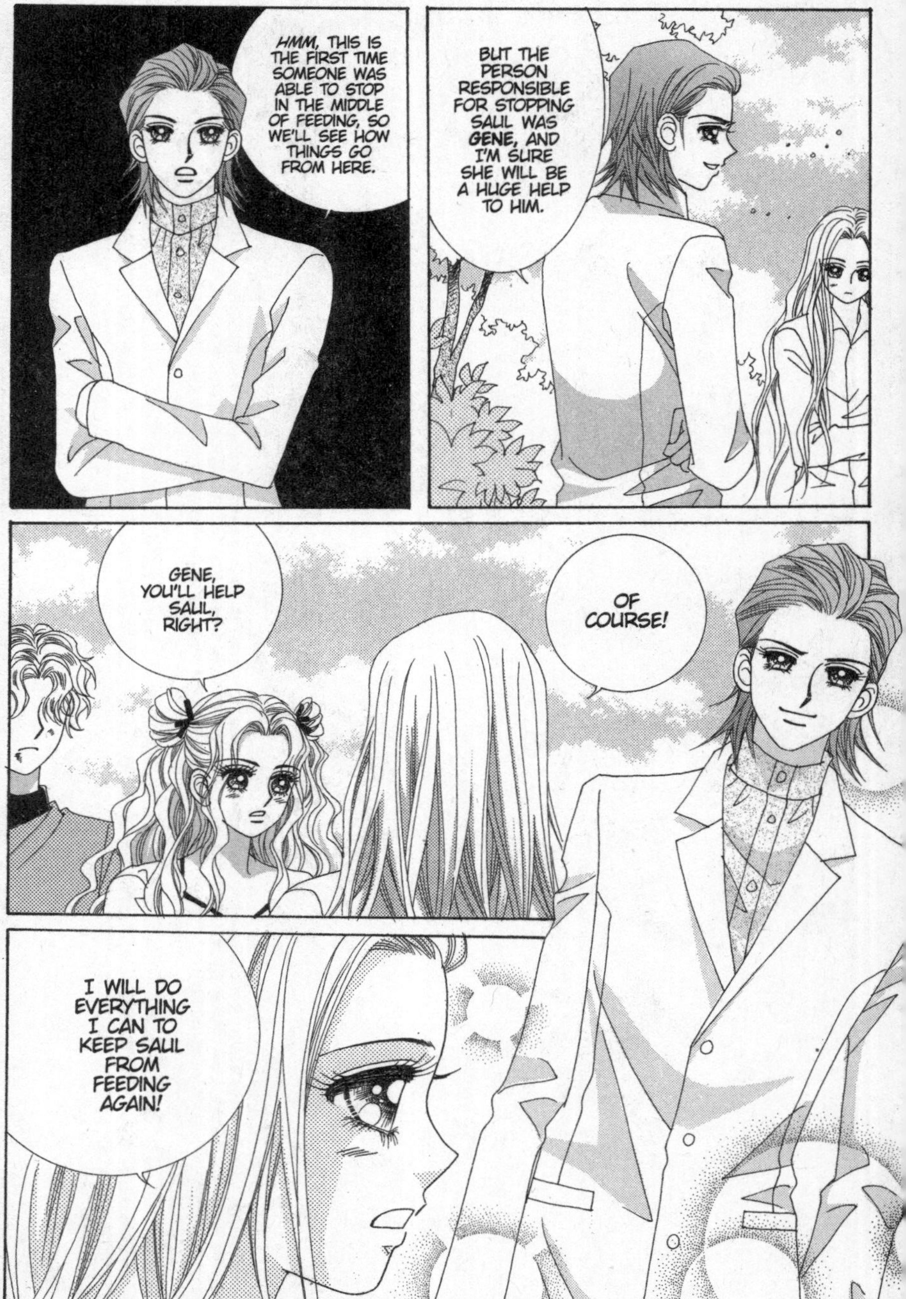
HMM, THIS IS THE FIRST TIME SOMEONE WAS ABLE TO STOP IN THE MIDDLE OF FEEDING, SO WE'LL SEE HOW THINGS GO FROM HERE.
BUT THE PERSON RESPONSIBLE FOR STOPPING SAUL WAS GENE, AND I'M SURE SHE WILL BE A HUGE HELP TO HIM.
GENE, YOU'LL HELP SAUL, RIGHT?
OF COURSE!
I WILL DO EVERYTHING I CAN TO KEEP SAUL FROM FEEDING AGAIN!

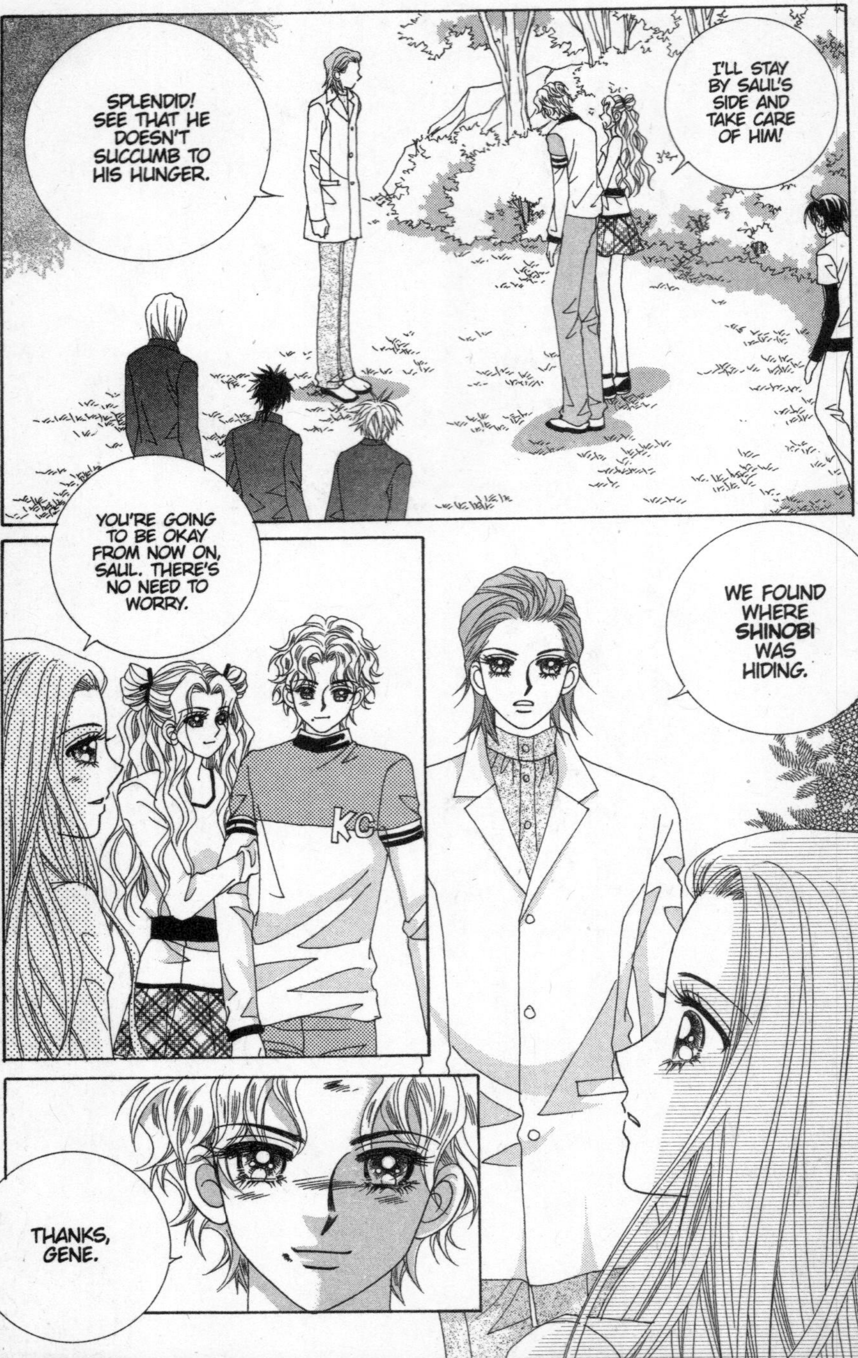
SPLENDID! SEE THAT HE DOESN'T SUCCUMB TO HIS HUNGER.
I'LL STAY BY SAUL'S SIDE AND TAKE CARE OF HIM!
YOU'RE GOING TO BE OKAY FROM NOW ON, SAUL. THERE'S NO NEED TO WORRY.
THANKS, GENE.
WE FOUND WHERE SHINOBI WAS HIDING.

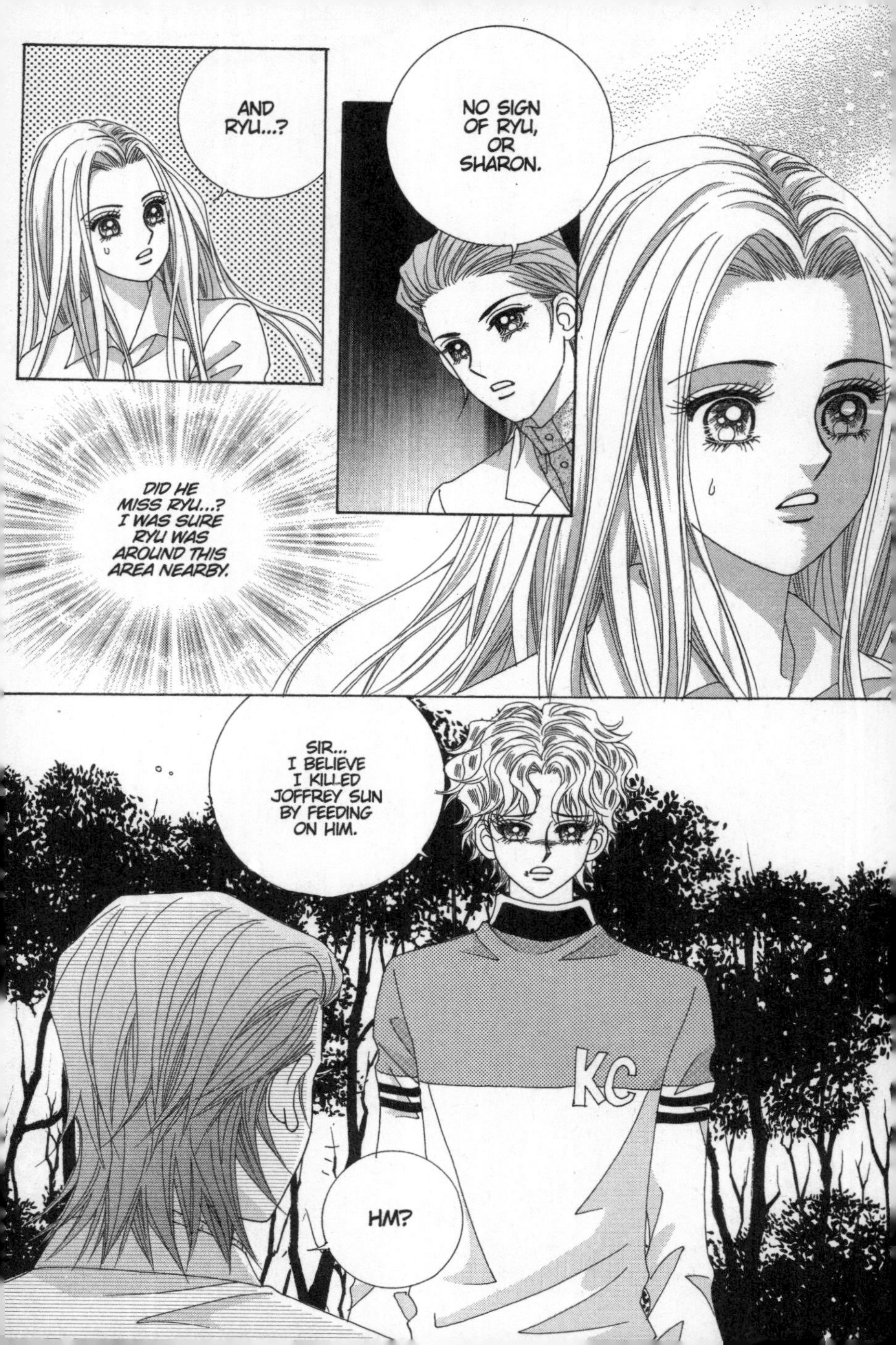
AND RYU...?
NO SIGN OF RYU, OR SHARON.
DID HE MISS RYU...? I WAS SURE RYU WAS AROUND THIS AREA NEARBY.
SIR... I BELIEVE I KILLED JOFFREY SUN BY FEEDING ON HIM.
HM?

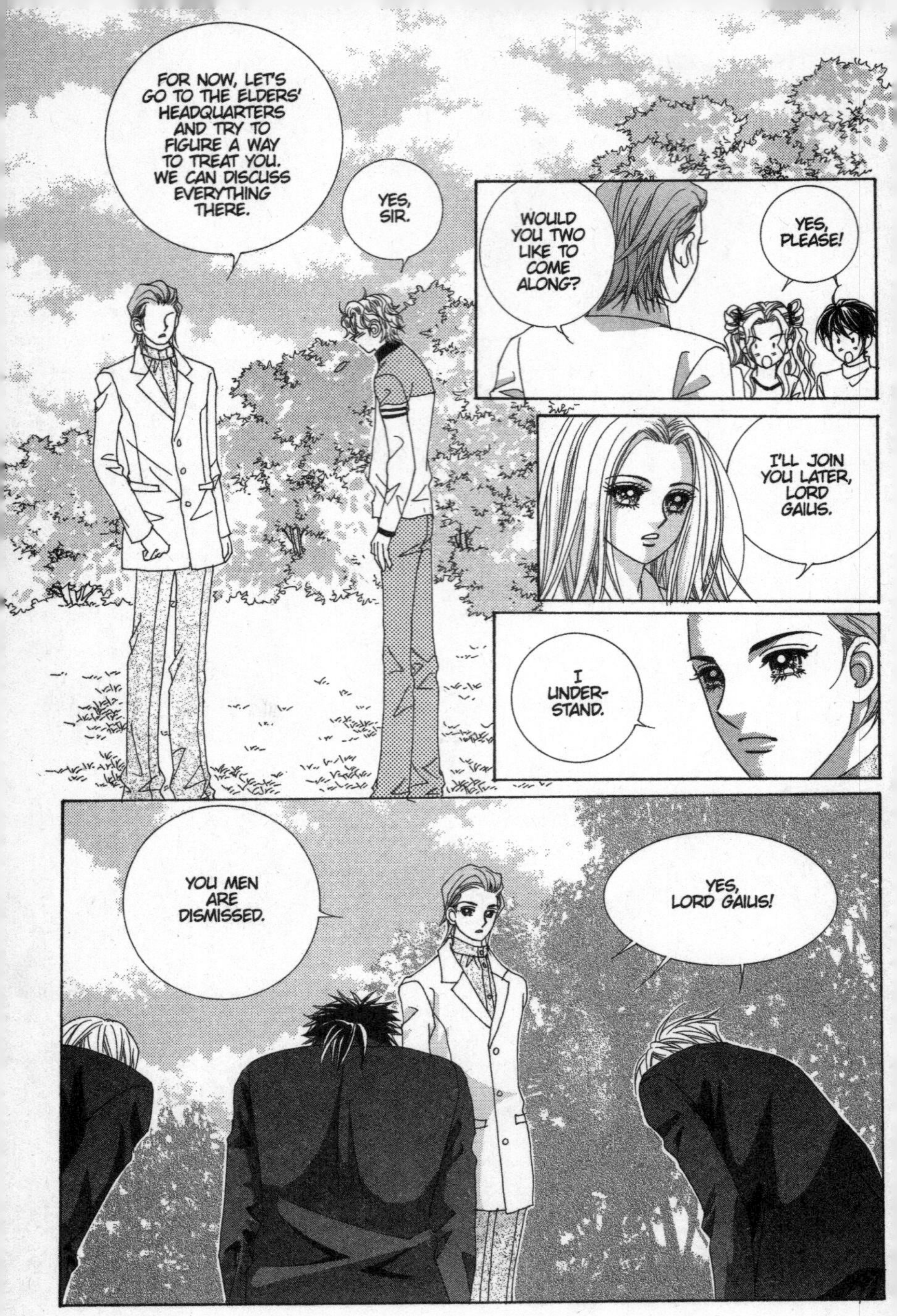
FOR NOW, LET'S GO TO THE ELDERS' HEADQUARTERS AND TRY TO FIGURE A WAY TO TREAT YOU. WE CAN DISCUSS EVERYTHING THERE.
YES, SIR.
WOULD YOU TWO LIKE TO COME ALONG?
YES, PLEASE!
I'LL JOIN YOU LATER, LORD GAIUS.
I UNDER-STAND.
YOU MEN ARE DISMISSED.
YES, LORD GAIUS!

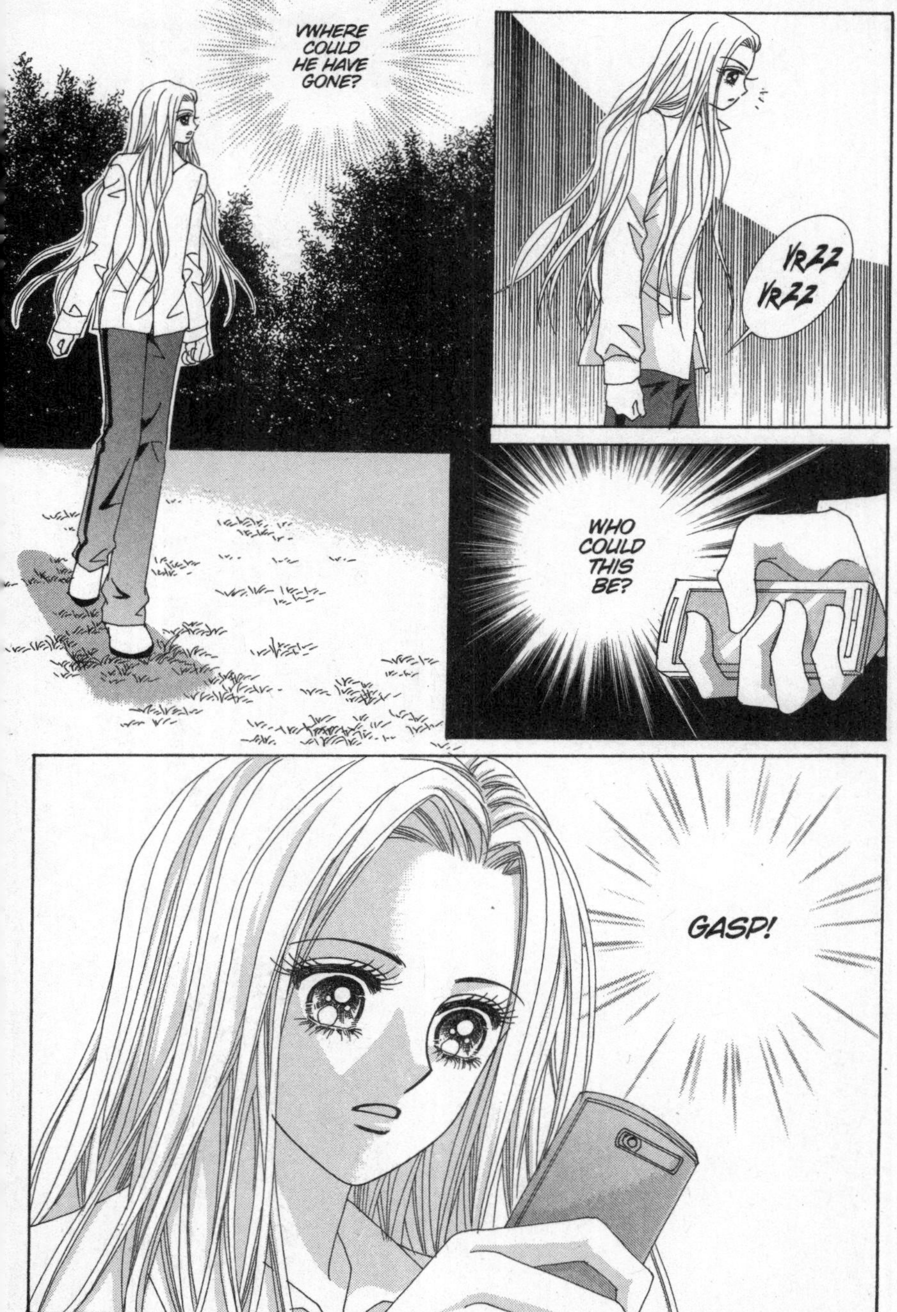
WHERE COULD HE HAVE GONE?
VRZZ VRZZ
WHO COULD THIS BE?
GASP!

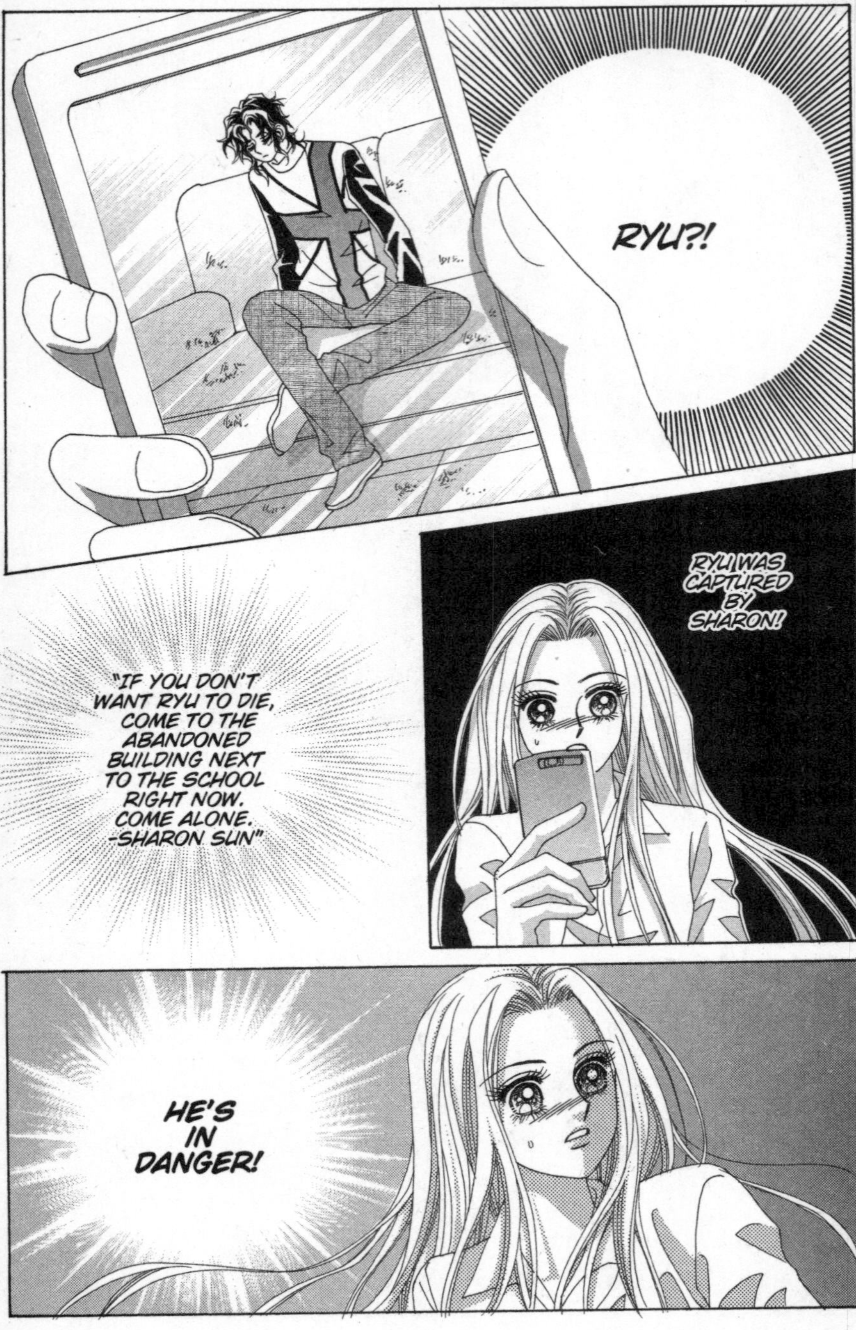
RYU?!
"IF YOU DON'T WANT RYU TO DIE, COME TO THE ABANDONED BUILDING NEXT TO THE SCHOOL RIGHT NOW. COME ALONE. -SHARON SUN"
RYU WAS CAPTURED BY SHARON!
HE'S IN DANGER!

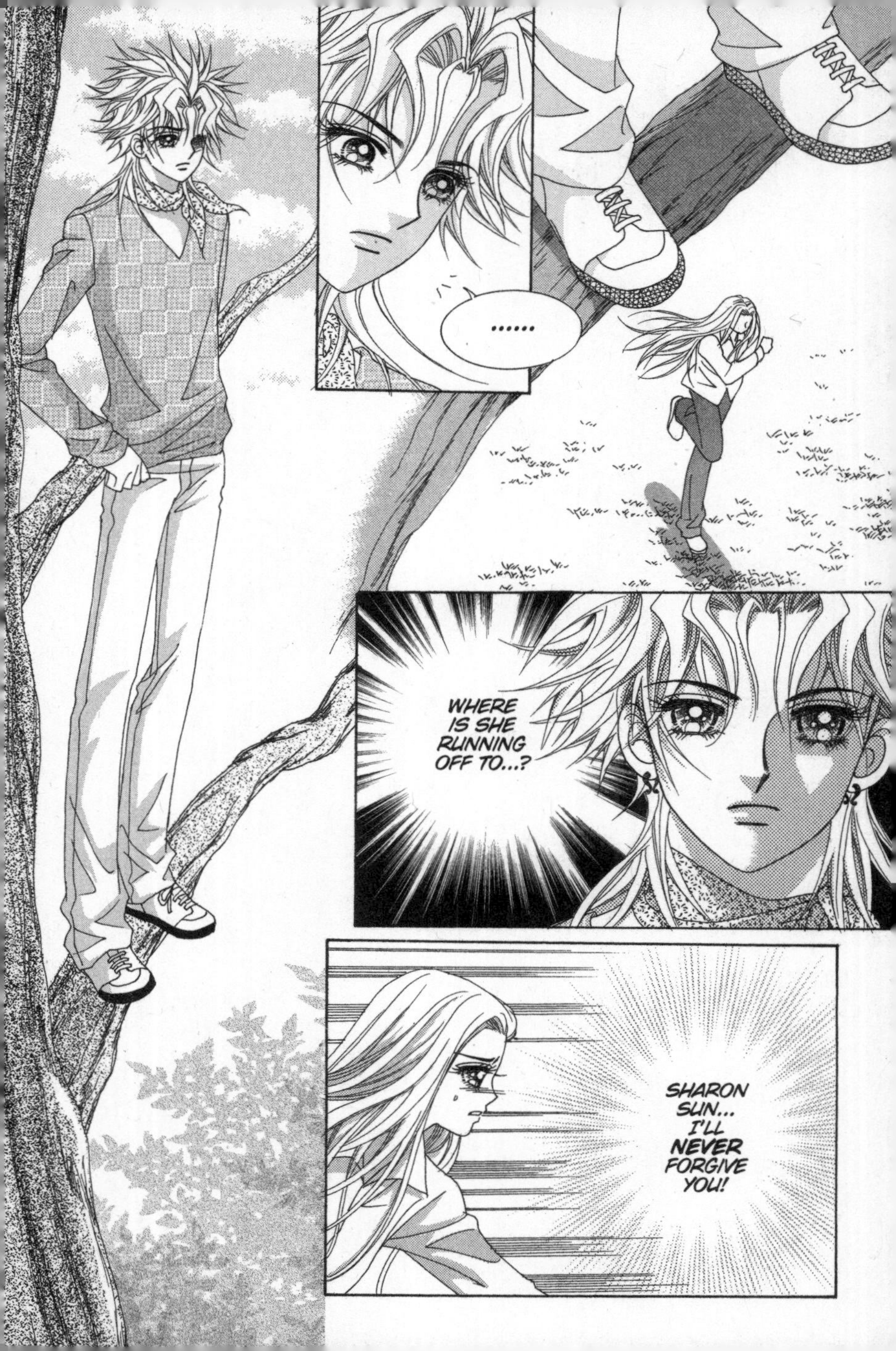
......
WHERE IS SHE RUNNING OFF TO...?
SHARON SUN... I'LL NEVER FORGIVE YOU!

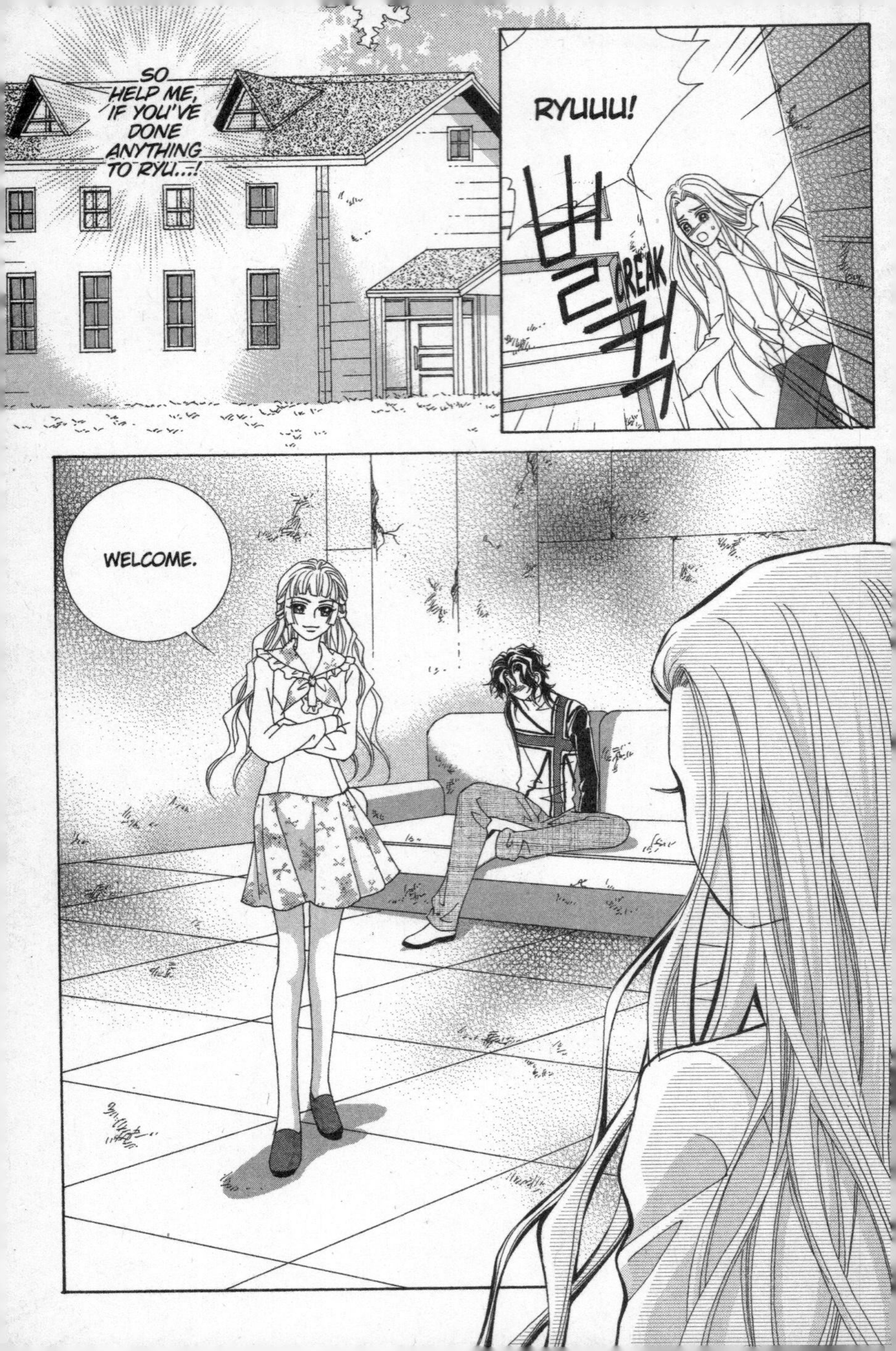
SO HELP ME, IF YOU'VE DONE ANYTHING TO RYU...!
RYUUU!
CREAK
WELCOME.

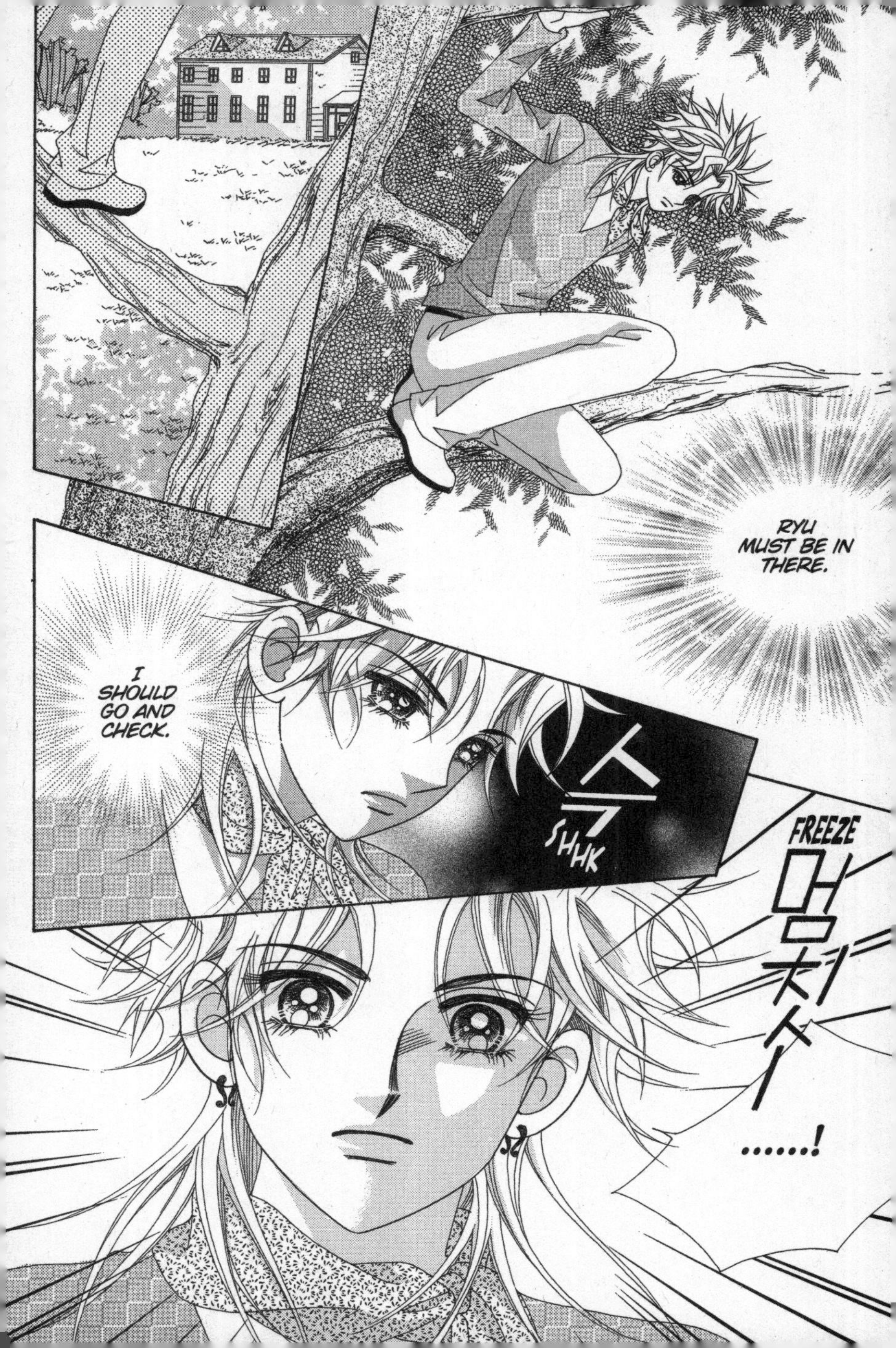
RYU MUST BE IN THERE.
I SHOULD GO AND CHECK.
SHHK
FREEZE
......!

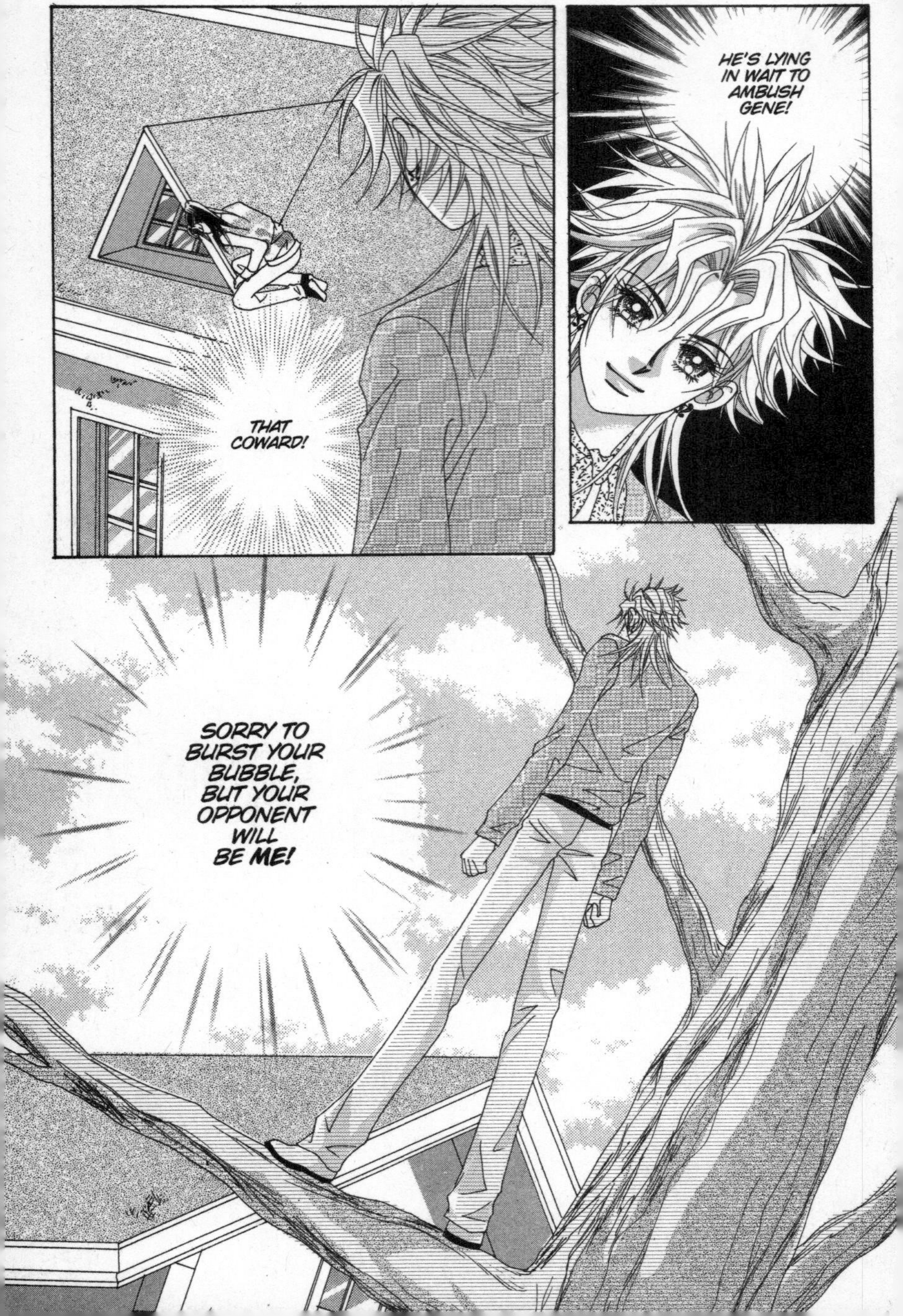
THAT COWARD!
HE'S LYING IN WAIT TO AMBUSH GENE!
SORRY TO BURST YOUR BUBBLE, BUT YOUR OPPONENT WILL BE ME!

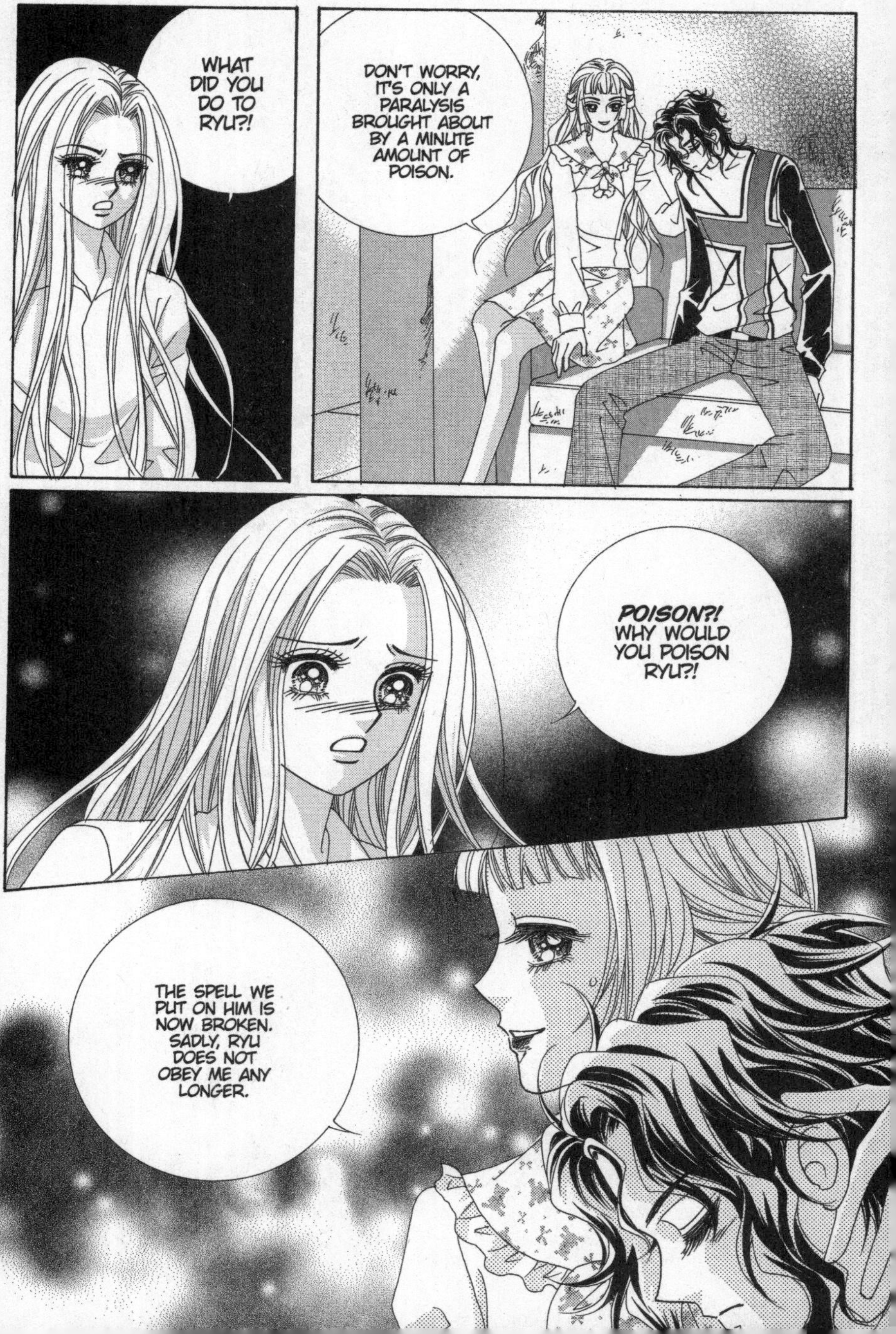
WHAT DID YOU DO TO RYU?!
DON'T WORRY, IT'S ONLY A PARALYSIS BROUGHT ABOUT BY A MINUTE AMOUNT OF POISON.
POISON?! WHY WOULD YOU POISON RYU?!
THE SPELL WE PUT ON HIM IS NOW BROKEN. SADLY, RYU DOES NOT OBEY ME ANY LONGER.

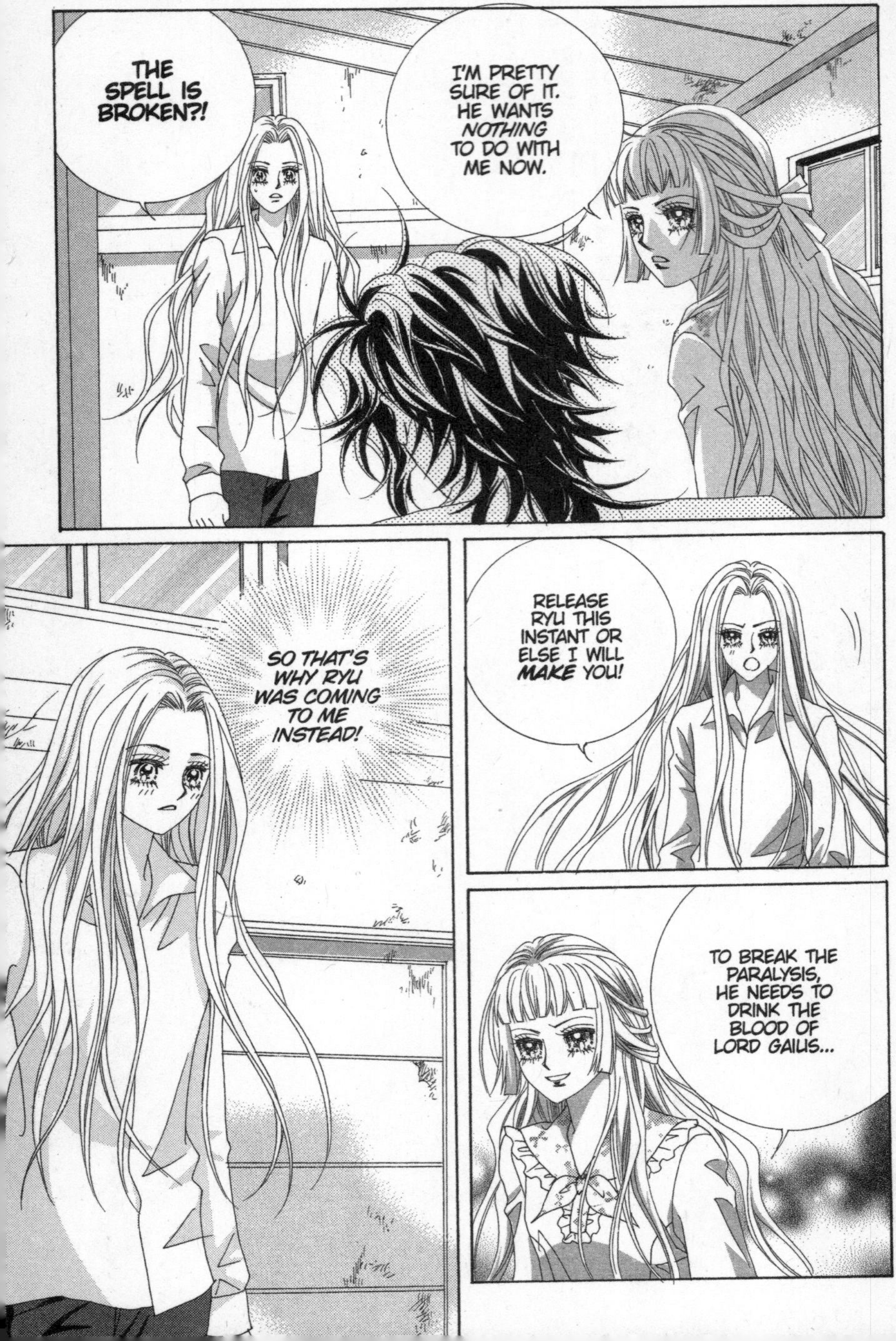
THE SPELL IS BROKEN?!
I'M PRETTY SURE OF IT. HE WANTS NOTHING TO DO WITH ME NOW.
SO THAT'S WHY RYU WAS COMING TO ME INSTEAD!
RELEASE RYU THIS INSTANT OR ELSE I WILL MAKE YOU!
TO BREAK THE PARALYSIS, HE NEEDS TO DRINK THE BLOOD OF LORD GAIUS...

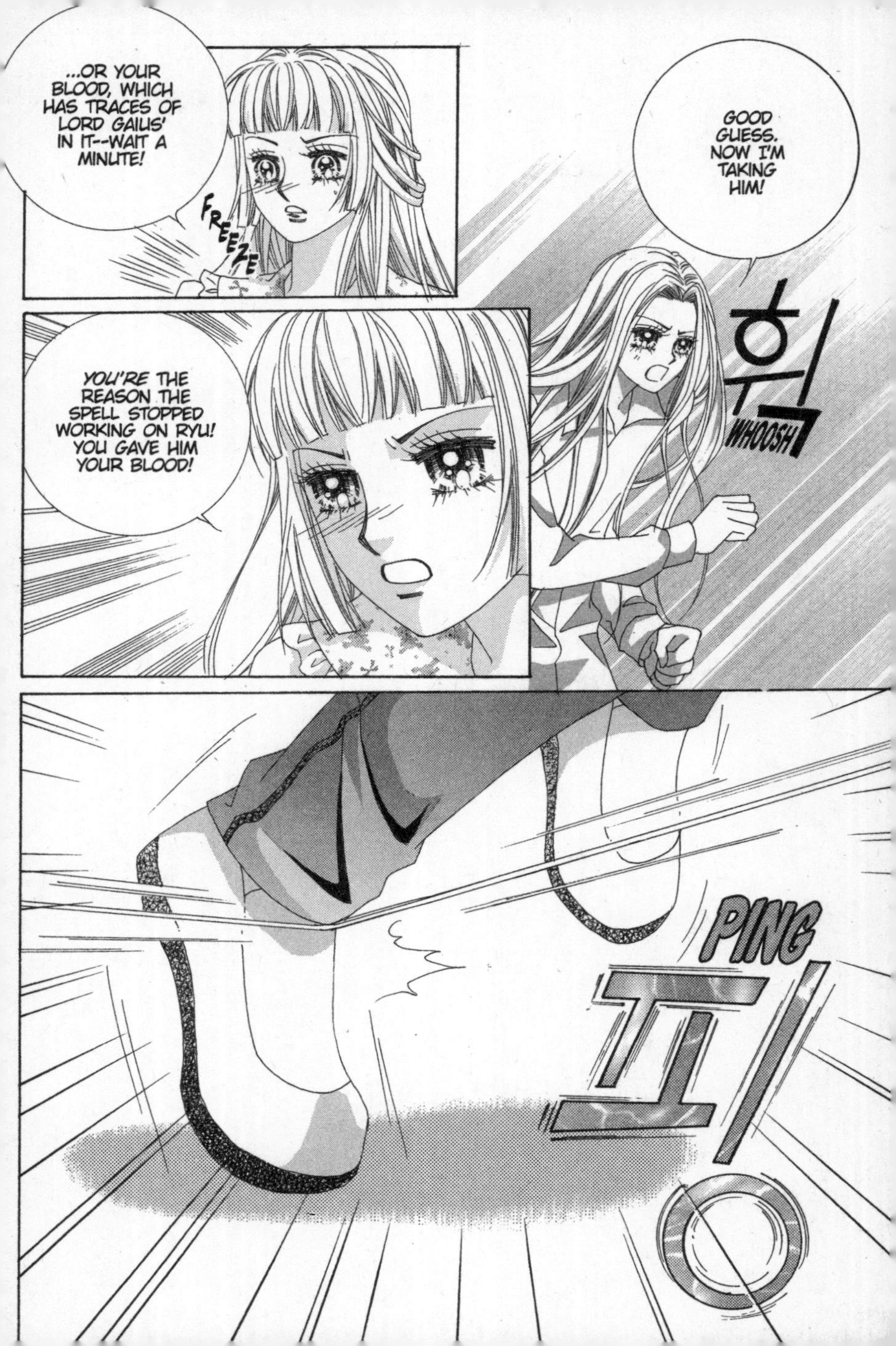
...OR YOUR BLOOD, WHICH HAS TRACES OF LORD GAIUS' IN IT--WAIT A MINUTE!
FREEZE
YOU'RE THE REASON THE SPELL STOPPED WORKING ON RYU! YOU GAVE HIM YOUR BLOOD!
GOOD GUESS. NOW I'M TAKING HIM!
휙
WHOOSH
PING
핑

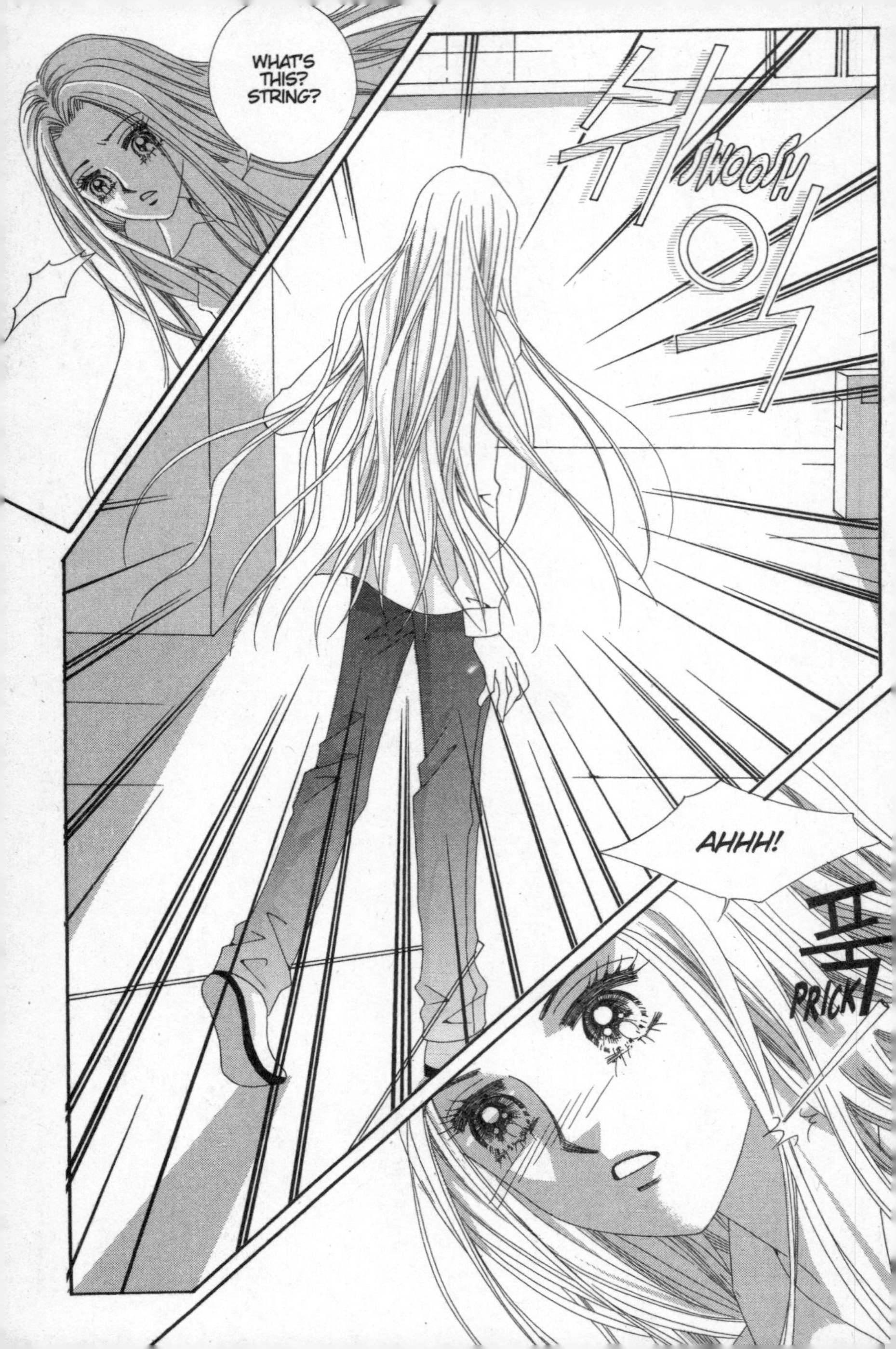
WHAT'S THIS? STRING?
SWOOSH
AHHH!
PRICK

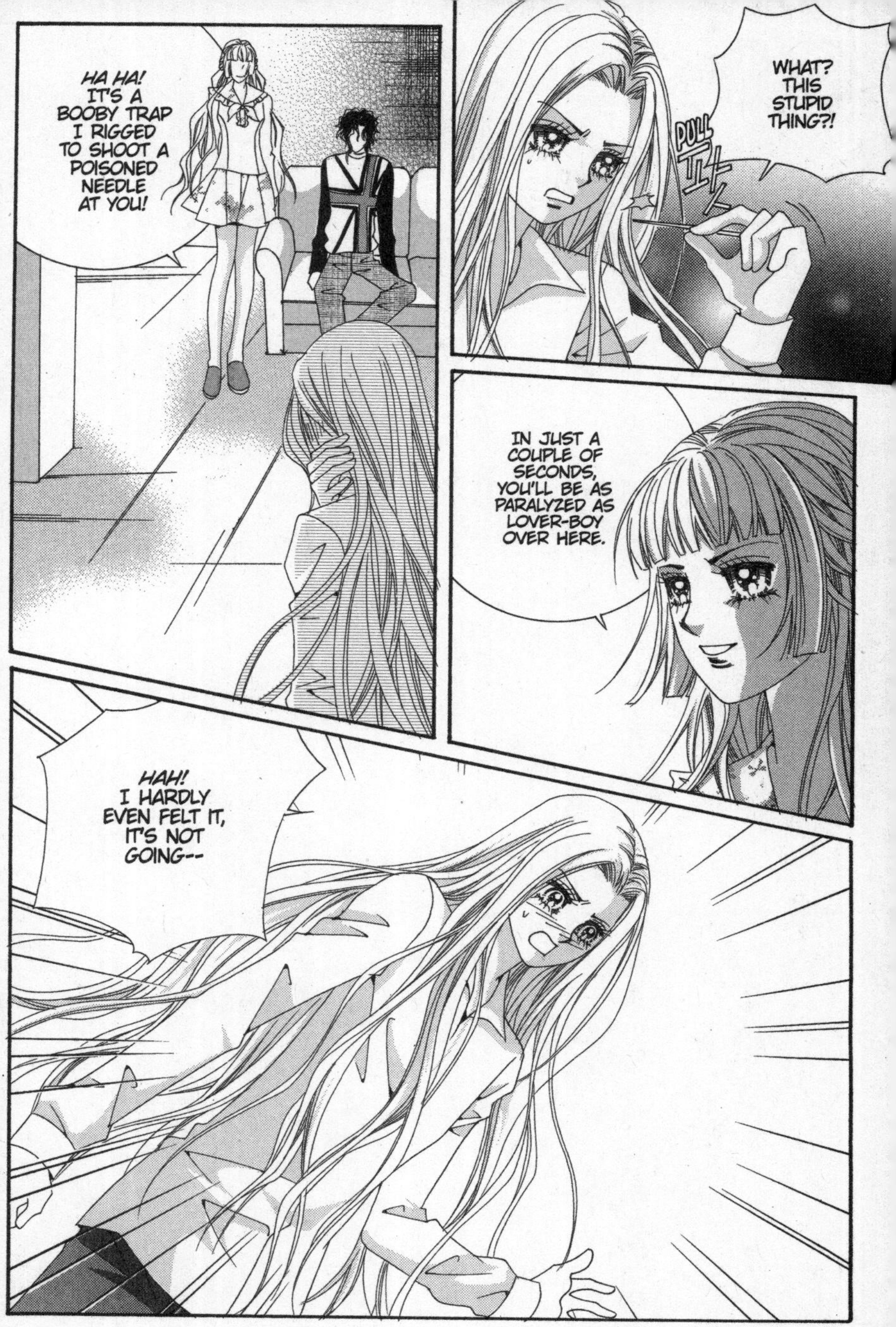

WHAT? THIS STUPID THING?!
PULL
HA HA! IT'S A BOOBY TRAP I RIGGED TO SHOOT A POISONED NEEDLE AT YOU!
IN JUST A COUPLE OF SECONDS, YOU'LL BE AS PARALYZED AS LOVER-BOY OVER HERE.
HAH! I HARDLY EVEN FELT IT, IT'S NOT GOING--

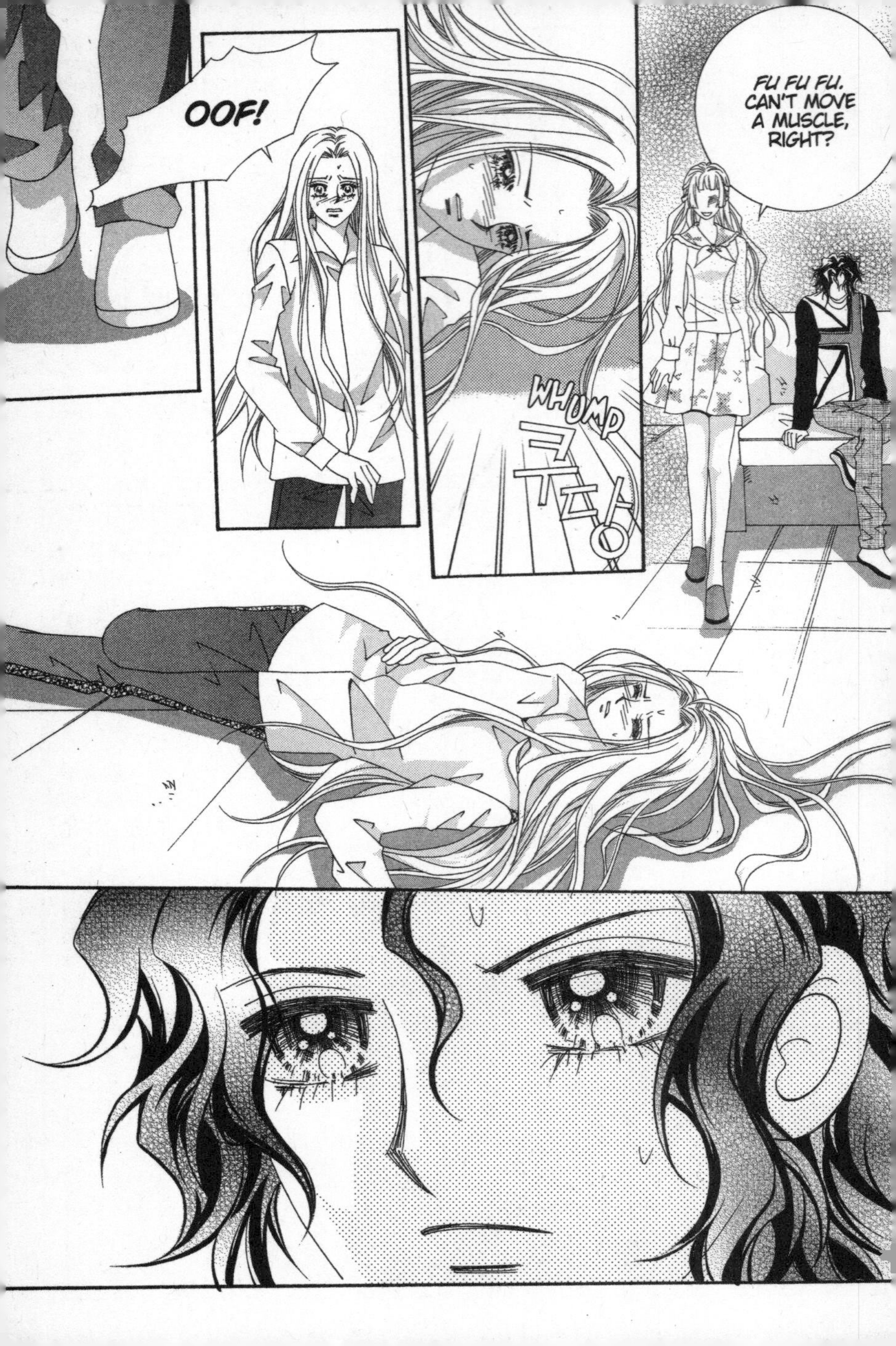

OOF!
WHUMP
FU FU FU. CAN'T MOVE A MUSCLE, RIGHT?

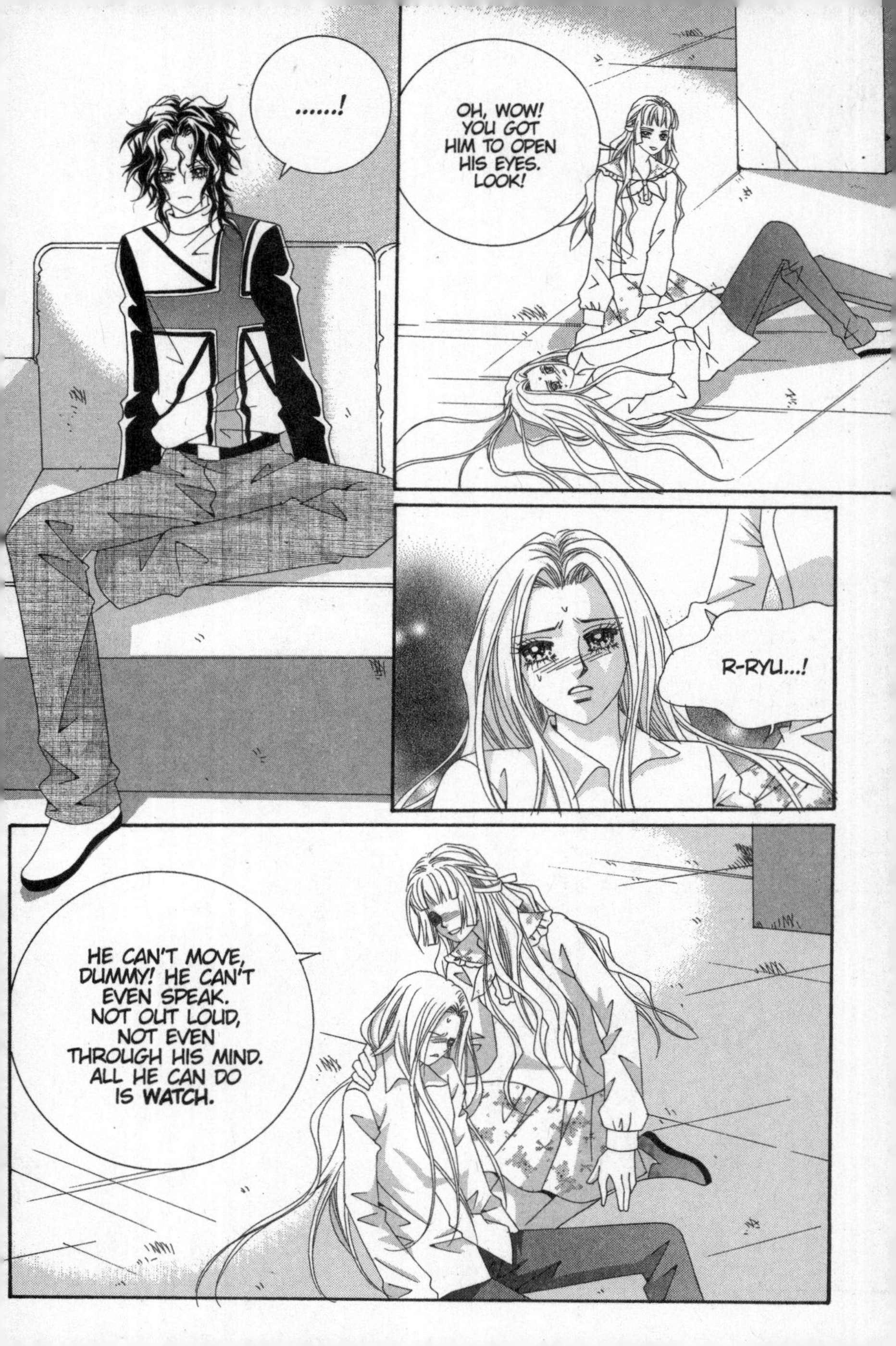
......!
OH, WOW! YOU GOT HIM TO OPEN HIS EYES. LOOK!
R-RYU...!
HE CAN'T MOVE, DUMMY! HE CAN'T EVEN SPEAK. NOT OUT LOUD, NOT EVEN THROUGH HIS MIND. ALL HE CAN DO IS WATCH.

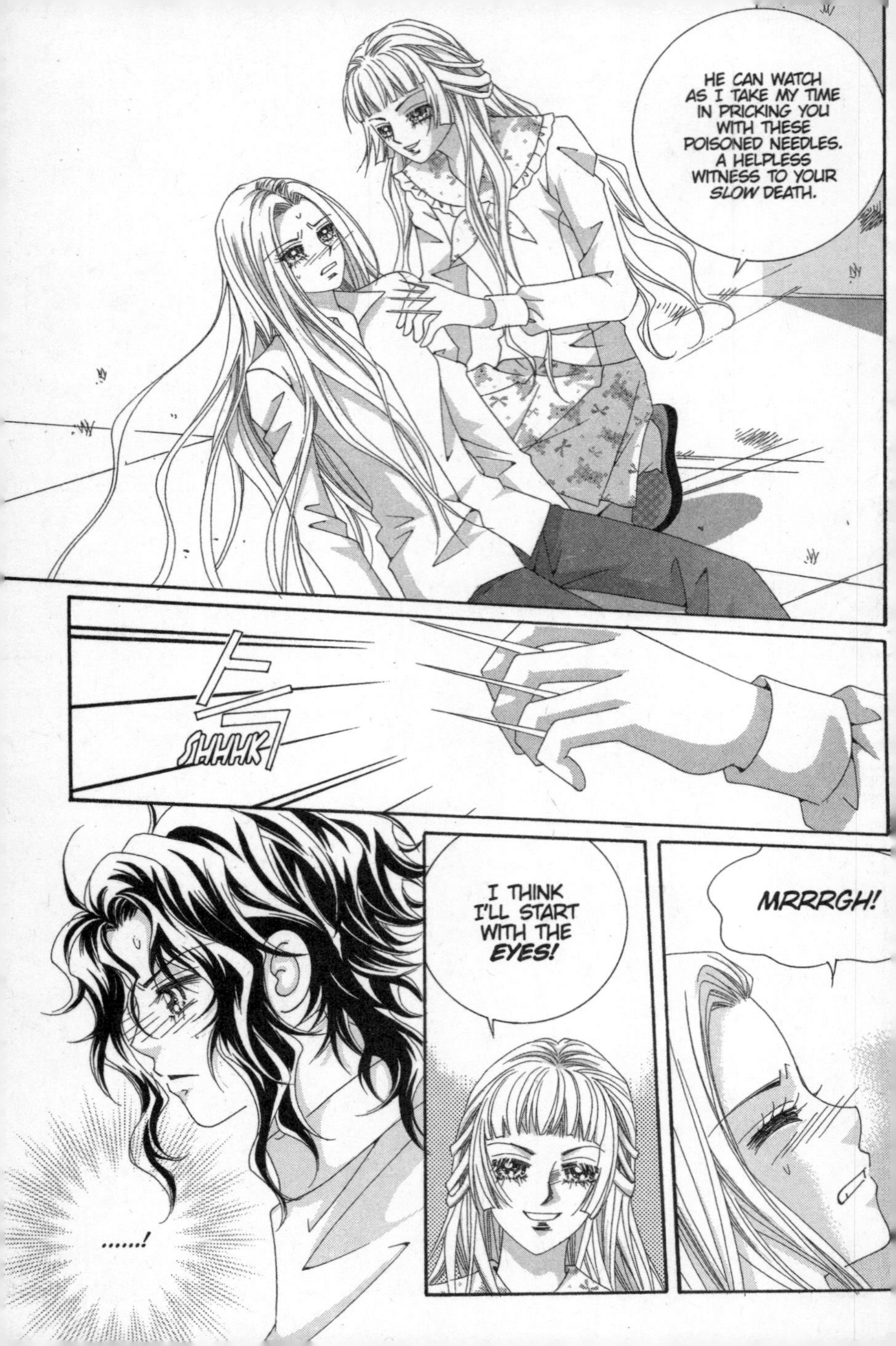
HE CAN WATCH AS I TAKE MY TIME IN PRICKING YOU WITH THESE POISONED NEEDLES. A HELPLESS WITNESS TO YOUR *SLOW* DEATH.
SHHHK
......!
I THINK I'LL START WITH THE *EYES!*
MRRRGH!

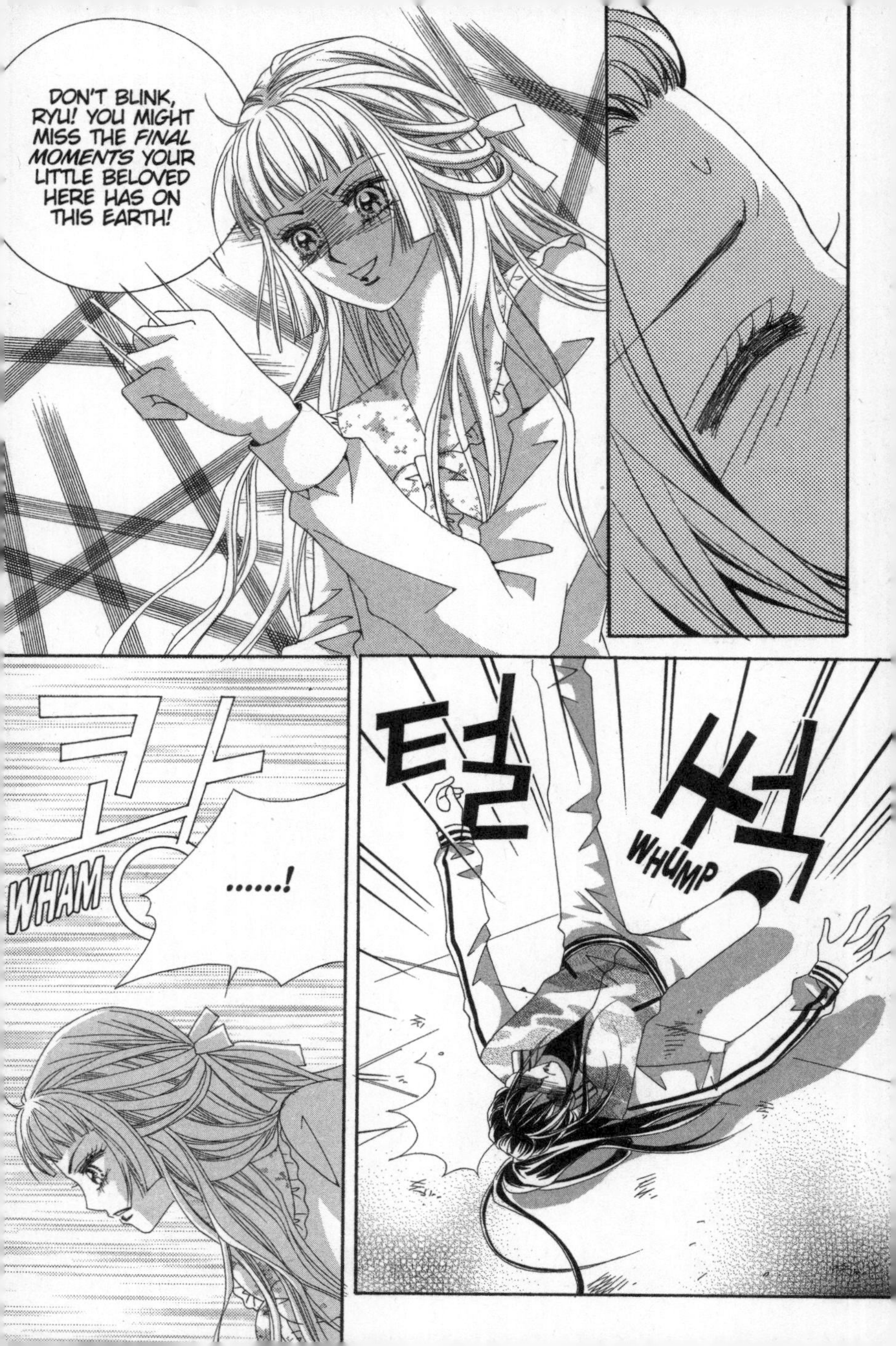
DON'T BLINK, RYU! YOU MIGHT MISS THE *FINAL MOMENTS* YOUR LITTLE BELOVED HERE HAS ON THIS EARTH!
WHAM
......!
WHUMP

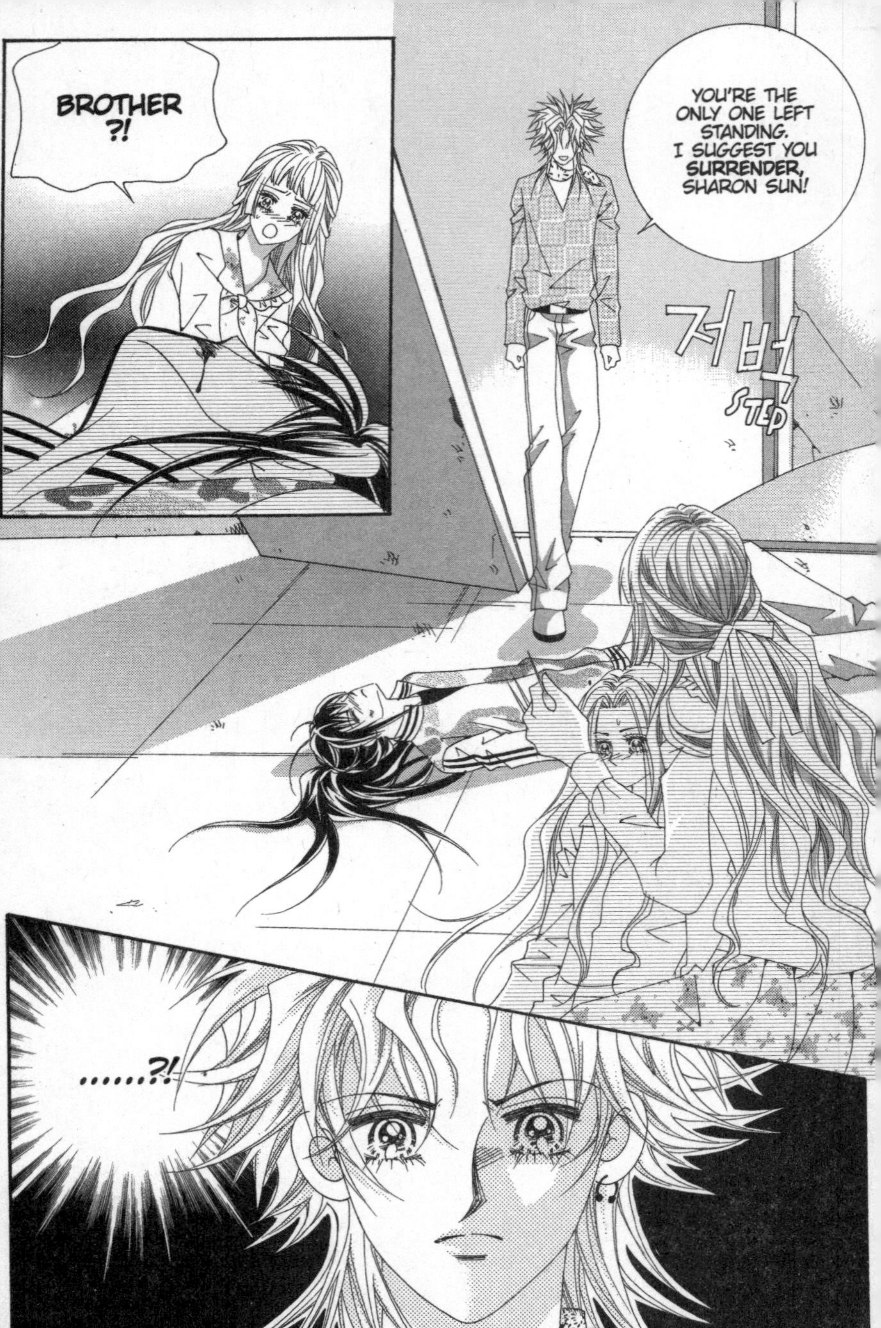
BROTHER ?!
YOU'RE THE ONLY ONE LEFT STANDING. I SUGGEST YOU SURRENDER, SHARON SUN!
저벅
STEP
......?!

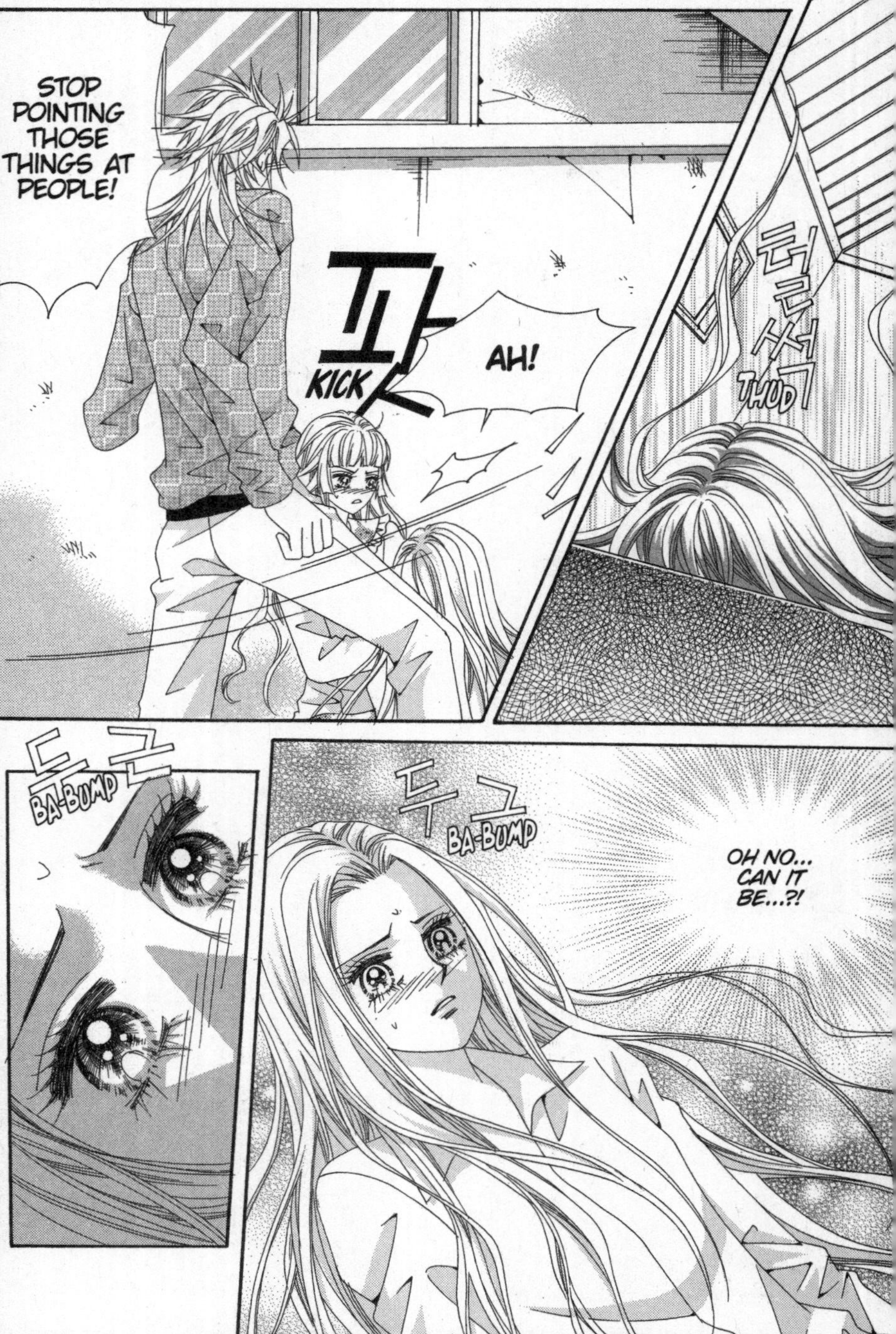

STOP POINTING THOSE THINGS AT PEOPLE!
파
KICK
AH!
털썩
THUD
두근
BA-BUMP
두근
BA-BUMP
OH NO... CAN IT BE...?!

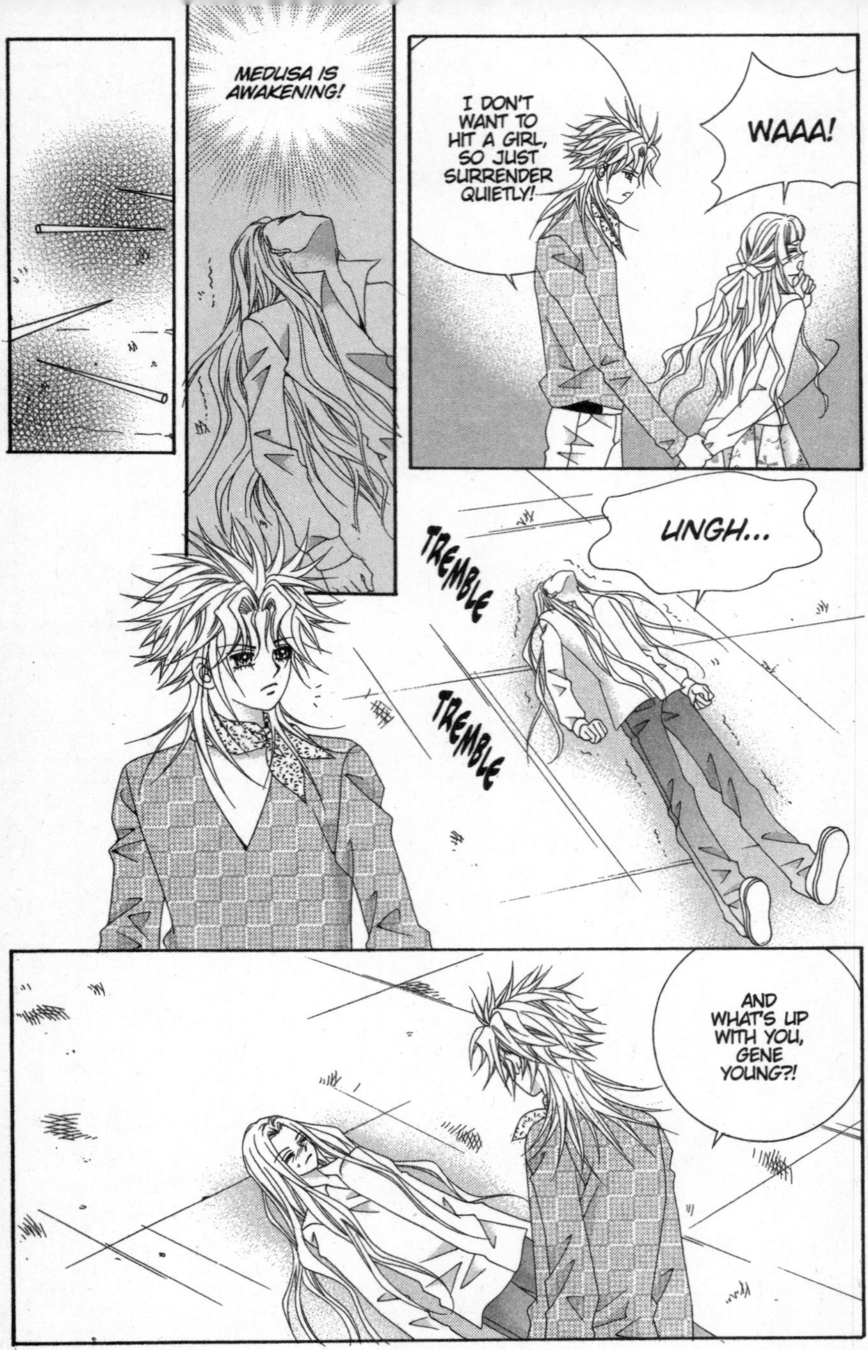
MEDUSA IS AWAKENING!
I DON'T WANT TO HIT A GIRL, SO JUST SURRENDER QUIETLY!
WAAA!
TREMBLE
TREMBLE
UNGH...
AND WHAT'S UP WITH YOU, GENE YOUNG?!

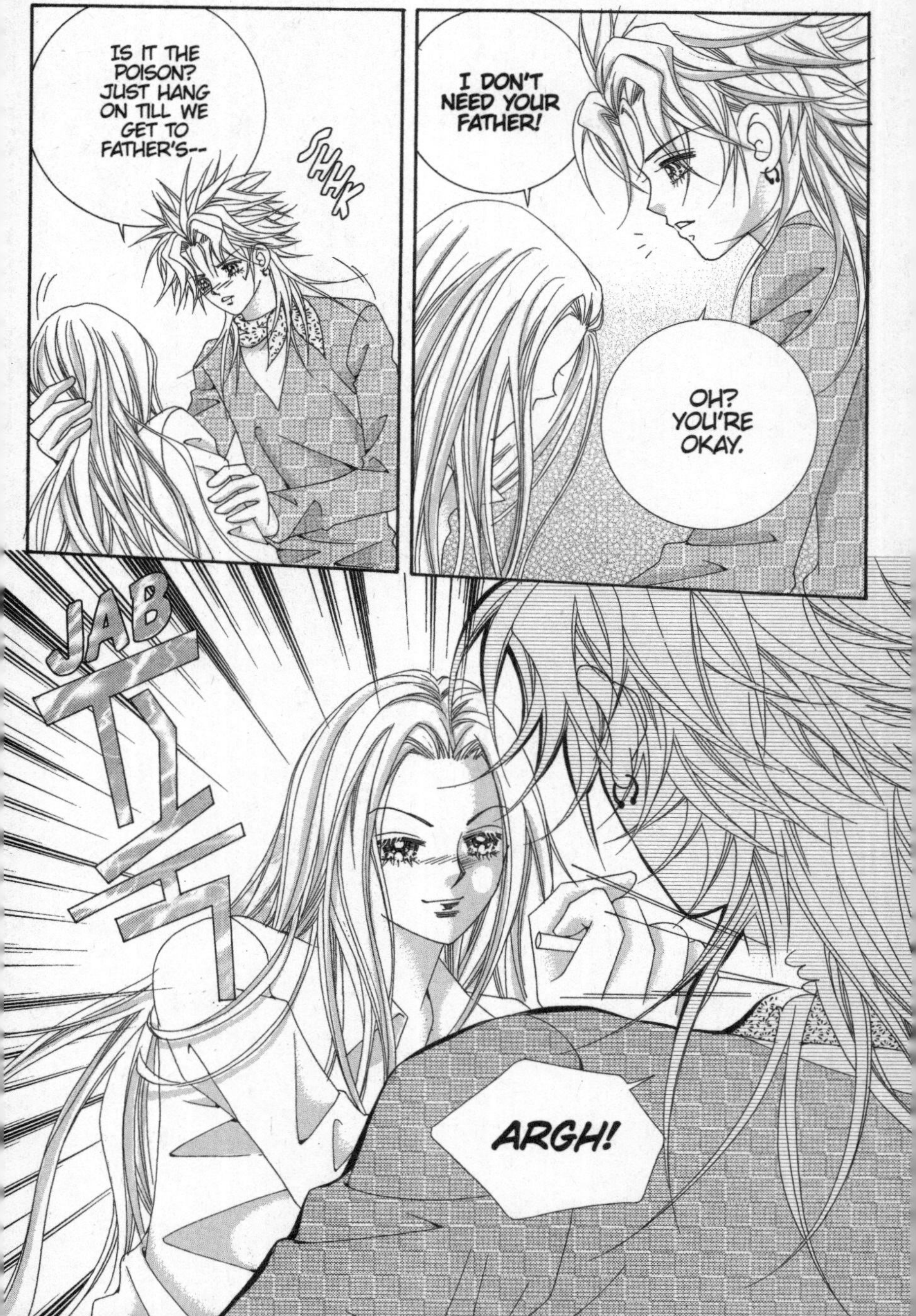
IS IT THE POISON? JUST HANG ON TILL WE GET TO FATHER'S--
SHHK
I DON'T NEED YOUR FATHER!
OH? YOU'RE OKAY.
JAB
ARGH!

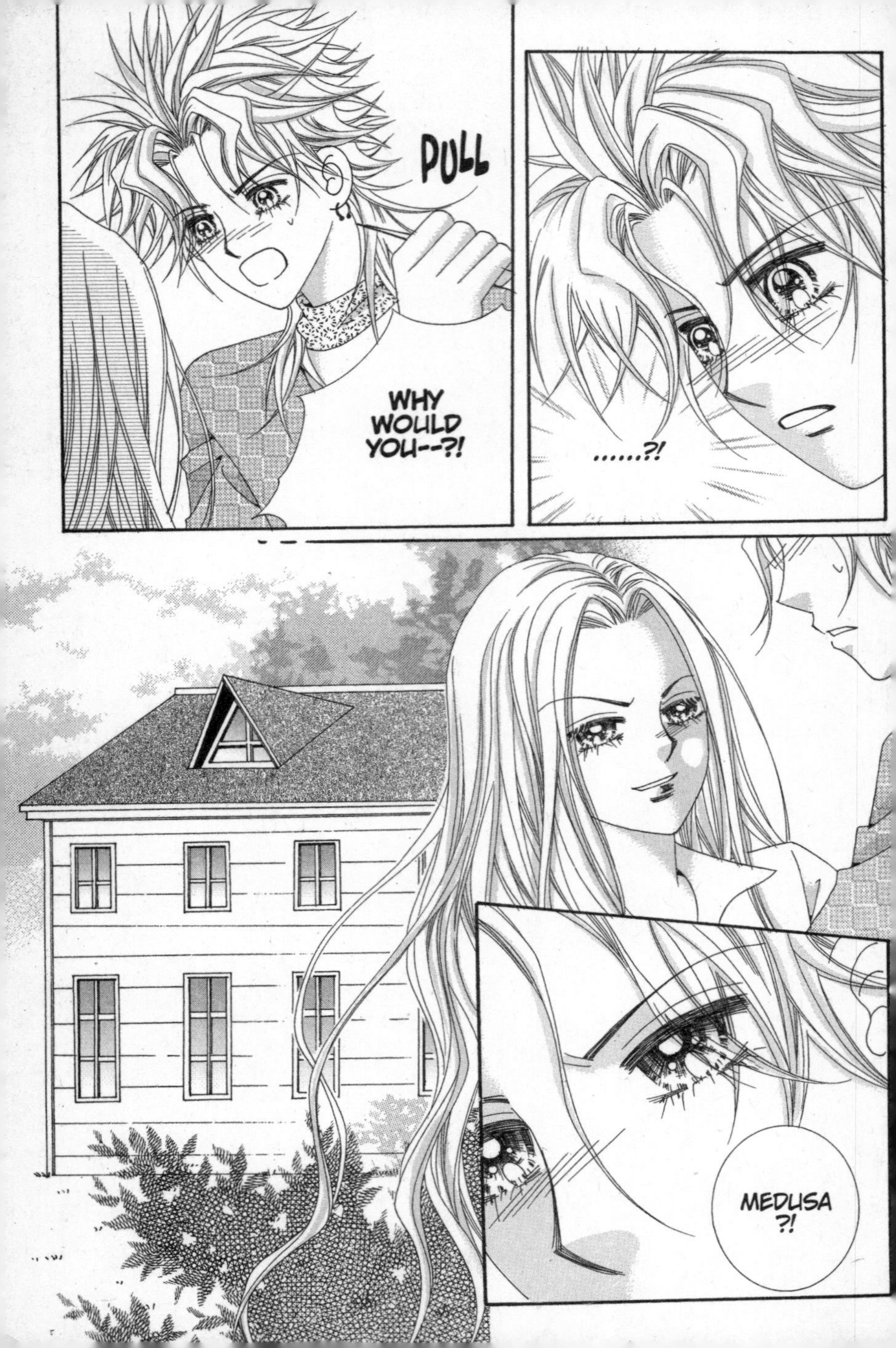
PULL
WHY WOULD YOU--?!
......?!
MEDUSA ?!

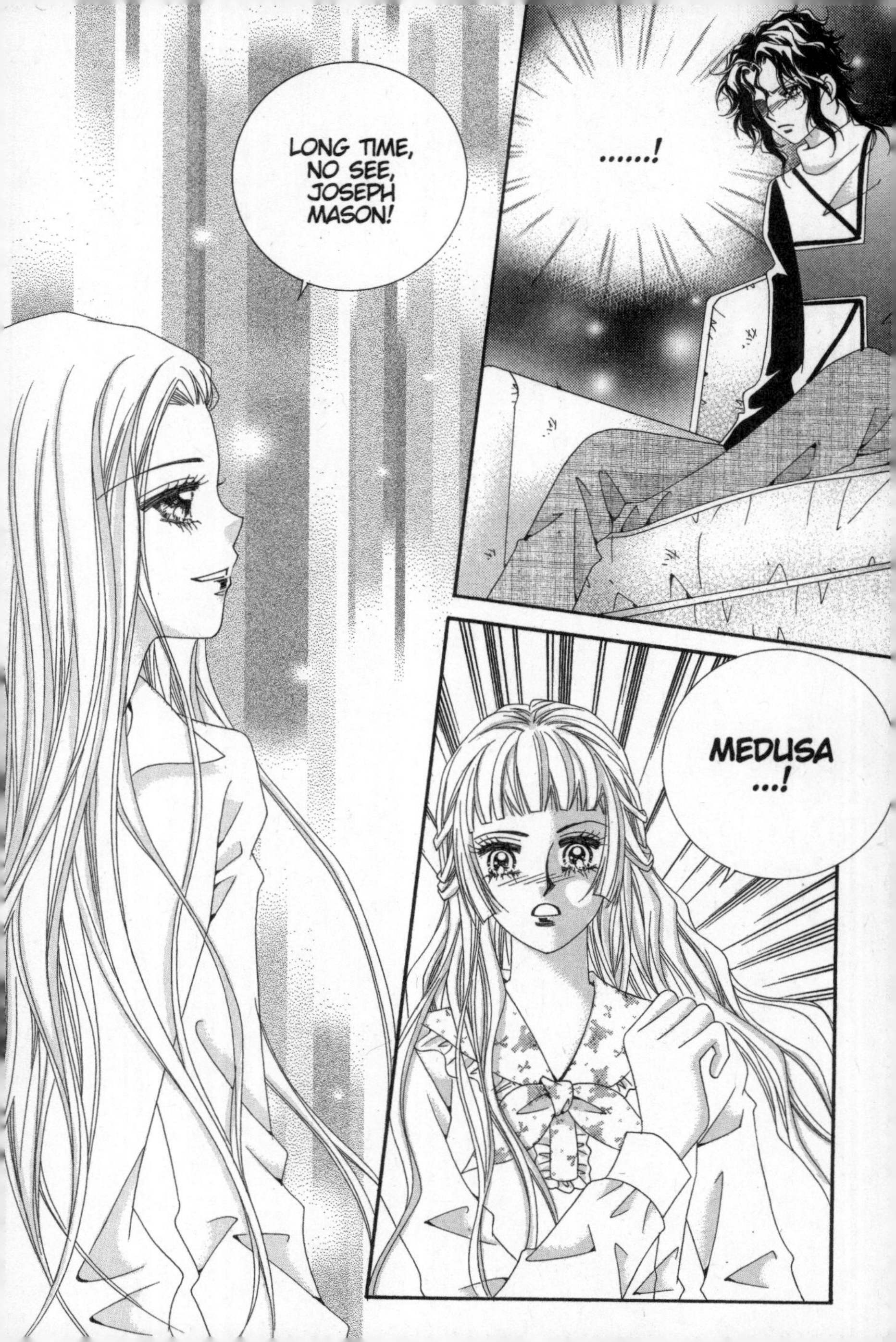
LONG TIME, NO SEE, JOSEPH MASON!
......!
MEDUSA ...!

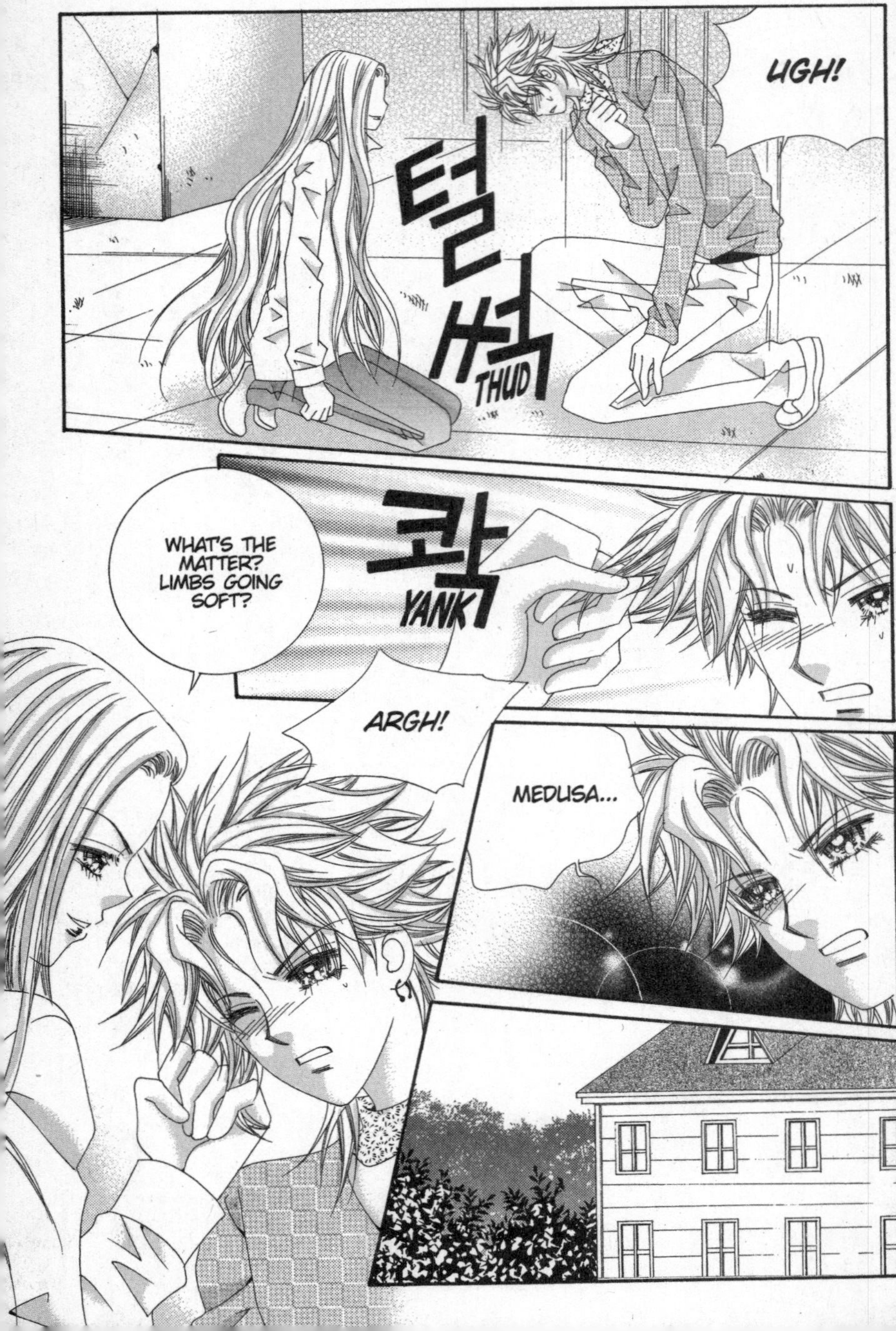
UGH!
털썩
THUD
WHAT'S THE MATTER? LIMBS GOING SOFT?
콱
YANK
ARGH!
MEDUSA...

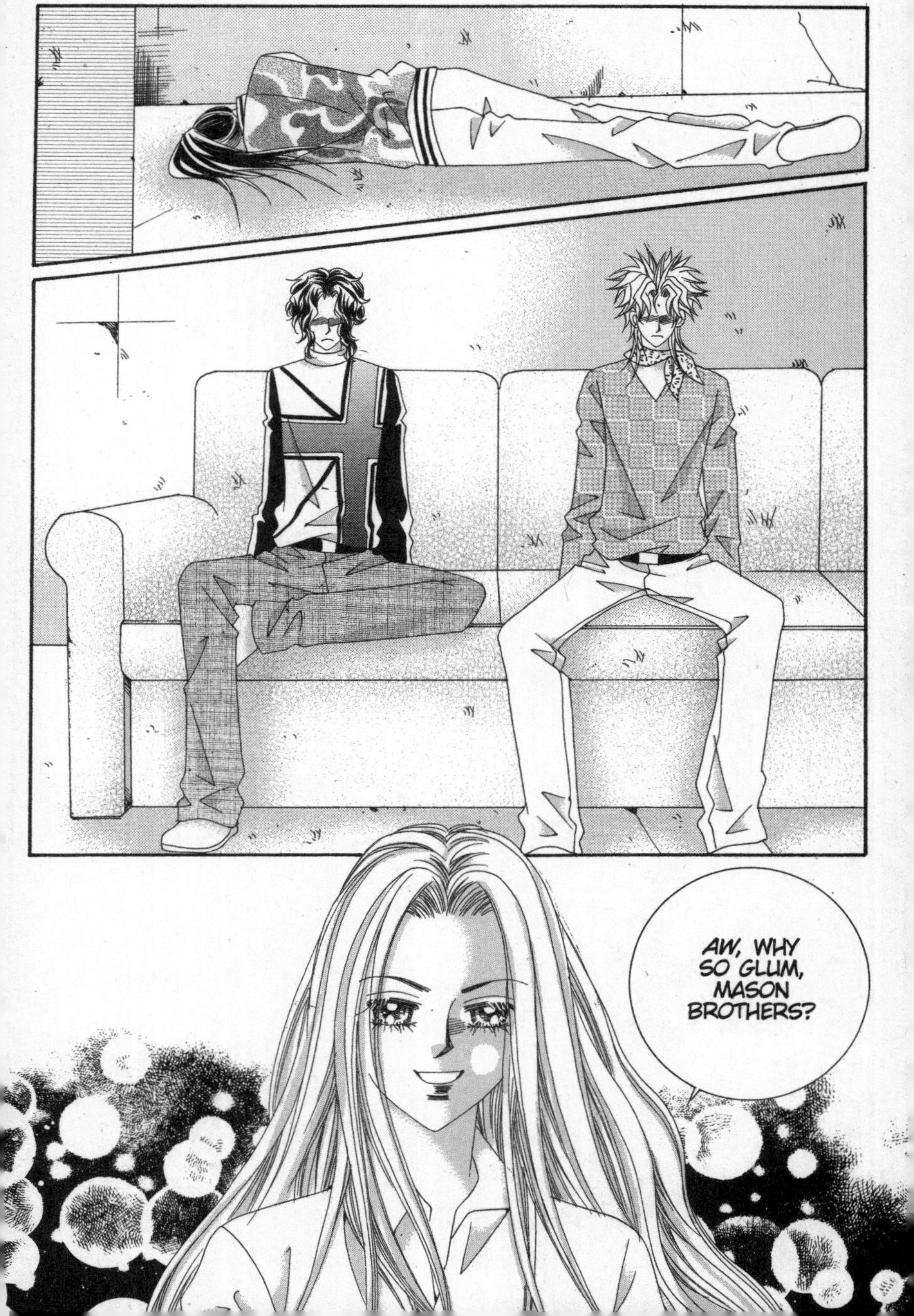
AW, WHY SO GLUM, MASON BROTHERS?

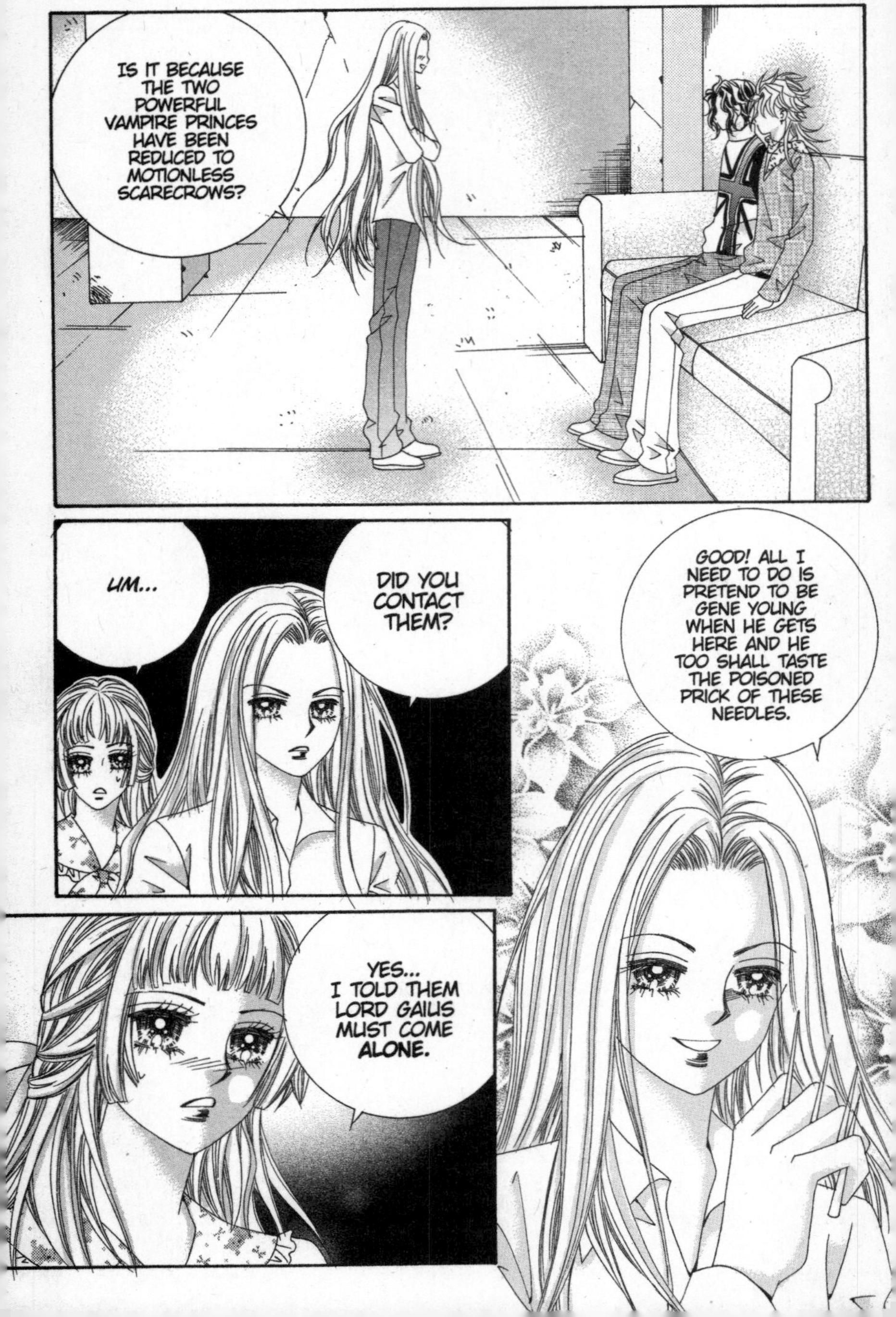

IS IT BECAUSE THE TWO POWERFUL VAMPIRE PRINCES HAVE BEEN REDUCED TO MOTIONLESS SCARECROWS?
UM...
DID YOU CONTACT THEM?
GOOD! ALL I NEED TO DO IS PRETEND TO BE GENE YOUNG WHEN HE GETS HERE AND HE TOO SHALL TASTE THE POISONED PRICK OF THESE NEEDLES.
YES... I TOLD THEM LORD GAIUS MUST COME ALONE.

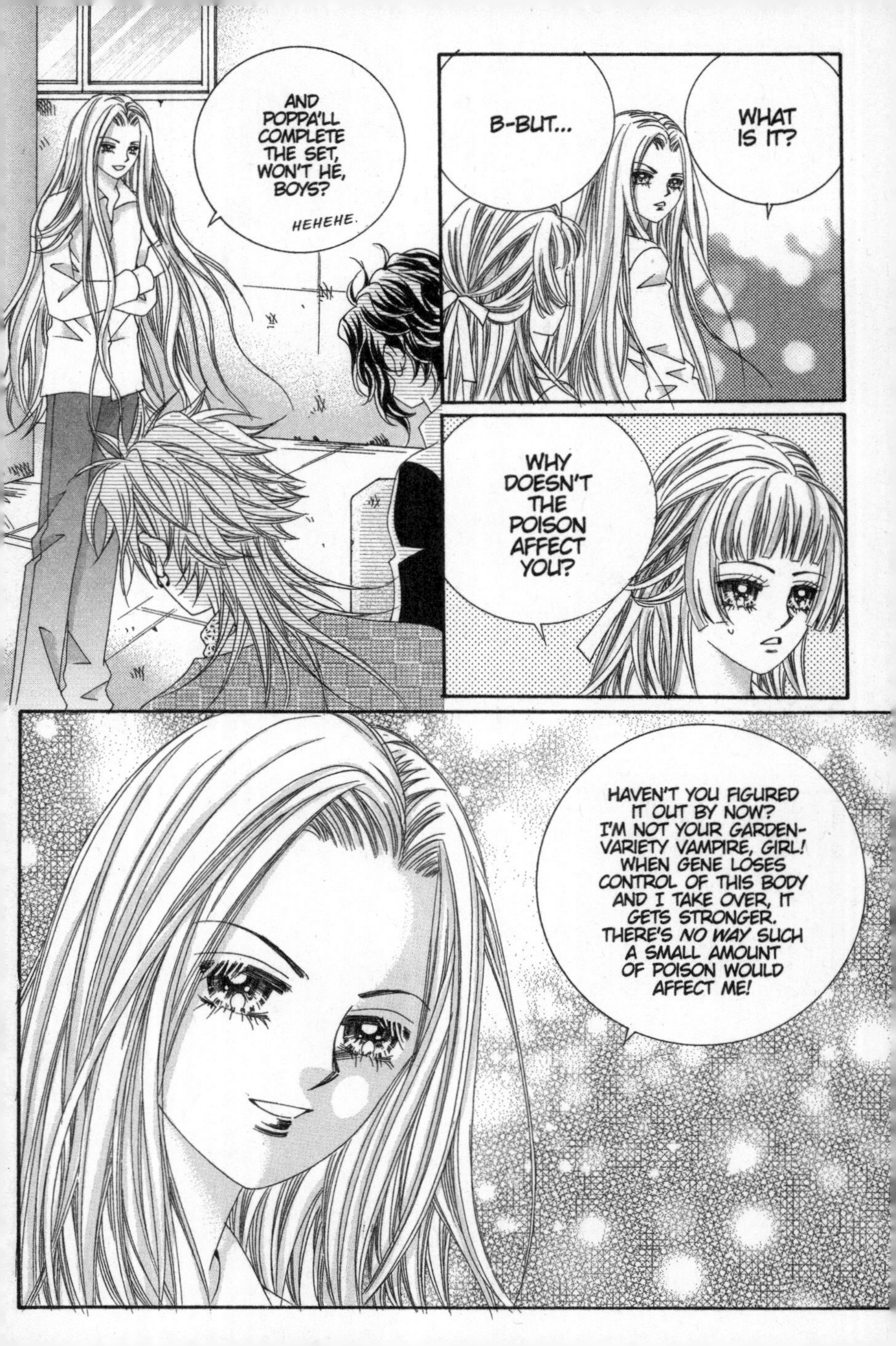
AND POPPA'LL COMPLETE THE SET, WON'T HE, BOYS?
HEHEHE.
B-BUT...
WHAT IS IT?
WHY DOESN'T THE POISON AFFECT YOU?
HAVEN'T YOU FIGURED IT OUT BY NOW? I'M NOT YOUR GARDEN-VARIETY VAMPIRE, GIRL! WHEN GENE LOSES CONTROL OF THIS BODY AND I TAKE OVER, IT GETS STRONGER. THERE'S *NO WAY* SUCH A SMALL AMOUNT OF POISON WOULD AFFECT ME!

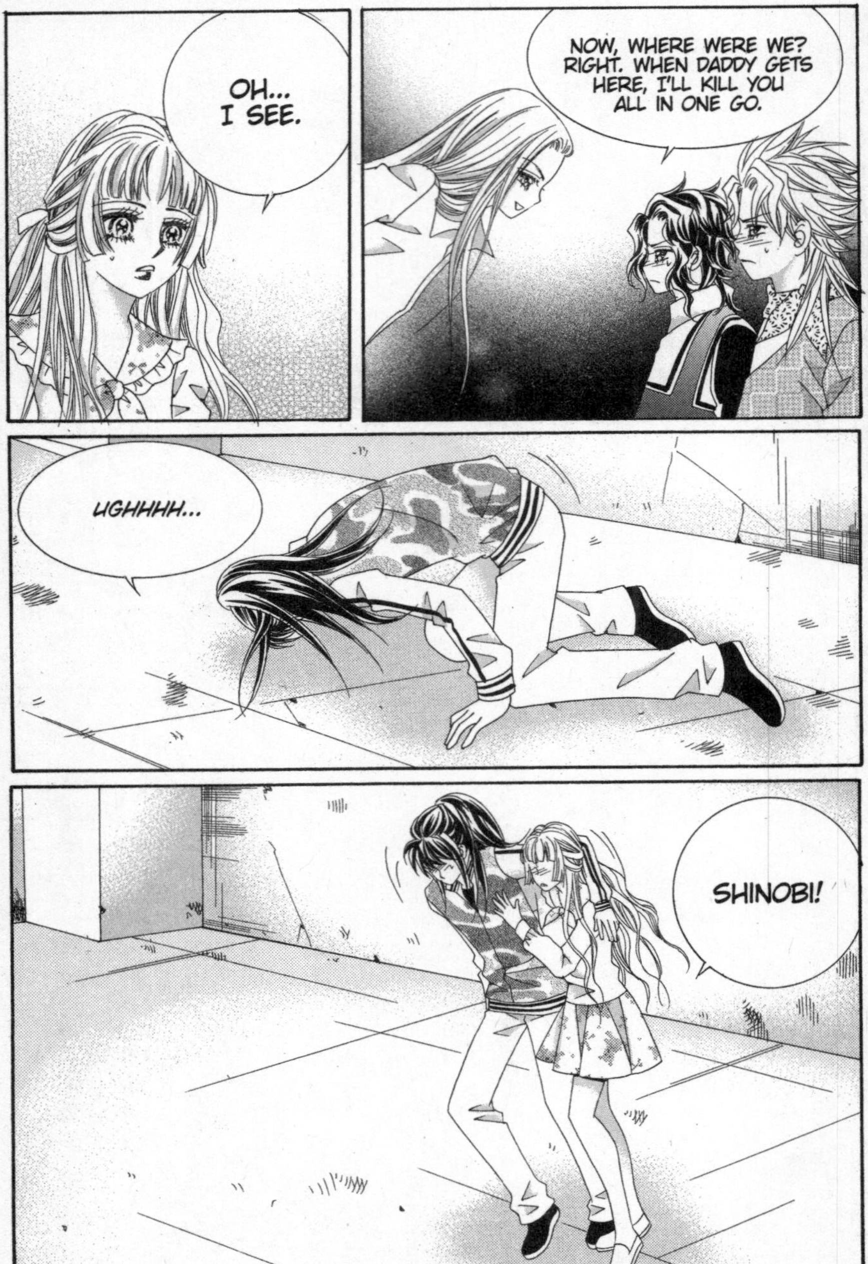
OH...
I SEE.
NOW, WHERE WERE WE? RIGHT. WHEN DADDY GETS HERE, I'LL KILL YOU ALL IN ONE GO.
UGHHHH...
SHINOBI!

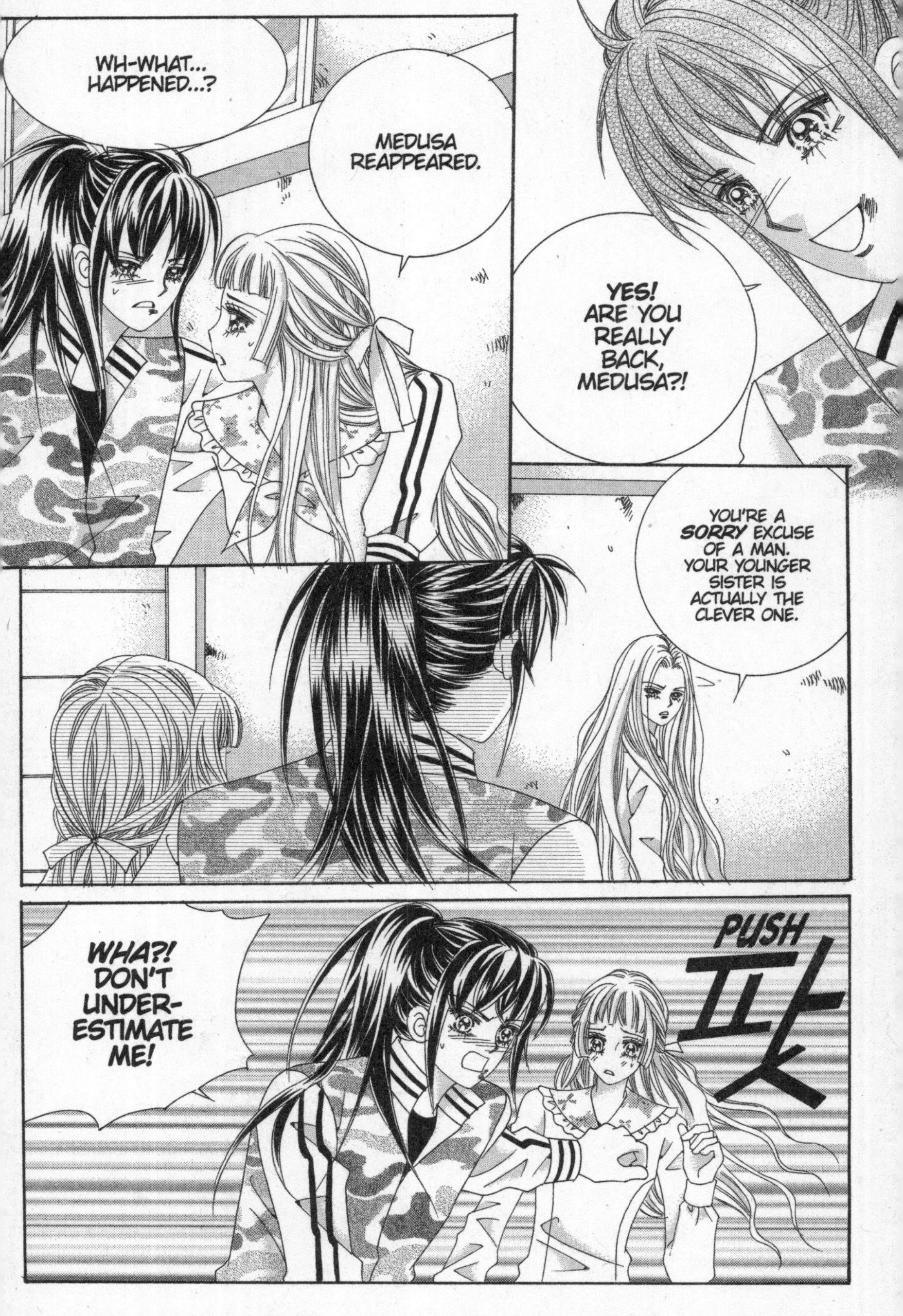
WH-WHAT... HAPPENED...?
MEDUSA REAPPEARED.
YES! ARE YOU REALLY BACK, MEDUSA?!
YOU'RE A **SORRY** EXCUSE OF A MAN. YOUR YOUNGER SISTER IS ACTUALLY THE CLEVER ONE.
WHA?! DON'T UNDER-ESTIMATE ME!
PUSH
팟

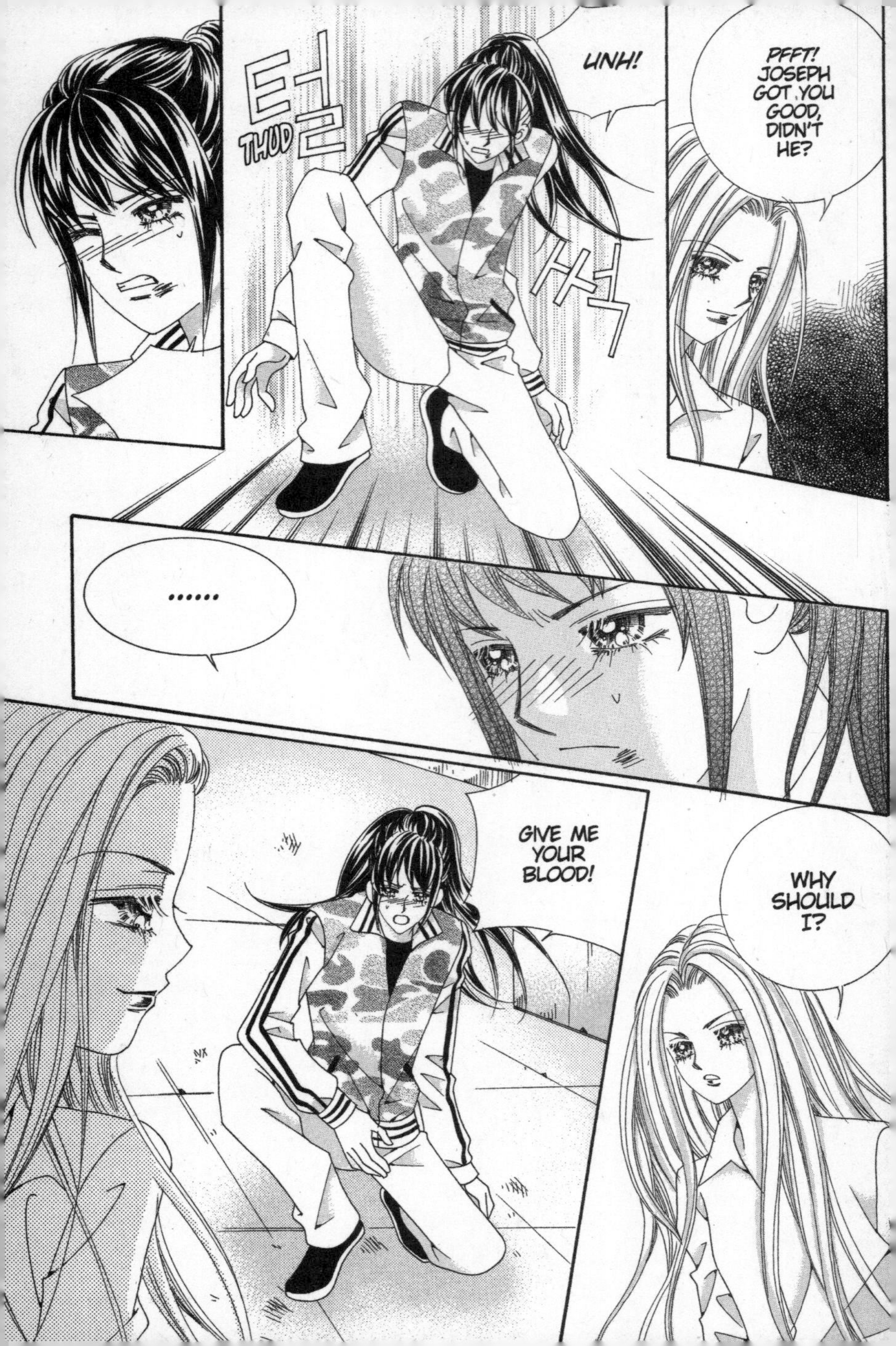

털
THUD
UNH!
썩
PFFT! JOSEPH GOT YOU GOOD, DIDN'T HE?
......
GIVE ME YOUR BLOOD!
WHY SHOULD I?

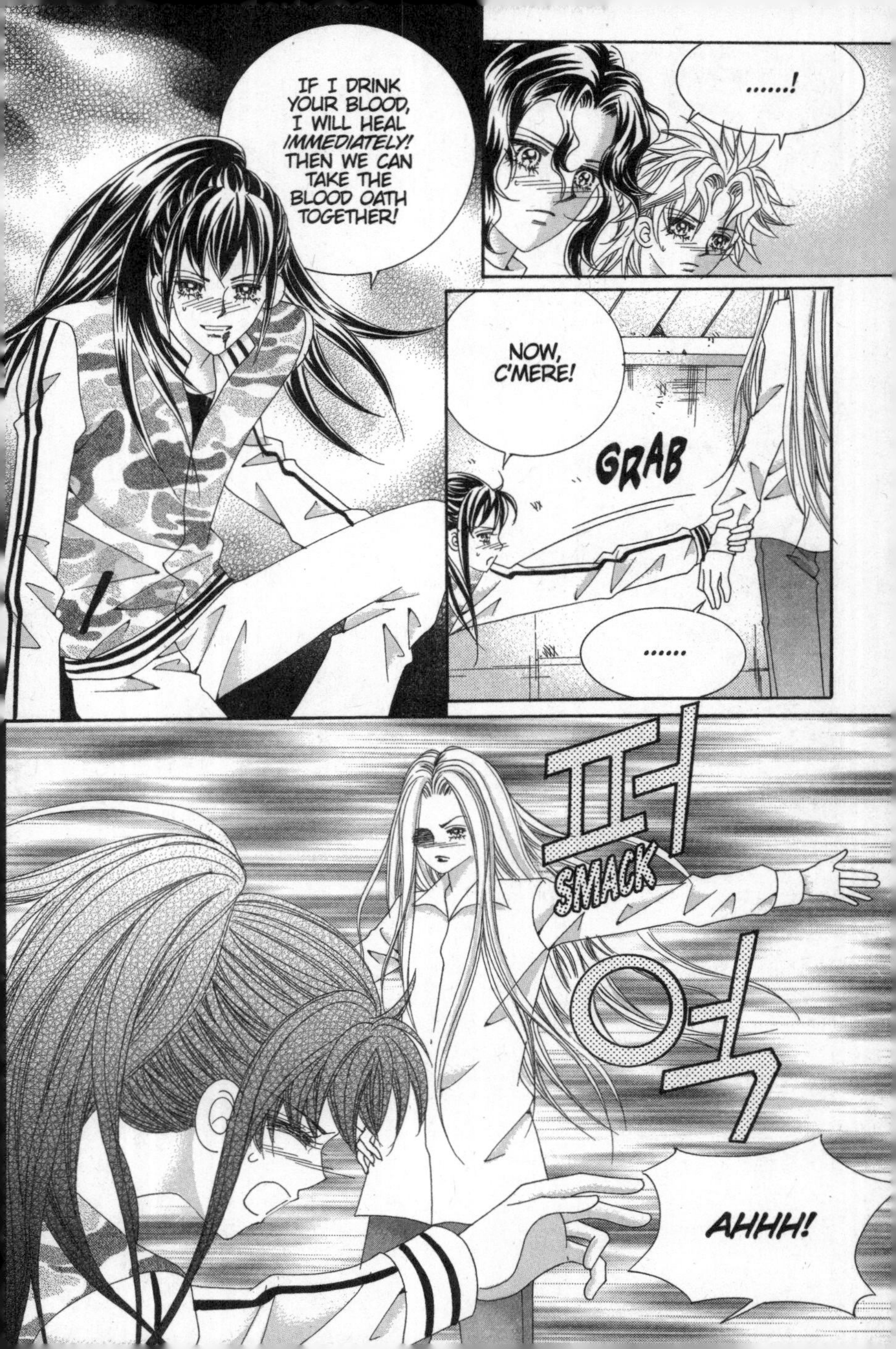
IF I DRINK YOUR BLOOD, I WILL HEAL *IMMEDIATELY!* THEN WE CAN TAKE THE BLOOD OATH TOGETHER!
......!
NOW, C'MERE!
GRAB
......
SMACK
AHHH!

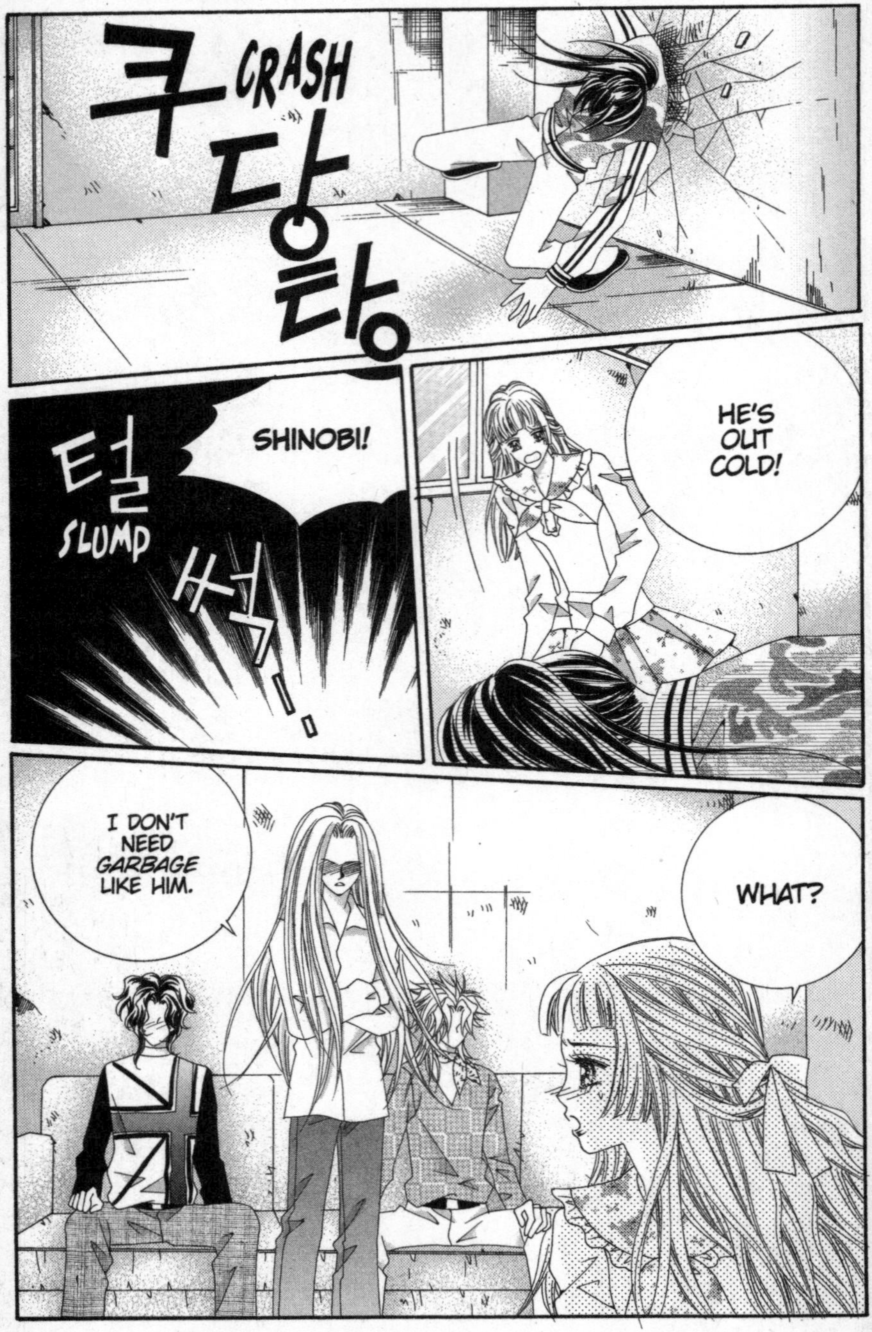
쿠당탕
CRASH
SHINOBI!
털썩
SLUMP
HE'S OUT COLD!
I DON'T NEED GARBAGE LIKE HIM.
WHAT?

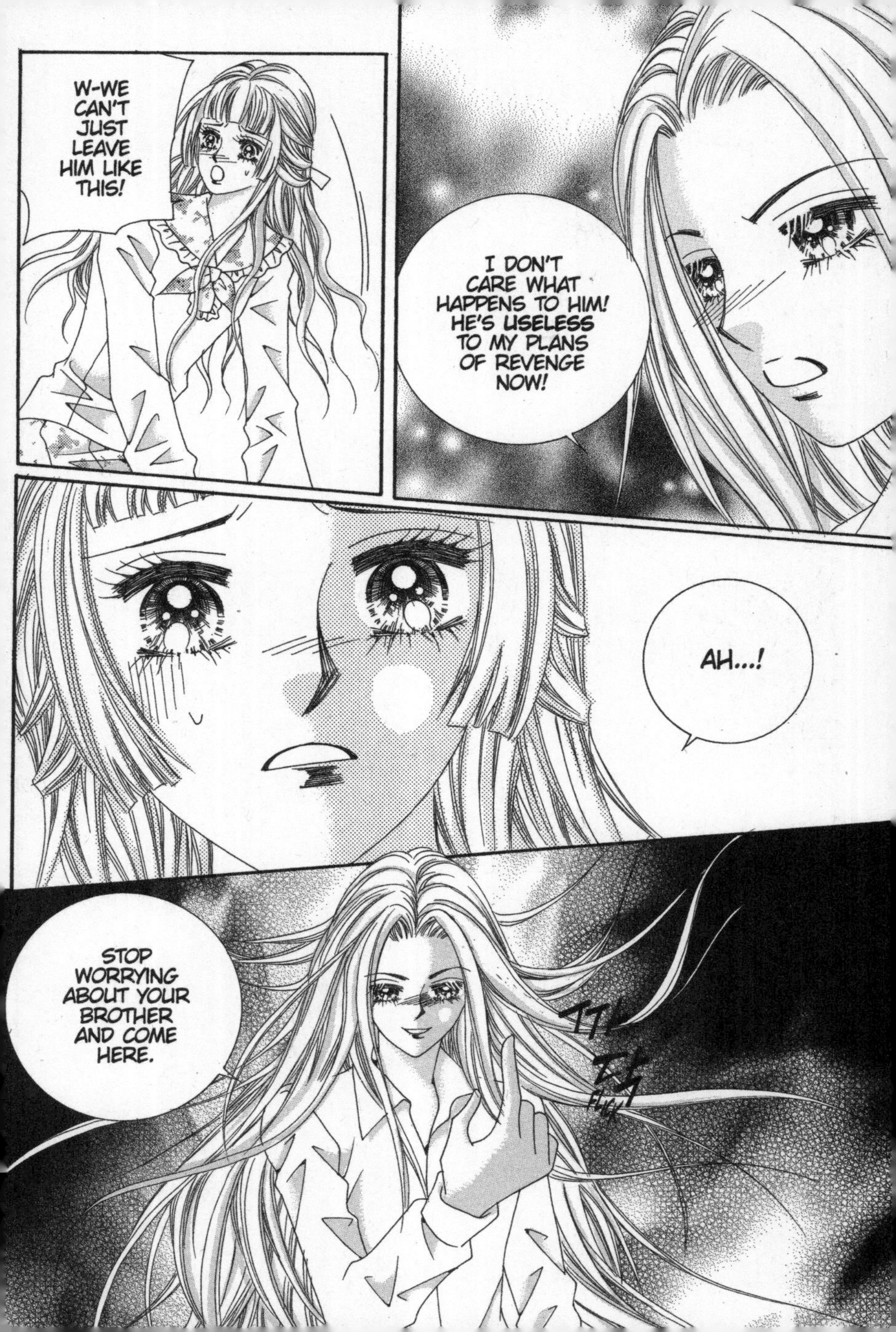
W-WE CAN'T JUST LEAVE HIM LIKE THIS!
I DON'T CARE WHAT HAPPENS TO HIM! HE'S USELESS TO MY PLANS OF REVENGE NOW!
AH...!
STOP WORRYING ABOUT YOUR BROTHER AND COME HERE.
FLICK

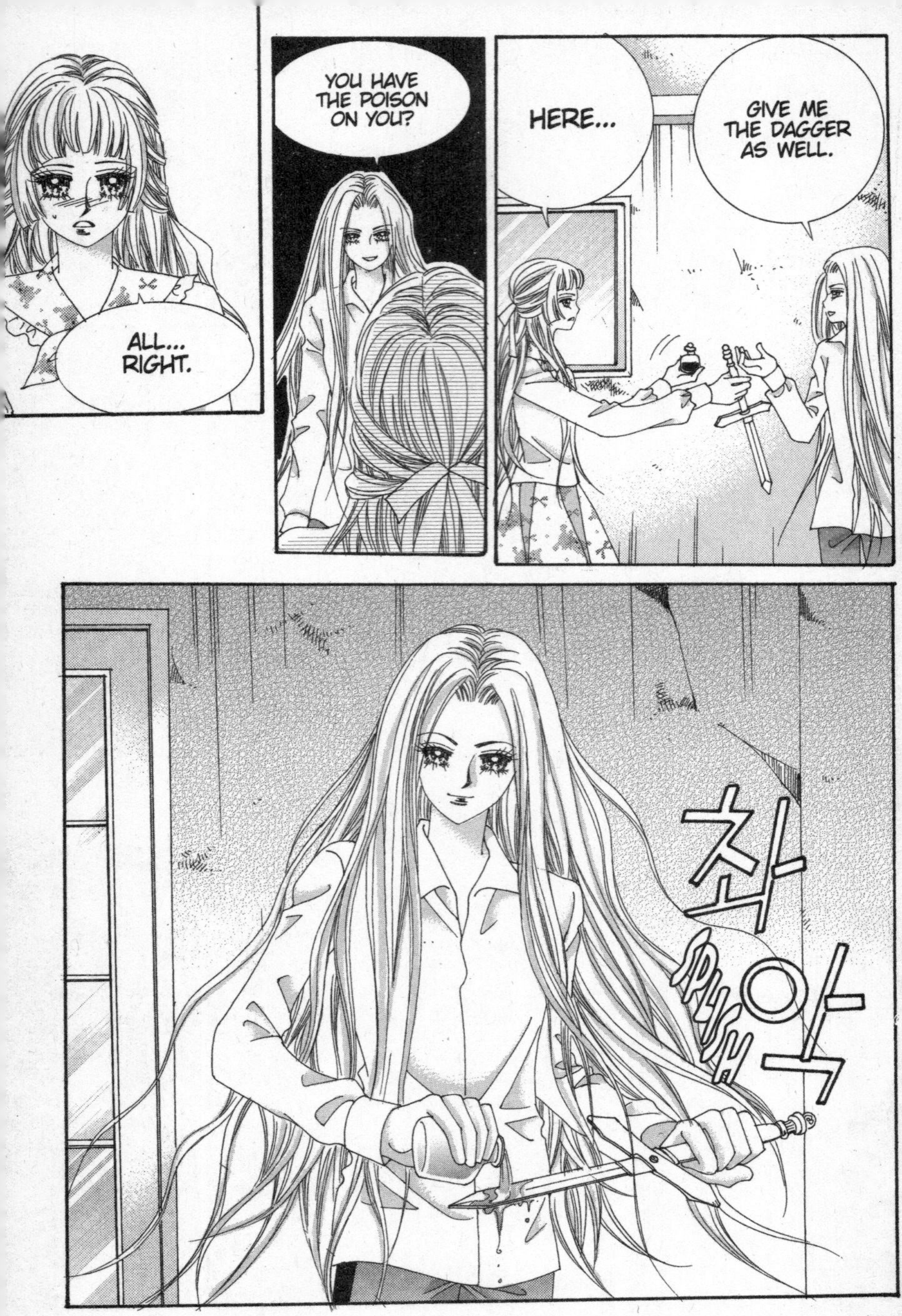
ALL... RIGHT.
YOU HAVE THE POISON ON YOU?
HERE...
GIVE ME THE DAGGER AS WELL.
촤악
SPLISH

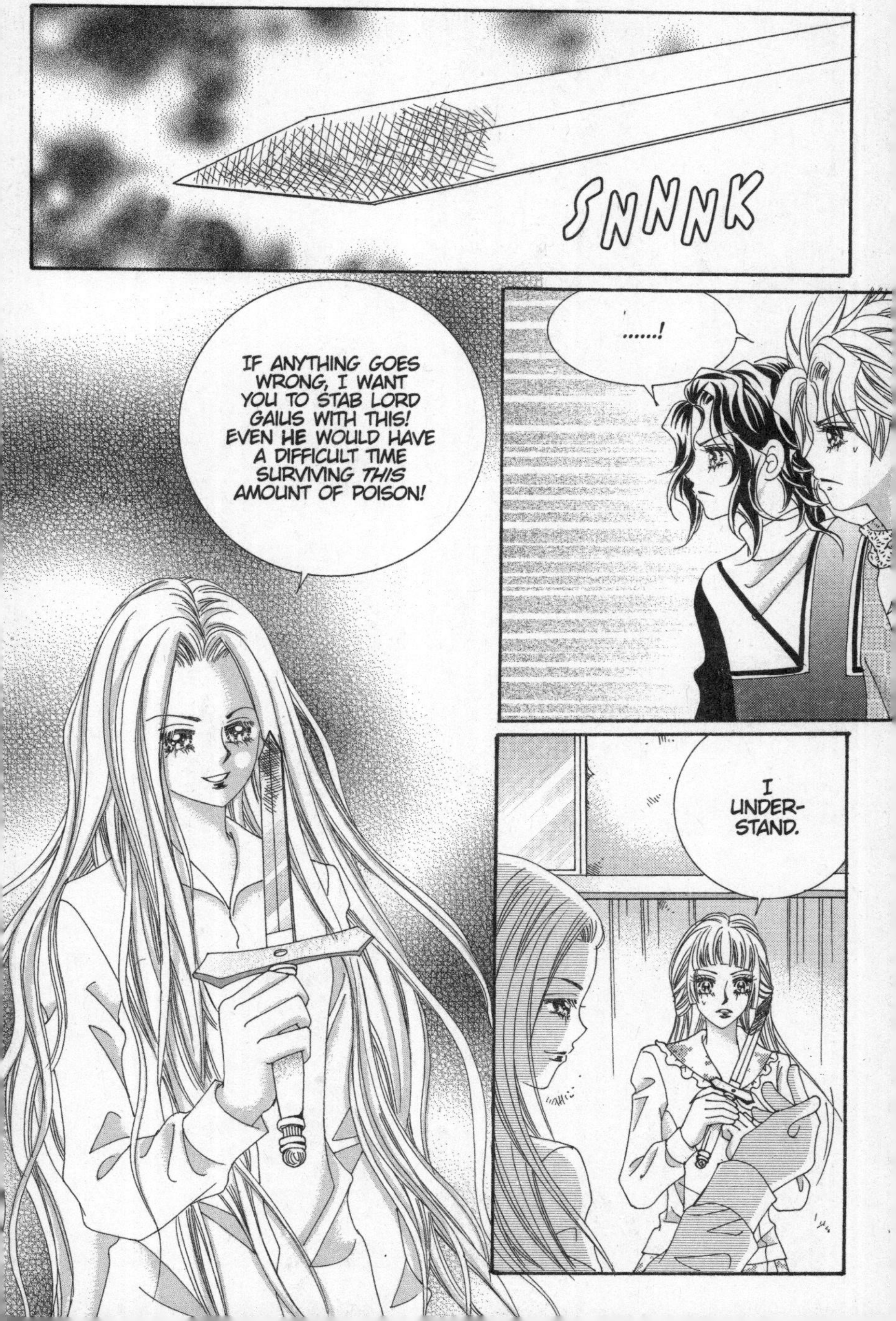
SNNNK
IF ANYTHING GOES WRONG, I WANT YOU TO STAB LORD GAIUS WITH THIS! EVEN HE WOULD HAVE A DIFFICULT TIME SURVIVING *THIS* AMOUNT OF POISON!
......!
I UNDER-STAND.

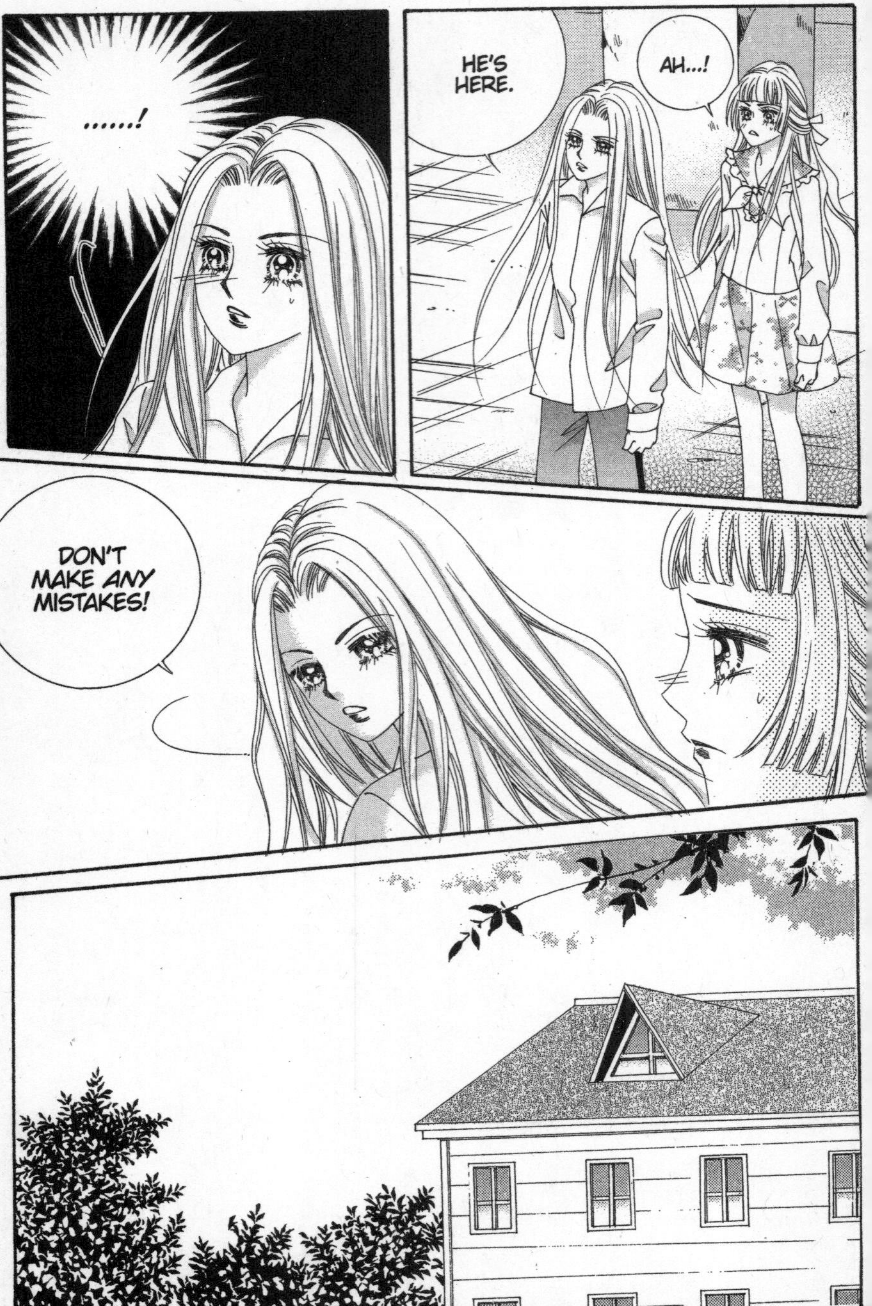
......!
HE'S HERE.
AH...!
DON'T MAKE ANY MISTAKES!

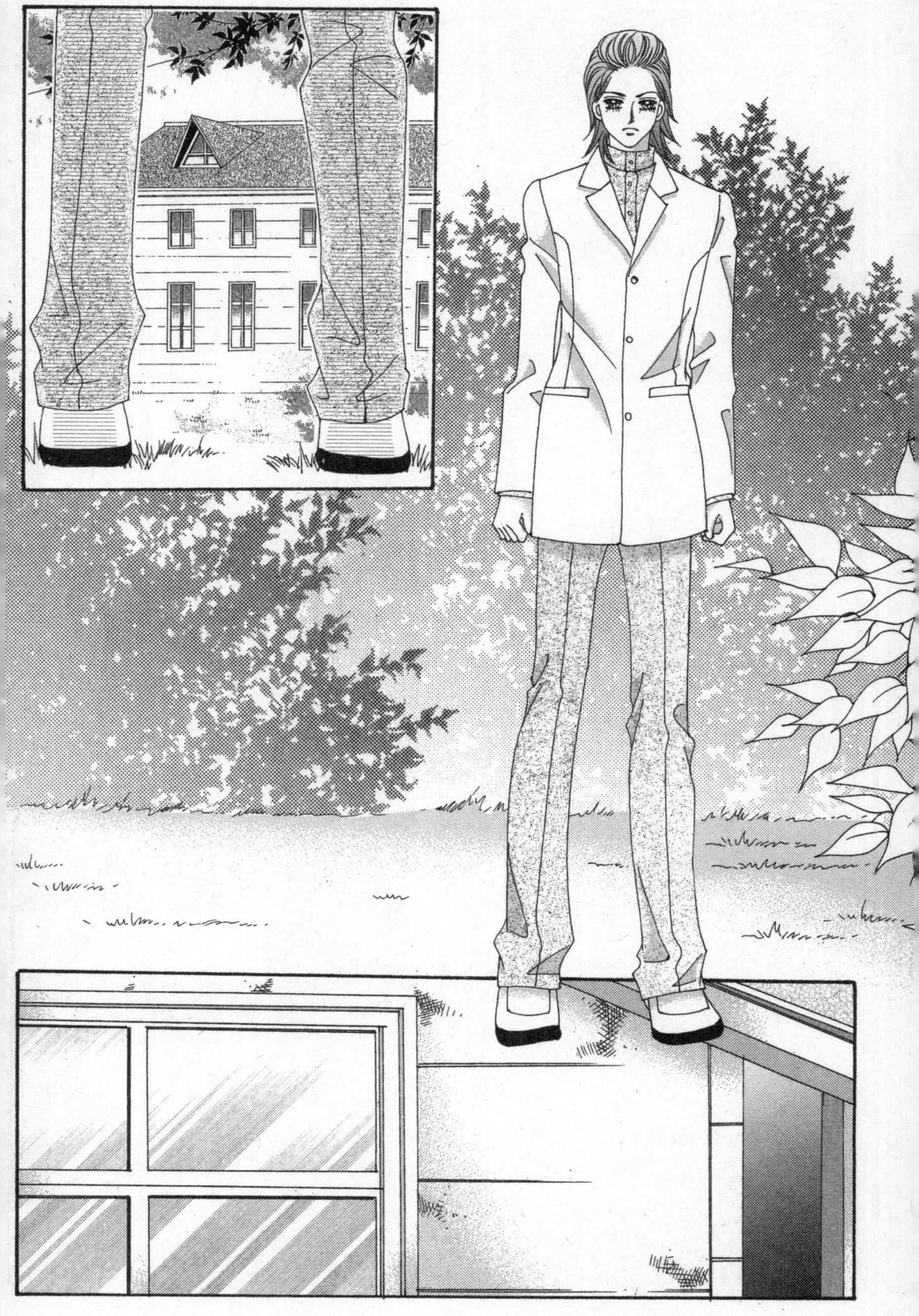

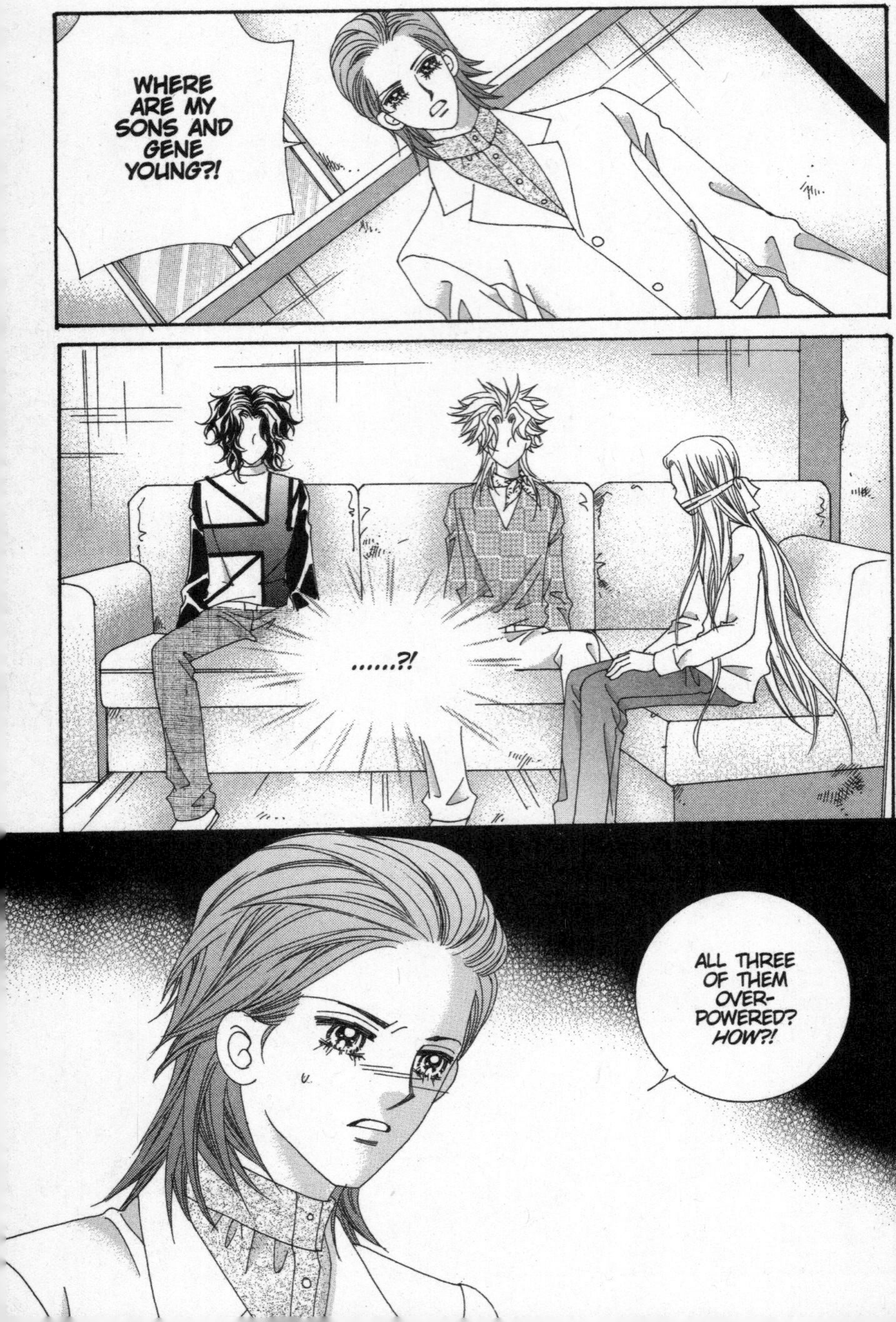
WHERE ARE MY SONS AND GENE YOUNG?!
......?!
ALL THREE OF THEM OVER-POWERED? HOW?!

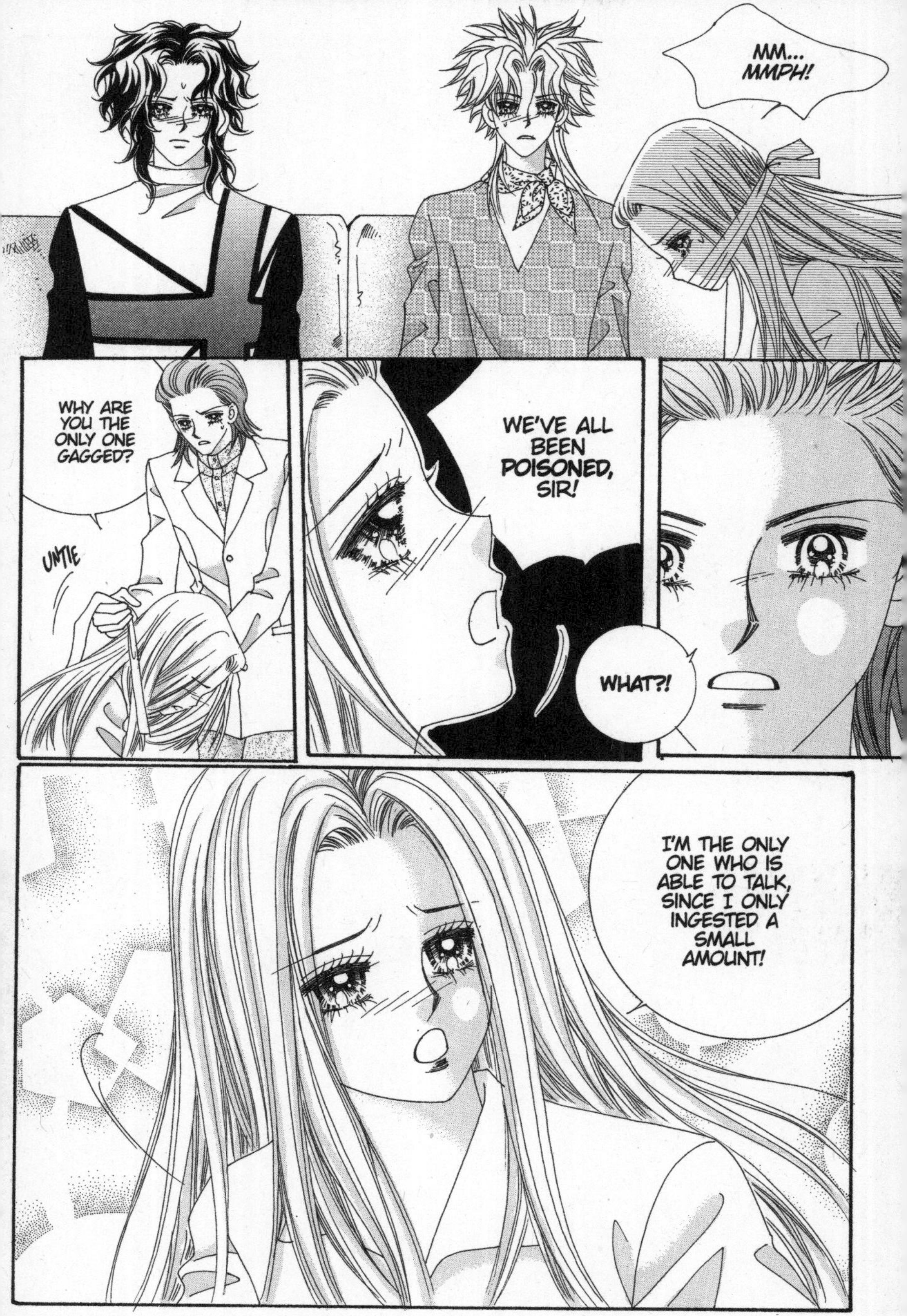
MM... MMPH!
WHY ARE YOU THE ONLY ONE GAGGED?
UNTIE
WE'VE ALL BEEN POISONED, SIR!
WHAT?!
I'M THE ONLY ONE WHO IS ABLE TO TALK, SINCE I ONLY INGESTED A SMALL AMOUNT!

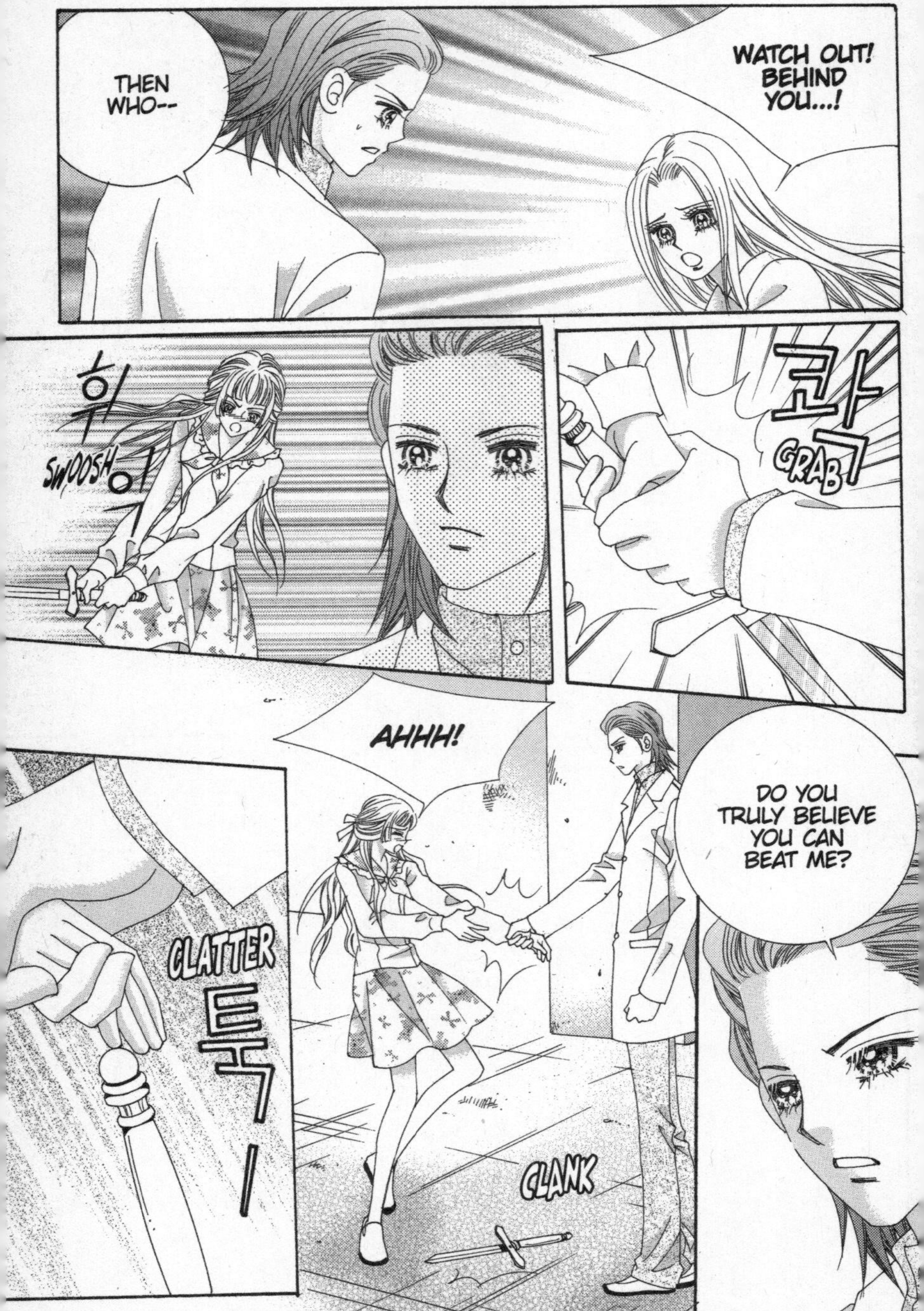

THEN WHO--
WATCH OUT! BEHIND YOU...!
휘익
SWOOSH
콱
GRAB
CLATTER
툭
AHHH!
CLANK
DO YOU TRULY BELIEVE YOU CAN BEAT ME?

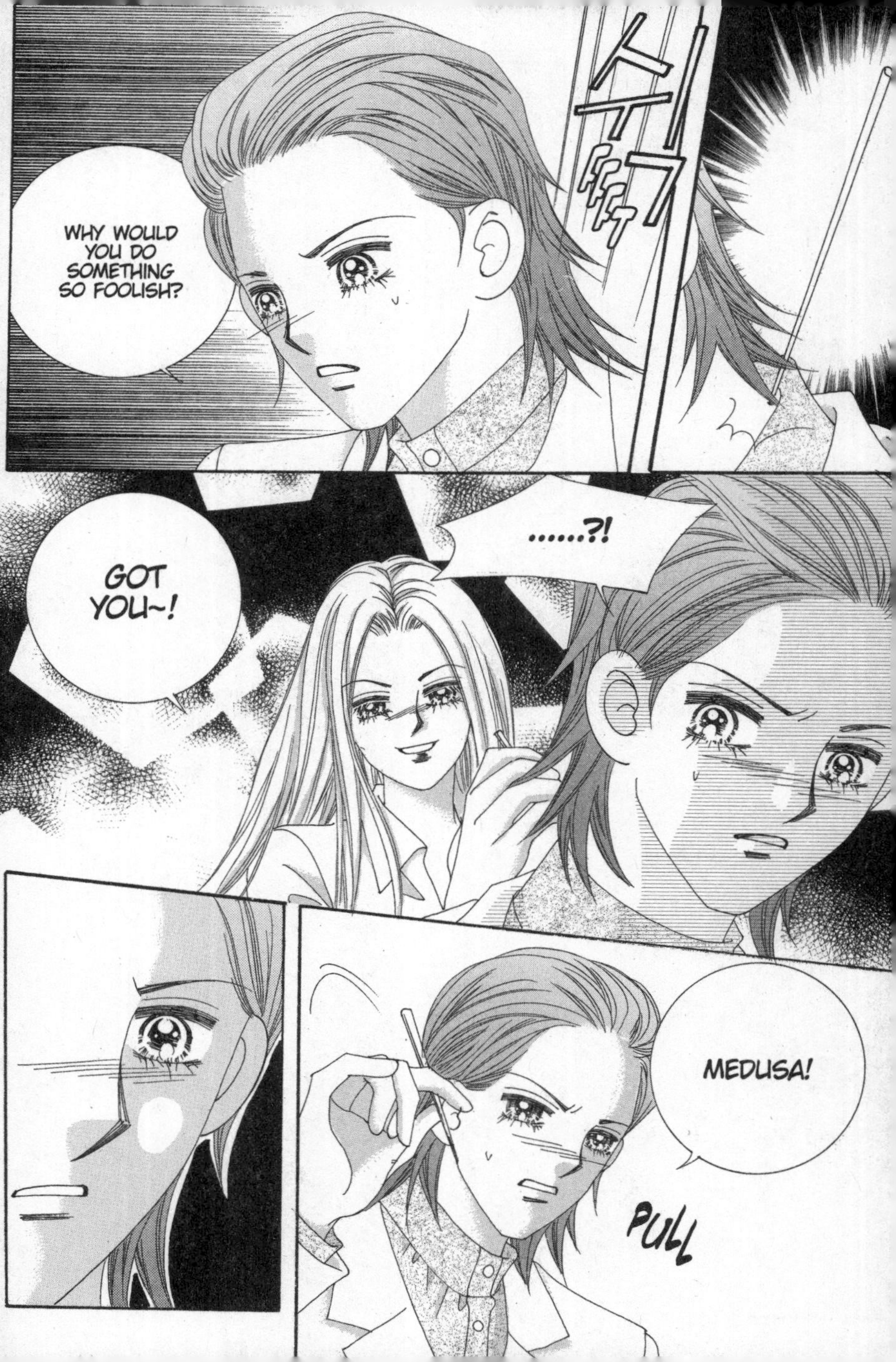
WHY WOULD YOU DO SOMETHING SO FOOLISH?
GOT YOU~!
......?!
MEDUSA!
PULL

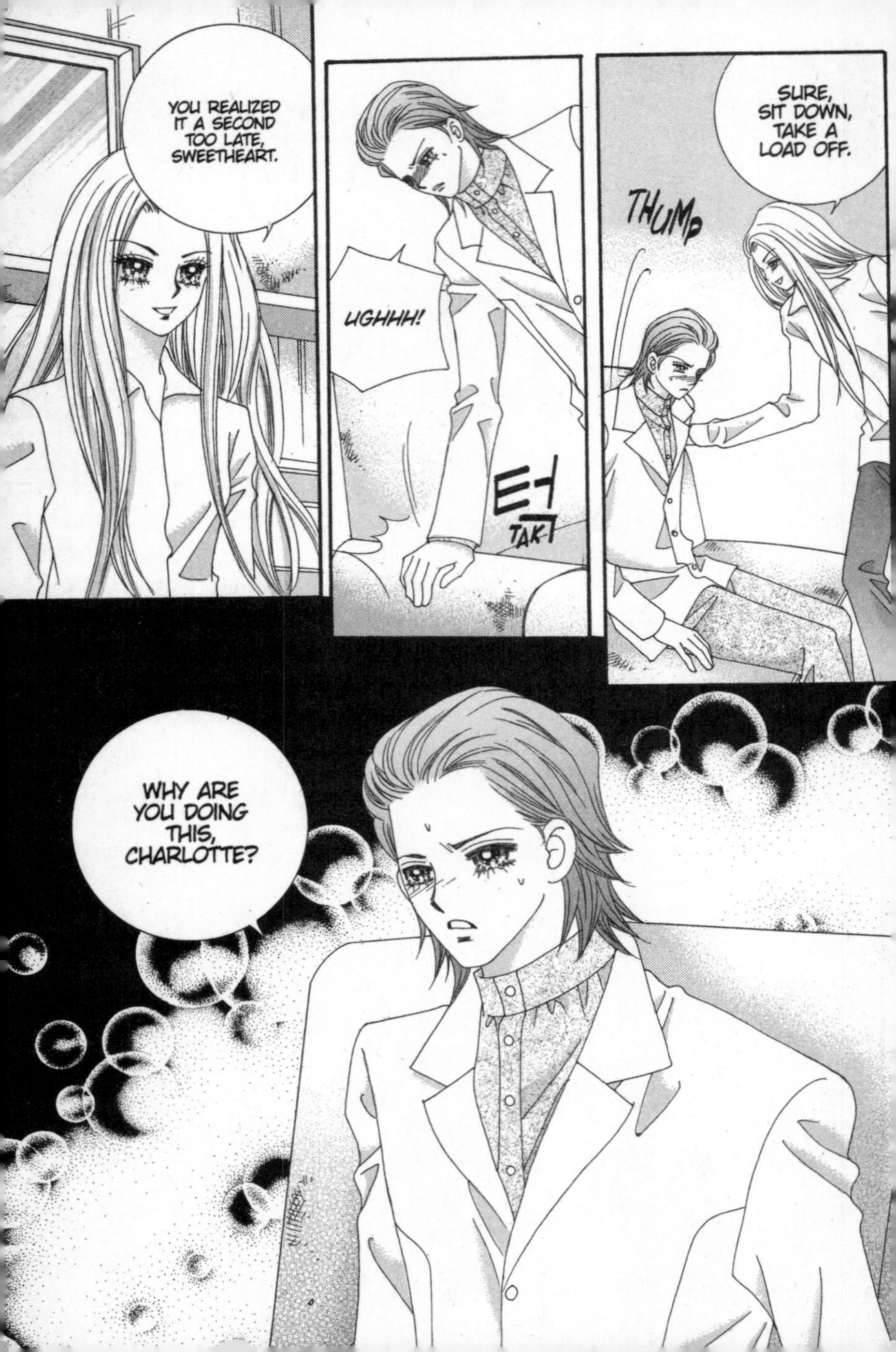
YOU REALIZED IT A SECOND TOO LATE, SWEETHEART.
UGHHH!
TAK
THUMP
SURE, SIT DOWN, TAKE A LOAD OFF.
WHY ARE YOU DOING THIS, CHARLOTTE?

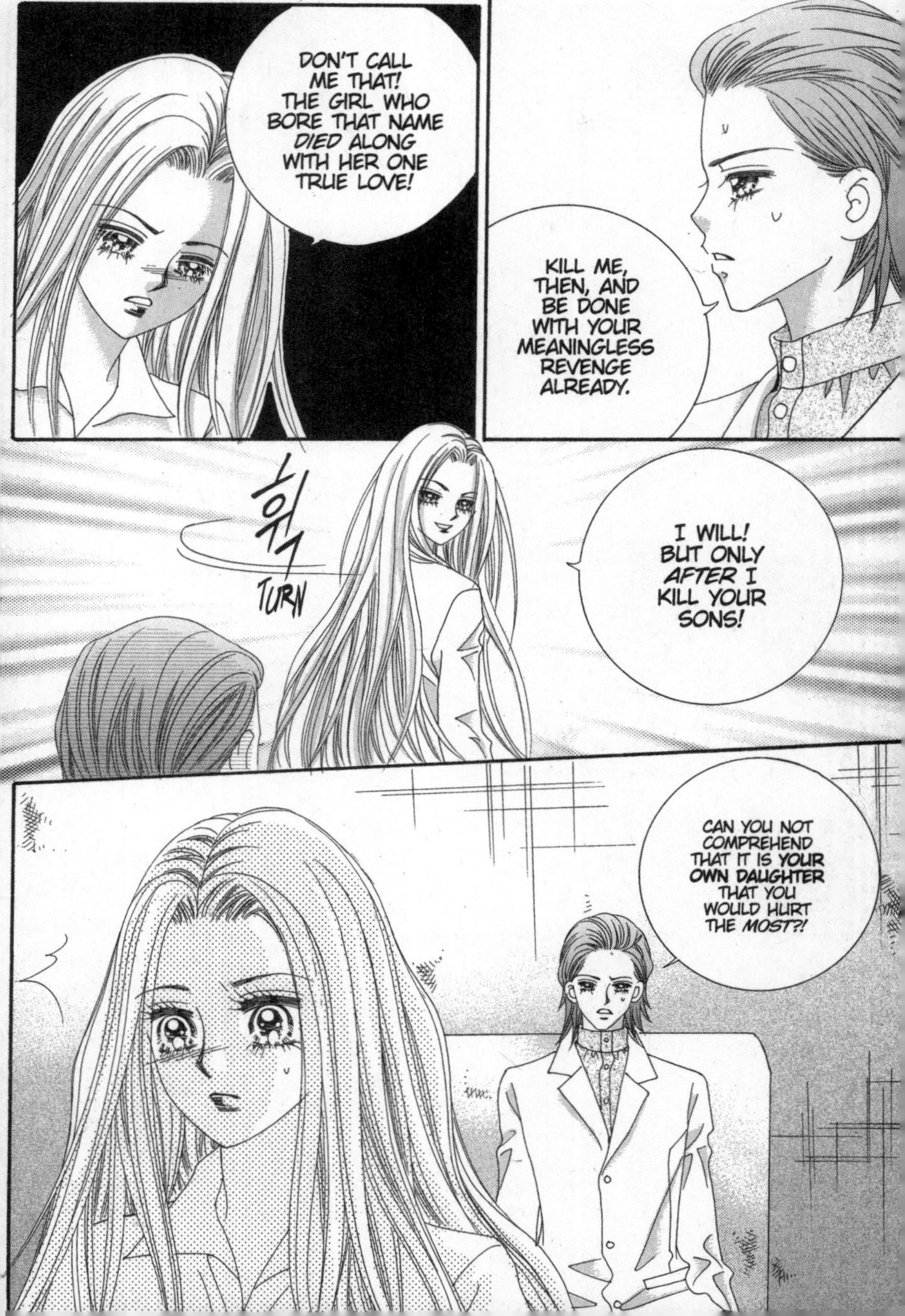
DON'T CALL ME THAT! THE GIRL WHO BORE THAT NAME *DIED* ALONG WITH HER ONE TRUE LOVE!
KILL ME, THEN, AND BE DONE WITH YOUR MEANINGLESS REVENGE ALREADY.
TURN
I WILL! BUT ONLY *AFTER* I KILL YOUR SONS!
CAN YOU NOT COMPREHEND THAT IT IS **YOUR OWN DAUGHTER** THAT YOU WOULD HURT THE *MOST?!*

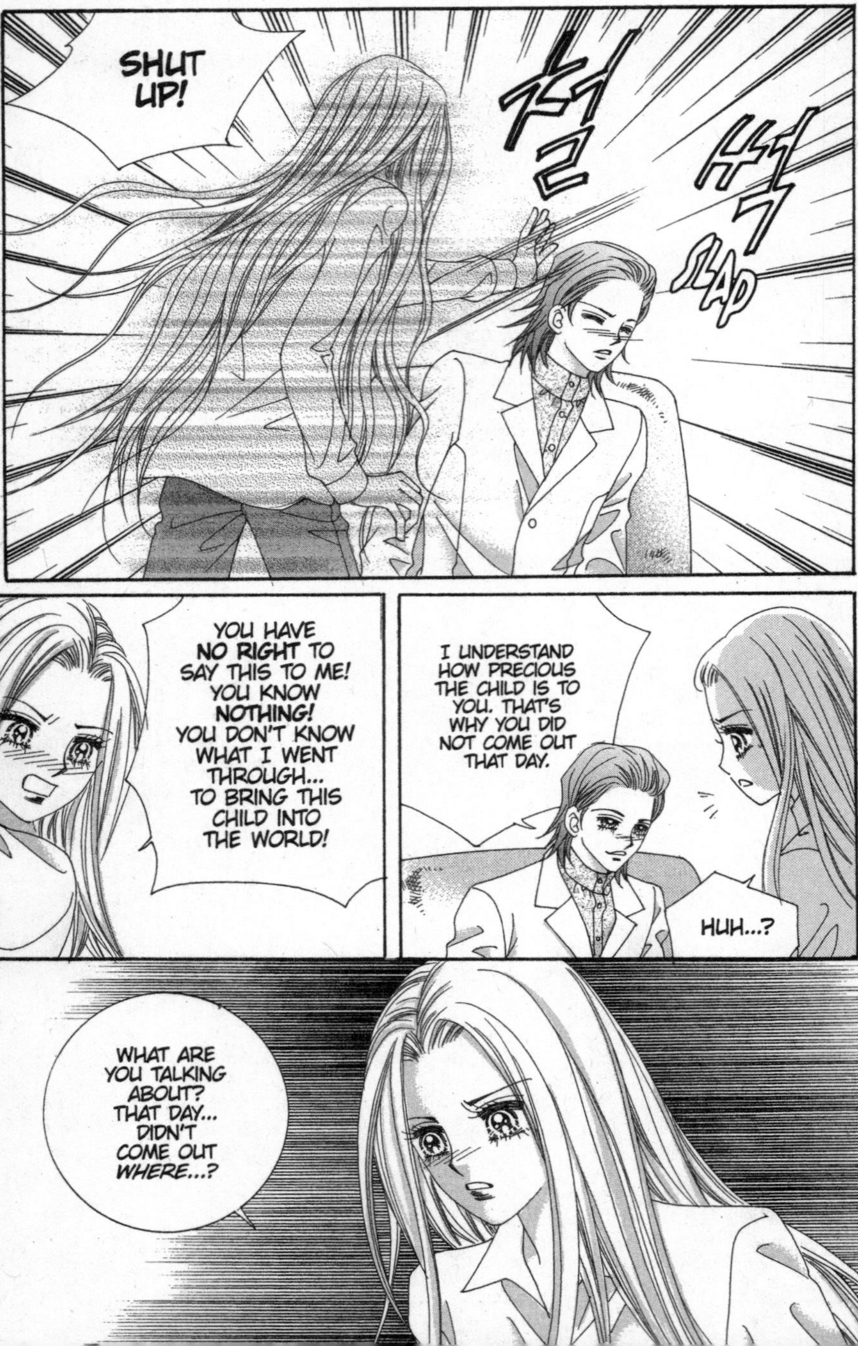
SHUT UP!
철
썩
SLAP
YOU HAVE NO RIGHT TO SAY THIS TO ME! YOU KNOW NOTHING! YOU DON'T KNOW WHAT I WENT THROUGH... TO BRING THIS CHILD INTO THE WORLD!
I UNDERSTAND HOW PRECIOUS THE CHILD IS TO YOU. THAT'S WHY YOU DID NOT COME OUT THAT DAY.
HUH...?
WHAT ARE YOU TALKING ABOUT? THAT DAY... DIDN'T COME OUT WHERE...?

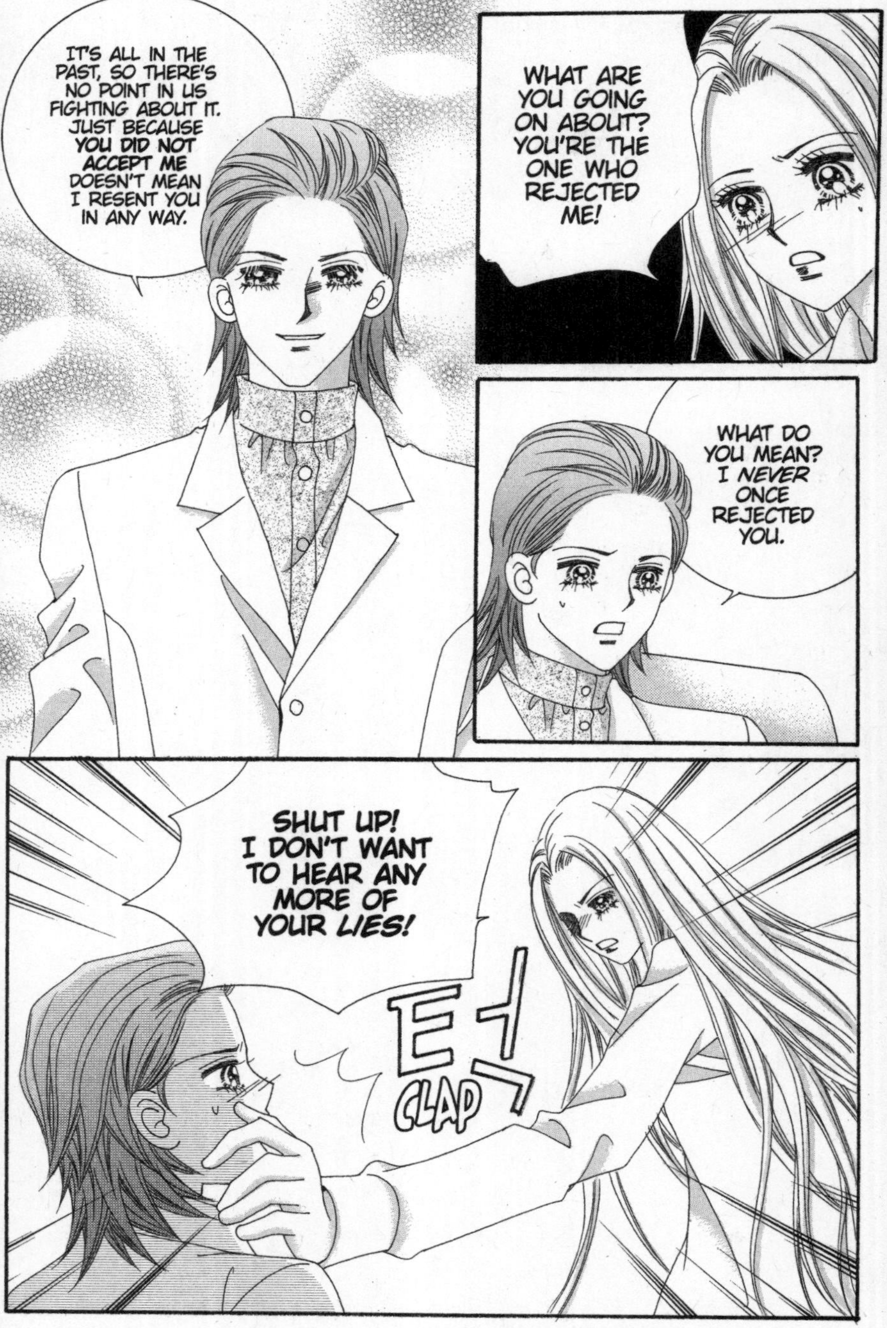
IT'S ALL IN THE PAST, SO THERE'S NO POINT IN US FIGHTING ABOUT IT. JUST BECAUSE YOU DID NOT ACCEPT ME DOESN'T MEAN I RESENT YOU IN ANY WAY.
WHAT ARE YOU GOING ON ABOUT? YOU'RE THE ONE WHO REJECTED ME!
WHAT DO YOU MEAN? I NEVER ONCE REJECTED YOU.
SHUT UP! I DON'T WANT TO HEAR ANY MORE OF YOUR LIES!
CLAP

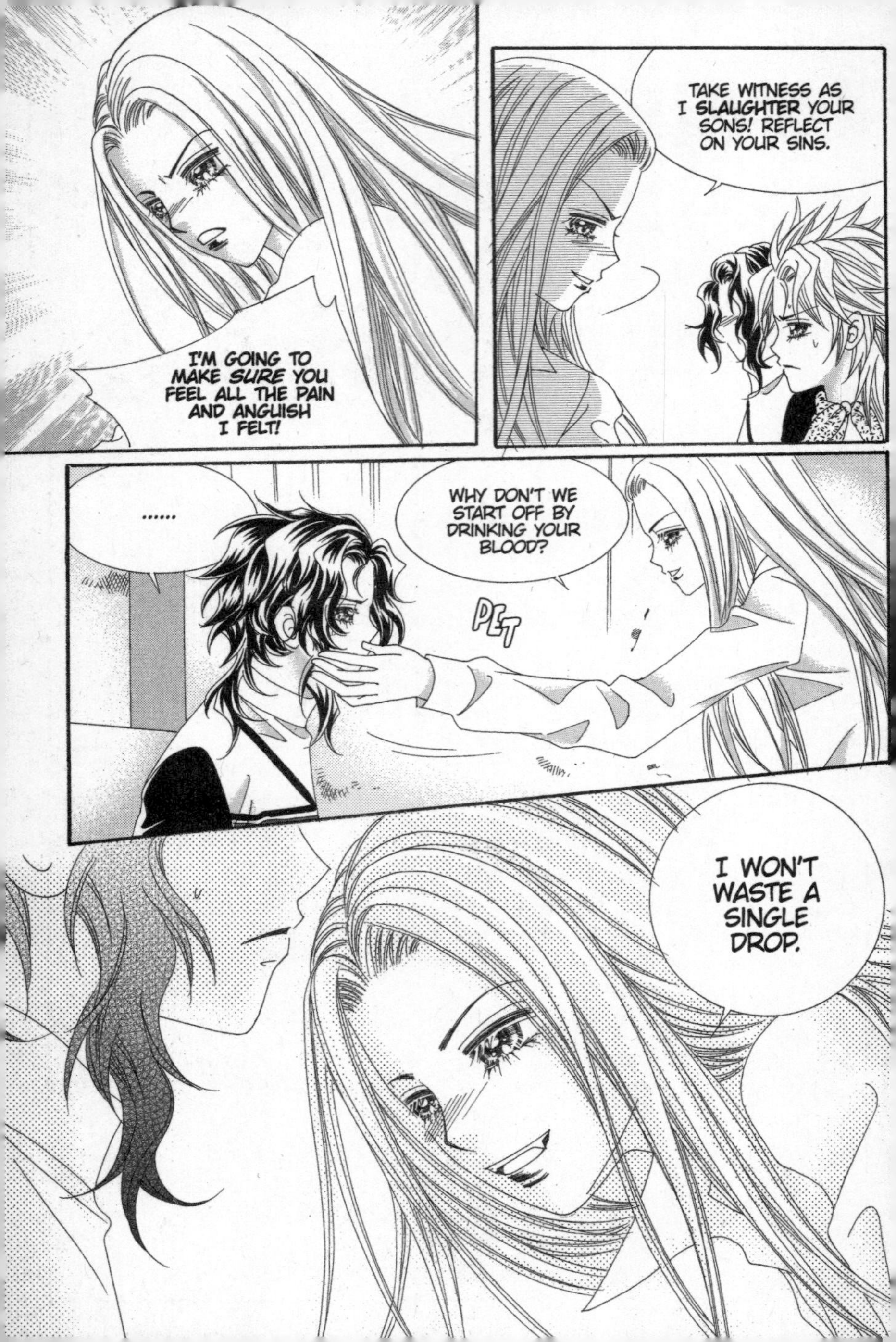
I'M GOING TO MAKE SURE YOU FEEL ALL THE PAIN AND ANGUISH I FELT!
TAKE WITNESS AS I SLAUGHTER YOUR SONS! REFLECT ON YOUR SINS.
......
WHY DON'T WE START OFF BY DRINKING YOUR BLOOD?
PET
I WON'T WASTE A SINGLE DROP.

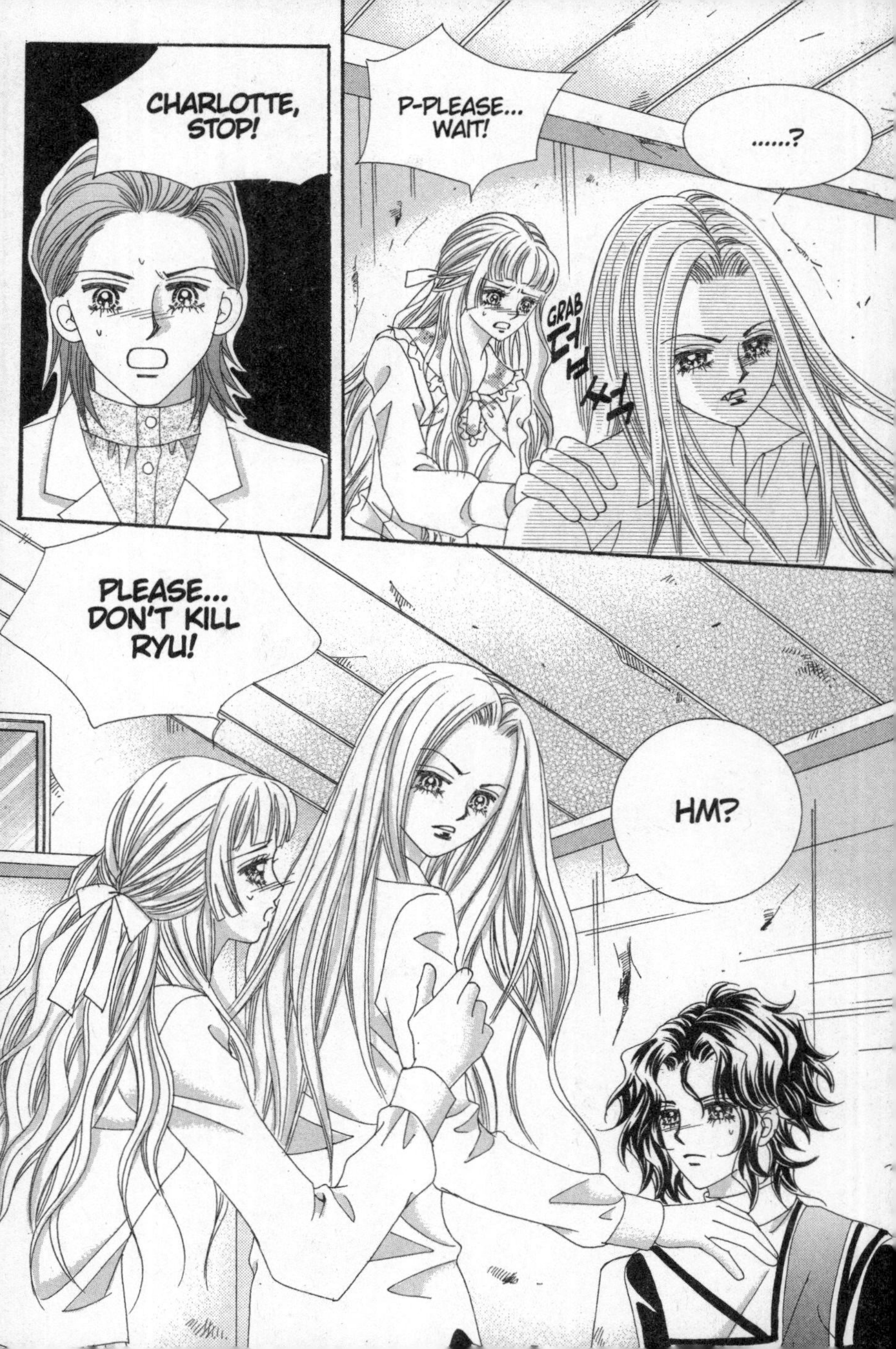

CHARLOTTE, STOP!
P-PLEASE... WAIT!
......?
GRAB
PLEASE... DON'T KILL RYU!
HM?

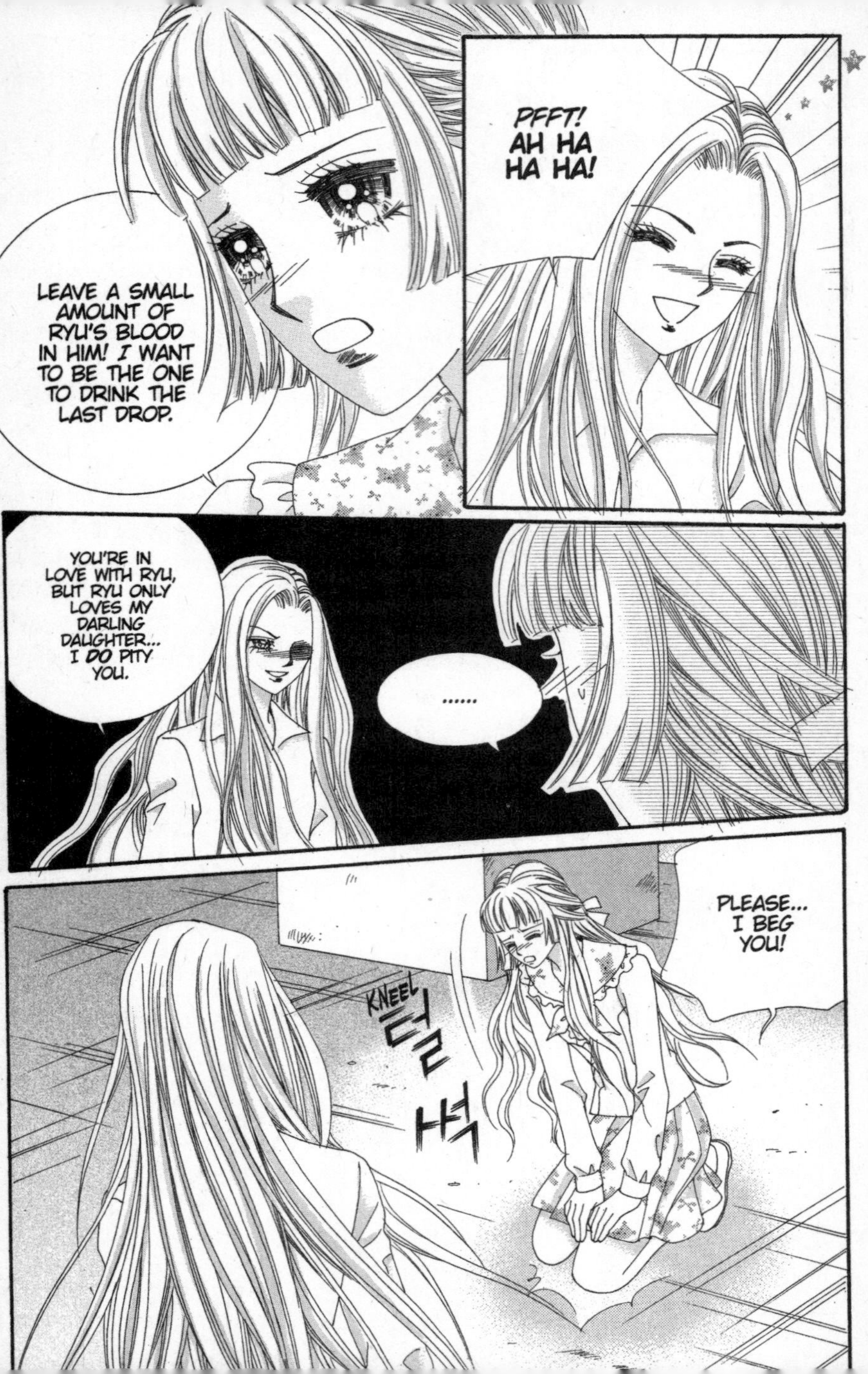
LEAVE A SMALL AMOUNT OF RYU'S BLOOD IN HIM! *I* WANT TO BE THE ONE TO DRINK THE LAST DROP.
PFFT! AH HA HA HA!
YOU'RE IN LOVE WITH RYU, BUT RYU ONLY LOVES MY DARLING DAUGHTER... I *DO* PITY YOU.
......
KNEEL
PLEASE... I BEG YOU!

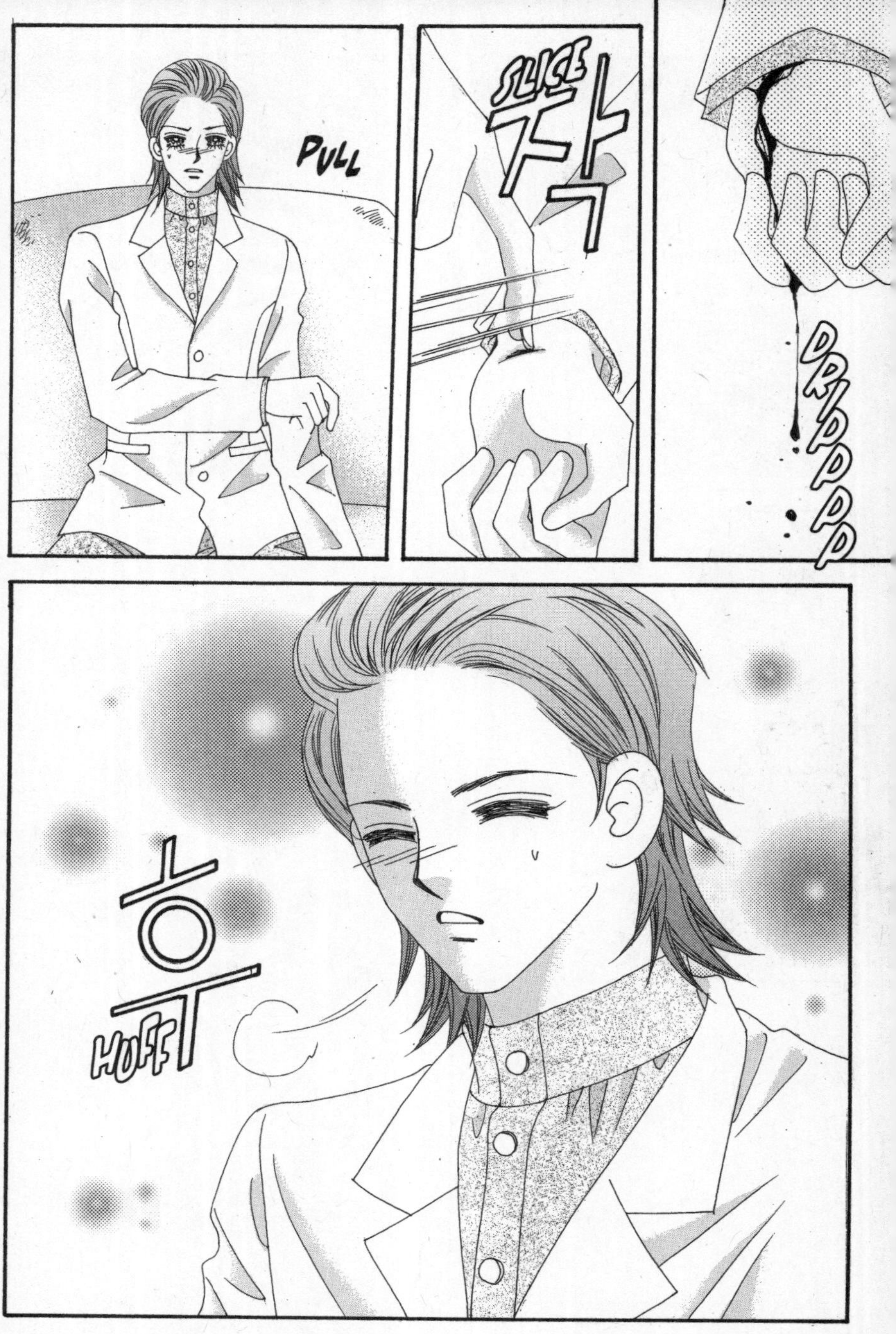
PULL
SLICE
DRIPPPP
HUFF

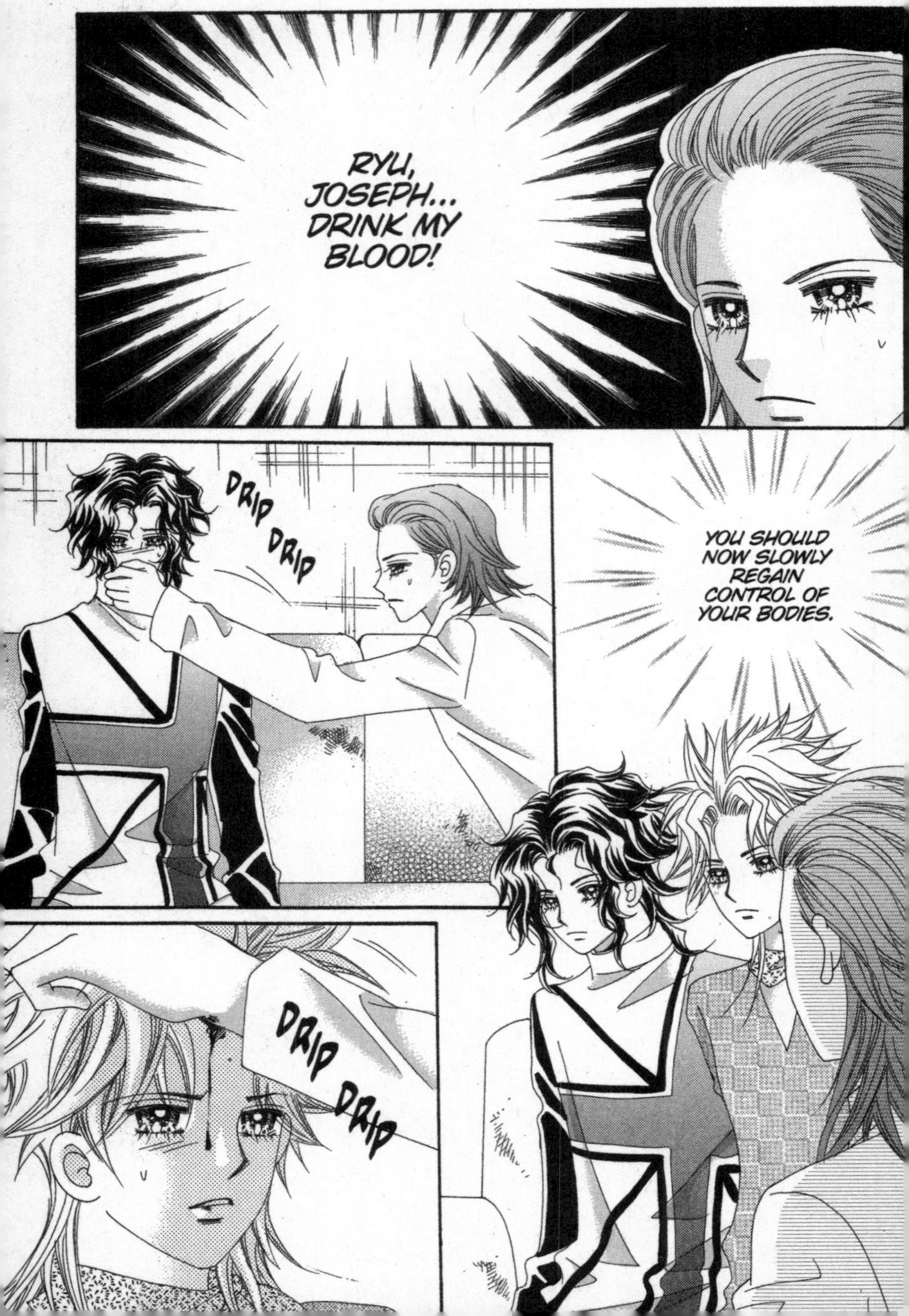
RYU, JOSEPH... DRINK MY BLOOD!
DRIP DRIP
YOU SHOULD NOW SLOWLY REGAIN CONTROL OF YOUR BODIES.
DRIP DRIP

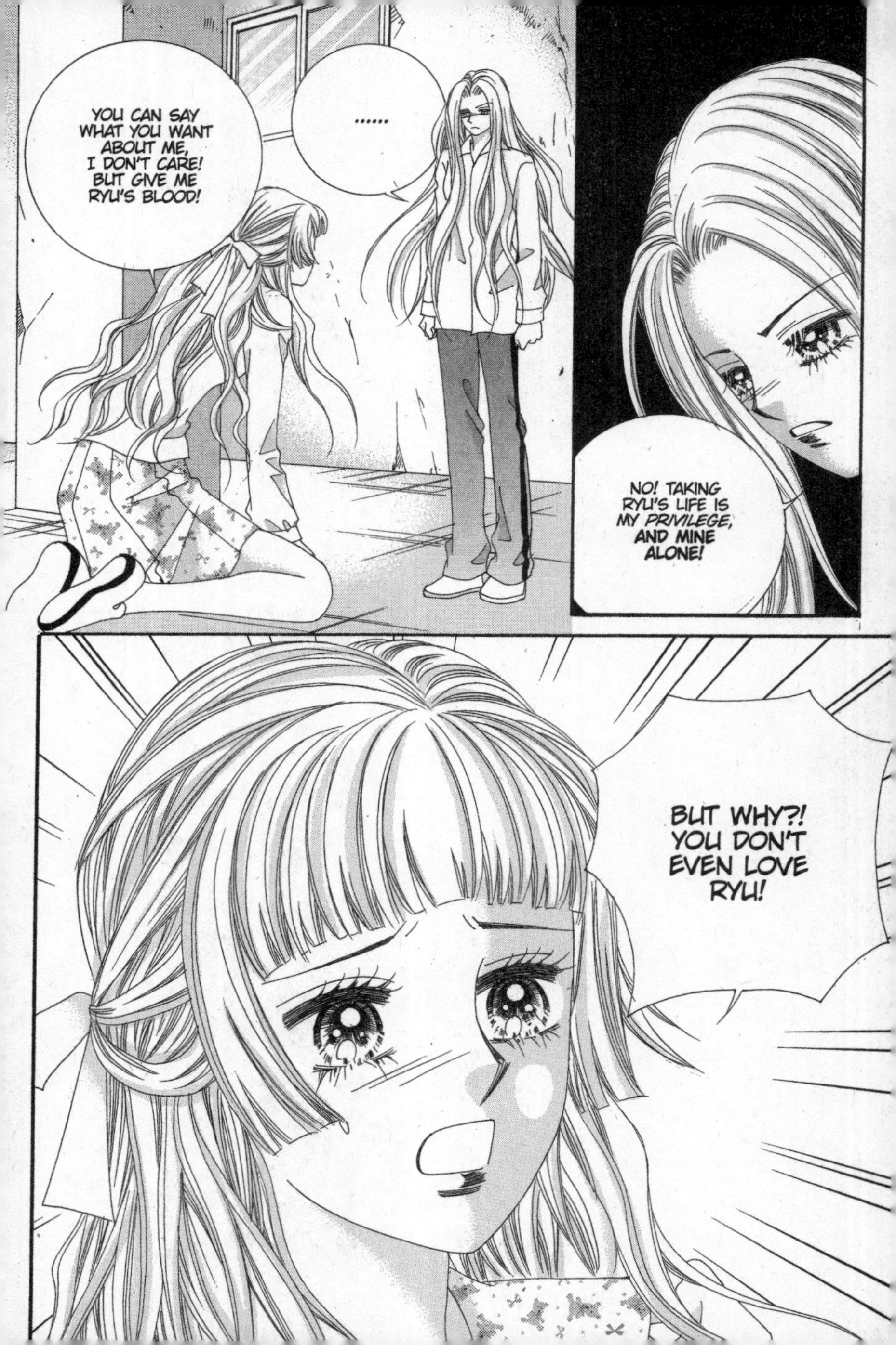
YOU CAN SAY WHAT YOU WANT ABOUT ME, I DON'T CARE! BUT GIVE ME RYU'S BLOOD!
......
NO! TAKING RYU'S LIFE IS MY *PRIVILEGE*, AND MINE ALONE!
BUT WHY?! YOU DON'T EVEN LOVE RYU!

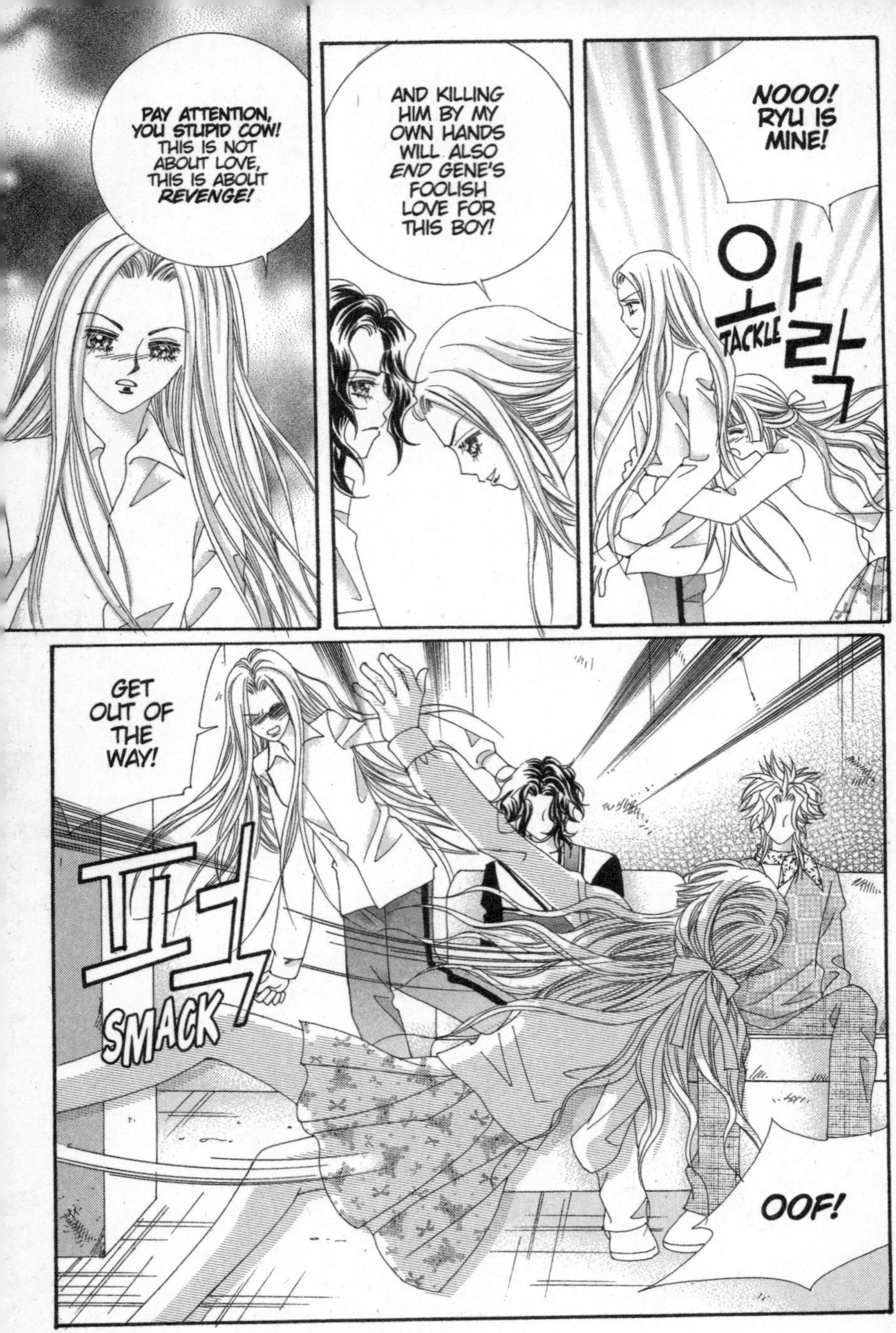
PAY ATTENTION, YOU STUPID COW! THIS IS NOT ABOUT LOVE, THIS IS ABOUT REVENGE!
AND KILLING HIM BY MY OWN HANDS WILL ALSO END GENE'S FOOLISH LOVE FOR THIS BOY!
NOOO! RYU IS MINE!
와락
TACKLE
GET OUT OF THE WAY!
퍽
SMACK
OOF!

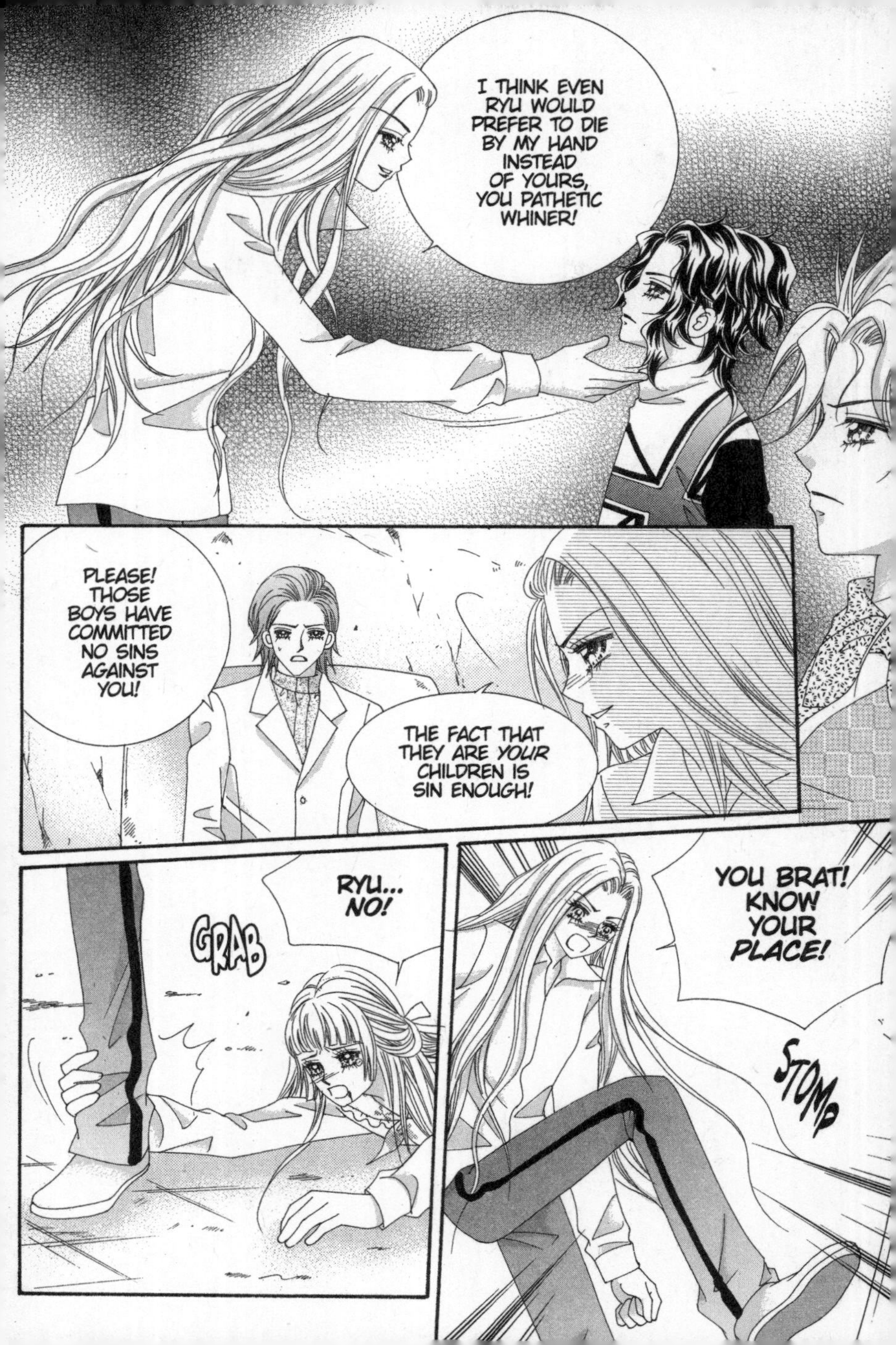
I THINK EVEN RYU WOULD PREFER TO DIE BY MY HAND INSTEAD OF YOURS, YOU PATHETIC WHINER!
PLEASE! THOSE BOYS HAVE COMMITTED NO SINS AGAINST YOU!
THE FACT THAT THEY ARE *YOUR* CHILDREN IS SIN ENOUGH!
GRAB
RYU... *NO!*
YOU BRAT! KNOW YOUR *PLACE!*
STOMP

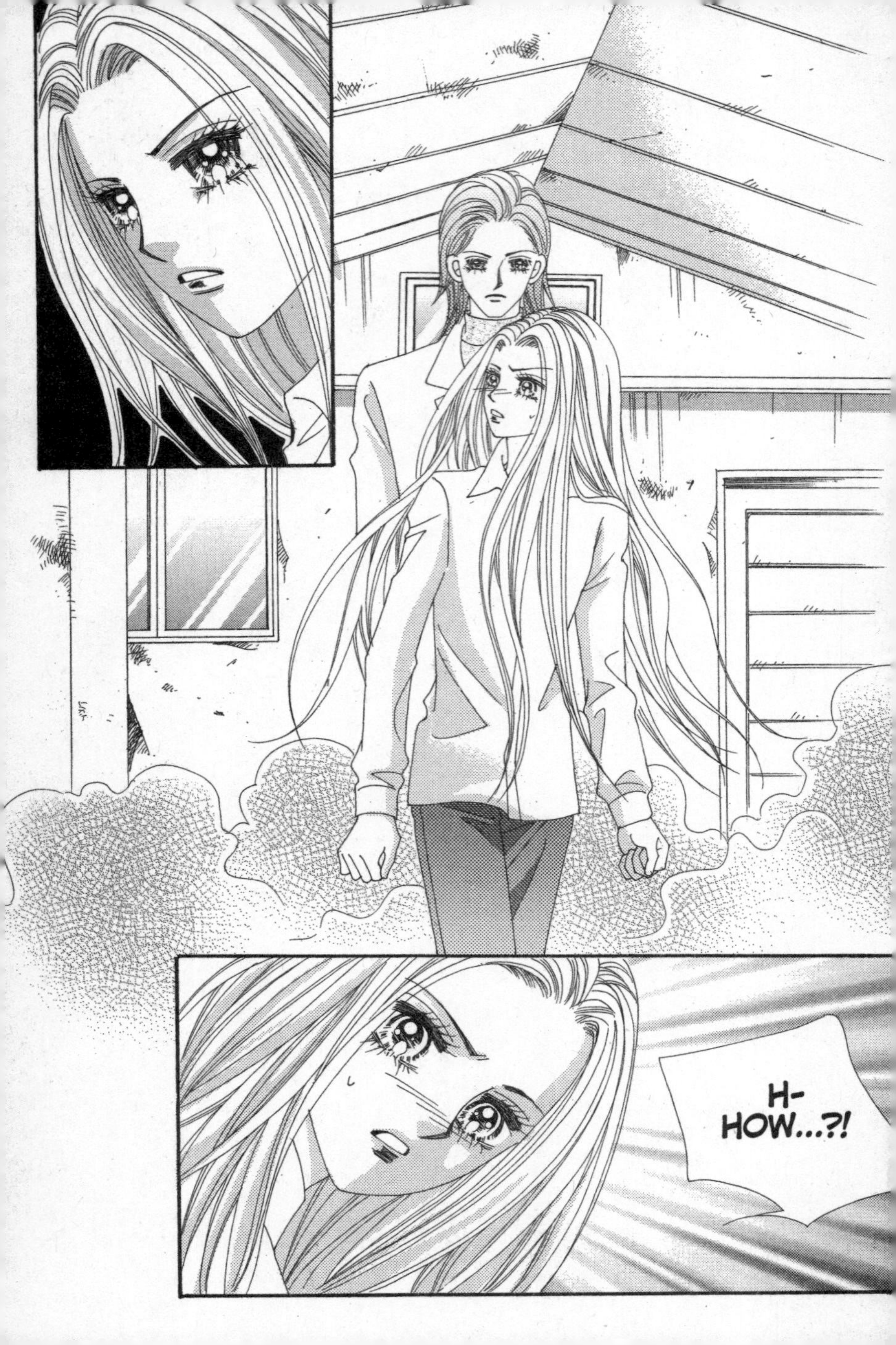
H-
HOW...?!

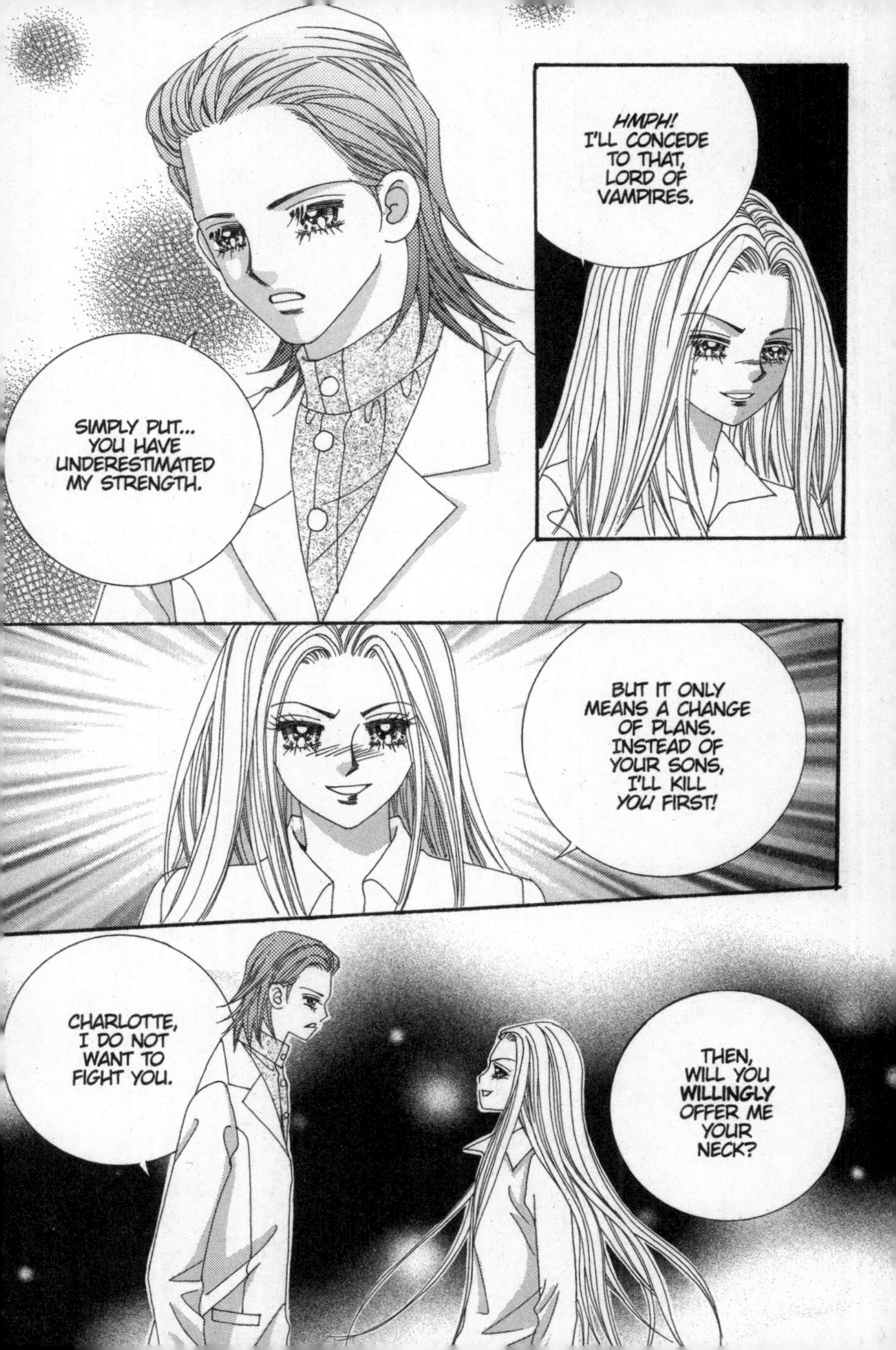
SIMPLY PUT... YOU HAVE UNDERESTIMATED MY STRENGTH.
HMPH! I'LL CONCEDE TO THAT, LORD OF VAMPIRES.
BUT IT ONLY MEANS A CHANGE OF PLANS. INSTEAD OF YOUR SONS, I'LL KILL *YOU* FIRST!
CHARLOTTE, I DO NOT WANT TO FIGHT YOU.
THEN, WILL YOU **WILLINGLY** OFFER ME YOUR NECK?

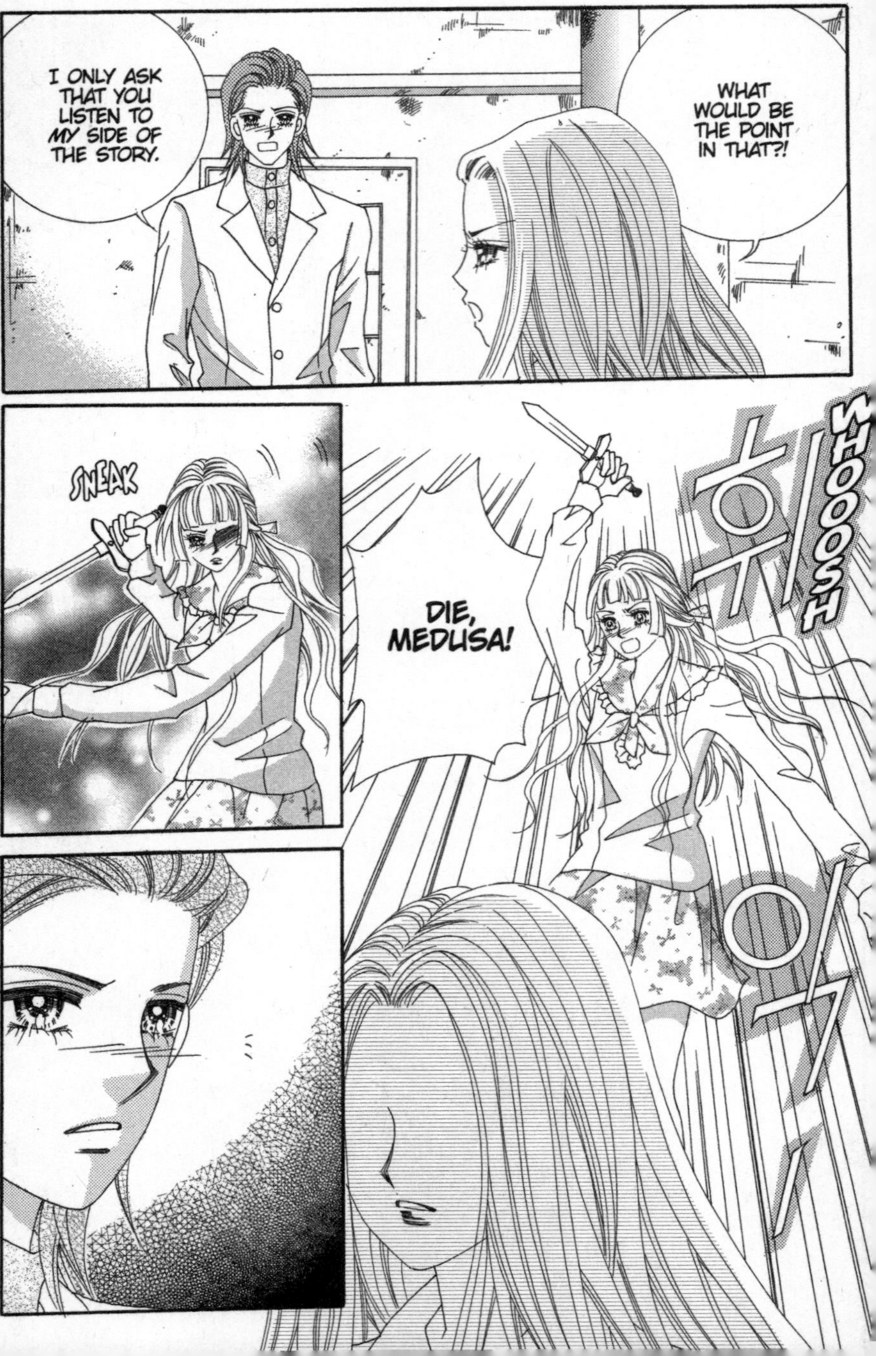
I ONLY ASK THAT YOU LISTEN TO MY SIDE OF THE STORY.
WHAT WOULD BE THE POINT IN THAT?!
SNEAK
DIE, MEDUSA!
WHOOOOSH

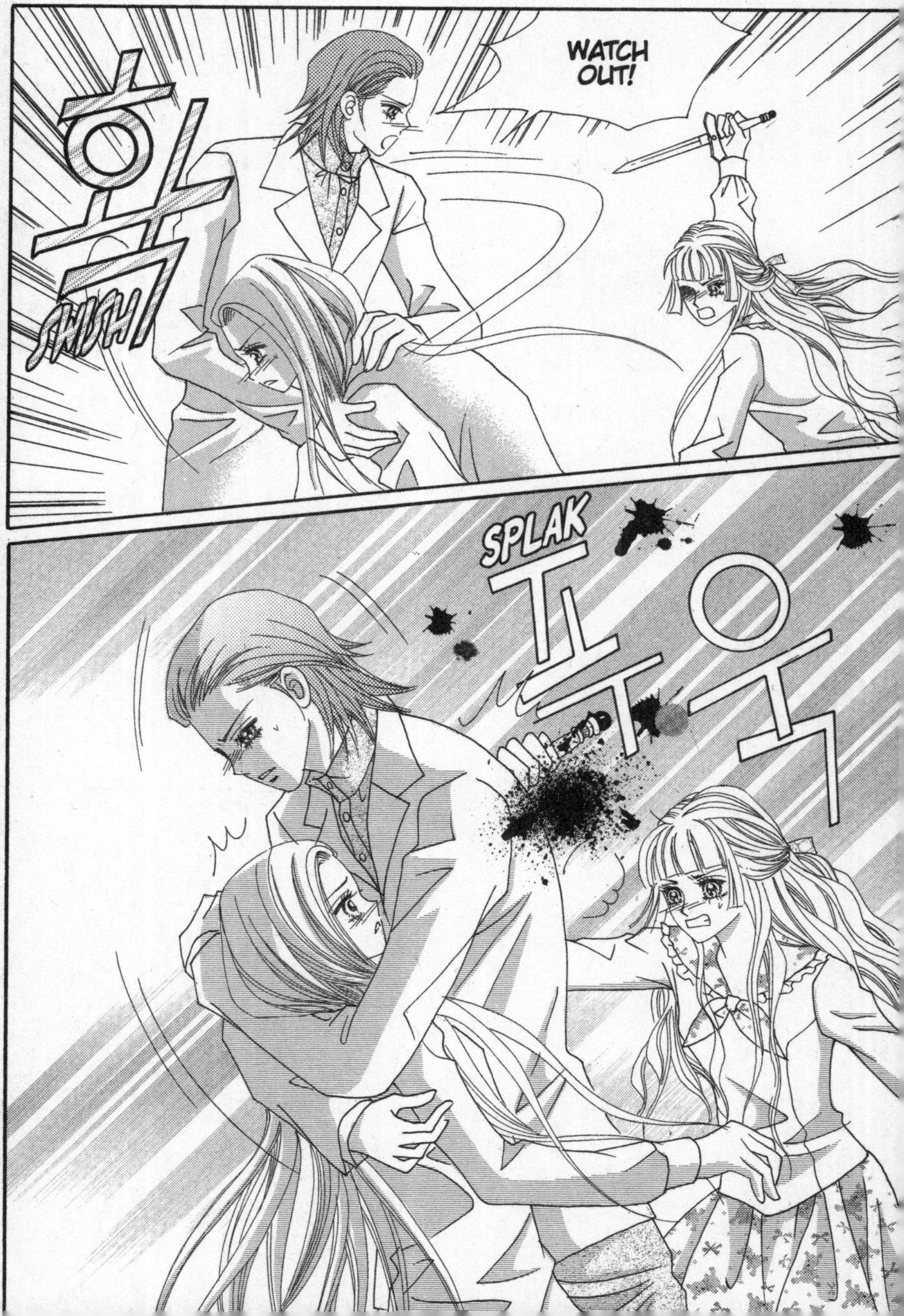
확
SWISH
WATCH OUT!
SPLAK
푸욱

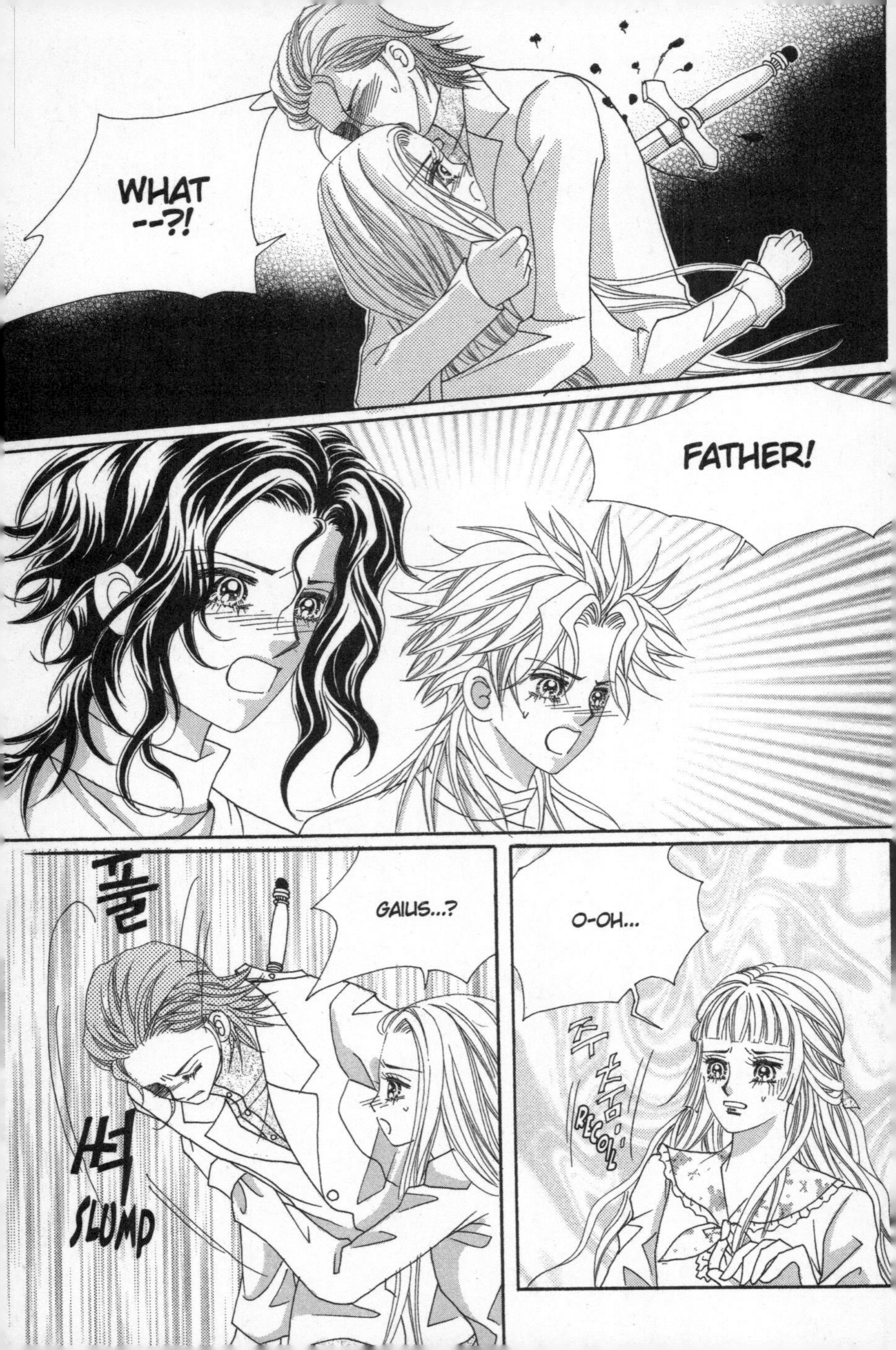
WHAT --?!
FATHER!
풀썩
SLUMP
GAIUS...?
O-OH...
주춤
RECOIL

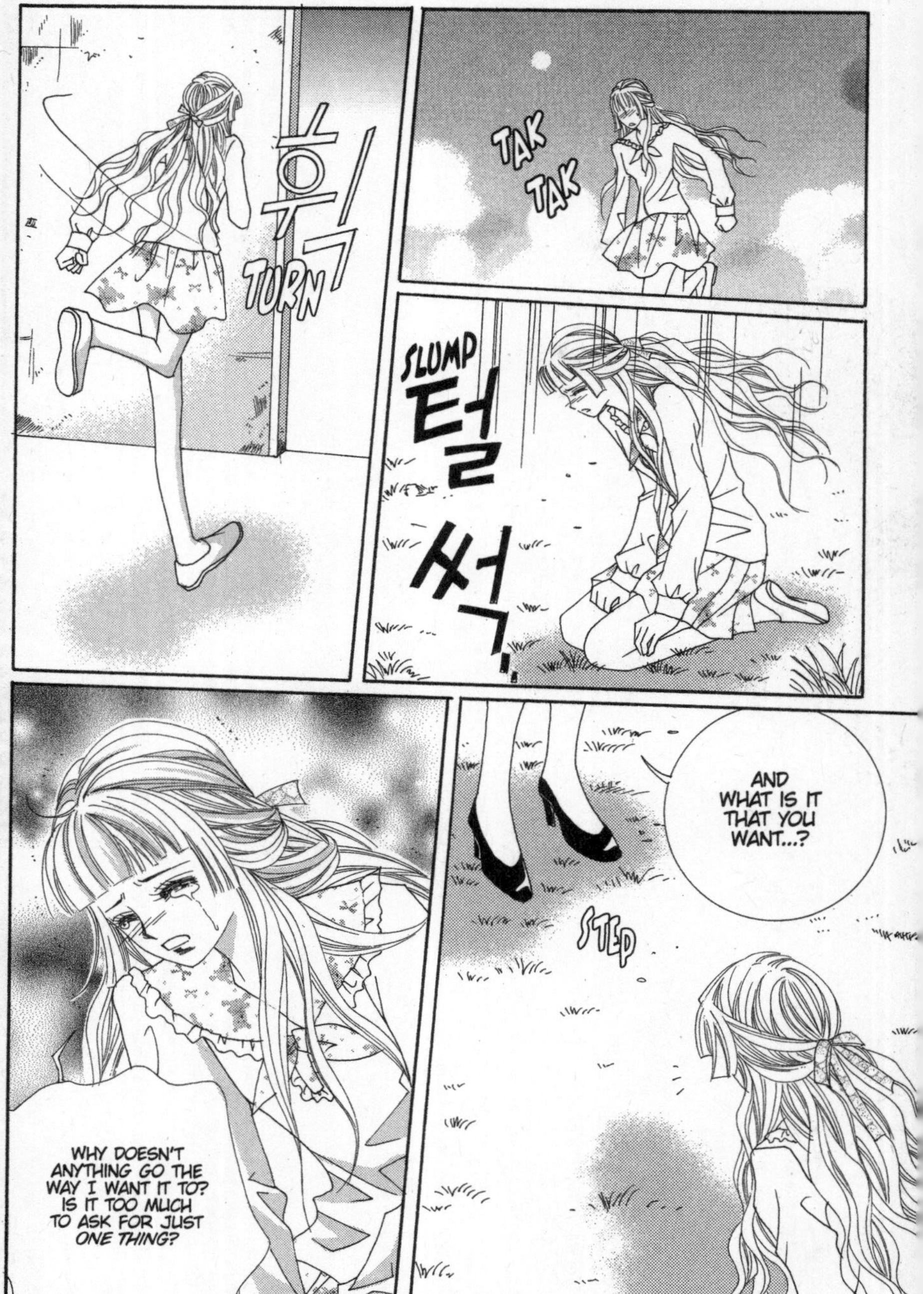
휙
TURN
TAK
TAK
SLUMP
털썩
WHY DOESN'T ANYTHING GO THE WAY I WANT IT TO? IS IT TOO MUCH TO ASK FOR JUST *ONE THING?*
AND WHAT IS IT THAT YOU WANT...?
STEP

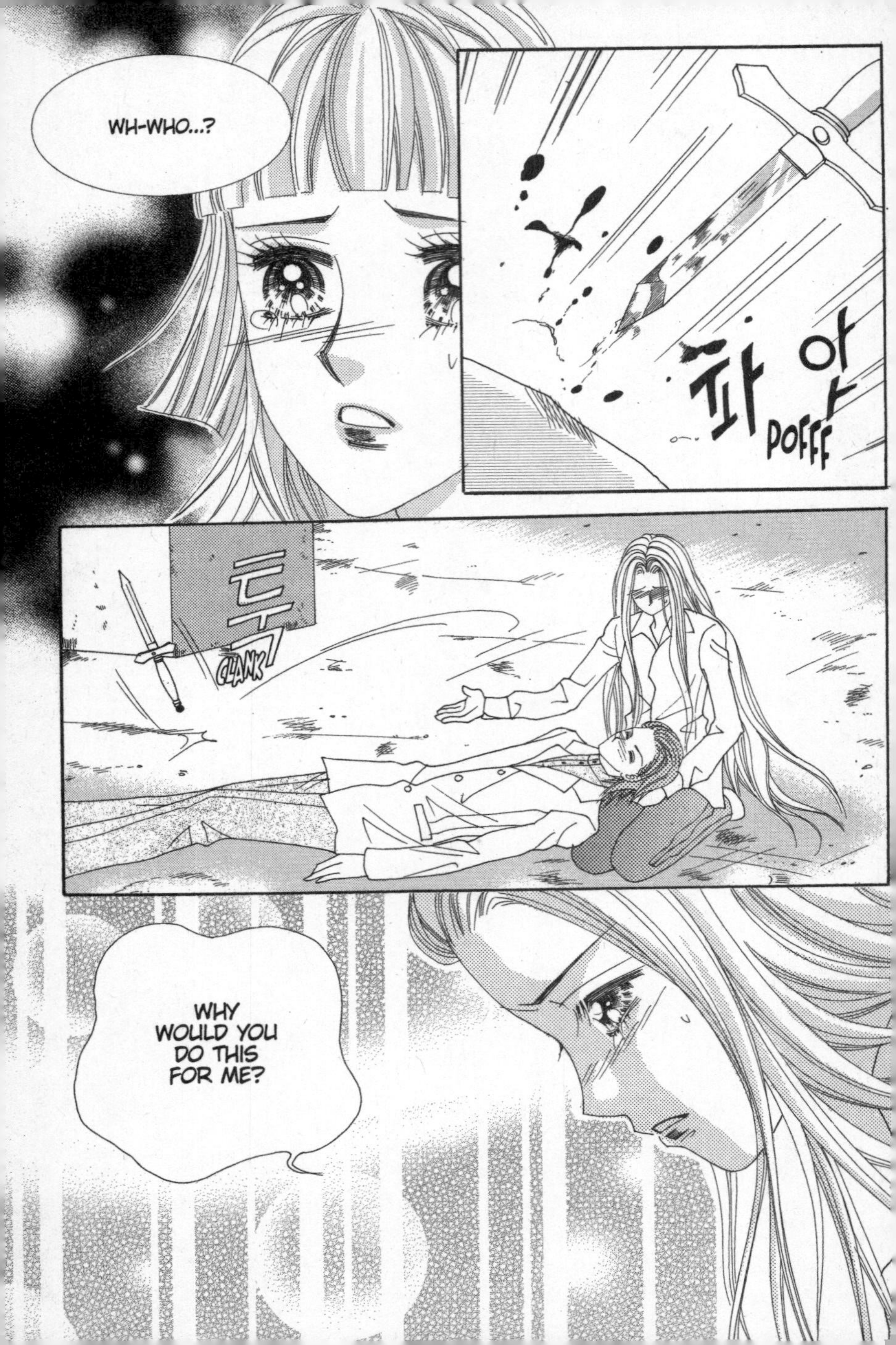
WH-WHO...?
POFFF
CLANK
WHY WOULD YOU DO THIS FOR ME?

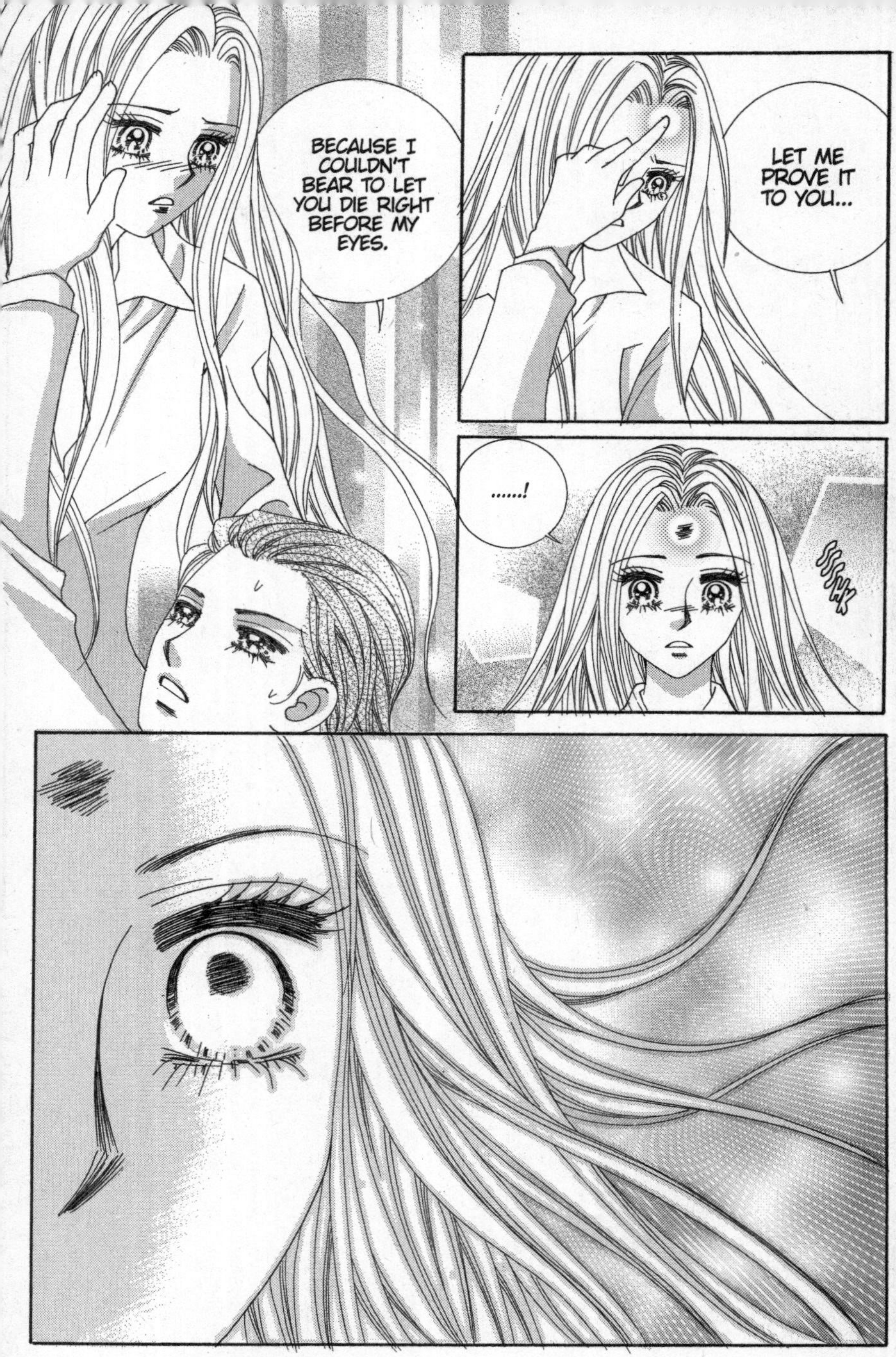
BECAUSE I COULDN'T BEAR TO LET YOU DIE RIGHT BEFORE MY EYES.
LET ME PROVE IT TO YOU...
......!
SSHK

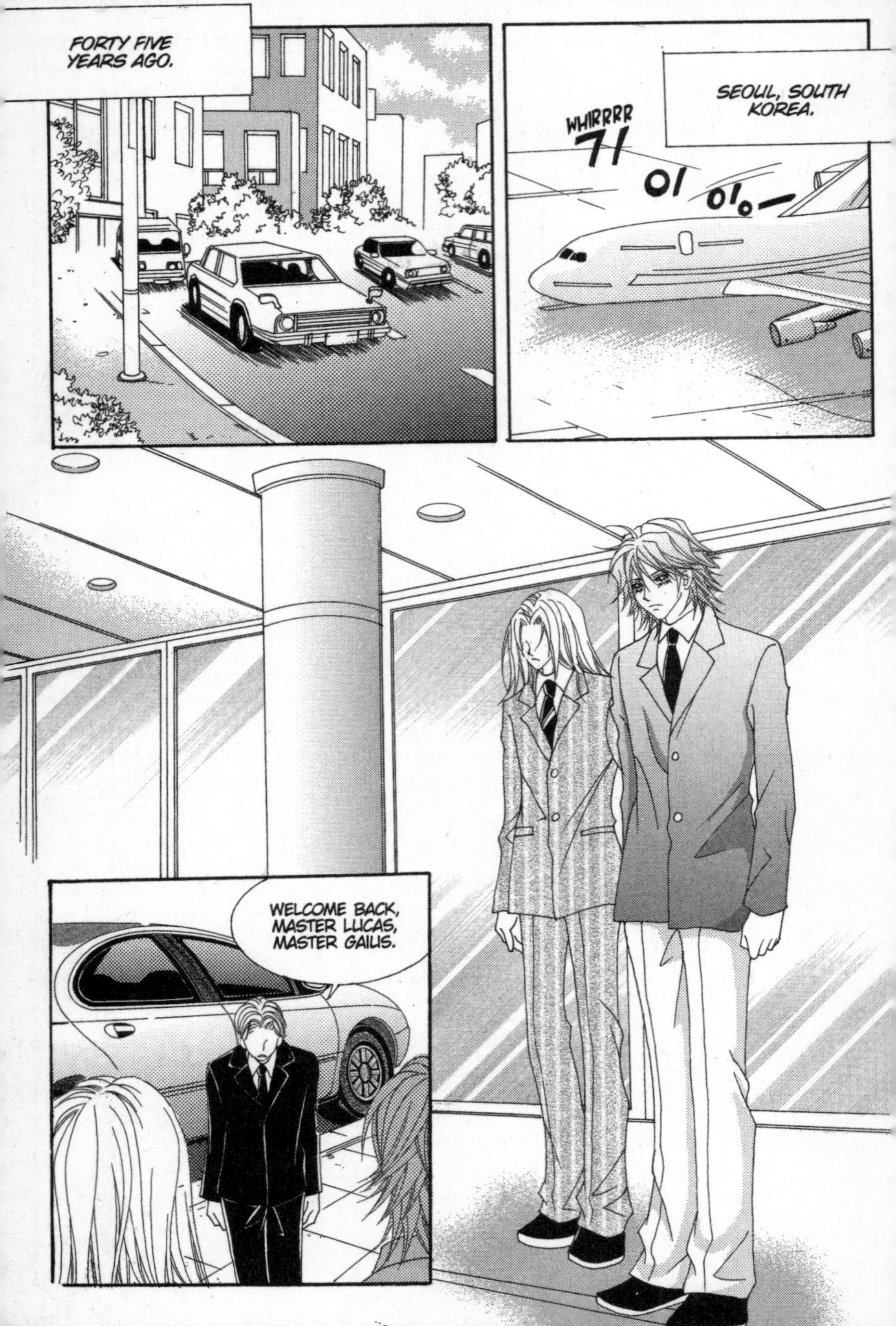
FORTY FIVE YEARS AGO.
SEOUL, SOUTH KOREA.
WHIRRRR
WELCOME BACK, MASTER LUCAS, MASTER GAIUS.

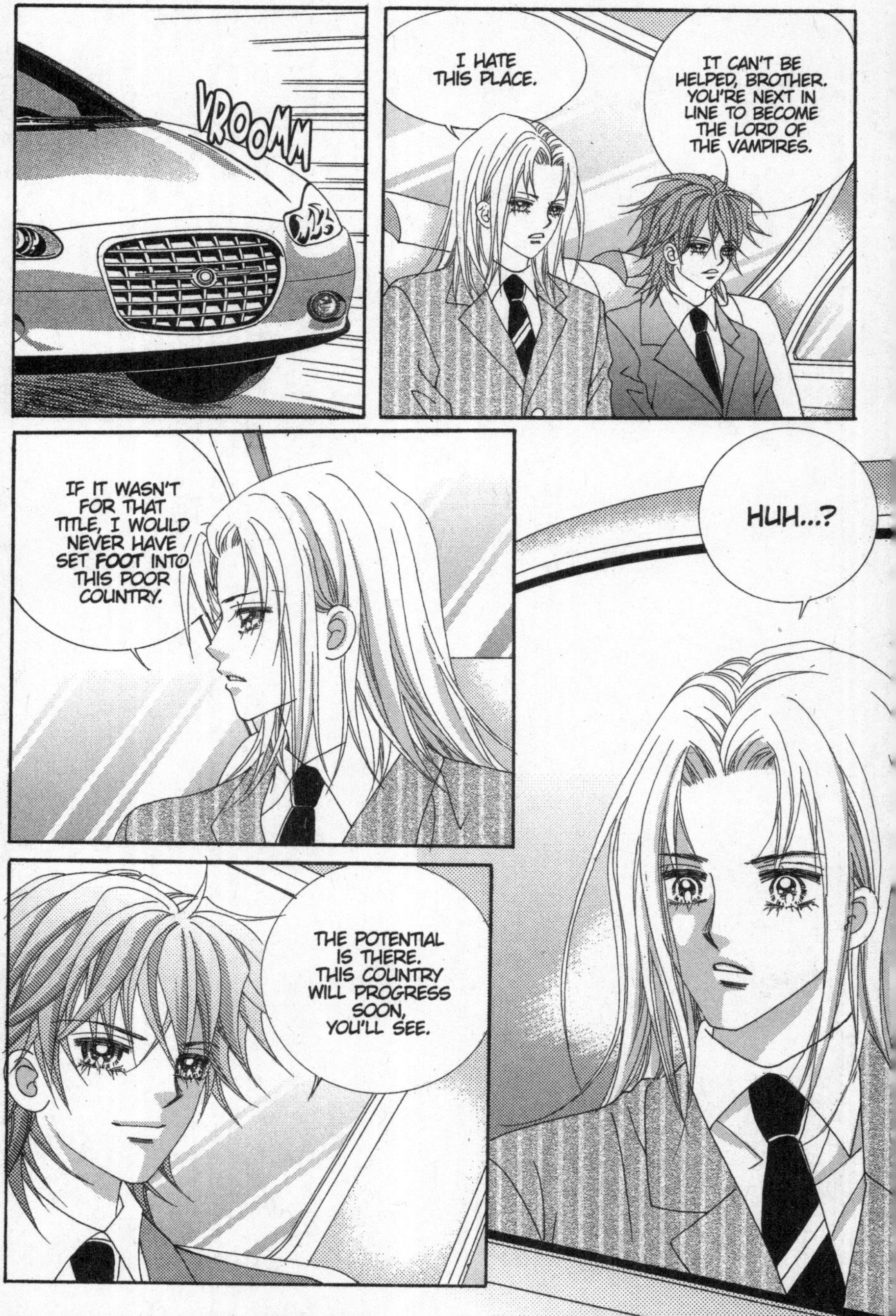
VROOMM
I HATE THIS PLACE.
IT CAN'T BE HELPED, BROTHER. YOU'RE NEXT IN LINE TO BECOME THE LORD OF THE VAMPIRES.
IF IT WASN'T FOR THAT TITLE, I WOULD NEVER HAVE SET FOOT INTO THIS POOR COUNTRY.
THE POTENTIAL IS THERE. THIS COUNTRY WILL PROGRESS SOON, YOU'LL SEE.
HUH...?

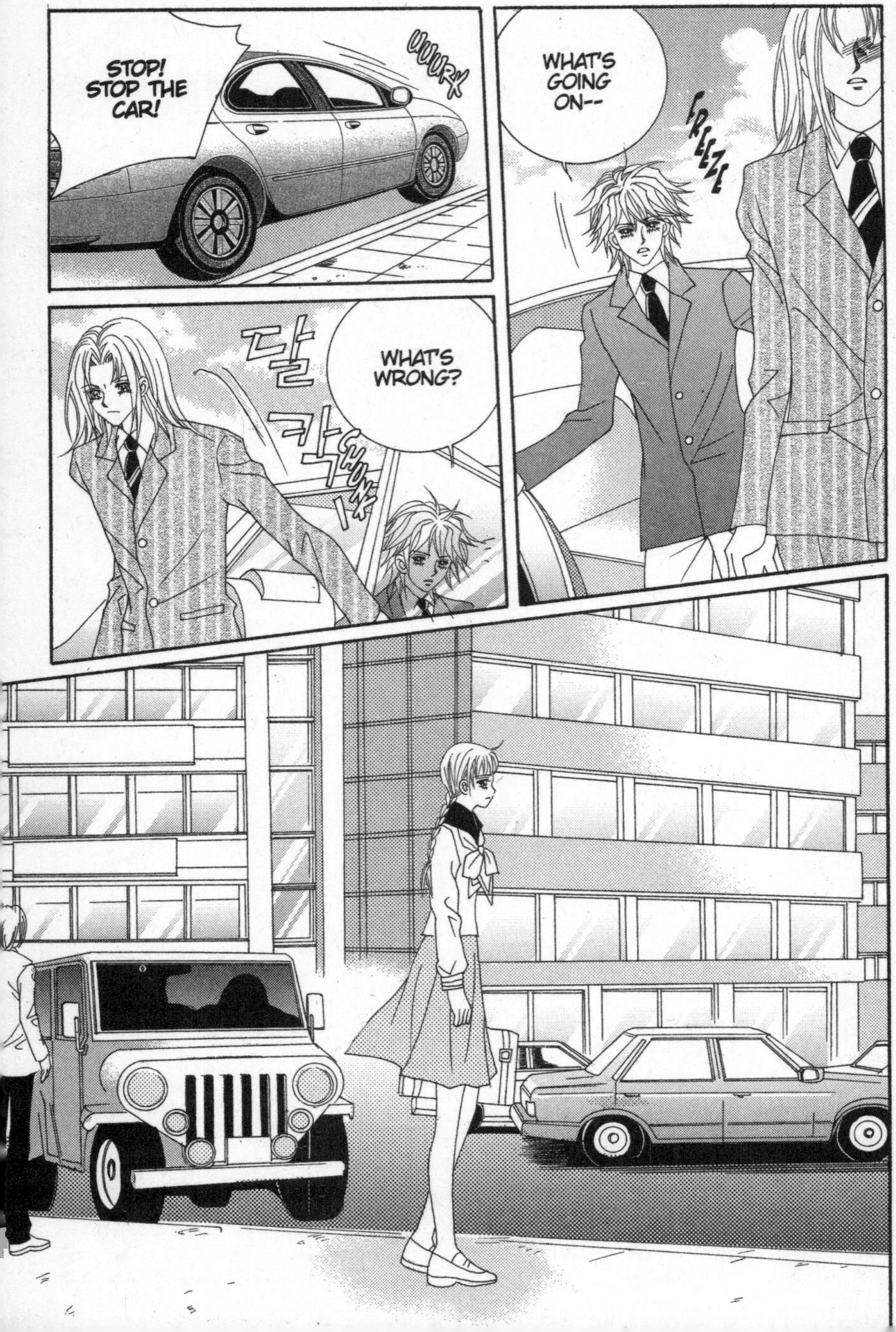
STOP! STOP THE CAR!
UUURK
달칵
CHUNK
WHAT'S WRONG?
WHAT'S GOING ON--
FREEZE

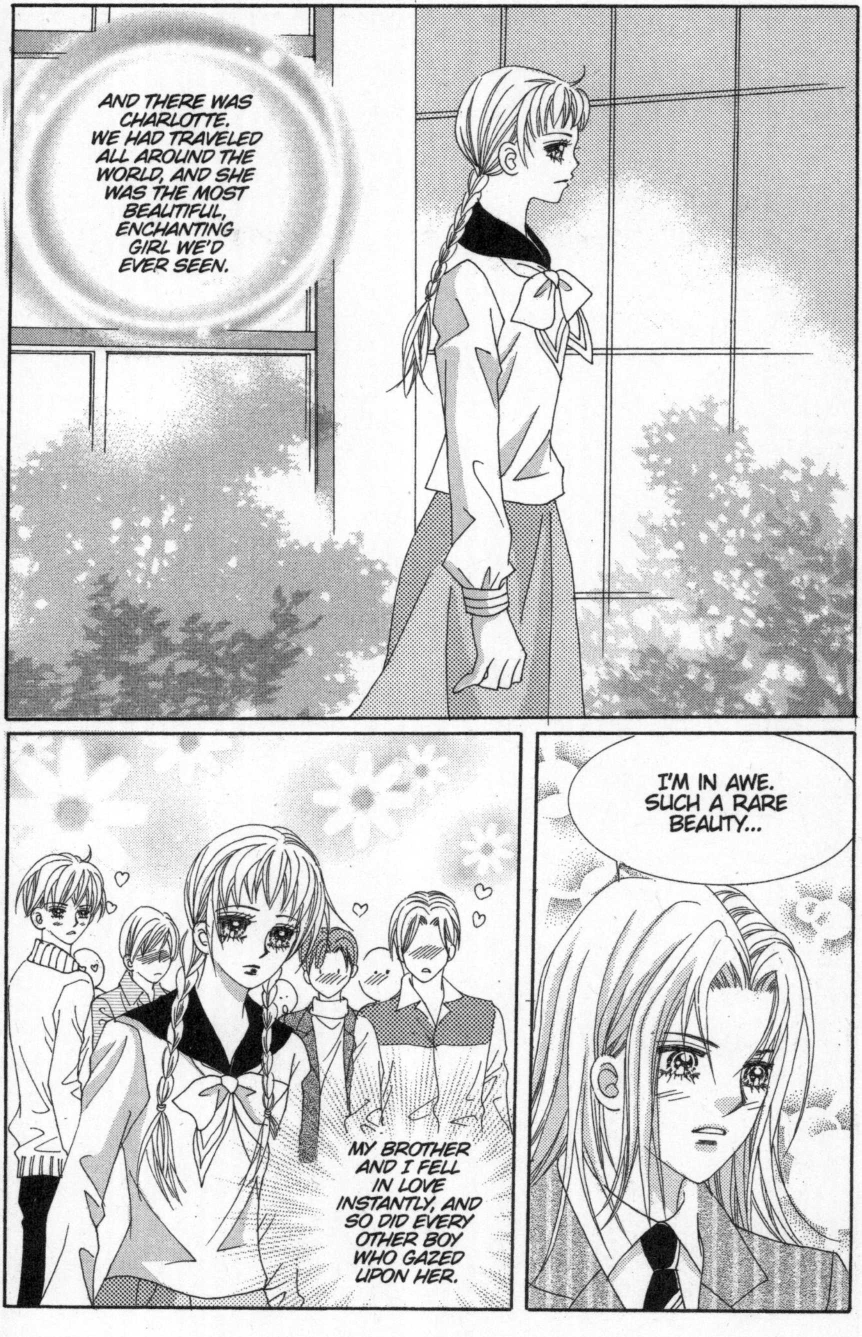
AND THERE WAS CHARLOTTE. WE HAD TRAVELED ALL AROUND THE WORLD, AND SHE WAS THE MOST BEAUTIFUL, ENCHANTING GIRL WE'D EVER SEEN.
MY BROTHER AND I FELL IN LOVE INSTANTLY, AND SO DID EVERY OTHER BOY WHO GAZED UPON HER.
I'M IN AWE. SUCH A RARE BEAUTY...

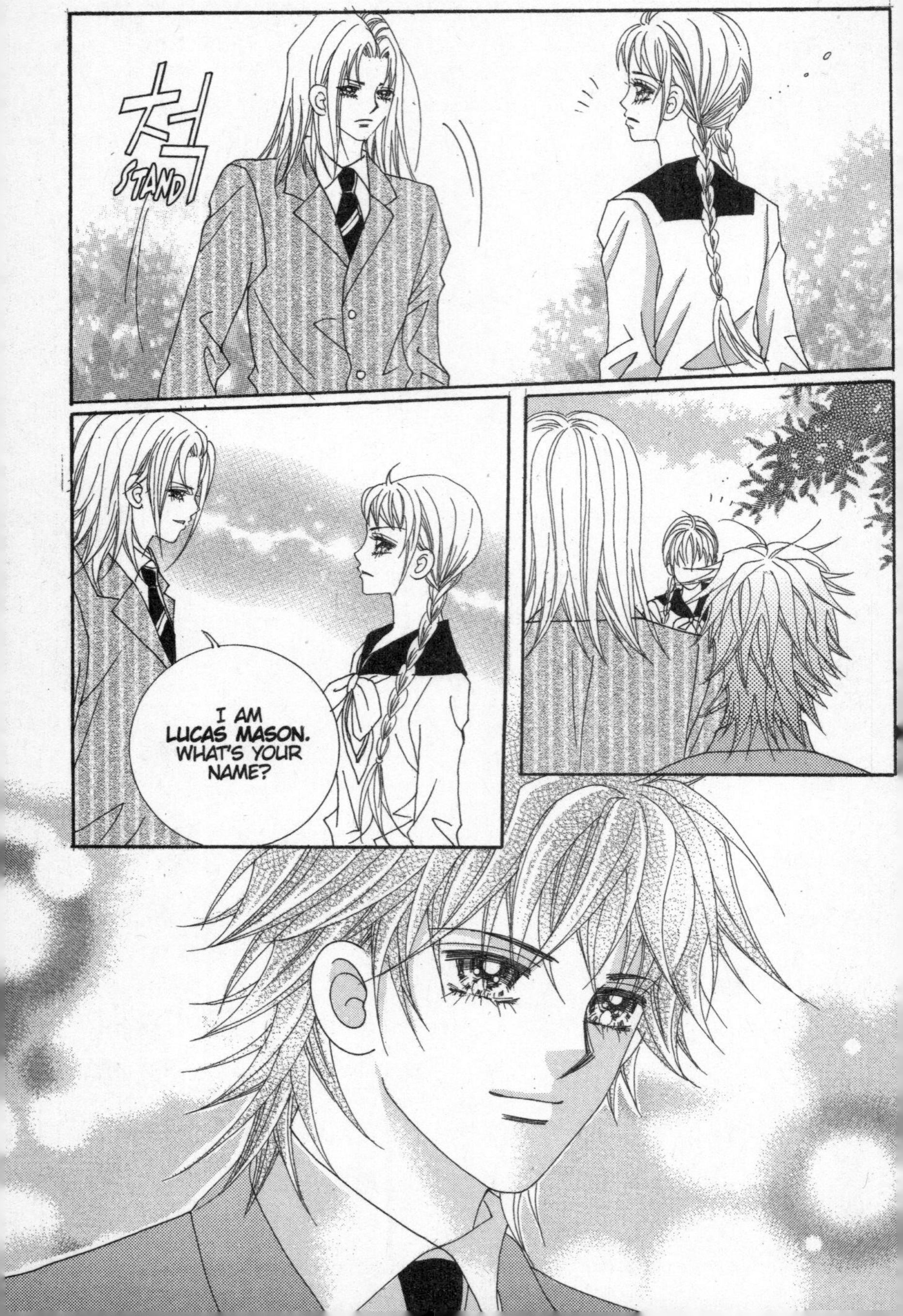
척
STAND
I AM LUCAS MASON. WHAT'S YOUR NAME?

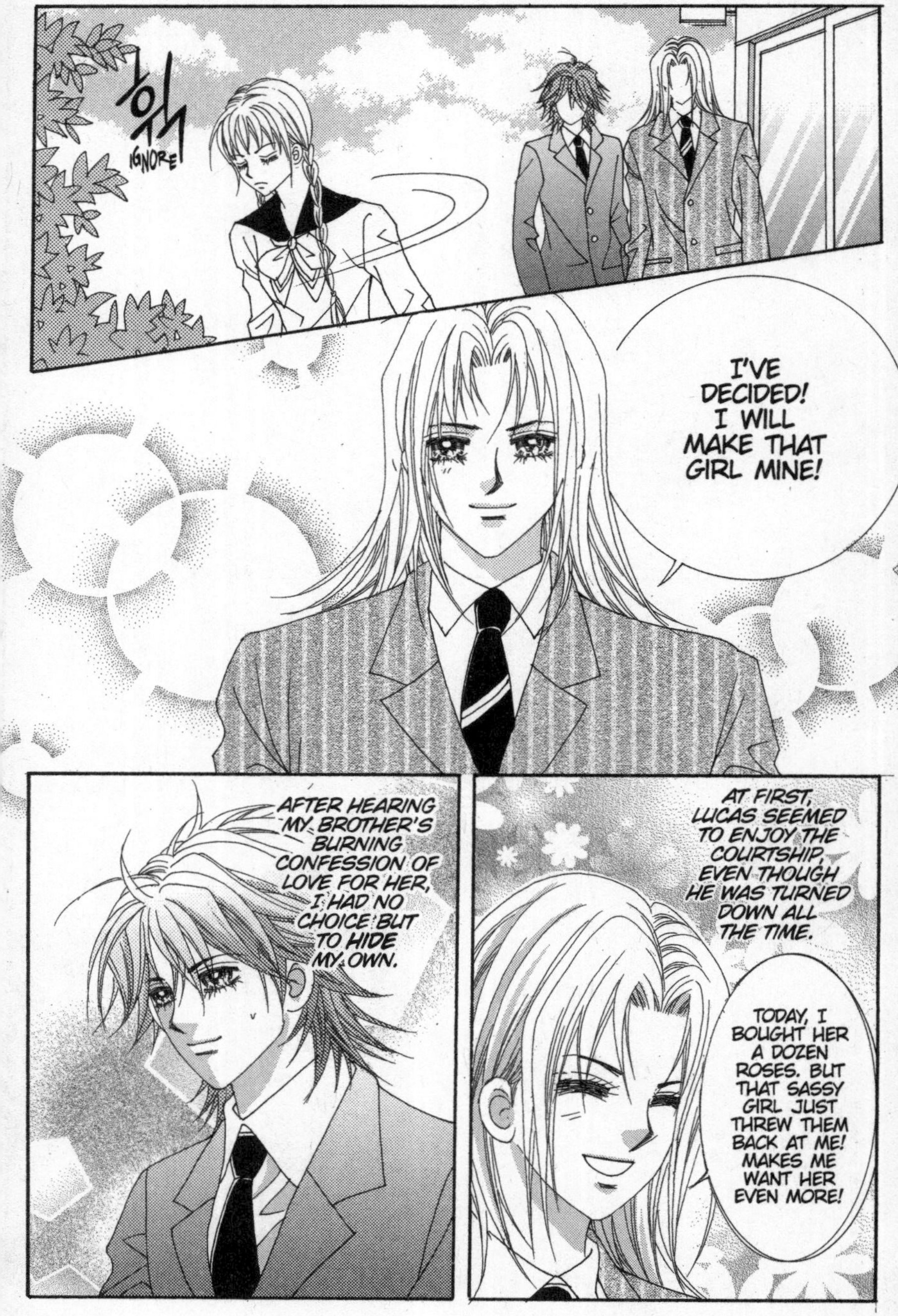

IGNORE
I'VE DECIDED! I WILL MAKE THAT GIRL MINE!
AFTER HEARING MY BROTHER'S BURNING CONFESSION OF LOVE FOR HER, I HAD NO CHOICE BUT TO HIDE MY OWN.
AT FIRST, LUCAS SEEMED TO ENJOY THE COURTSHIP, EVEN THOUGH HE WAS TURNED DOWN ALL THE TIME.
TODAY, I BOUGHT HER A DOZEN ROSES. BUT THAT SASSY GIRL JUST THREW THEM BACK AT ME! MAKES ME WANT HER EVEN MORE!

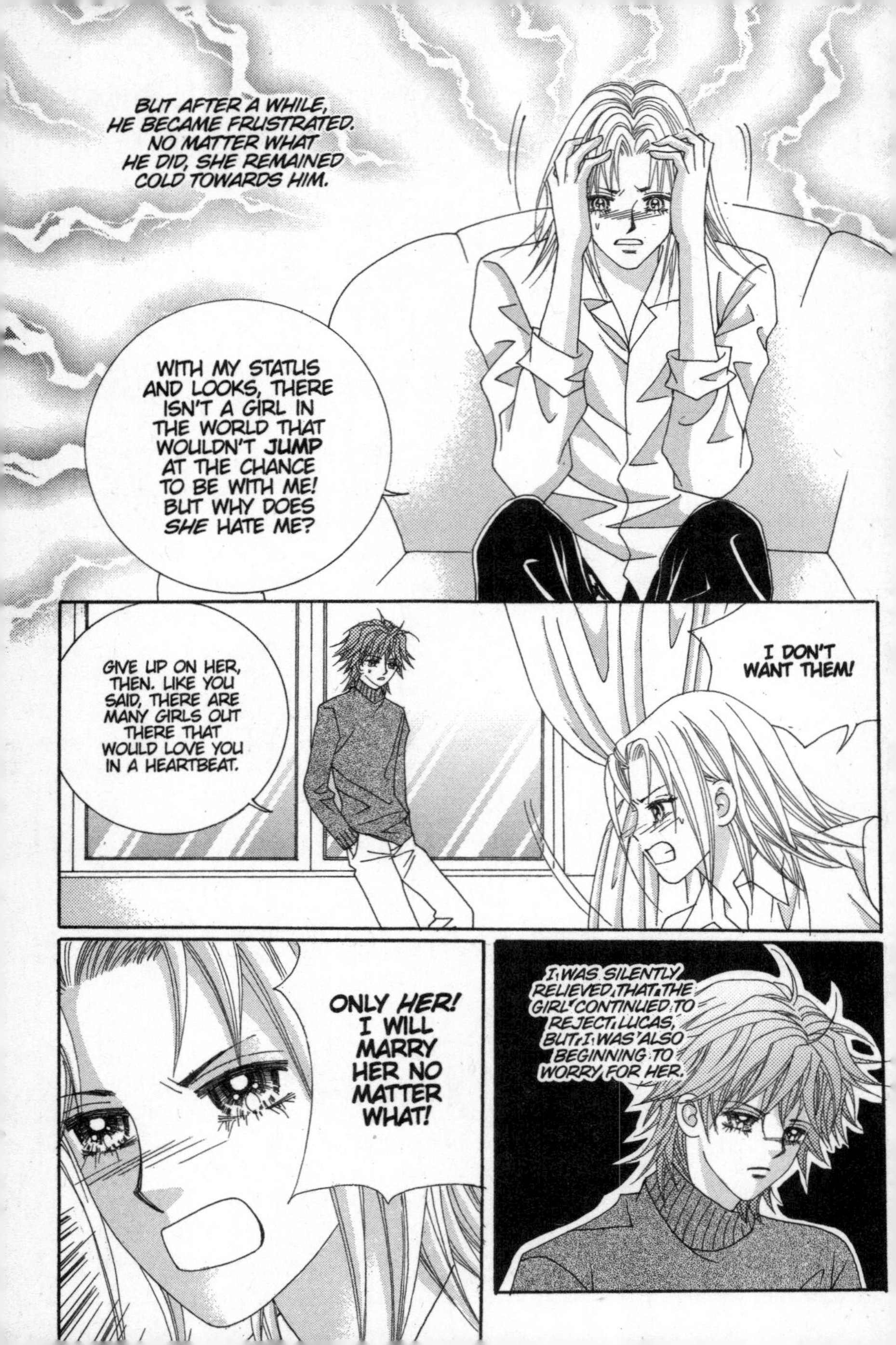
BUT AFTER A WHILE, HE BECAME FRUSTRATED. NO MATTER WHAT HE DID, SHE REMAINED COLD TOWARDS HIM.
WITH MY STATUS AND LOOKS, THERE ISN'T A GIRL IN THE WORLD THAT WOULDN'T JUMP AT THE CHANCE TO BE WITH ME! BUT WHY DOES SHE HATE ME?
GIVE UP ON HER, THEN. LIKE YOU SAID, THERE ARE MANY GIRLS OUT THERE THAT WOULD LOVE YOU IN A HEARTBEAT.
I DON'T WANT THEM!
ONLY HER! I WILL MARRY HER NO MATTER WHAT!
I WAS SILENTLY RELIEVED THAT THE GIRL CONTINUED TO REJECT LUCAS, BUT I WAS ALSO BEGINNING TO WORRY FOR HER.

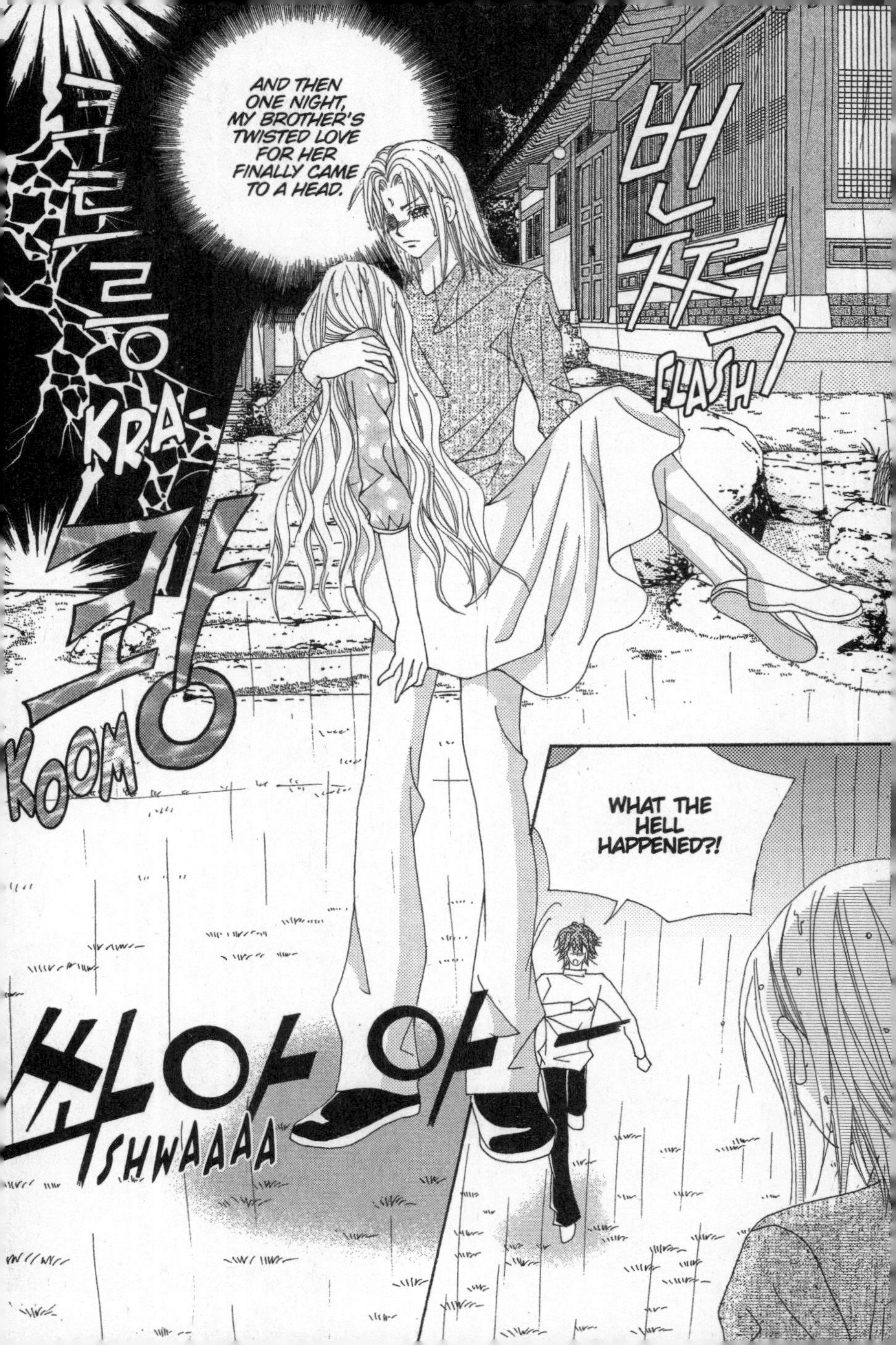

AND THEN ONE NIGHT, MY BROTHER'S TWISTED LOVE FOR HER FINALLY CAME TO A HEAD.
KRA-
번쩍
FLASH
KOOM
WHAT THE HELL HAPPENED?!
쏴아아
SHWAAAA

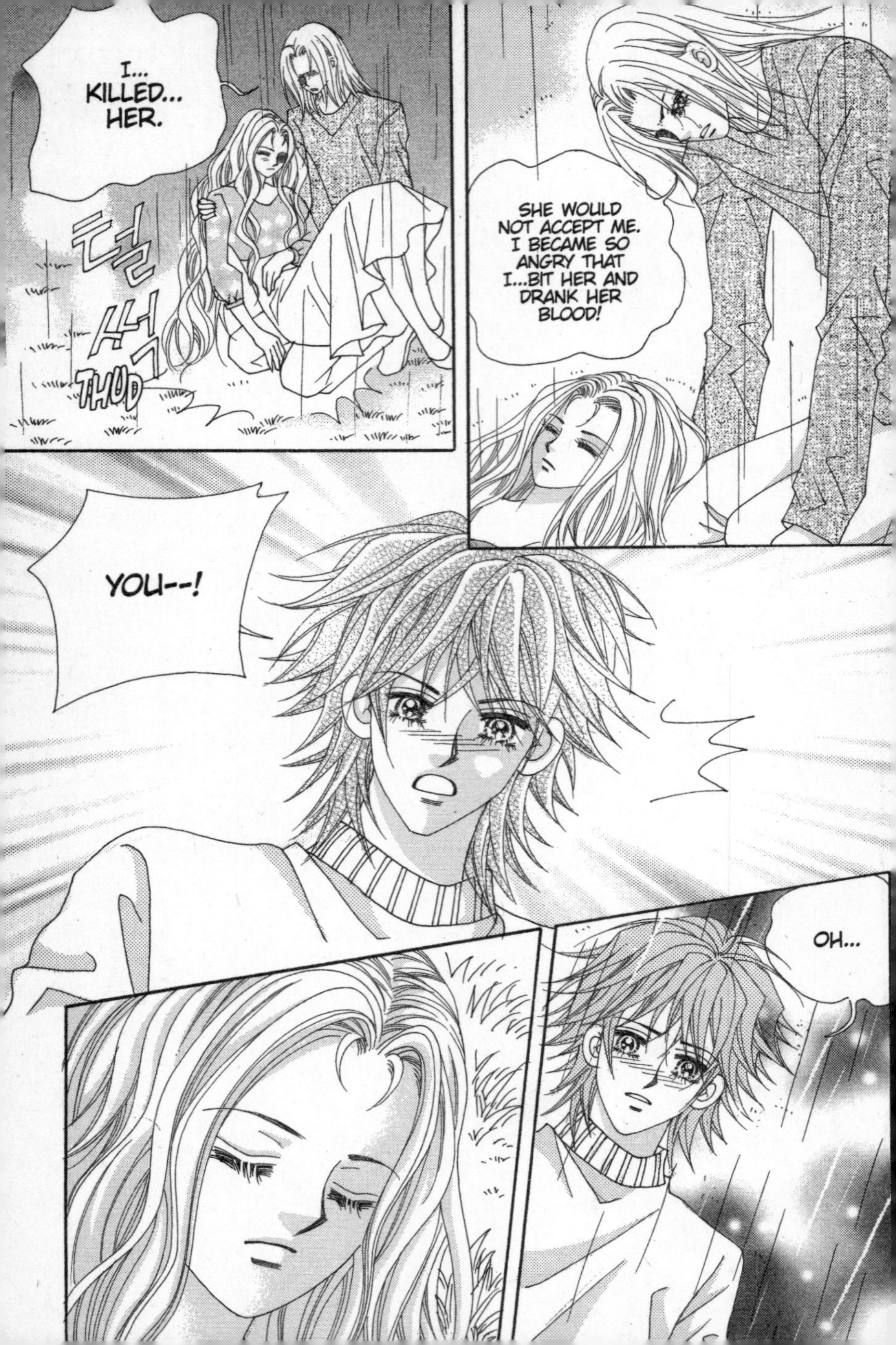
I... KILLED... HER.
털썩
THUD
SHE WOULD NOT ACCEPT ME. I BECAME SO ANGRY THAT I...BIT HER AND DRANK HER BLOOD!
YOU--!
OH...

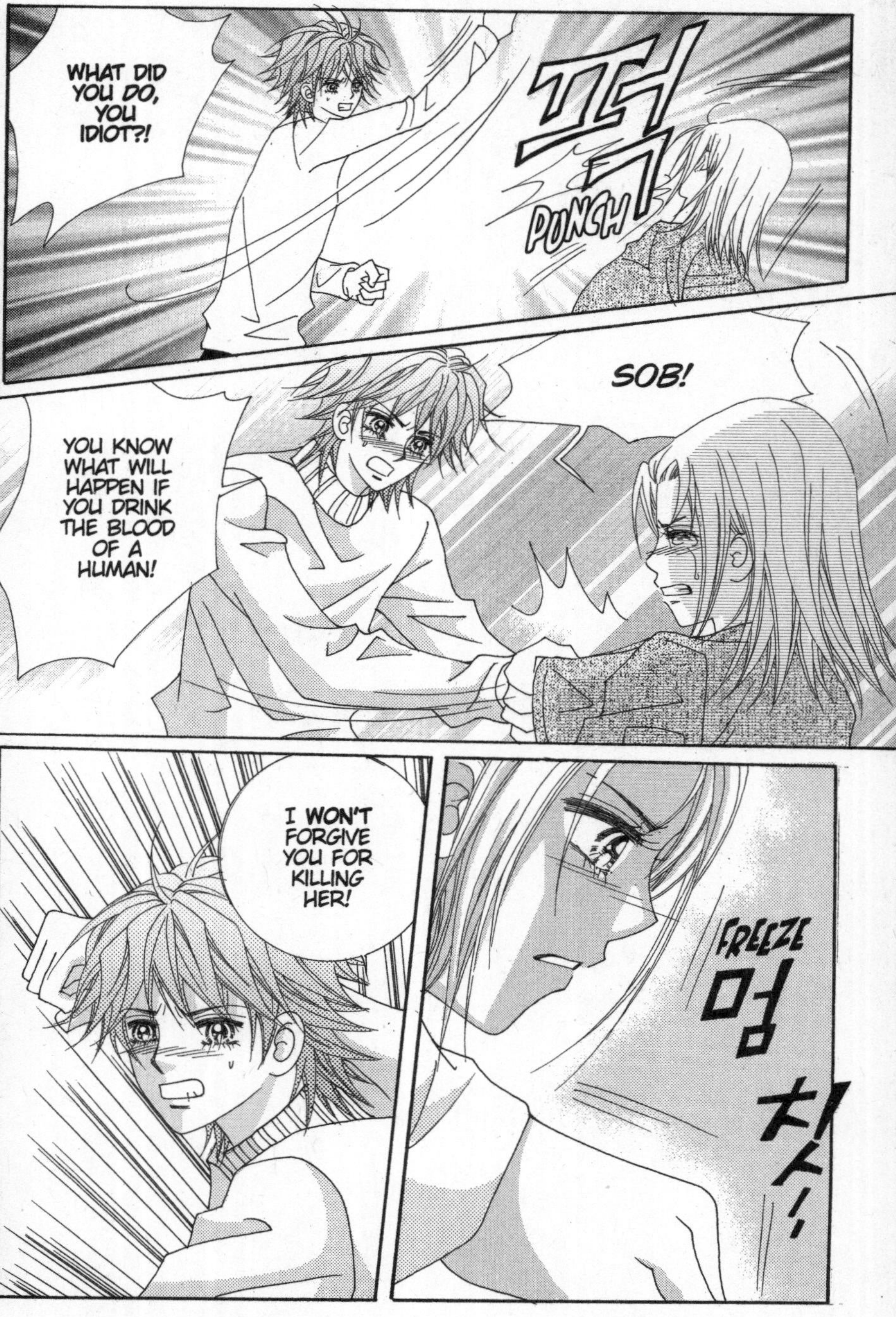
WHAT DID YOU DO, YOU IDIOT?!
퍽
PUNCH
YOU KNOW WHAT WILL HAPPEN IF YOU DRINK THE BLOOD OF A HUMAN!
SOB!
I WON'T FORGIVE YOU FOR KILLING HER!
FREEZE
멈칫!!

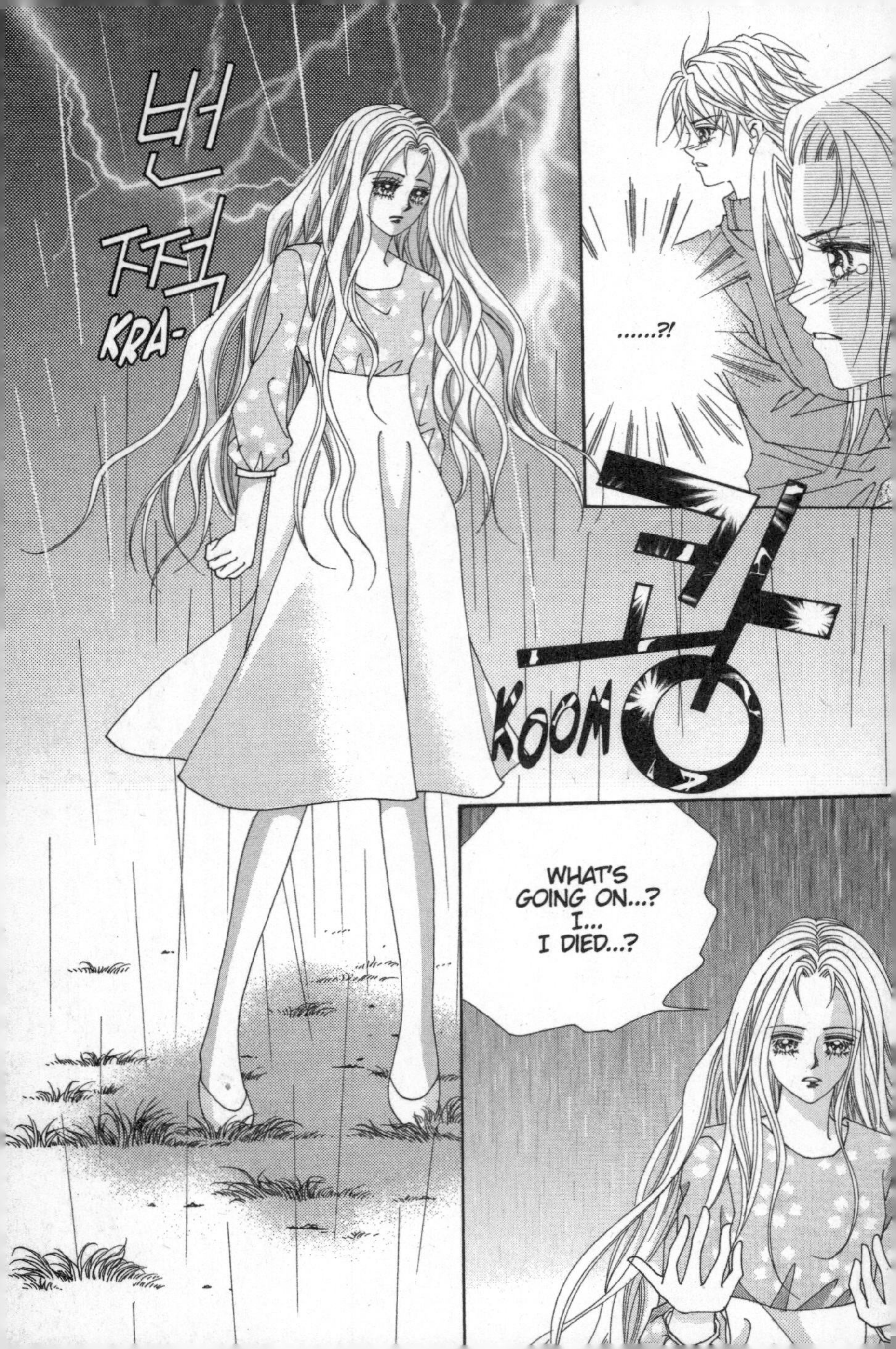

번쩍
KRA-
......?!
쾅
KOOM
WHAT'S GOING ON...? I... I DIED...?

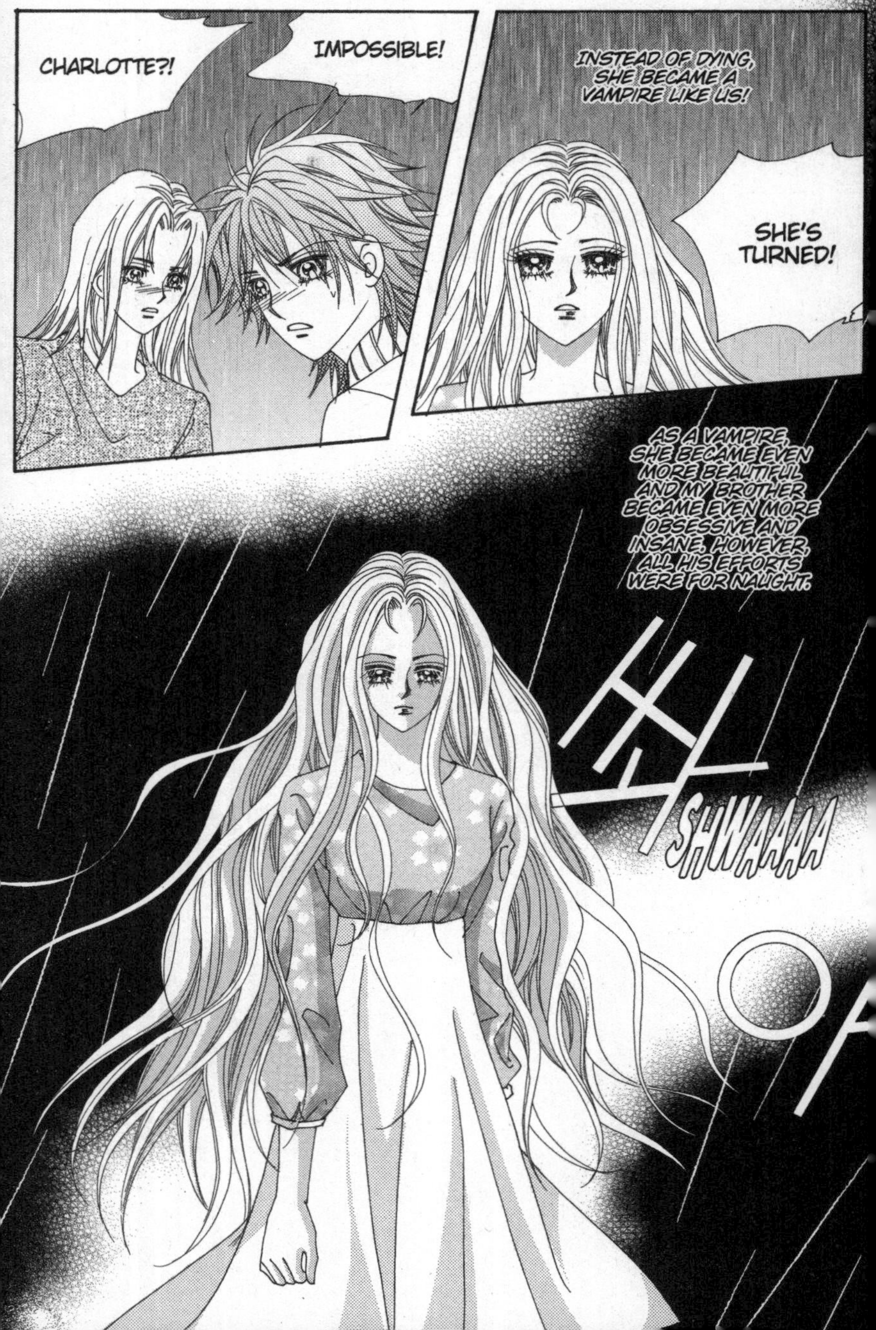
CHARLOTTE?!
IMPOSSIBLE!
INSTEAD OF DYING, SHE BECAME A VAMPIRE LIKE US!
SHE'S TURNED!
AS A VAMPIRE, SHE BECAME EVEN MORE BEAUTIFUL AND MY BROTHER BECAME EVEN MORE OBSESSIVE AND INSANE. HOWEVER, ALL HIS EFFORTS WERE FOR NAUGHT.
SHWAAAA

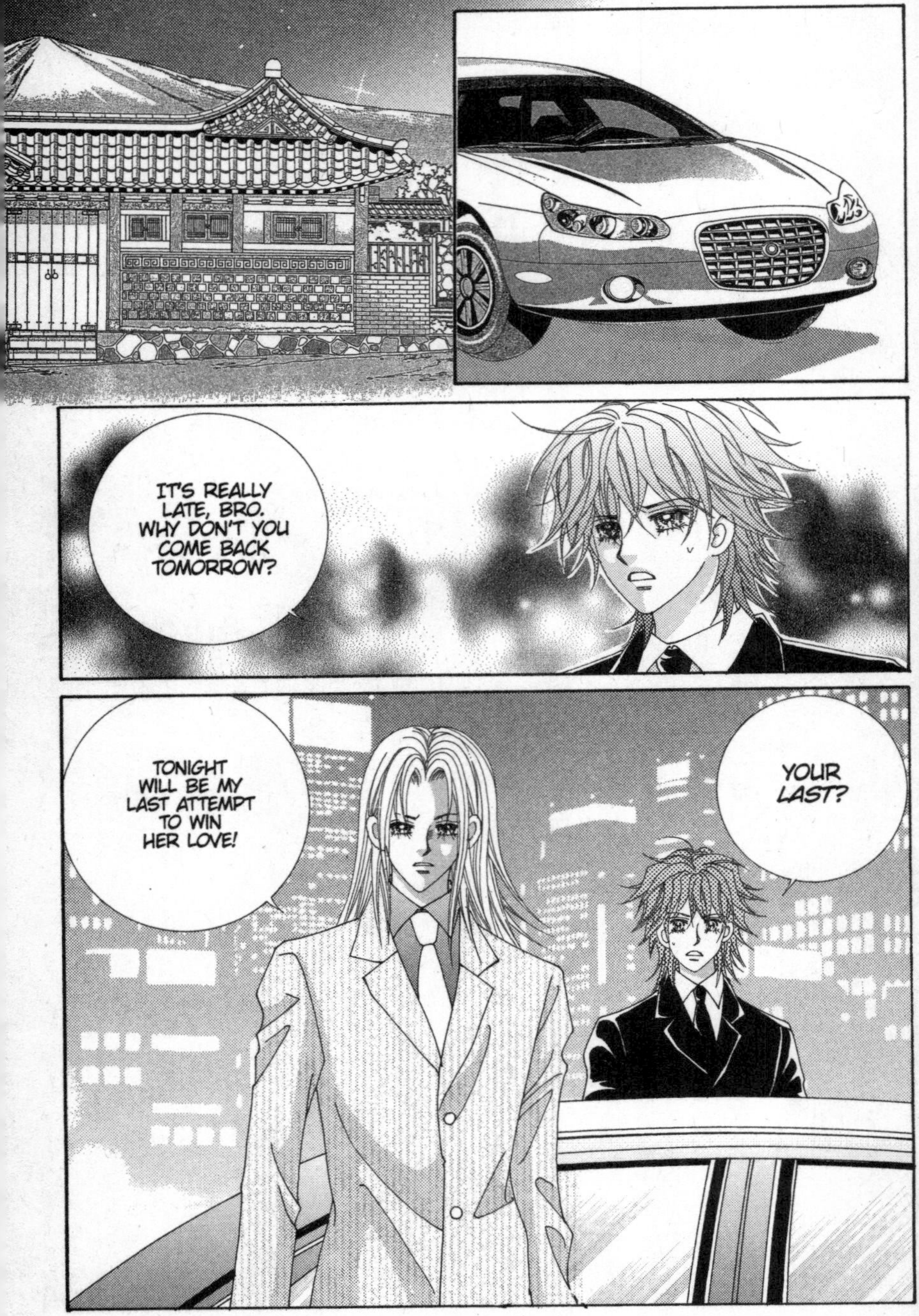
IT'S REALLY LATE, BRO. WHY DON'T YOU COME BACK TOMORROW?
TONIGHT WILL BE MY LAST ATTEMPT TO WIN HER LOVE!
YOUR LAST?

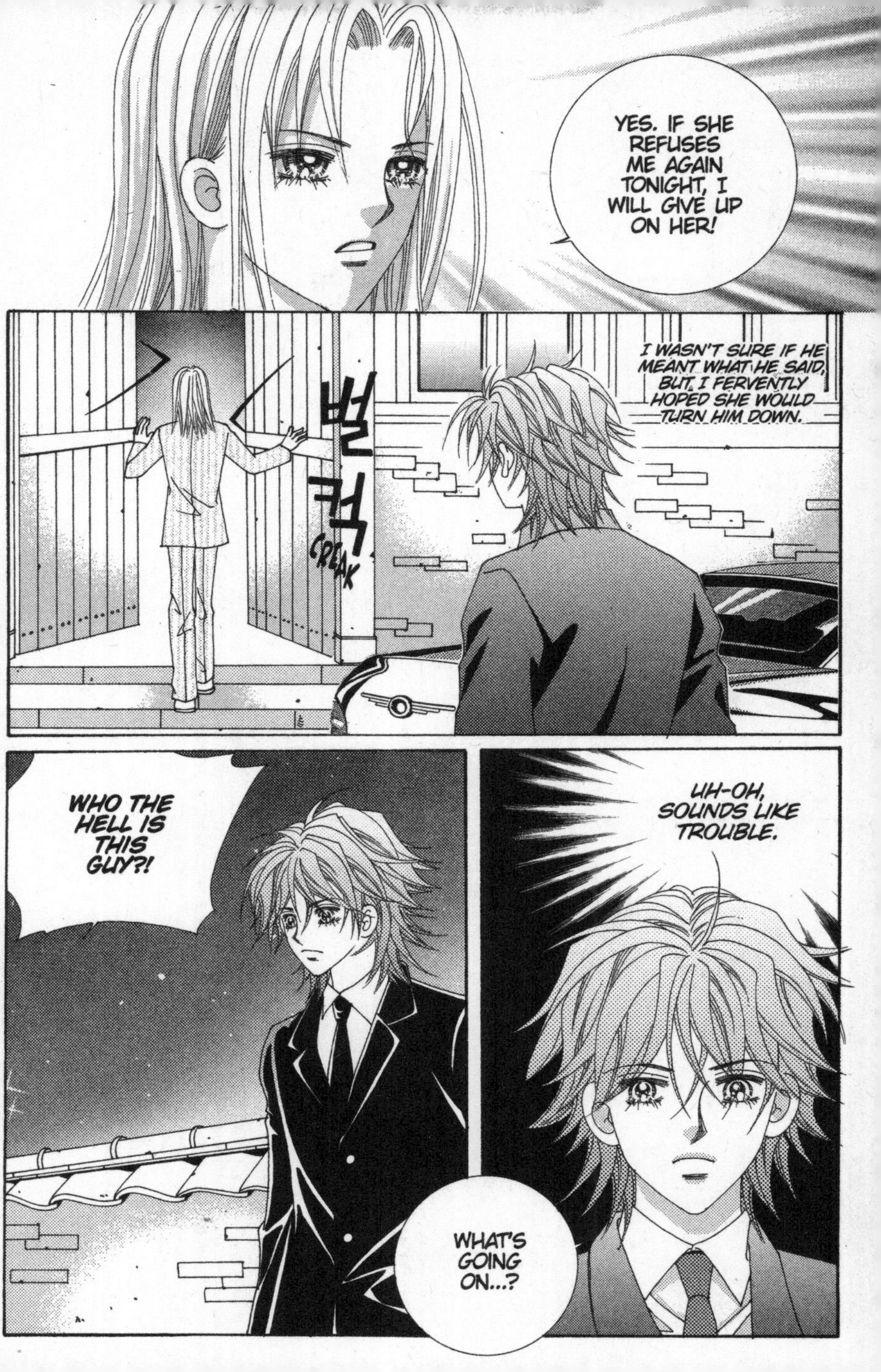

YES. IF SHE REFUSES ME AGAIN TONIGHT, I WILL GIVE UP ON HER!
벌컥
CREAK
I WASN'T SURE IF HE MEANT WHAT HE SAID, BUT I FERVENTLY HOPED SHE WOULD TURN HIM DOWN.
WHO THE HELL IS THIS GUY?!
UH-OH, SOUNDS LIKE TROUBLE.
WHAT'S GOING ON...?

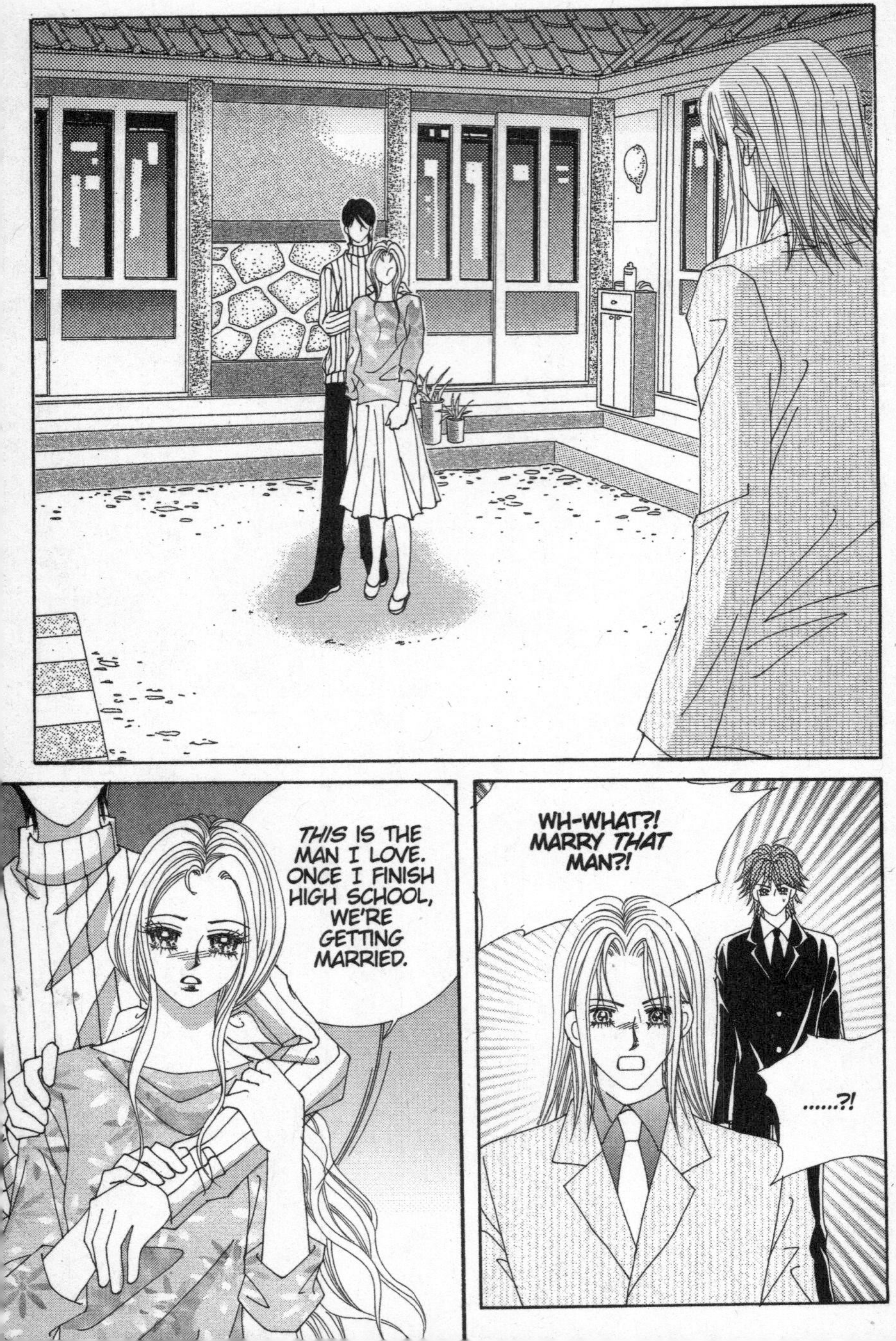
THIS IS THE MAN I LOVE. ONCE I FINISH HIGH SCHOOL, WE'RE GETTING MARRIED.
WH-WHAT?! MARRY *THAT* MAN?!
......?!

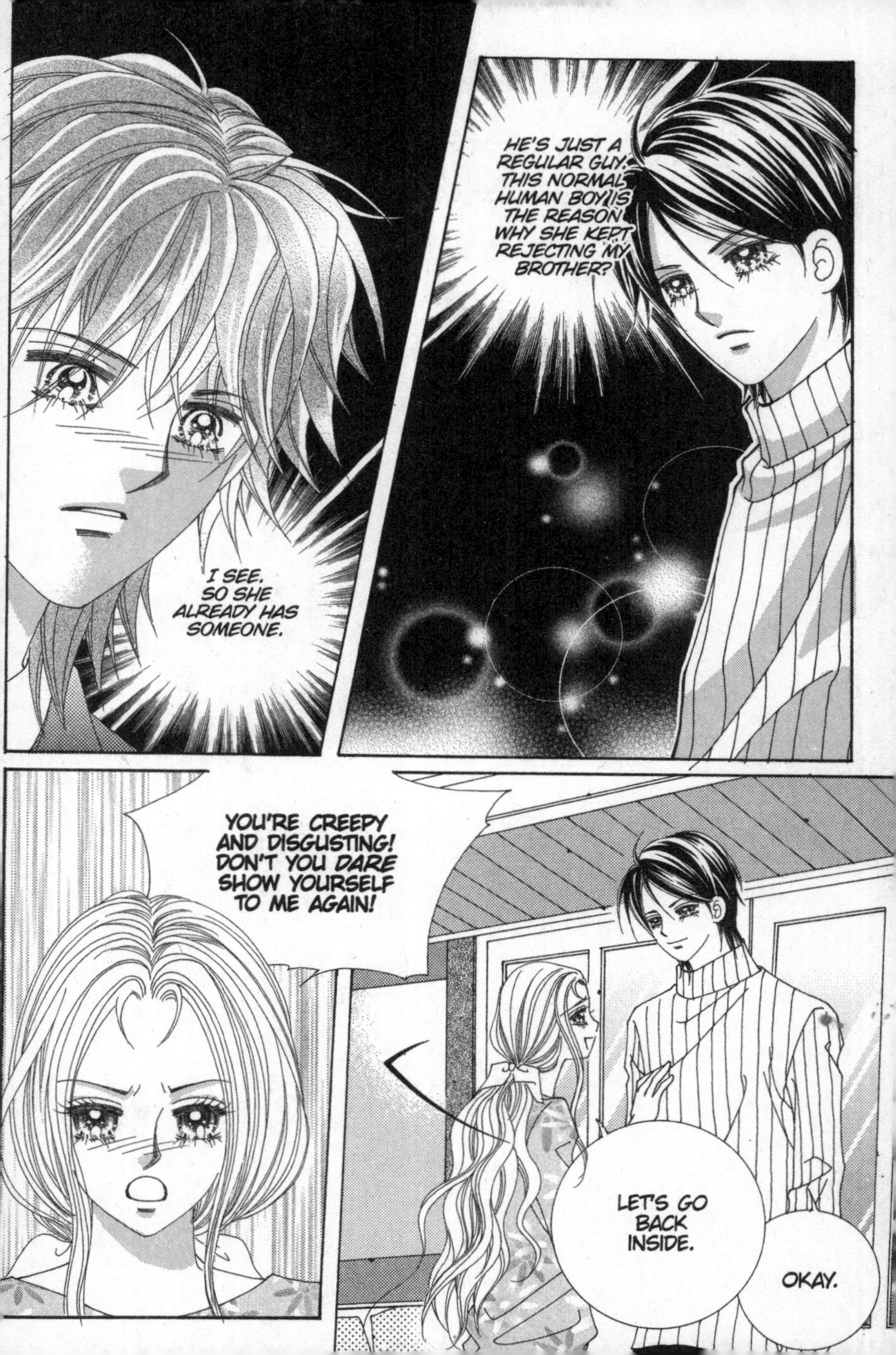
I SEE. SO SHE ALREADY HAS SOMEONE.
HE'S JUST A REGULAR GUY. THIS NORMAL HUMAN BOY IS THE REASON WHY SHE KEPT REJECTING MY BROTHER?
YOU'RE CREEPY AND DISGUSTING! DON'T YOU DARE SHOW YOURSELF TO ME AGAIN!
LET'S GO BACK INSIDE.
OKAY.

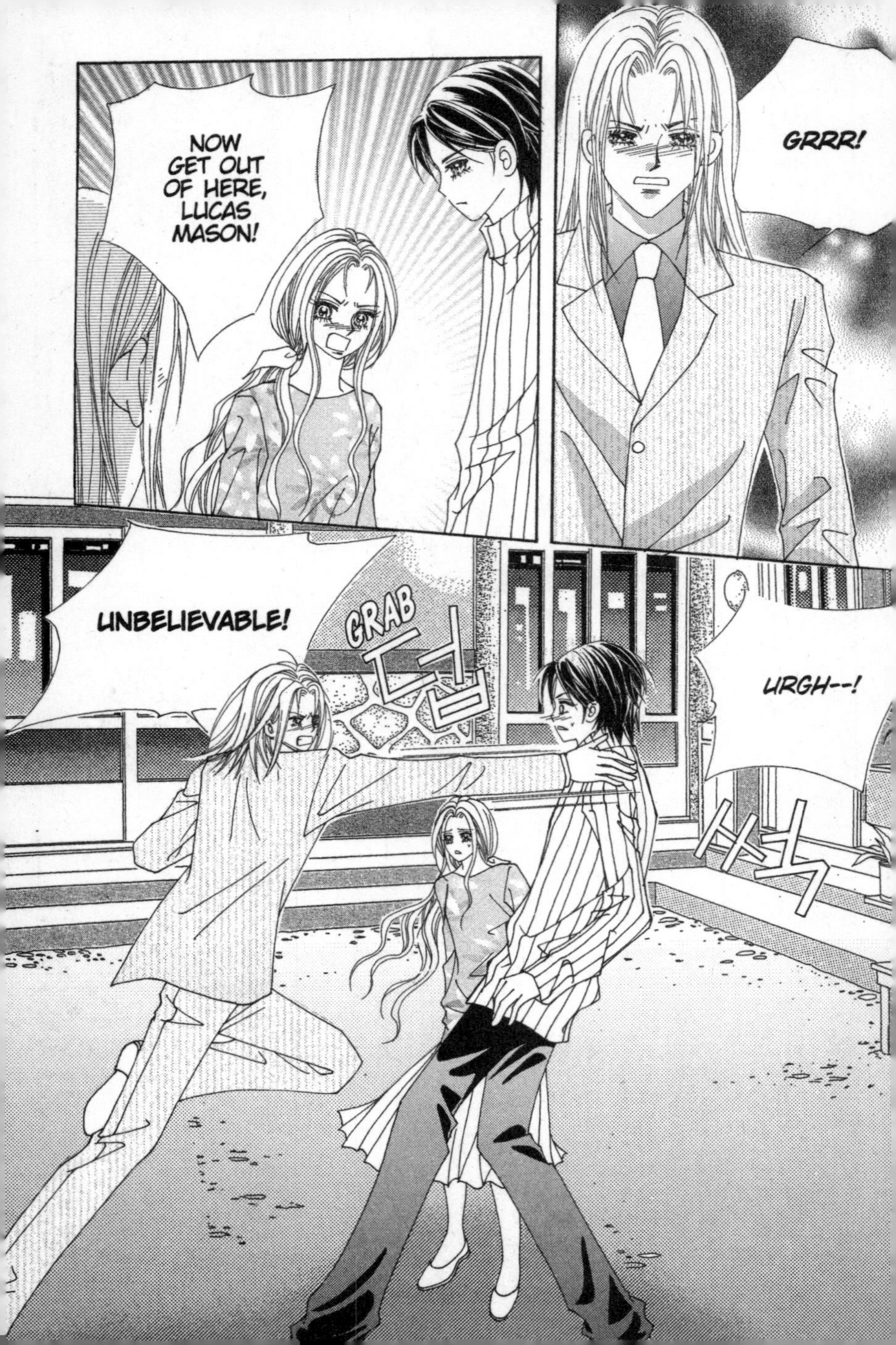
NOW GET OUT OF HERE, LUCAS MASON!
GRRR!
UNBELIEVABLE!
GRAB
URGH--!

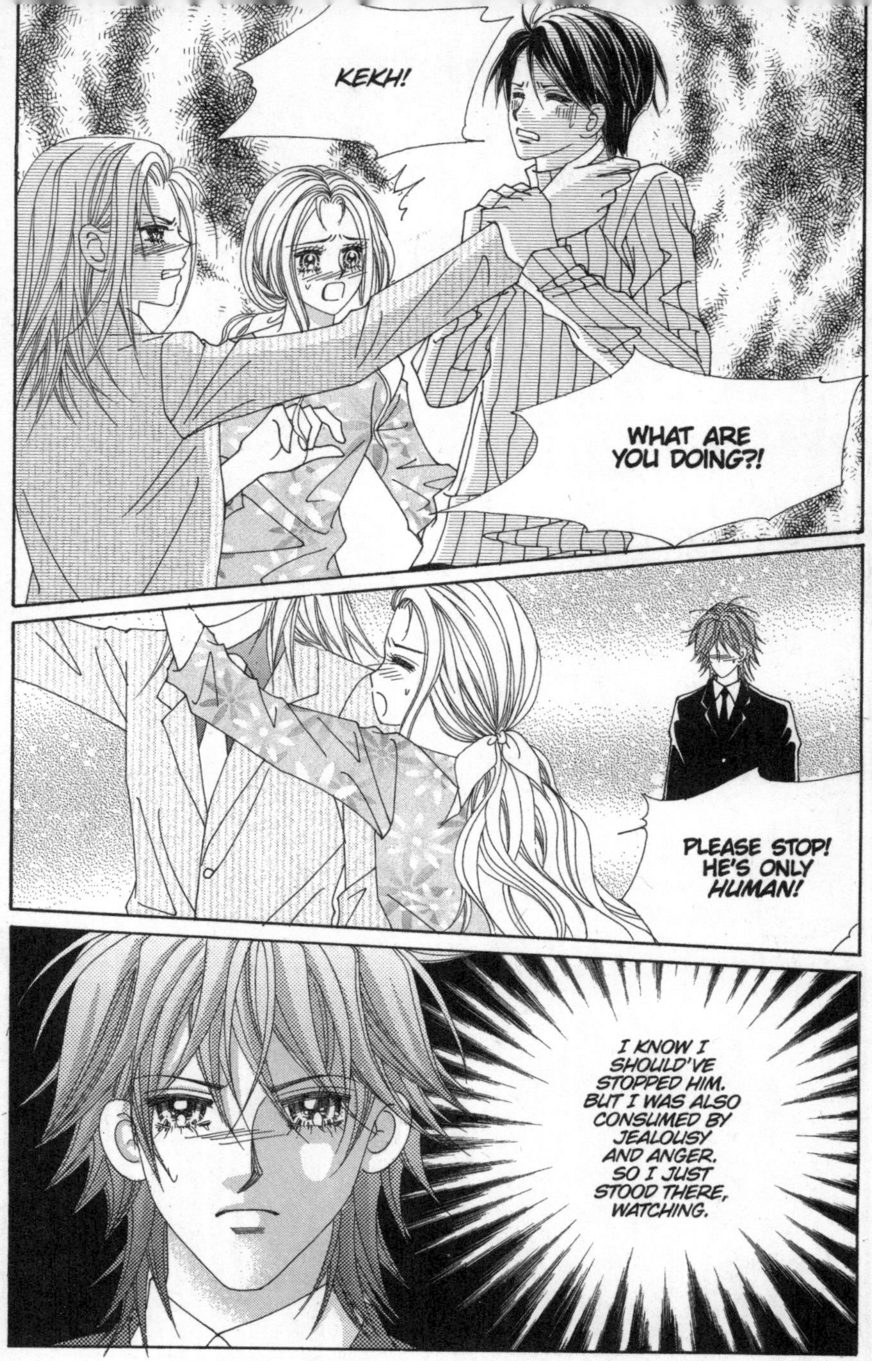
KEKH!
WHAT ARE YOU DOING?!
PLEASE STOP! HE'S ONLY *HUMAN!*
I KNOW I SHOULD'VE STOPPED HIM. BUT I WAS ALSO CONSUMED BY JEALOUSY AND ANGER. SO I JUST STOOD THERE, WATCHING.

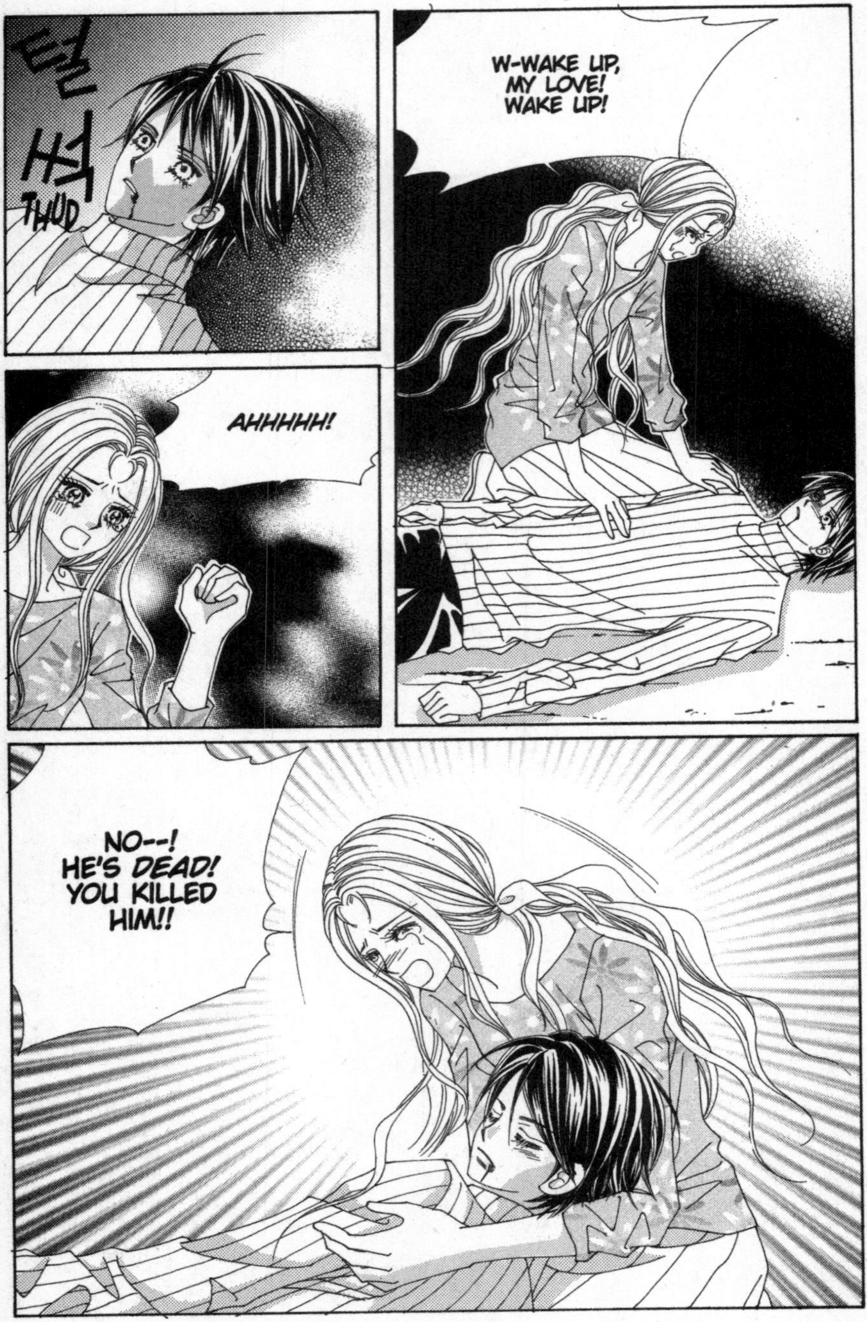
털썩
THUD
AHHHHH!
W-WAKE UP, MY LOVE! WAKE UP!
NO--! HE'S *DEAD!* YOU KILLED HIM!!

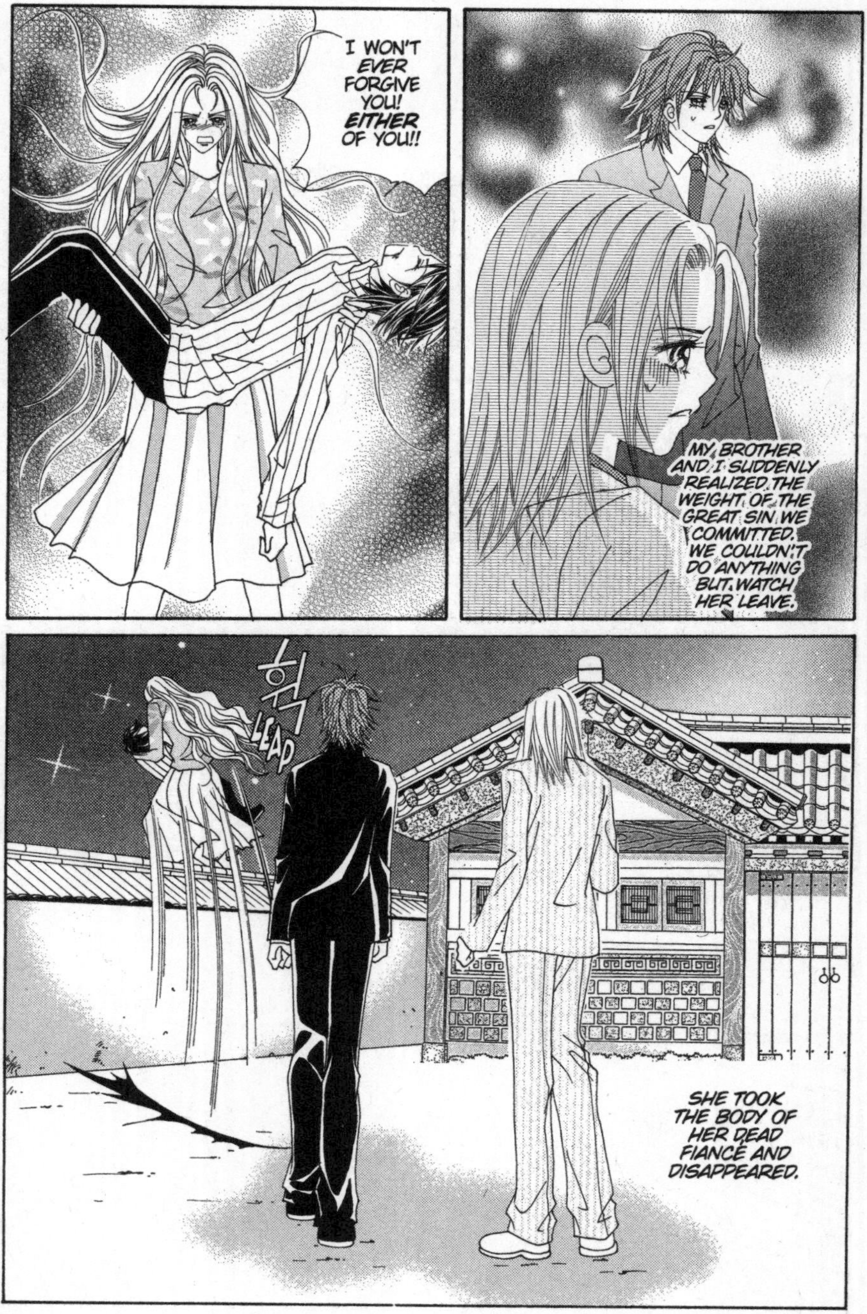
I WON'T EVER FORGIVE YOU! EITHER OF YOU!!
MY BROTHER AND I SUDDENLY REALIZED THE WEIGHT OF THE GREAT SIN WE COMMITTED. WE COULDN'T DO ANYTHING BUT WATCH HER LEAVE.
LEAP
SHE TOOK THE BODY OF HER DEAD FIANCE AND DISAPPEARED.

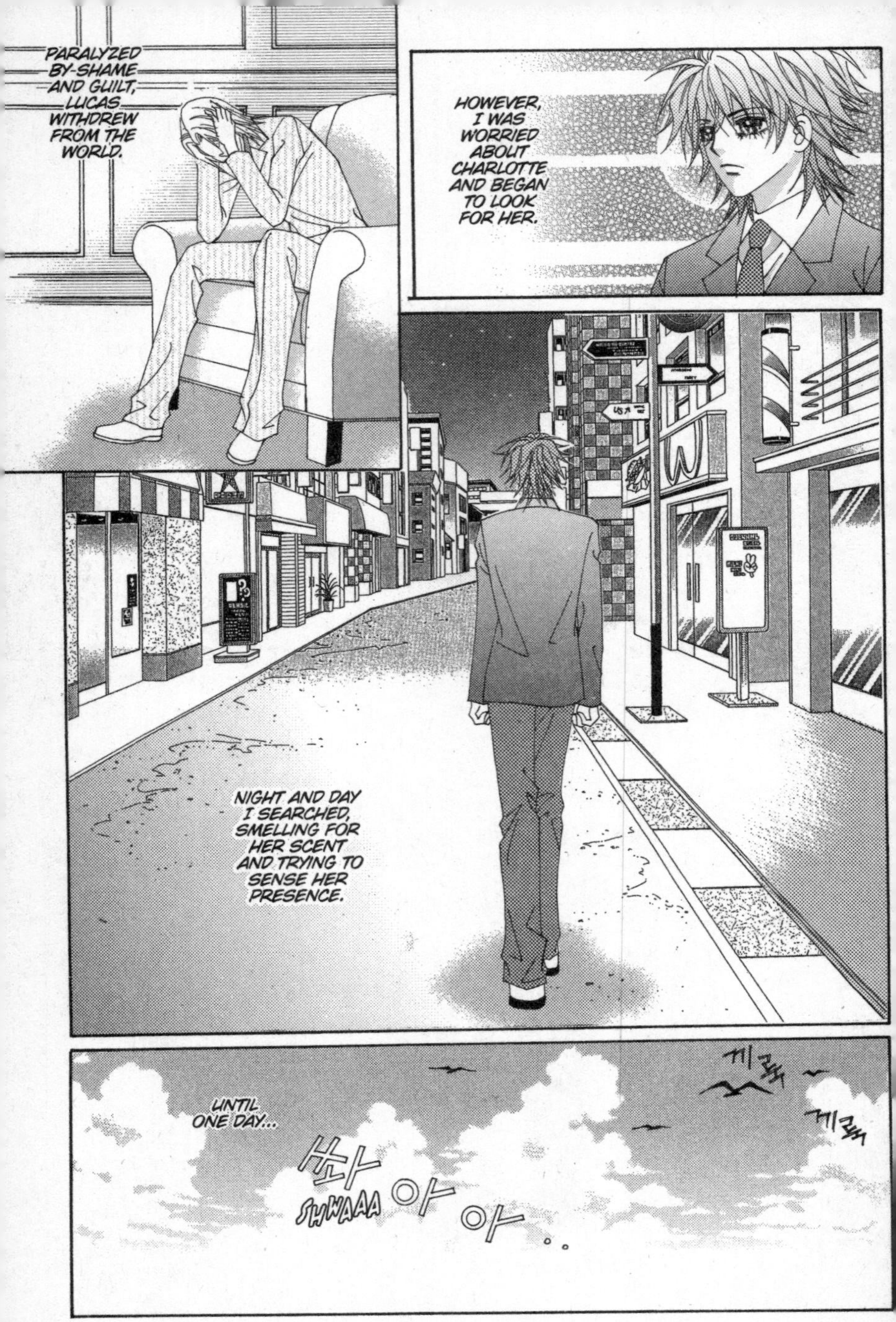
PARALYZED BY-SHAME AND GUILT, LUCAS WITHDREW FROM THE WORLD.
HOWEVER, I WAS WORRIED ABOUT CHARLOTTE AND BEGAN TO LOOK FOR HER.
NIGHT AND DAY I SEARCHED, SMELLING FOR HER SCENT AND TRYING TO SENSE HER PRESENCE.
UNTIL ONE DAY...
쏴아아..
SHWAAA
끼룩
끼룩

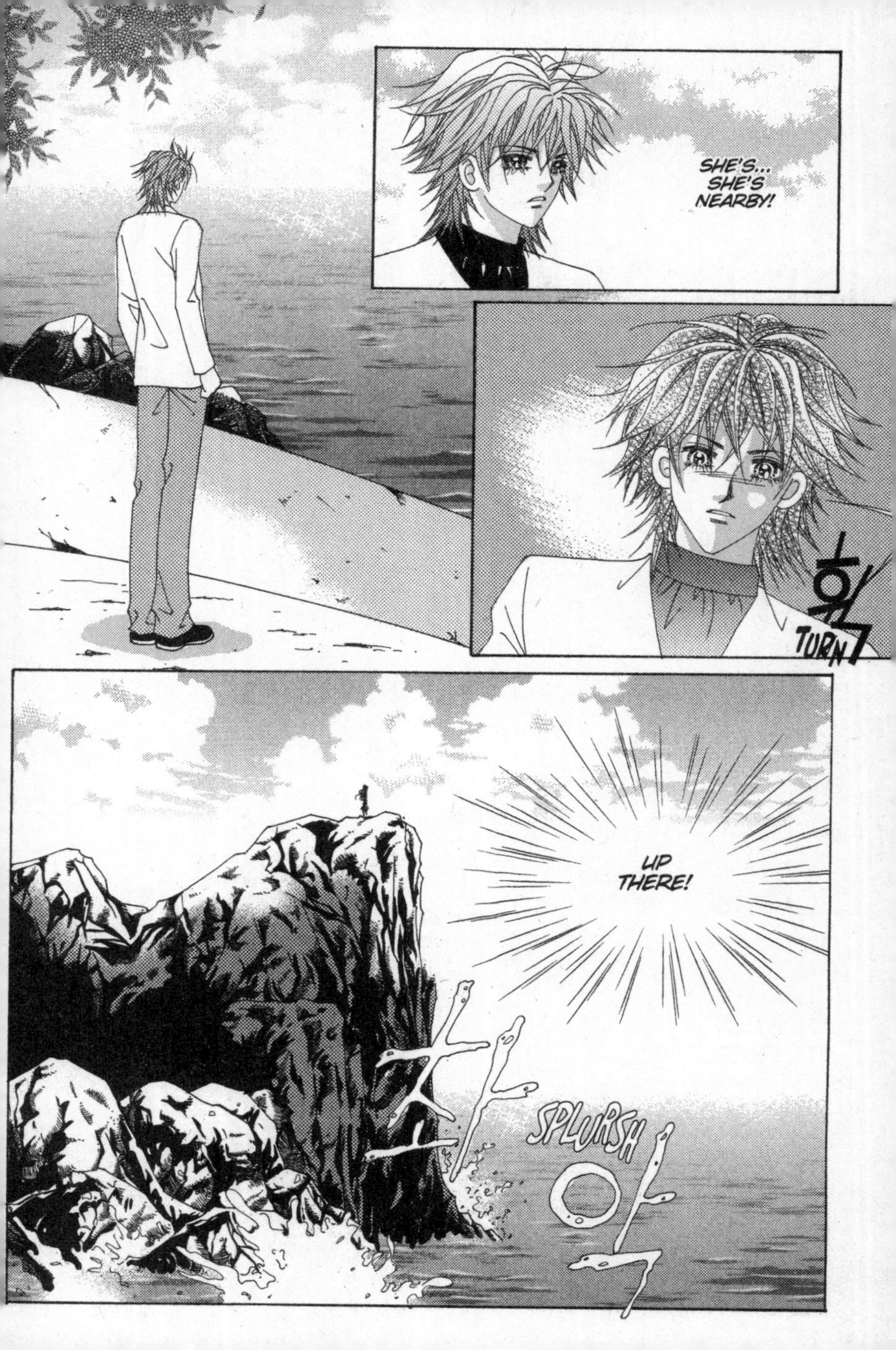
SHE'S...
SHE'S
NEARBY!
TURN
UP
THERE!
SPLURSH

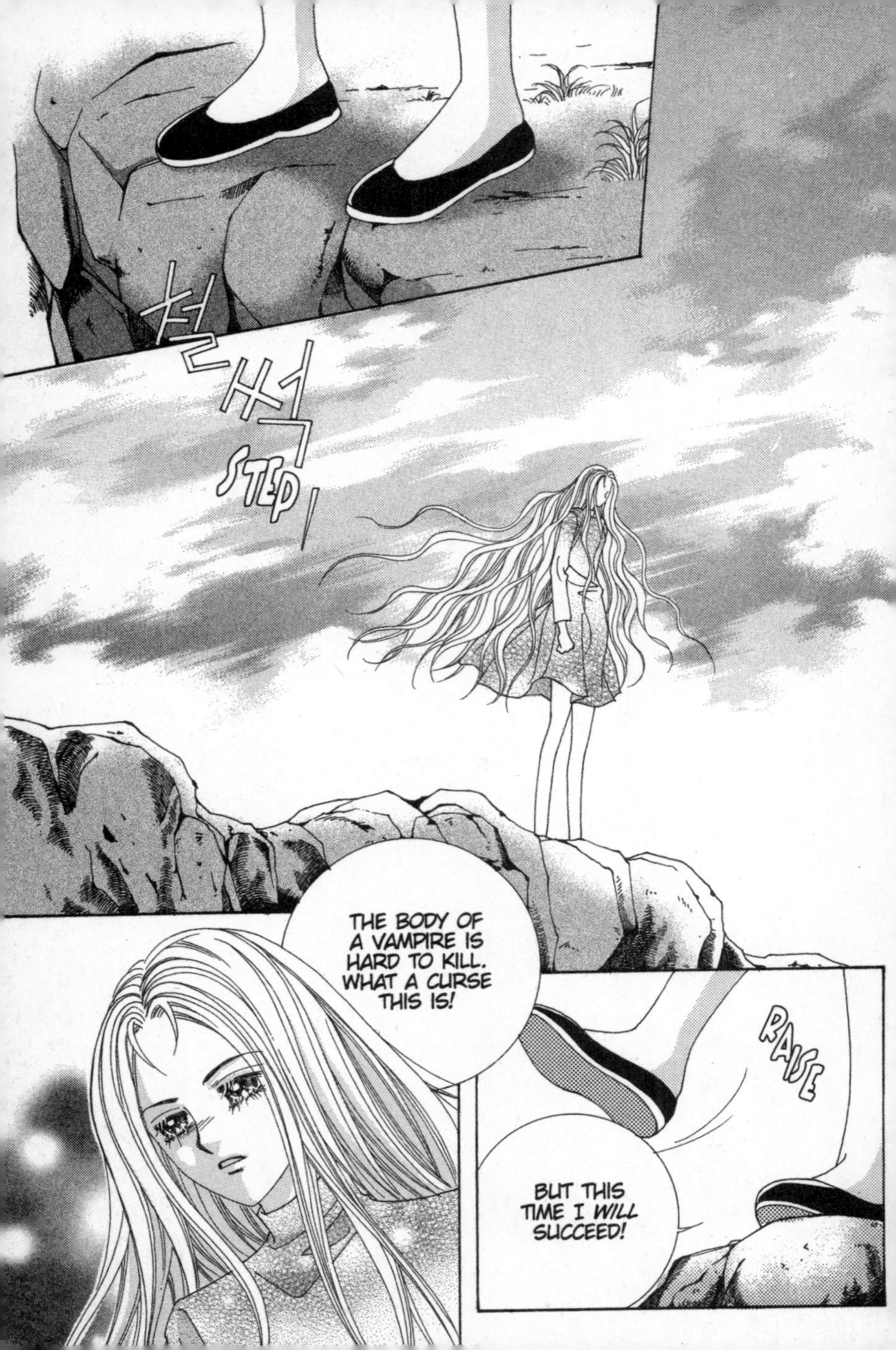
STEP
THE BODY OF A VAMPIRE IS HARD TO KILL. WHAT A CURSE THIS IS!
RAISE
BUT THIS TIME I WILL SUCCEED!

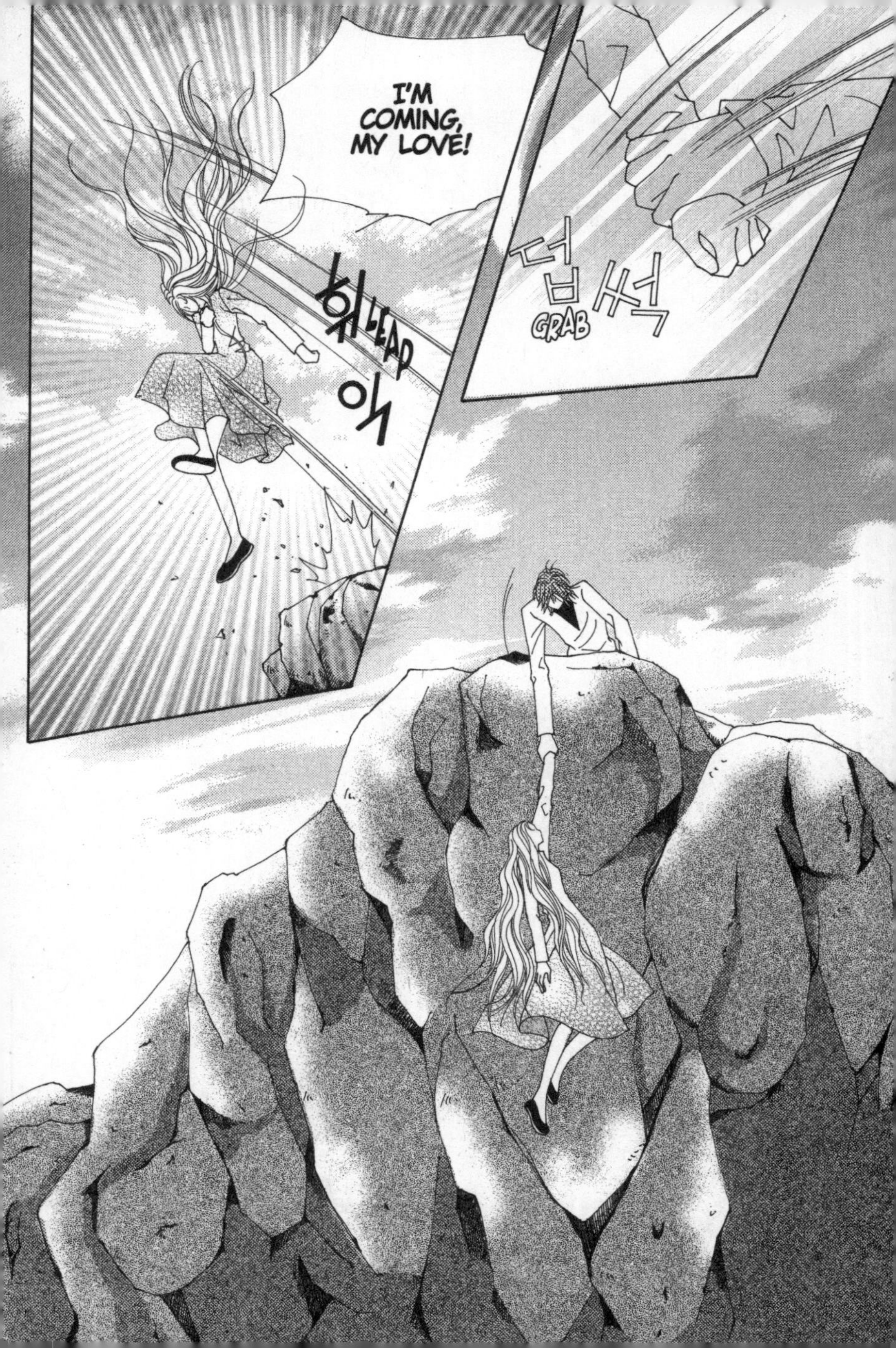
I'M COMING, MY LOVE!
LEAP
GRAB

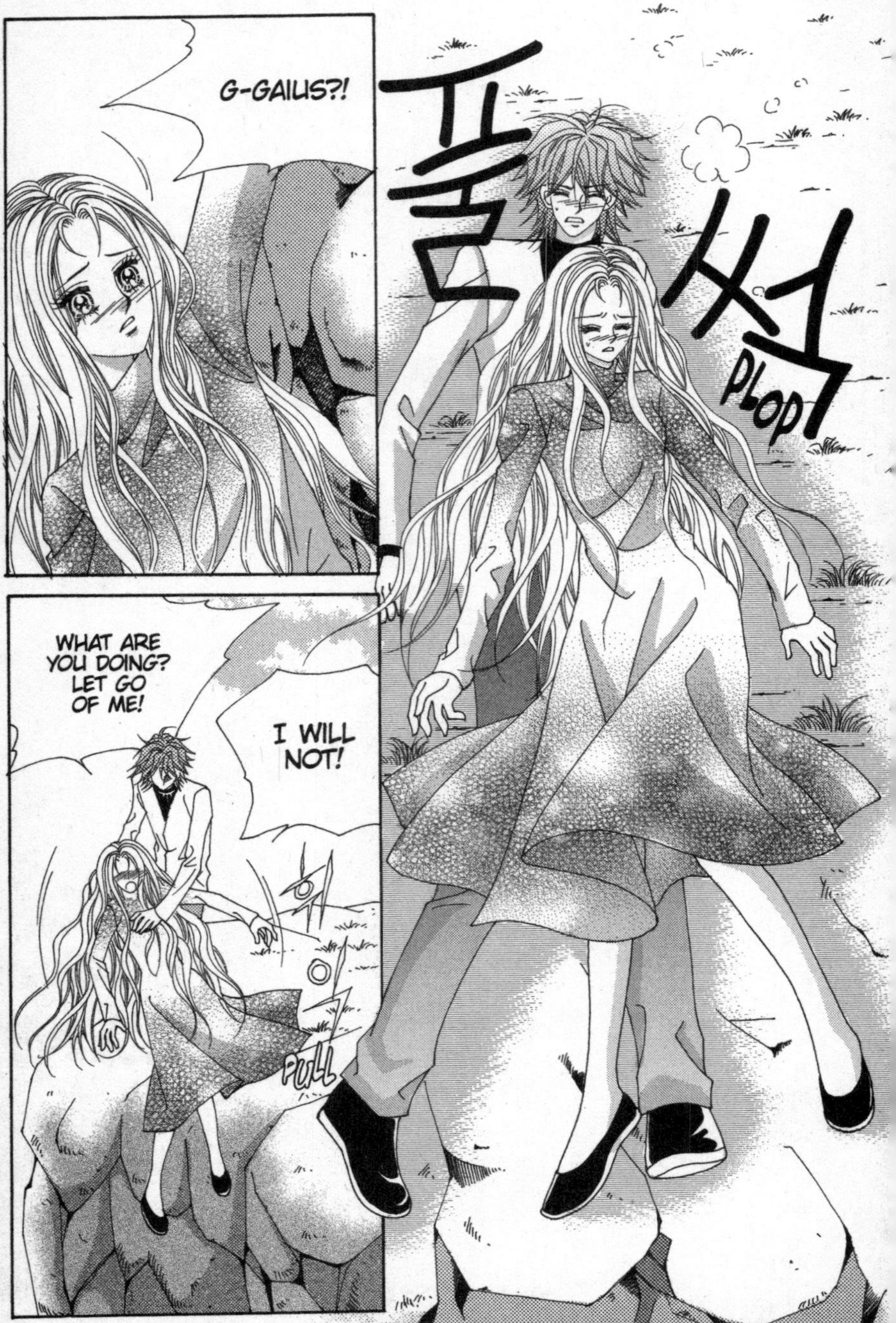
G-GAIUS?!
WHAT ARE YOU DOING? LET GO OF ME!
I WILL NOT!
PULL
풀썩
PLOP

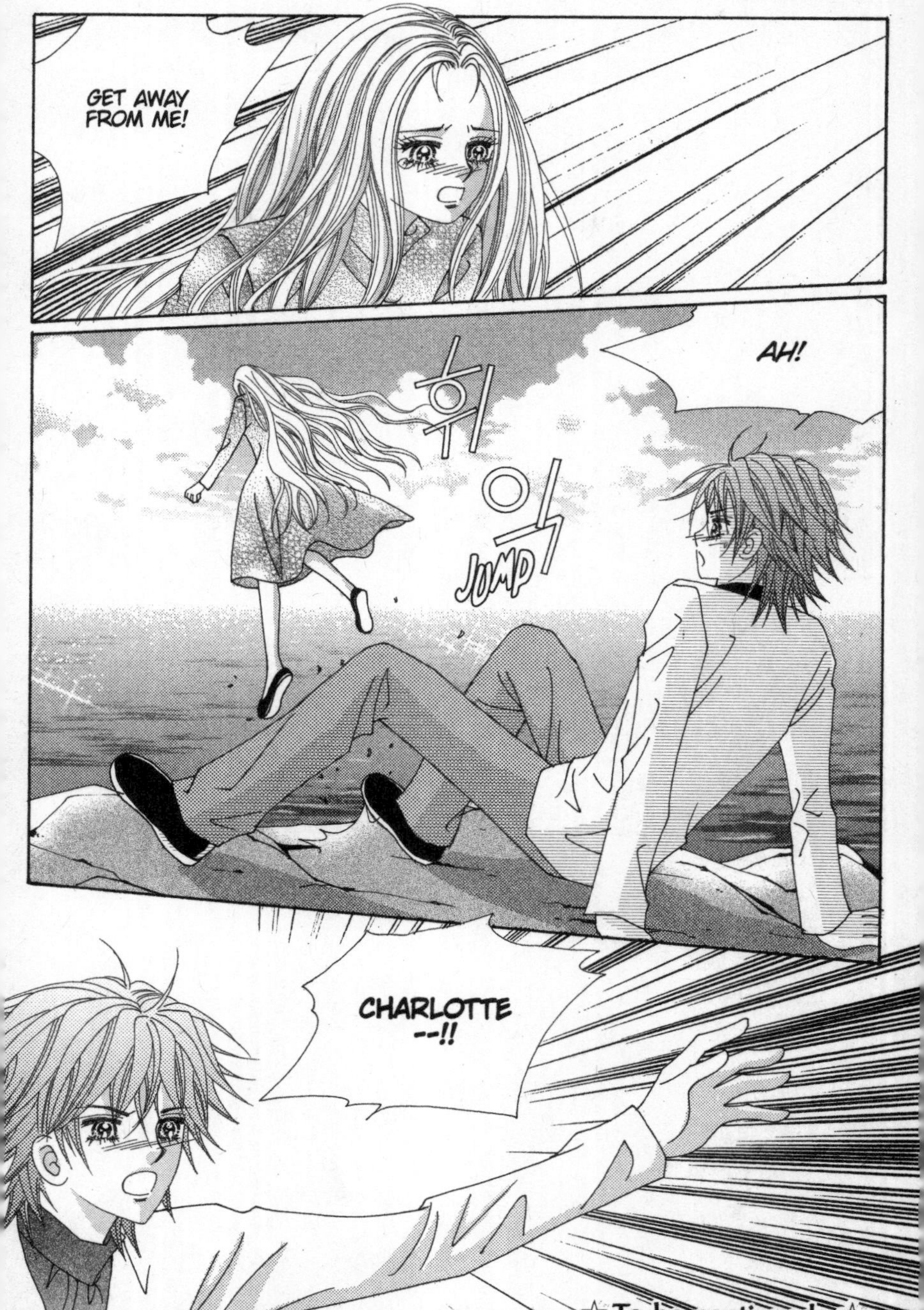
GET AWAY FROM ME!
휘익
JUMP
AH!
CHARLOTTE --!!

☆To be continued...☆

My Boyfriend is a

VAM PIRE

BOOK 14

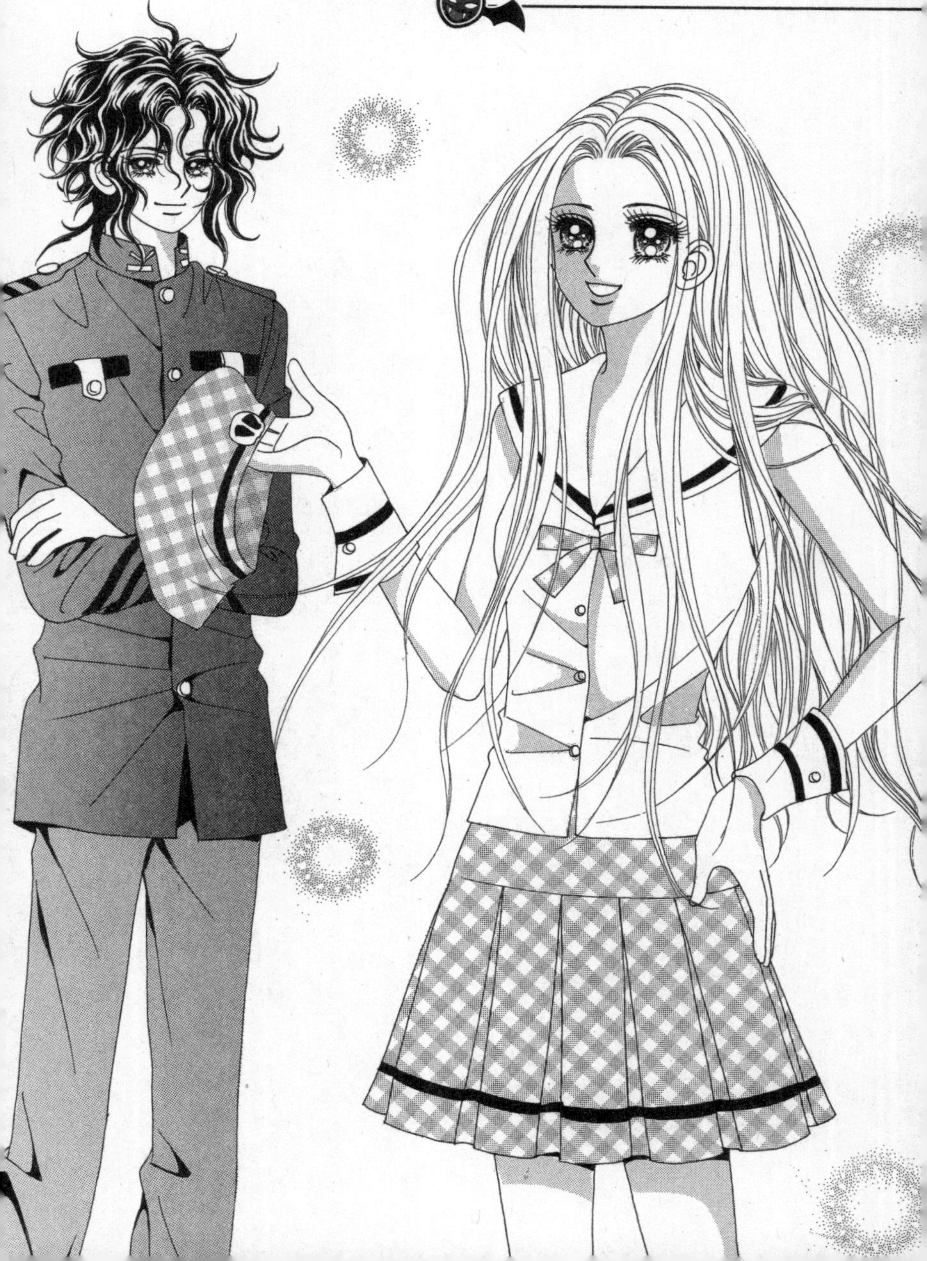

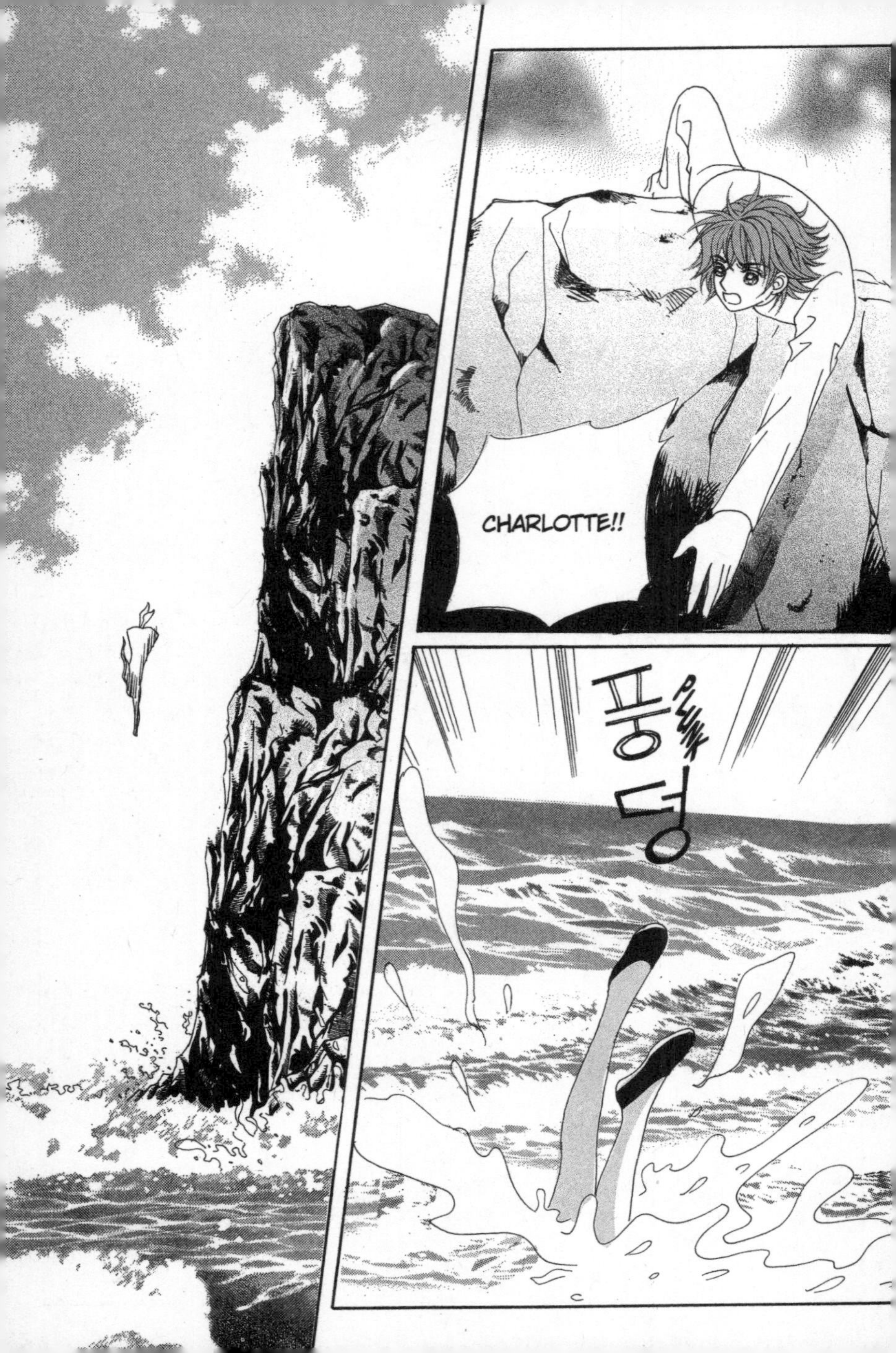
CHARLOTTE!!
풍덩
PLUNK

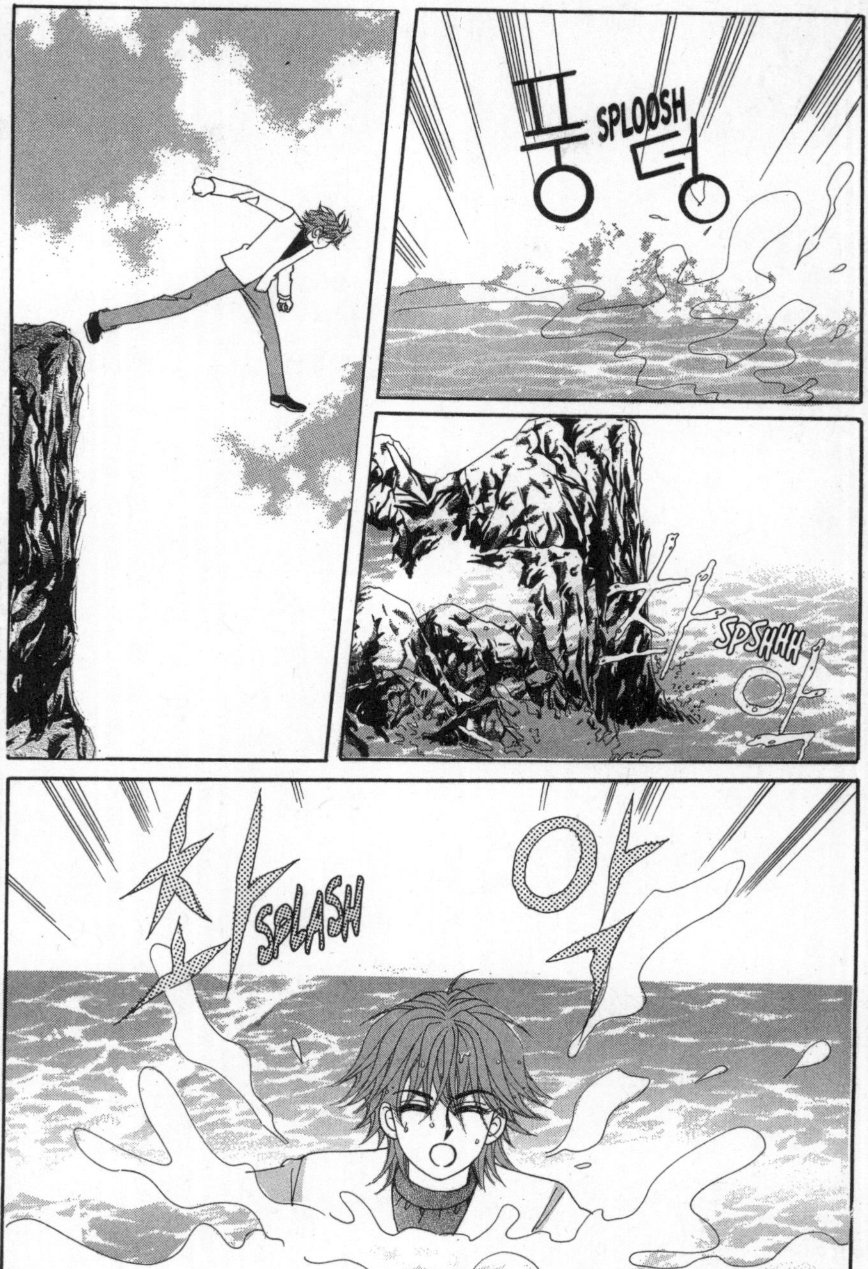
풍덩
SPLOOSH
SPSHHH
SPLASH

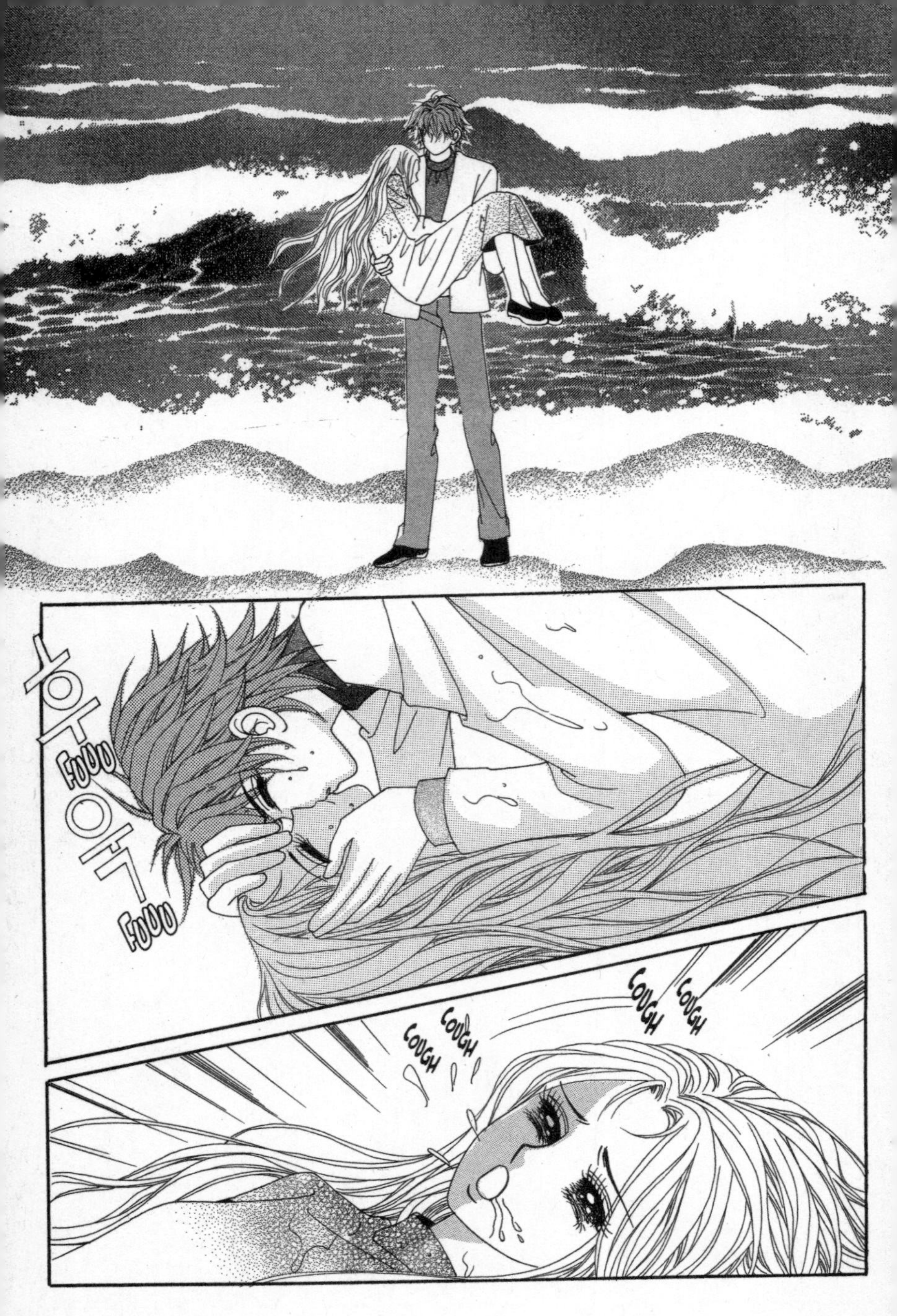
FUUU
FUUU
COUGH
COUGH
COUGH
COUGH

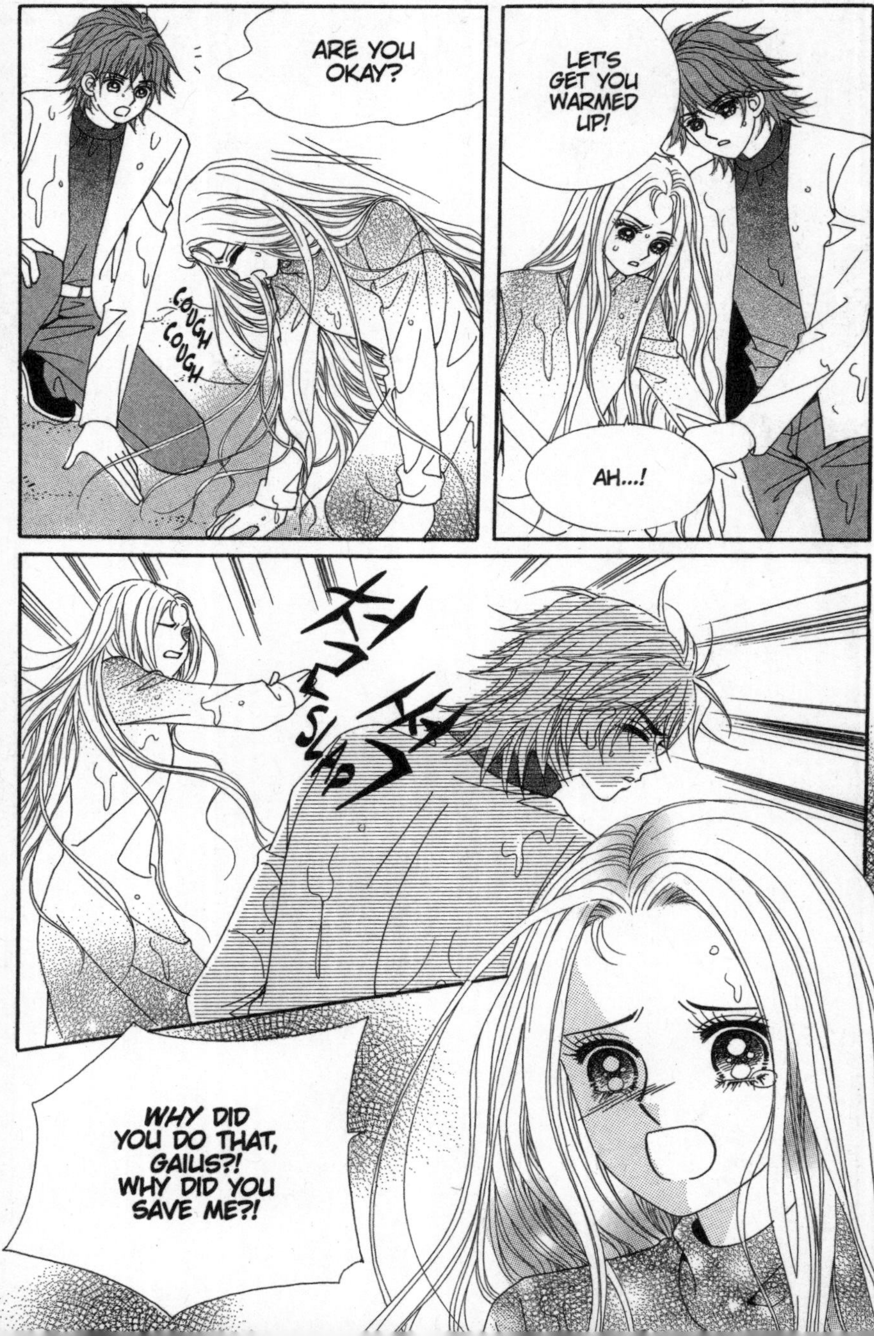
ARE YOU OKAY?
COUGH COUGH
LET'S GET YOU WARMED UP!
AH...!
SLAP
WHY DID YOU DO THAT, GAILUS?! WHY DID YOU SAVE ME?!

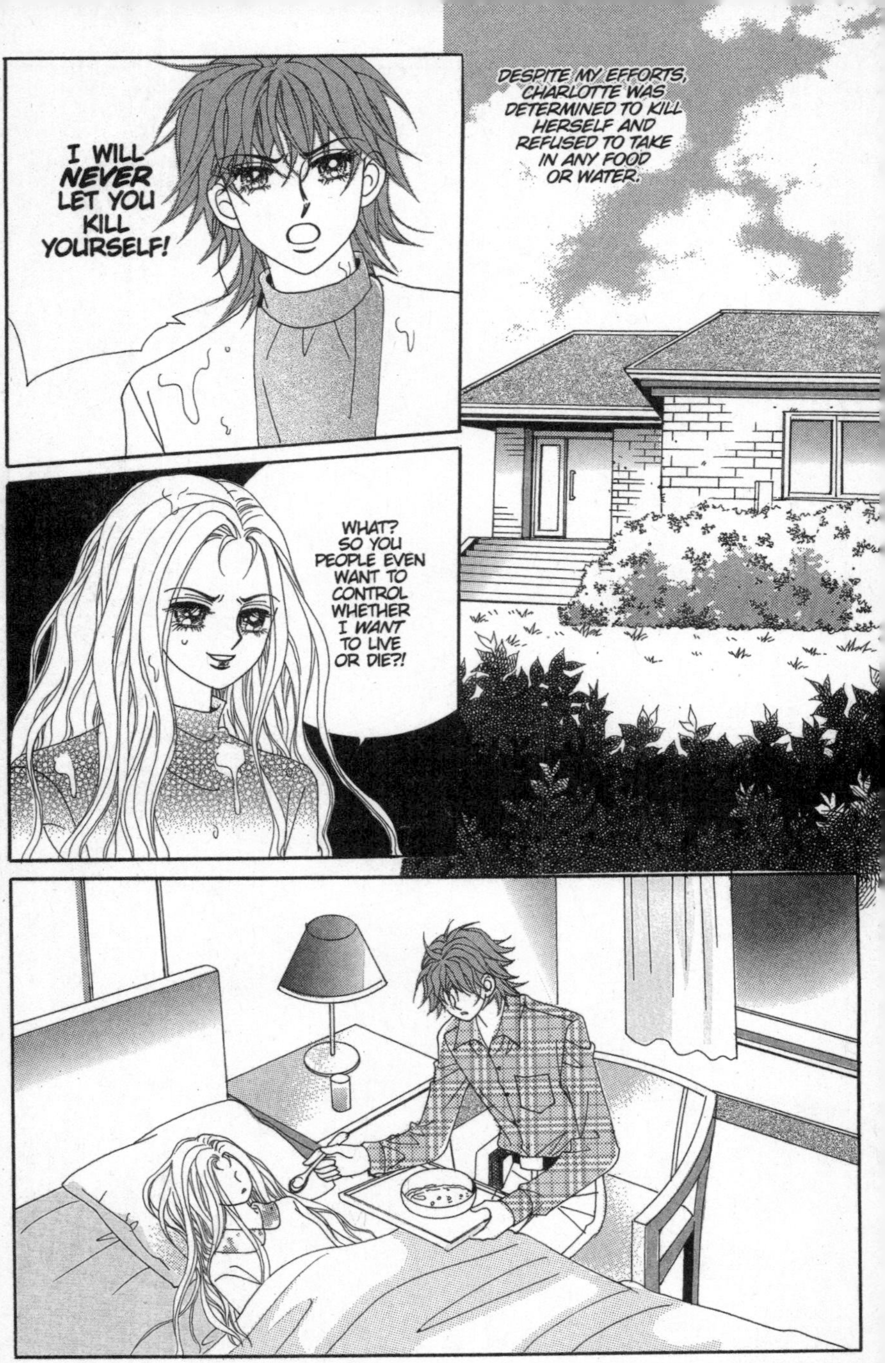
I WILL NEVER LET YOU KILL YOURSELF!
WHAT? SO YOU PEOPLE EVEN WANT TO CONTROL WHETHER I WANT TO LIVE OR DIE?!
DESPITE MY EFFORTS, CHARLOTTE WAS DETERMINED TO KILL HERSELF AND REFUSED TO TAKE IN ANY FOOD OR WATER.

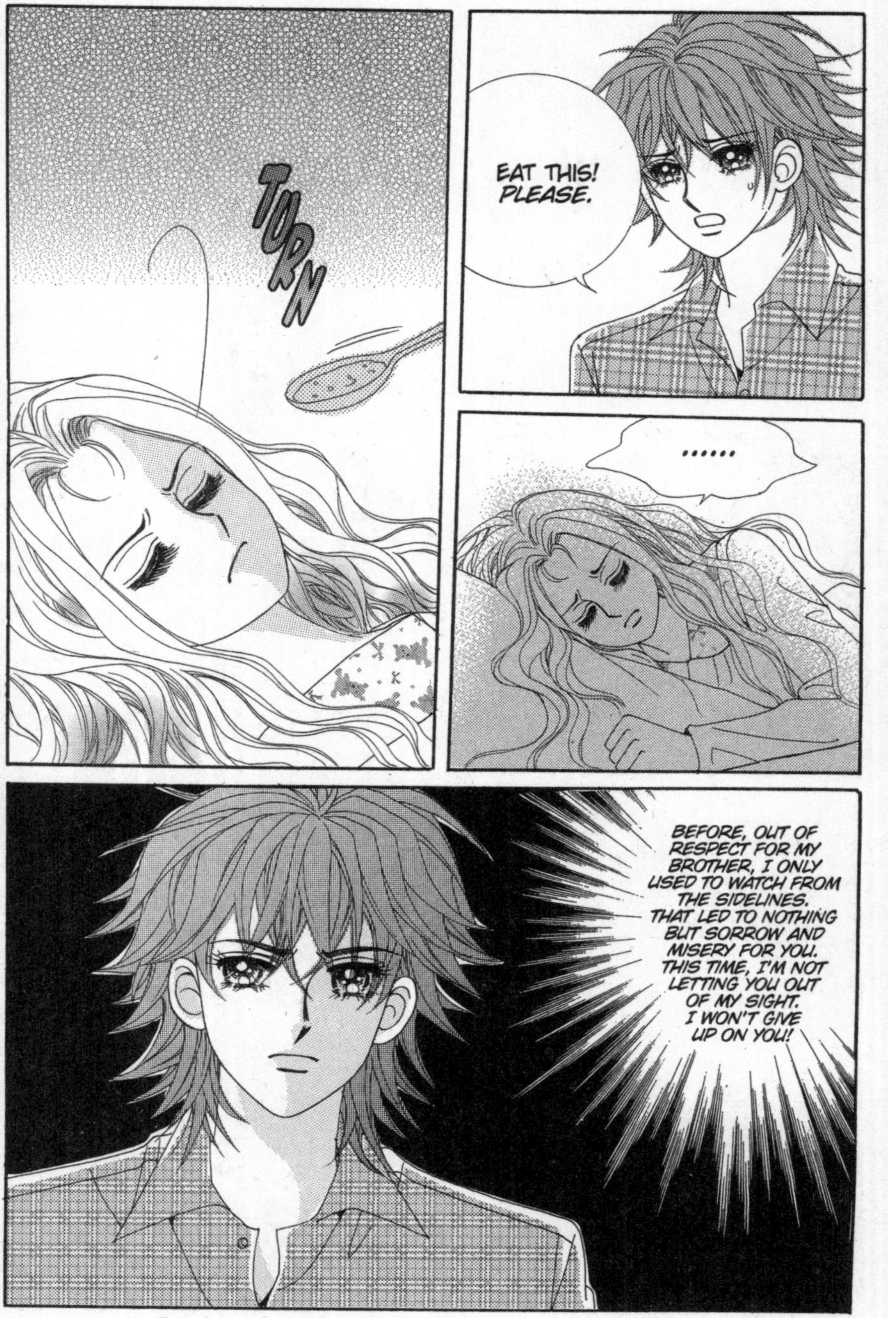
TURN
EAT THIS! PLEASE.
......
BEFORE, OUT OF RESPECT FOR MY BROTHER, I ONLY USED TO WATCH FROM THE SIDELINES. THAT LED TO NOTHING BUT SORROW AND MISERY FOR YOU. THIS TIME, I'M NOT LETTING YOU OUT OF MY SIGHT. I WON'T GIVE UP ON YOU!

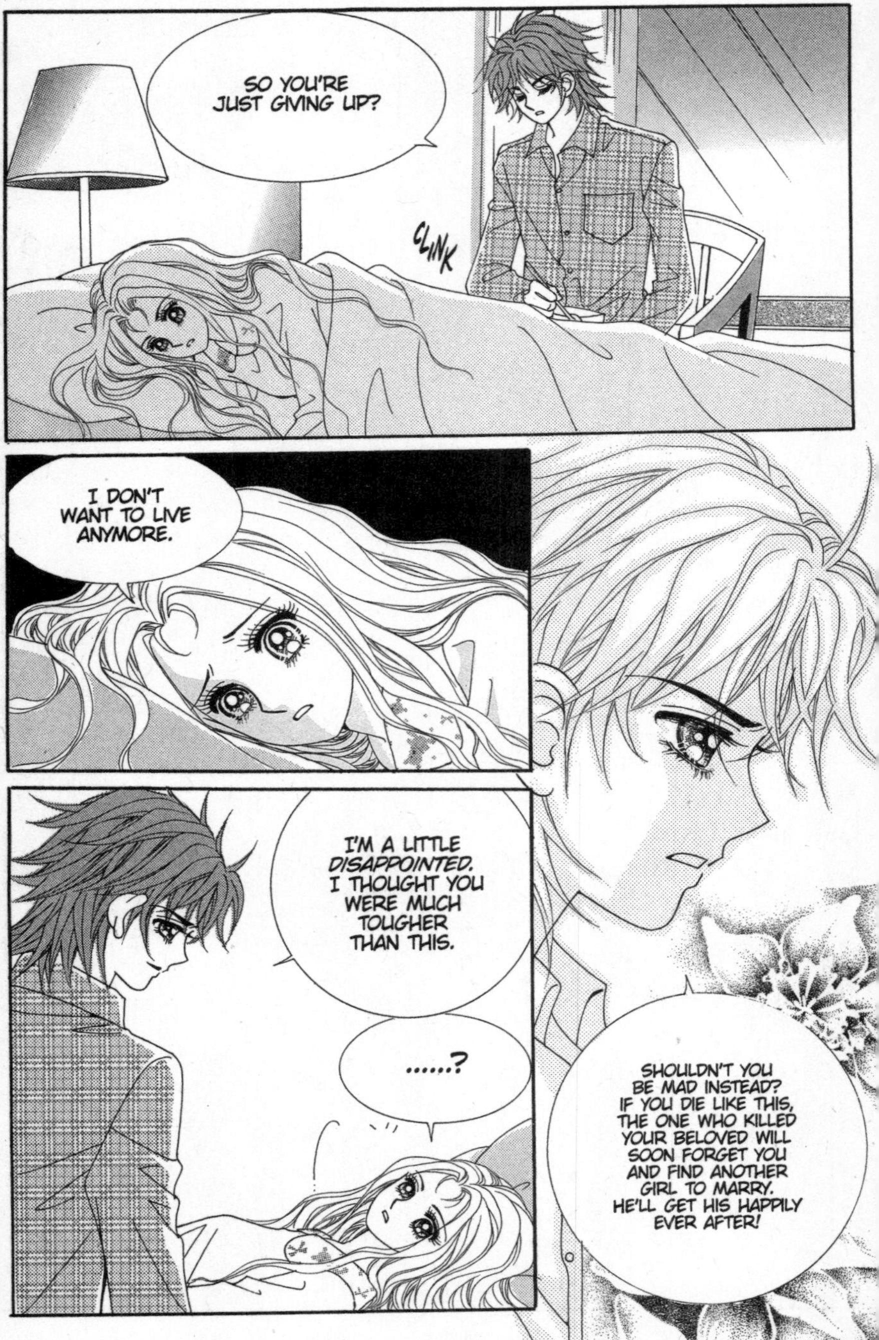
SO YOU'RE JUST GIVING UP?
CLINK
I DON'T WANT TO LIVE ANYMORE.
I'M A LITTLE *DISAPPOINTED.* I THOUGHT YOU WERE MUCH TOUGHER THAN THIS.
......?
SHOULDN'T YOU BE MAD INSTEAD? IF YOU DIE LIKE THIS, THE ONE WHO KILLED YOUR BELOVED WILL SOON FORGET YOU AND FIND ANOTHER GIRL TO MARRY. HE'LL GET HIS HAPPILY EVER AFTER!

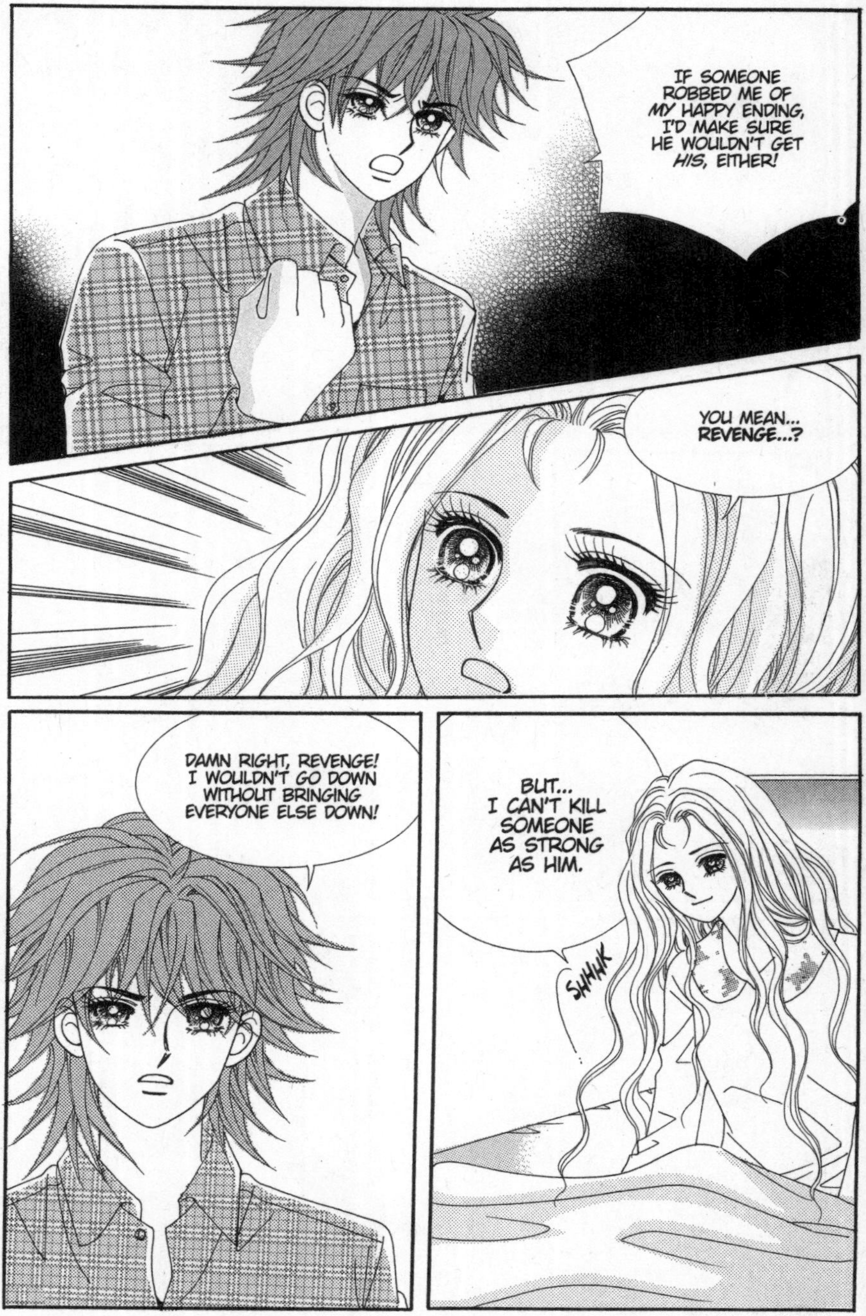
IF SOMEONE ROBBED ME OF *MY* HAPPY ENDING, I'D MAKE SURE HE WOULDN'T GET *HIS*, EITHER!
YOU MEAN... REVENGE...?
DAMN RIGHT, REVENGE! I WOULDN'T GO DOWN WITHOUT BRINGING EVERYONE ELSE DOWN!
BUT... I CAN'T KILL SOMEONE AS STRONG AS HIM.
SHHHK
...

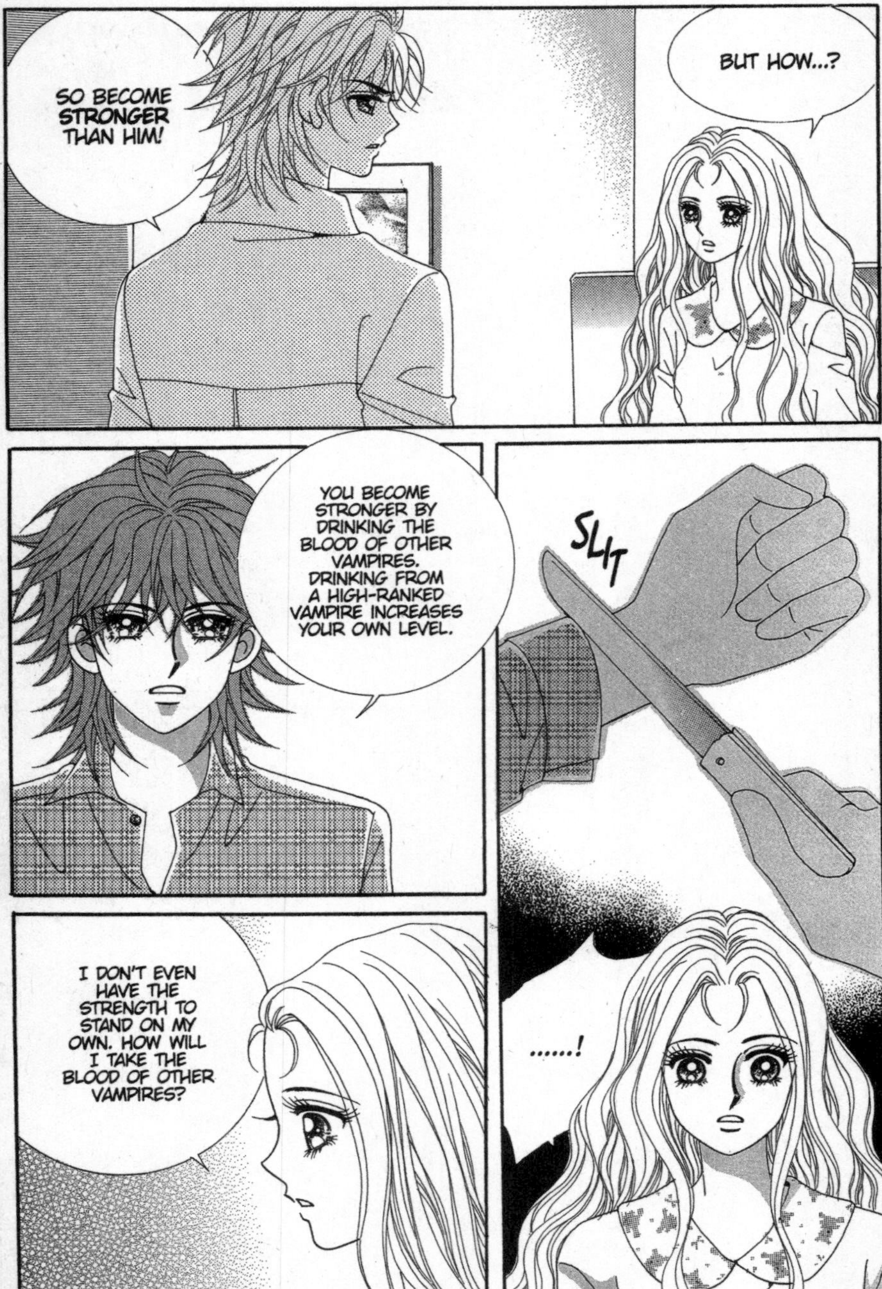
SO BECOME STRONGER THAN HIM!
BUT HOW...?
YOU BECOME STRONGER BY DRINKING THE BLOOD OF OTHER VAMPIRES. DRINKING FROM A HIGH-RANKED VAMPIRE INCREASES YOUR OWN LEVEL.
I DON'T EVEN HAVE THE STRENGTH TO STAND ON MY OWN. HOW WILL I TAKE THE BLOOD OF OTHER VAMPIRES?
SLIT
......!

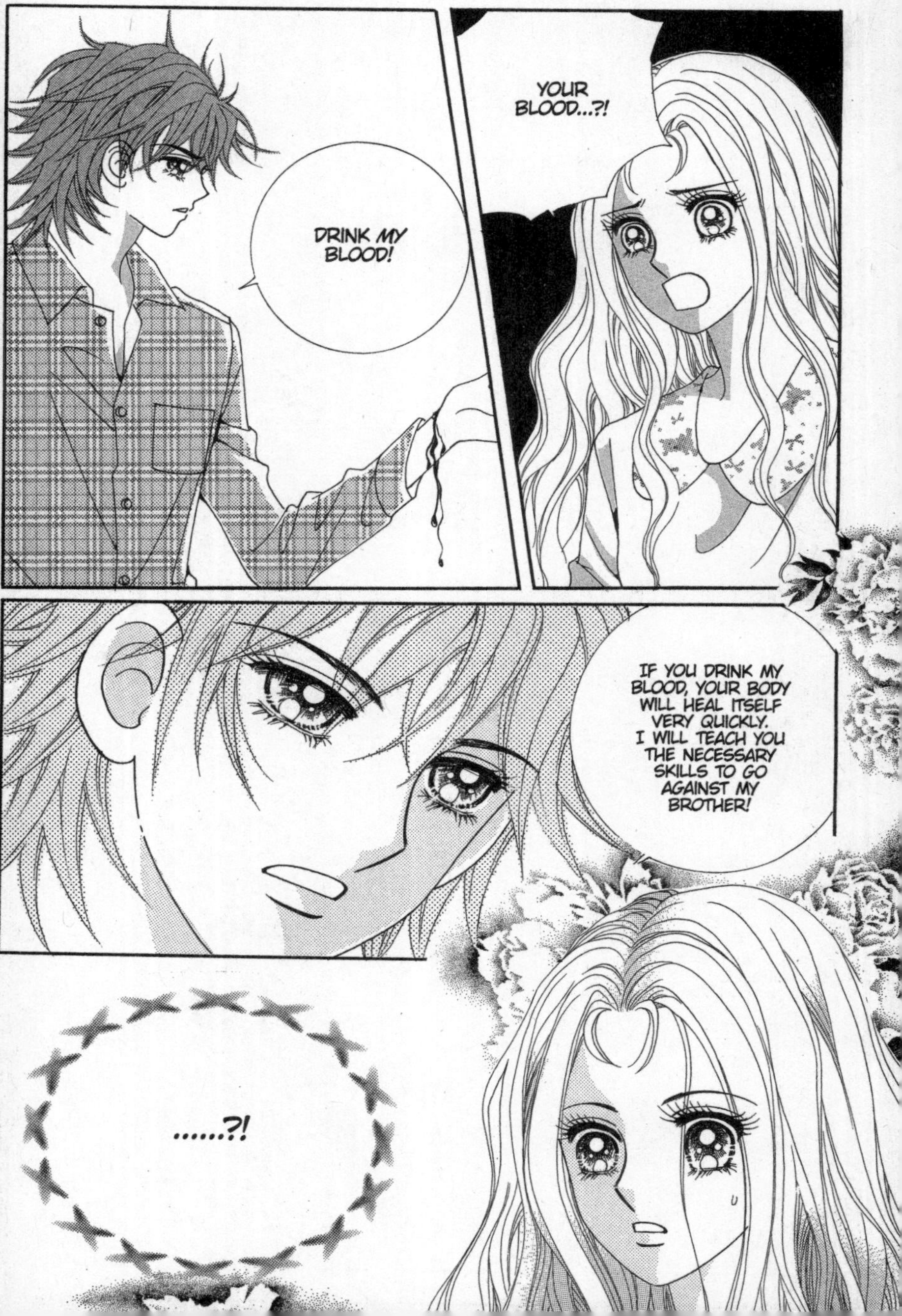
DRINK MY BLOOD!
YOUR BLOOD...?!
IF YOU DRINK MY BLOOD, YOUR BODY WILL HEAL ITSELF VERY QUICKLY. I WILL TEACH YOU THE NECESSARY SKILLS TO GO AGAINST MY BROTHER!
......?!

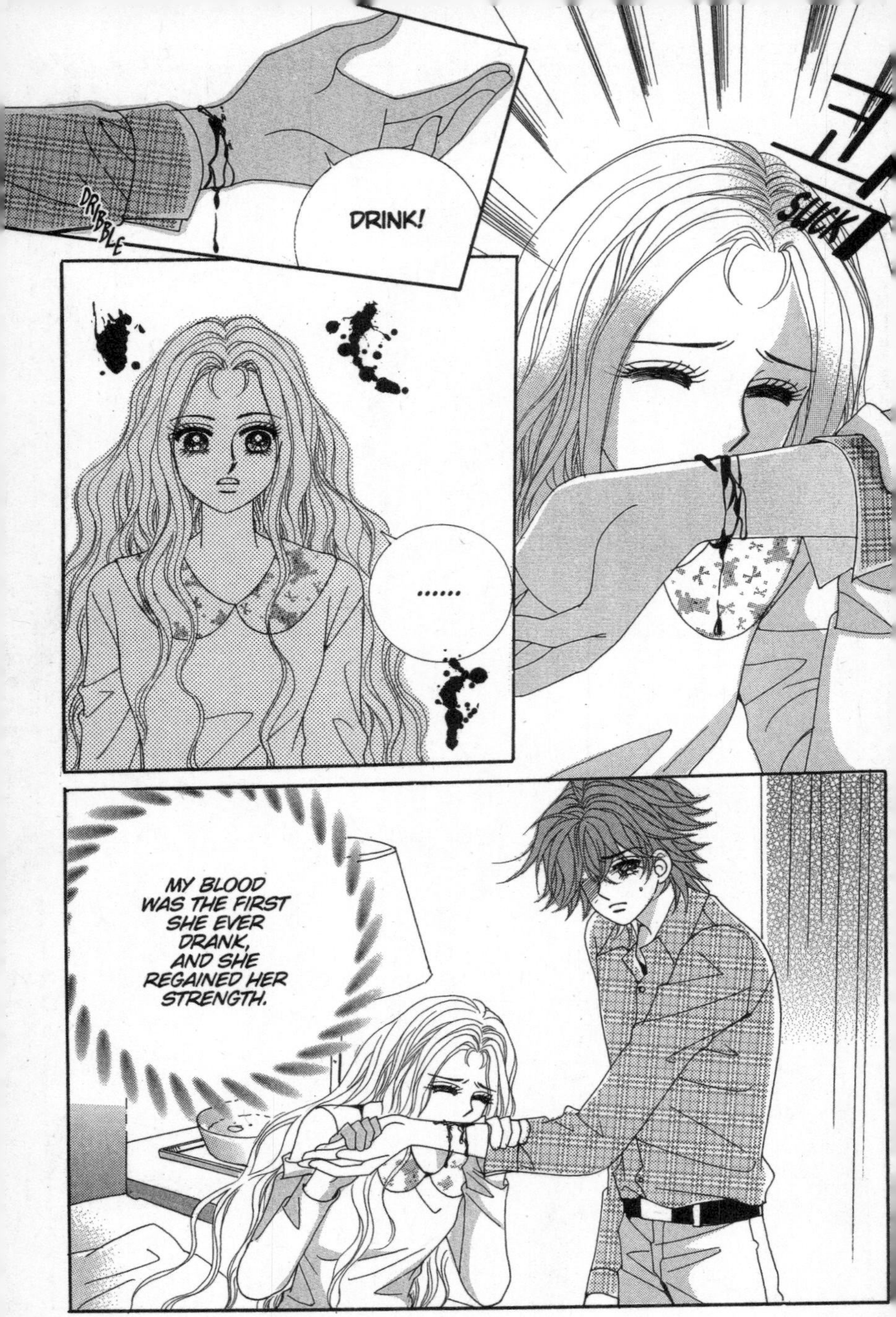
DRIBBLE
DRINK!
......
SUCK
MY BLOOD WAS THE FIRST SHE EVER DRANK, AND SHE REGAINED HER STRENGTH.

AND...THEN I TAUGHT HER ALL THE DIFFERENT VAMPIRE FIGHTING TECHNIQUES.

AGILITY AND SPEED ARE VERY IMPORTANT. TO BEGIN TODAY'S TRAINING, I WANT YOU TO JUMP ON THAT HIGH BRANCH.

POFF

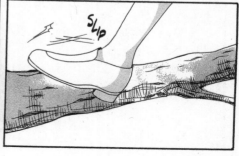

SLIP

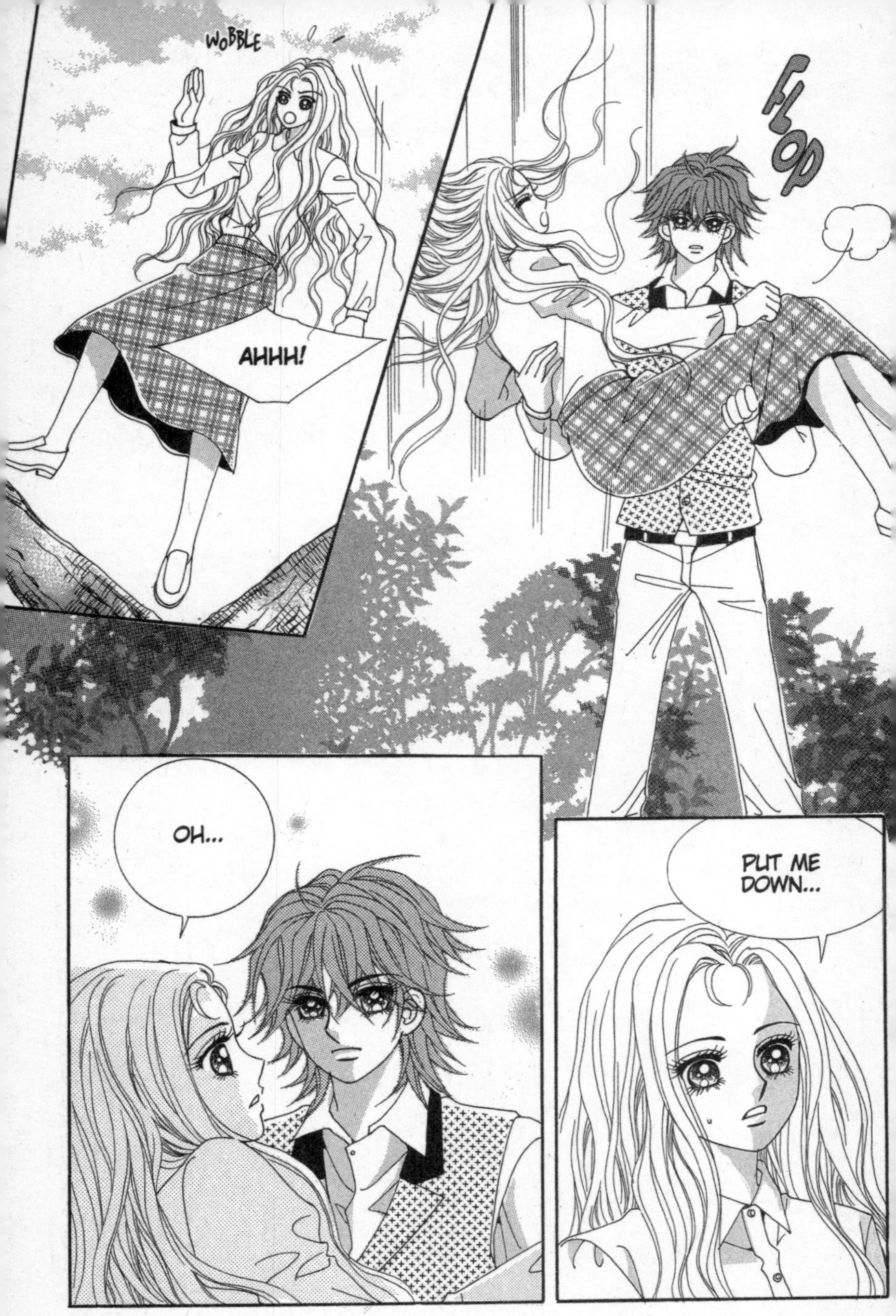
WOBBLE
AHHH!
FLOP
OH...
PUT ME DOWN...

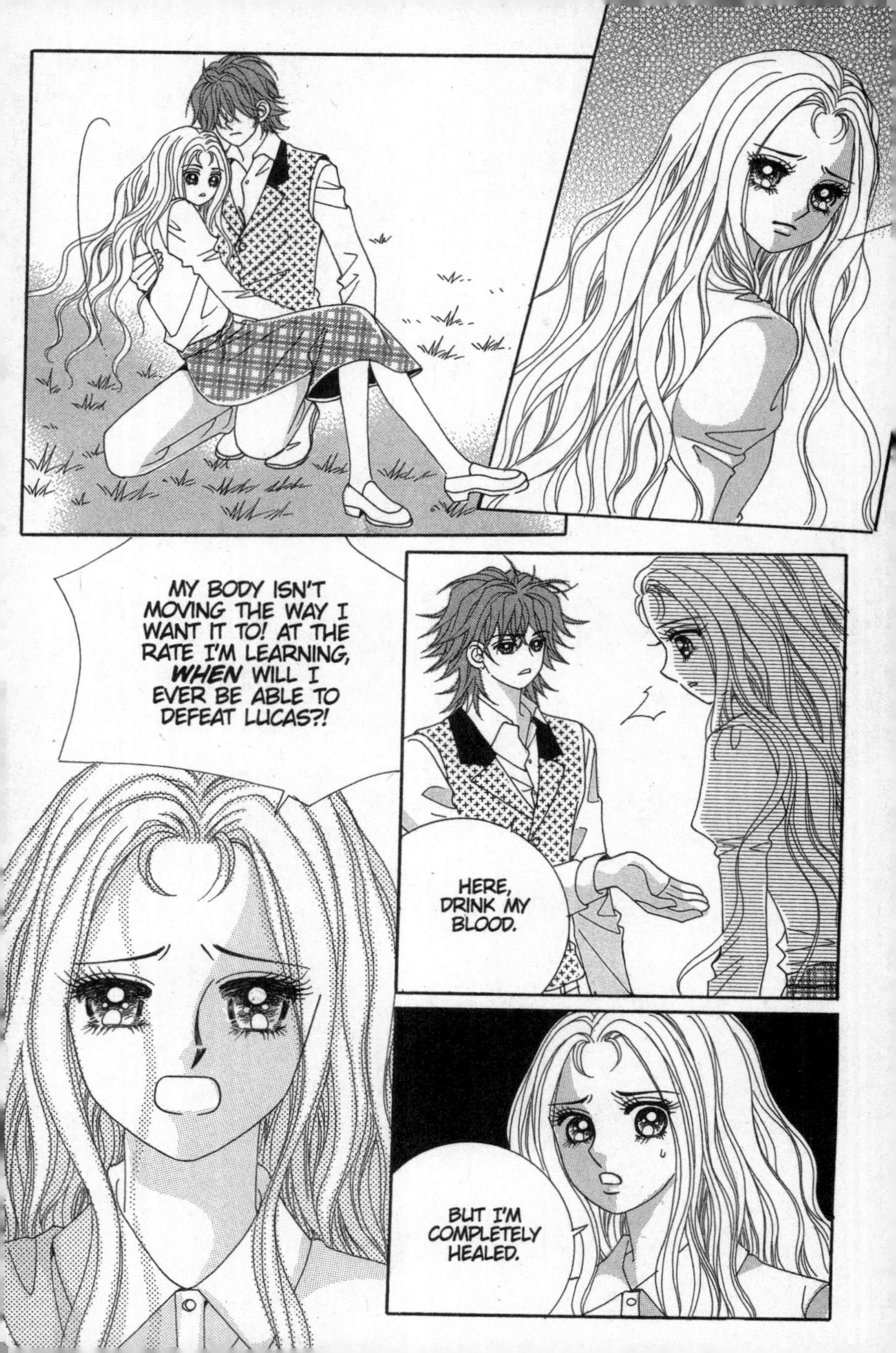
MY BODY ISN'T MOVING THE WAY I WANT IT TO! AT THE RATE I'M LEARNING, *WHEN* WILL I EVER BE ABLE TO DEFEAT LUCAS?!
HERE, DRINK MY BLOOD.
BUT I'M COMPLETELY HEALED.

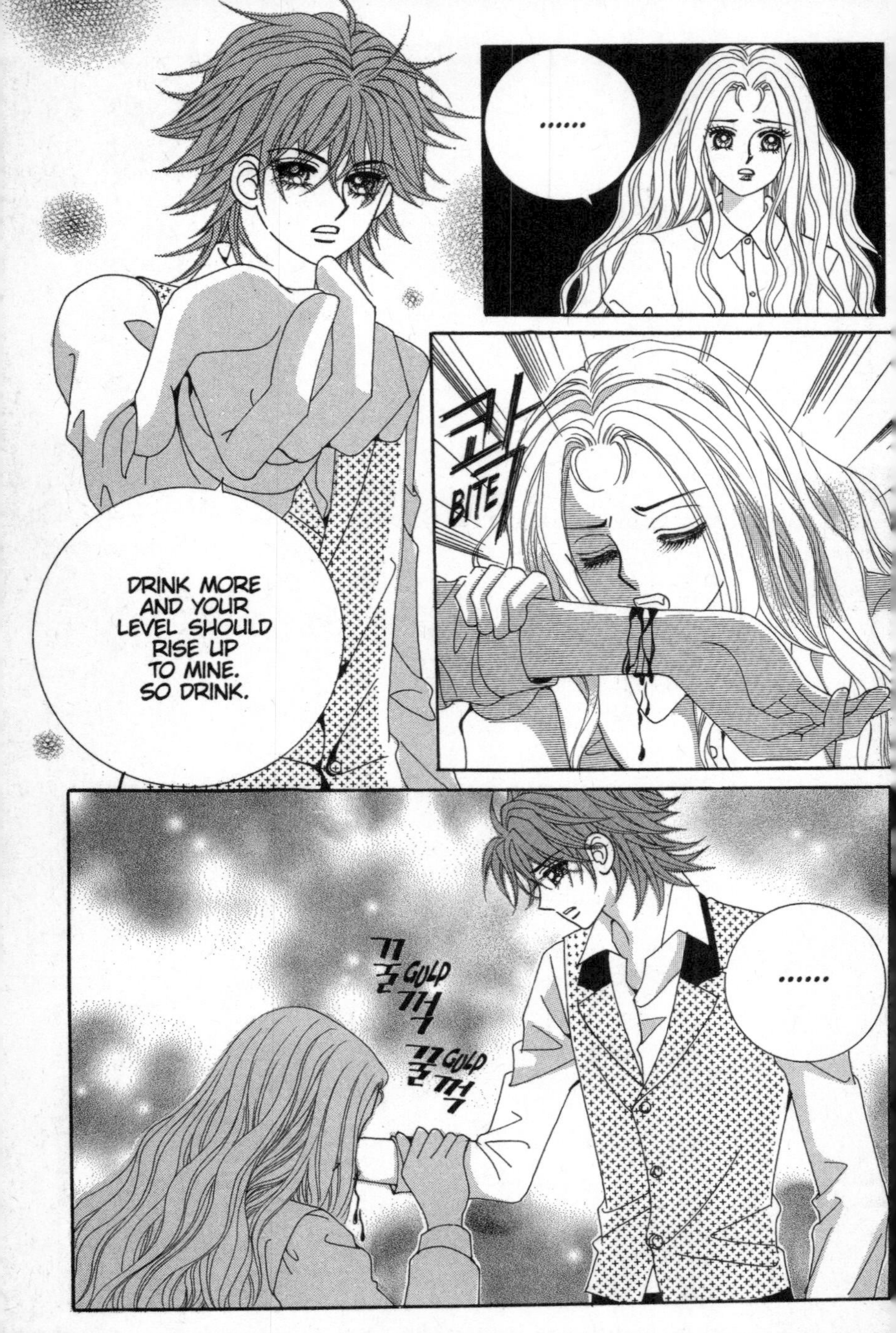
DRINK MORE AND YOUR LEVEL SHOULD RISE UP TO MINE. SO DRINK.
......
콱 BITE
꿀꺽 GULP
꿀꺽 GULP
......

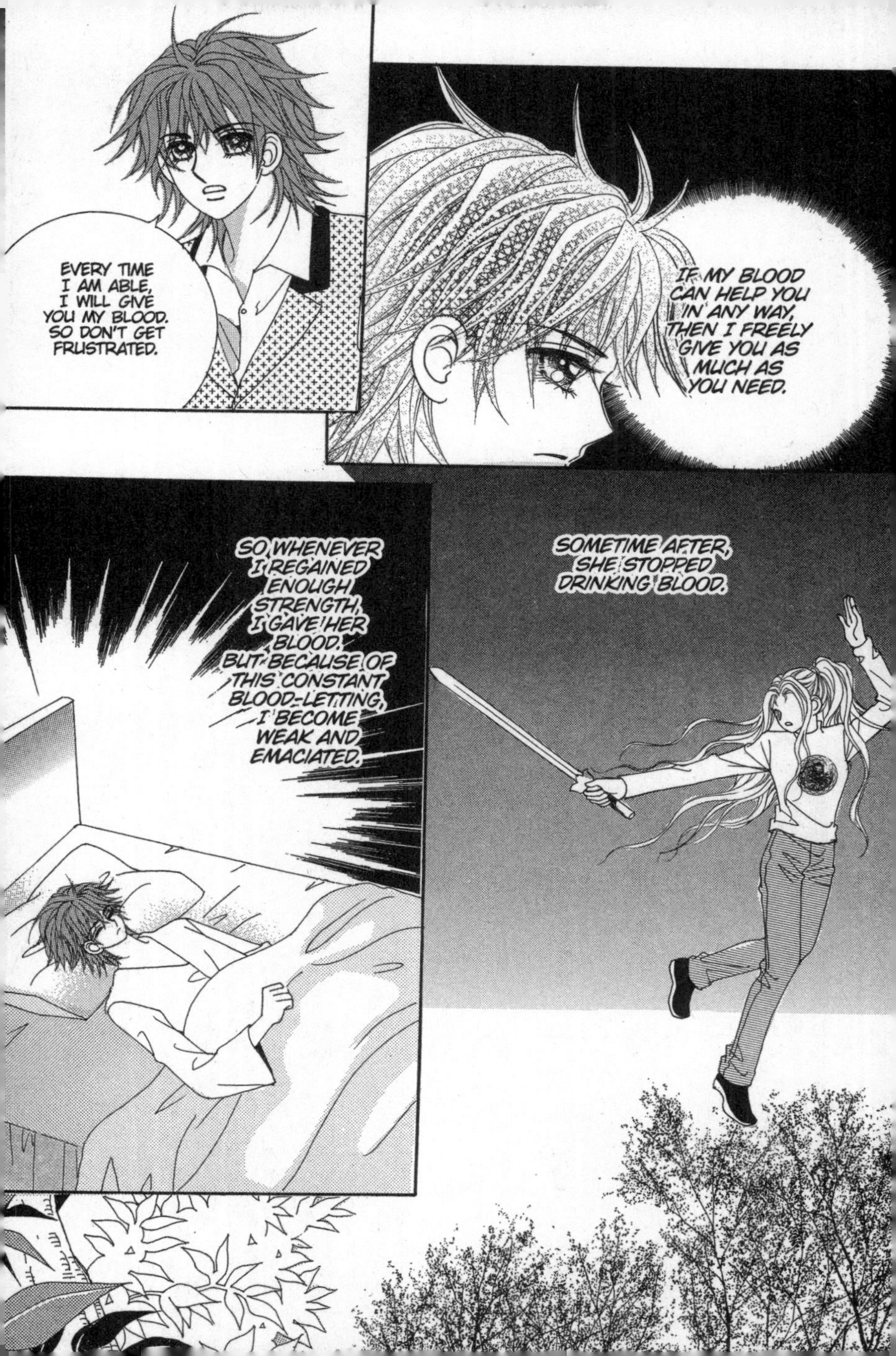
EVERY TIME I AM ABLE, I WILL GIVE YOU MY BLOOD. SO DON'T GET FRUSTRATED.
IF MY BLOOD CAN HELP YOU IN ANY WAY, THEN I FREELY GIVE YOU AS MUCH AS YOU NEED.
SO WHENEVER I REGAINED ENOUGH STRENGTH, I GAVE HER BLOOD. BUT BECAUSE OF THIS CONSTANT BLOOD-LETTING, I BECOME WEAK AND EMACIATED.
SOMETIME AFTER, SHE STOPPED DRINKING BLOOD.

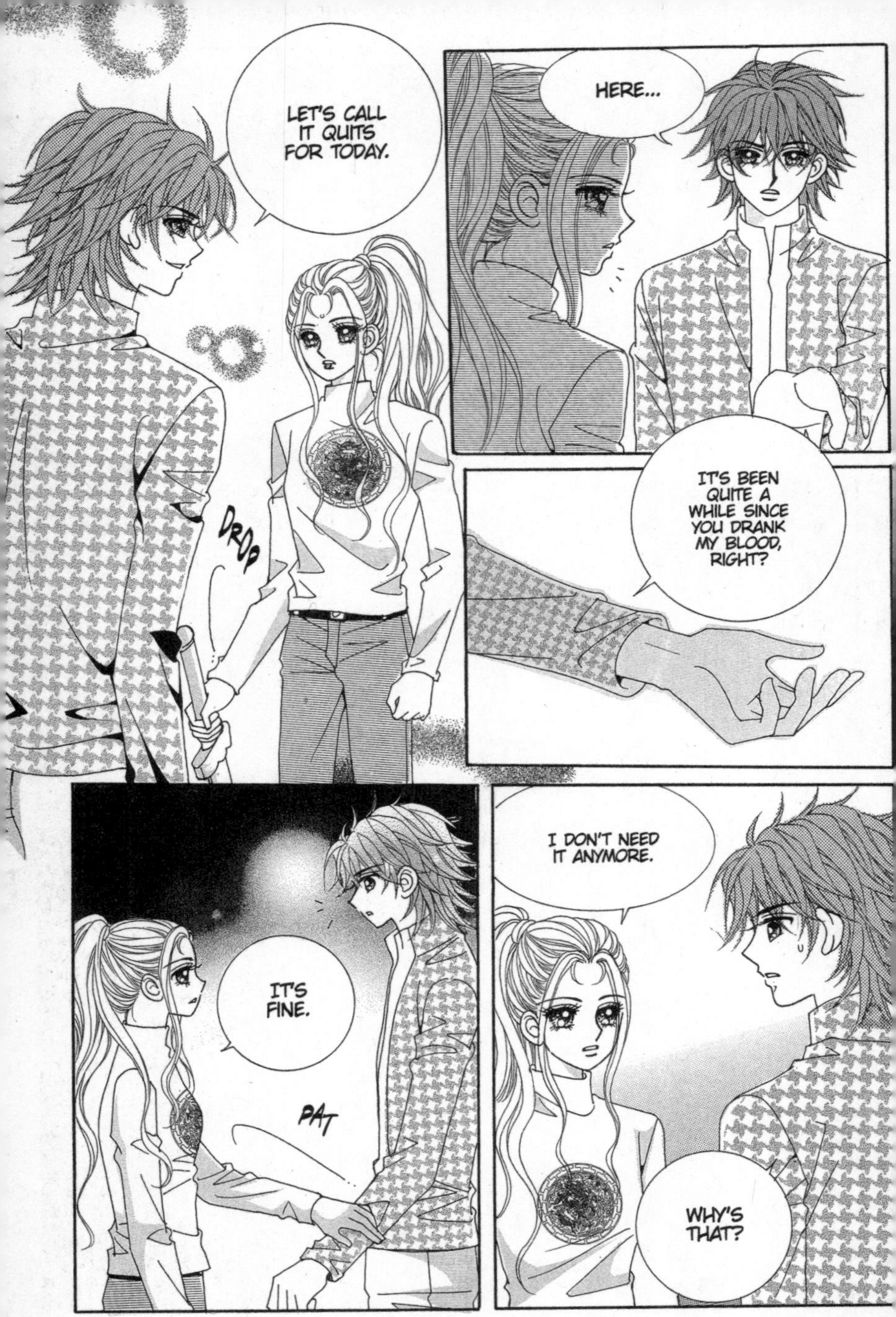
LET'S CALL IT QUITS FOR TODAY.
DROP
HERE...
IT'S BEEN QUITE A WHILE SINCE YOU DRANK MY BLOOD, RIGHT?
IT'S FINE.
PAT
I DON'T NEED IT ANYMORE.
WHY'S THAT?

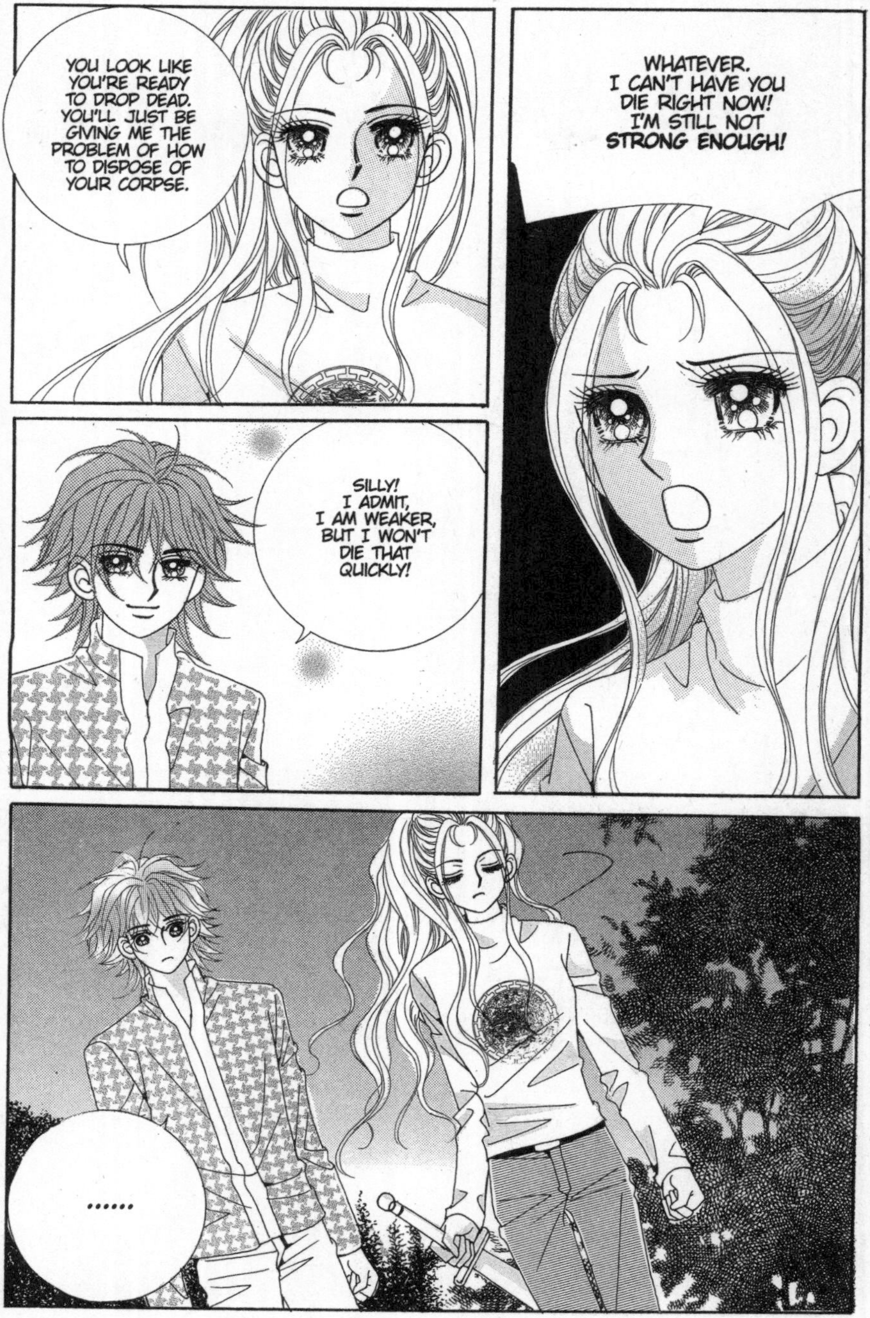
YOU LOOK LIKE YOU'RE READY TO DROP DEAD. YOU'LL JUST BE GIVING ME THE PROBLEM OF HOW TO DISPOSE OF YOUR CORPSE.
SILLY! I ADMIT, I AM WEAKER, BUT I WON'T DIE THAT QUICKLY!
WHATEVER. I CAN'T HAVE YOU DIE RIGHT NOW! I'M STILL NOT STRONG ENOUGH!
......

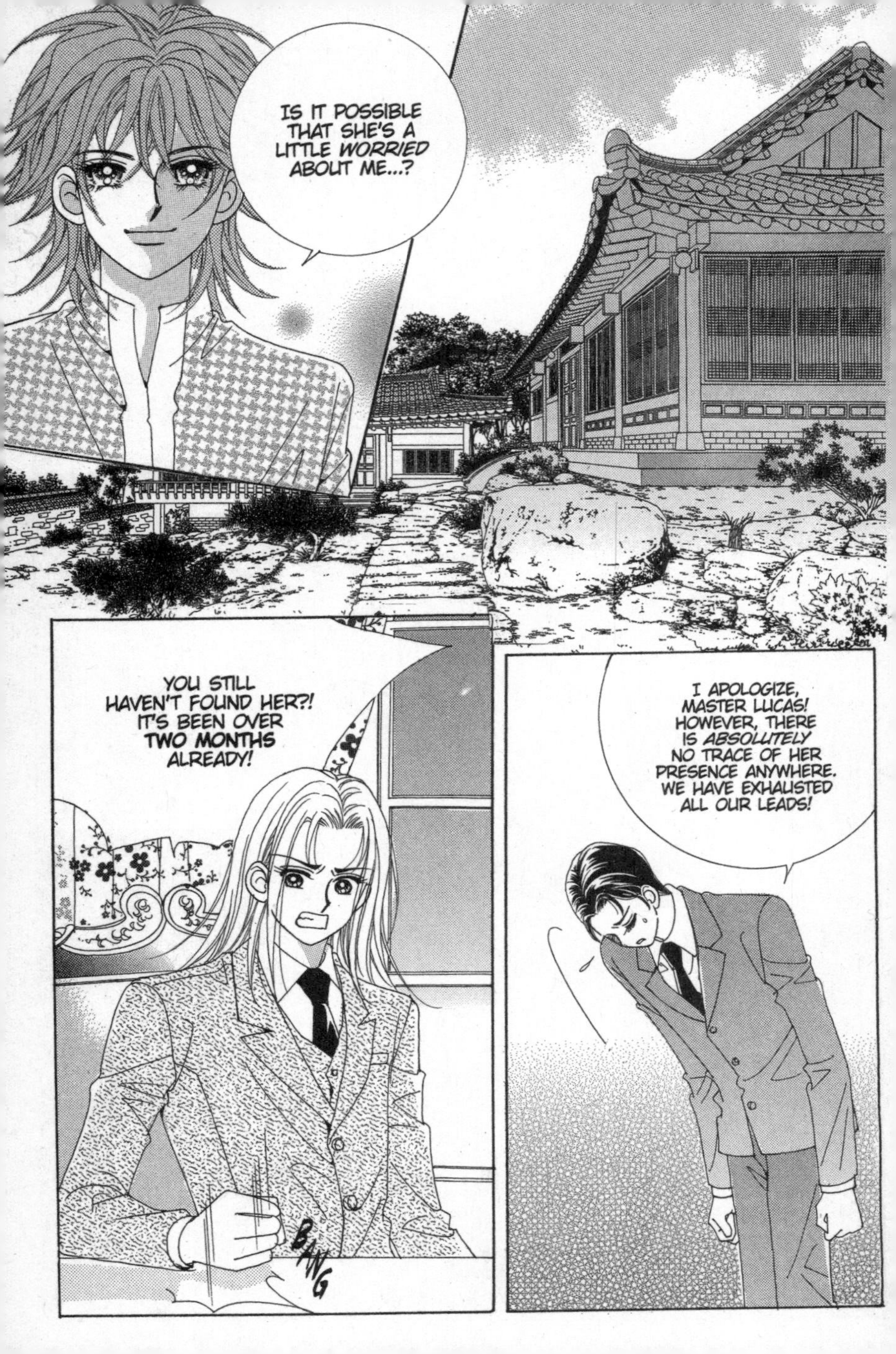
IS IT POSSIBLE THAT SHE'S A LITTLE *WORRIED* ABOUT ME...?
YOU STILL HAVEN'T FOUND HER?! IT'S BEEN OVER **TWO MONTHS** ALREADY!
BANG
I APOLOGIZE, MASTER LUCAS! HOWEVER, THERE IS *ABSOLUTELY* NO TRACE OF HER PRESENCE ANYWHERE. WE HAVE EXHAUSTED ALL OUR LEADS!

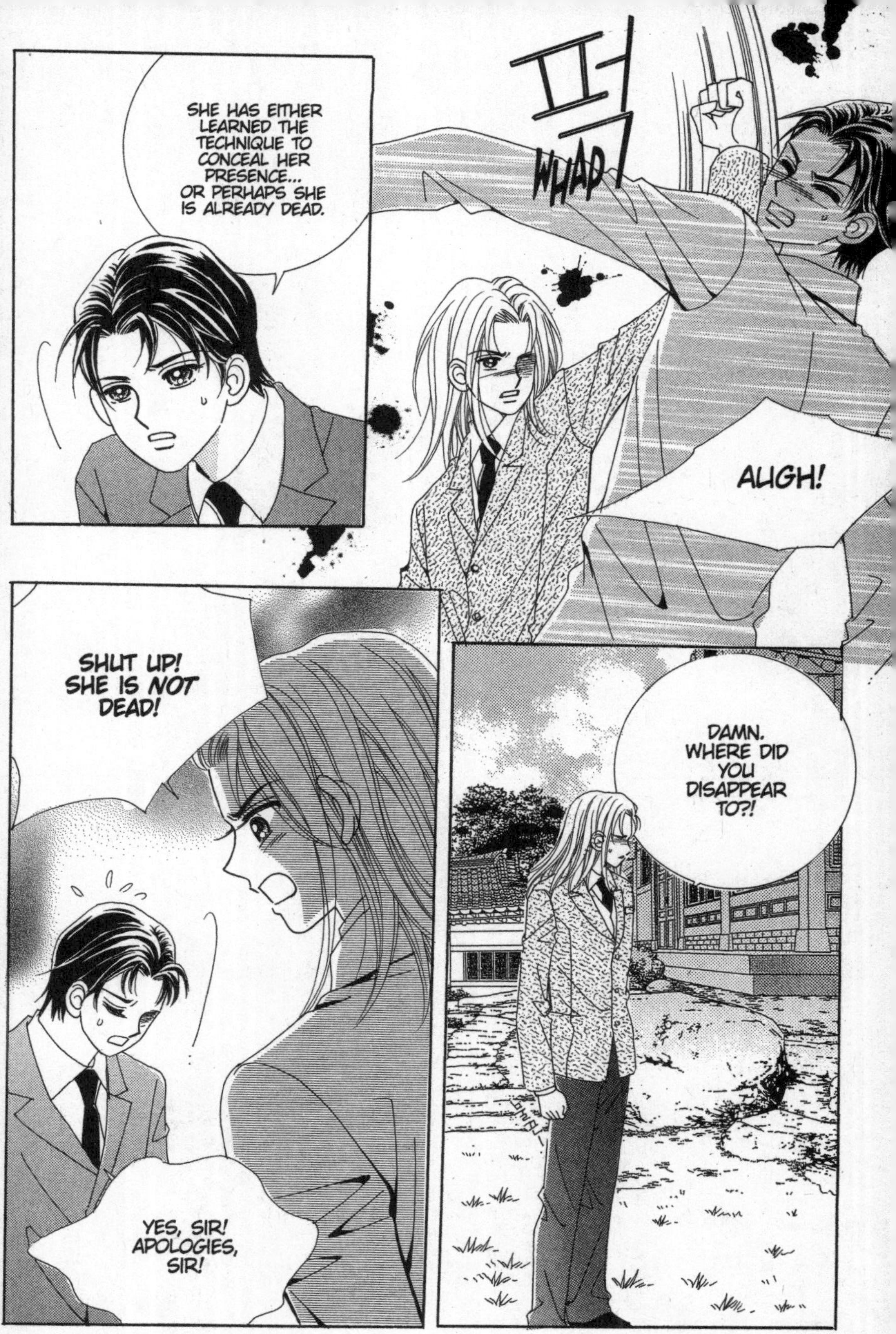
SHE HAS EITHER LEARNED THE TECHNIQUE TO CONCEAL HER PRESENCE... OR PERHAPS SHE IS ALREADY DEAD.
퍽
WHAP
AUGH!
SHUT UP! SHE IS *NOT* DEAD!
YES, SIR! APOLOGIES, SIR!
DAMN. WHERE DID YOU DISAPPEAR TO?!

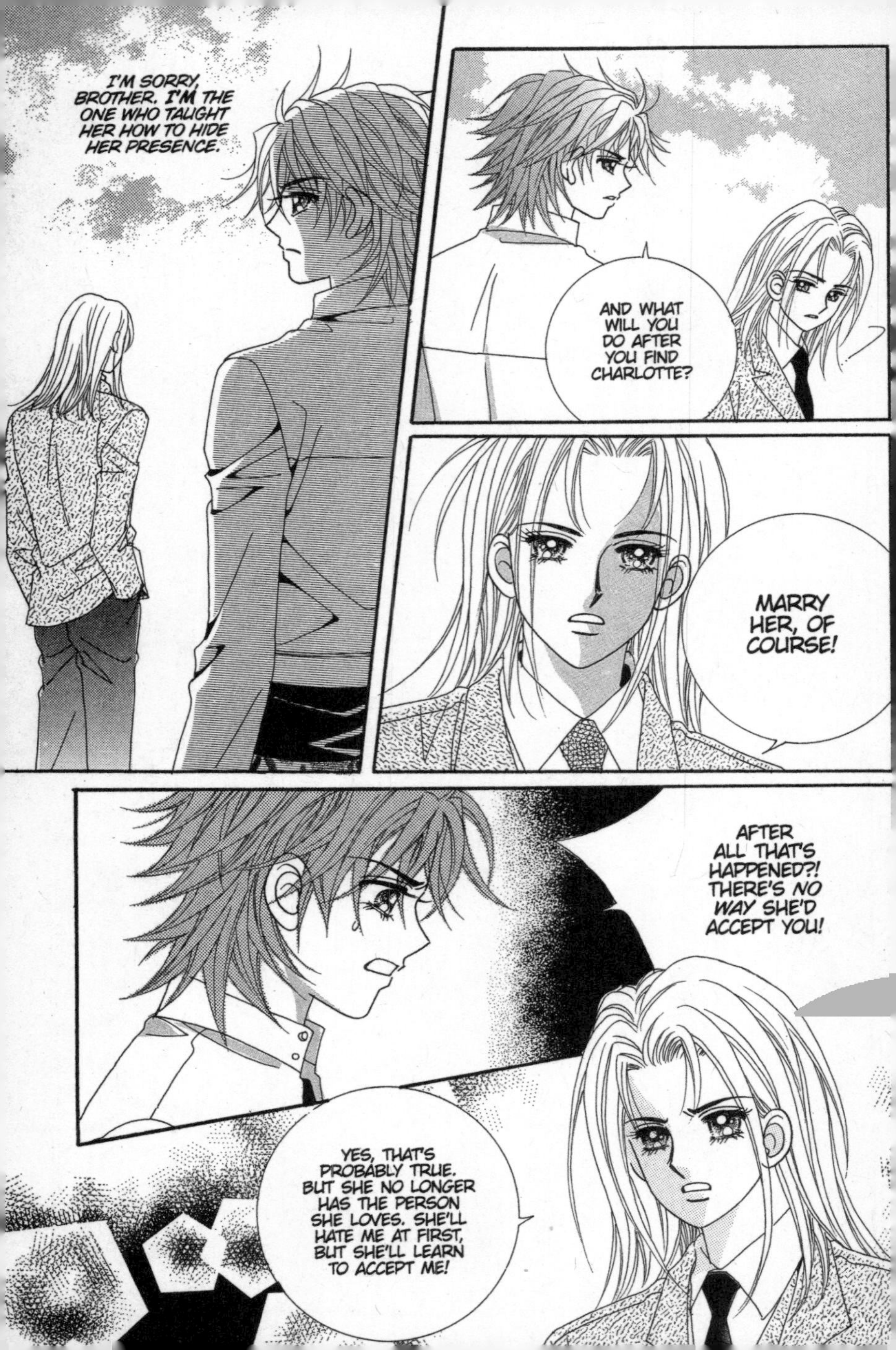
I'M SORRY, BROTHER. I'M THE ONE WHO TAUGHT HER HOW TO HIDE HER PRESENCE.
AND WHAT WILL YOU DO AFTER YOU FIND CHARLOTTE?
MARRY HER, OF COURSE!
AFTER ALL THAT'S HAPPENED?! THERE'S NO WAY SHE'D ACCEPT YOU!
YES, THAT'S PROBABLY TRUE. BUT SHE NO LONGER HAS THE PERSON SHE LOVES. SHE'LL HATE ME AT FIRST, BUT SHE'LL LEARN TO ACCEPT ME!

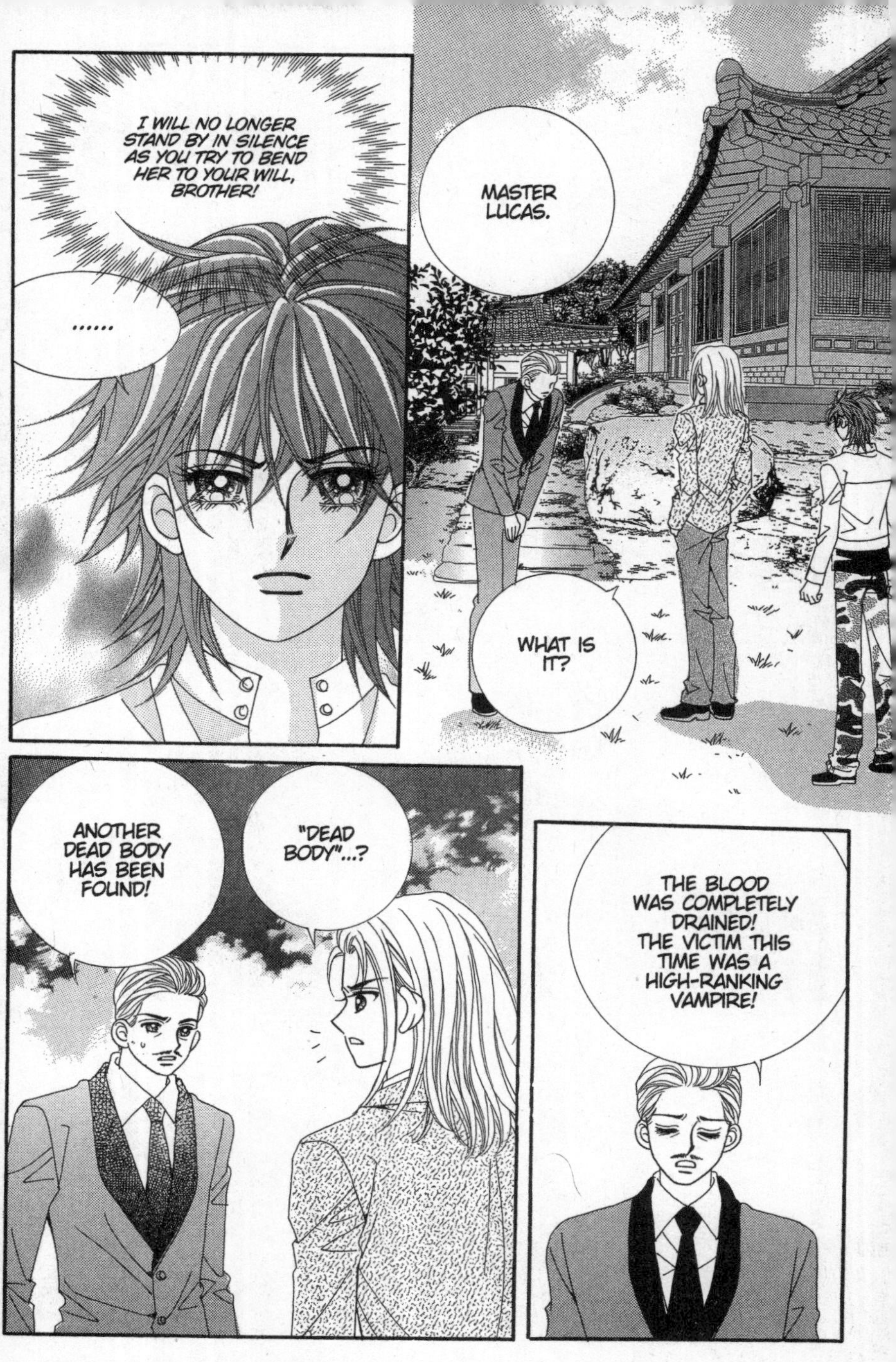
I WILL NO LONGER STAND BY IN SILENCE AS YOU TRY TO BEND HER TO YOUR WILL, BROTHER!
......
MASTER LUCAS.
WHAT IS IT?
ANOTHER DEAD BODY HAS BEEN FOUND!
"DEAD BODY"...?
THE BLOOD WAS COMPLETELY DRAINED! THE VICTIM THIS TIME WAS A HIGH-RANKING VAMPIRE!

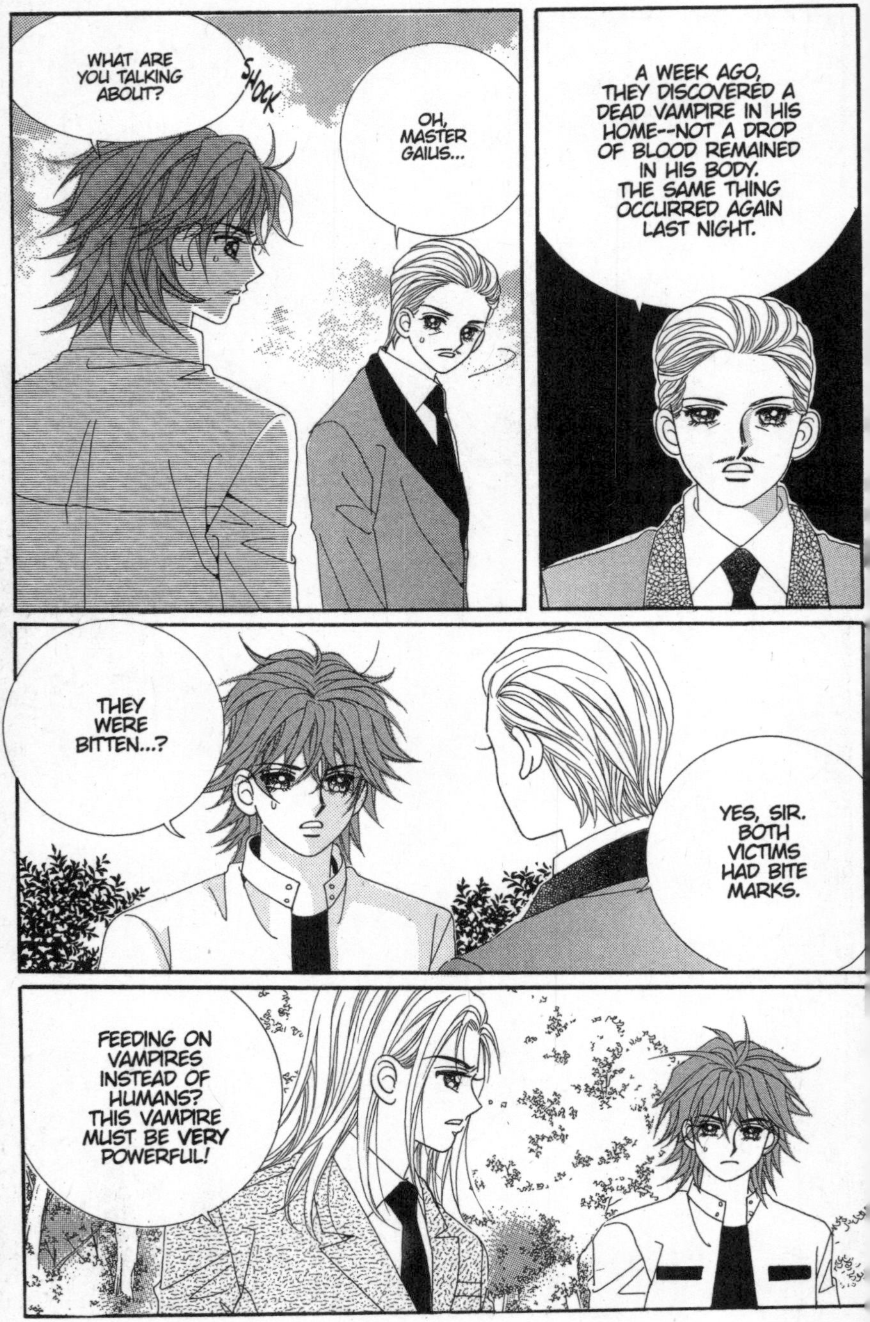
WHAT ARE YOU TALKING ABOUT?
SHOCK
OH, MASTER GAIUS...
A WEEK AGO, THEY DISCOVERED A DEAD VAMPIRE IN HIS HOME--NOT A DROP OF BLOOD REMAINED IN HIS BODY. THE SAME THING OCCURRED AGAIN LAST NIGHT.
THEY WERE BITTEN...?
YES, SIR. BOTH VICTIMS HAD BITE MARKS.
FEEDING ON VAMPIRES INSTEAD OF HUMANS? THIS VAMPIRE MUST BE VERY POWERFUL!

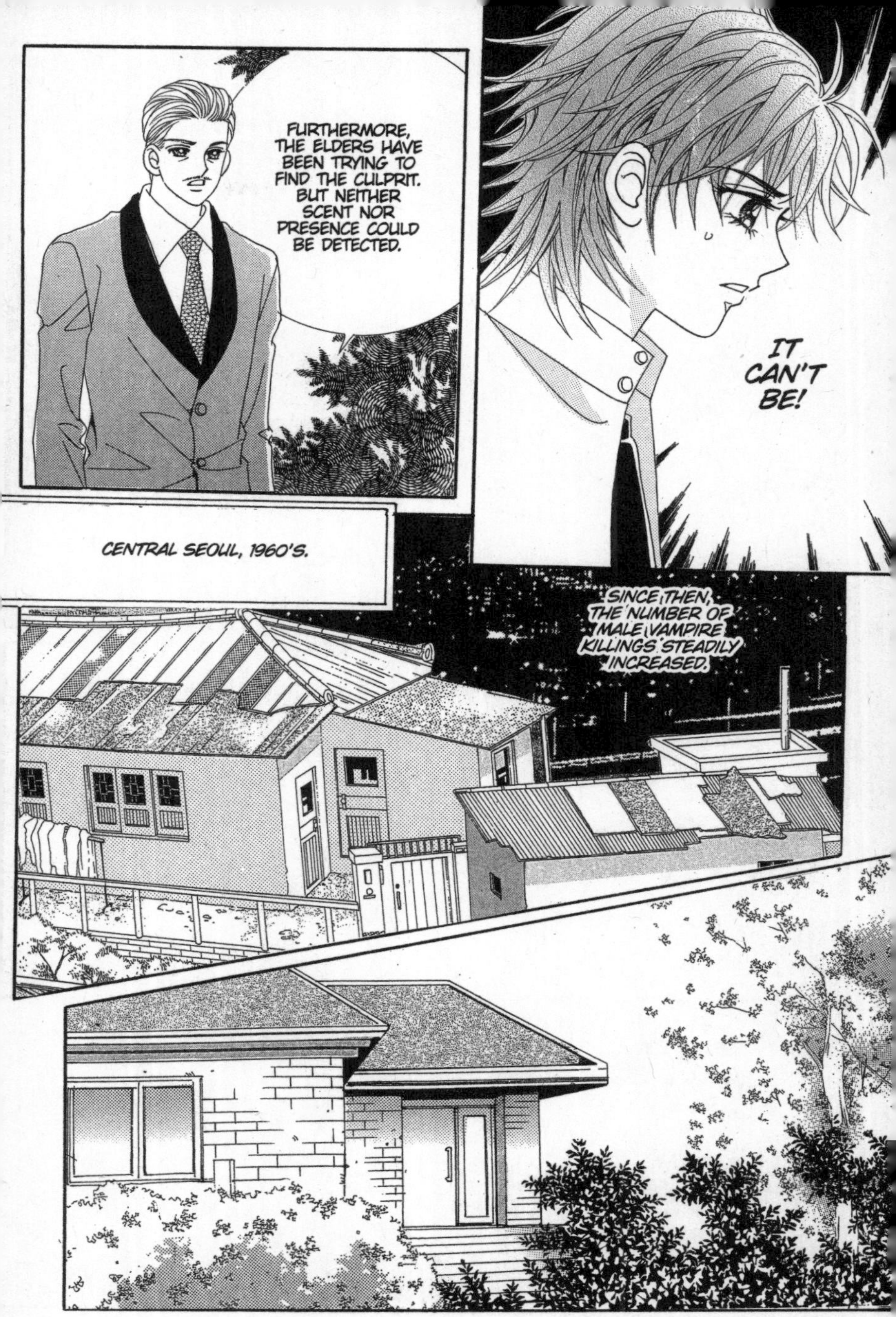
FURTHERMORE, THE ELDERS HAVE BEEN TRYING TO FIND THE CULPRIT. BUT NEITHER SCENT NOR PRESENCE COULD BE DETECTED.
IT CAN'T BE!
CENTRAL SEOUL, 1960'S.
SINCE THEN, THE NUMBER OF MALE VAMPIRE KILLINGS STEADILY INCREASED.

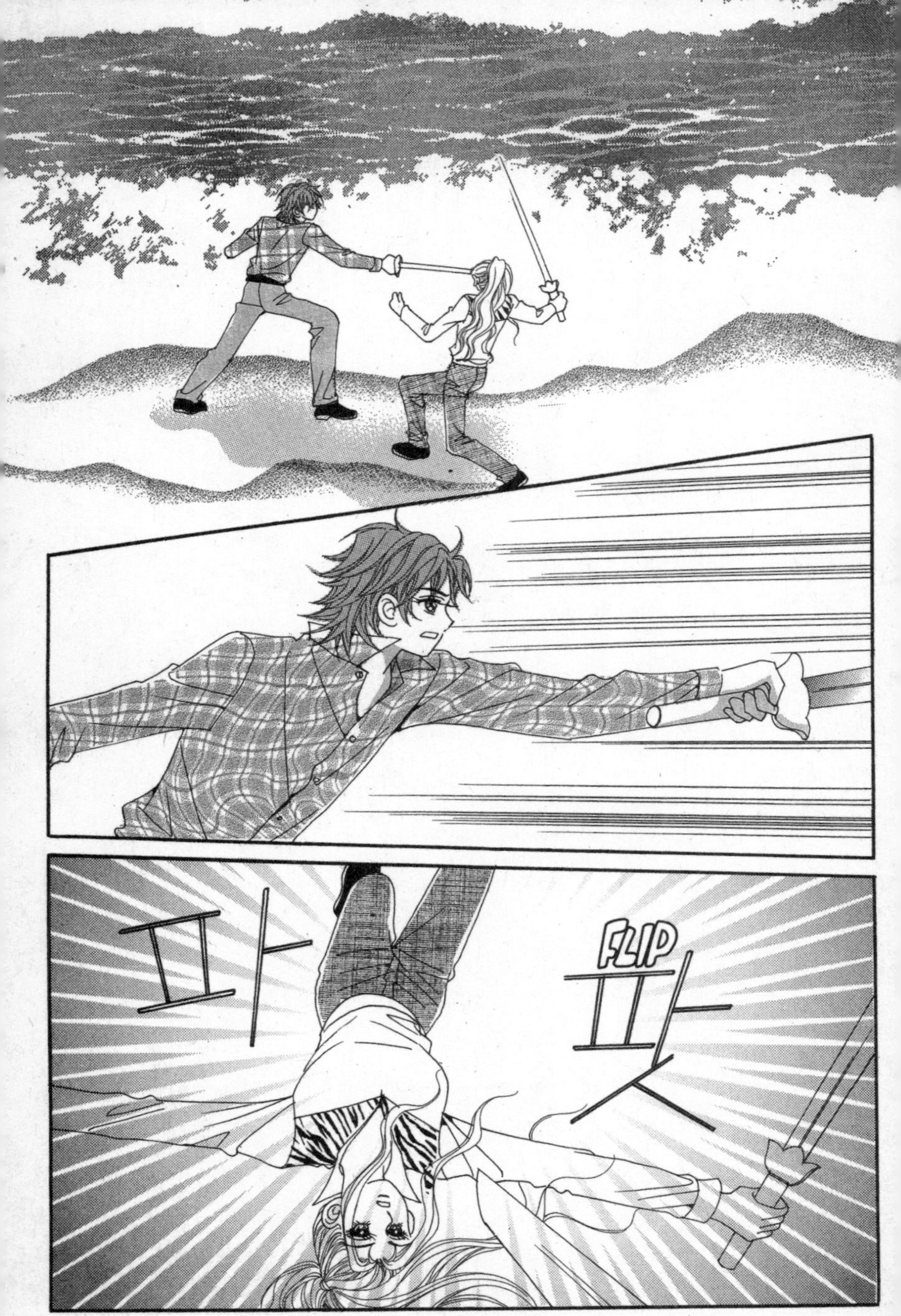
파
FLIP
팟

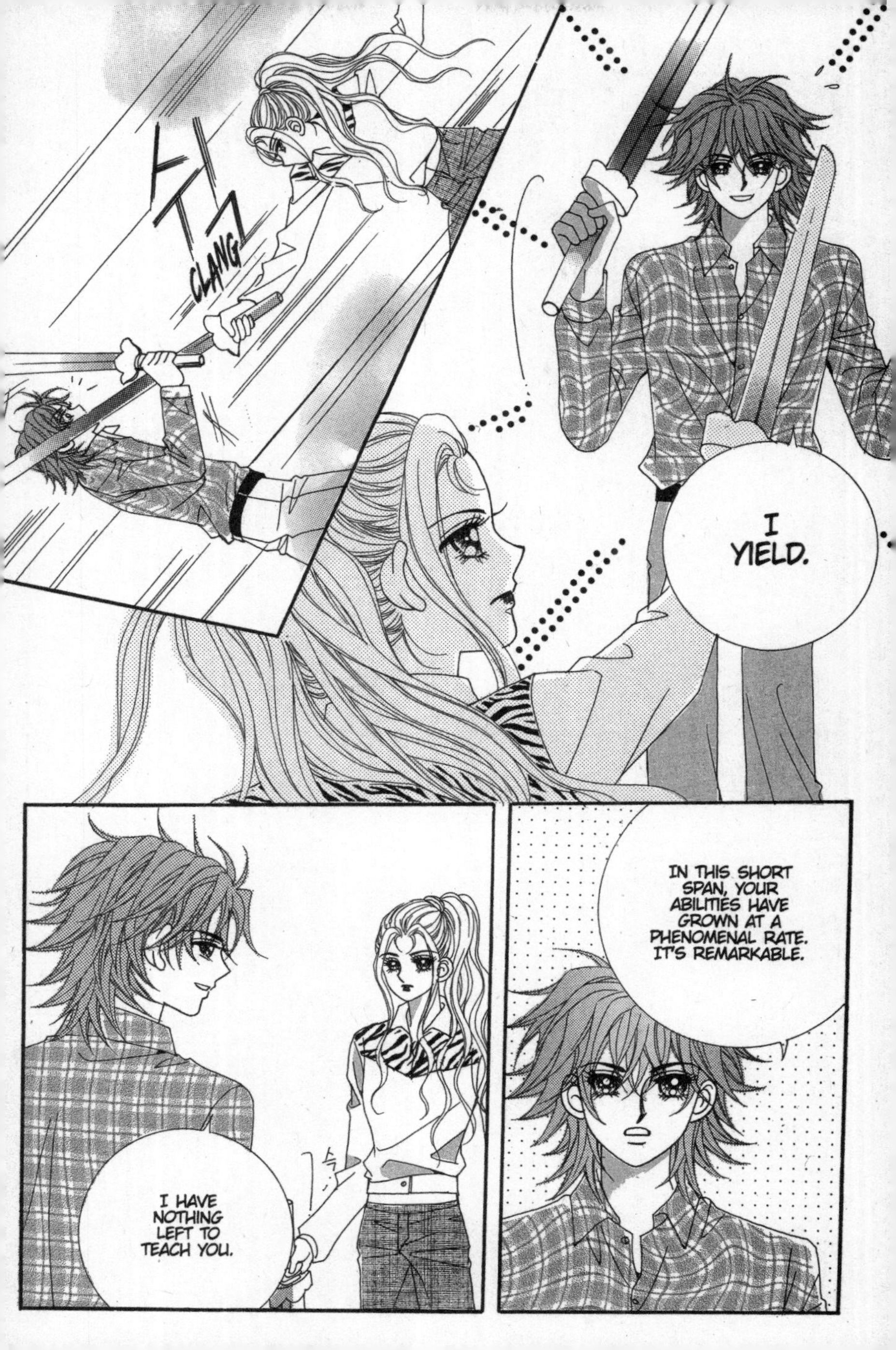
CLANG
I YIELD.
I HAVE NOTHING LEFT TO TEACH YOU.
IN THIS SHORT SPAN, YOUR ABILITIES HAVE GROWN AT A PHENOMENAL RATE. IT'S REMARKABLE.

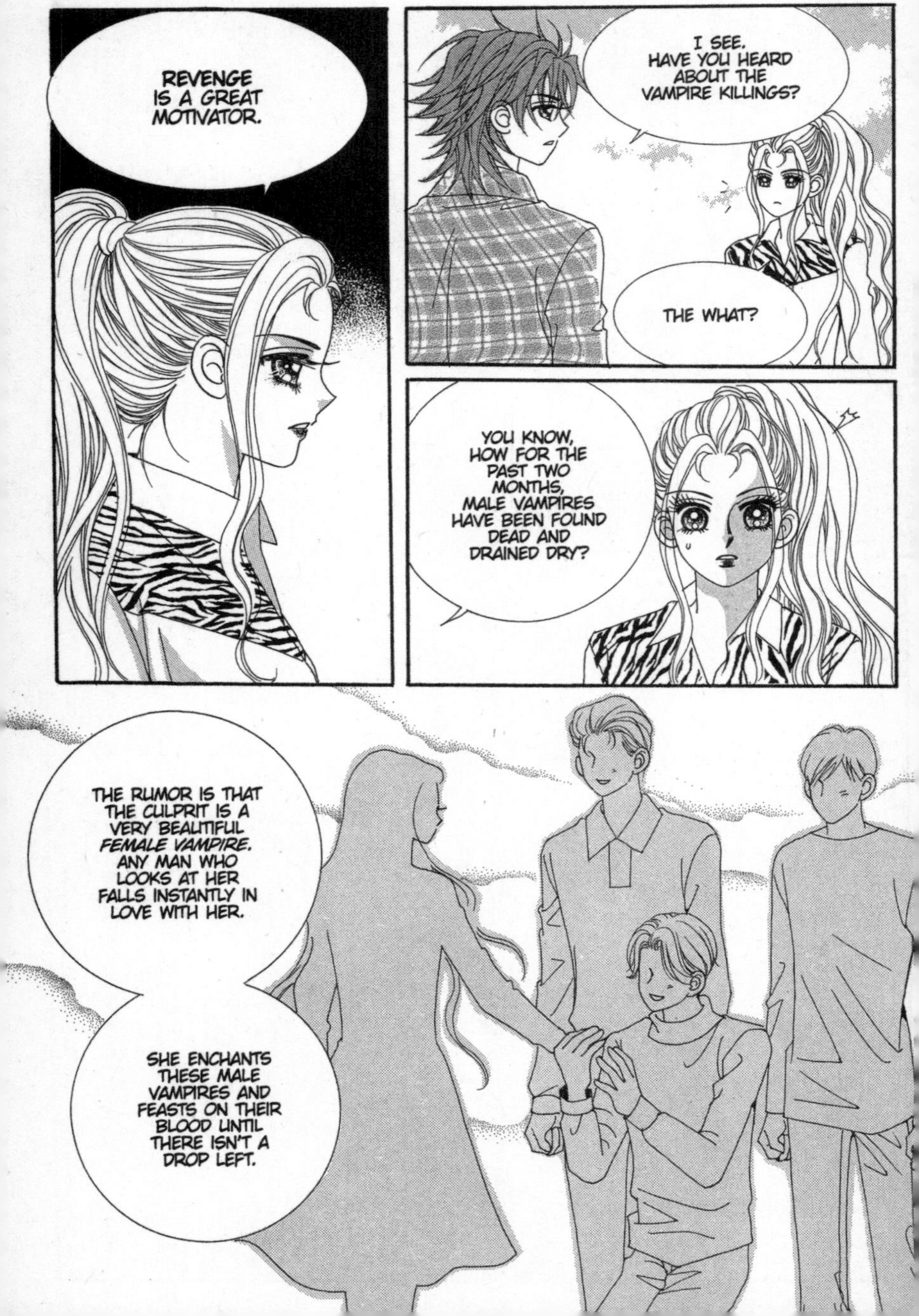
REVENGE IS A GREAT MOTIVATOR.
I SEE. HAVE YOU HEARD ABOUT THE VAMPIRE KILLINGS?
THE WHAT?
YOU KNOW, HOW FOR THE PAST TWO MONTHS, MALE VAMPIRES HAVE BEEN FOUND DEAD AND DRAINED DRY?
THE RUMOR IS THAT THE CULPRIT IS A VERY BEAUTIFUL *FEMALE VAMPIRE.* ANY MAN WHO LOOKS AT HER FALLS INSTANTLY IN LOVE WITH HER.
SHE ENCHANTS THESE MALE VAMPIRES AND FEASTS ON THEIR BLOOD UNTIL THERE ISN'T A DROP LEFT.

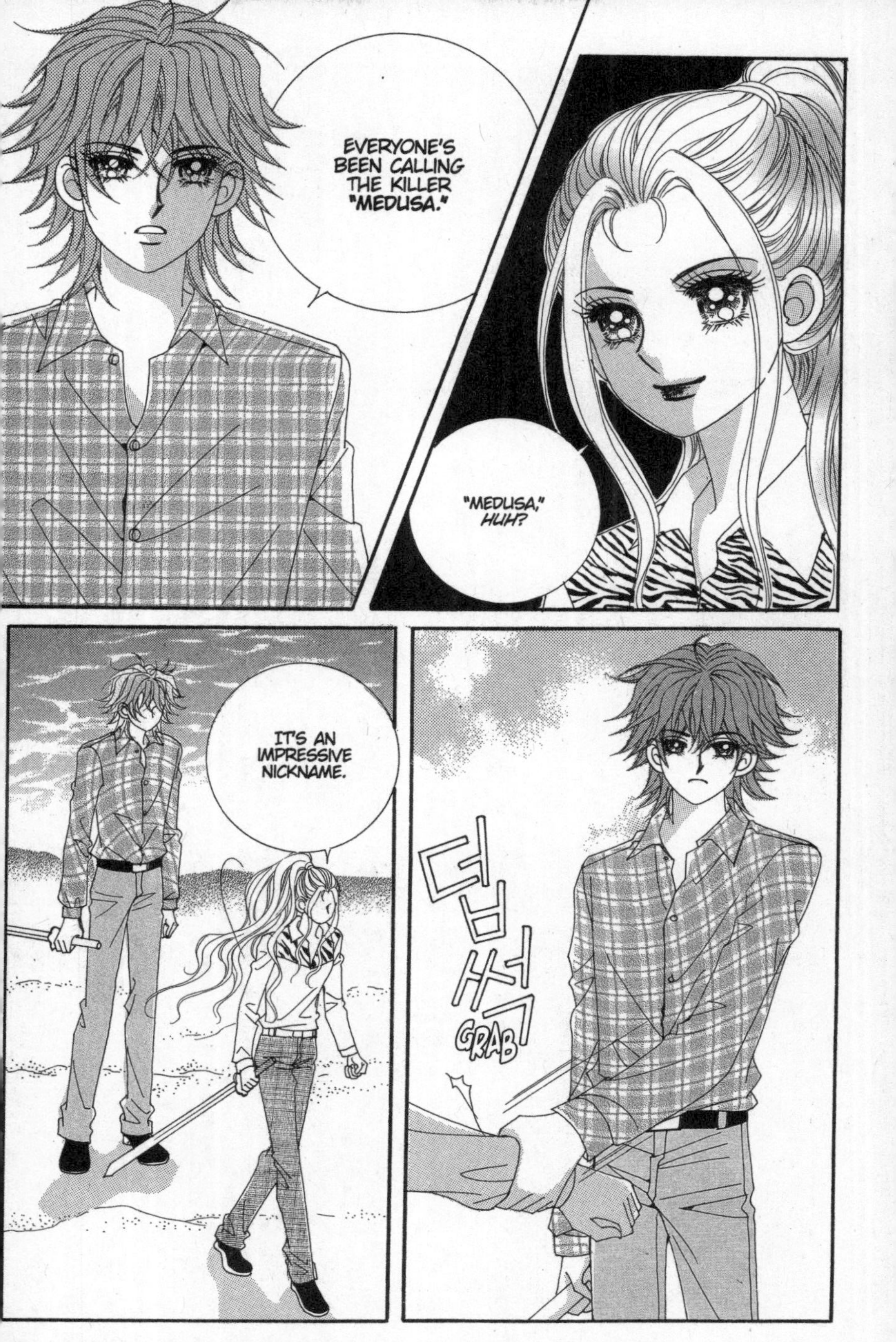
EVERYONE'S BEEN CALLING THE KILLER "MEDUSA."
"MEDUSA," HUH?
IT'S AN IMPRESSIVE NICKNAME.
덥석
GRAB

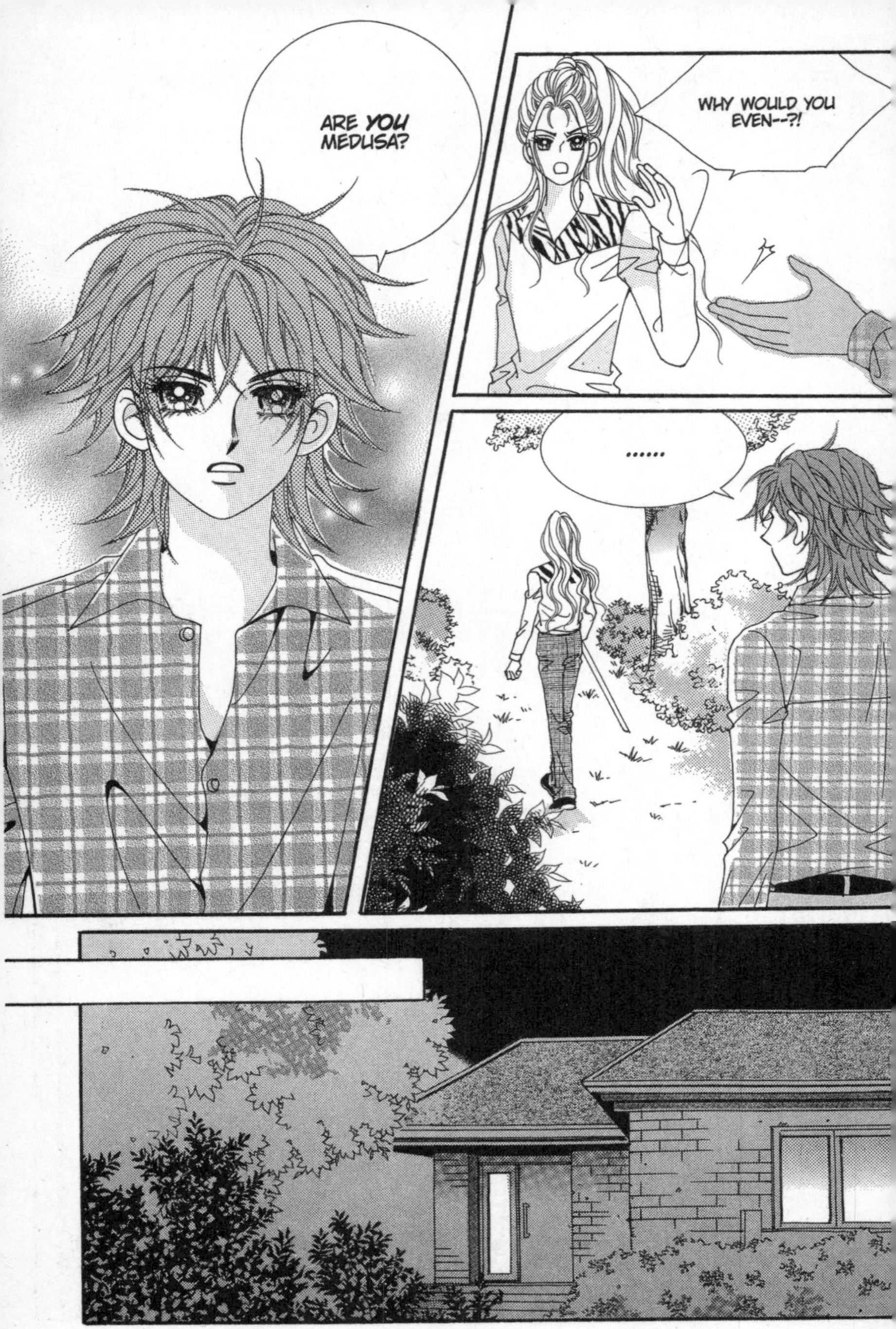
ARE *YOU* MEDUSA?
WHY WOULD YOU EVEN--?!
......

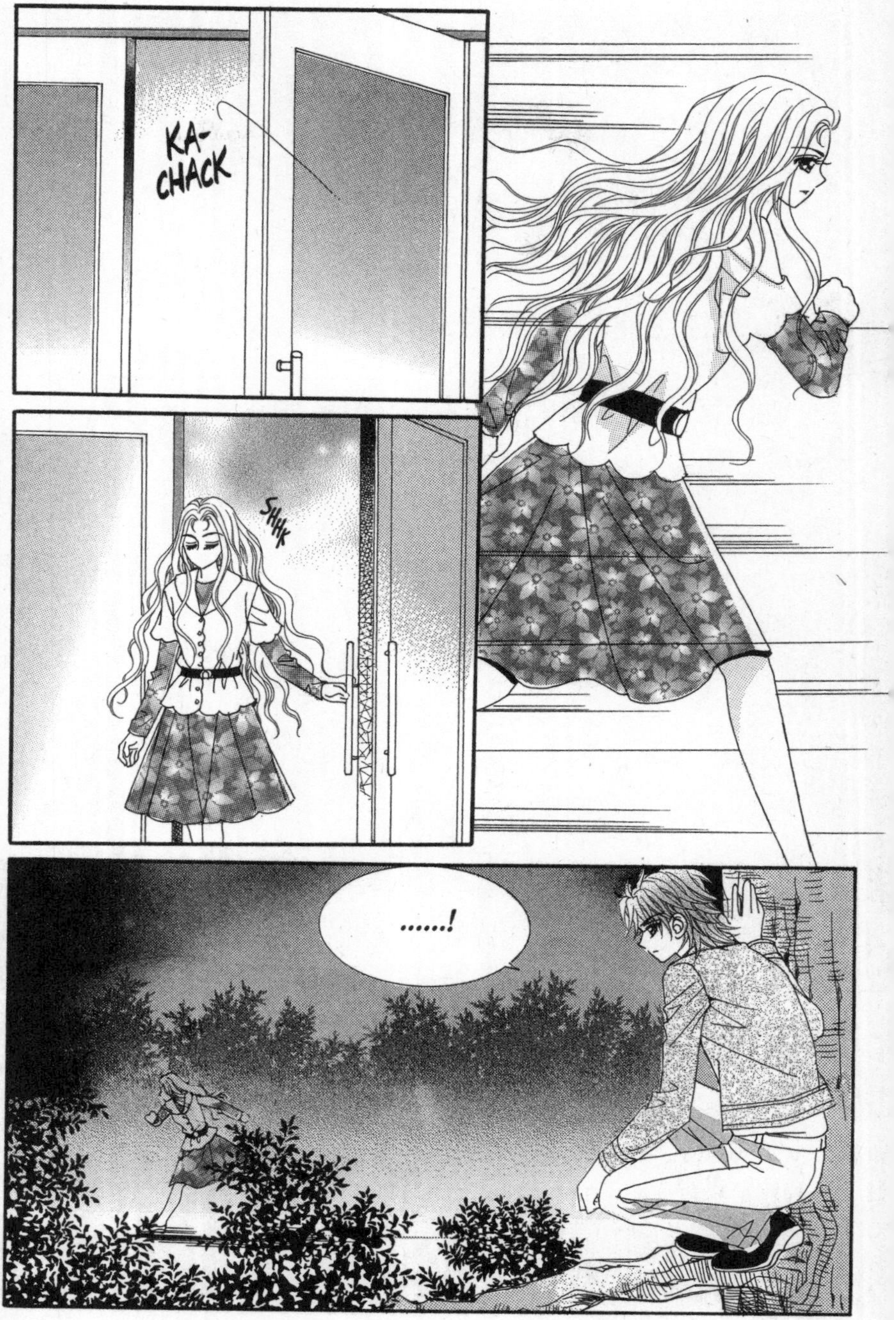
KA-
CHACK
SHHK
......!

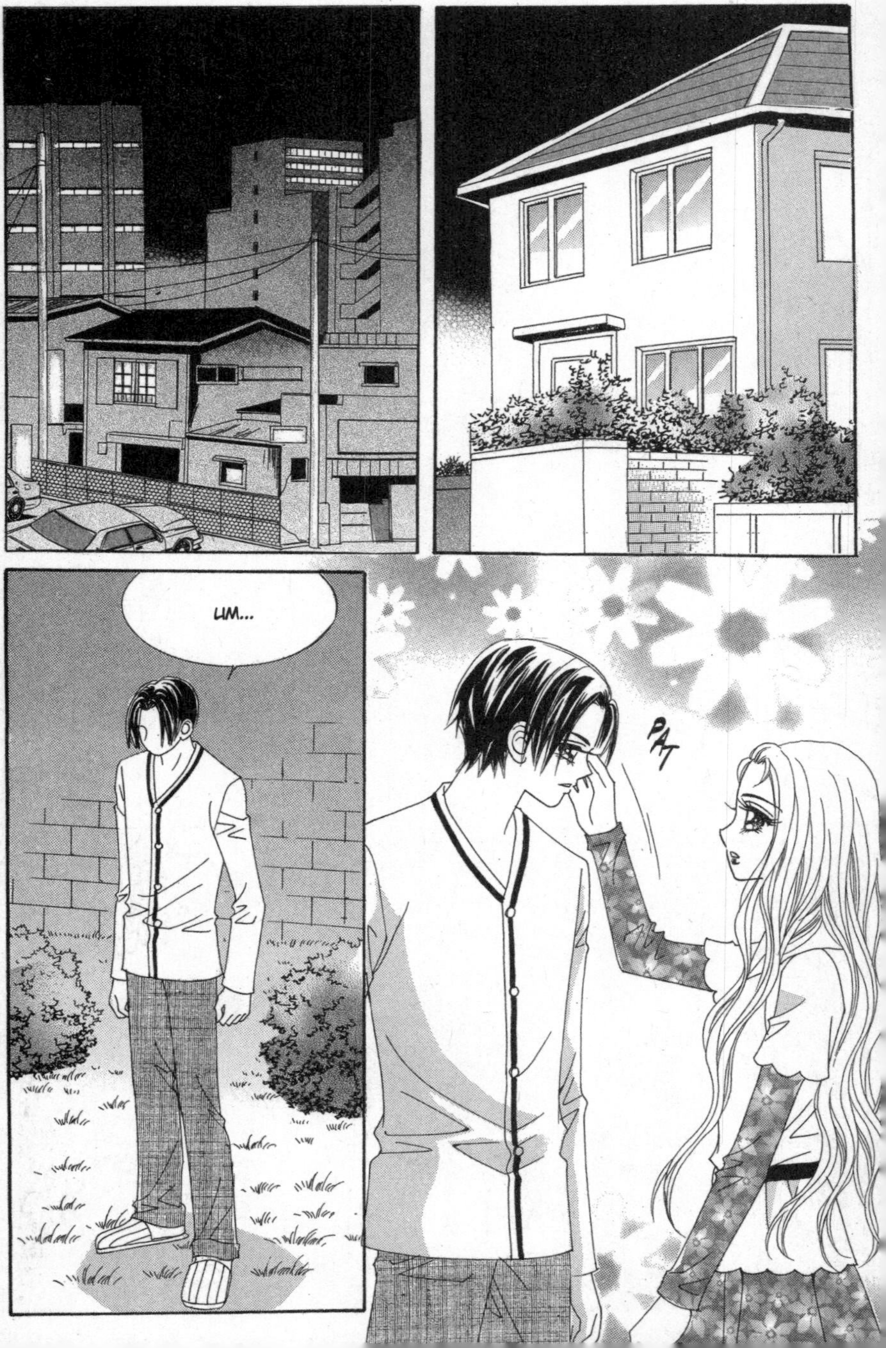
UM...
PAT

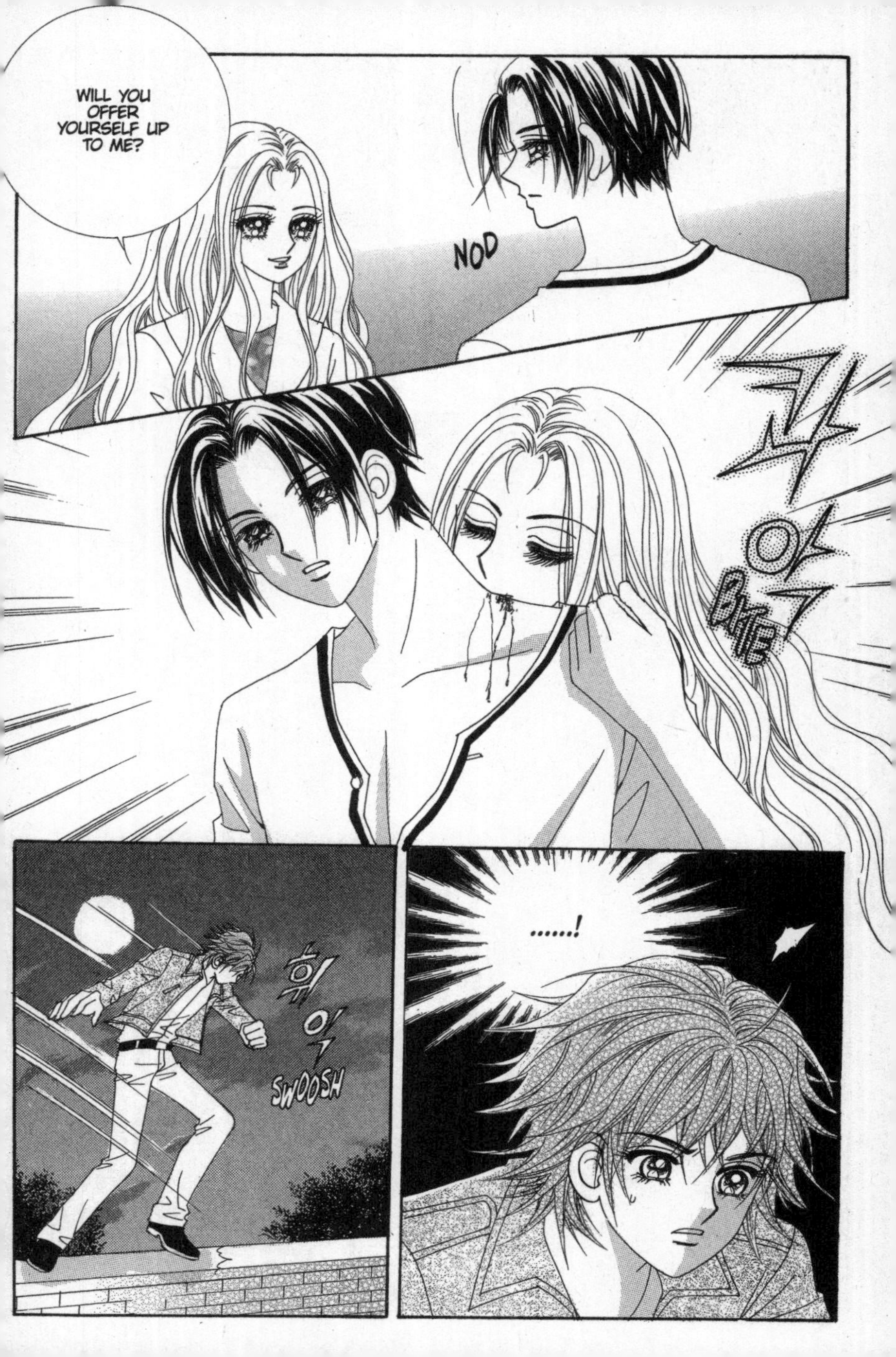
WILL YOU OFFER YOURSELF UP TO ME?
NOD
BITE
SWOOSH
......!

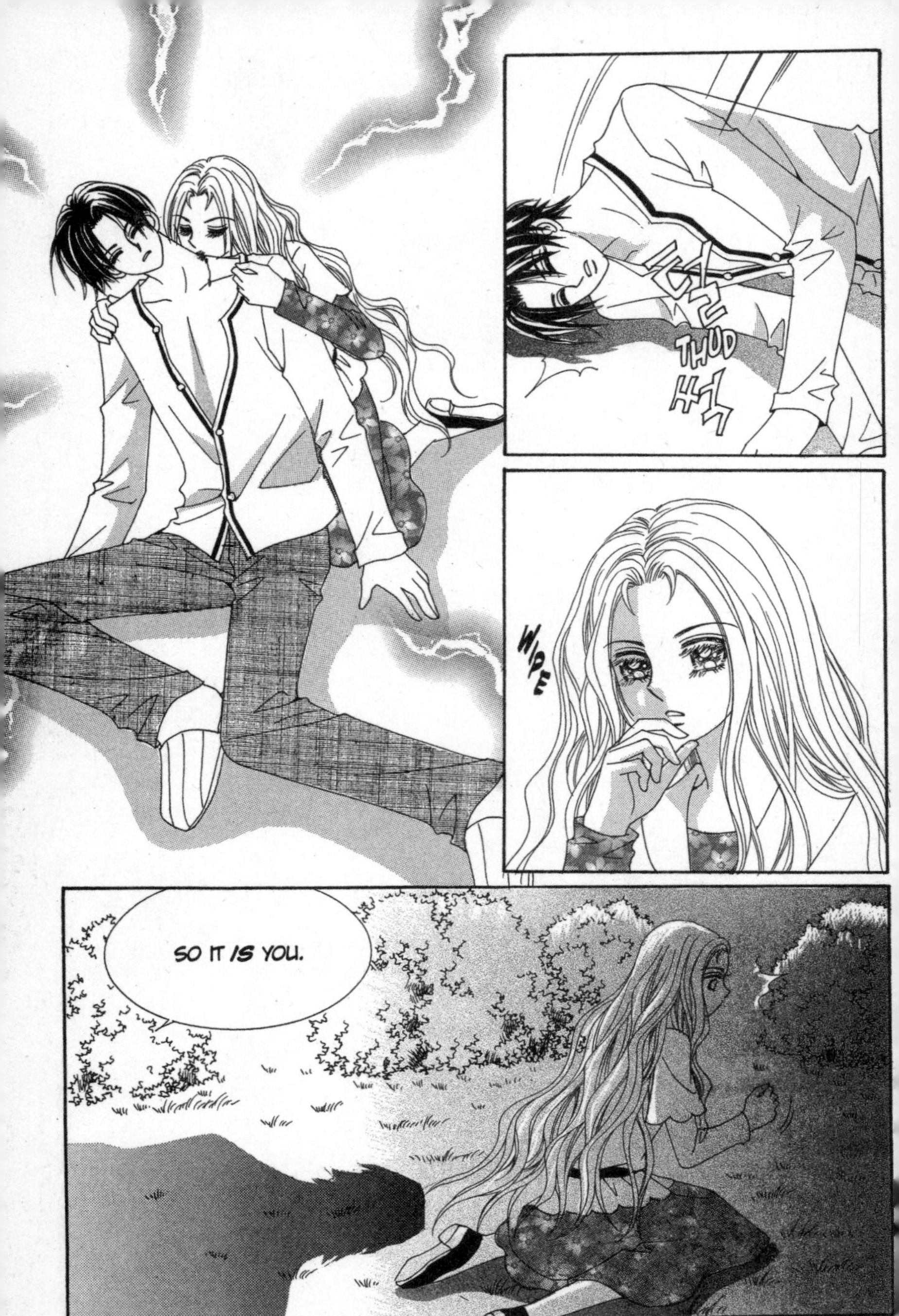
THUD
WIPE
SO IT *IS* YOU.

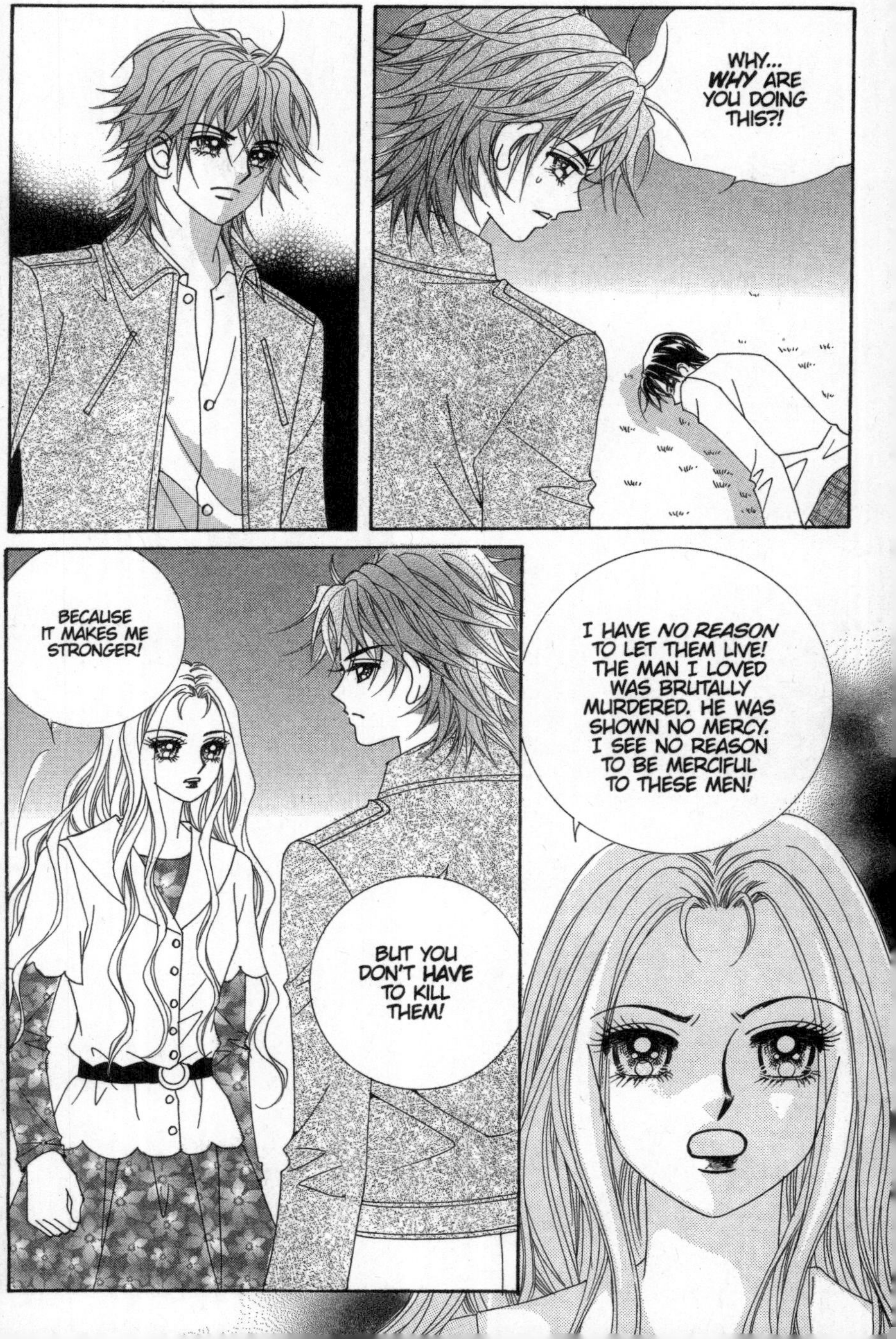
WHY... *WHY* ARE YOU DOING THIS?!
BECAUSE IT MAKES ME STRONGER!
BUT YOU DON'T HAVE TO KILL THEM!
I HAVE *NO REASON* TO LET THEM LIVE! THE MAN I LOVED WAS BRUTALLY MURDERED. HE WAS SHOWN NO MERCY. I SEE NO REASON TO BE MERCIFUL TO THESE MEN!

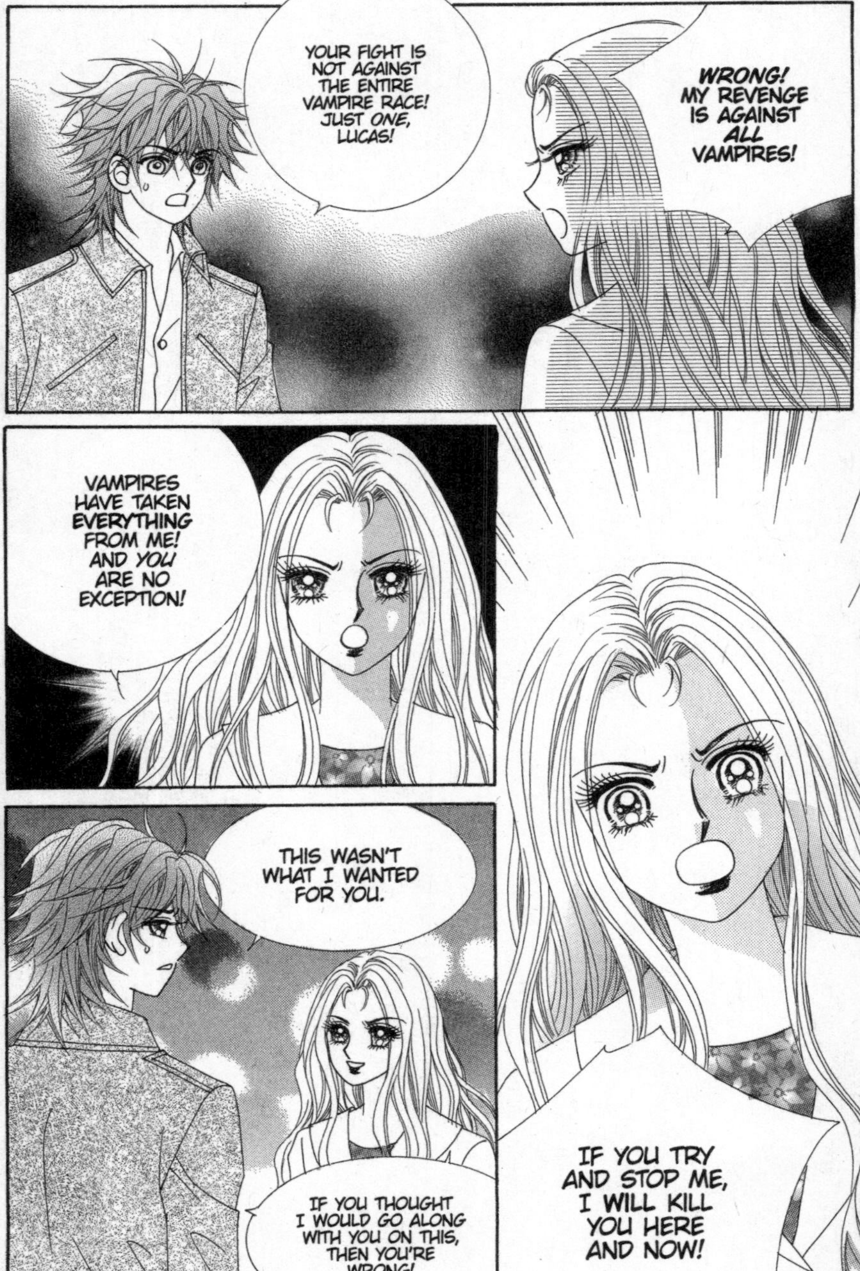
YOUR FIGHT IS NOT AGAINST THE ENTIRE VAMPIRE RACE! JUST *ONE*, LUCAS!
WRONG! MY REVENGE IS AGAINST *ALL* VAMPIRES!
VAMPIRES HAVE TAKEN EVERYTHING FROM ME! AND *YOU* ARE NO EXCEPTION!
THIS WASN'T WHAT I WANTED FOR YOU.
IF YOU THOUGHT I WOULD GO ALONG WITH YOU ON THIS, THEN YOU'RE WRONG!
IF YOU TRY AND STOP ME, I WILL KILL YOU HERE AND NOW!

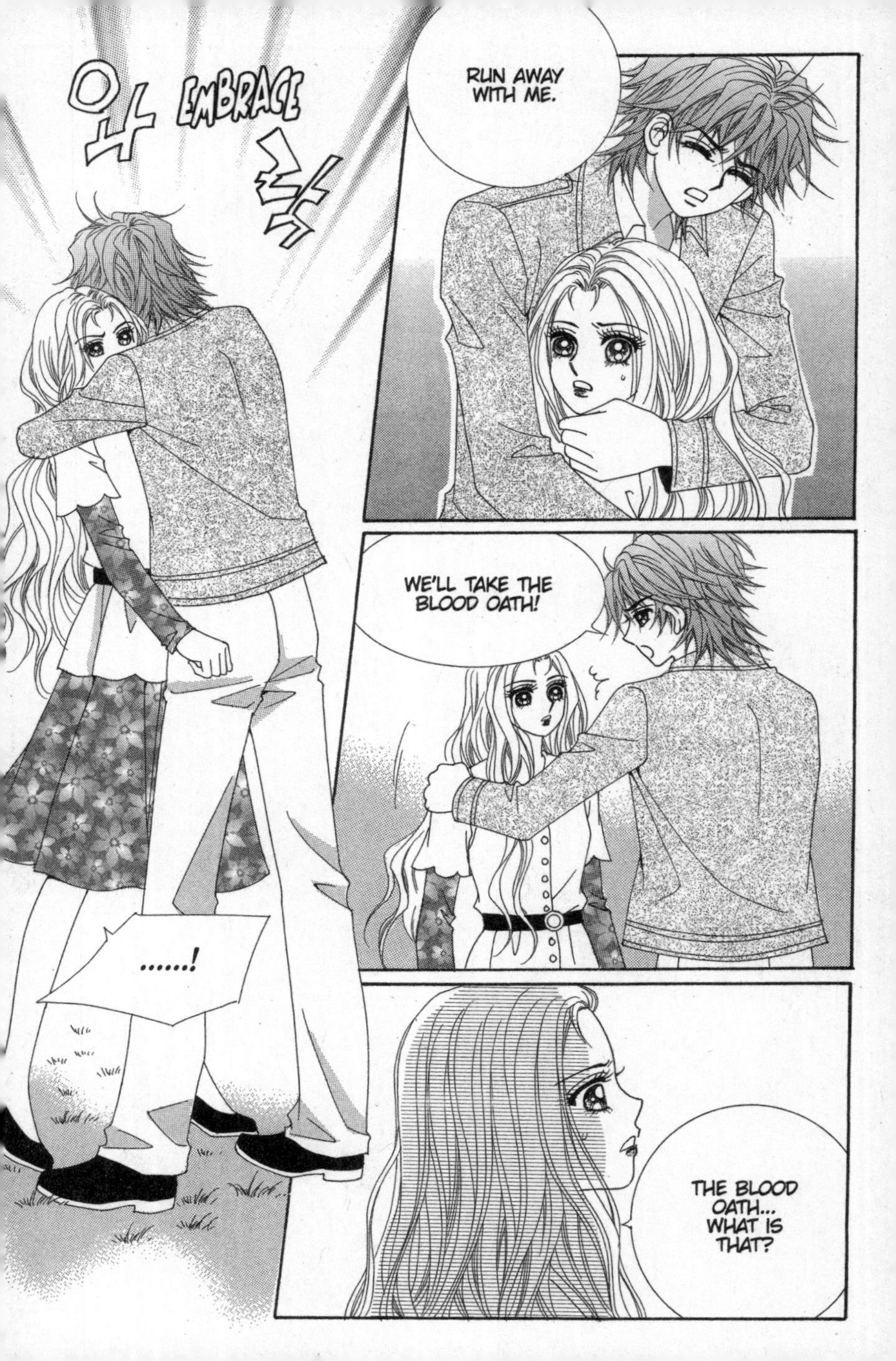
EMBRACE
......!
RUN AWAY WITH ME.
WE'LL TAKE THE BLOOD OATH!
THE BLOOD OATH... WHAT IS THAT?

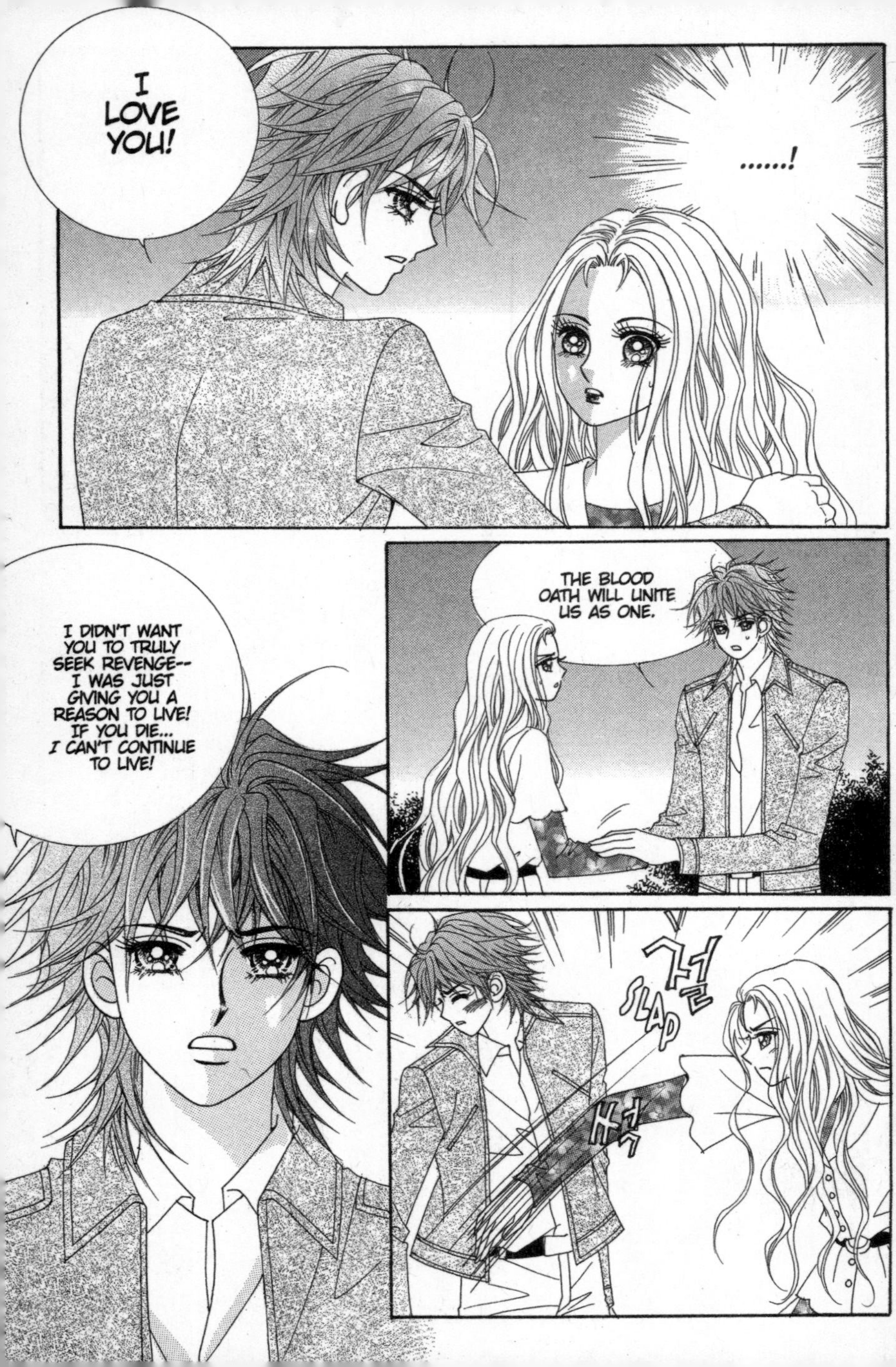

I LOVE YOU!
......!
I DIDN'T WANT YOU TO TRULY SEEK REVENGE-- I WAS JUST GIVING YOU A REASON TO LIVE! IF YOU DIE... I CAN'T CONTINUE TO LIVE!
THE BLOOD OATH WILL UNITE US AS ONE.
SLAP

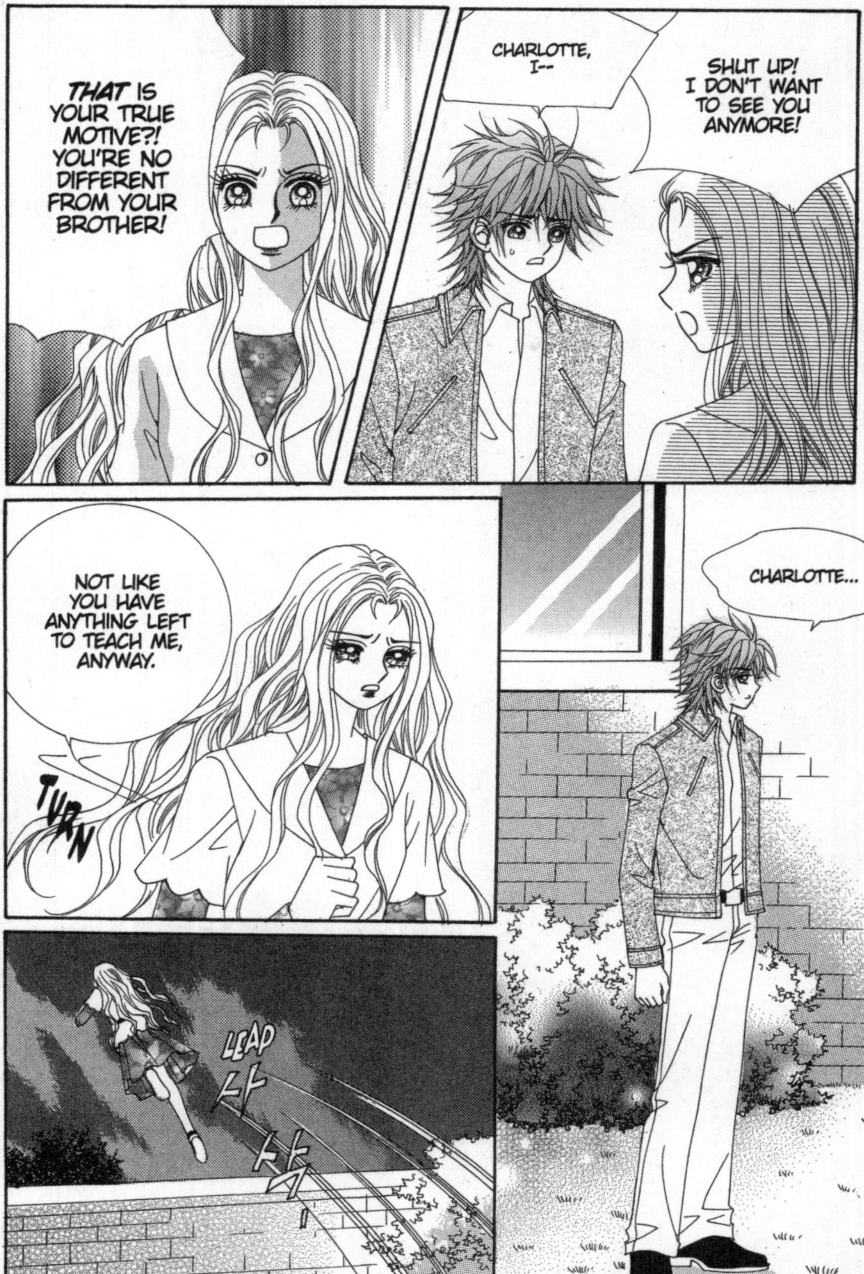
THAT IS YOUR TRUE MOTIVE?! YOU'RE NO DIFFERENT FROM YOUR BROTHER!
CHARLOTTE, I--
SHUT UP! I DON'T WANT TO SEE YOU ANYMORE!
NOT LIKE YOU HAVE ANYTHING LEFT TO TEACH ME, ANYWAY.
TURN
LEAP
CHARLOTTE...

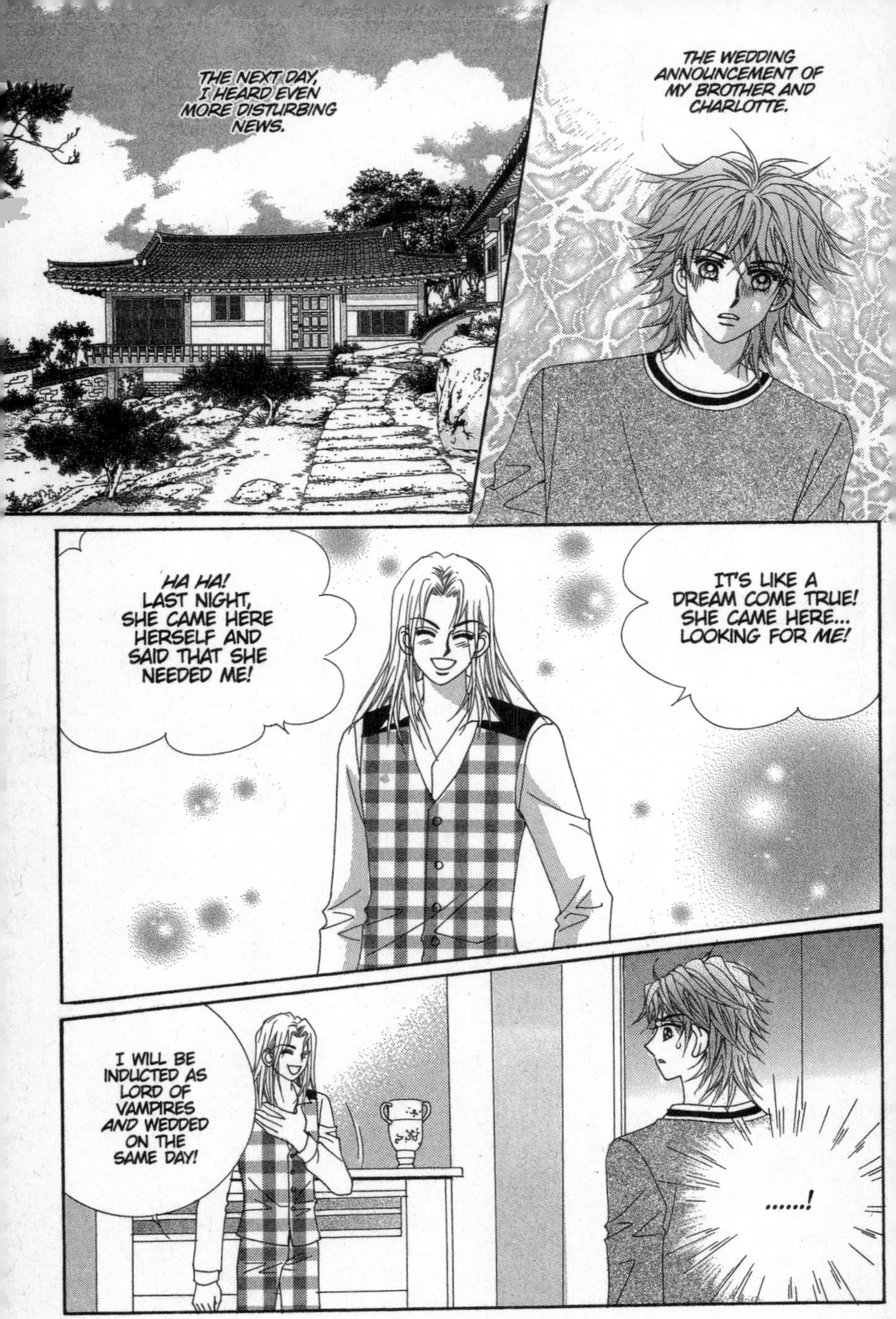
THE NEXT DAY, I HEARD EVEN MORE DISTURBING NEWS.
THE WEDDING ANNOUNCEMENT OF MY BROTHER AND CHARLOTTE.
HA HA! LAST NIGHT, SHE CAME HERE HERSELF AND SAID THAT SHE NEEDED ME!
IT'S LIKE A DREAM COME TRUE! SHE CAME HERE... LOOKING FOR ME!
I WILL BE INDUCTED AS LORD OF VAMPIRES AND WEDDED ON THE SAME DAY!
......!

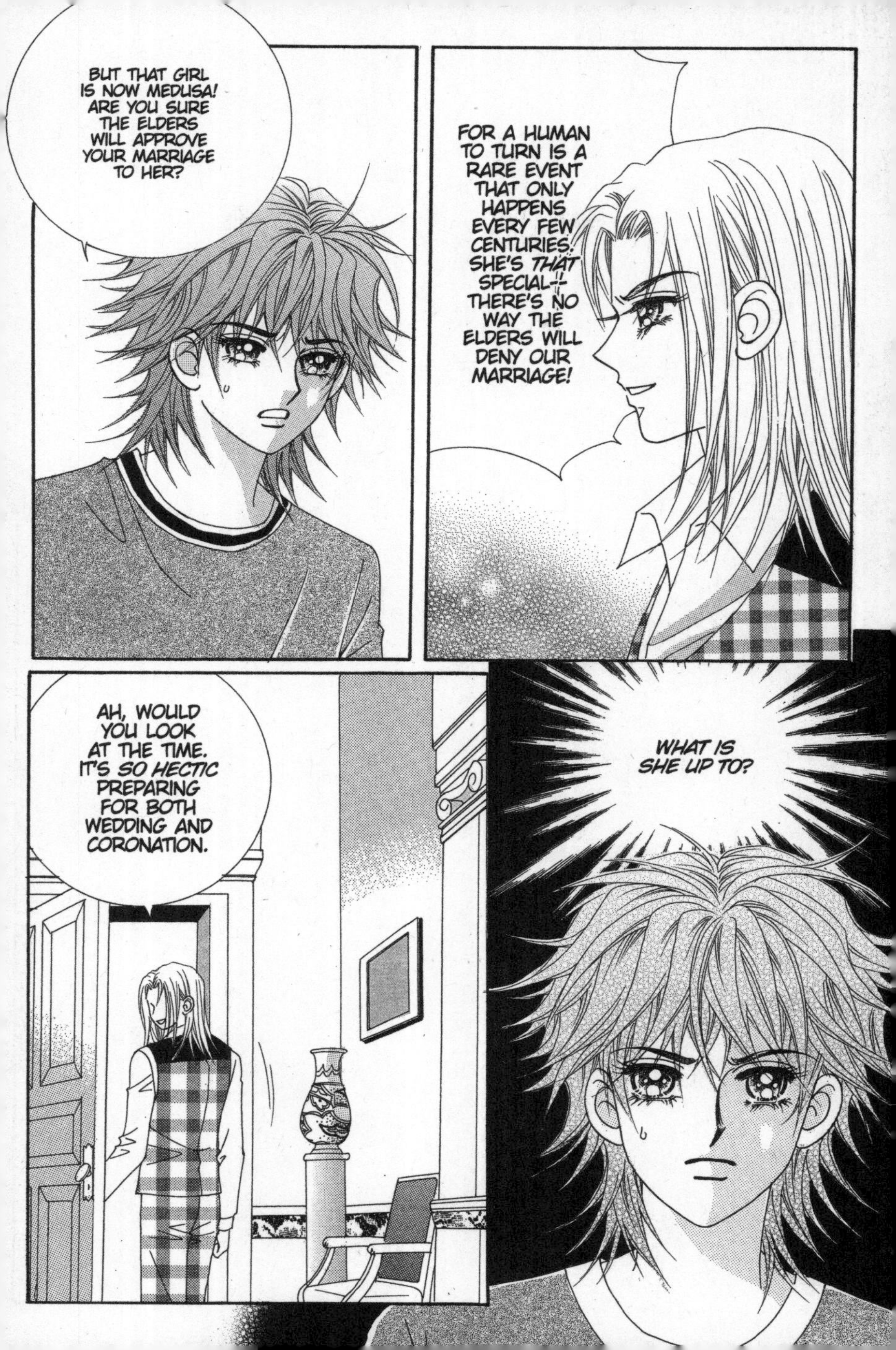

BUT THAT GIRL IS NOW MEDUSA! ARE YOU SURE THE ELDERS WILL APPROVE YOUR MARRIAGE TO HER?
FOR A HUMAN TO TURN IS A RARE EVENT THAT ONLY HAPPENS EVERY FEW CENTURIES. SHE'S *THAT* SPECIAL-- THERE'S NO WAY THE ELDERS WILL DENY OUR MARRIAGE!
AH, WOULD YOU LOOK AT THE TIME. IT'S *SO HECTIC* PREPARING FOR BOTH WEDDING AND CORONATION.
WHAT IS SHE UP TO?

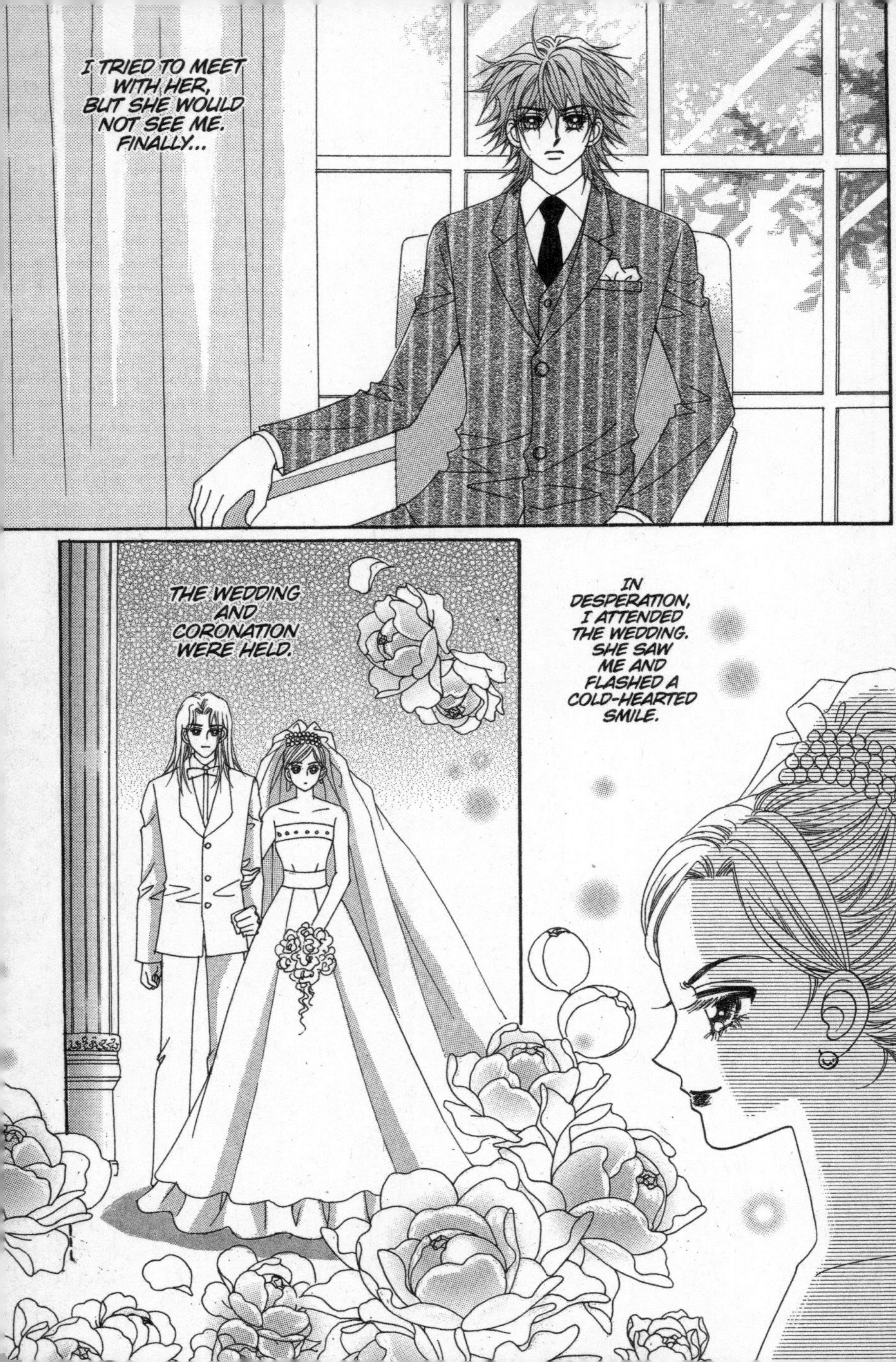
I TRIED TO MEET WITH HER, BUT SHE WOULD NOT SEE ME. FINALLY...
THE WEDDING AND CORONATION WERE HELD.
IN DESPERATION, I ATTENDED THE WEDDING. SHE SAW ME AND FLASHED A COLD-HEARTED SMILE.

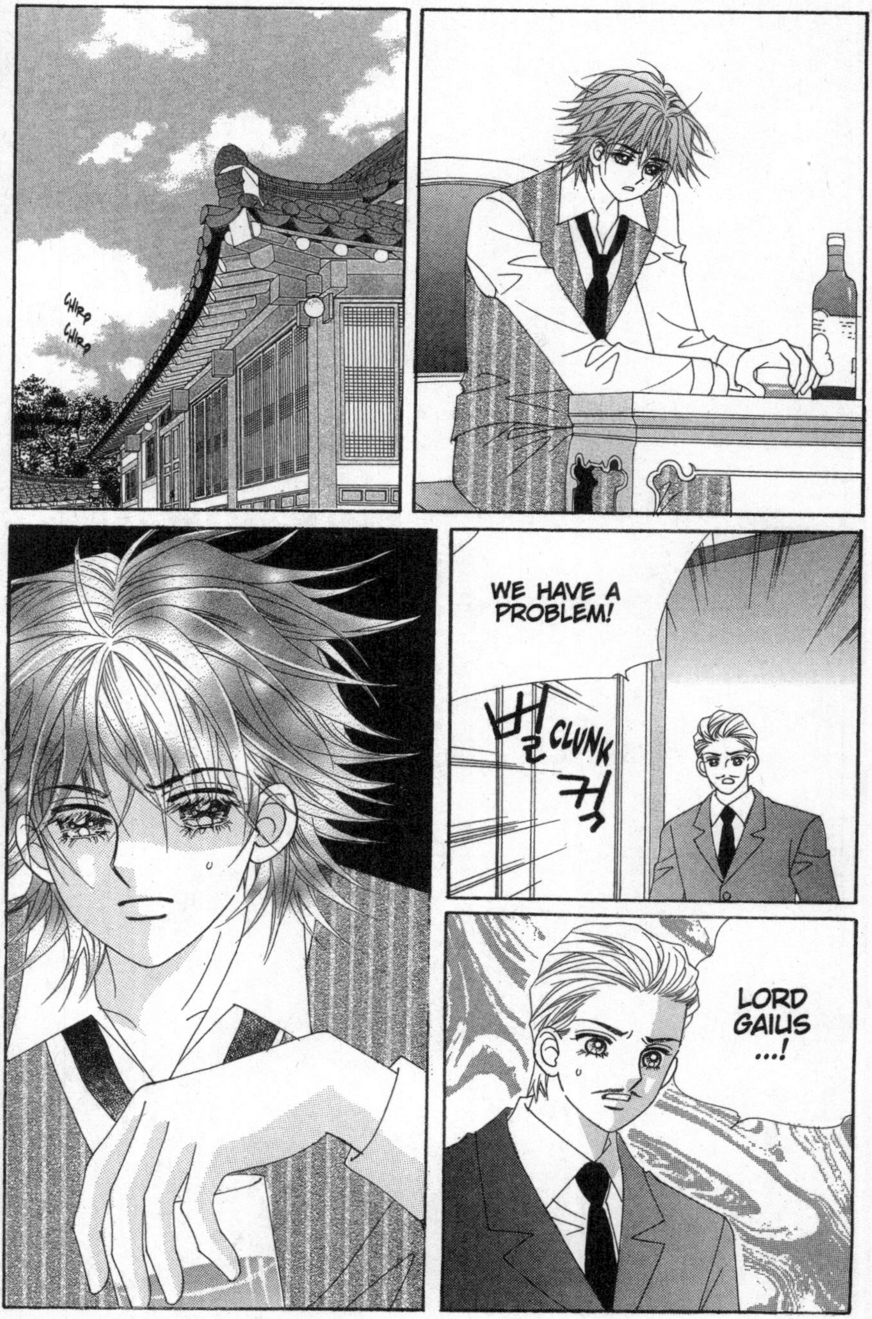
CHIRP
CHIRP
WE HAVE A PROBLEM!
벌 CLUNK 컥
LORD GAIUS ...!

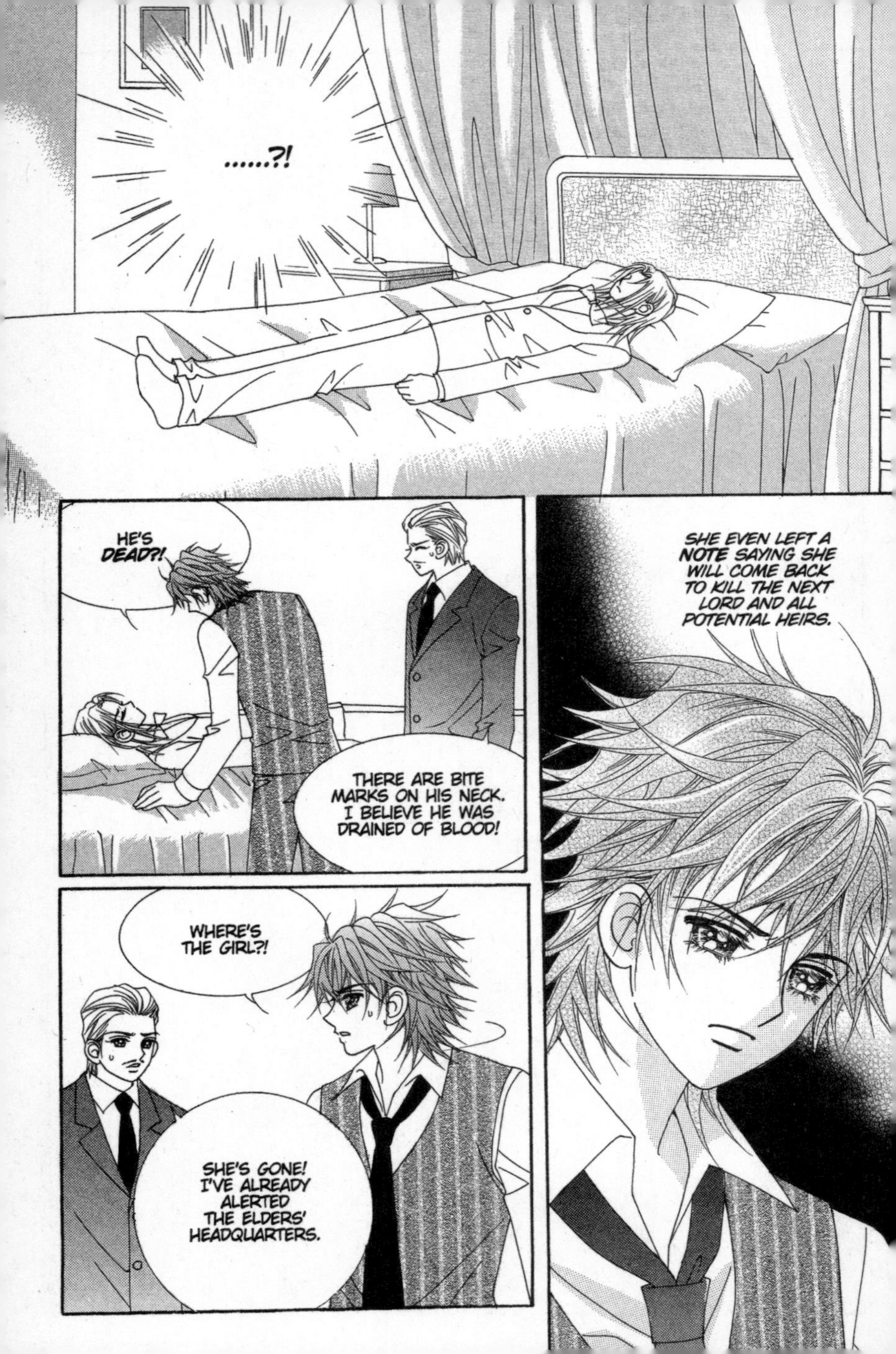
......?!
HE'S DEAD?!
THERE ARE BITE MARKS ON HIS NECK. I BELIEVE HE WAS DRAINED OF BLOOD!
WHERE'S THE GIRL?!
SHE'S GONE! I'VE ALREADY ALERTED THE ELDERS' HEADQUARTERS.
SHE EVEN LEFT A NOTE SAYING SHE WILL COME BACK TO KILL THE NEXT LORD AND ALL POTENTIAL HEIRS.

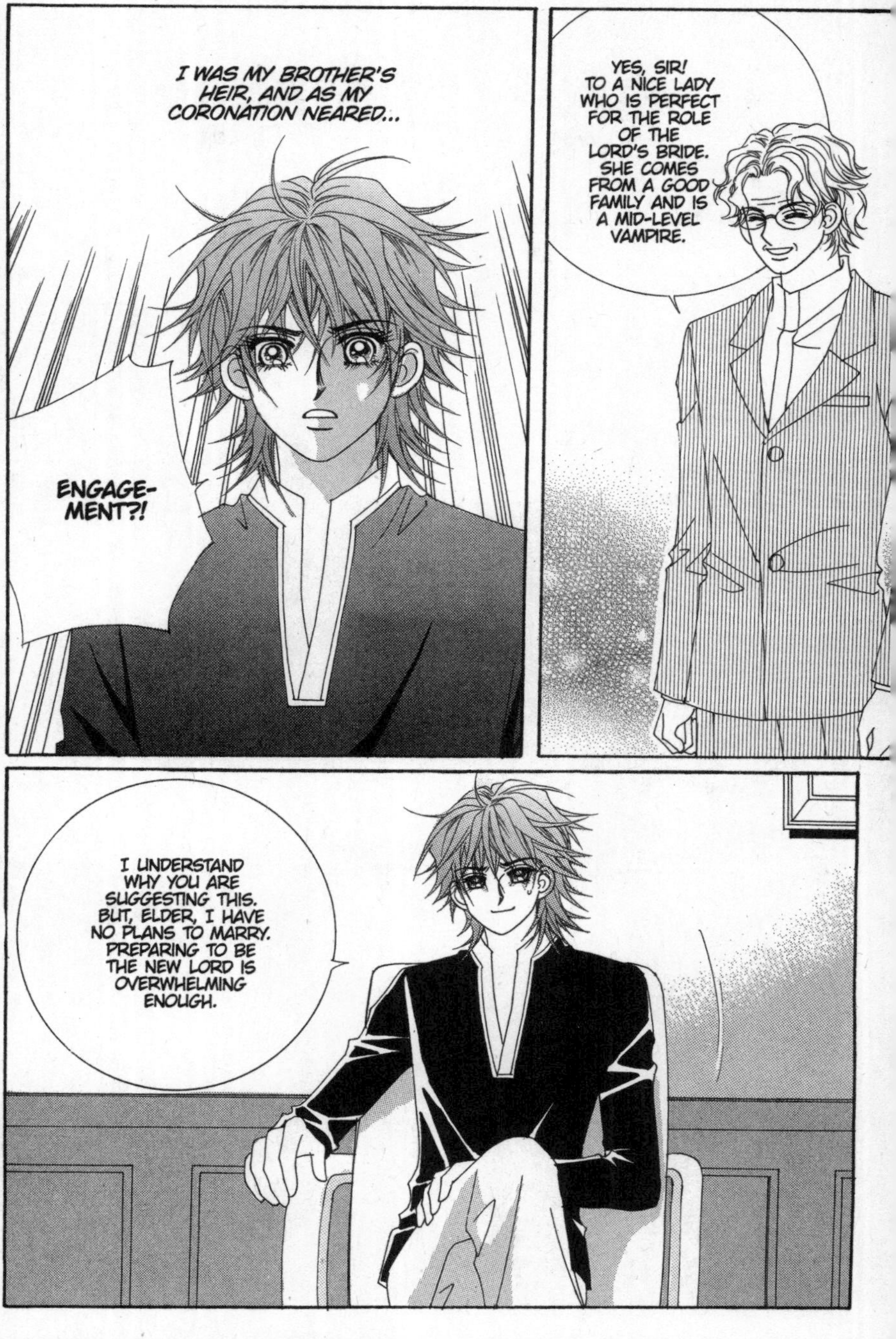
I WAS MY BROTHER'S HEIR, AND AS MY CORONATION NEARED...
ENGAGE-MENT?!
YES, SIR! TO A NICE LADY WHO IS PERFECT FOR THE ROLE OF THE LORD'S BRIDE. SHE COMES FROM A GOOD FAMILY AND IS A MID-LEVEL VAMPIRE.
I UNDERSTAND WHY YOU ARE SUGGESTING THIS. BUT, ELDER, I HAVE NO PLANS TO MARRY. PREPARING TO BE THE NEW LORD IS OVERWHELMING ENOUGH.

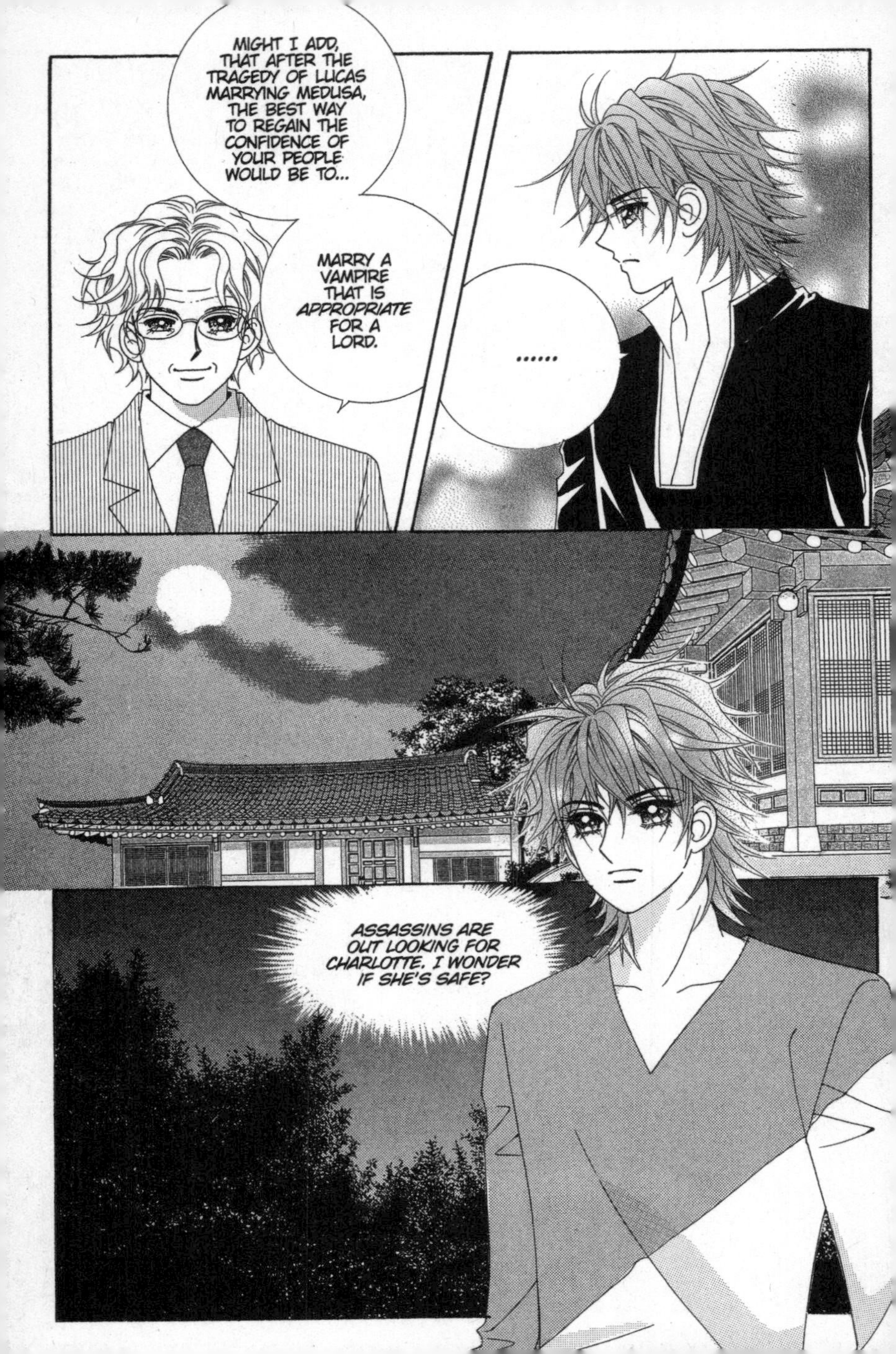
MIGHT I ADD, THAT AFTER THE TRAGEDY OF LUCAS MARRYING MEDUSA, THE BEST WAY TO REGAIN THE CONFIDENCE OF YOUR PEOPLE WOULD BE TO...
MARRY A VAMPIRE THAT IS APPROPRIATE FOR A LORD.
......
ASSASSINS ARE OUT LOOKING FOR CHARLOTTE. I WONDER IF SHE'S SAFE?

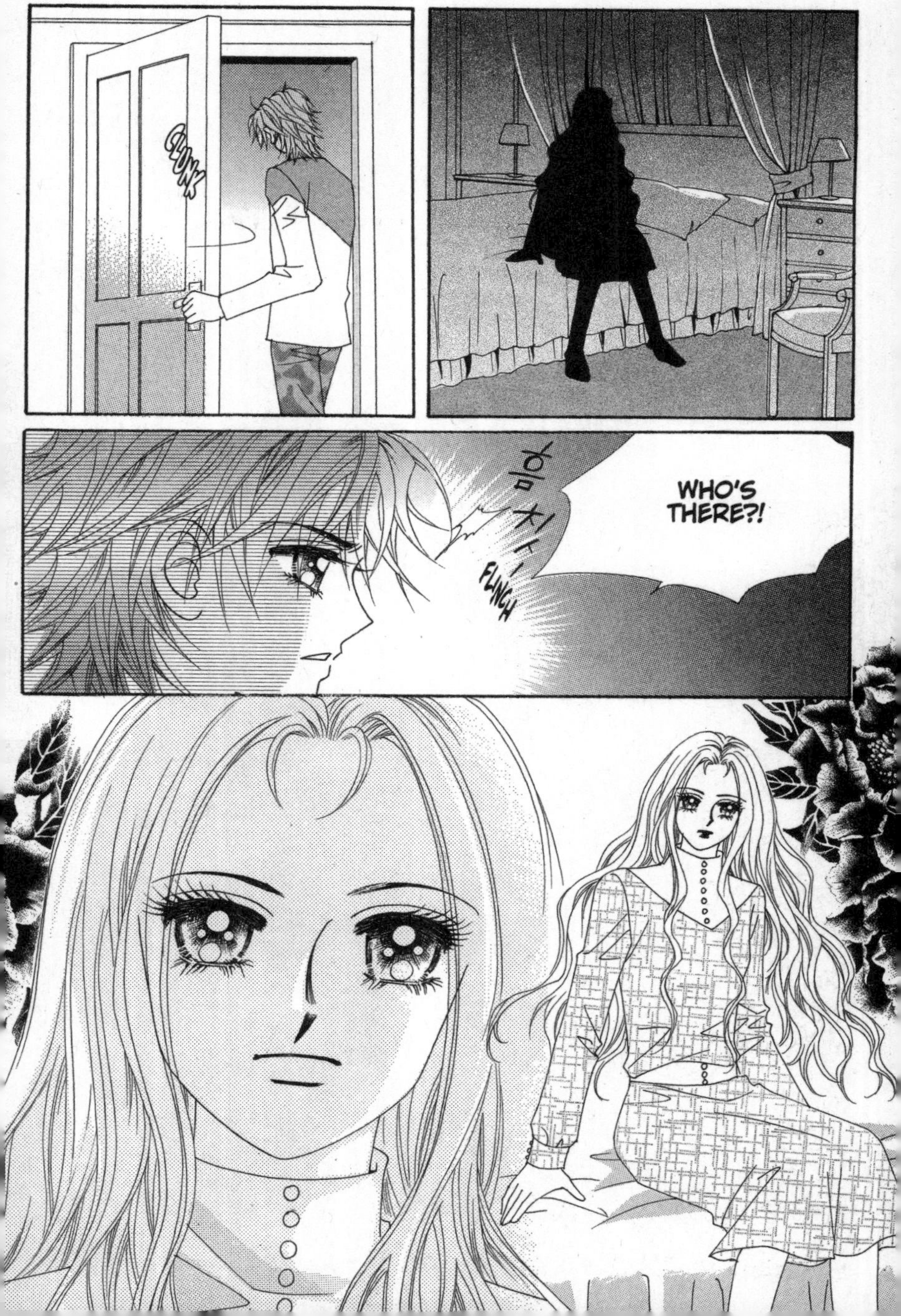
CLUNK
흠칫!
FLINCH
WHO'S THERE?!

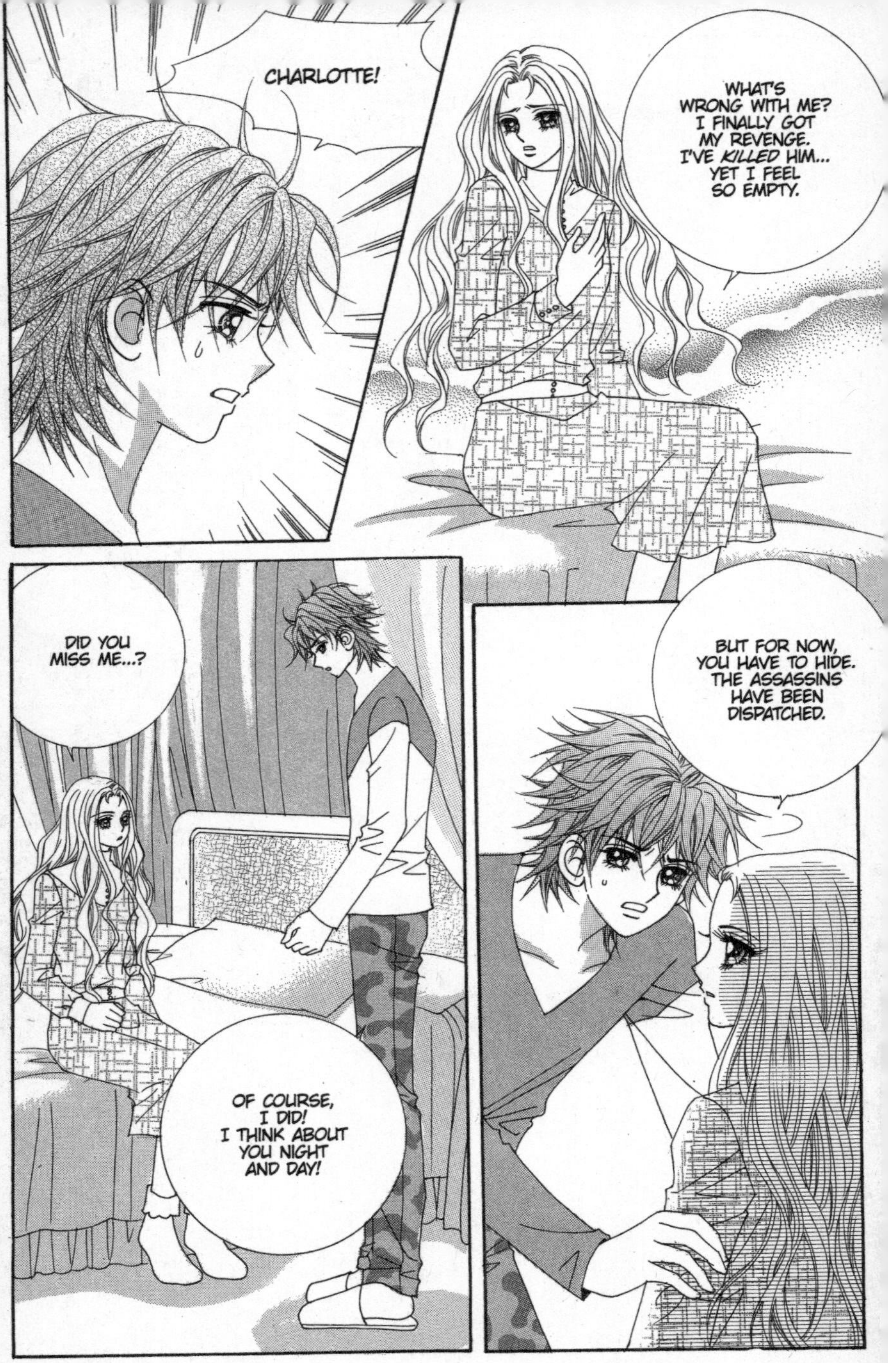
CHARLOTTE!
WHAT'S WRONG WITH ME? I FINALLY GOT MY REVENGE. I'VE *KILLED* HIM... YET I FEEL SO EMPTY.
DID YOU MISS ME...?
OF COURSE, I DID! I THINK ABOUT YOU NIGHT AND DAY!
BUT FOR NOW, YOU HAVE TO HIDE. THE ASSASSINS HAVE BEEN DISPATCHED.

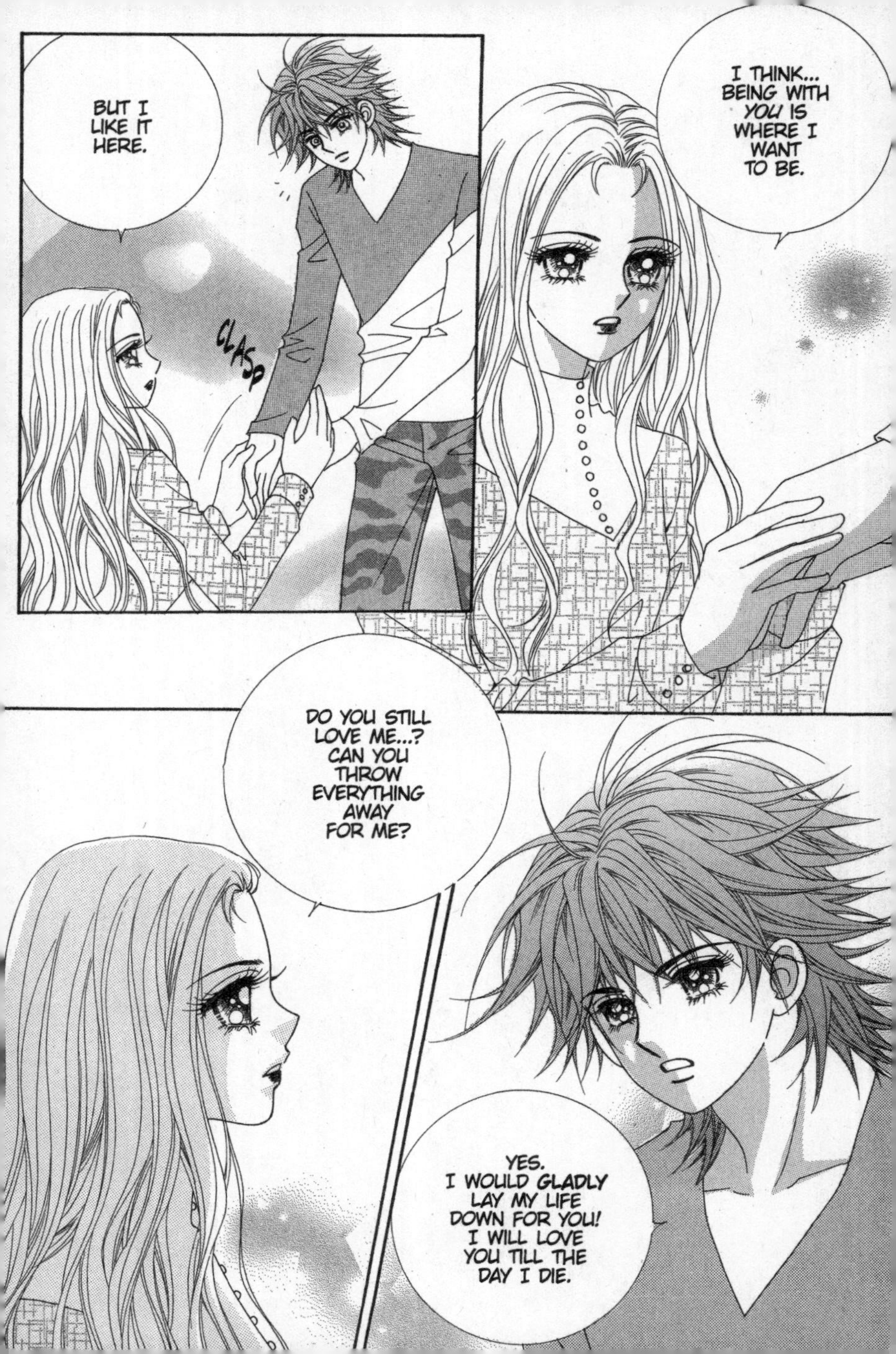
BUT I LIKE IT HERE.
CLASP
I THINK... BEING WITH YOU IS WHERE I WANT TO BE.
DO YOU STILL LOVE ME...? CAN YOU THROW EVERYTHING AWAY FOR ME?
YES. I WOULD GLADLY LAY MY LIFE DOWN FOR YOU! I WILL LOVE YOU TILL THE DAY I DIE.

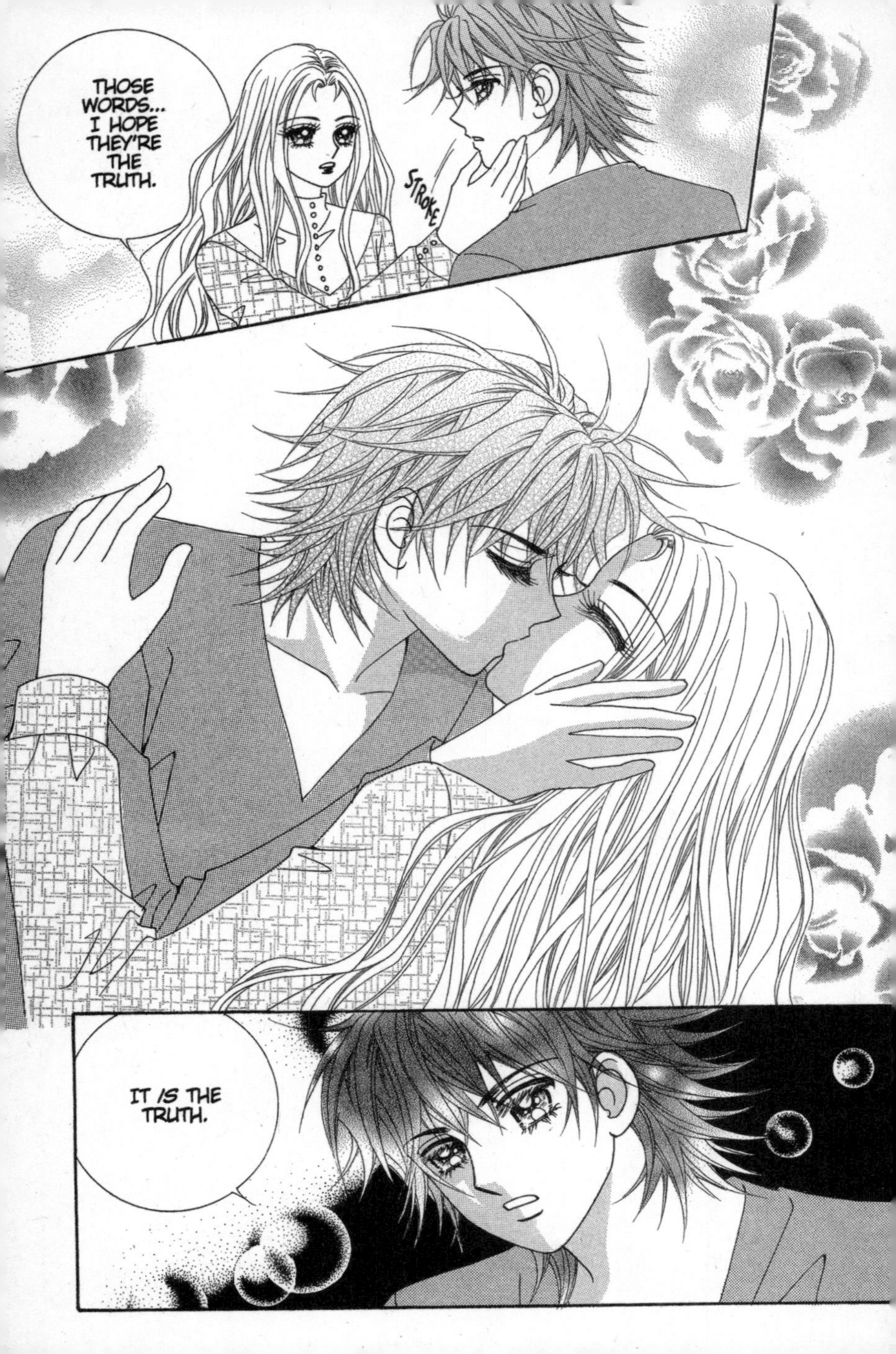
THOSE WORDS... I HOPE THEY'RE THE TRUTH.
STROKE
IT IS THE TRUTH.

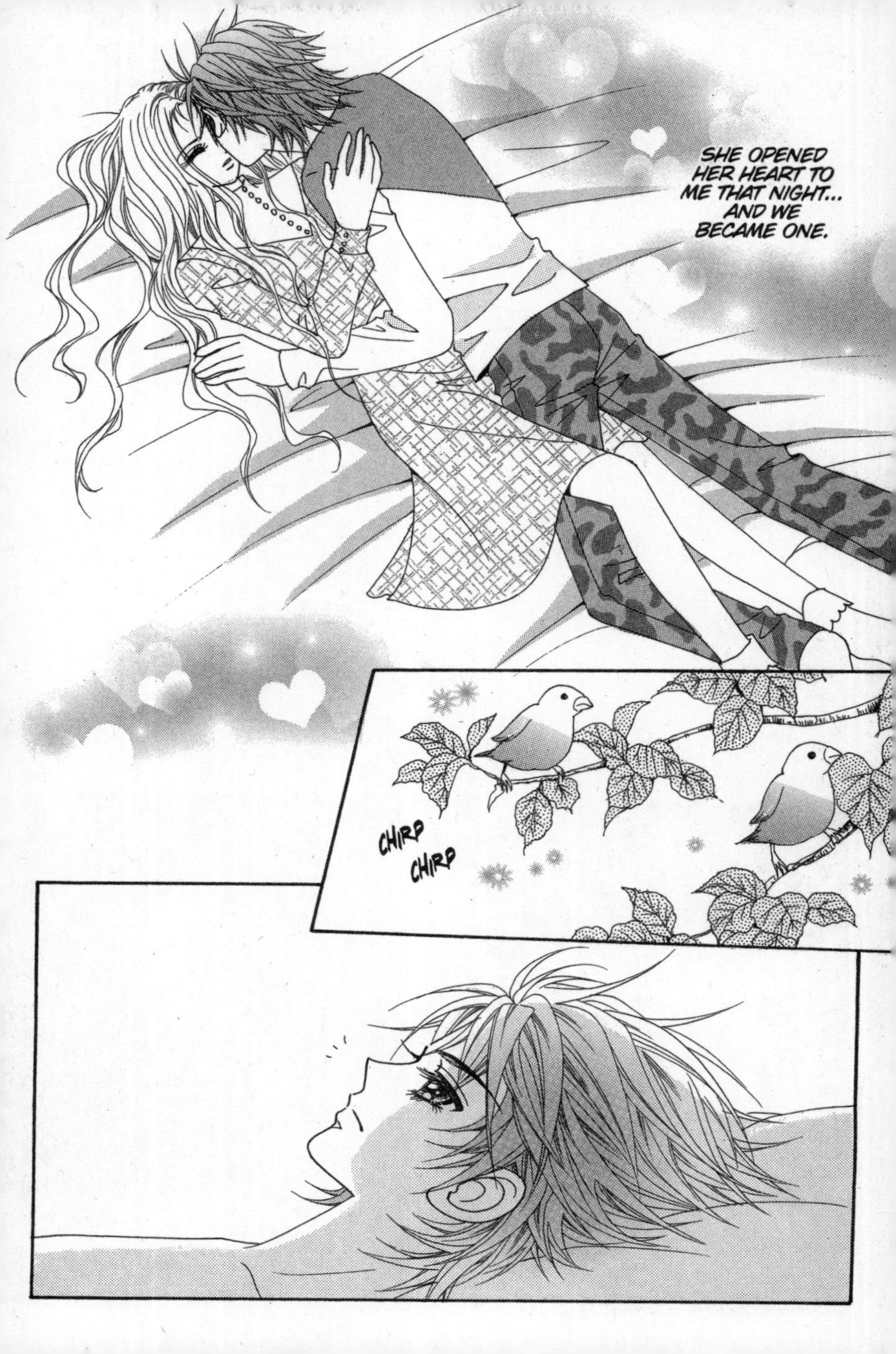
SHE OPENED HER HEART TO ME THAT NIGHT... AND WE BECAME ONE.
CHIRP
CHIRP

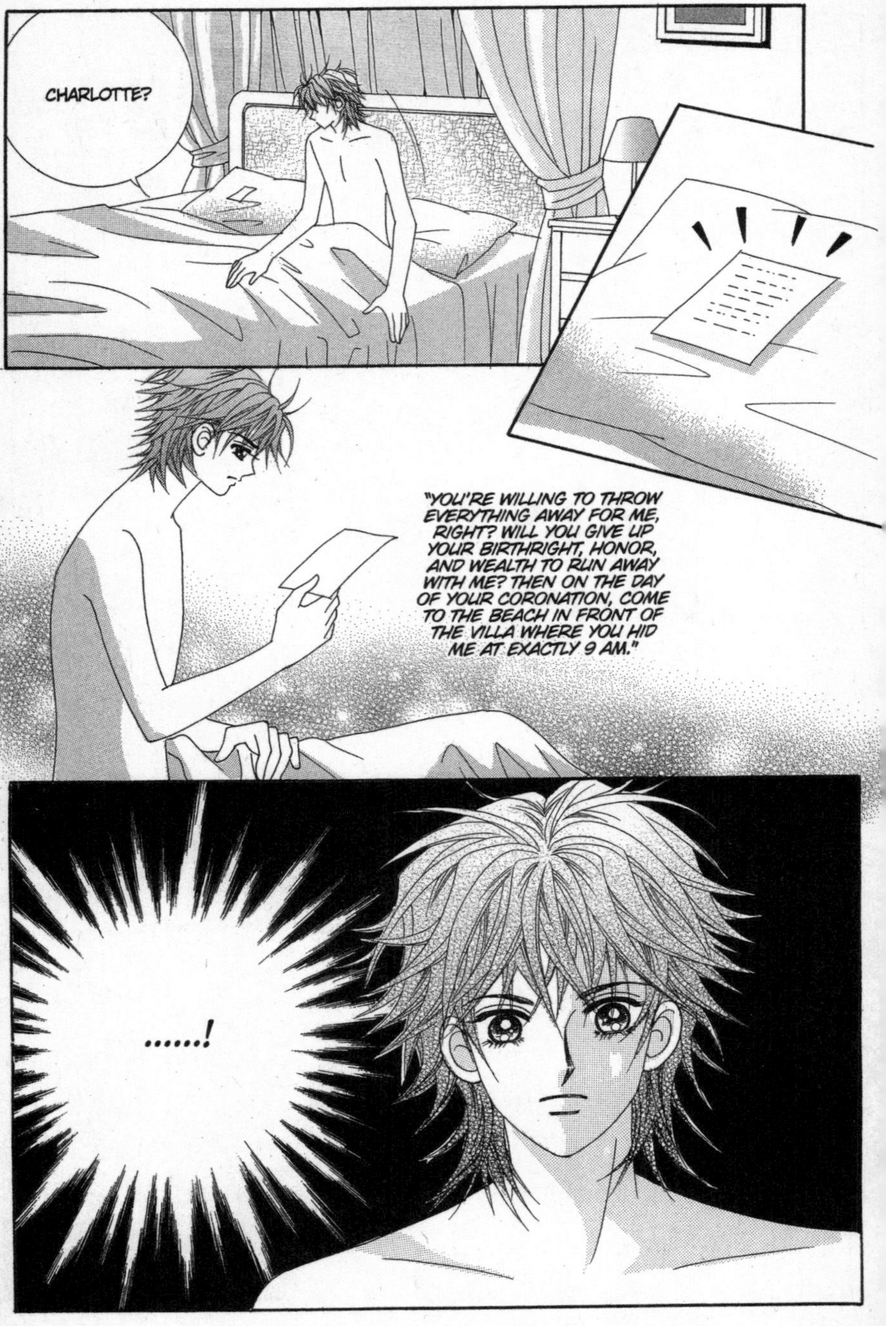
CHARLOTTE?
"YOU'RE WILLING TO THROW EVERYTHING AWAY FOR ME, RIGHT? WILL YOU GIVE UP YOUR BIRTHRIGHT, HONOR, AND WEALTH TO RUN AWAY WITH ME? THEN ON THE DAY OF YOUR CORONATION, COME TO THE BEACH IN FRONT OF THE VILLA WHERE YOU HID ME AT EXACTLY 9 AM."
......!

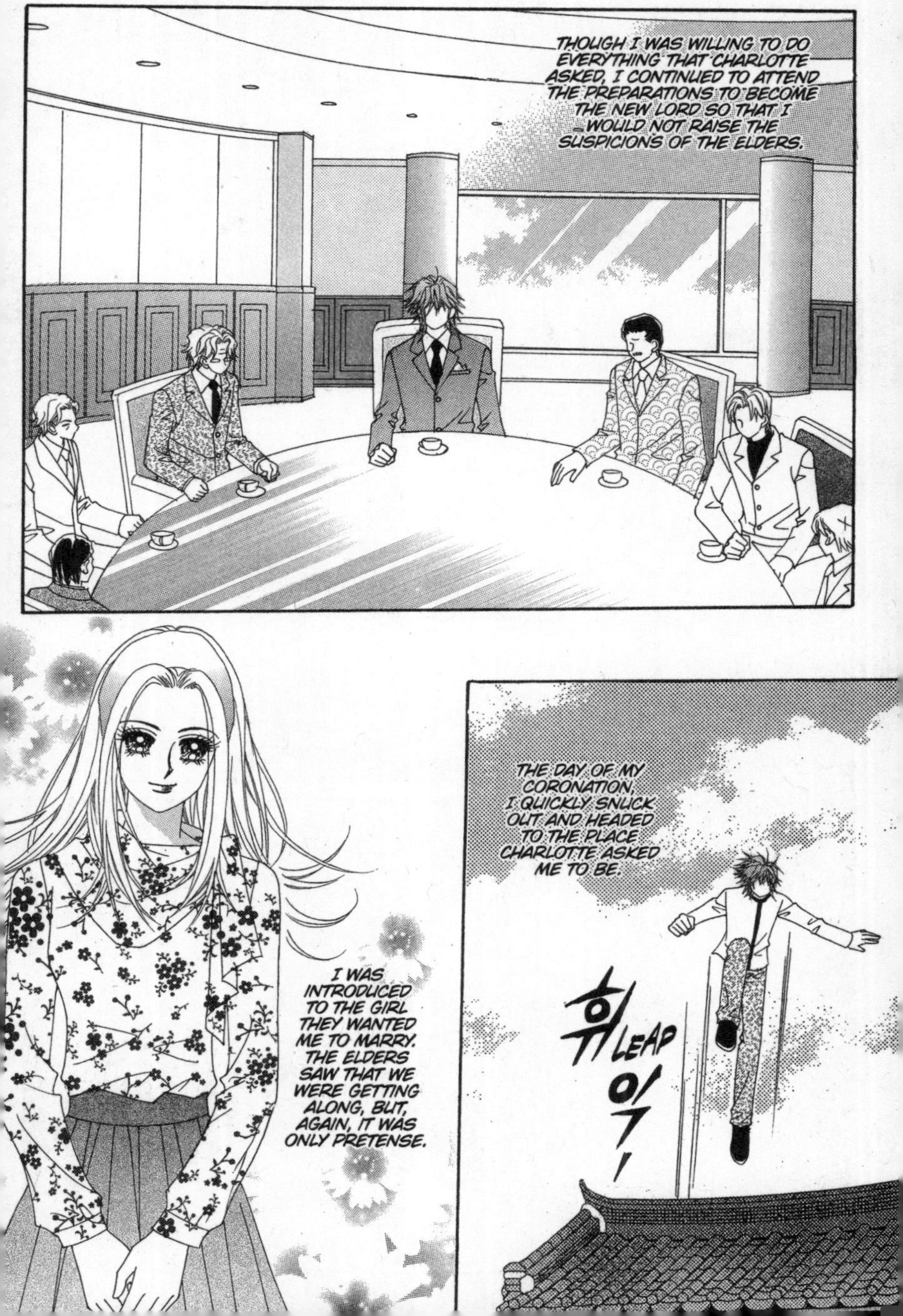
THOUGH I WAS WILLING TO DO EVERYTHING THAT CHARLOTTE ASKED, I CONTINUED TO ATTEND THE PREPARATIONS TO BECOME THE NEW LORD SO THAT I WOULD NOT RAISE THE SUSPICIONS OF THE ELDERS.
I WAS INTRODUCED TO THE GIRL THEY WANTED ME TO MARRY. THE ELDERS SAW THAT WE WERE GETTING ALONG, BUT, AGAIN, IT WAS ONLY PRETENSE.
THE DAY OF MY CORONATION, I QUICKLY SNUCK OUT AND HEADED TO THE PLACE CHARLOTTE ASKED ME TO BE.
휘익!
LEAP

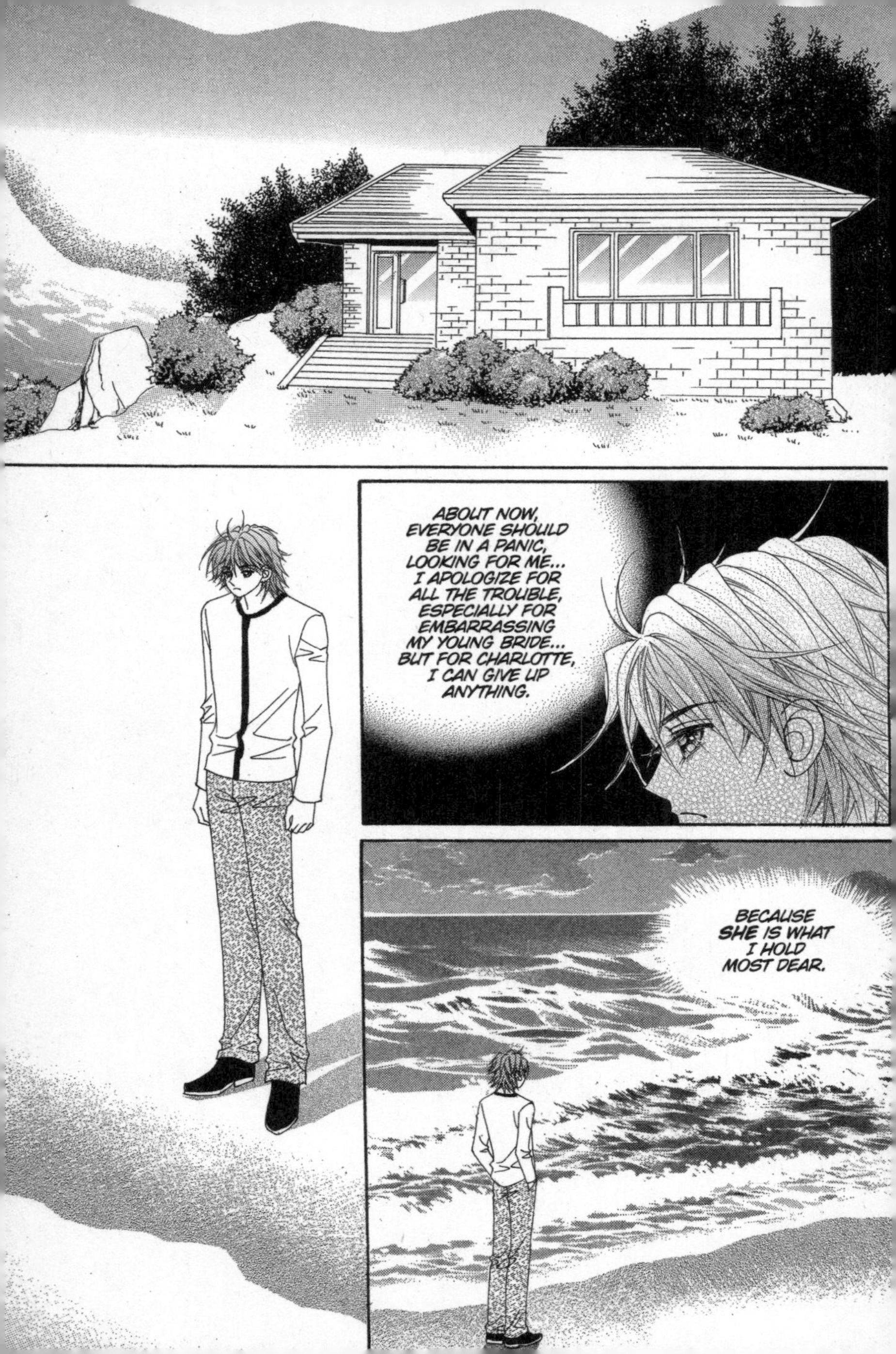
ABOUT NOW, EVERYONE SHOULD BE IN A PANIC, LOOKING FOR ME... I APOLOGIZE FOR ALL THE TROUBLE, ESPECIALLY FOR EMBARRASSING MY YOUNG BRIDE... BUT FOR CHARLOTTE, I CAN GIVE UP ANYTHING.
BECAUSE SHE IS WHAT I HOLD MOST DEAR.

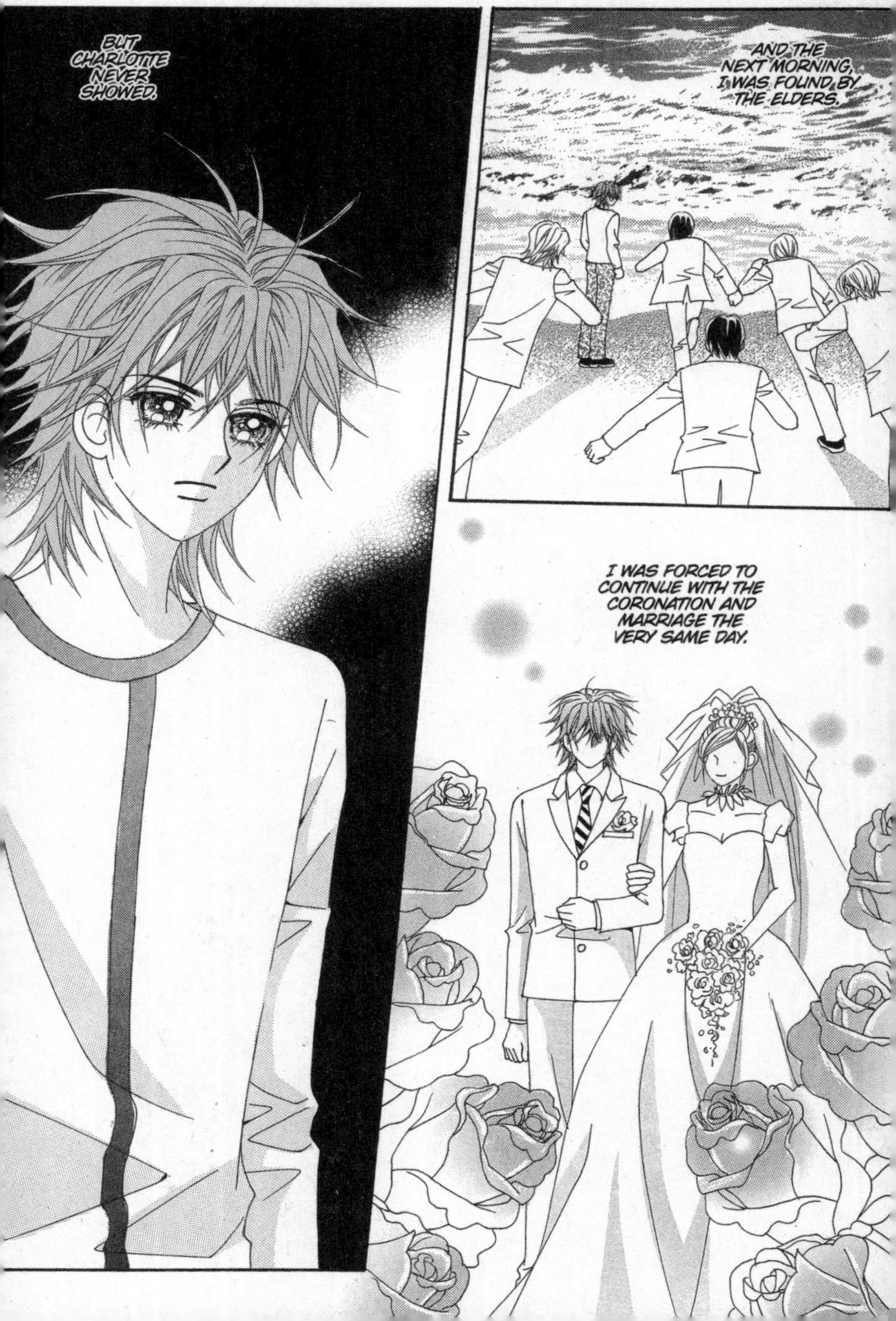
BUT CHARLOTTE NEVER SHOWED.
AND THE NEXT MORNING, I WAS FOUND BY THE ELDERS.
I WAS FORCED TO CONTINUE WITH THE CORONATION AND MARRIAGE THE VERY SAME DAY.

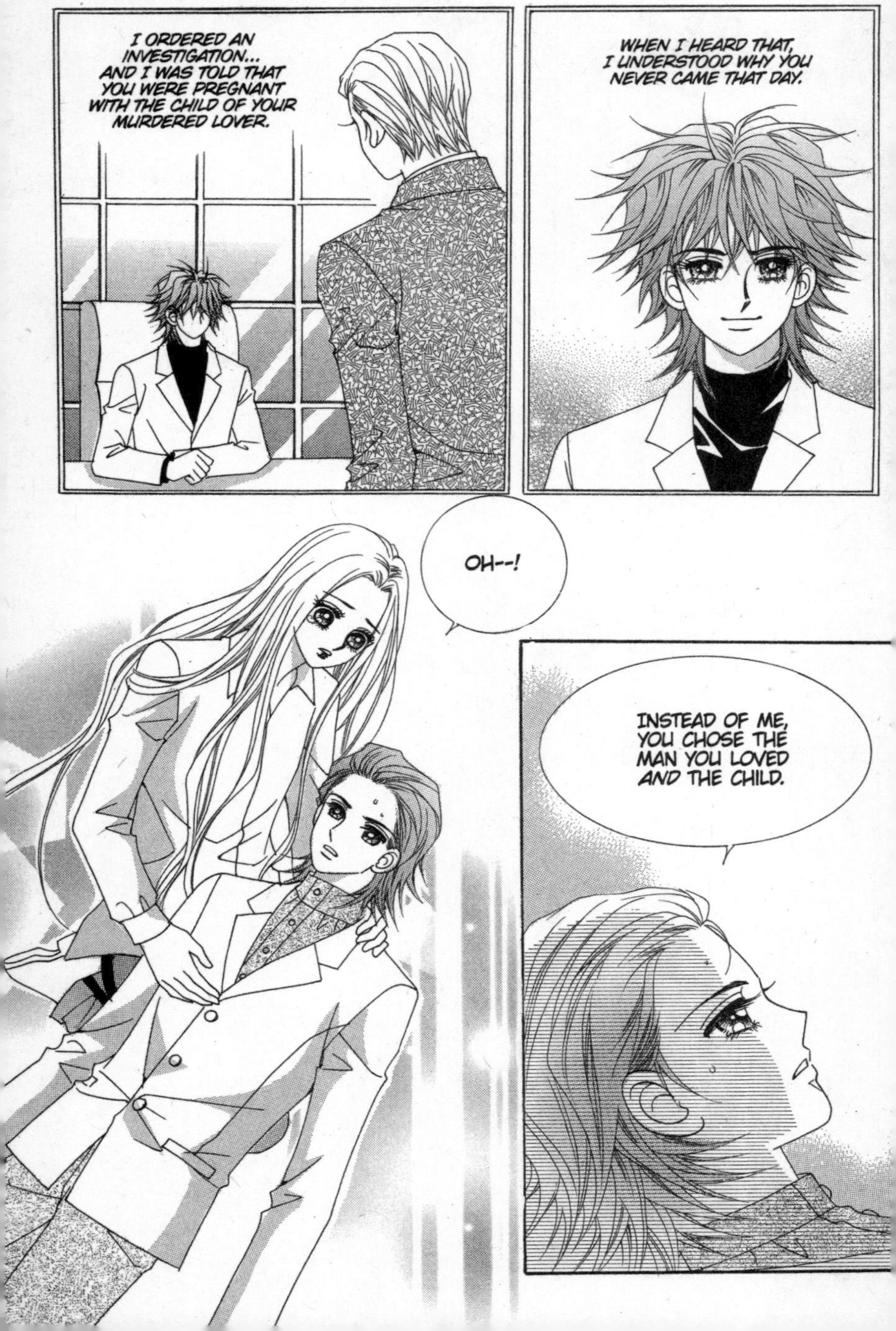
I ORDERED AN INVESTIGATION... AND I WAS TOLD THAT YOU WERE PREGNANT WITH THE CHILD OF YOUR MURDERED LOVER.
WHEN I HEARD THAT, I UNDERSTOOD WHY YOU NEVER CAME THAT DAY.
OH--!
INSTEAD OF ME, YOU CHOSE THE MAN YOU LOVED AND THE CHILD.

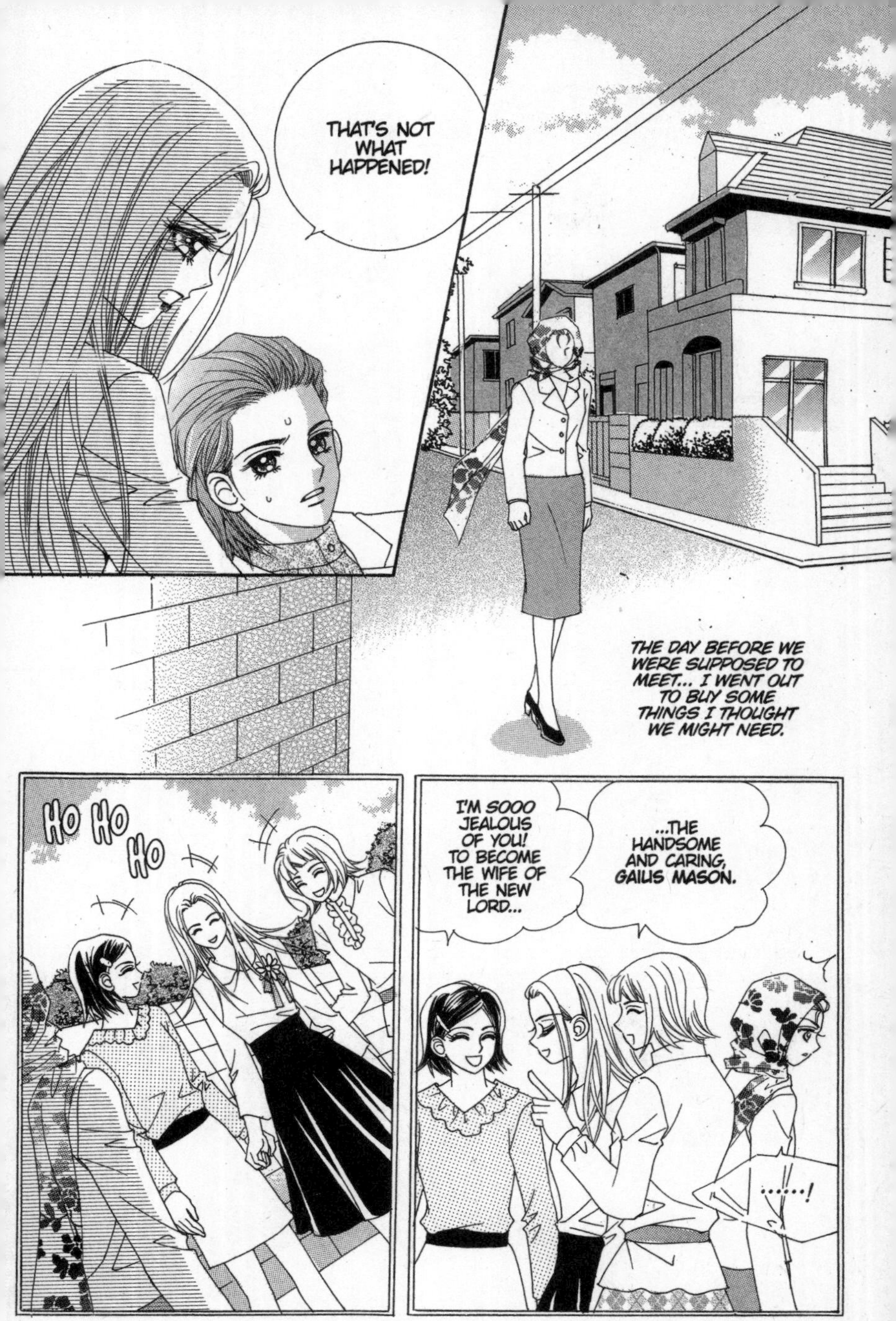
THAT'S NOT WHAT HAPPENED!
THE DAY BEFORE WE WERE SUPPOSED TO MEET... I WENT OUT TO BUY SOME THINGS I THOUGHT WE MIGHT NEED.
HO HO HO
I'M *SOOO* JEALOUS OF YOU! TO BECOME THE WIFE OF THE NEW LORD...
...THE HANDSOME AND CARING, GAIUS MASON.
......!

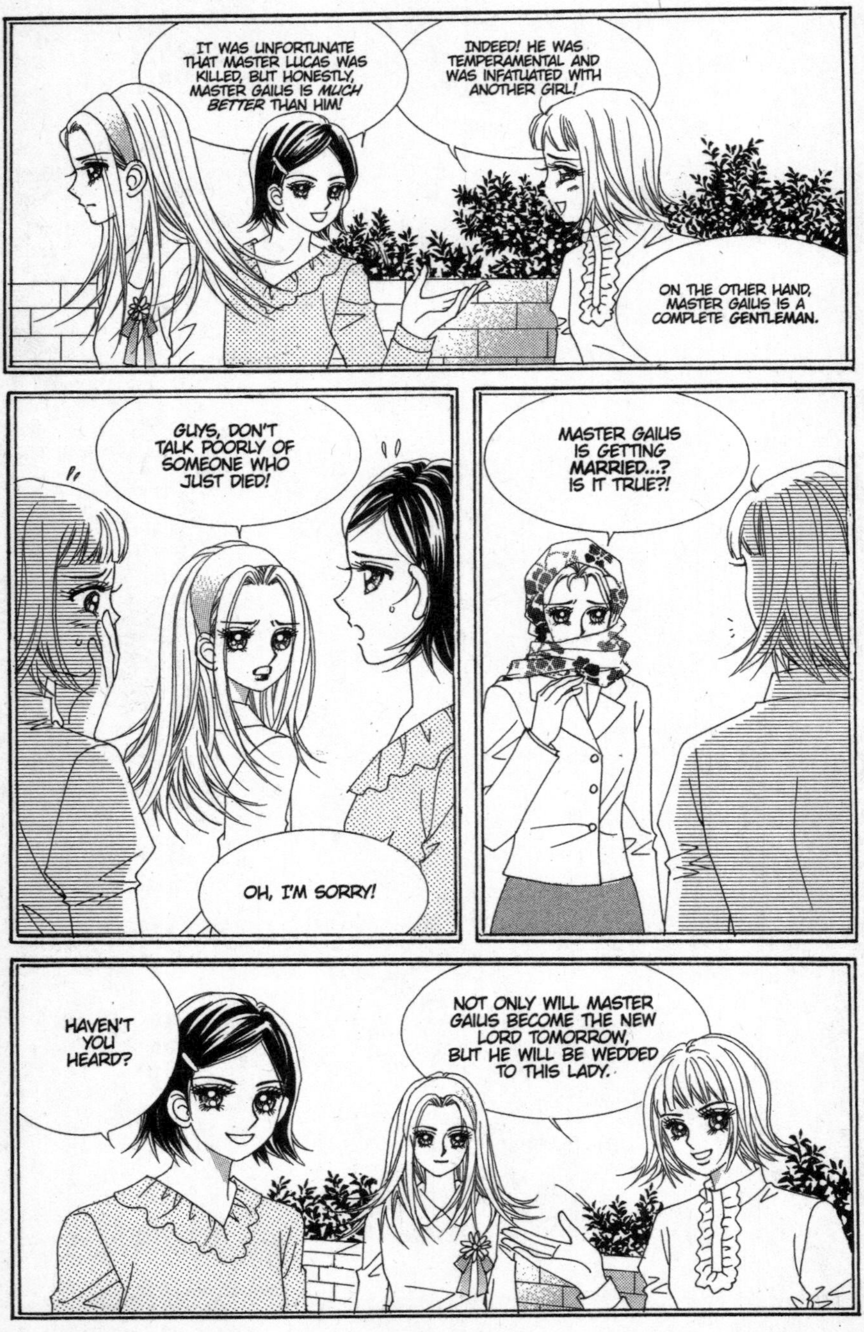
IT WAS UNFORTUNATE THAT MASTER LUCAS WAS KILLED, BUT HONESTLY, MASTER GAIUS IS *MUCH BETTER* THAN HIM!
INDEED! HE WAS TEMPERAMENTAL AND WAS INFATUATED WITH ANOTHER GIRL!
ON THE OTHER HAND, MASTER GAIUS IS A COMPLETE GENTLEMAN.
GUYS, DON'T TALK POORLY OF SOMEONE WHO JUST DIED!
OH, I'M SORRY!
MASTER GAIUS IS GETTING MARRIED...? IS IT TRUE?!
HAVEN'T YOU HEARD?
NOT ONLY WILL MASTER GAIUS BECOME THE NEW LORD TOMORROW, BUT HE WILL BE WEDDED TO THIS LADY.

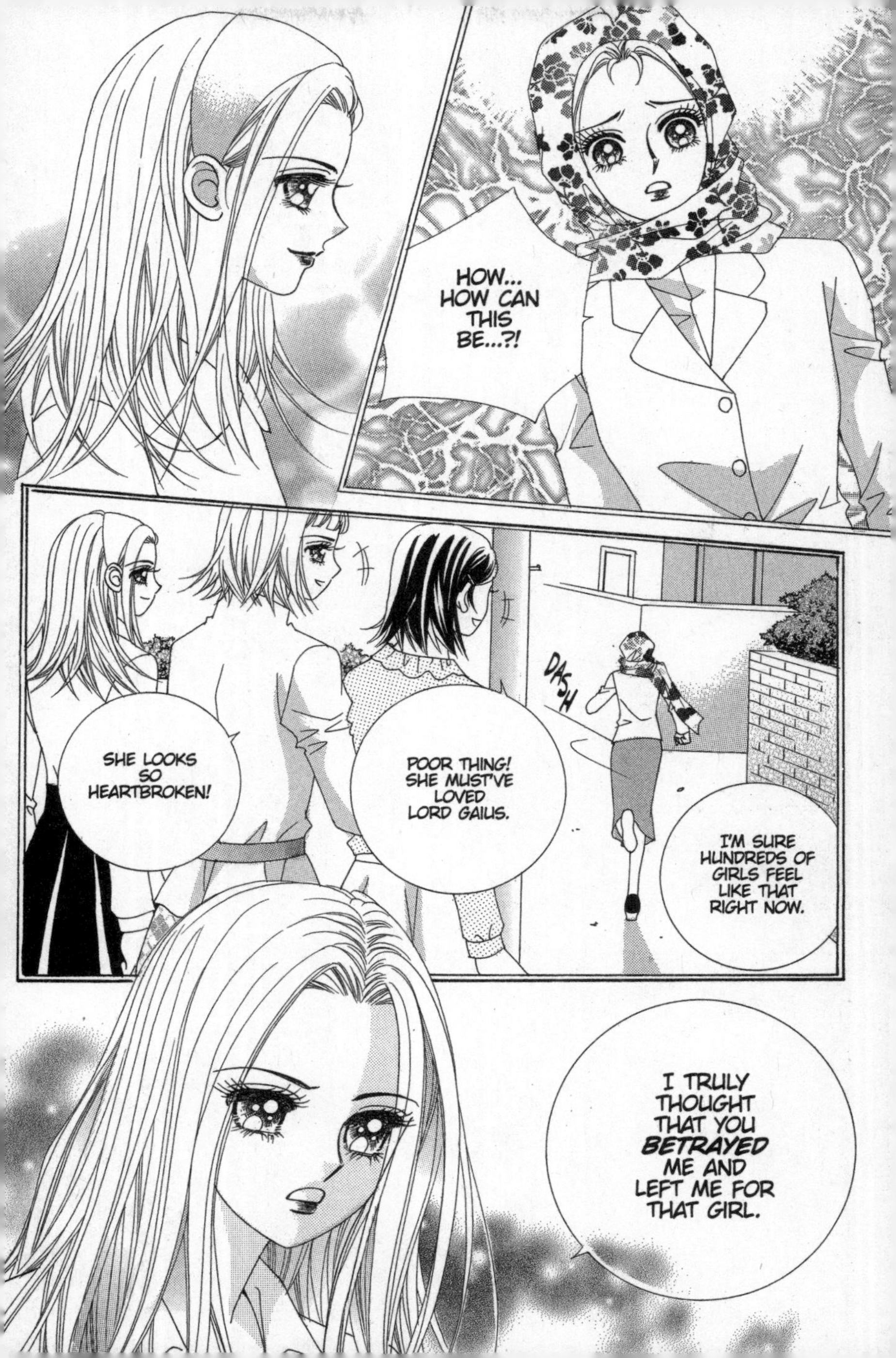
HOW... HOW CAN THIS BE...?!
SHE LOOKS SO HEARTBROKEN!
POOR THING! SHE MUST'VE LOVED LORD GAIUS.
DASH
I'M SURE HUNDREDS OF GIRLS FEEL LIKE THAT RIGHT NOW.
I TRULY THOUGHT THAT YOU ***BETRAYED*** ME AND LEFT ME FOR THAT GIRL.

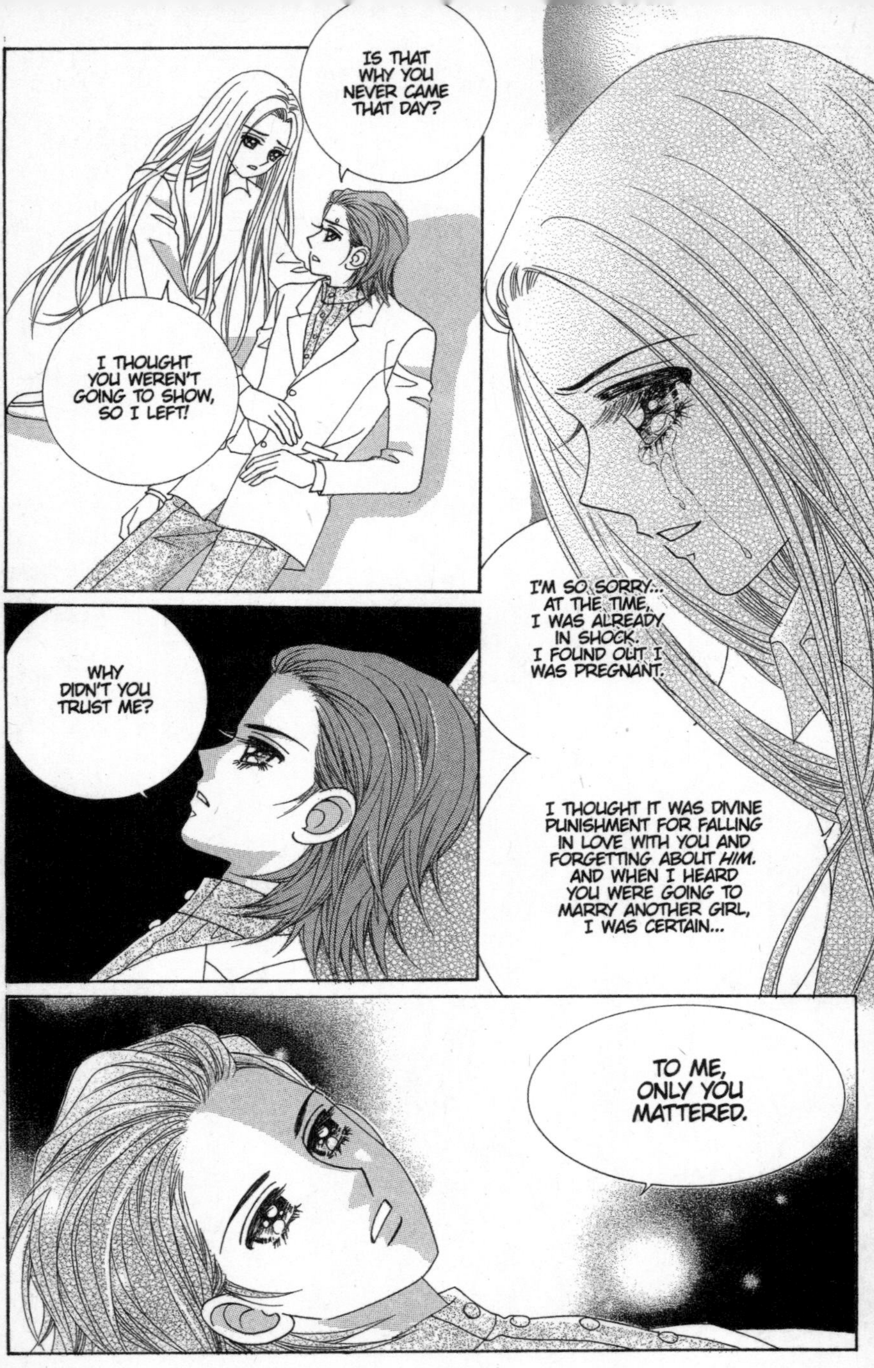
IS THAT WHY YOU NEVER CAME THAT DAY?
I THOUGHT YOU WEREN'T GOING TO SHOW, SO I LEFT!
WHY DIDN'T YOU TRUST ME?
I'M SO SORRY... AT THE TIME, I WAS ALREADY IN SHOCK. I FOUND OUT I WAS PREGNANT.
I THOUGHT IT WAS DIVINE PUNISHMENT FOR FALLING IN LOVE WITH YOU AND FORGETTING ABOUT *HIM*. AND WHEN I HEARD YOU WERE GOING TO MARRY ANOTHER GIRL, I WAS CERTAIN...
TO ME, ONLY YOU MATTERED.

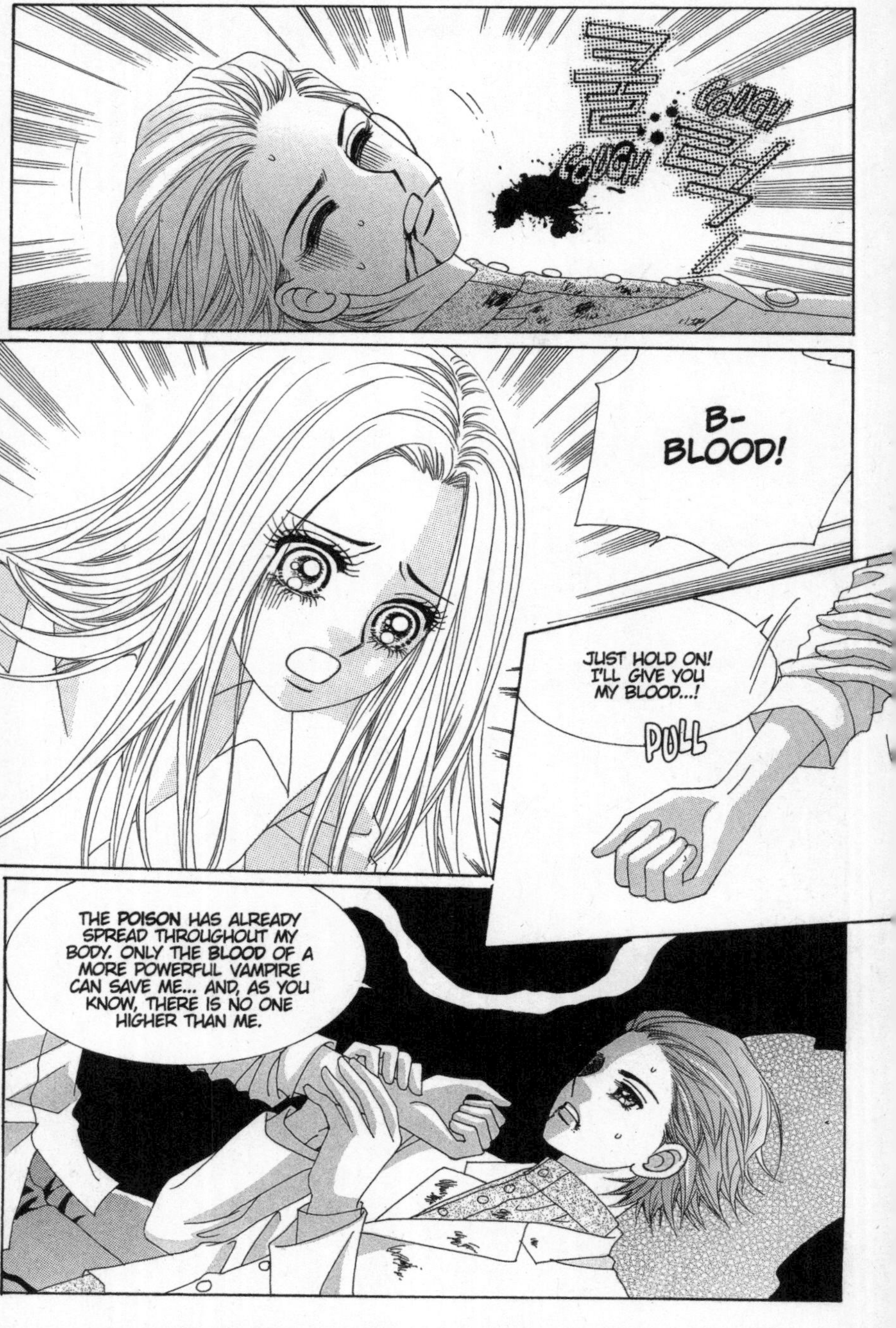
COUGH!
COUGH!
B-BLOOD!
JUST HOLD ON! I'LL GIVE YOU MY BLOOD...!
PULL
THE POISON HAS ALREADY SPREAD THROUGHOUT MY BODY. ONLY THE BLOOD OF A MORE POWERFUL VAMPIRE CAN SAVE ME... AND, AS YOU KNOW, THERE IS NO ONE HIGHER THAN ME.

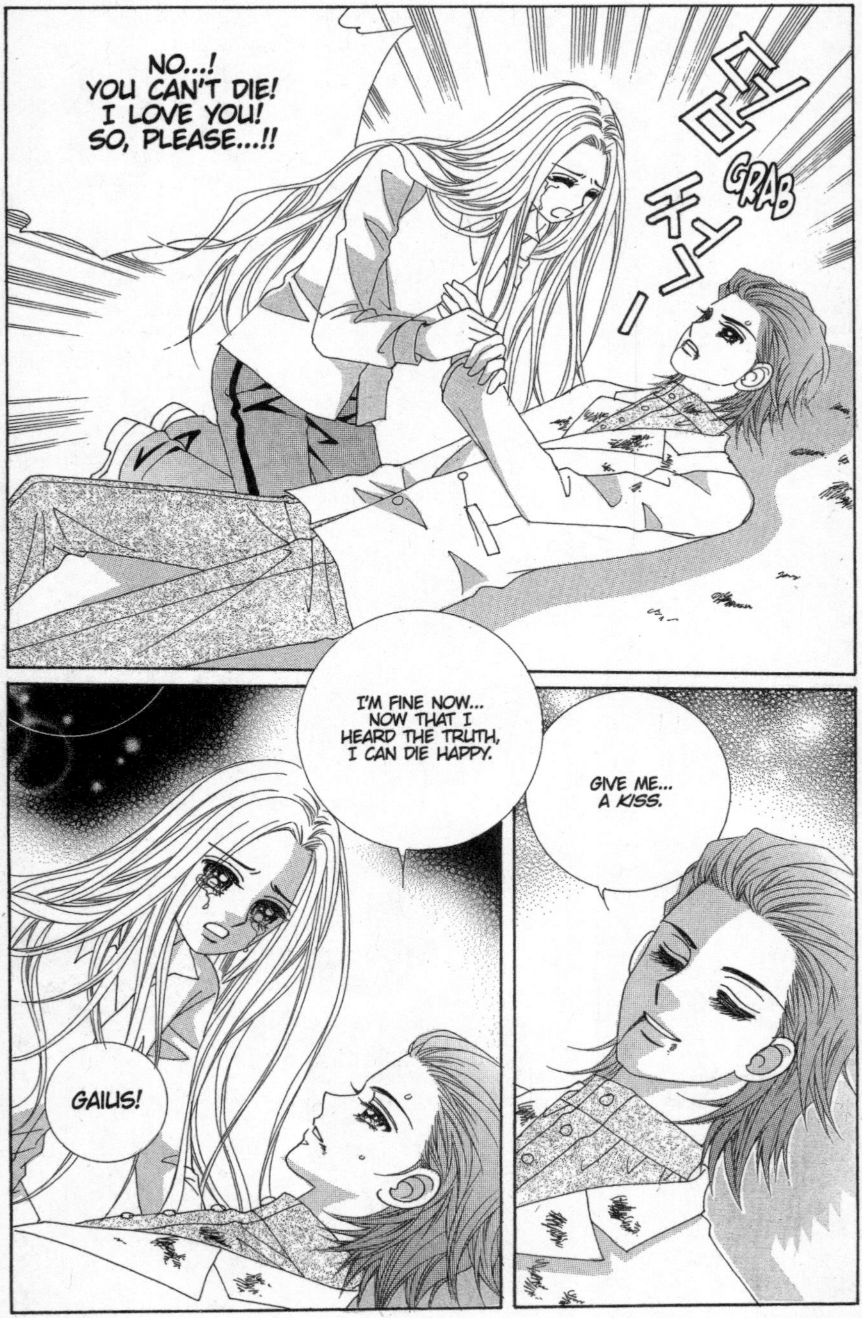
NO...! YOU CAN'T DIE! I LOVE YOU! SO, PLEASE...!!
GRAB
I'M FINE NOW... NOW THAT I HEARD THE TRUTH, I CAN DIE HAPPY.
GAIUS!
GIVE ME... A KISS.

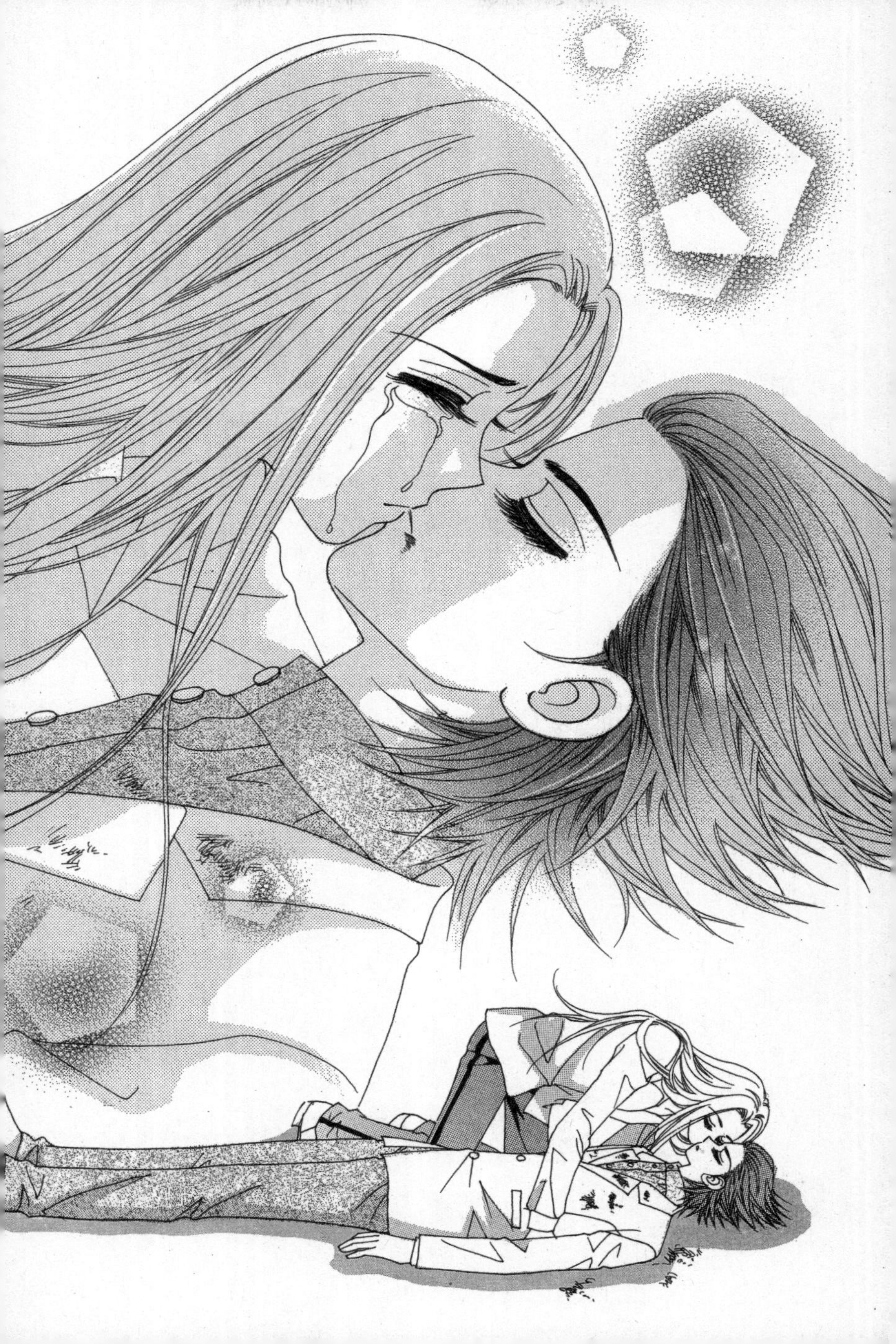

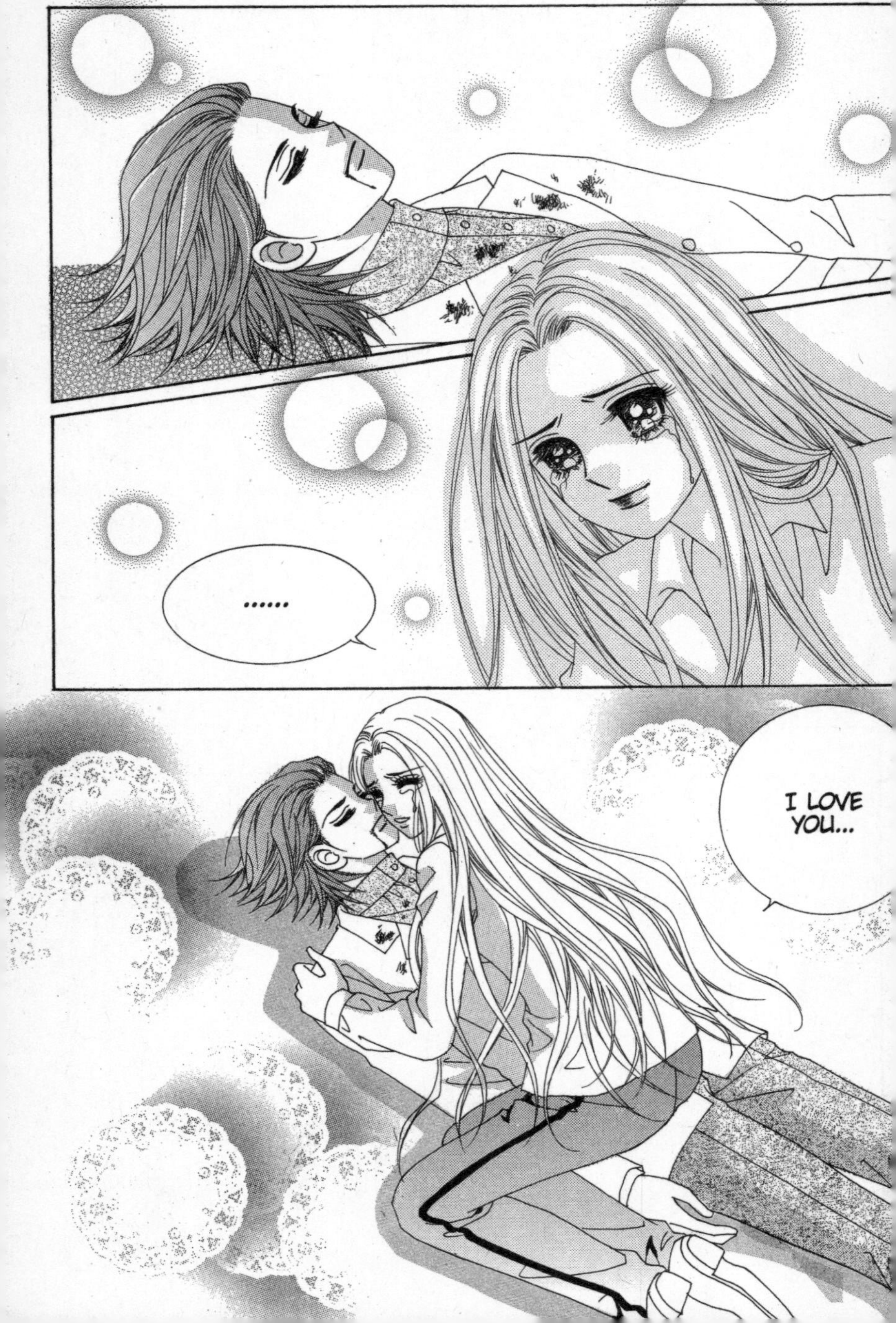
......
I LOVE YOU...

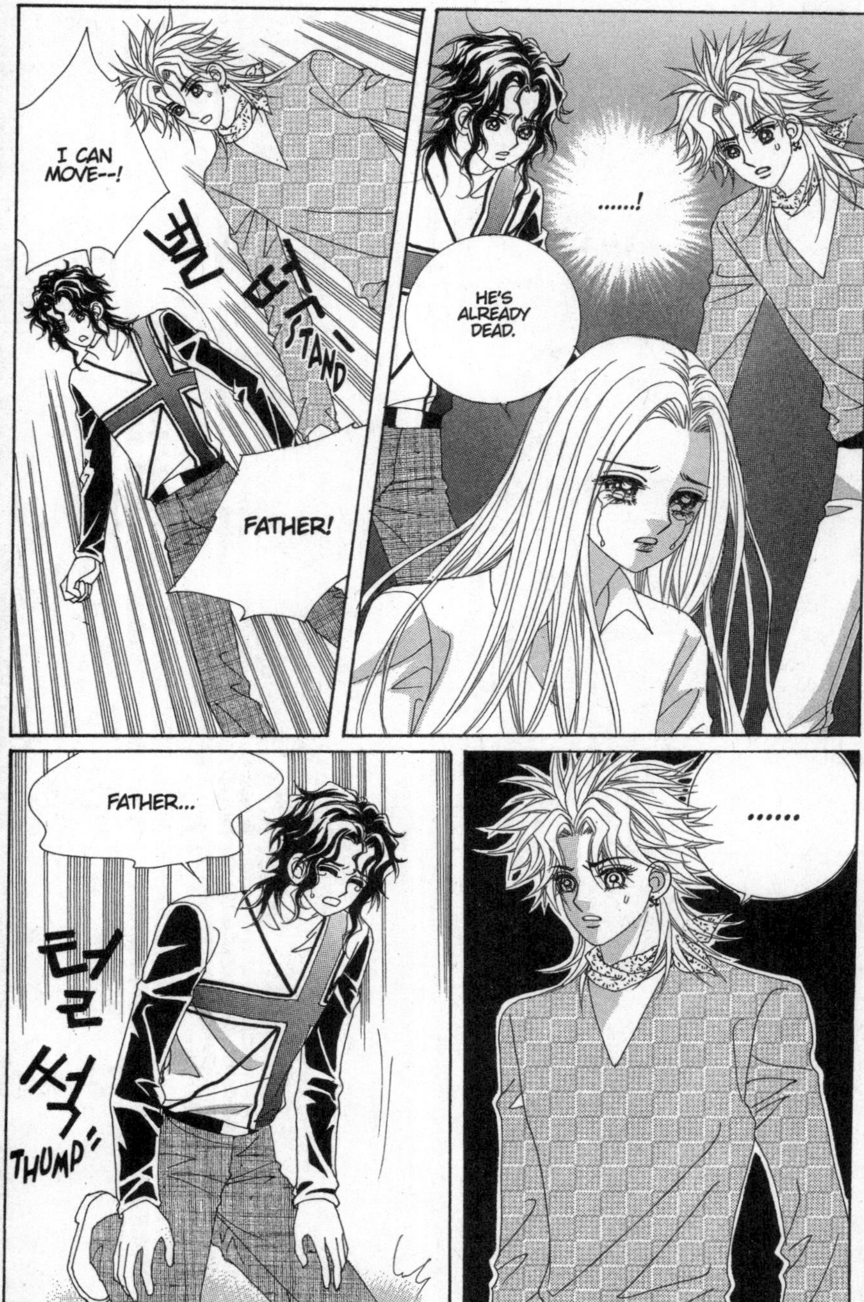
I CAN MOVE--!
STAND
FATHER!
......!
HE'S ALREADY DEAD.
FATHER...
털썩
THUMP
......

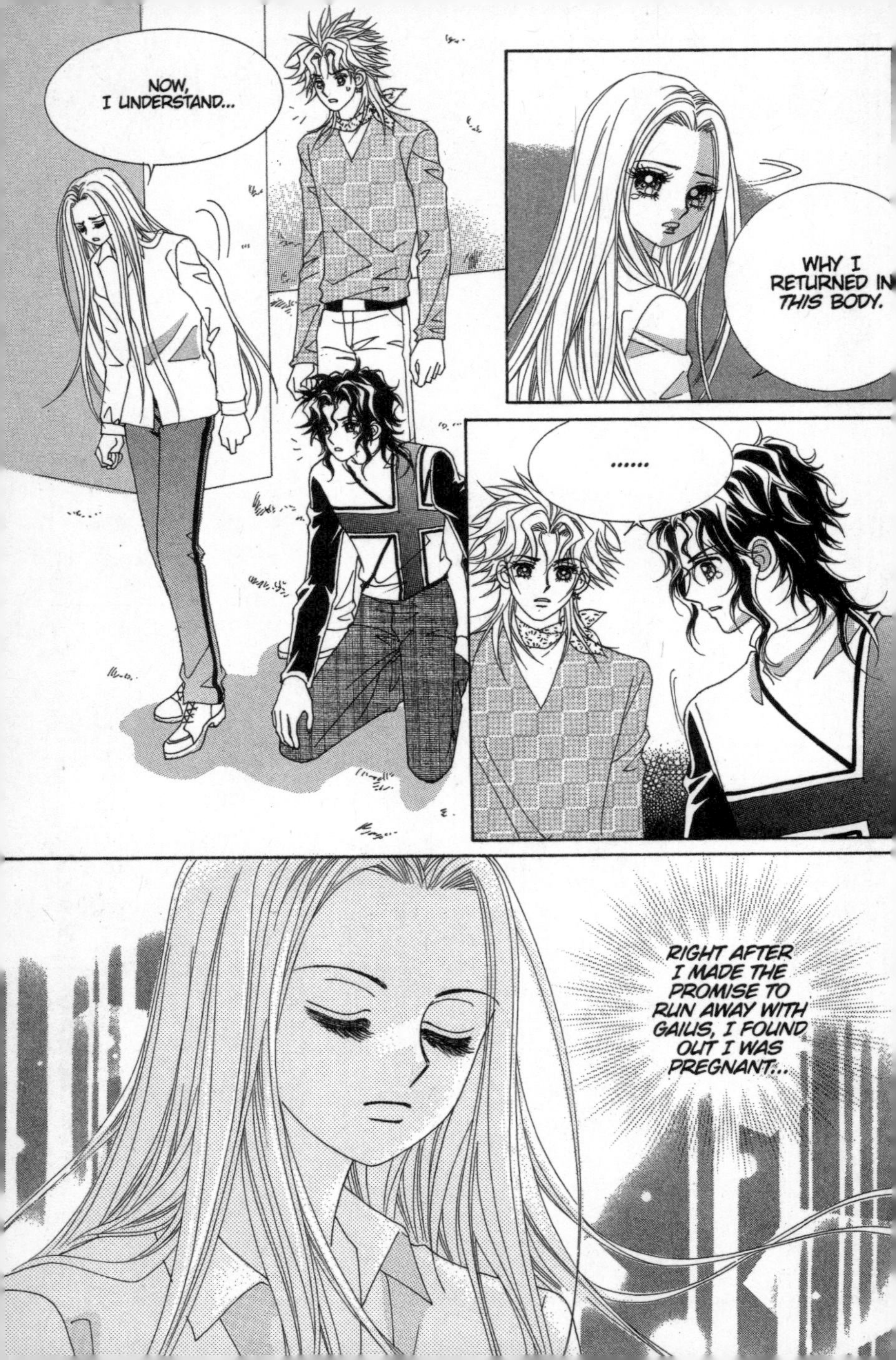
NOW, I UNDERSTAND...
WHY I RETURNED IN *THIS* BODY.
......
RIGHT AFTER I MADE THE PROMISE TO RUN AWAY WITH GAIUS, I FOUND OUT I WAS PREGNANT...

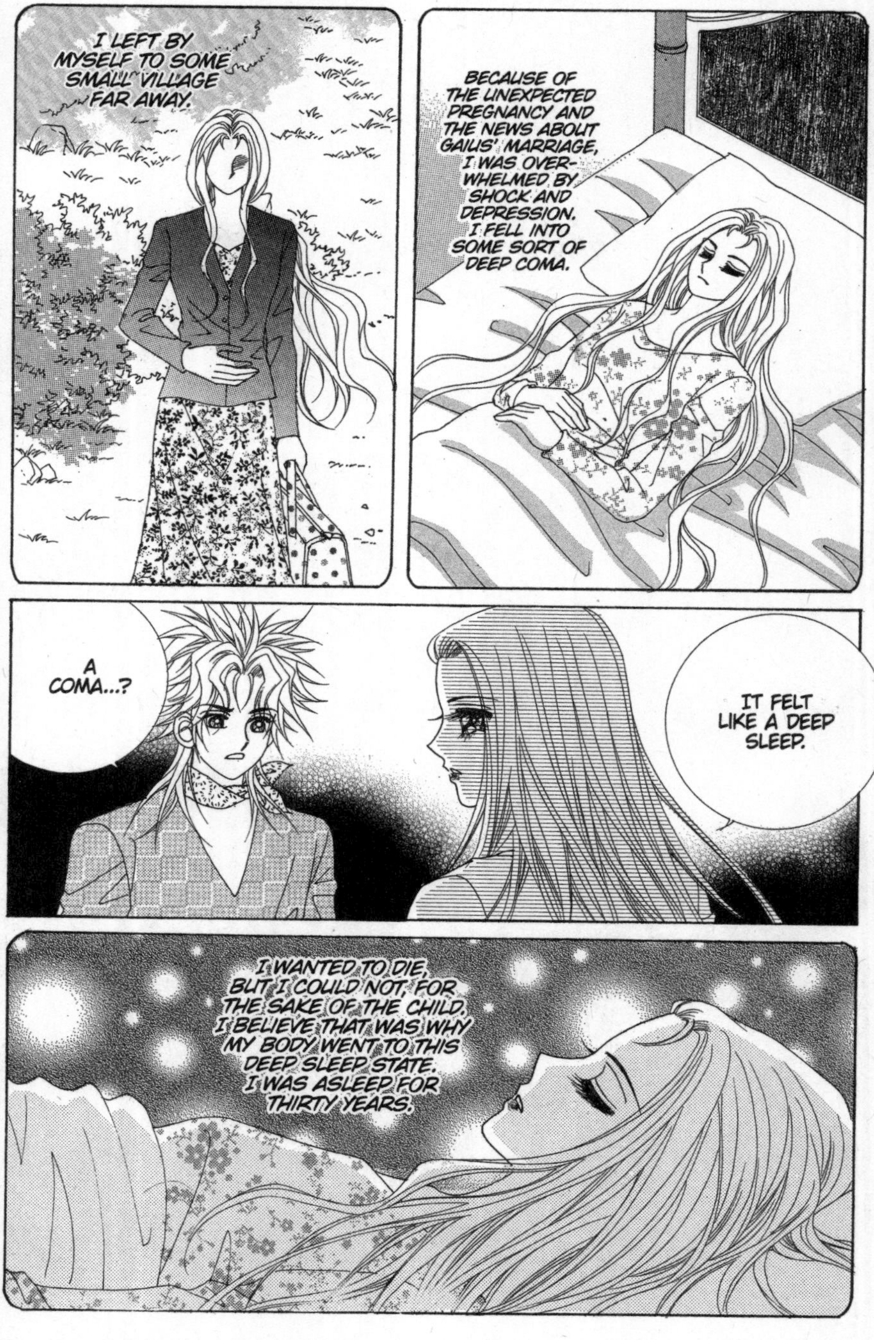
I LEFT BY MYSELF TO SOME SMALL VILLAGE FAR AWAY.
BECAUSE OF THE UNEXPECTED PREGNANCY AND THE NEWS ABOUT GAILIS' MARRIAGE, I WAS OVER-WHELMED BY SHOCK AND DEPRESSION. I FELL INTO SOME SORT OF DEEP COMA.
A COMA...?
IT FELT LIKE A DEEP SLEEP.
I WANTED TO DIE, BUT I COULD NOT, FOR THE SAKE OF THE CHILD. I BELIEVE THAT WAS WHY MY BODY WENT TO THIS DEEP SLEEP STATE. I WAS ASLEEP FOR THIRTY YEARS.

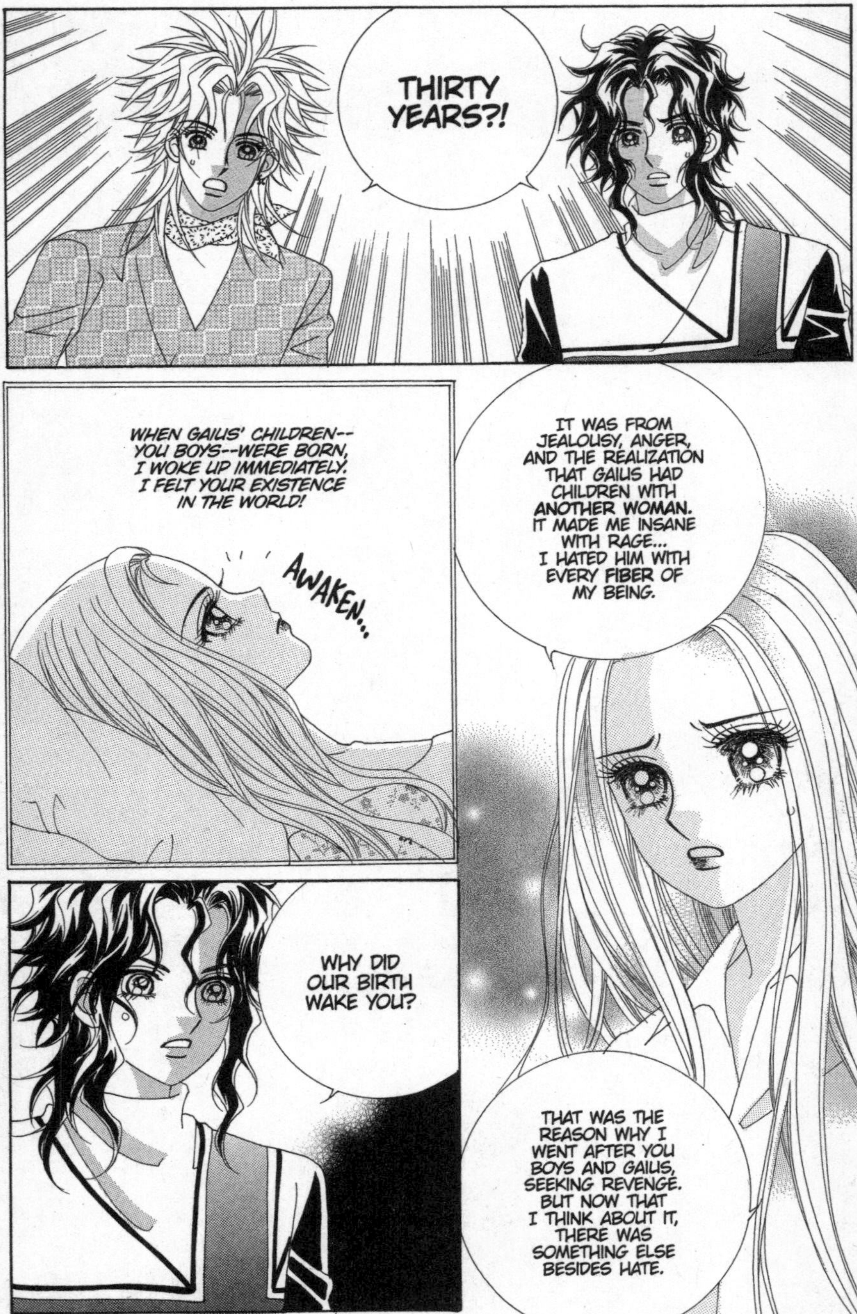
THIRTY YEARS?!
WHEN GAIUS' CHILDREN-- YOU BOYS--WERE BORN, I WOKE UP IMMEDIATELY. I FELT YOUR EXISTENCE IN THE WORLD!
AWAKEN...
WHY DID OUR BIRTH WAKE YOU?
IT WAS FROM JEALOUSY, ANGER, AND THE REALIZATION THAT GAIUS HAD CHILDREN WITH ANOTHER WOMAN. IT MADE ME INSANE WITH RAGE... I HATED HIM WITH EVERY FIBER OF MY BEING.
THAT WAS THE REASON WHY I WENT AFTER YOU BOYS AND GAIUS, SEEKING REVENGE. BUT NOW THAT I THINK ABOUT IT, THERE WAS SOMETHING ELSE BESIDES HATE.

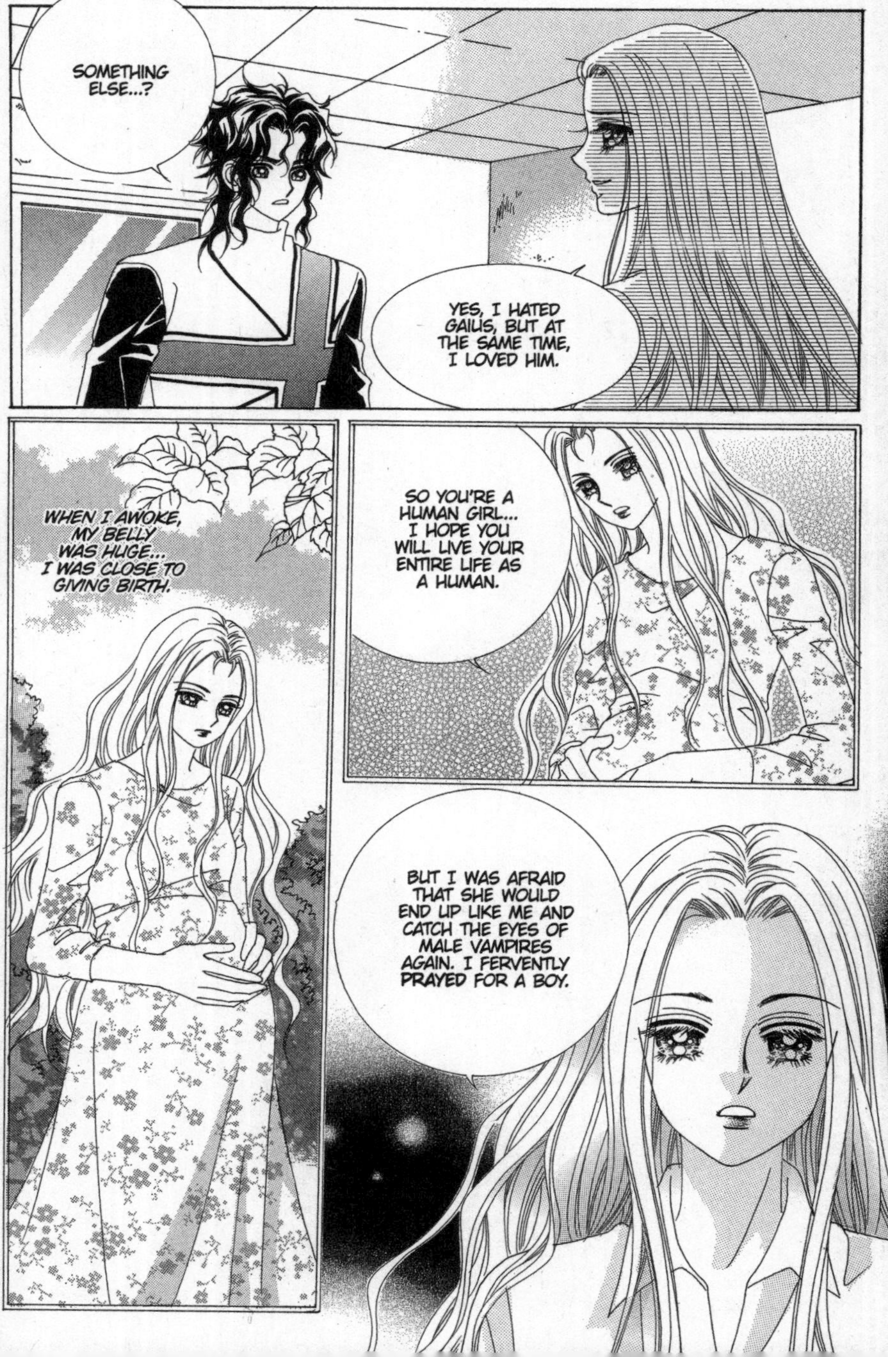
SOMETHING ELSE...?
YES, I HATED GAIUS, BUT AT THE SAME TIME, I LOVED HIM.
WHEN I AWOKE, MY BELLY WAS HUGE... I WAS CLOSE TO GIVING BIRTH.
SO YOU'RE A HUMAN GIRL... I HOPE YOU WILL LIVE YOUR ENTIRE LIFE AS A HUMAN.
BUT I WAS AFRAID THAT SHE WOULD END UP LIKE ME AND CATCH THE EYES OF MALE VAMPIRES AGAIN. I FERVENTLY PRAYED FOR A BOY.

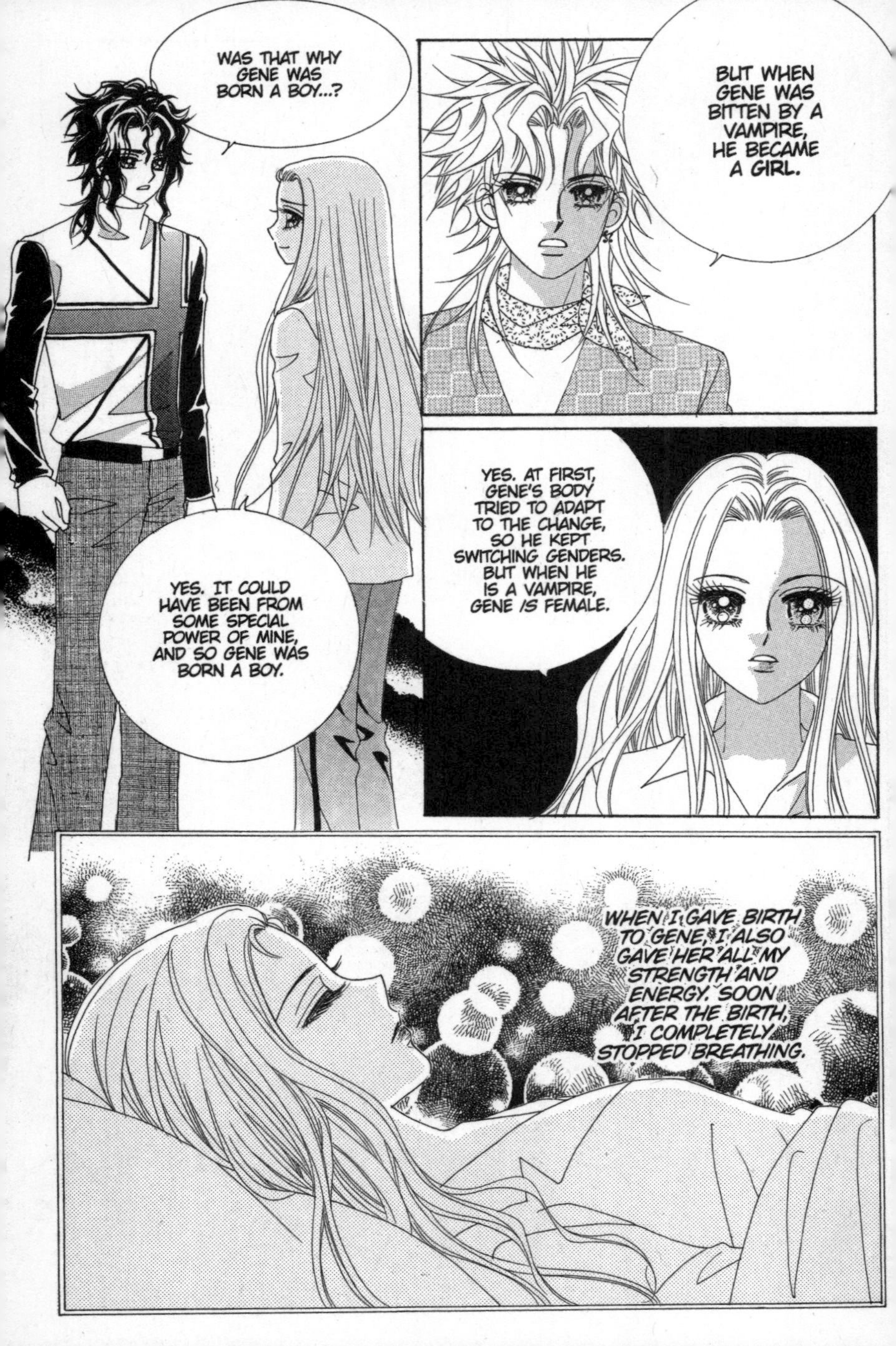
WAS THAT WHY GENE WAS BORN A BOY...?
YES. IT COULD HAVE BEEN FROM SOME SPECIAL POWER OF MINE, AND SO GENE WAS BORN A BOY.
BUT WHEN GENE WAS BITTEN BY A VAMPIRE, HE BECAME A GIRL.
YES. AT FIRST, GENE'S BODY TRIED TO ADAPT TO THE CHANGE, SO HE KEPT SWITCHING GENDERS. BUT WHEN HE IS A VAMPIRE, GENE *IS* FEMALE.
WHEN I GAVE BIRTH TO GENE, I ALSO GAVE HER ALL MY STRENGTH AND ENERGY. SOON AFTER THE BIRTH, I COMPLETELY STOPPED BREATHING.

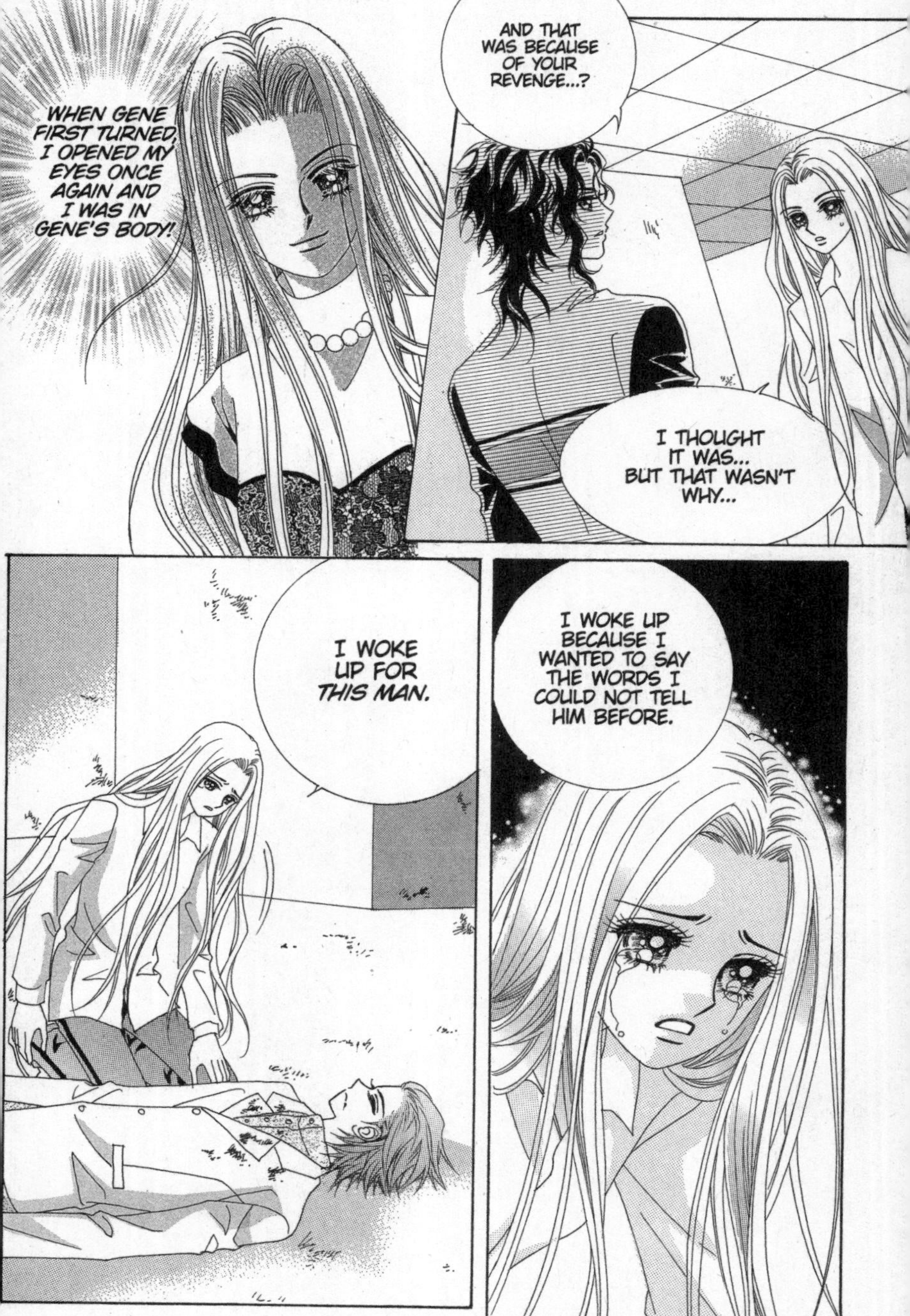
WHEN GENE FIRST TURNED, I OPENED MY EYES ONCE AGAIN AND I WAS IN GENE'S BODY!
AND THAT WAS BECAUSE OF YOUR REVENGE...?
I THOUGHT IT WAS... BUT THAT WASN'T WHY...
I WOKE UP FOR *THIS MAN.*
I WOKE UP BECAUSE I WANTED TO SAY THE WORDS I COULD NOT TELL HIM BEFORE.

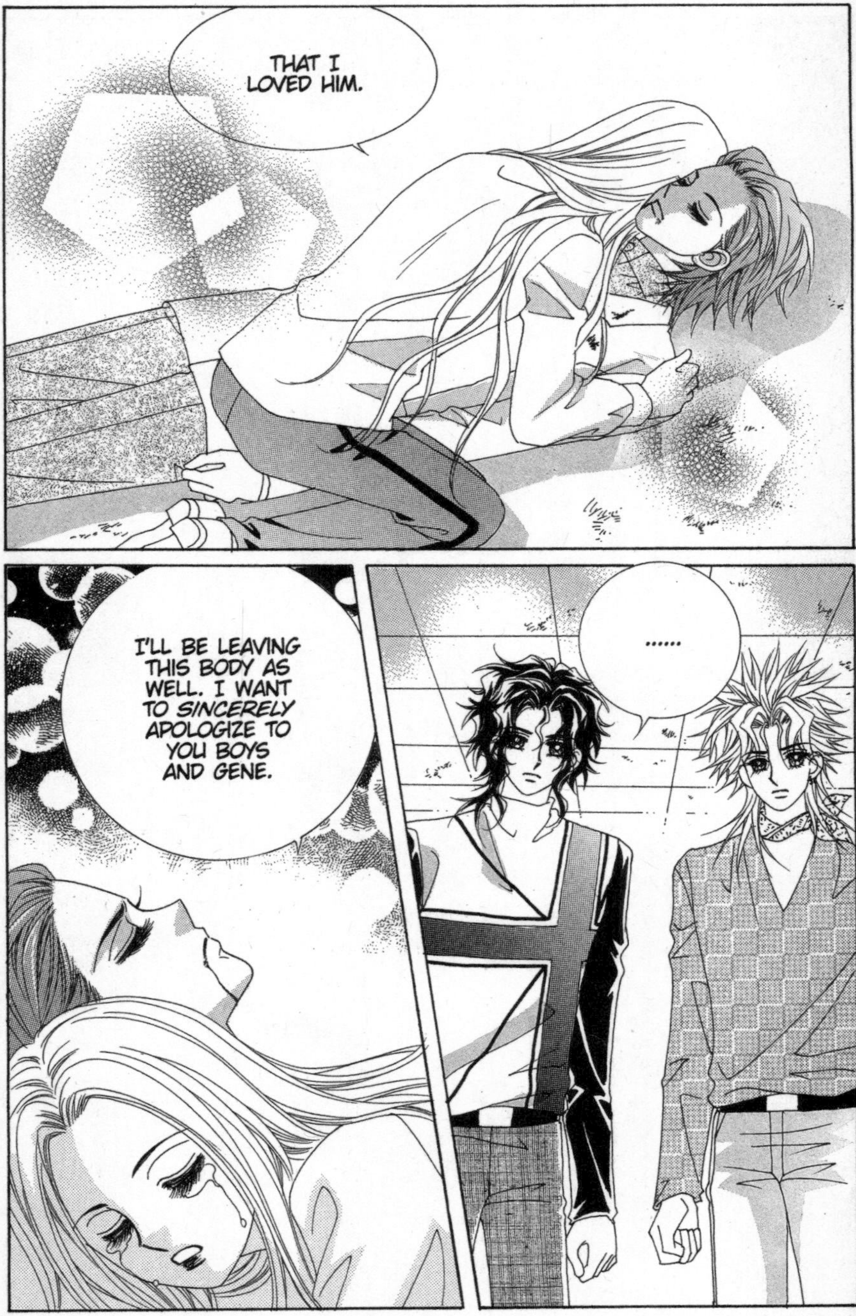
THAT I LOVED HIM.
I'LL BE LEAVING THIS BODY AS WELL. I WANT TO *SINCERELY* APOLOGIZE TO YOU BOYS AND GENE.
......

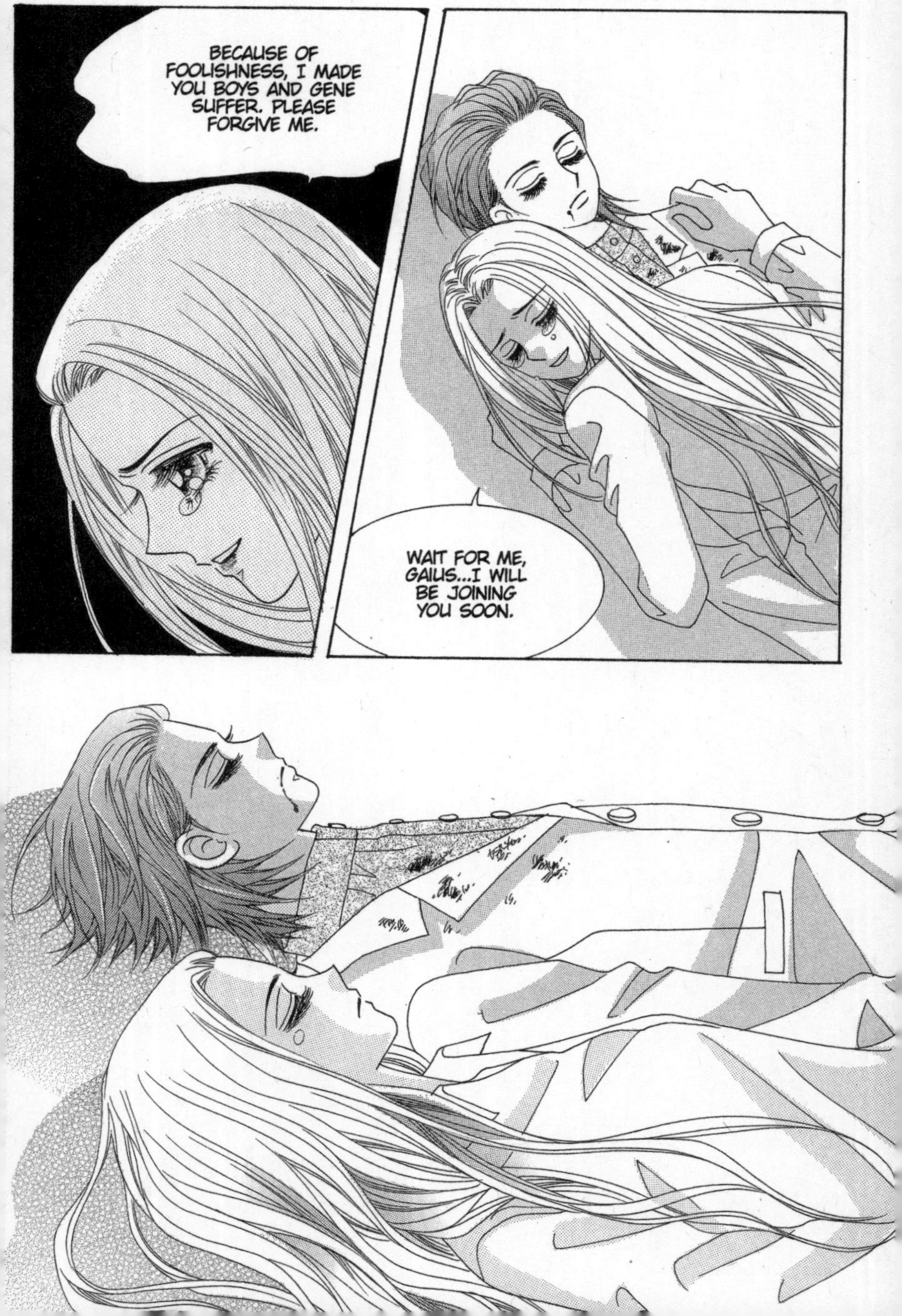
BECAUSE OF FOOLISHNESS, I MADE YOU BOYS AND GENE SUFFER. PLEASE FORGIVE ME.
WAIT FOR ME, GAIUS...I WILL BE JOINING YOU SOON.

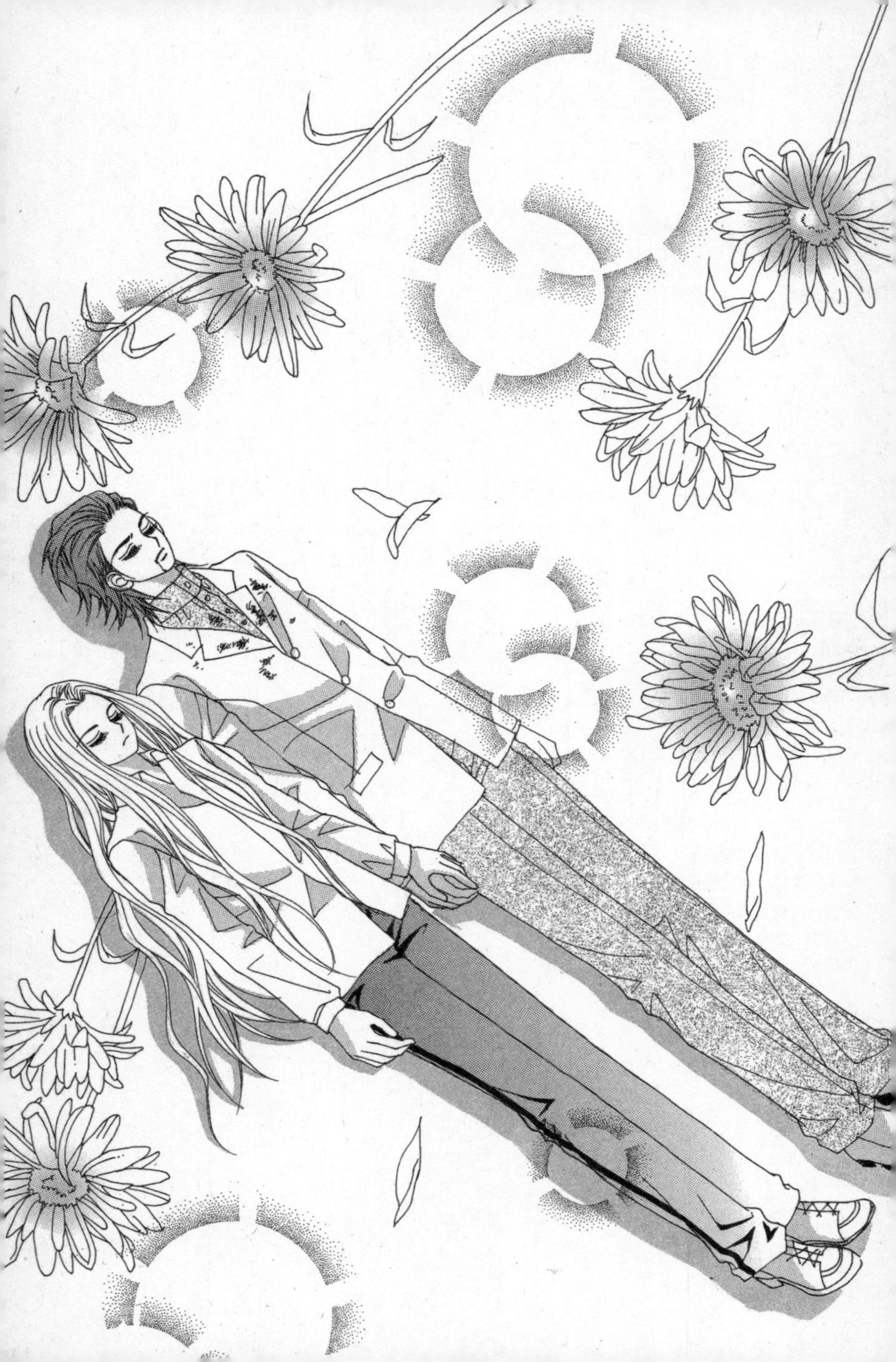

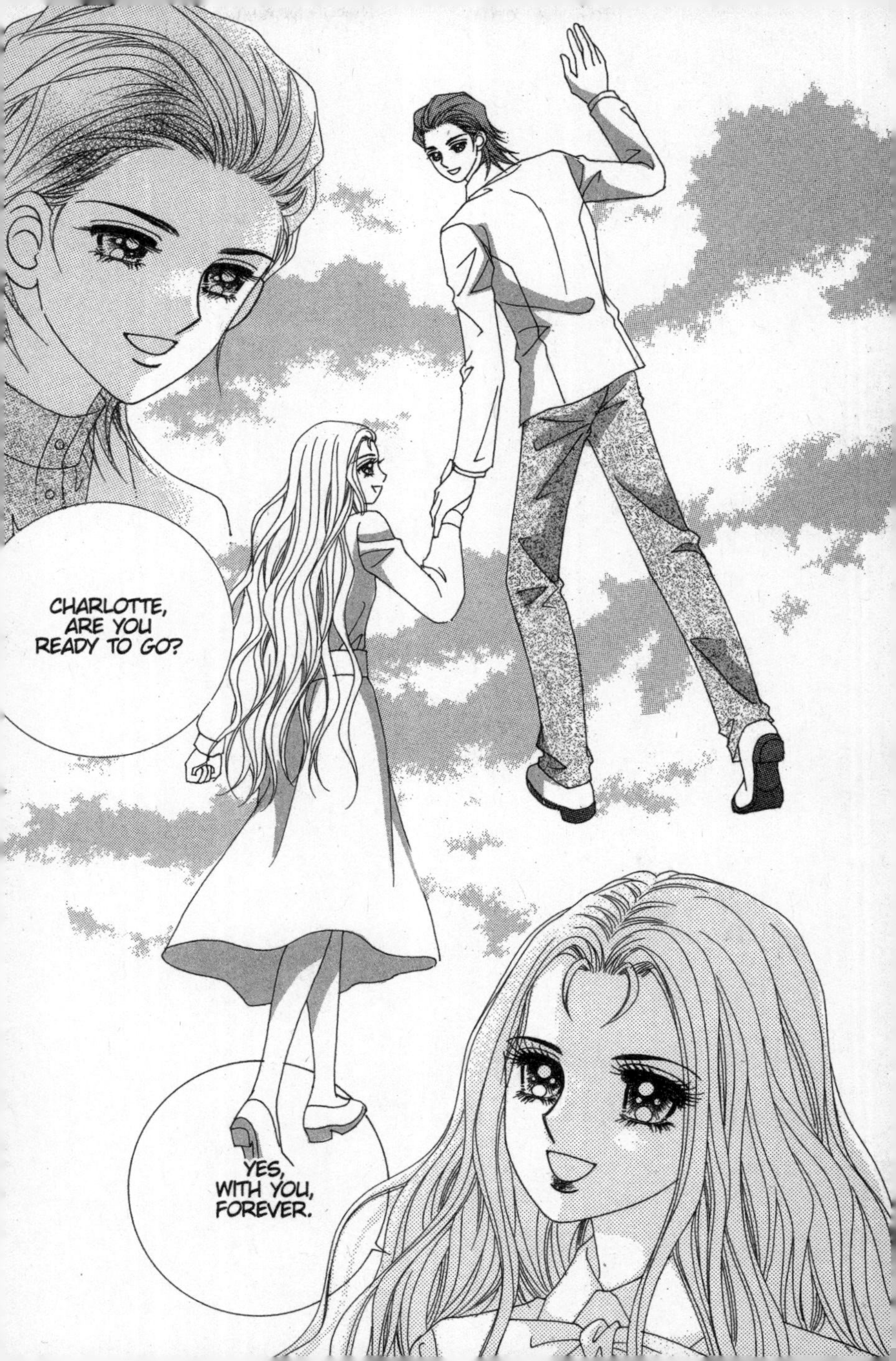
CHARLOTTE, ARE YOU READY TO GO?
YES, WITH YOU, FOREVER.

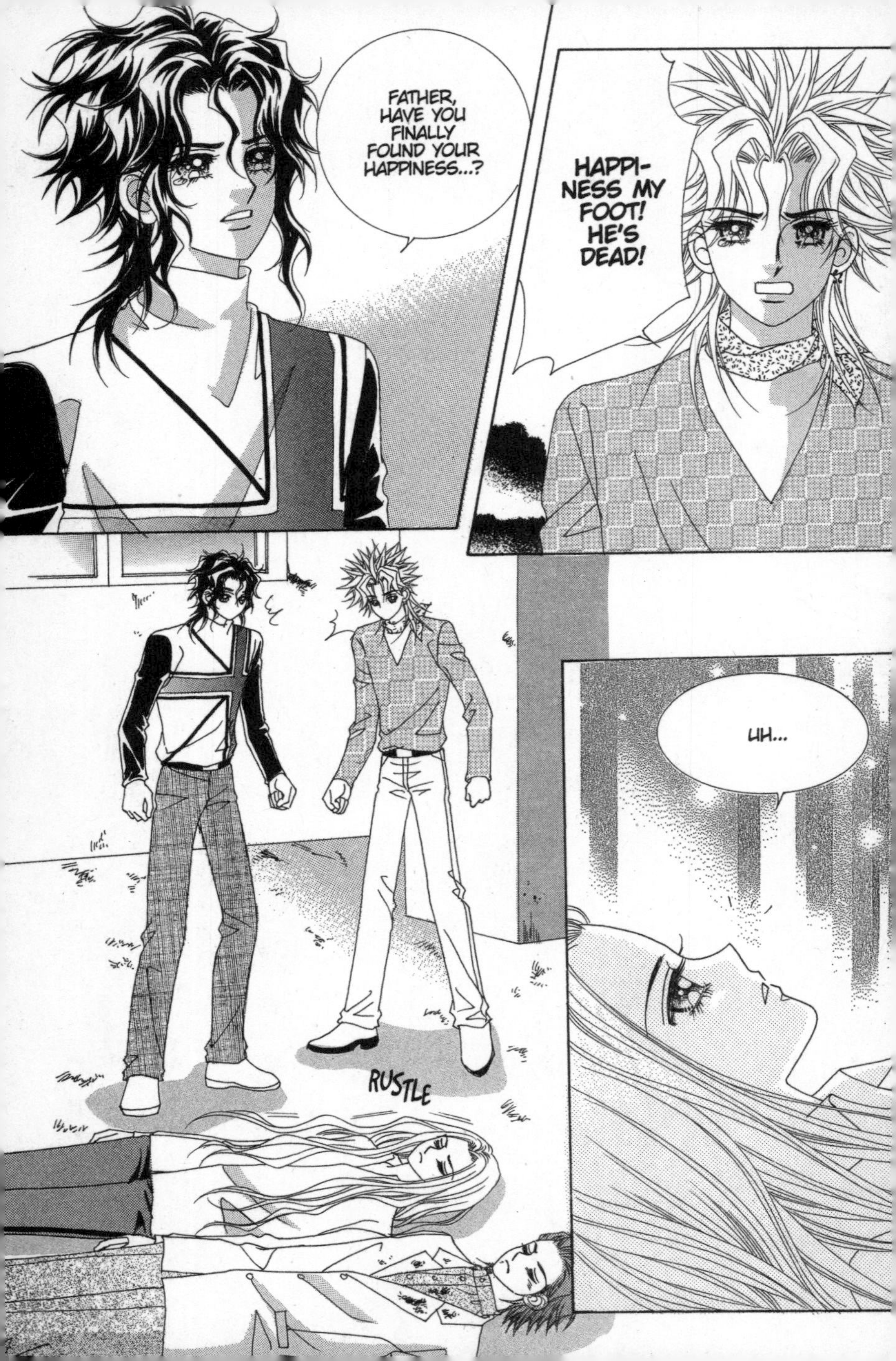

FATHER, HAVE YOU FINALLY FOUND YOUR HAPPINESS...?
HAPPI-NESS MY FOOT! HE'S DEAD!
RUSTLE
UH...

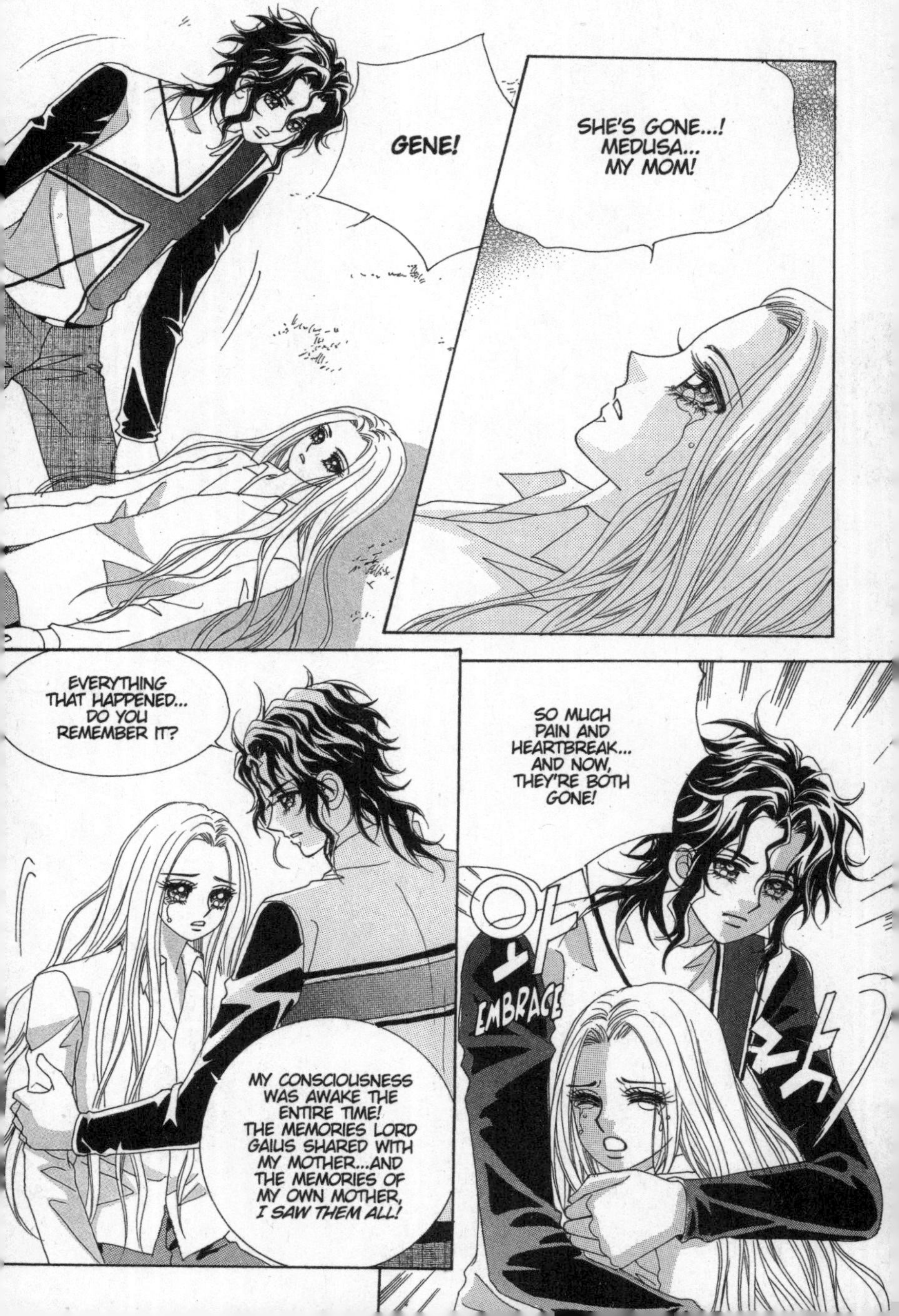
GENE!
SHE'S GONE...! MEDUSA... MY MOM!
EVERYTHING THAT HAPPENED... DO YOU REMEMBER IT?
MY CONSCIOUSNESS WAS AWAKE THE ENTIRE TIME! THE MEMORIES LORD GAIUS SHARED WITH MY MOTHER...AND THE MEMORIES OF MY OWN MOTHER, *I SAW THEM ALL!*
SO MUCH PAIN AND HEARTBREAK... AND NOW, THEY'RE BOTH GONE!
EMBRACE

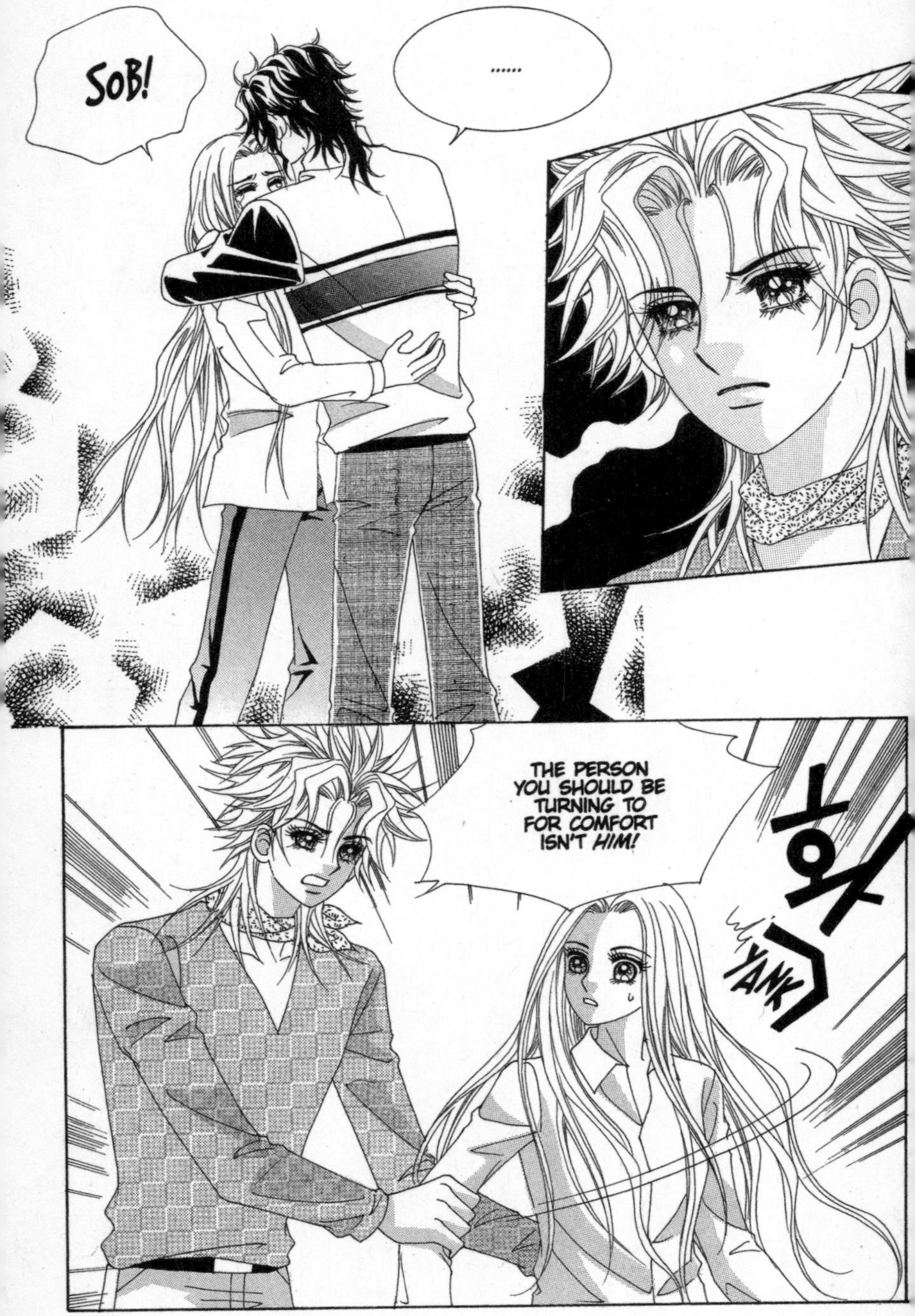
SOB!
......
THE PERSON YOU SHOULD BE TURNING TO FOR COMFORT ISN'T *HIM!*
YANK

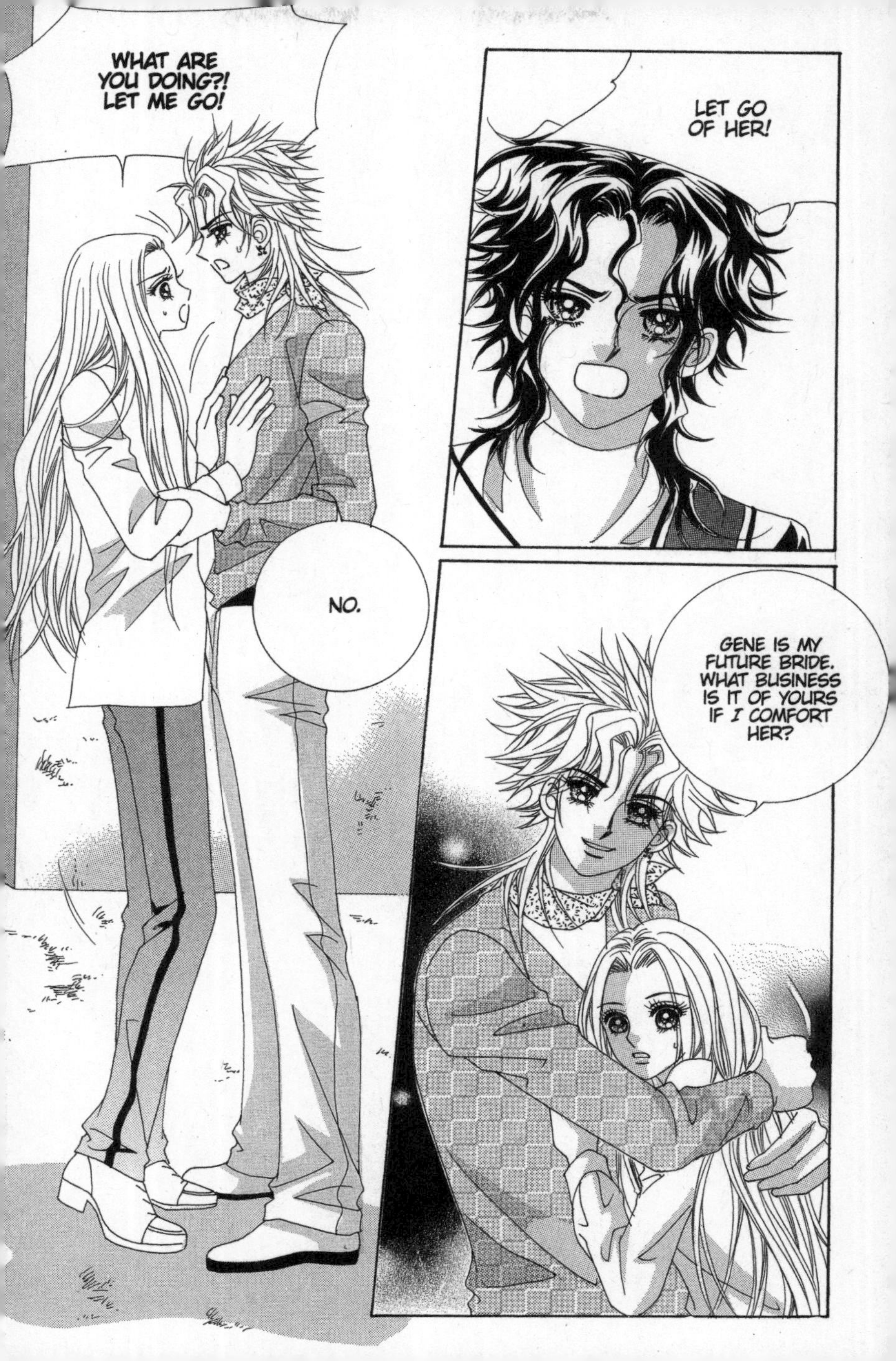
WHAT ARE YOU DOING?! LET ME GO!
NO.
LET GO OF HER!
GENE IS MY FUTURE BRIDE. WHAT BUSINESS IS IT OF YOURS IF *I* COMFORT HER?

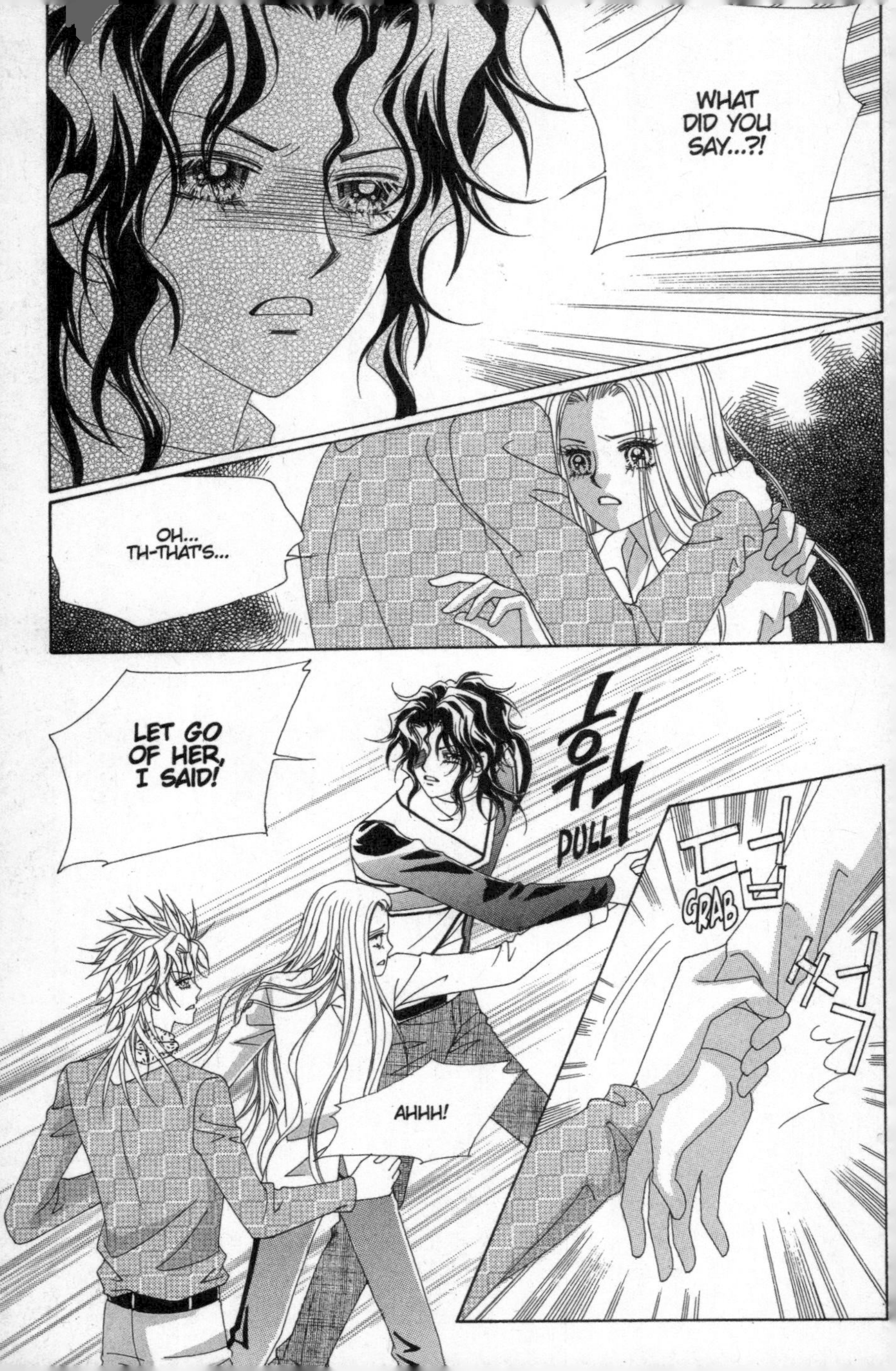
WHAT DID YOU SAY...?!
OH... TH-THAT'S...
LET GO OF HER, I SAID!
휙
PULL
GRAB
AHHH!

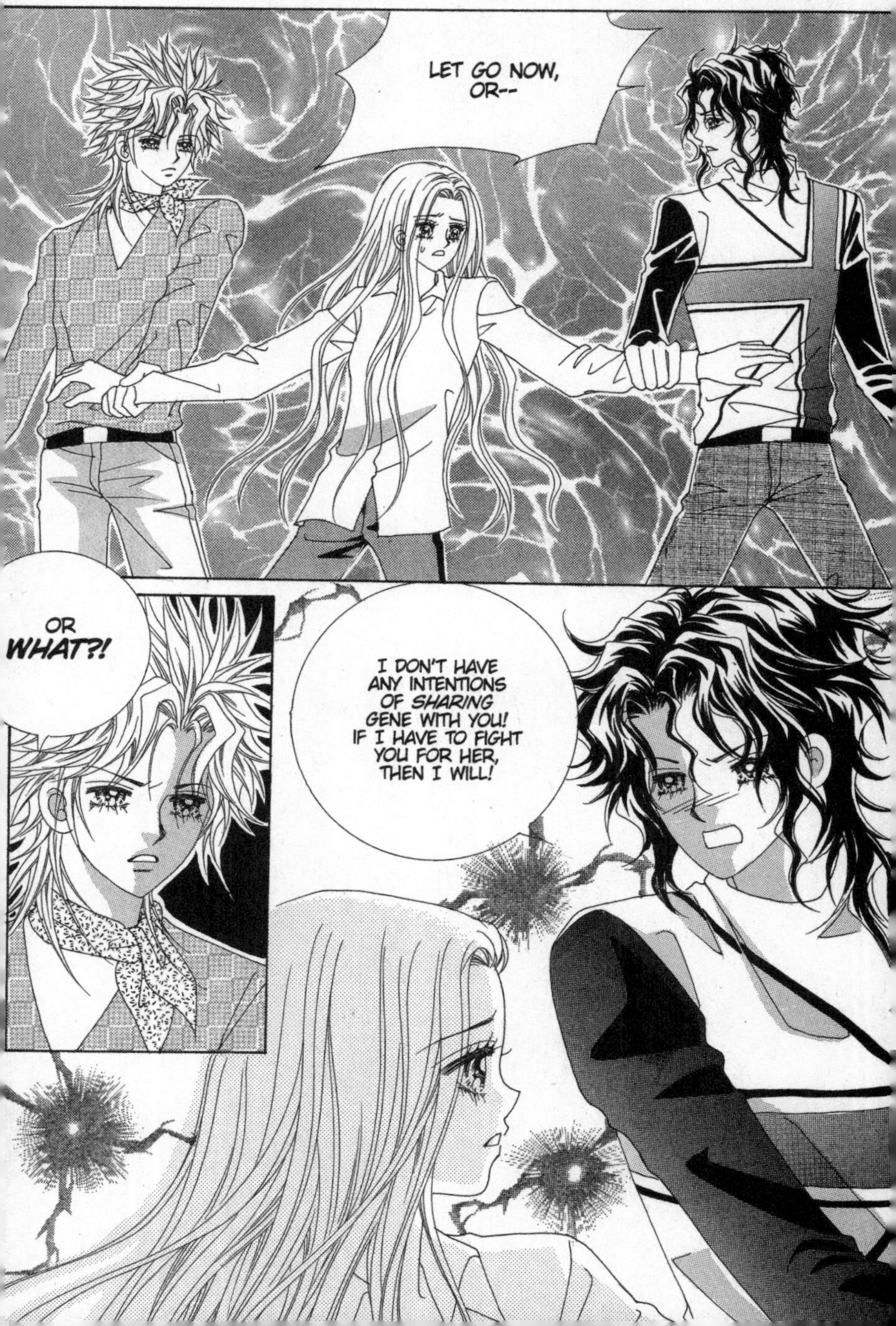
LET GO NOW, OR--
OR WHAT?!
I DON'T HAVE ANY INTENTIONS OF SHARING GENE WITH YOU! IF I HAVE TO FIGHT YOU FOR HER, THEN I WILL!

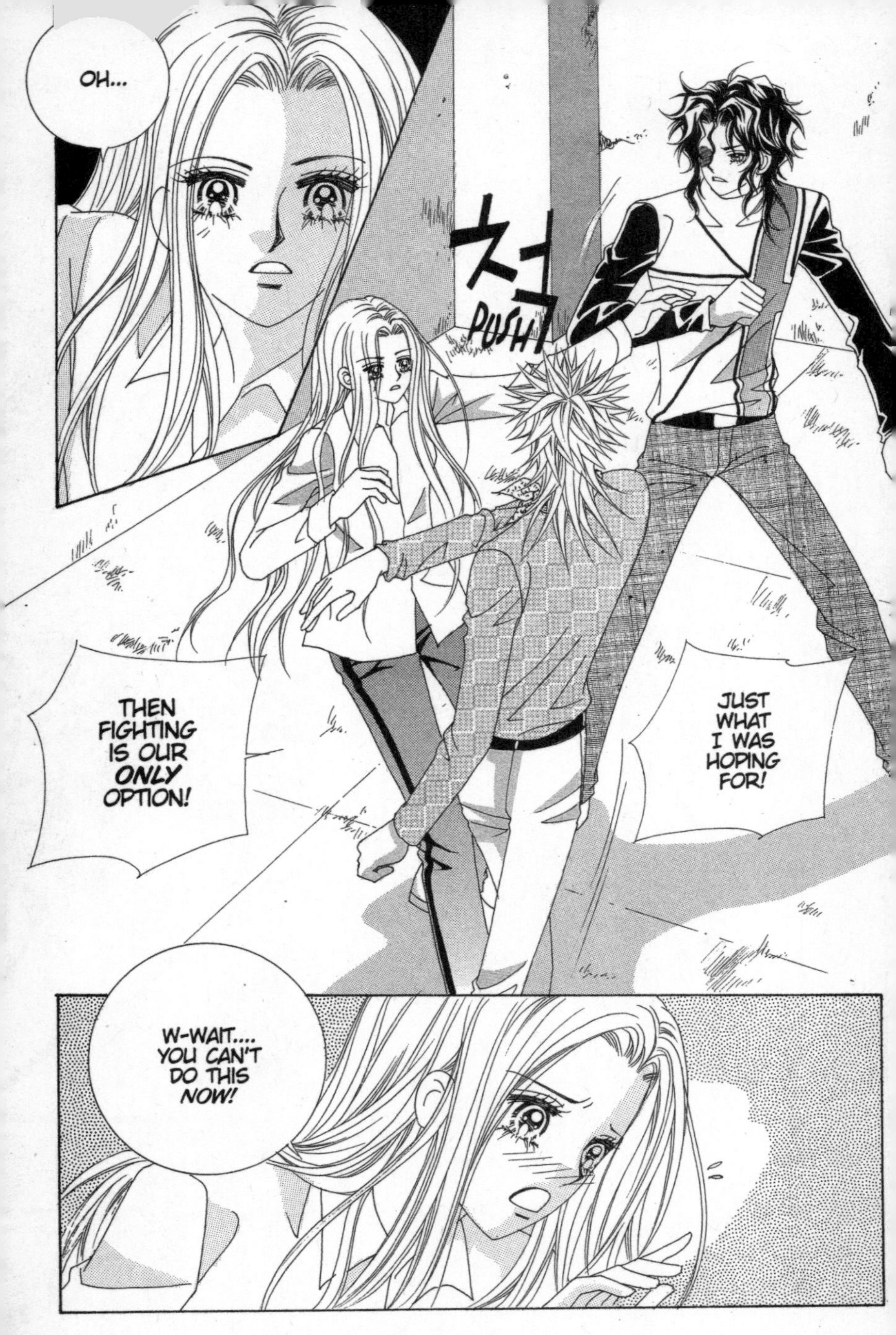

OH...
척
PUSH
THEN FIGHTING IS OUR *ONLY* OPTION!
JUST WHAT I WAS HOPING FOR!
W-WAIT.... YOU CAN'T DO THIS *NOW!*

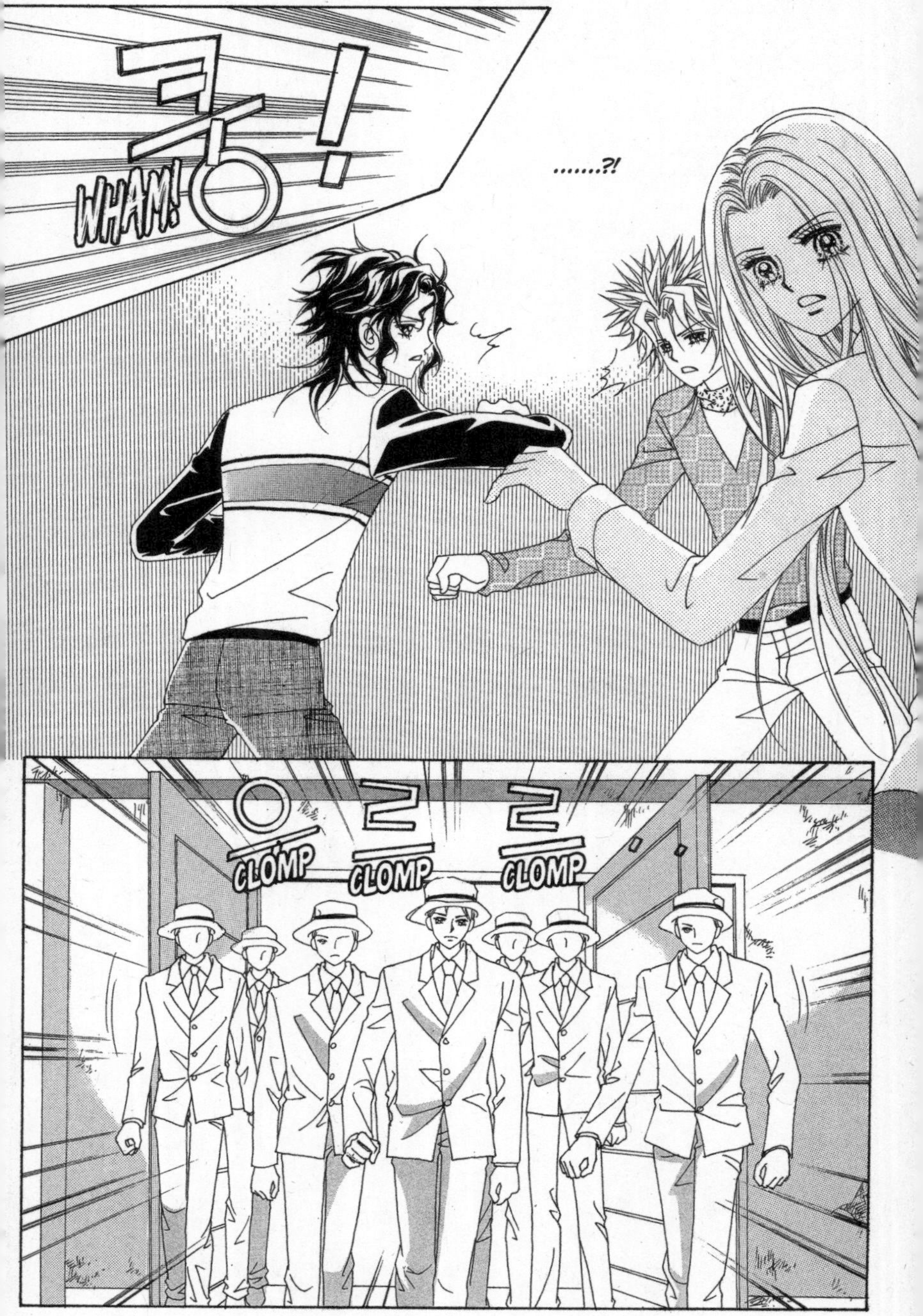
WHAM!
.......?!
CLOMP
CLOMP
CLOMP

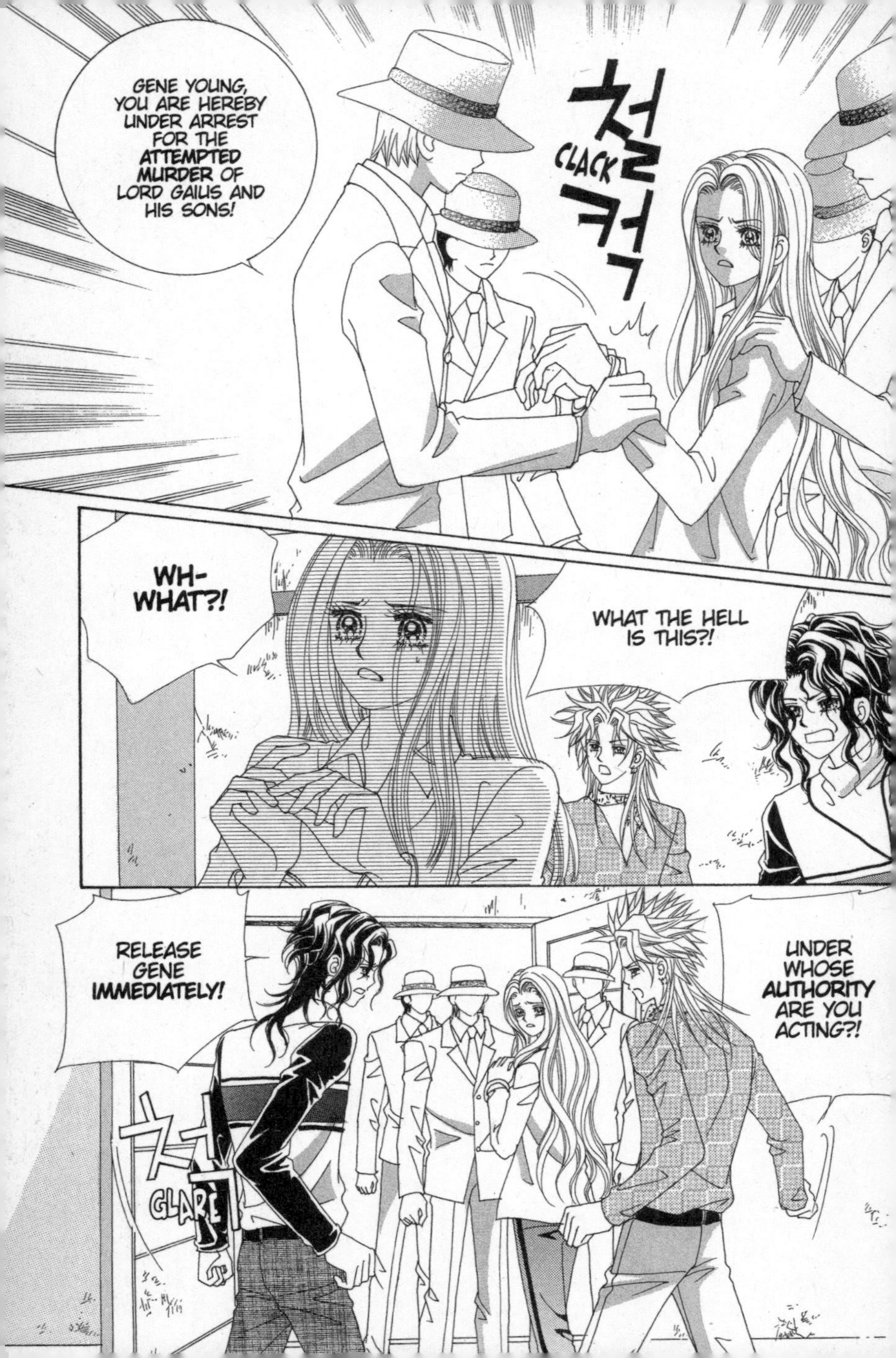
GENE YOUNG, YOU ARE HEREBY UNDER ARREST FOR THE ATTEMPTED MURDER OF LORD GAIUS AND HIS SONS!
철컥
CLACK
WH- WHAT?!
WHAT THE HELL IS THIS?!
RELEASE GENE IMMEDIATELY!
UNDER WHOSE AUTHORITY ARE YOU ACTING?!
GLARE

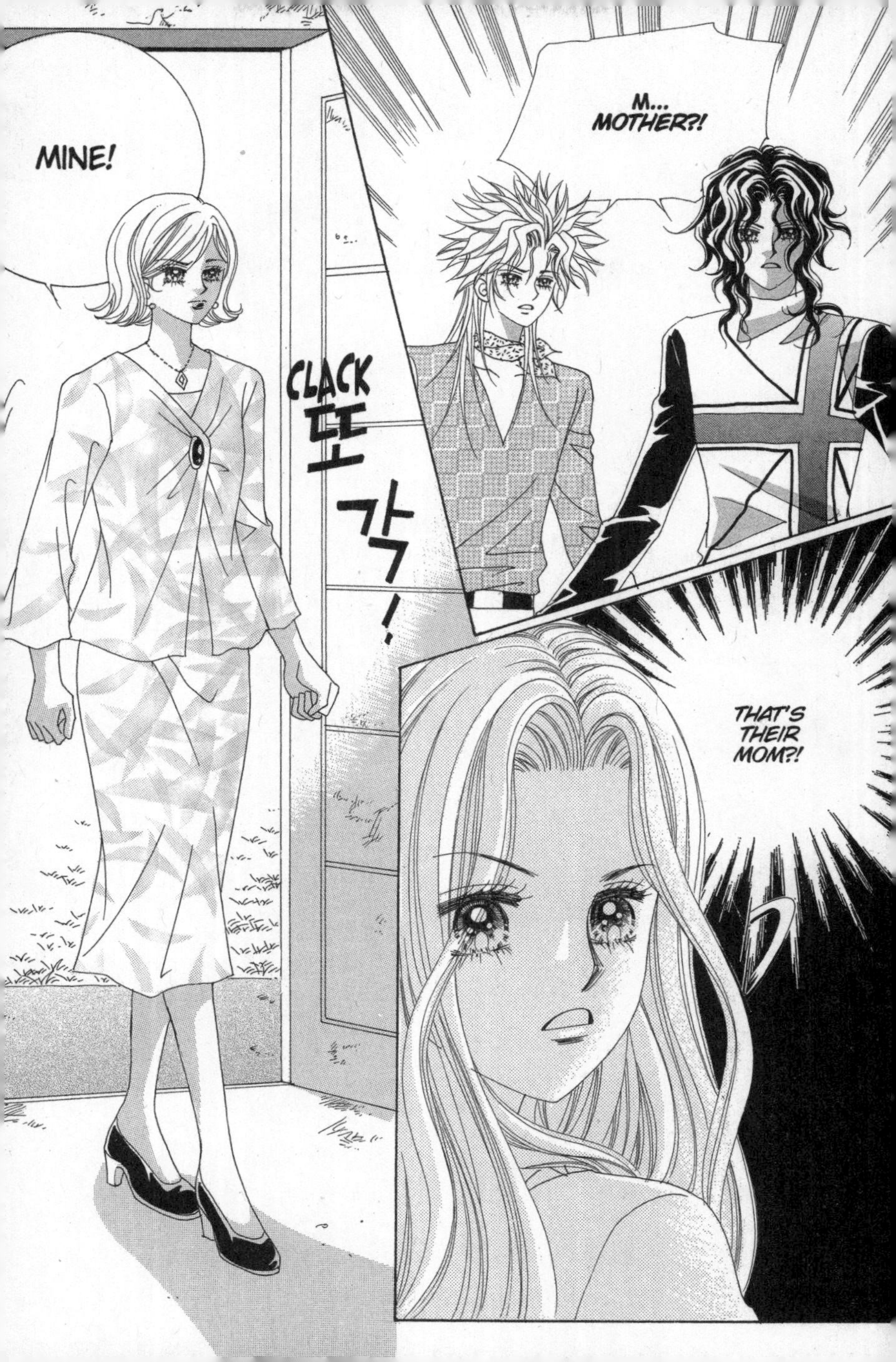
MINE!
CLACK
또각!
M... MOTHER?!
THAT'S THEIR MOM?!

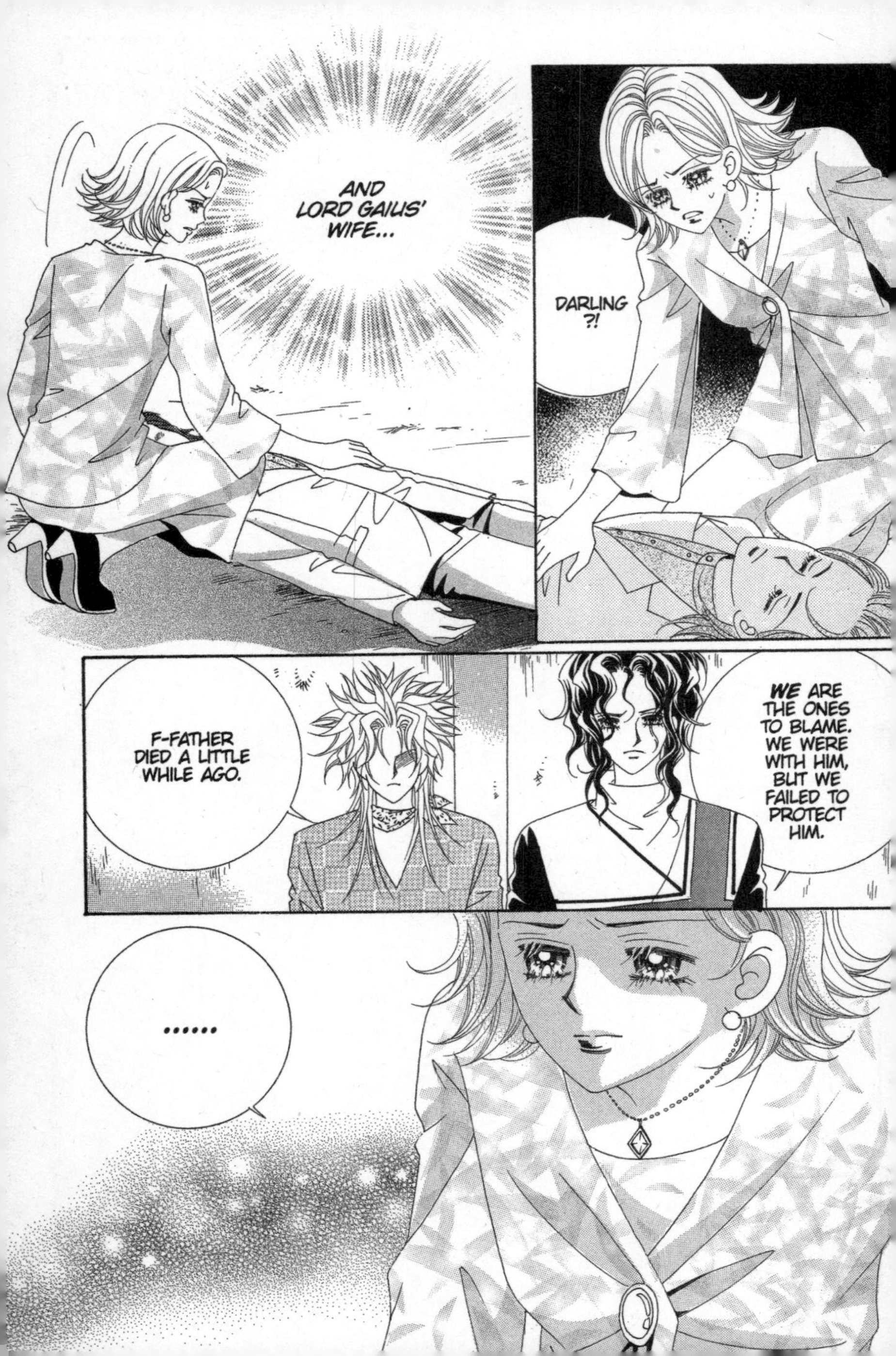
AND LORD GAIUS' WIFE...
DARLING ?!
F-FATHER DIED A LITTLE WHILE AGO.
WE ARE THE ONES TO BLAME. WE WERE WITH HIM, BUT WE FAILED TO PROTECT HIM.
......

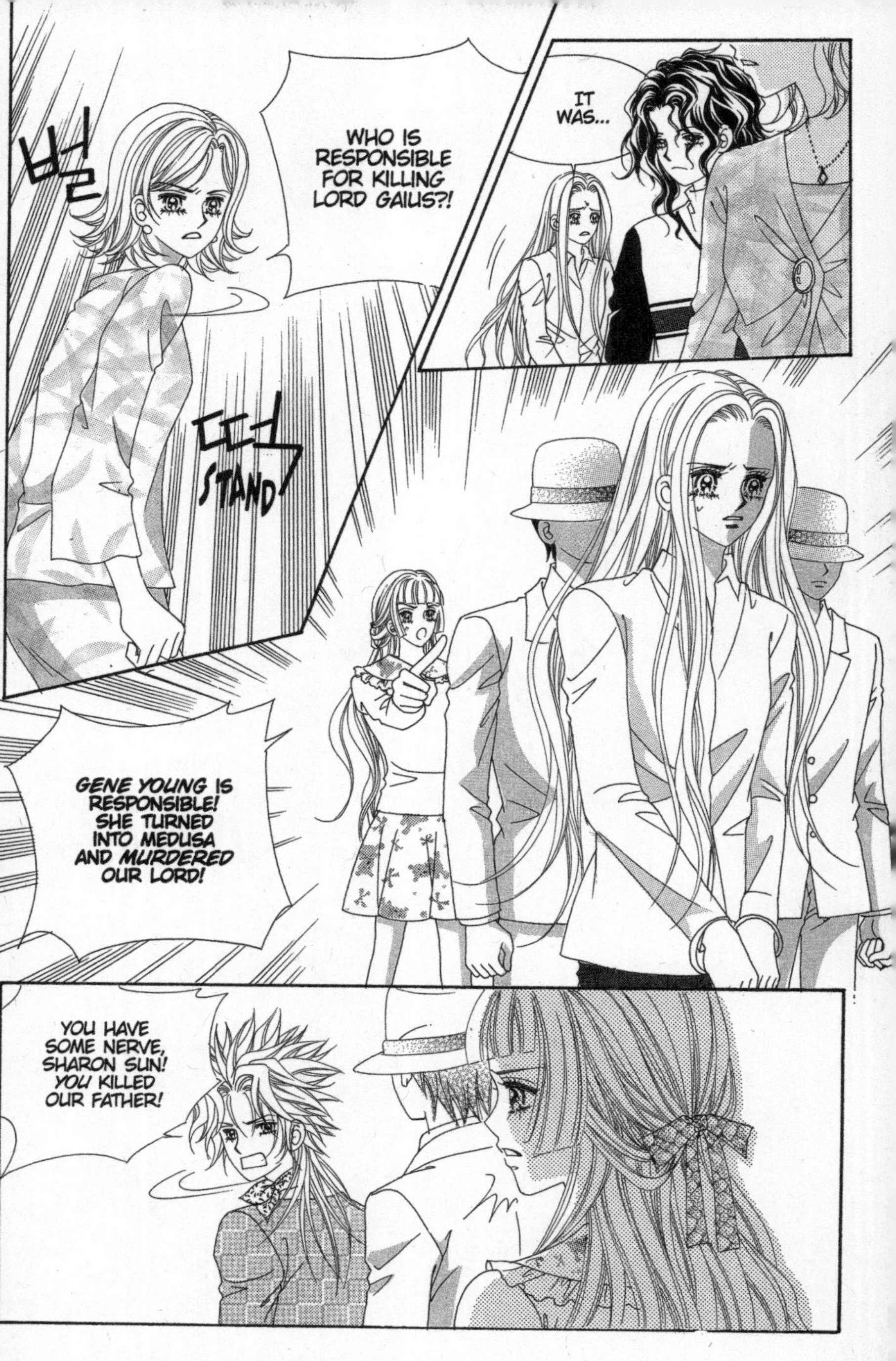
WHO IS RESPONSIBLE FOR KILLING LORD GAIUS?!
STAND
IT WAS...
GENE YOUNG IS RESPONSIBLE! SHE TURNED INTO MEDUSA AND MURDERED OUR LORD!
YOU HAVE SOME NERVE, SHARON SUN! YOU KILLED OUR FATHER!

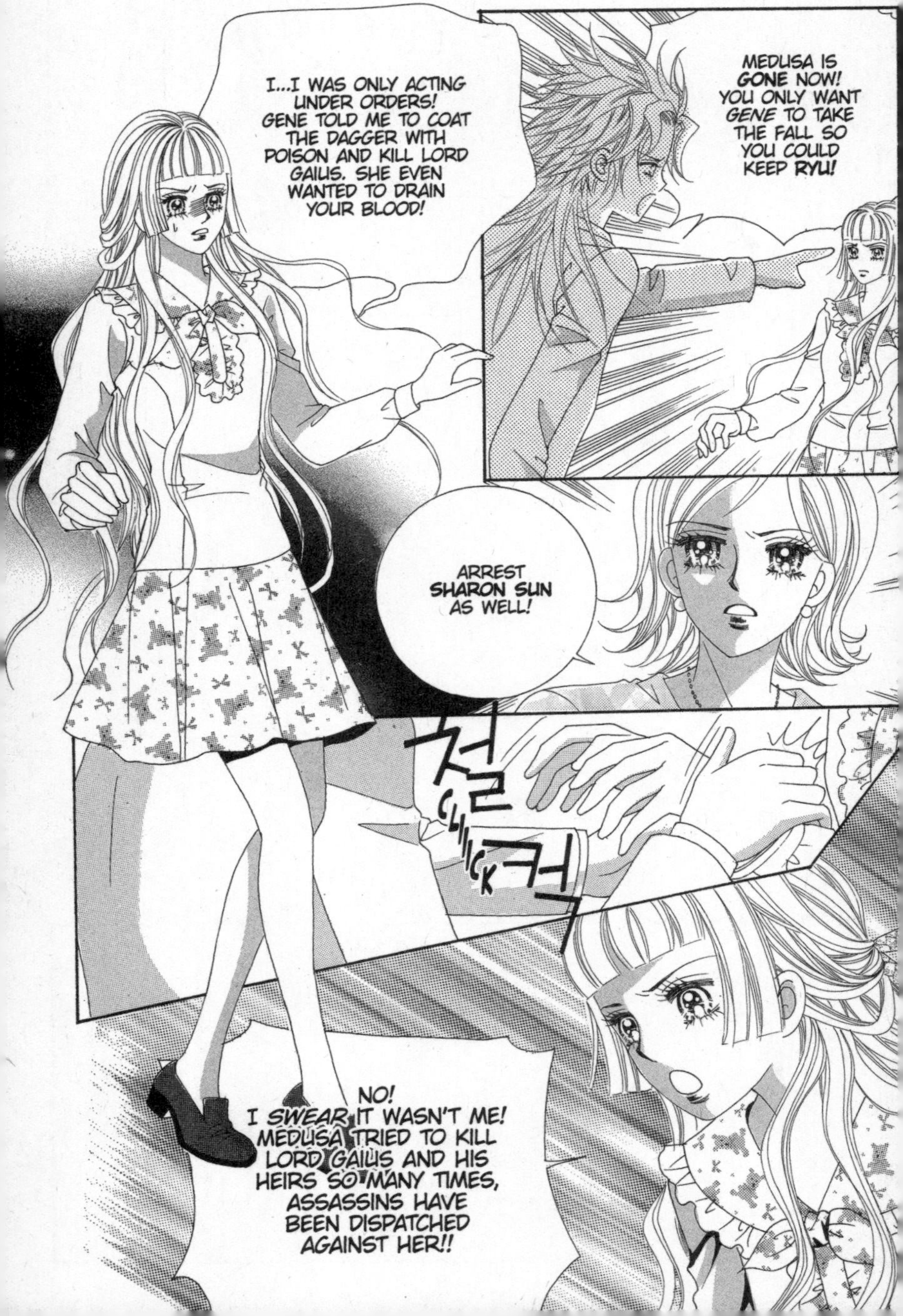
I...I WAS ONLY ACTING UNDER ORDERS! GENE TOLD ME TO COAT THE DAGGER WITH POISON AND KILL LORD GAIUS. SHE EVEN WANTED TO DRAIN YOUR BLOOD!
MEDUSA IS GONE NOW! YOU ONLY WANT GENE TO TAKE THE FALL SO YOU COULD KEEP RYU!
ARREST SHARON SUN AS WELL!
철컥
CLIICK
NO! I SWEAR IT WASN'T ME! MEDUSA TRIED TO KILL LORD GAIUS AND HIS HEIRS SO MANY TIMES, ASSASSINS HAVE BEEN DISPATCHED AGAINST HER!!

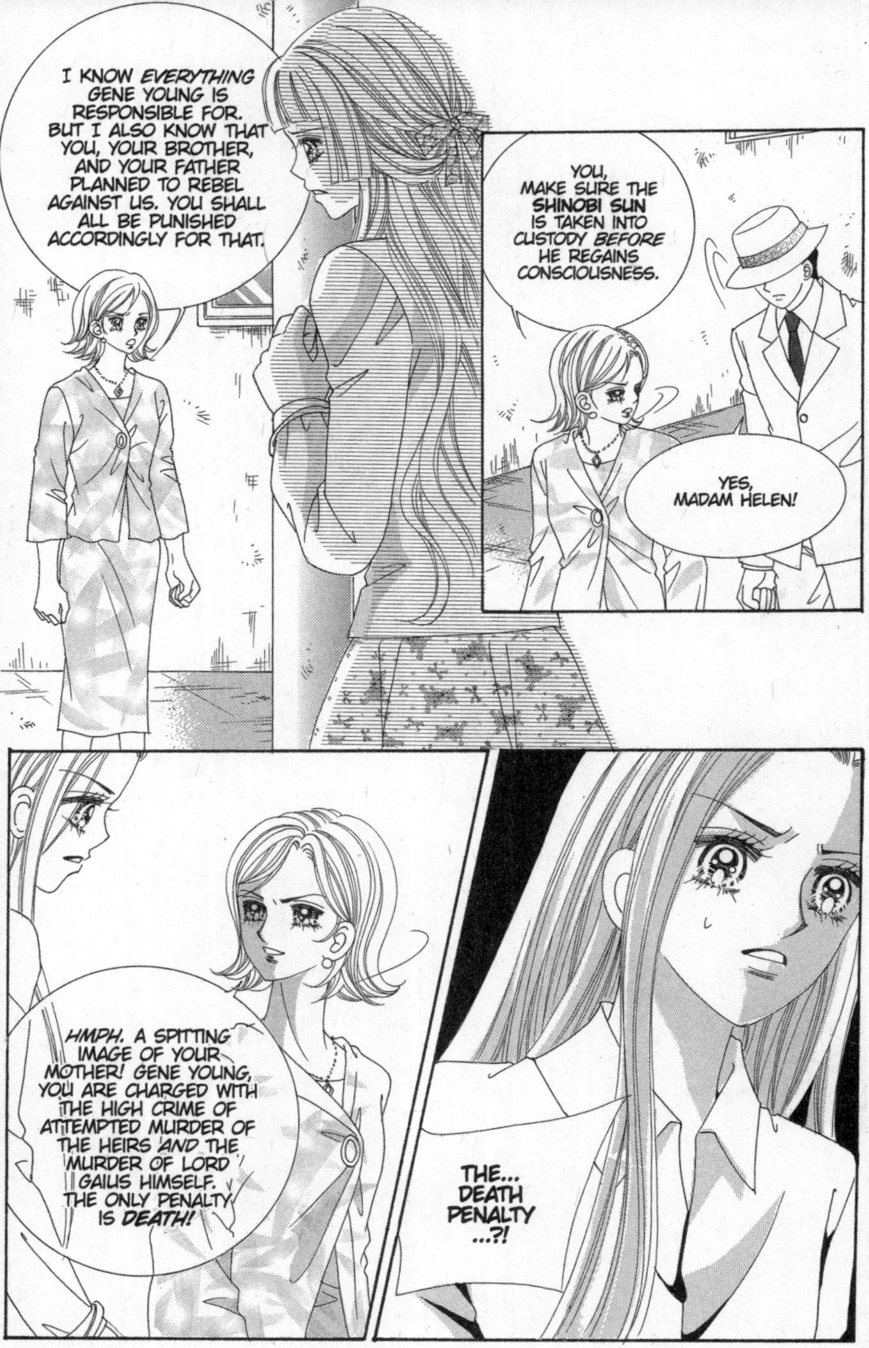
I KNOW *EVERYTHING* GENE YOUNG IS RESPONSIBLE FOR. BUT I ALSO KNOW THAT YOU, YOUR BROTHER, AND YOUR FATHER PLANNED TO REBEL AGAINST US. YOU SHALL ALL BE PUNISHED ACCORDINGLY FOR THAT.
YOU, MAKE SURE THE **SHINOBI SUN** IS TAKEN INTO CUSTODY *BEFORE* HE REGAINS CONSCIOUSNESS.
YES, MADAM HELEN!
HMPH. A SPITTING IMAGE OF YOUR MOTHER! GENE YOUNG, YOU ARE CHARGED WITH THE HIGH CRIME OF ATTEMPTED MURDER OF THE HEIRS *AND* THE MURDER OF LORD GAIUS HIMSELF. THE ONLY PENALTY IS ***DEATH!***
THE... DEATH PENALTY ...?!

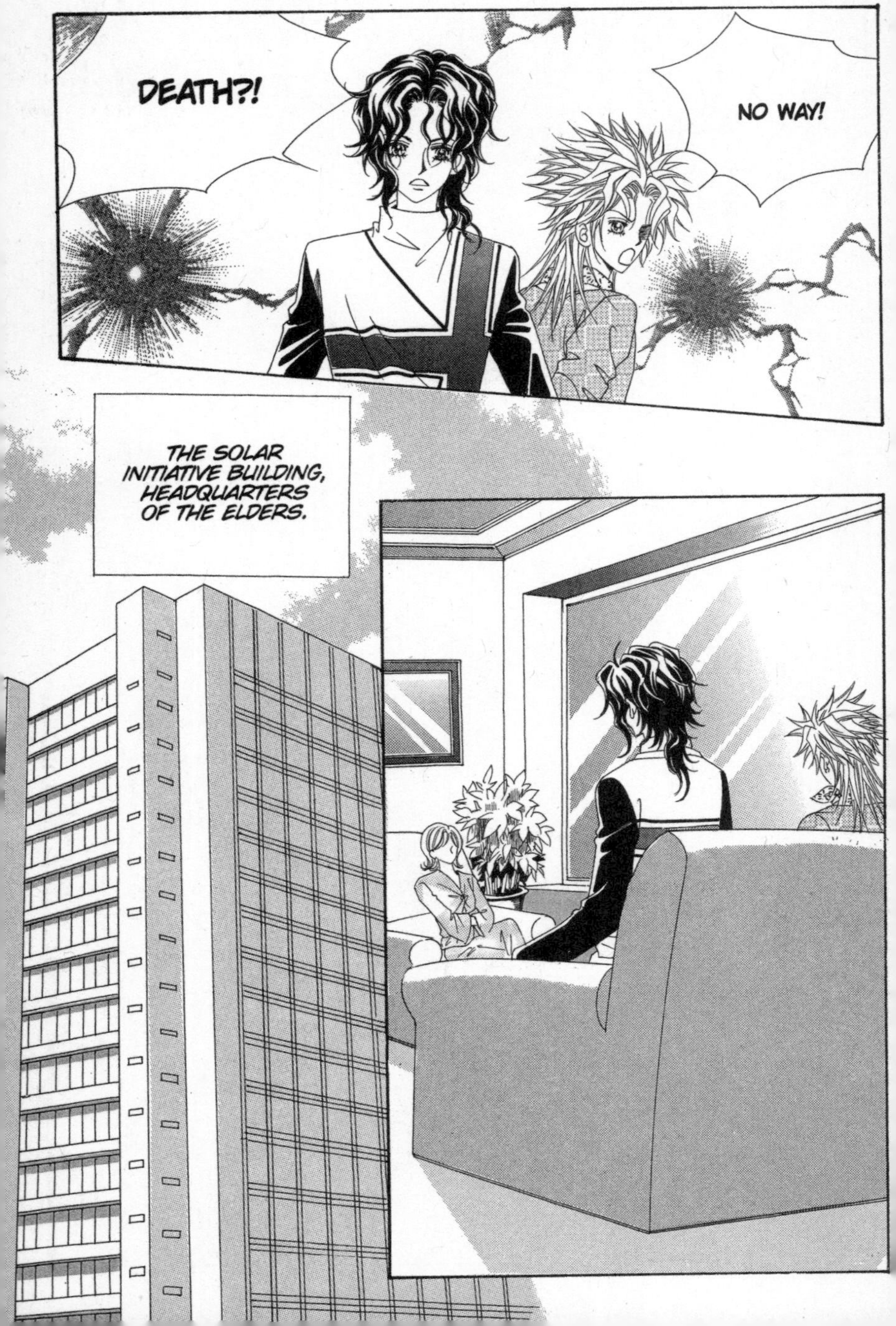
DEATH?!
NO WAY!
THE SOLAR INITIATIVE BUILDING, HEADQUARTERS OF THE ELDERS.

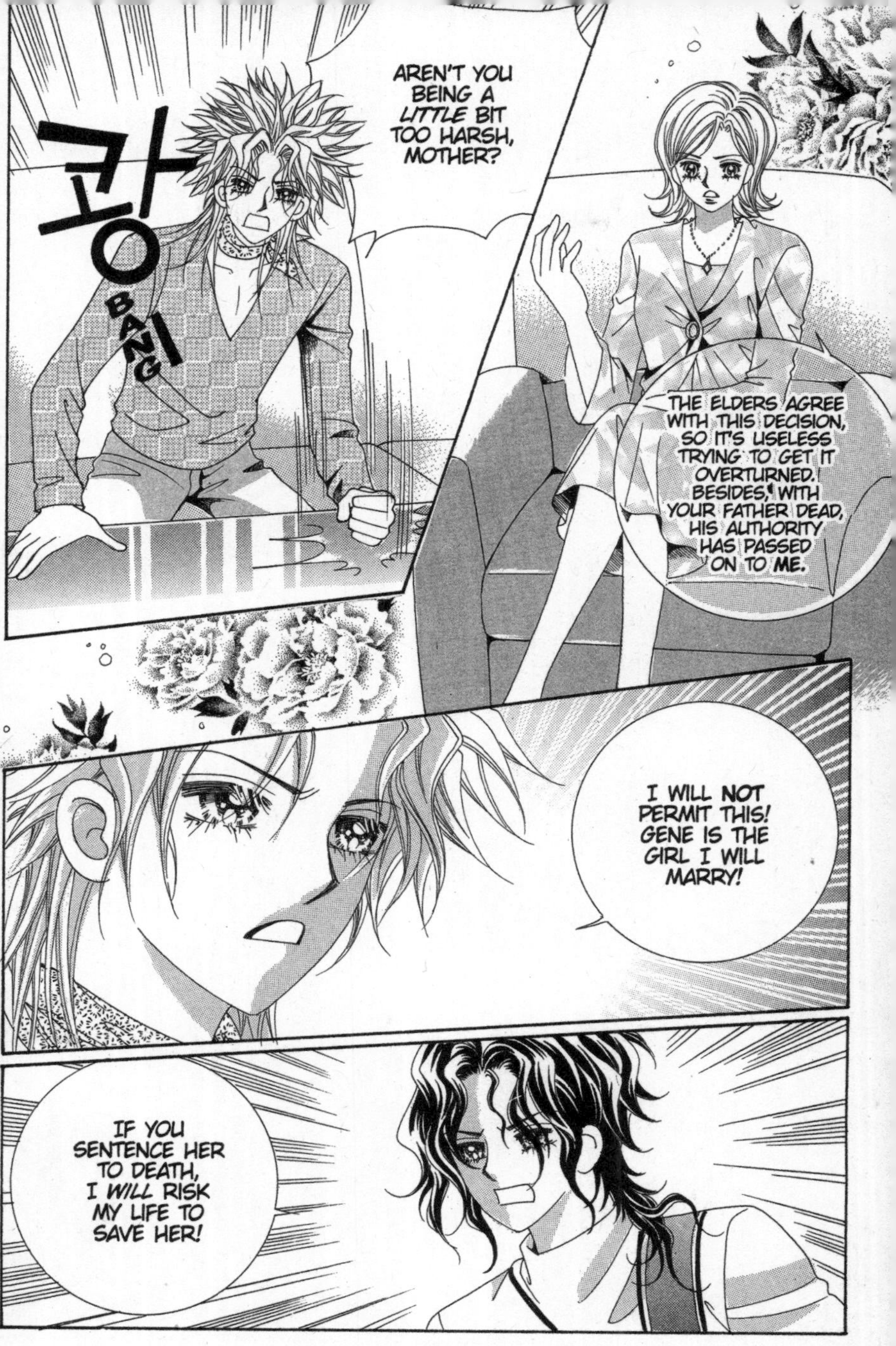

쾅
BANG
AREN'T YOU BEING A *LITTLE* BIT TOO HARSH, MOTHER?
THE ELDERS AGREE WITH THIS DECISION, SO IT'S USELESS TRYING TO GET IT OVERTURNED. BESIDES, WITH YOUR FATHER DEAD, HIS AUTHORITY HAS PASSED ON TO ME.
I WILL NOT PERMIT THIS! GENE IS THE GIRL I WILL MARRY!
IF YOU SENTENCE HER TO DEATH, I *WILL* RISK MY LIFE TO SAVE HER!

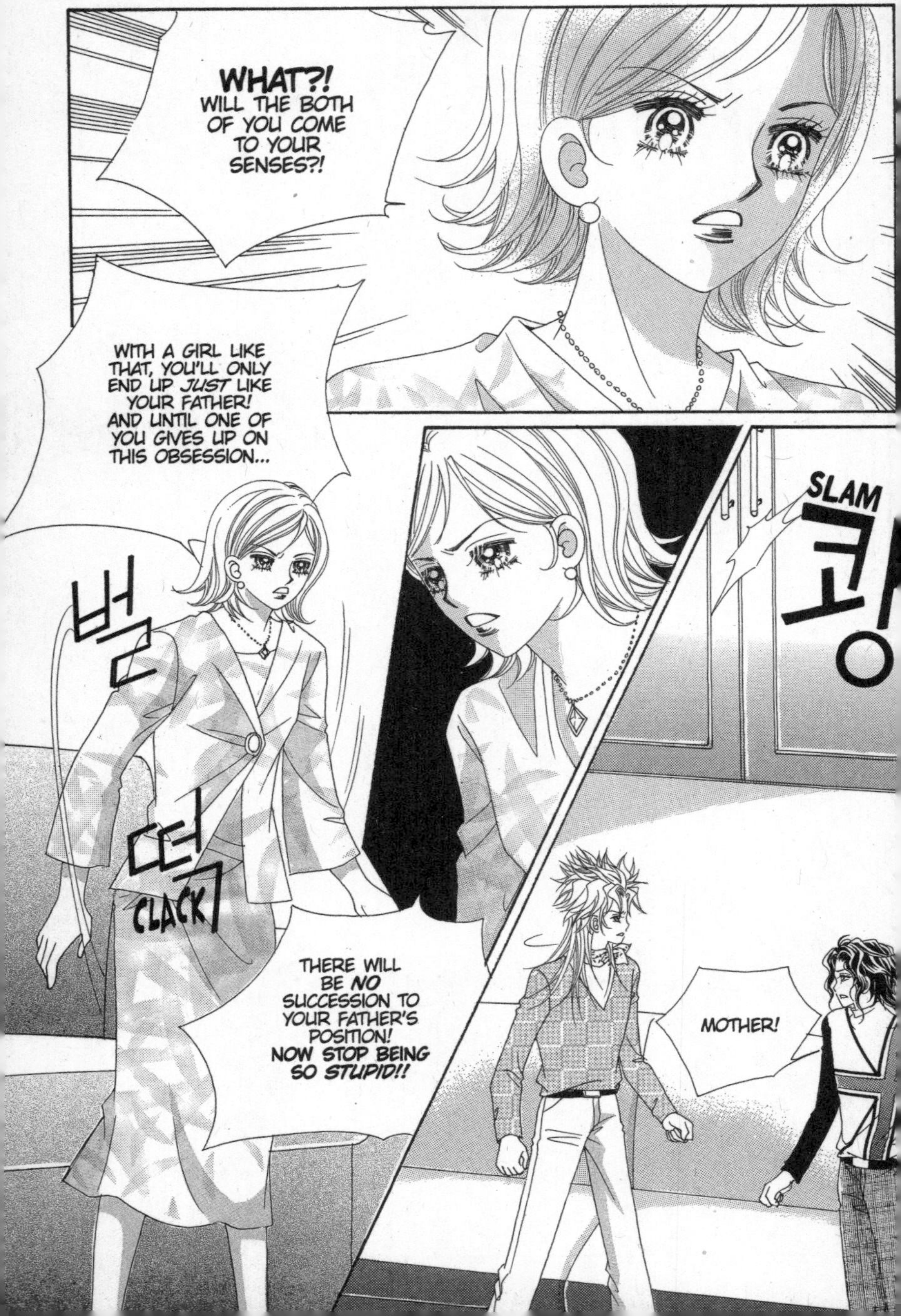

WHAT?! WILL THE BOTH OF YOU COME TO YOUR SENSES?!
WITH A GIRL LIKE THAT, YOU'LL ONLY END UP *JUST* LIKE YOUR FATHER! AND UNTIL ONE OF YOU GIVES UP ON THIS OBSESSION...
벌근
떡
CLACK
THERE WILL BE *NO* SUCCESSION TO YOUR FATHER'S POSITION! NOW STOP BEING SO *STUPID*!!
SLAM
쾅
MOTHER!

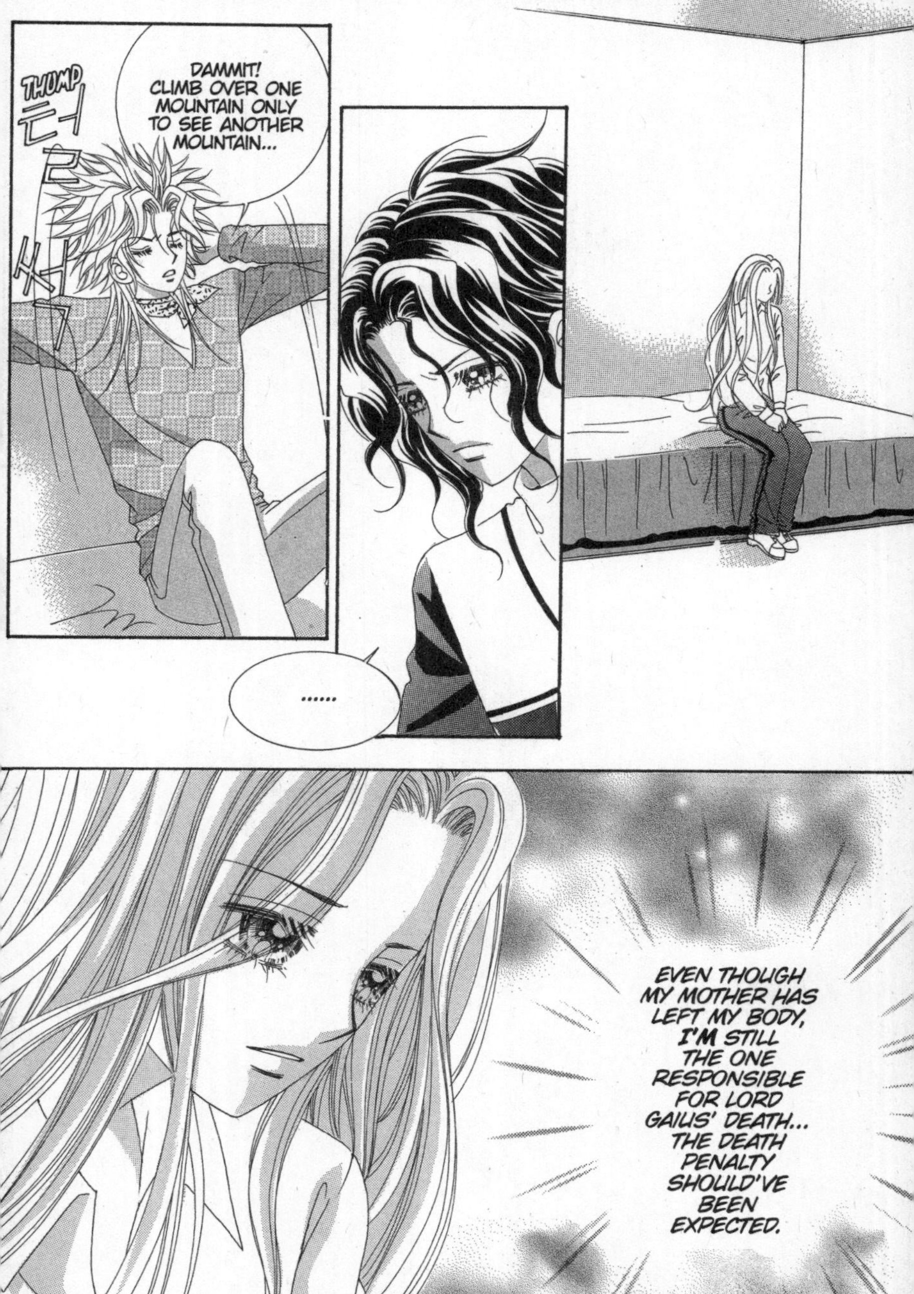
THUMP
DAMMIT! CLIMB OVER ONE MOUNTAIN ONLY TO SEE ANOTHER MOUNTAIN...
......
EVEN THOUGH MY MOTHER HAS LEFT MY BODY, **I'M** STILL THE ONE RESPONSIBLE FOR LORD GAIUS' DEATH... THE DEATH PENALTY SHOULD'VE BEEN EXPECTED.

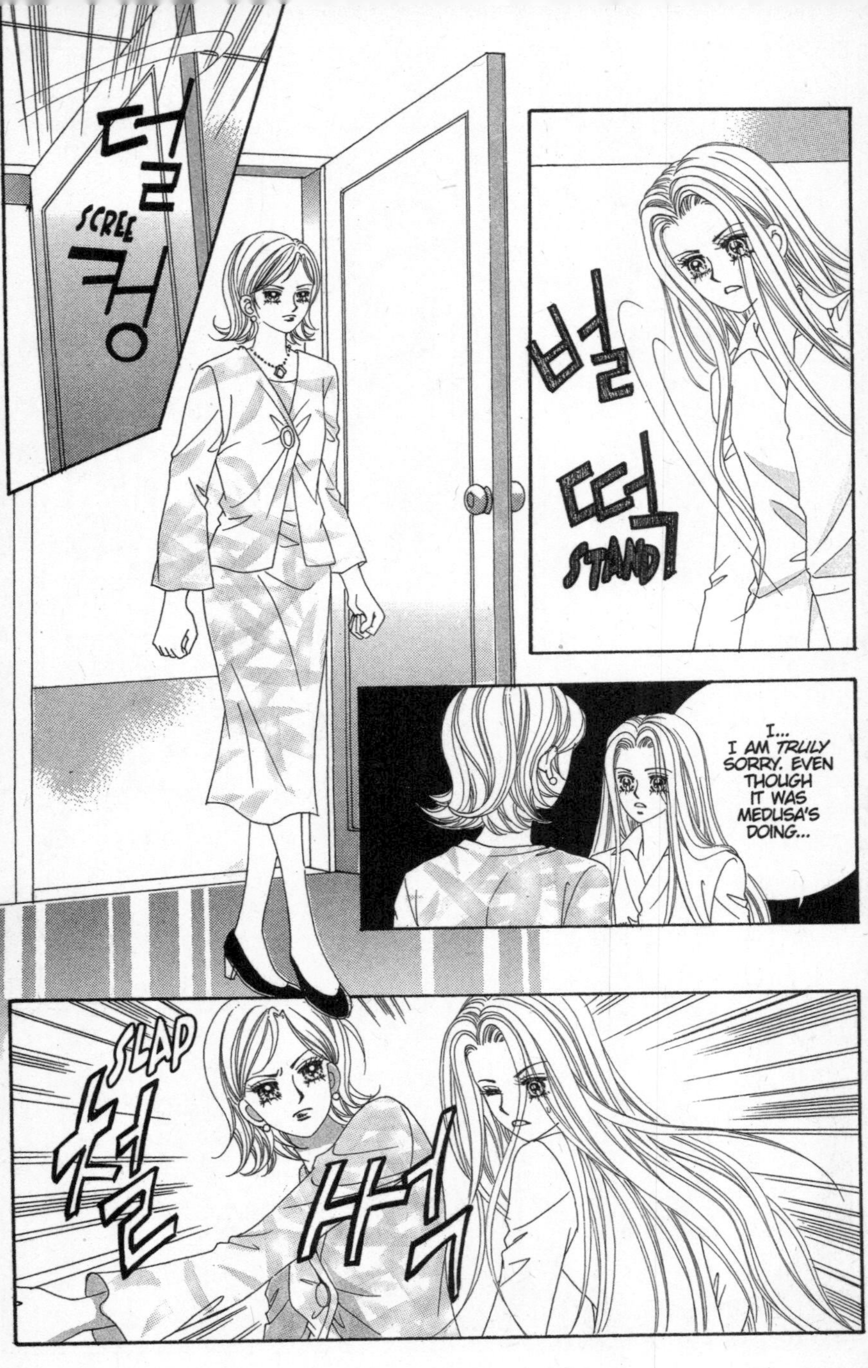

덜컹
SCREE
벌떡
STAND
I...
I AM *TRULY* SORRY. EVEN THOUGH IT WAS MEDUSA'S DOING...
SLAP

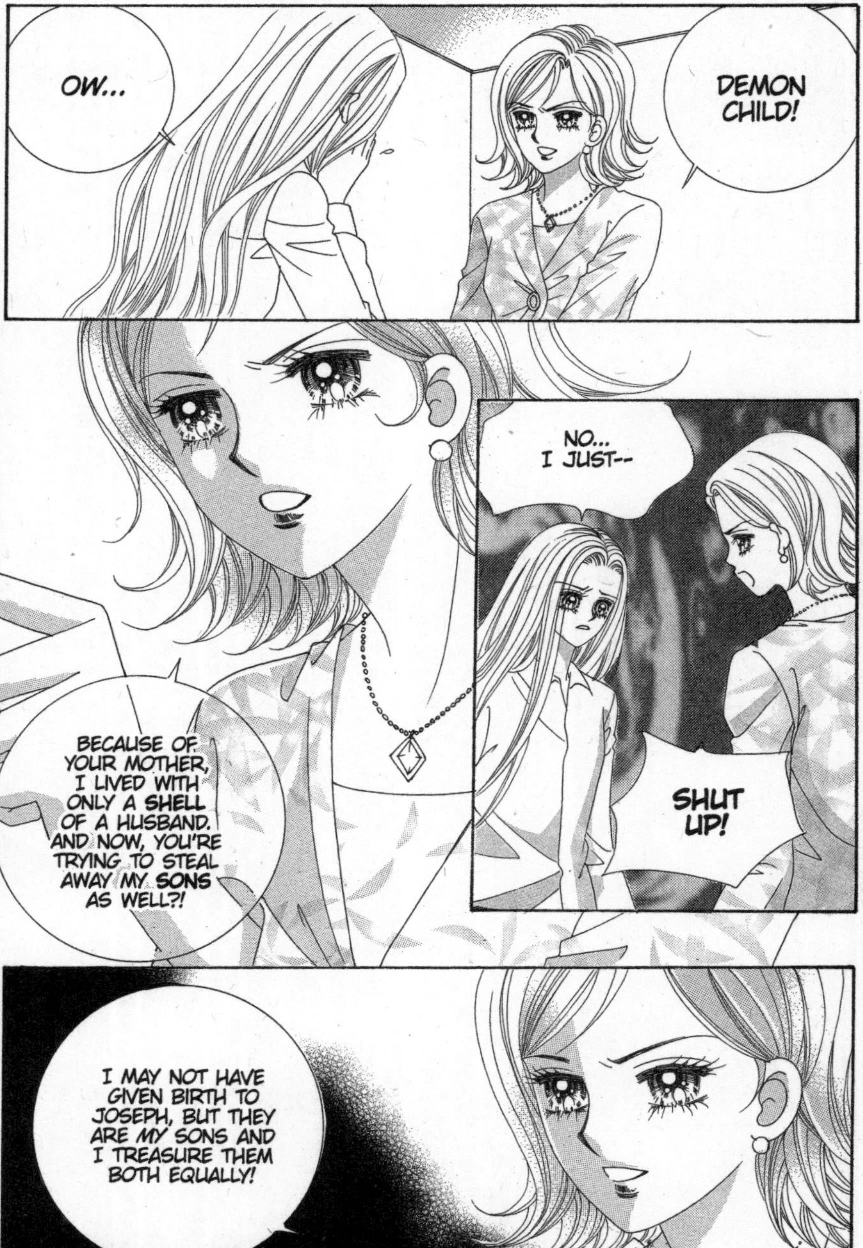
OW...
DEMON CHILD!
NO... I JUST--
SHUT UP!
BECAUSE OF YOUR MOTHER, I LIVED WITH ONLY A SHELL OF A HUSBAND. AND NOW, YOU'RE TRYING TO STEAL AWAY MY SONS AS WELL?!
I MAY NOT HAVE GIVEN BIRTH TO JOSEPH, BUT THEY ARE MY SONS AND I TREASURE THEM BOTH EQUALLY!

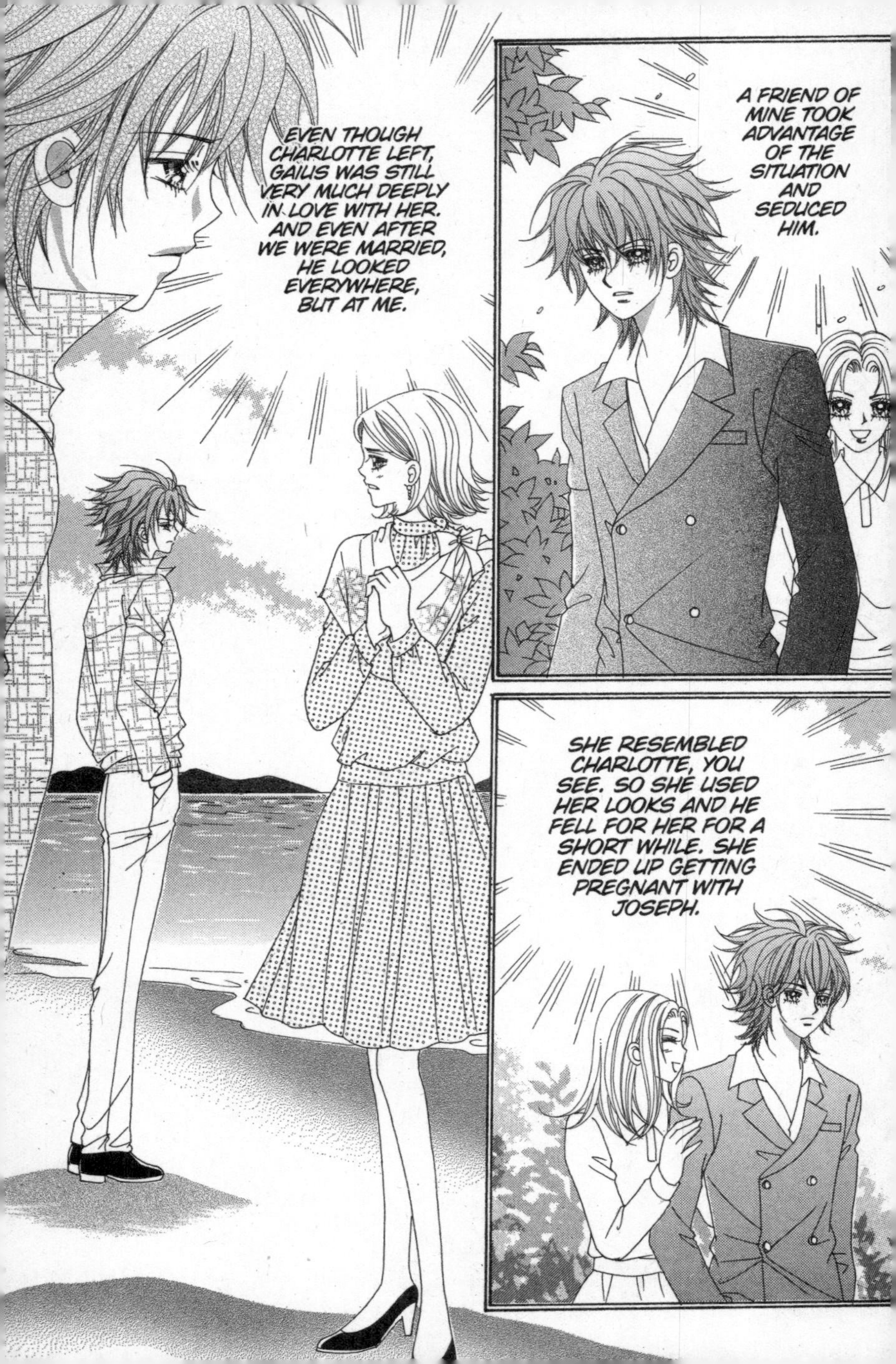
EVEN THOUGH CHARLOTTE LEFT, GAIUS WAS STILL VERY MUCH DEEPLY IN LOVE WITH HER. AND EVEN AFTER WE WERE MARRIED, HE LOOKED EVERYWHERE, BUT AT ME.
A FRIEND OF MINE TOOK ADVANTAGE OF THE SITUATION AND SEDUCED HIM.
SHE RESEMBLED CHARLOTTE, YOU SEE. SO SHE USED HER LOOKS AND HE FELL FOR HER FOR A SHORT WHILE. SHE ENDED UP GETTING PREGNANT WITH JOSEPH.

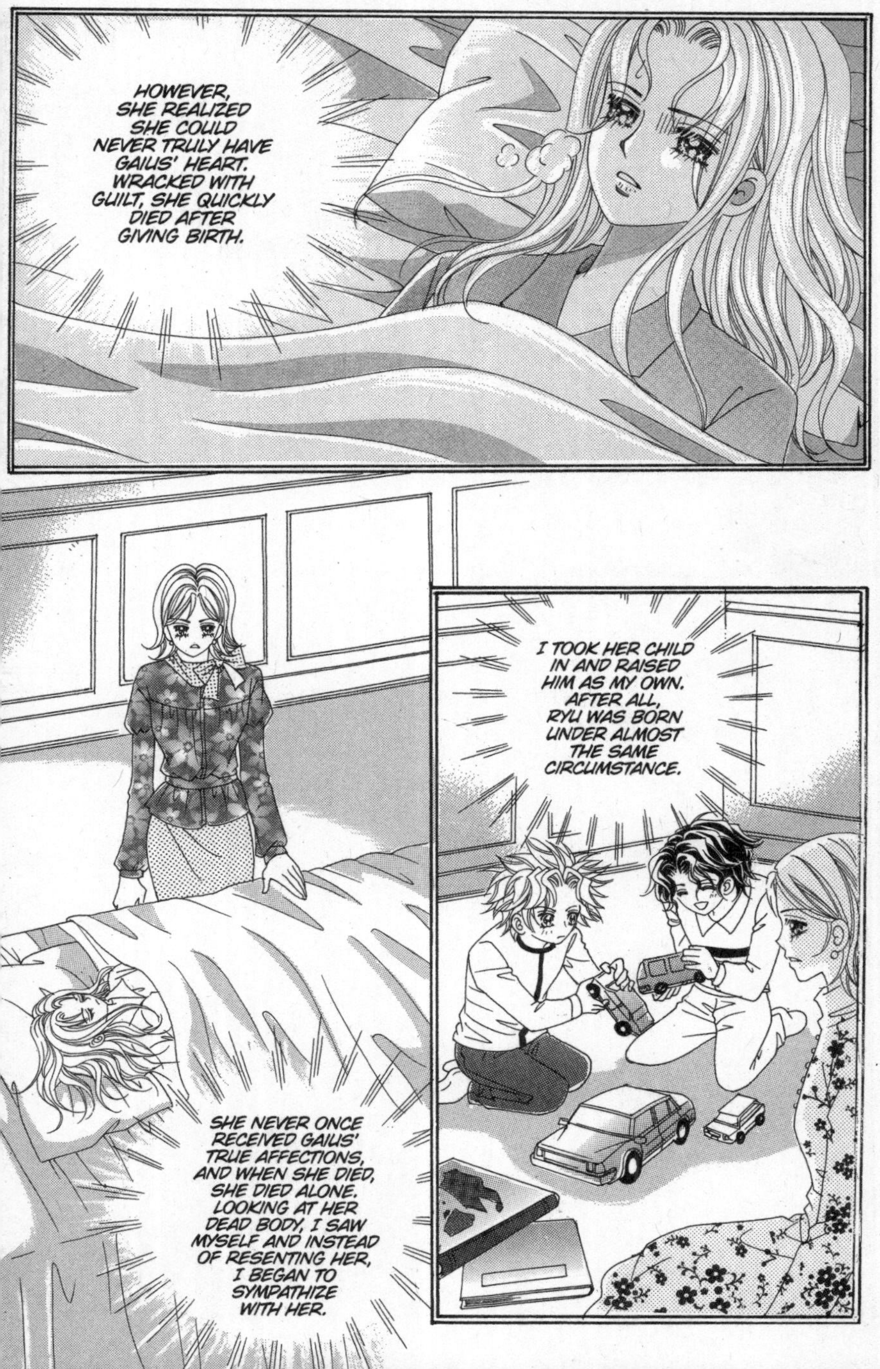
HOWEVER, SHE REALIZED SHE COULD NEVER TRULY HAVE GAIUS' HEART. WRACKED WITH GUILT, SHE QUICKLY DIED AFTER GIVING BIRTH.
SHE NEVER ONCE RECEIVED GAIUS' TRUE AFFECTIONS, AND WHEN SHE DIED, SHE DIED ALONE. LOOKING AT HER DEAD BODY, I SAW MYSELF AND INSTEAD OF RESENTING HER, I BEGAN TO SYMPATHIZE WITH HER.
I TOOK HER CHILD IN AND RAISED HIM AS MY OWN. AFTER ALL, RYU WAS BORN UNDER ALMOST THE SAME CIRCUMSTANCE.

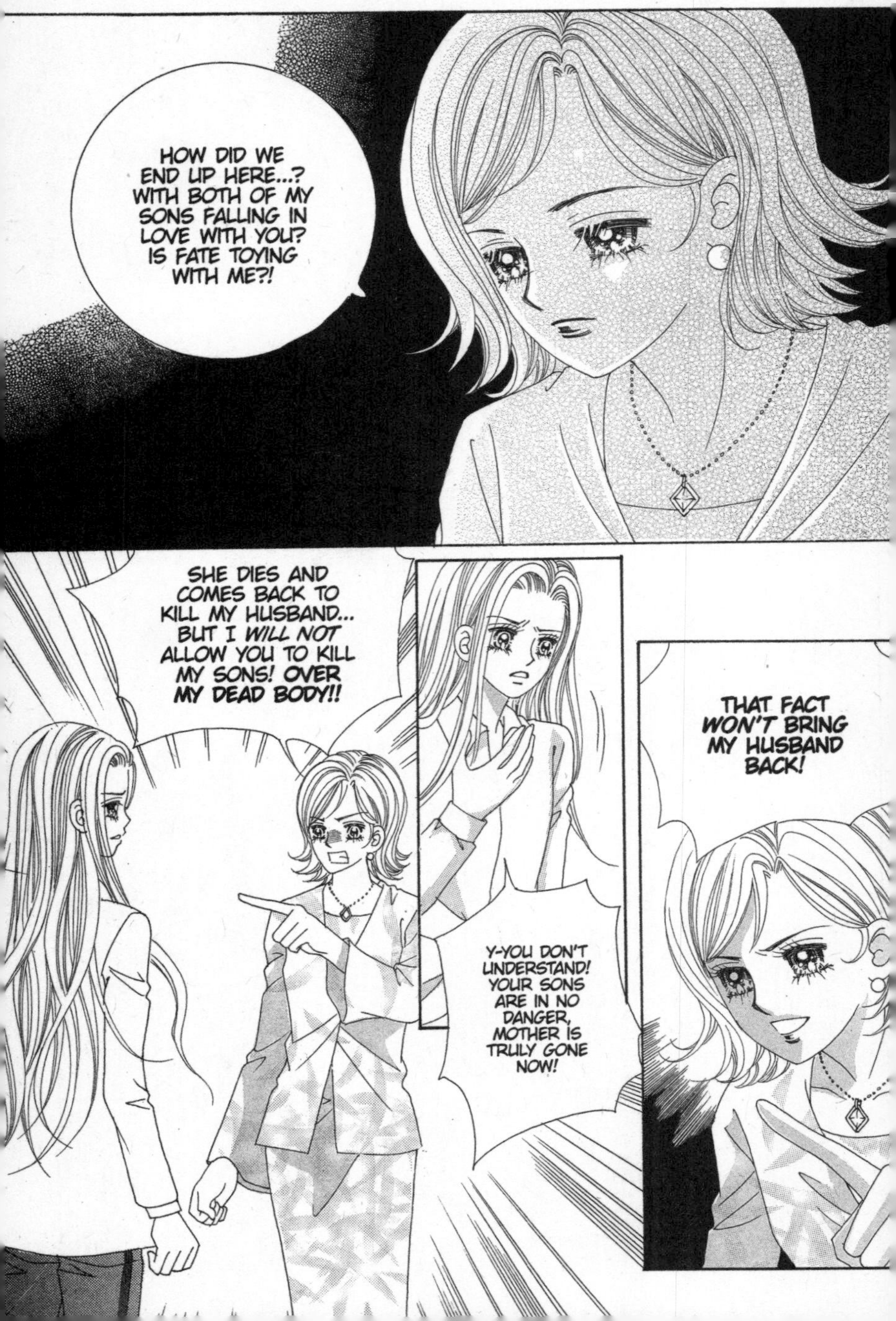
HOW DID WE END UP HERE...? WITH BOTH OF MY SONS FALLING IN LOVE WITH YOU? IS FATE TOYING WITH ME?!
SHE DIES AND COMES BACK TO KILL MY HUSBAND... BUT I WILL NOT ALLOW YOU TO KILL MY SONS! OVER MY DEAD BODY!!
Y-YOU DON'T UNDERSTAND! YOUR SONS ARE IN NO DANGER, MOTHER IS TRULY GONE NOW!
THAT FACT WON'T BRING MY HUSBAND BACK!

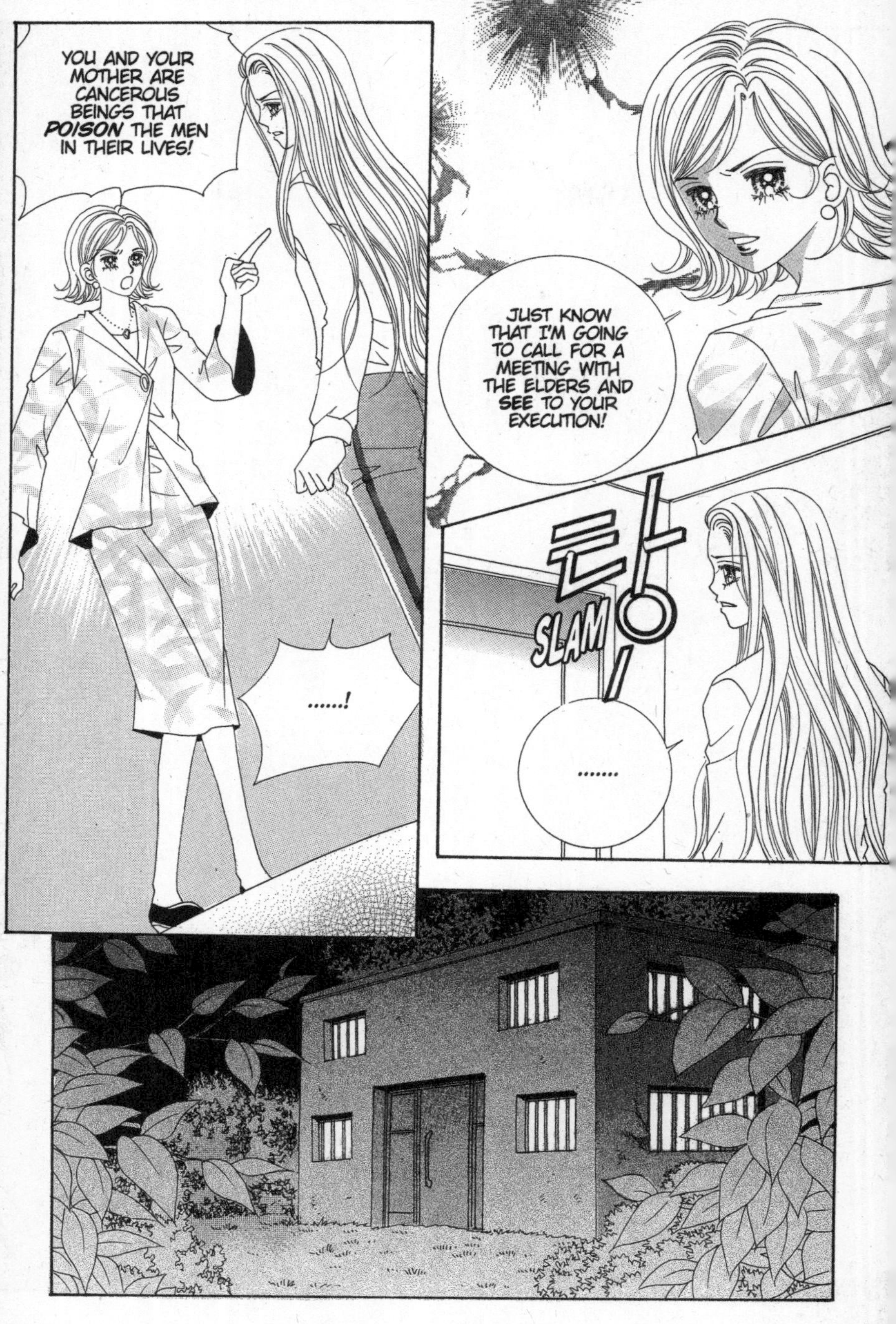
YOU AND YOUR MOTHER ARE CANCEROUS BEINGS THAT **POISON** THE MEN IN THEIR LIVES!
......!
JUST KNOW THAT I'M GOING TO CALL FOR A MEETING WITH THE ELDERS AND SEE TO YOUR EXECUTION!
SLAM
....

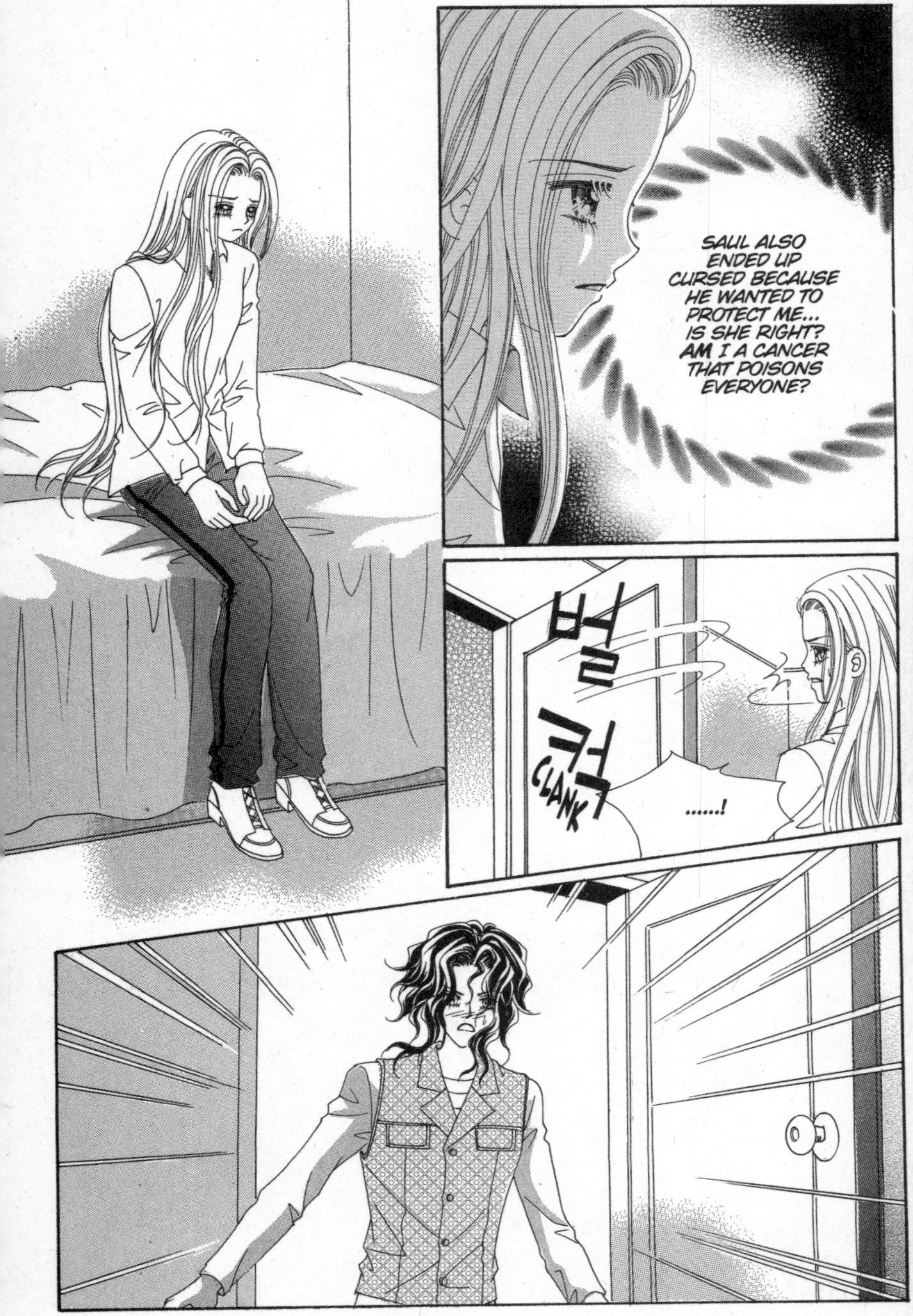
SAUL ALSO ENDED UP CURSED BECAUSE HE WANTED TO PROTECT ME... IS SHE RIGHT? AM I A CANCER THAT POISONS EVERYONE?
벌컥
CLANK
......!

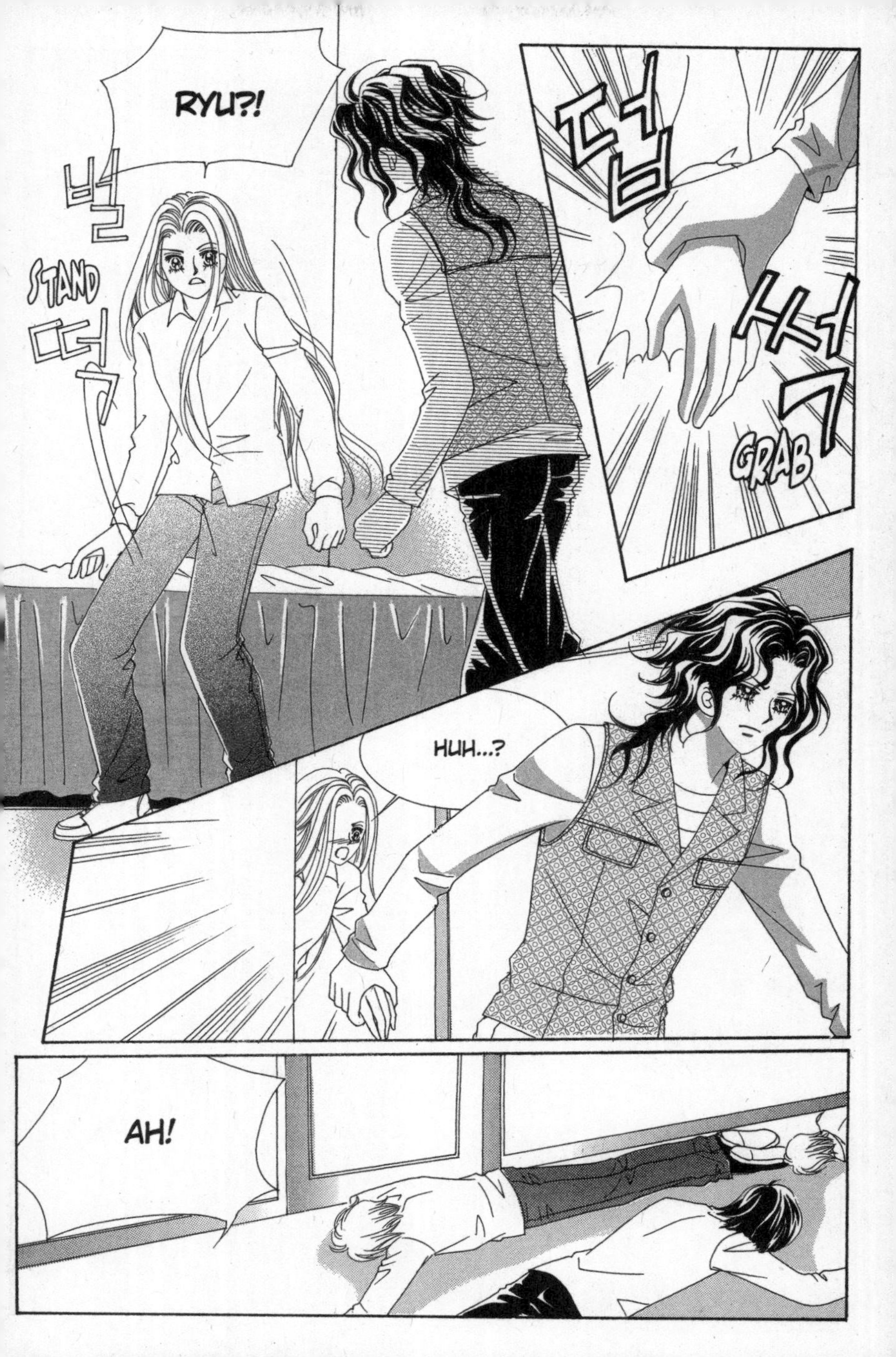
RYU?!
벌떡
STAND
덥석
GRAB
HUH...?
AH!

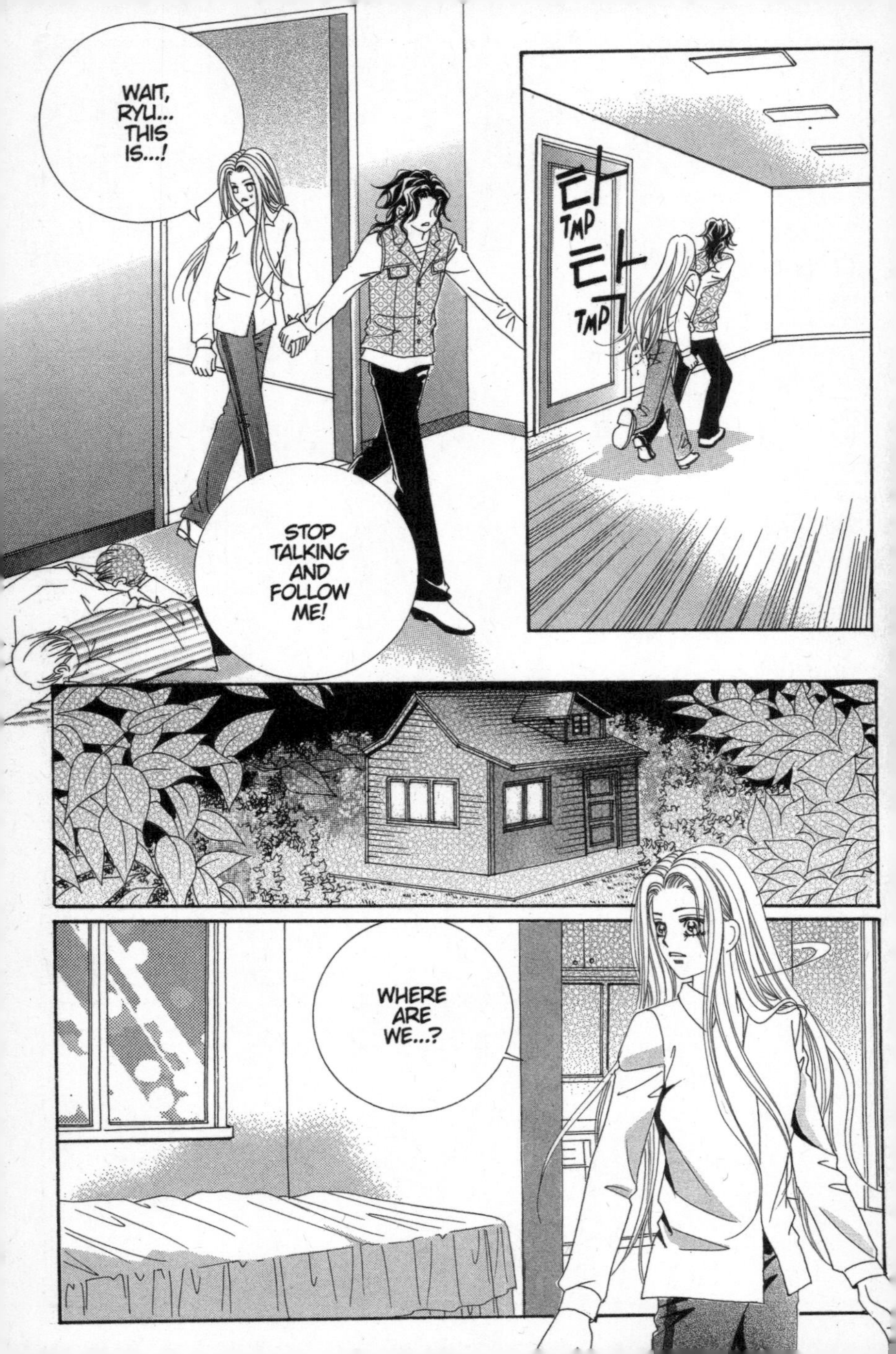
WAIT, RYU... THIS IS...!
STOP TALKING AND FOLLOW ME!
타 TMP
탁 TMP
WHERE ARE WE...?

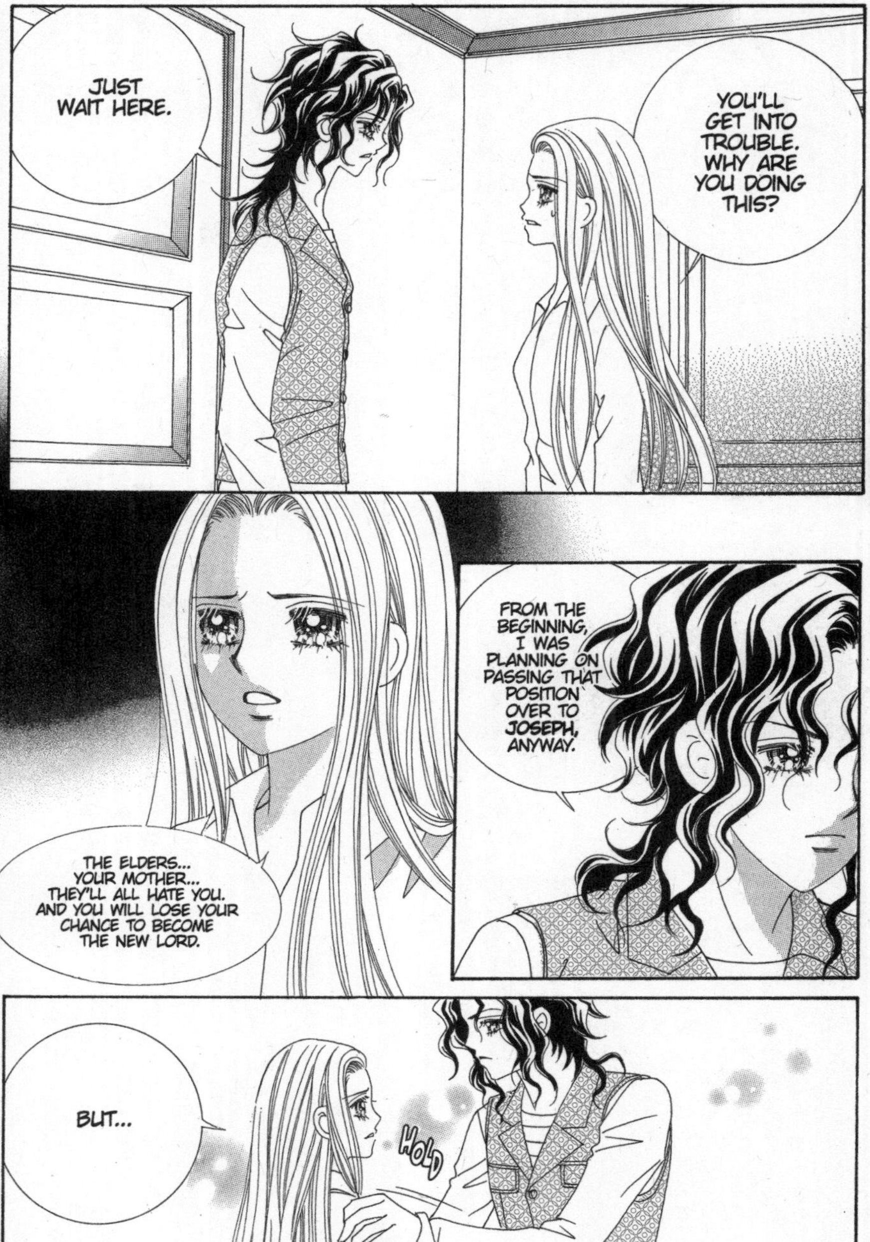
JUST WAIT HERE.
YOU'LL GET INTO TROUBLE. WHY ARE YOU DOING THIS?
THE ELDERS... YOUR MOTHER... THEY'LL ALL HATE YOU. AND YOU WILL LOSE YOUR CHANCE TO BECOME THE NEW LORD.
FROM THE BEGINNING, I WAS PLANNING ON PASSING THAT POSITION OVER TO JOSEPH, ANYWAY.
BUT...
HOLD

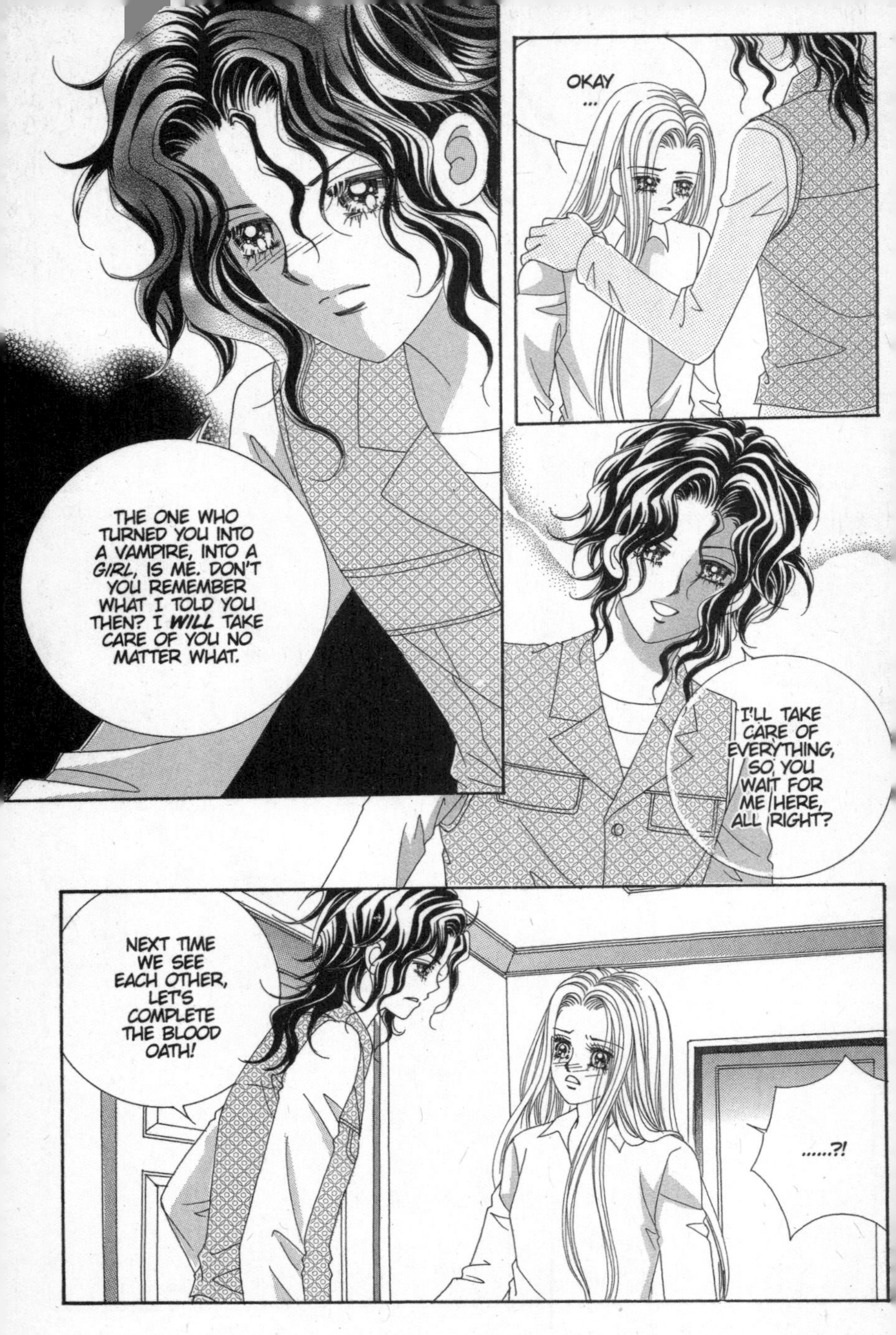

THE ONE WHO TURNED YOU INTO A VAMPIRE, INTO A *GIRL*, IS ME. DON'T YOU REMEMBER WHAT I TOLD YOU THEN? I **WILL** TAKE CARE OF YOU NO MATTER WHAT.
OKAY ...
I'LL TAKE CARE OF EVERYTHING, SO, YOU WAIT FOR ME HERE, ALL RIGHT?
NEXT TIME WE SEE EACH OTHER, LET'S COMPLETE THE BLOOD OATH!
......?!

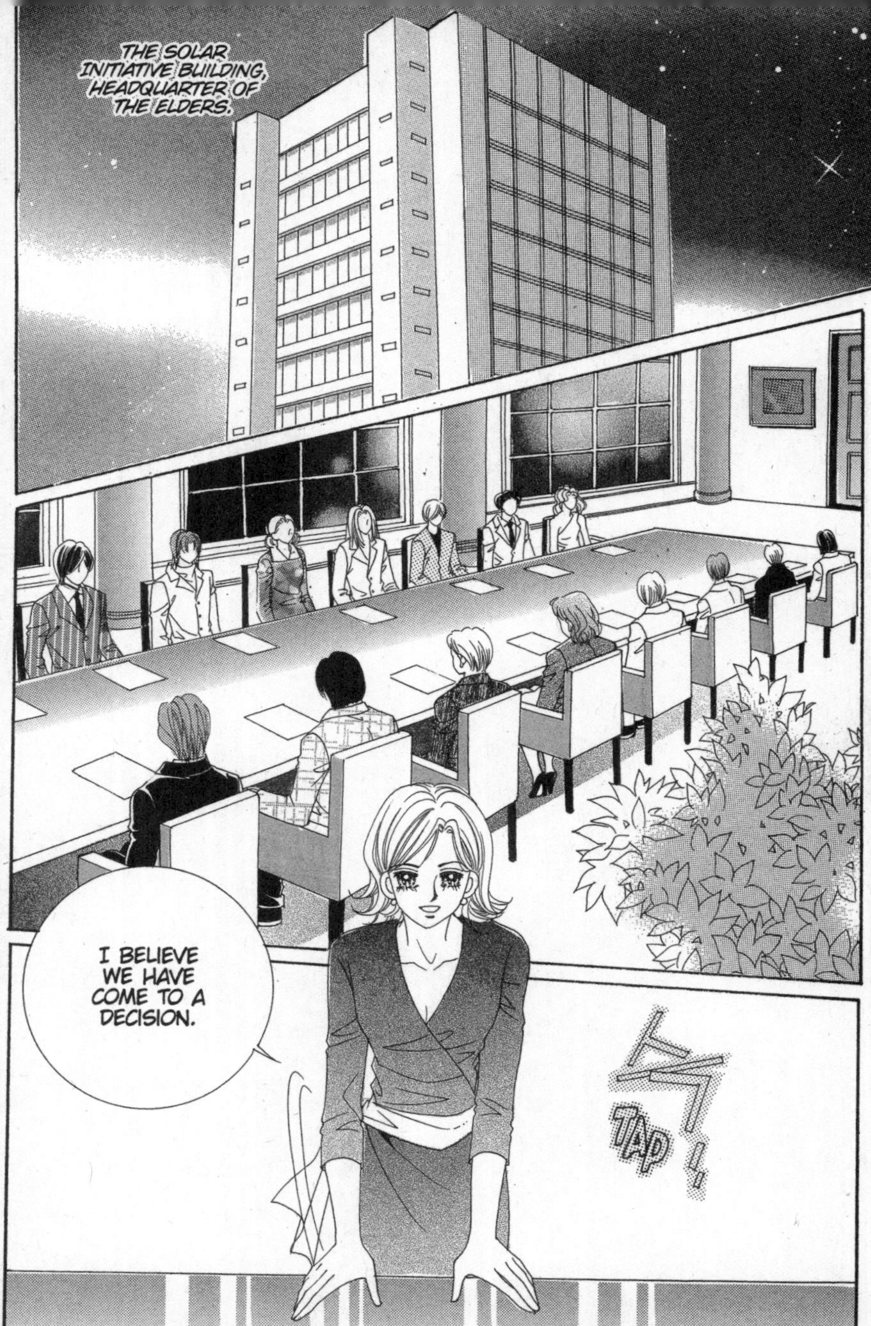
THE SOLAR INITIATIVE BUILDING, HEADQUARTER OF THE ELDERS.
I BELIEVE WE HAVE COME TO A DECISION.
TAP

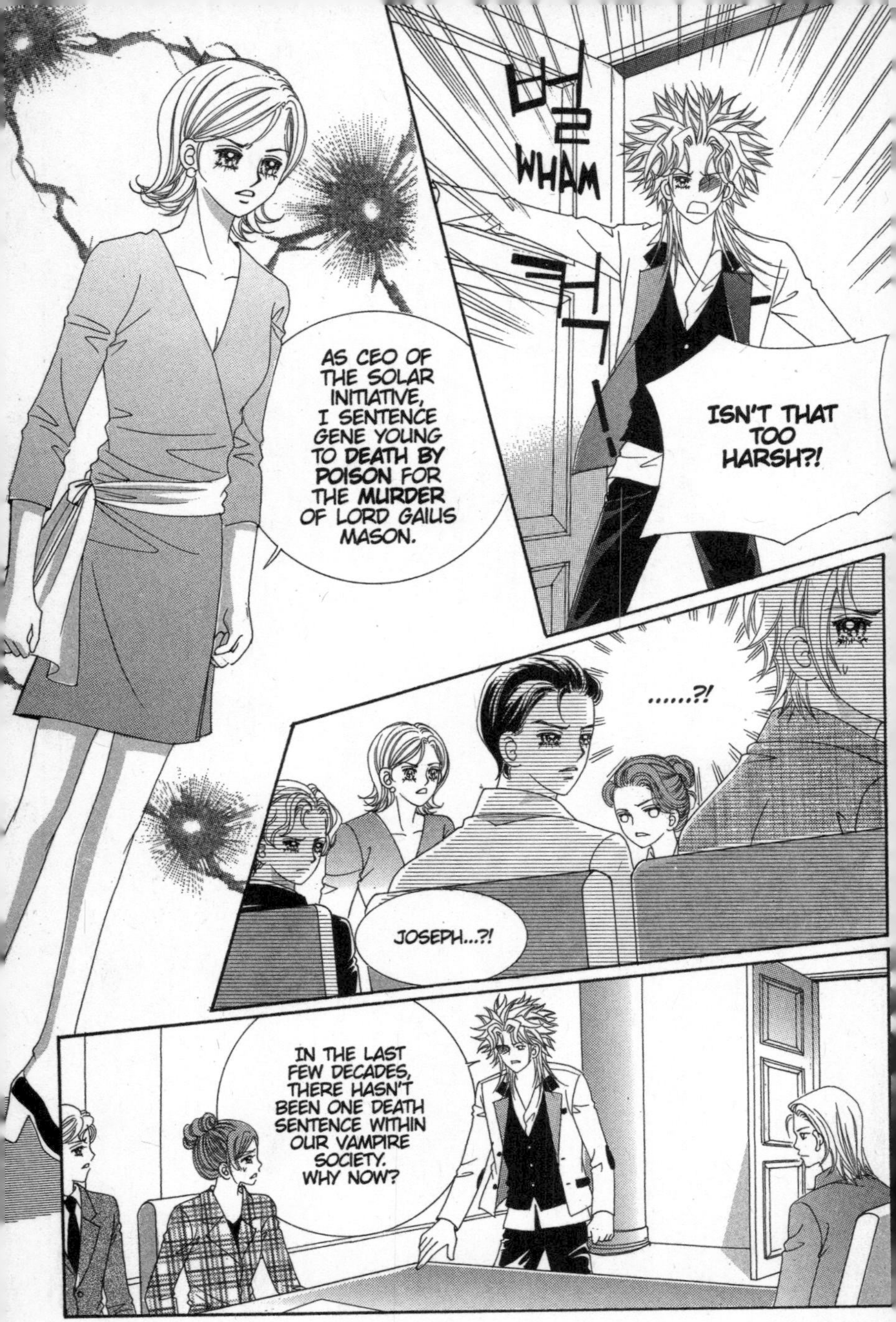
AS CEO OF THE SOLAR INITIATIVE, I SENTENCE GENE YOUNG TO DEATH BY POISON FOR THE MURDER OF LORD GAIUS MASON.
벌
WHAM
컥
ISN'T THAT TOO HARSH?!
......?!
JOSEPH...?!
IN THE LAST FEW DECADES, THERE HASN'T BEEN ONE DEATH SENTENCE WITHIN OUR VAMPIRE SOCIETY. WHY NOW?

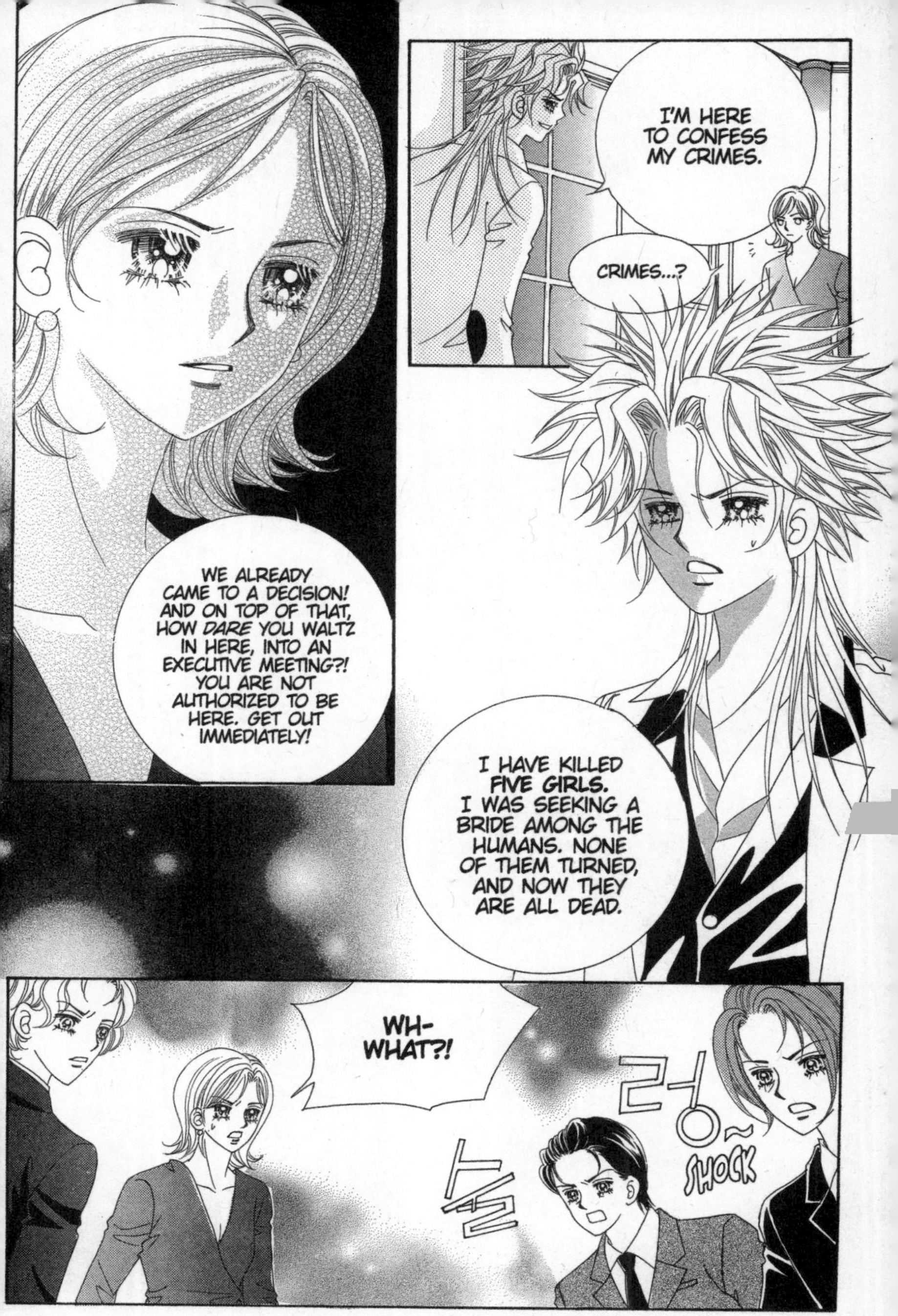
WE ALREADY CAME TO A DECISION! AND ON TOP OF THAT, HOW *DARE* YOU WALTZ IN HERE, INTO AN EXECUTIVE MEETING?! YOU ARE NOT AUTHORIZED TO BE HERE. GET OUT IMMEDIATELY!
I'M HERE TO CONFESS MY CRIMES.
CRIMES...?
I HAVE KILLED **FIVE GIRLS.** I WAS SEEKING A BRIDE AMONG THE HUMANS. NONE OF THEM TURNED, AND NOW THEY ARE ALL DEAD.
WH- WHAT?!
SHOCK

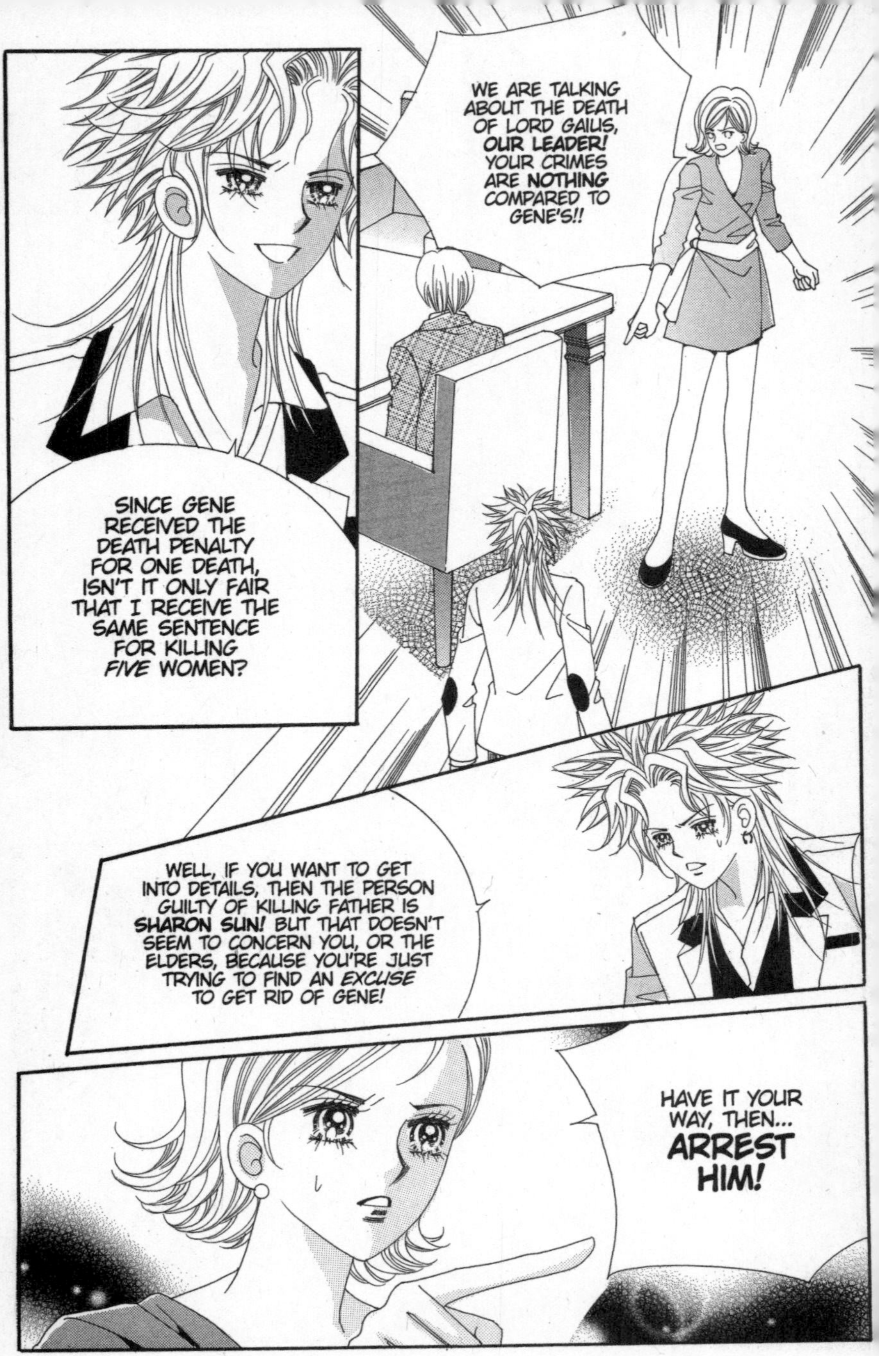
SINCE GENE RECEIVED THE DEATH PENALTY FOR ONE DEATH, ISN'T IT ONLY FAIR THAT I RECEIVE THE SAME SENTENCE FOR KILLING *FIVE* WOMEN?
WE ARE TALKING ABOUT THE DEATH OF LORD GAIUS, **OUR LEADER!** YOUR CRIMES ARE **NOTHING** COMPARED TO GENE'S!!
WELL, IF YOU WANT TO GET INTO DETAILS, THEN THE PERSON GUILTY OF KILLING FATHER IS **SHARON SUN!** BUT THAT DOESN'T SEEM TO CONCERN YOU, OR THE ELDERS, BECAUSE YOU'RE JUST TRYING TO FIND AN *EXCUSE* TO GET RID OF GENE!
HAVE IT YOUR WAY, THEN... **ARREST HIM!**

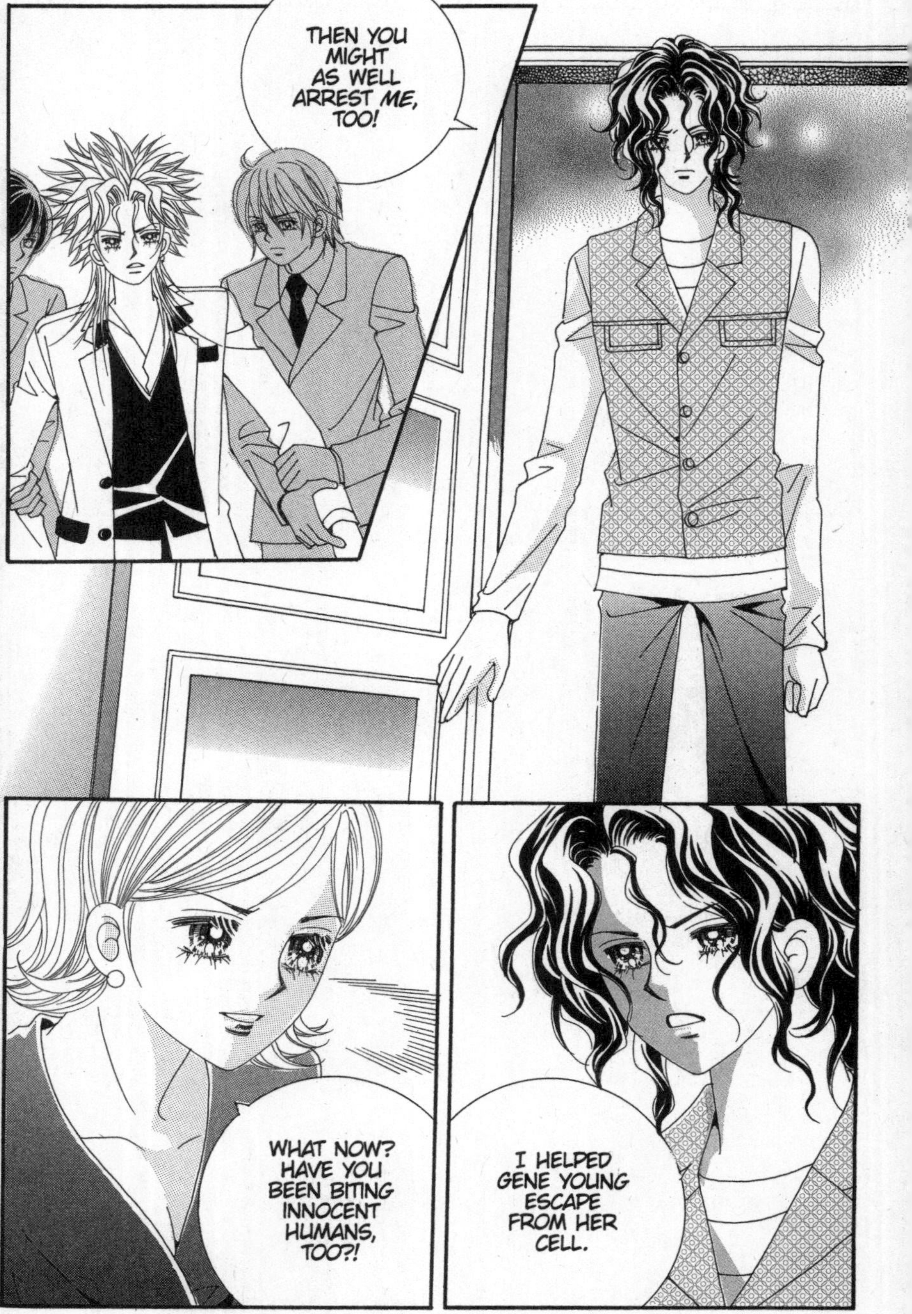
THEN YOU MIGHT AS WELL ARREST ME, TOO!
WHAT NOW? HAVE YOU BEEN BITING INNOCENT HUMANS, TOO?!
I HELPED GENE YOUNG ESCAPE FROM HER CELL.

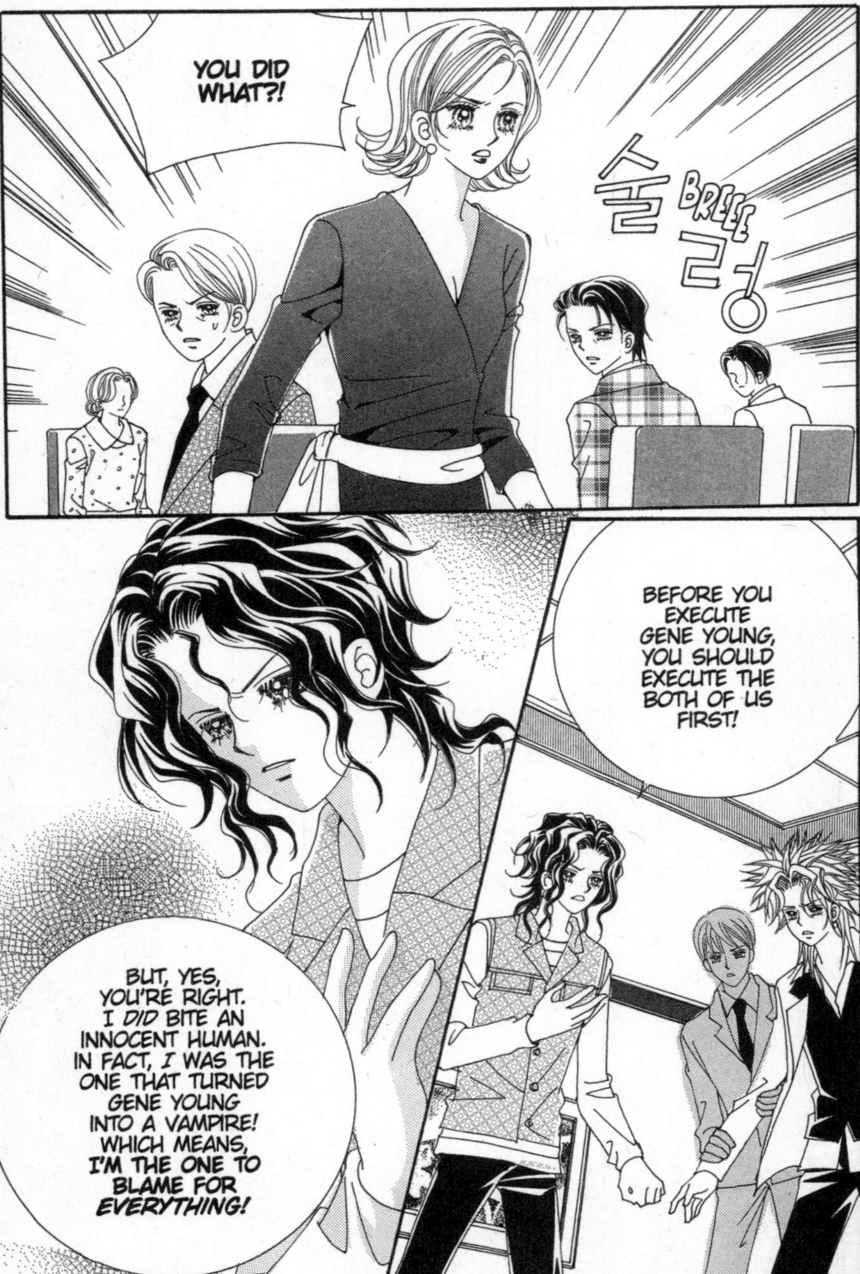
YOU DID WHAT?!
솔 BREEE 르릉
BUT, YES, YOU'RE RIGHT. I *DID* BITE AN INNOCENT HUMAN. IN FACT, *I* WAS THE ONE THAT TURNED GENE YOUNG INTO A VAMPIRE! WHICH MEANS, I'M THE ONE TO BLAME FOR *EVERYTHING!*
BEFORE YOU EXECUTE GENE YOUNG, YOU SHOULD EXECUTE THE BOTH OF US FIRST!

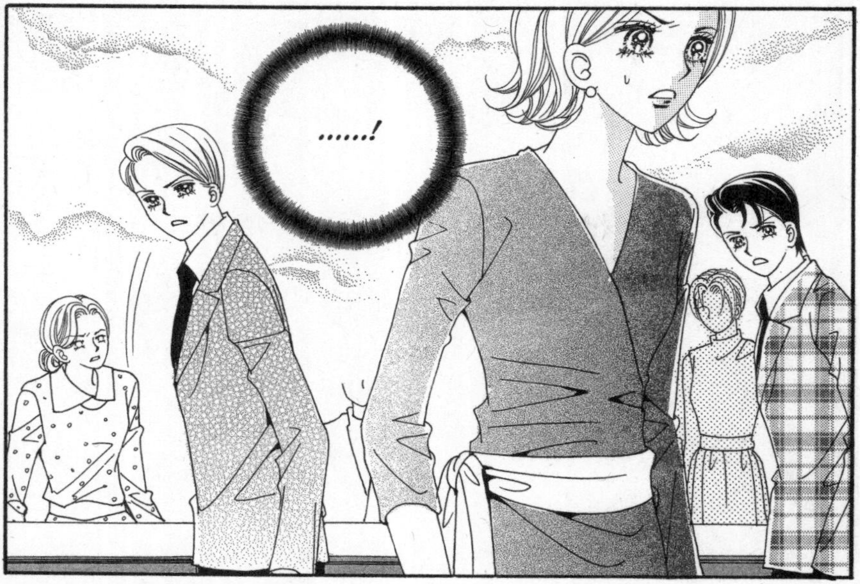
......!

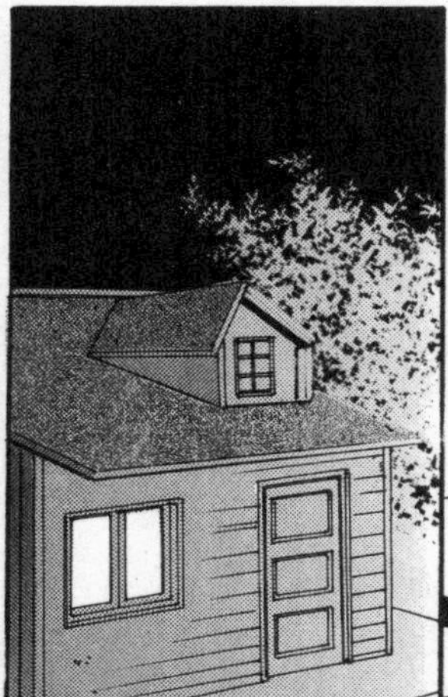

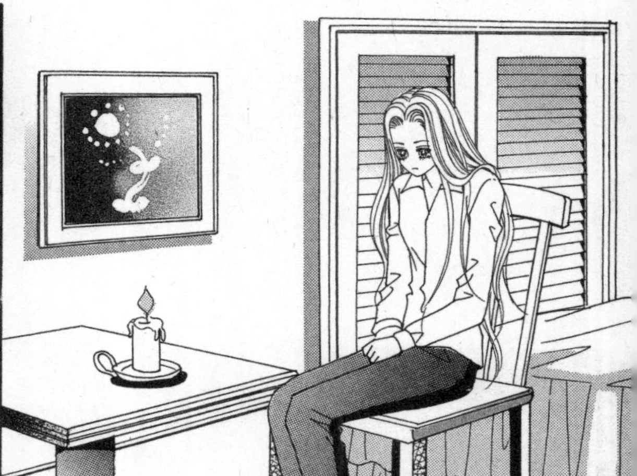

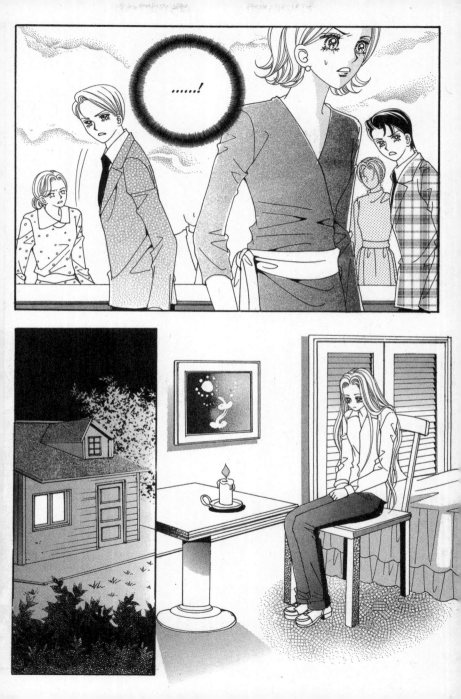

"YOU AND YOUR MOTHER ARE CANCEROUS BEINGS THAT POISON THE MEN IN THEIR LIVES!"

THE MEN WHO LOVED MY MOTHER ALL HAD UNFORTUNATE DEATHS.

I KEEP HEARING HER WORDS IN MY HEAD.

RYU AND JOSEPH CAN END UP LIKE THEM...

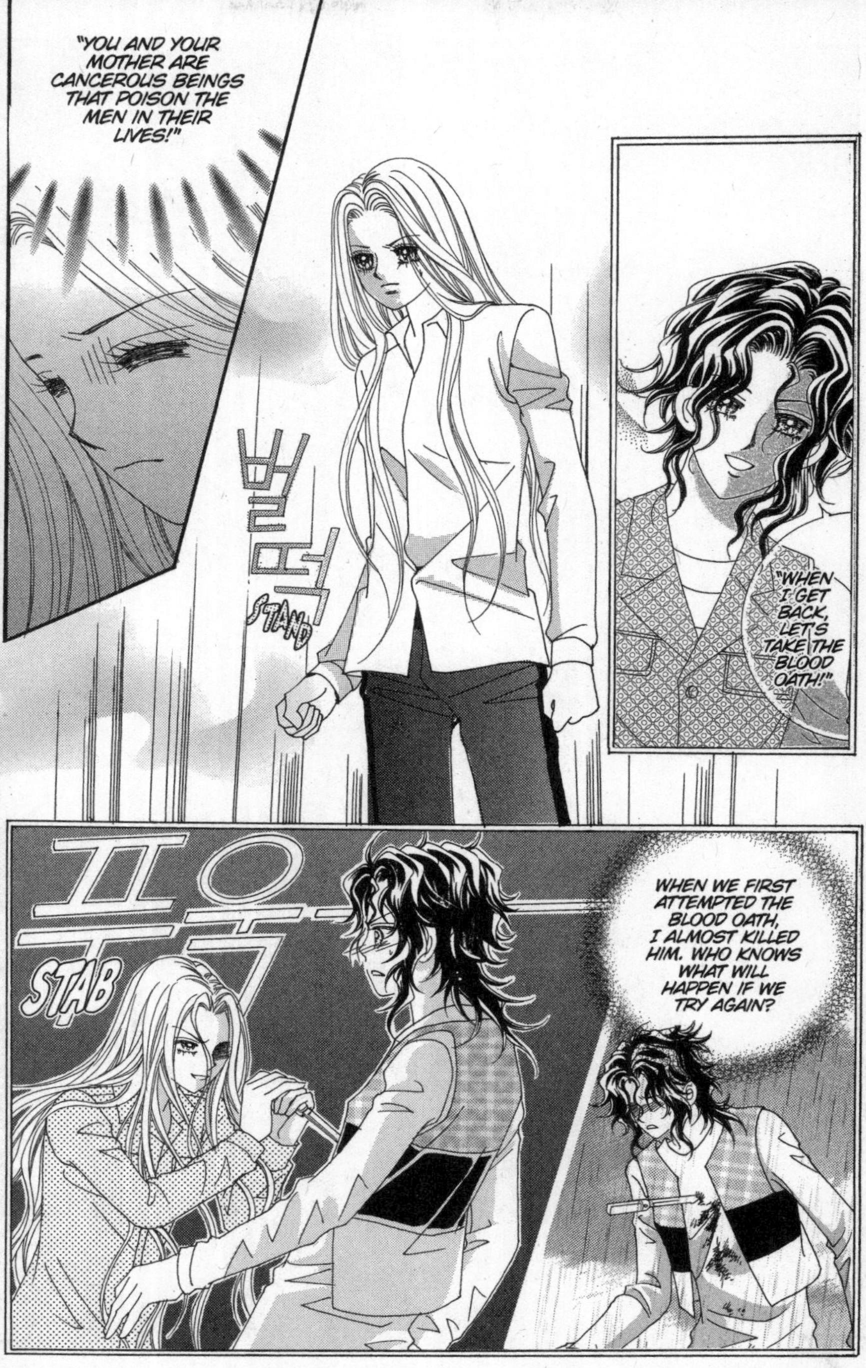
"YOU AND YOUR MOTHER ARE CANCEROUS BEINGS THAT POISON THE MEN IN THEIR LIVES!"
벌떡
STAND
"WHEN I GET BACK, LET'S TAKE THE BLOOD OATH!"
STAB
WHEN WE FIRST ATTEMPTED THE BLOOD OATH, I ALMOST KILLED HIM. WHO KNOWS WHAT WILL HAPPEN IF WE TRY AGAIN?

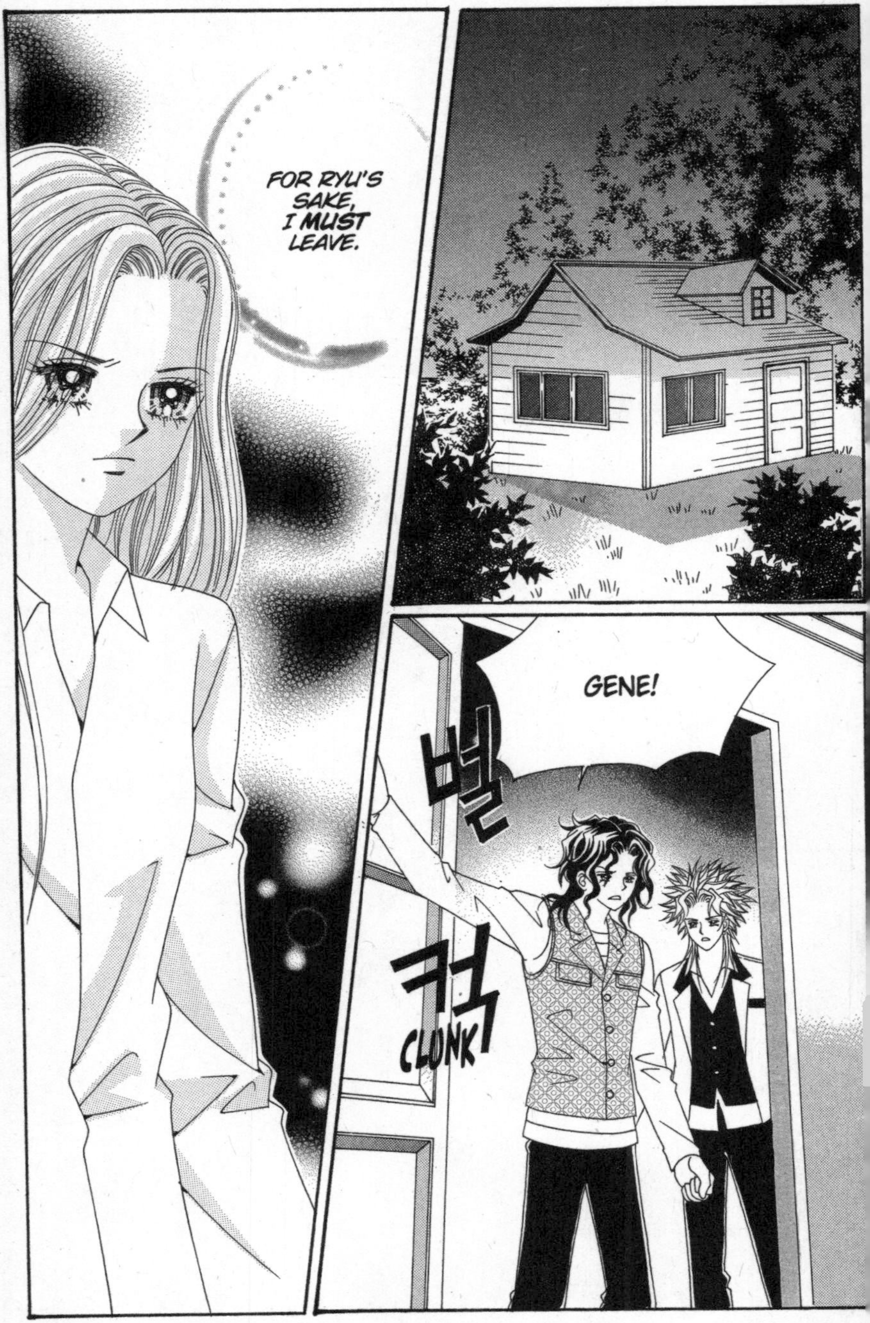
FOR RYU'S SAKE, I MUST LEAVE.
GENE!
벌컥
CLONK

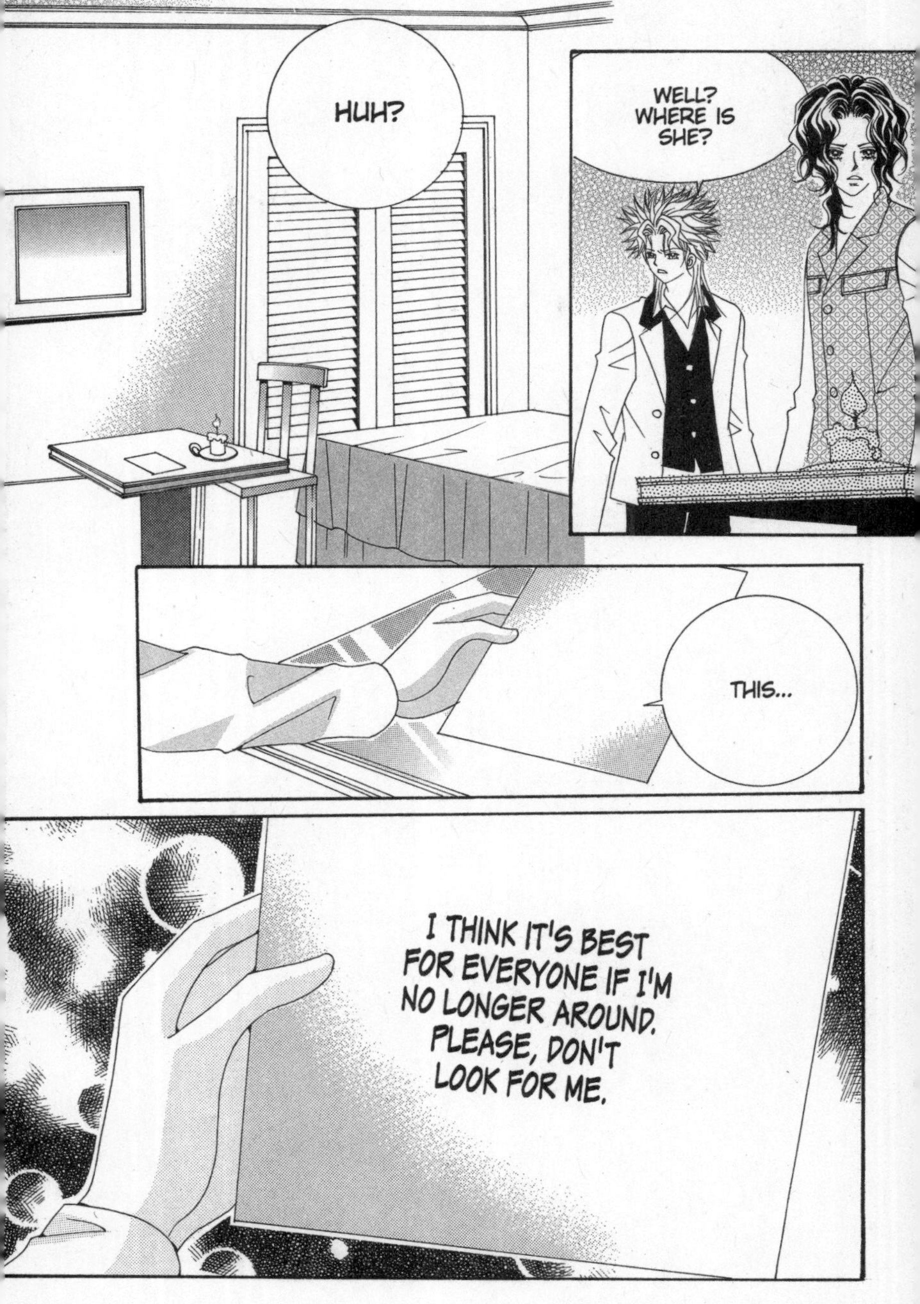
HUH?
WELL? WHERE IS SHE?
THIS...
I THINK IT'S BEST FOR EVERYONE IF I'M NO LONGER AROUND. PLEASE, DON'T LOOK FOR ME.

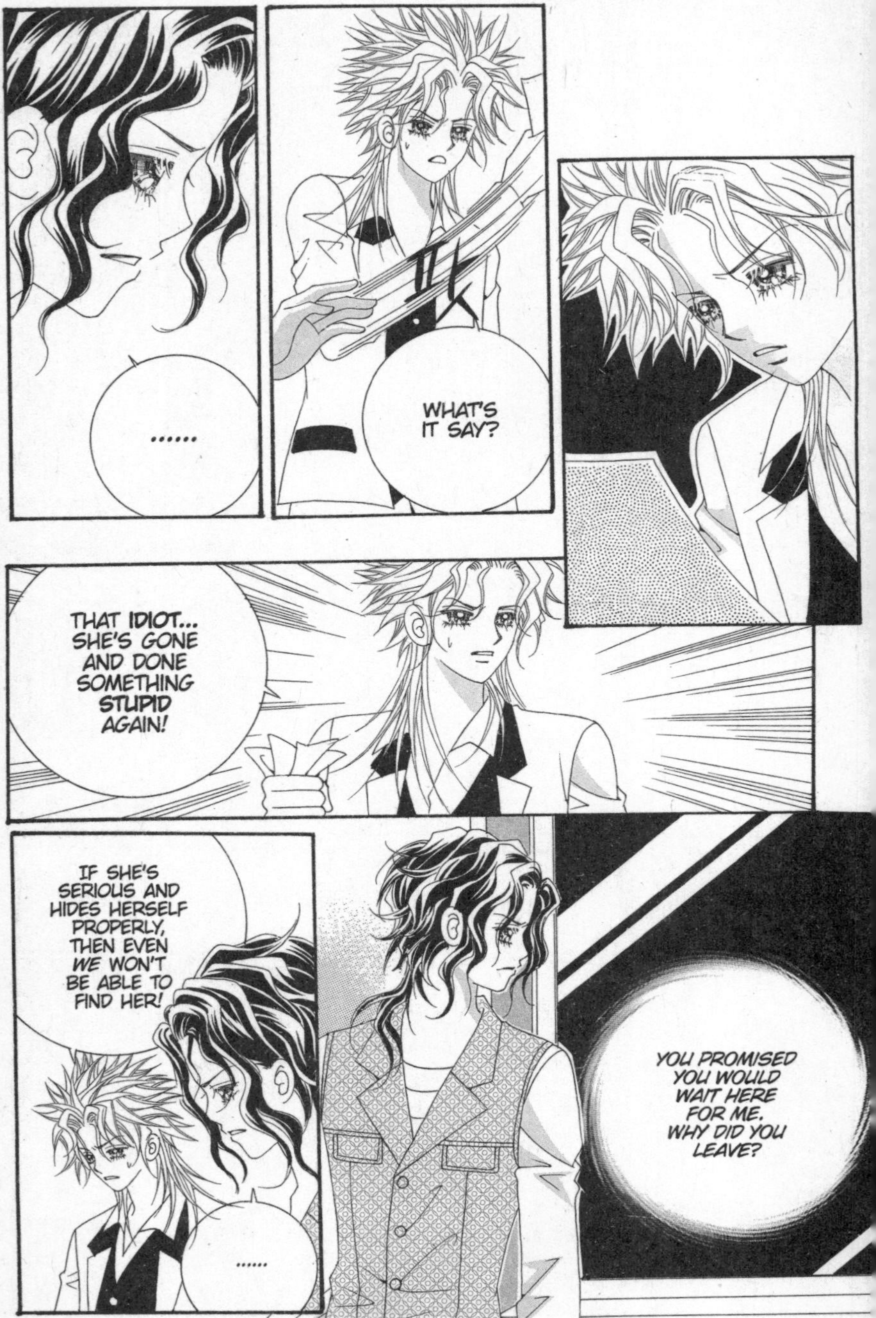
......
WHAT'S IT SAY?
THAT IDIOT... SHE'S GONE AND DONE SOMETHING STUPID AGAIN!
IF SHE'S SERIOUS AND HIDES HERSELF PROPERLY, THEN EVEN WE WON'T BE ABLE TO FIND HER!
......
YOU PROMISED YOU WOULD WAIT HERE FOR ME. WHY DID YOU LEAVE?

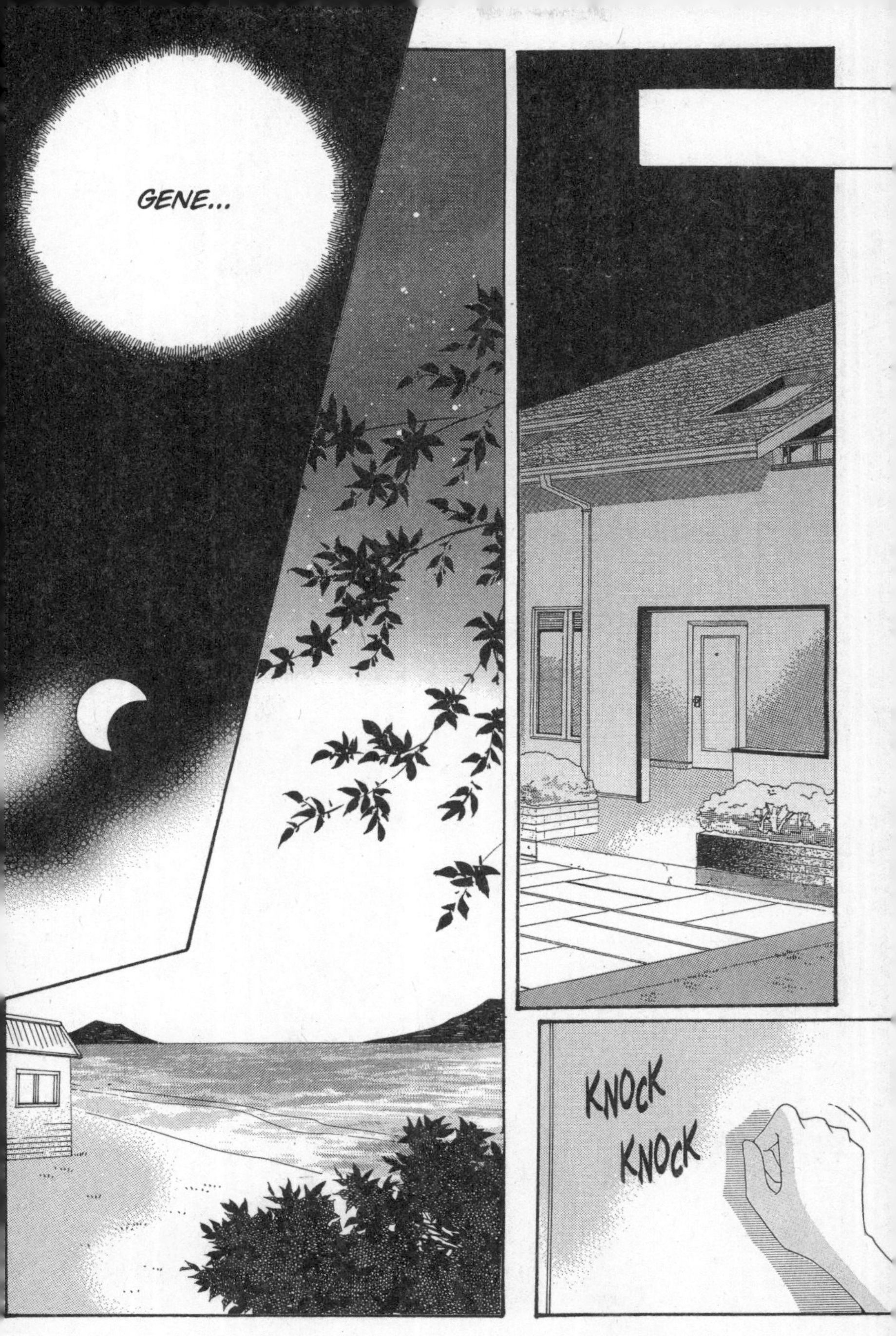
GENE...
KNOCK
KNOCK

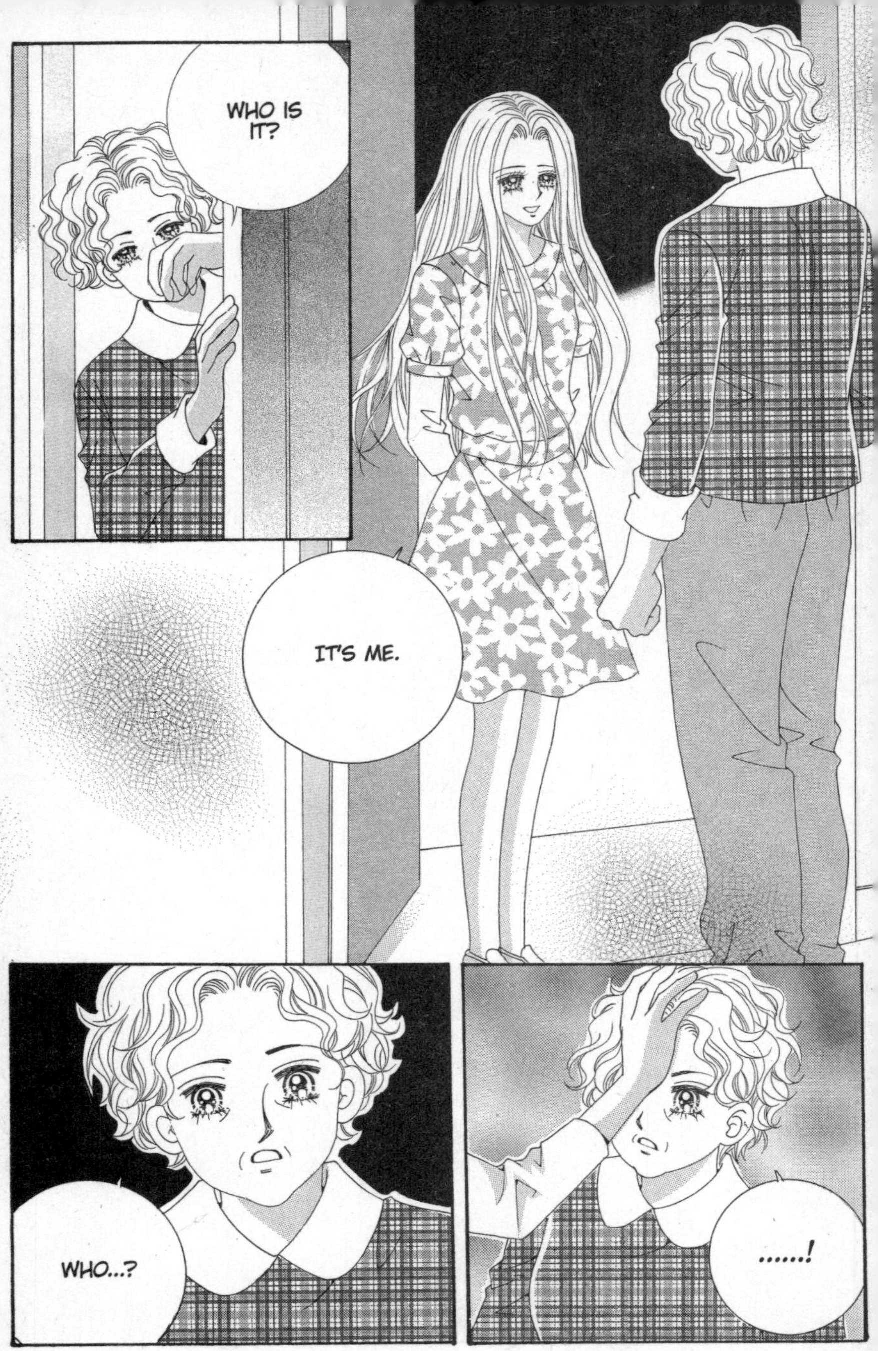
WHO IS IT?
IT'S ME.
WHO...?
......!

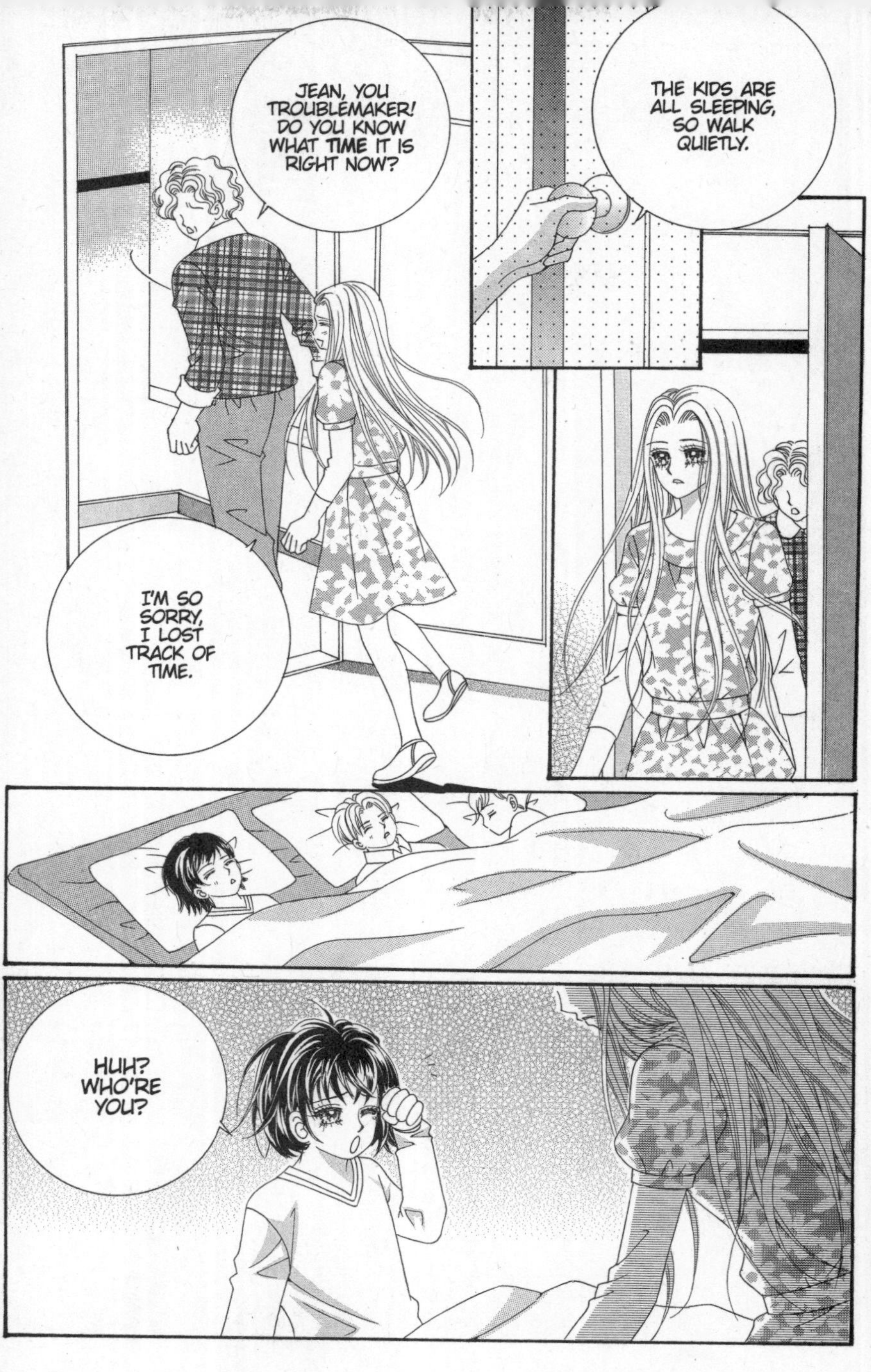
JEAN, YOU TROUBLEMAKER! DO YOU KNOW WHAT TIME IT IS RIGHT NOW?
I'M SO SORRY, I LOST TRACK OF TIME.
THE KIDS ARE ALL SLEEPING, SO WALK QUIETLY.
HUH? WHO'RE YOU?

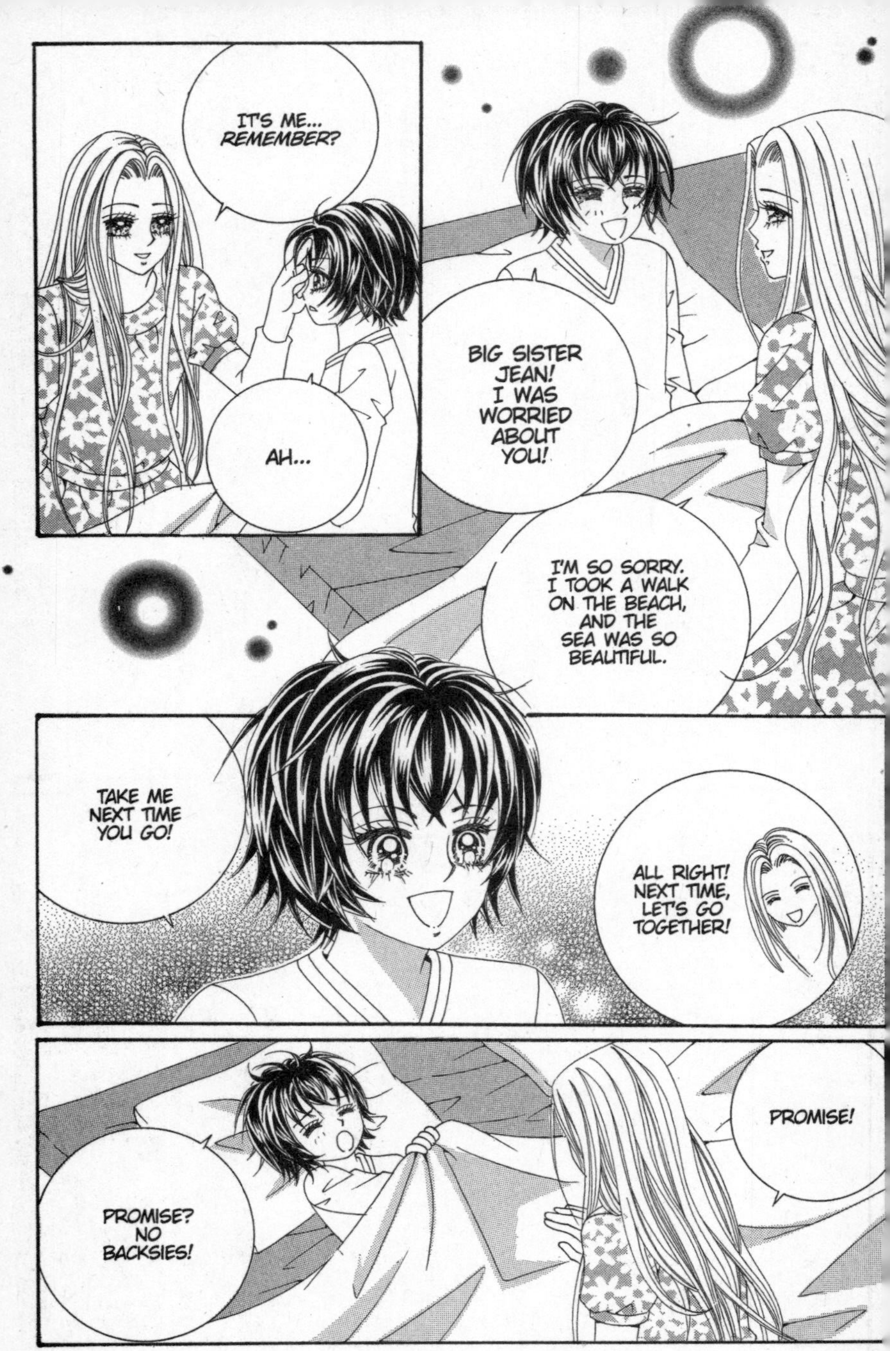
IT'S ME... REMEMBER?
AH...
BIG SISTER JEAN! I WAS WORRIED ABOUT YOU!
I'M SO SORRY. I TOOK A WALK ON THE BEACH, AND THE SEA WAS SO BEAUTIFUL.
TAKE ME NEXT TIME YOU GO!
ALL RIGHT! NEXT TIME, LET'S GO TOGETHER!
PROMISE? NO BACKSIES!
PROMISE!

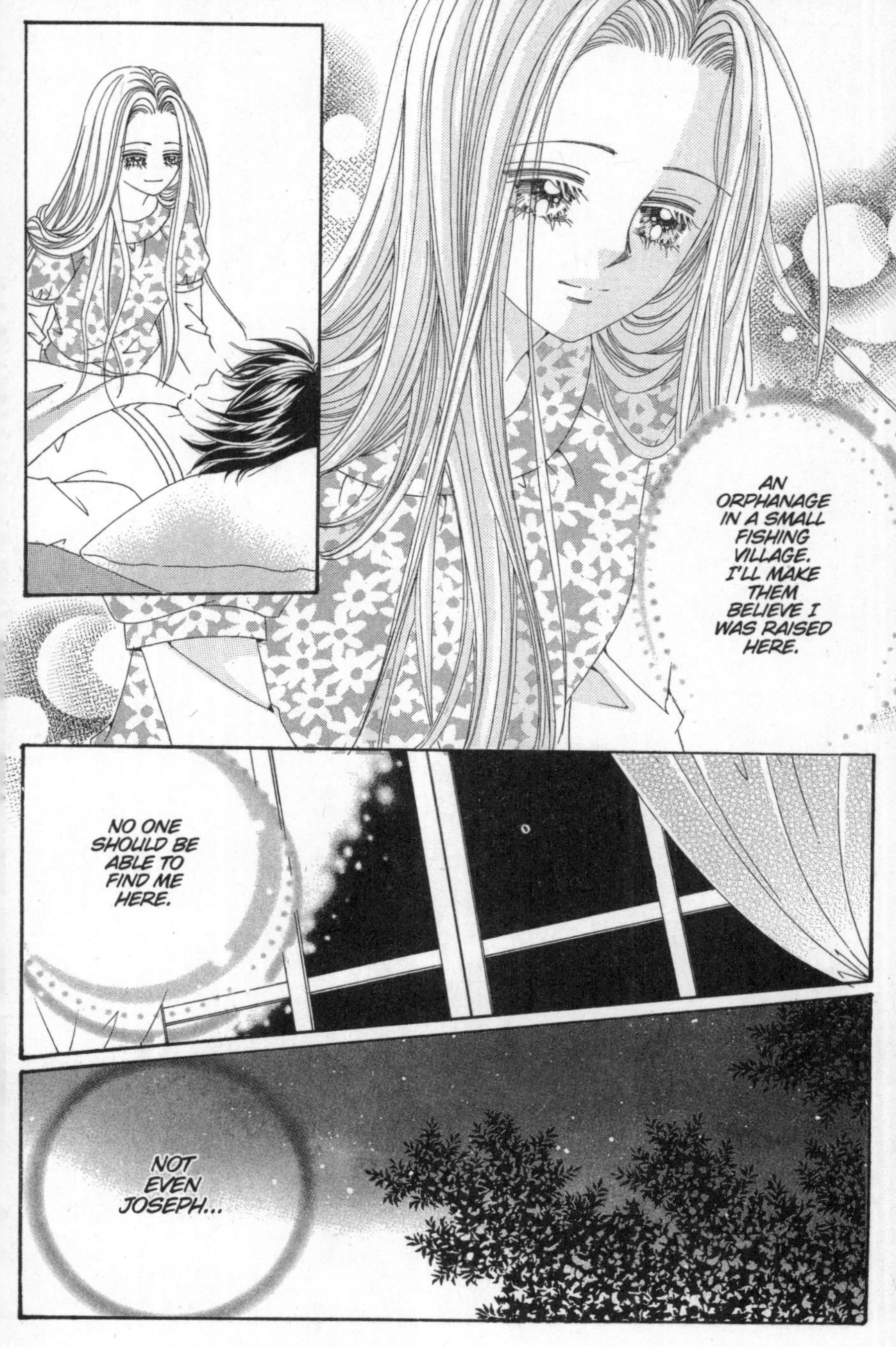
AN ORPHANAGE IN A SMALL FISHING VILLAGE. I'LL MAKE THEM BELIEVE I WAS RAISED HERE.
NO ONE SHOULD BE ABLE TO FIND ME HERE.
NOT EVEN JOSEPH...

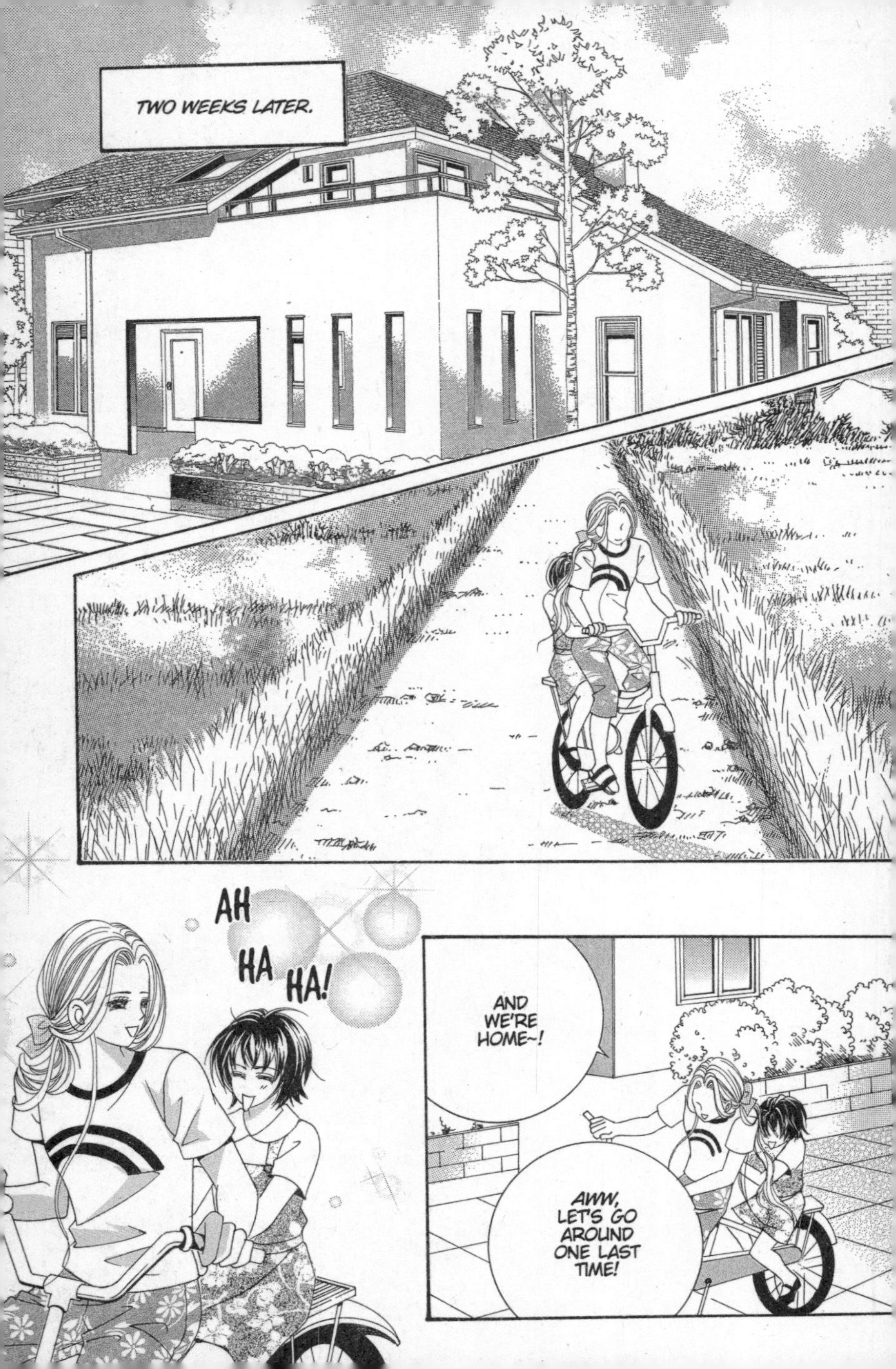
TWO WEEKS LATER.
AH HA HA!
AND WE'RE HOME~!
AWW, LET'S GO AROUND ONE LAST TIME!

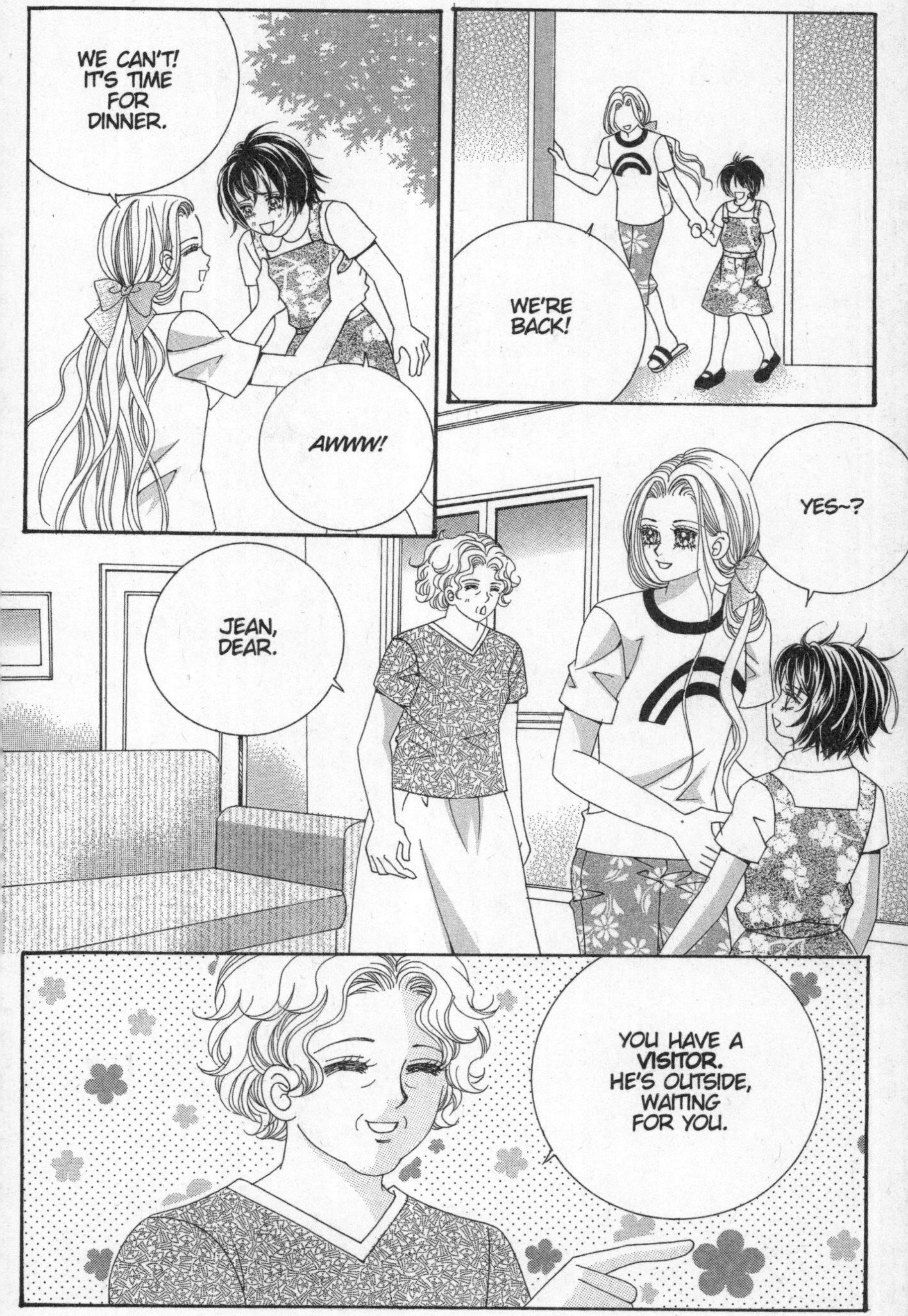
WE CAN'T! IT'S TIME FOR DINNER.
AWWW!
WE'RE BACK!
JEAN, DEAR.
YES~?
YOU HAVE A VISITOR. HE'S OUTSIDE, WAITING FOR YOU.

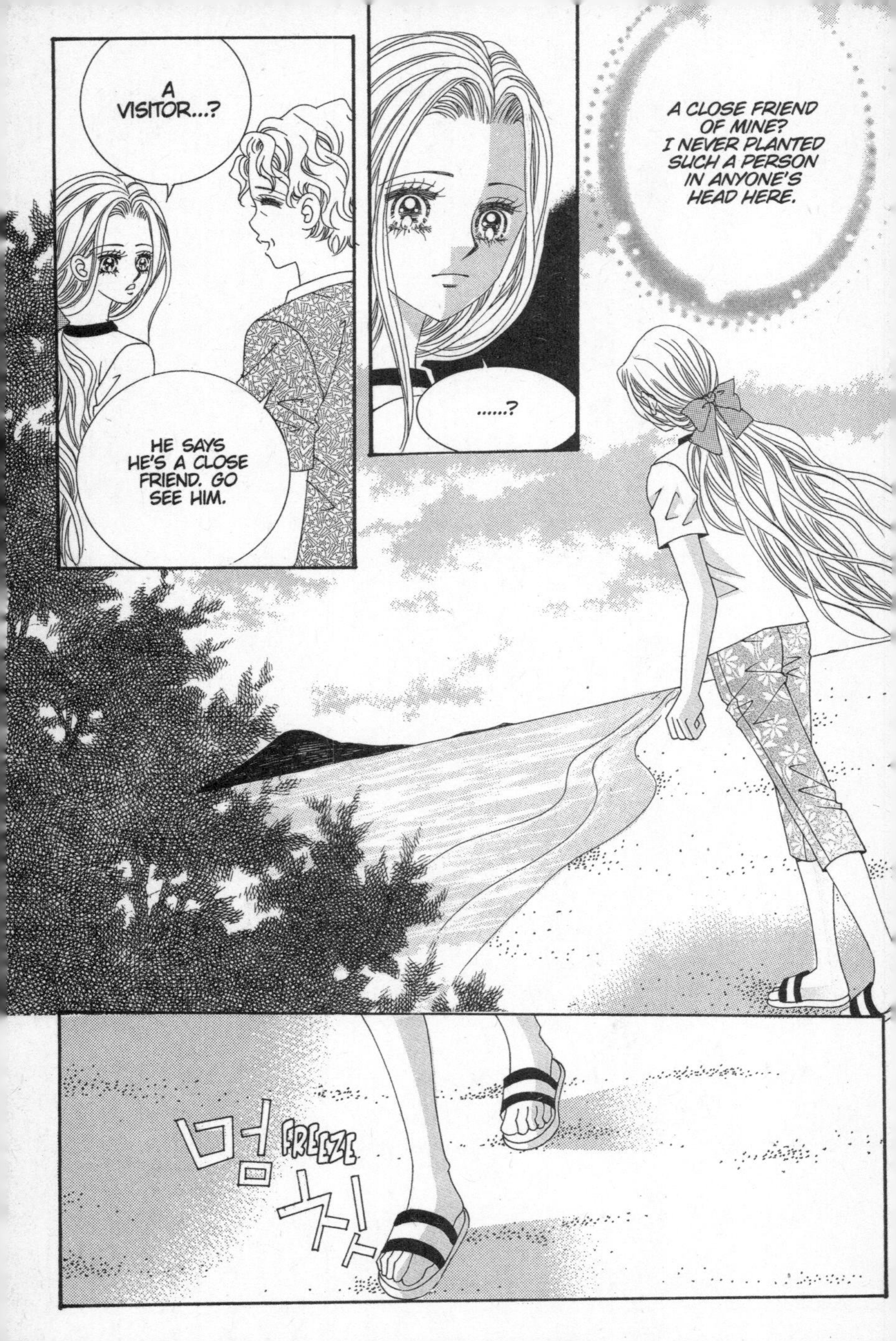
A VISITOR...?
HE SAYS HE'S A CLOSE FRIEND. GO SEE HIM.
......?
A CLOSE FRIEND OF MINE? I NEVER PLANTED SUCH A PERSON IN ANYONE'S HEAD HERE.
멈칫
FREEZE

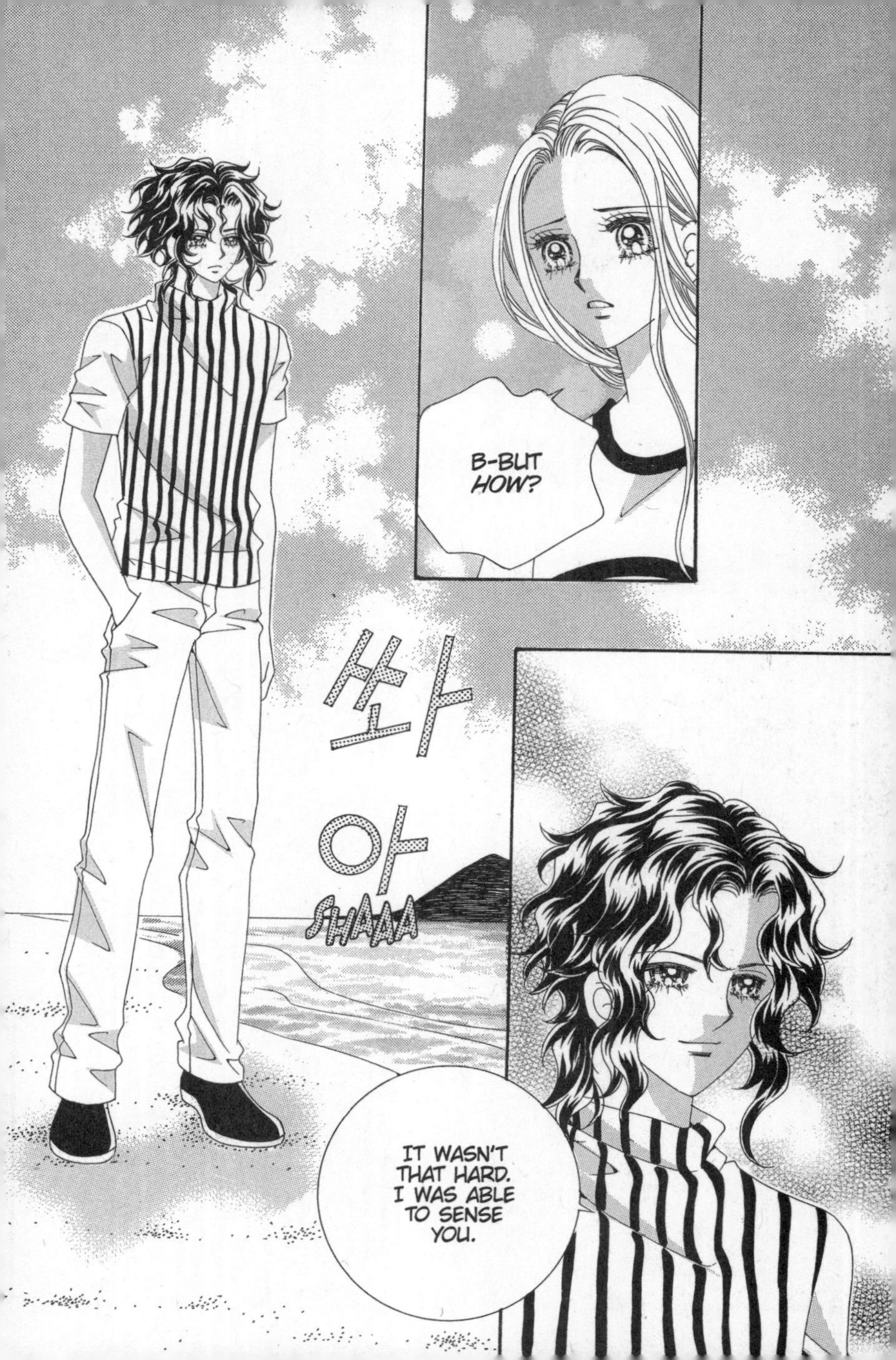
B-BUT HOW?
쏴아
SHAAA
IT WASN'T THAT HARD. I WAS ABLE TO SENSE YOU.

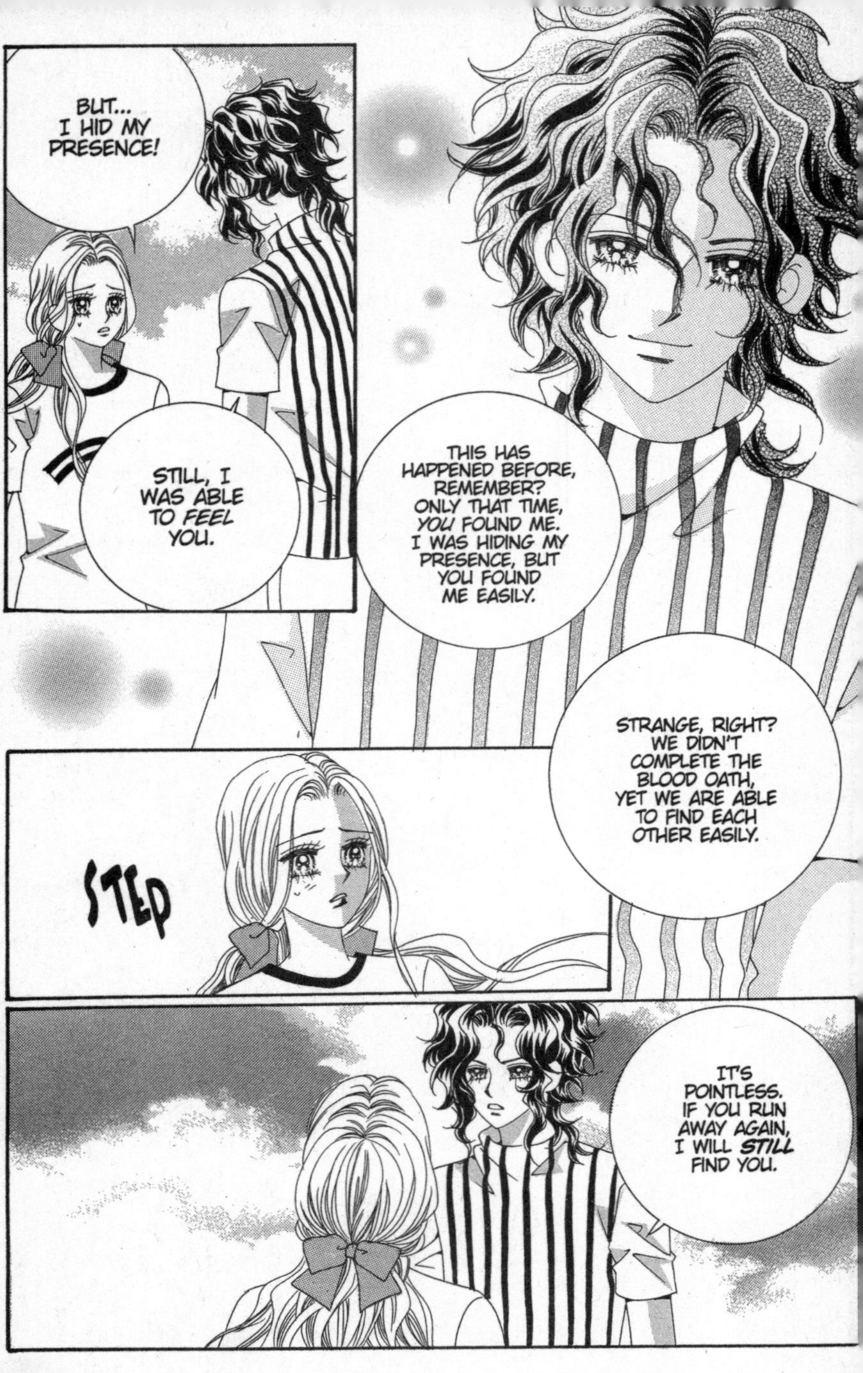
BUT... I HID MY PRESENCE!
STILL, I WAS ABLE TO *FEEL* YOU.
STEP
THIS HAS HAPPENED BEFORE, REMEMBER? ONLY THAT TIME, *YOU* FOUND ME. I WAS HIDING MY PRESENCE, BUT YOU FOUND ME EASILY.
STRANGE, RIGHT? WE DIDN'T COMPLETE THE BLOOD OATH, YET WE ARE ABLE TO FIND EACH OTHER EASILY.
IT'S POINTLESS. IF YOU RUN AWAY AGAIN, I WILL *STILL* FIND YOU.

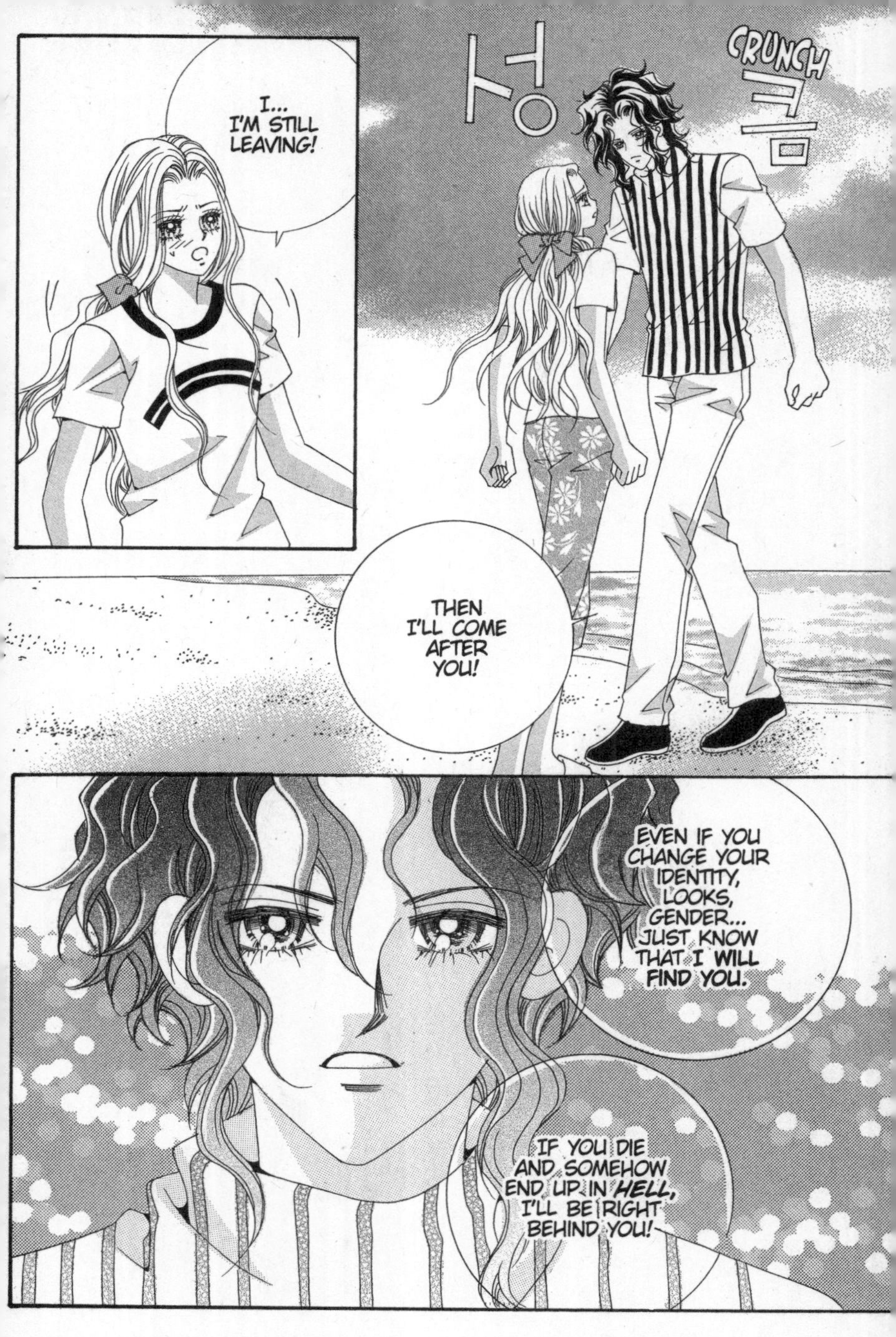
I... I'M STILL LEAVING!
CRUNCH
성큼
THEN I'LL COME AFTER YOU!
EVEN IF YOU CHANGE YOUR IDENTITY, LOOKS, GENDER... JUST KNOW THAT I WILL FIND YOU.
IF YOU DIE AND SOMEHOW END UP IN HELL, I'LL BE RIGHT BEHIND YOU!

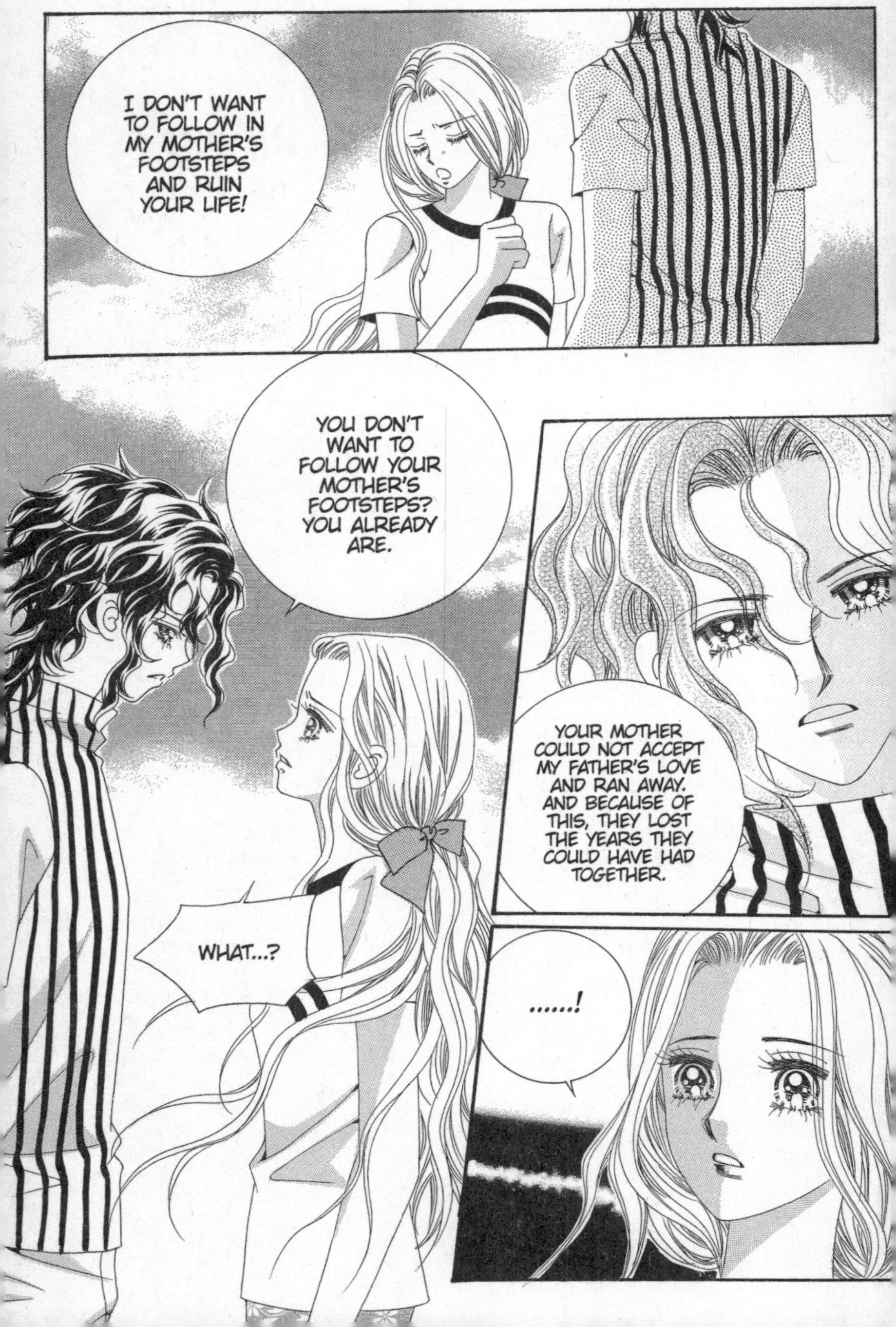
I DON'T WANT TO FOLLOW IN MY MOTHER'S FOOTSTEPS AND RUIN YOUR LIFE!
YOU DON'T WANT TO FOLLOW YOUR MOTHER'S FOOTSTEPS? YOU ALREADY ARE.
WHAT...?
YOUR MOTHER COULD NOT ACCEPT MY FATHER'S LOVE AND RAN AWAY. AND BECAUSE OF THIS, THEY LOST THE YEARS THEY COULD HAVE HAD TOGETHER.
......!

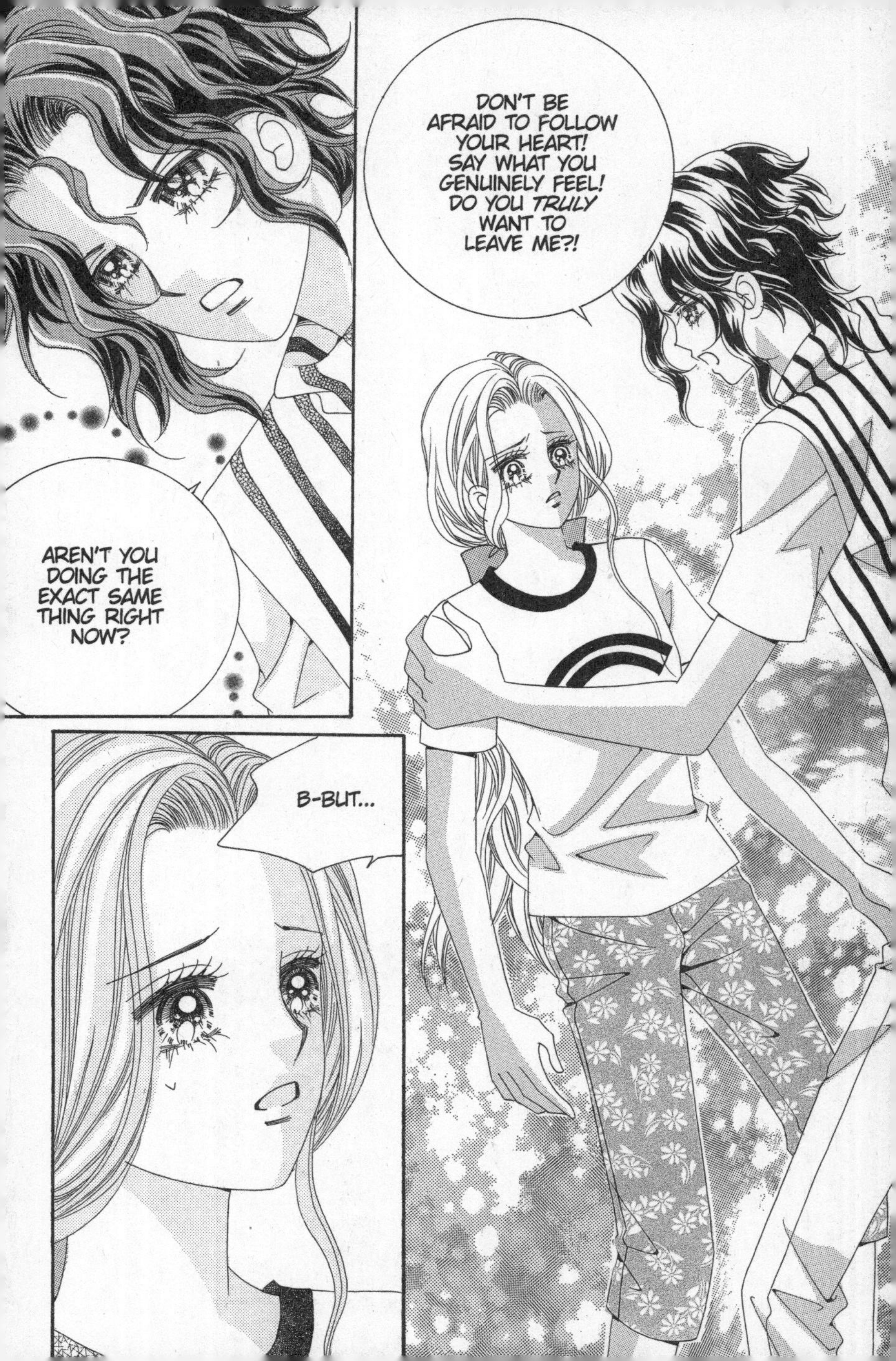
AREN'T YOU DOING THE EXACT SAME THING RIGHT NOW?
B-BUT...
DON'T BE AFRAID TO FOLLOW YOUR HEART! SAY WHAT YOU GENUINELY FEEL! DO YOU *TRULY* WANT TO LEAVE ME?!

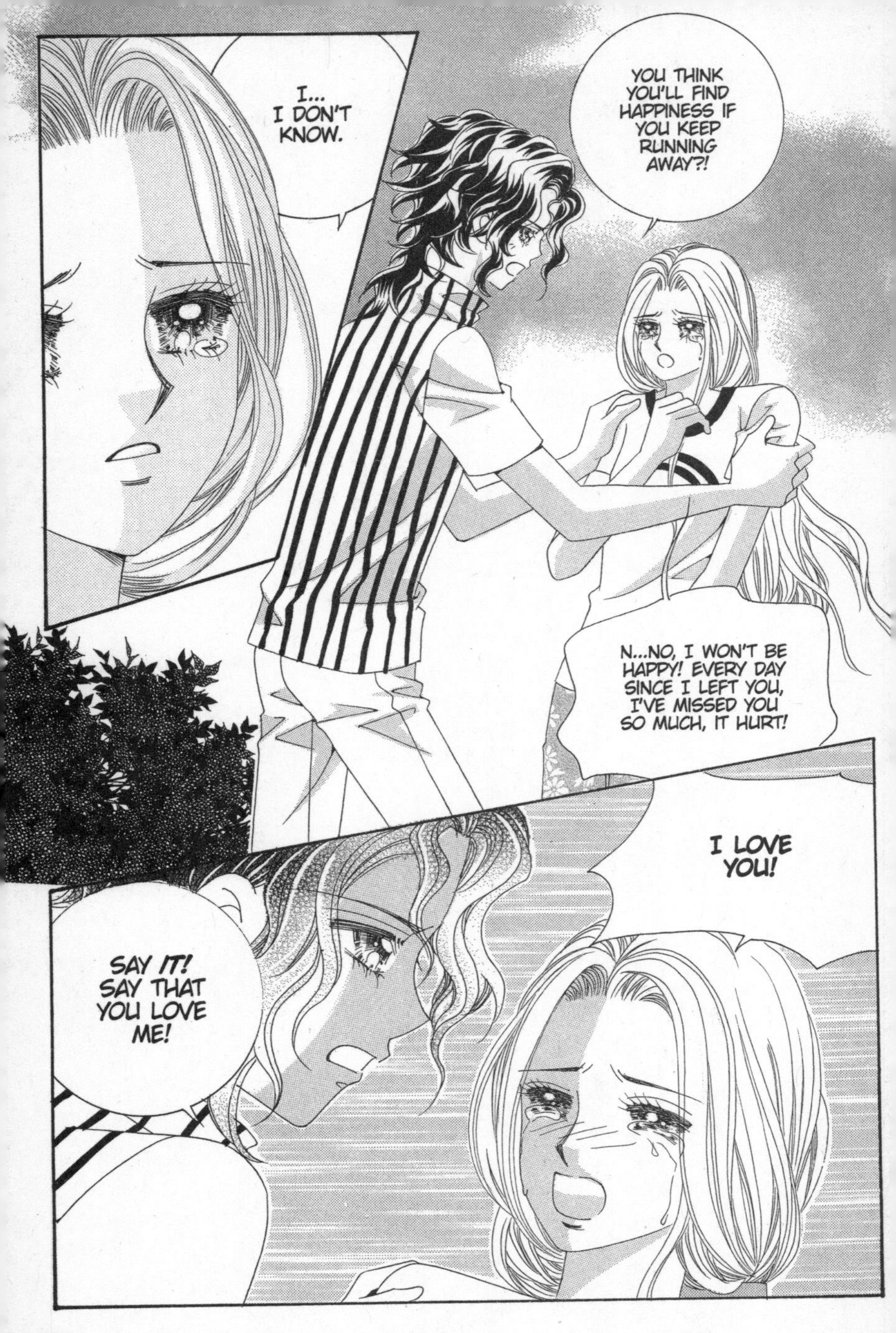
I... I DON'T KNOW.
YOU THINK YOU'LL FIND HAPPINESS IF YOU KEEP RUNNING AWAY?!
N...NO, I WON'T BE HAPPY! EVERY DAY SINCE I LEFT YOU, I'VE MISSED YOU SO MUCH, IT HURT!
SAY *IT!* SAY THAT YOU LOVE ME!
I LOVE YOU!

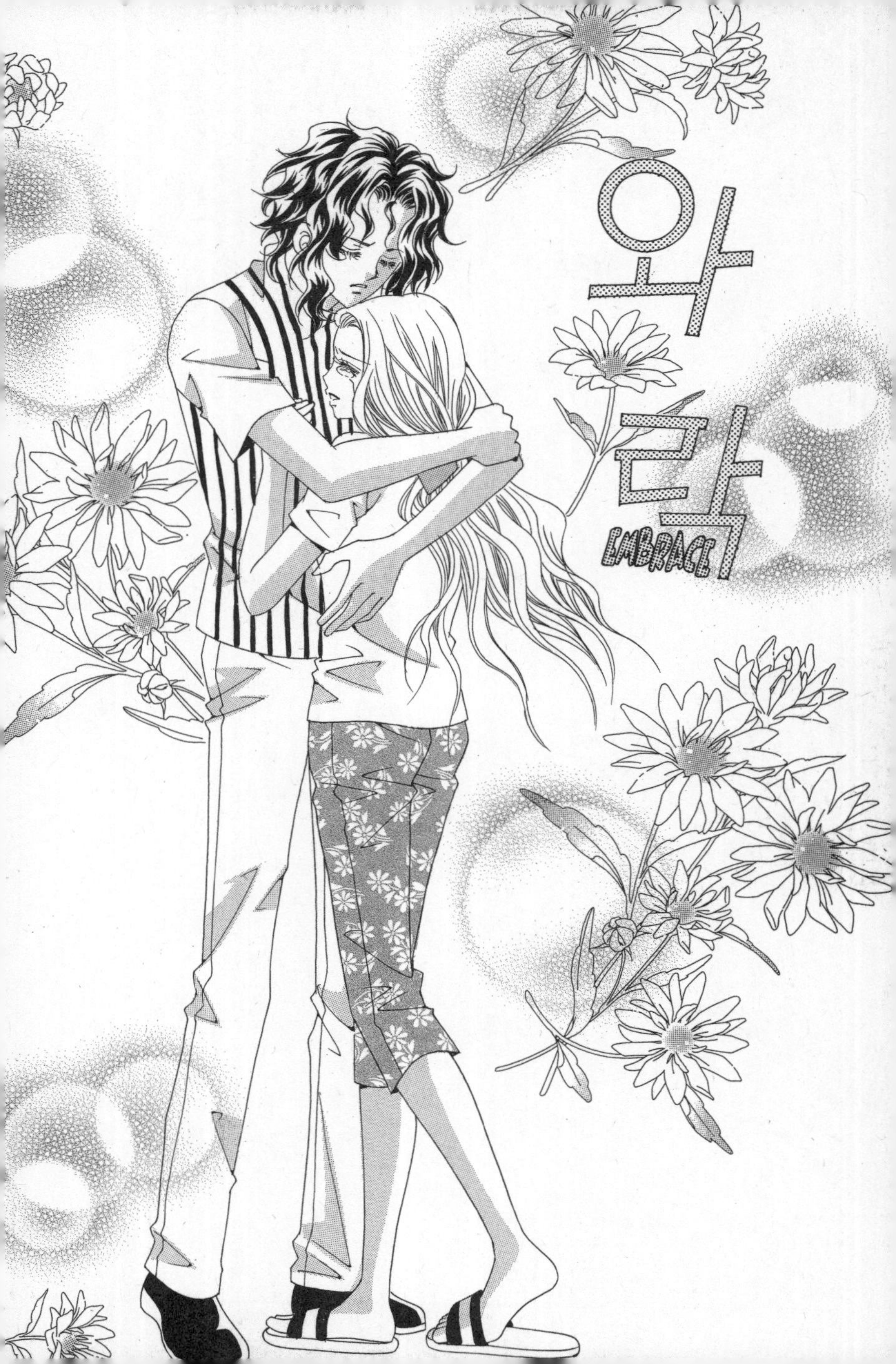
포옹
EMBRACE

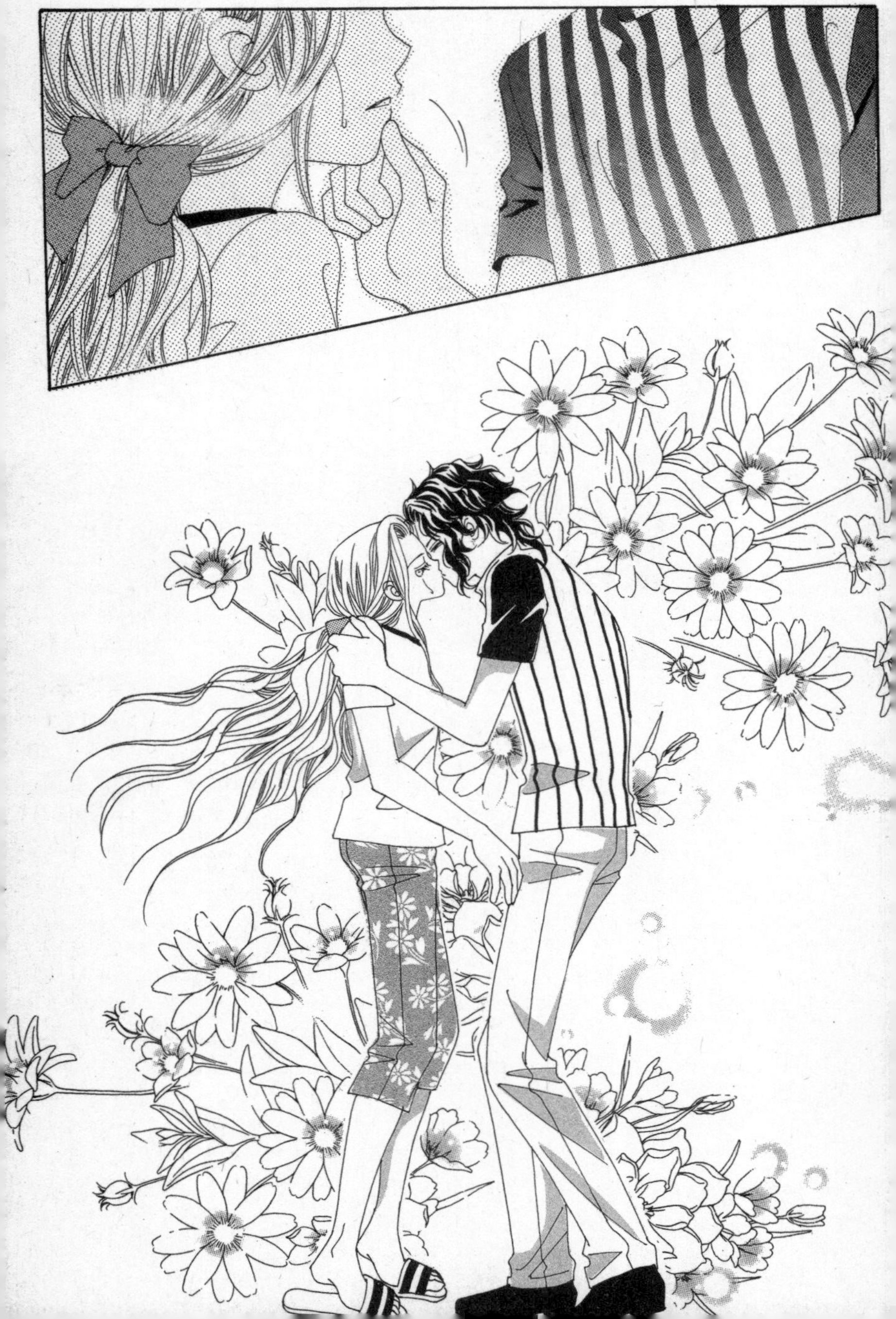

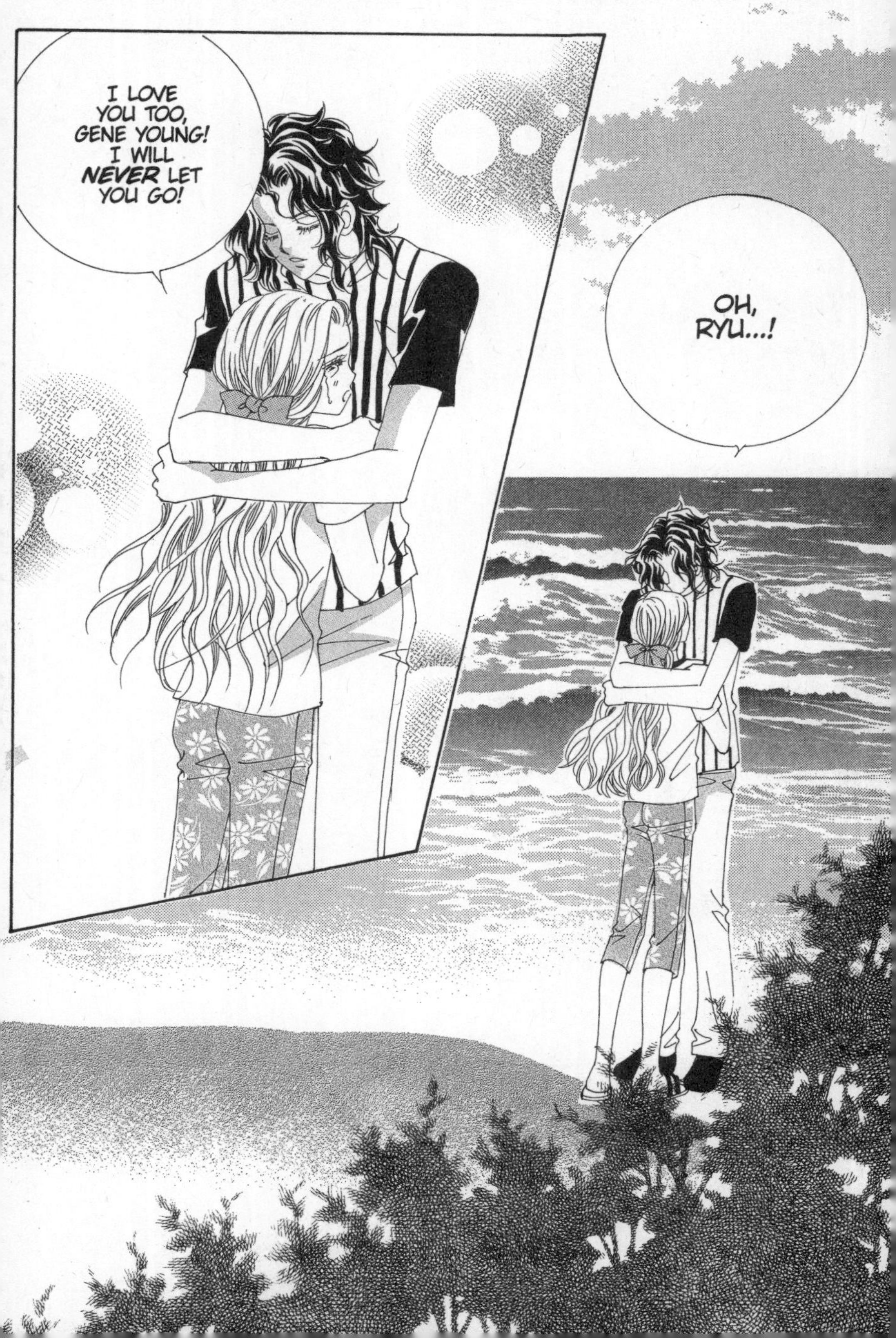
I LOVE YOU TOO, GENE YOUNG! I WILL NEVER LET YOU GO!
OH, RYU...!

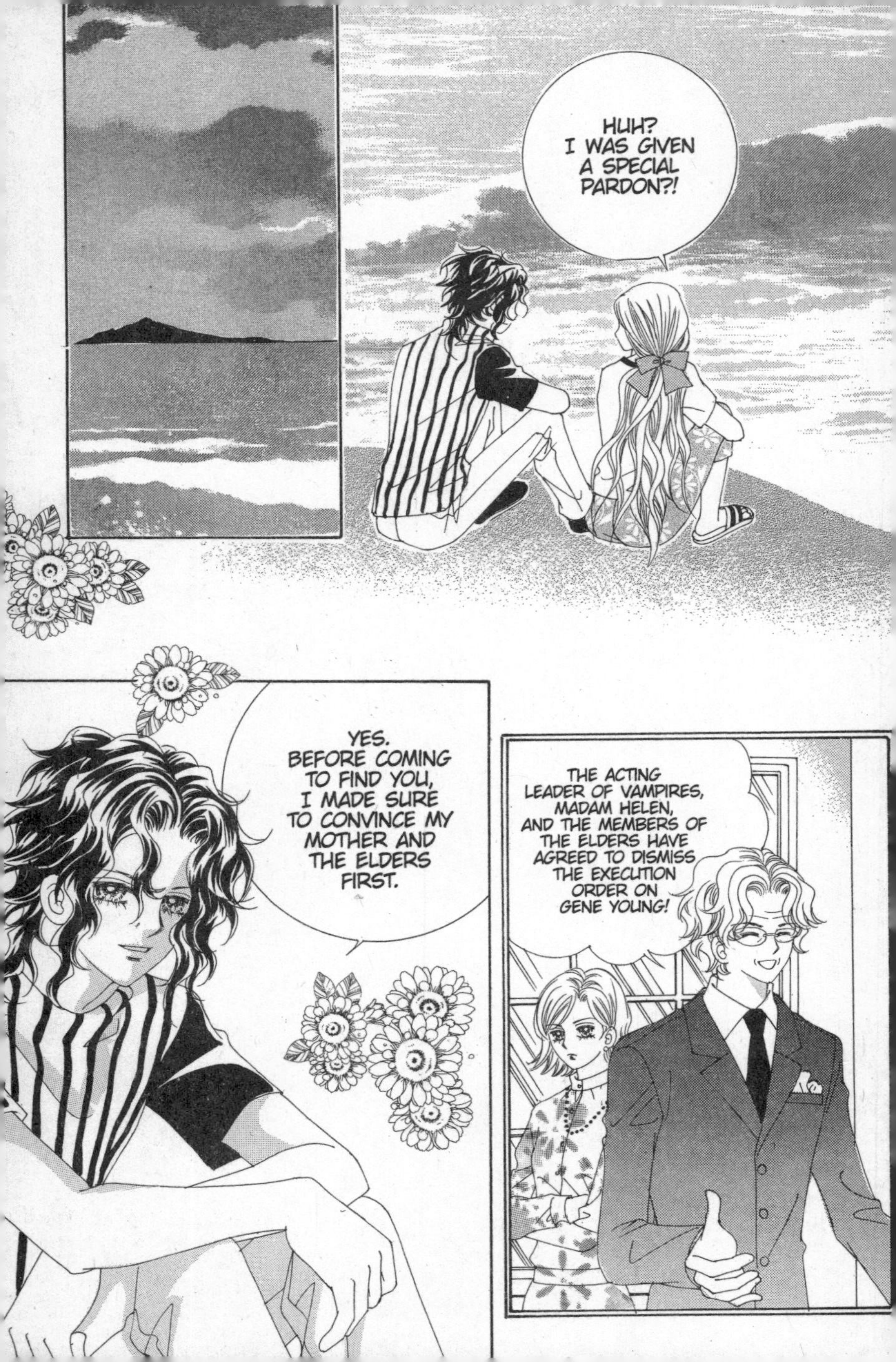
HUH?
I WAS GIVEN A SPECIAL PARDON?!
YES. BEFORE COMING TO FIND YOU, I MADE SURE TO CONVINCE MY MOTHER AND THE ELDERS FIRST.
THE ACTING LEADER OF VAMPIRES, MADAM HELEN, AND THE MEMBERS OF THE ELDERS HAVE AGREED TO DISMISS THE EXECUTION ORDER ON GENE YOUNG!

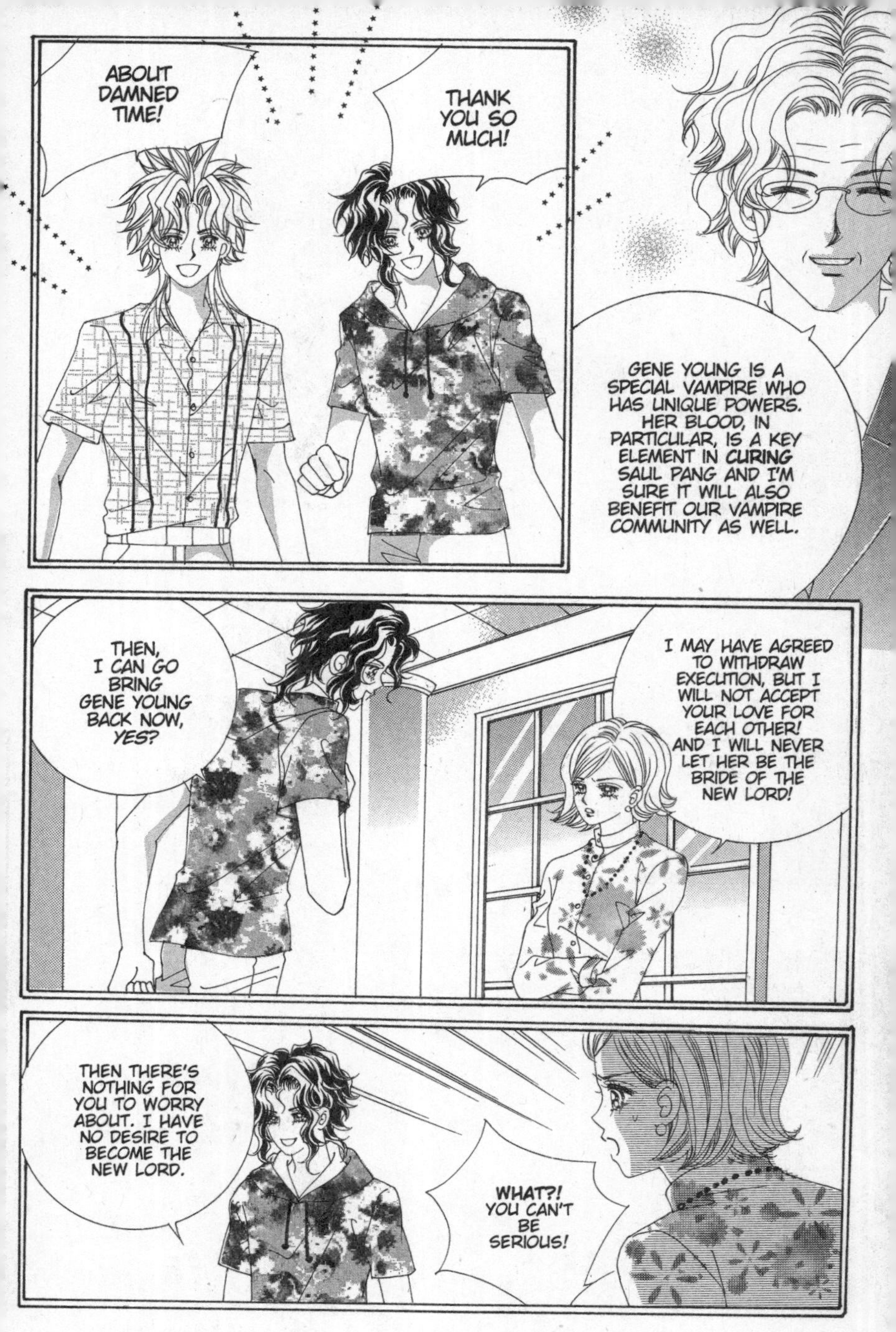
ABOUT DAMNED TIME!
THANK YOU SO MUCH!
GENE YOUNG IS A SPECIAL VAMPIRE WHO HAS UNIQUE POWERS. HER BLOOD, IN PARTICULAR, IS A KEY ELEMENT IN **CURING** SAUL PANG AND I'M SURE IT WILL ALSO BENEFIT OUR VAMPIRE COMMUNITY AS WELL.
THEN, I CAN GO BRING GENE YOUNG BACK NOW, *YES?*
I MAY HAVE AGREED TO WITHDRAW EXECUTION, BUT I WILL NOT ACCEPT YOUR LOVE FOR EACH OTHER! AND I WILL NEVER LET HER BE THE BRIDE OF THE NEW LORD!
THEN THERE'S NOTHING FOR YOU TO WORRY ABOUT. I HAVE NO DESIRE TO BECOME THE NEW LORD.
WHAT?! YOU CAN'T BE SERIOUS!

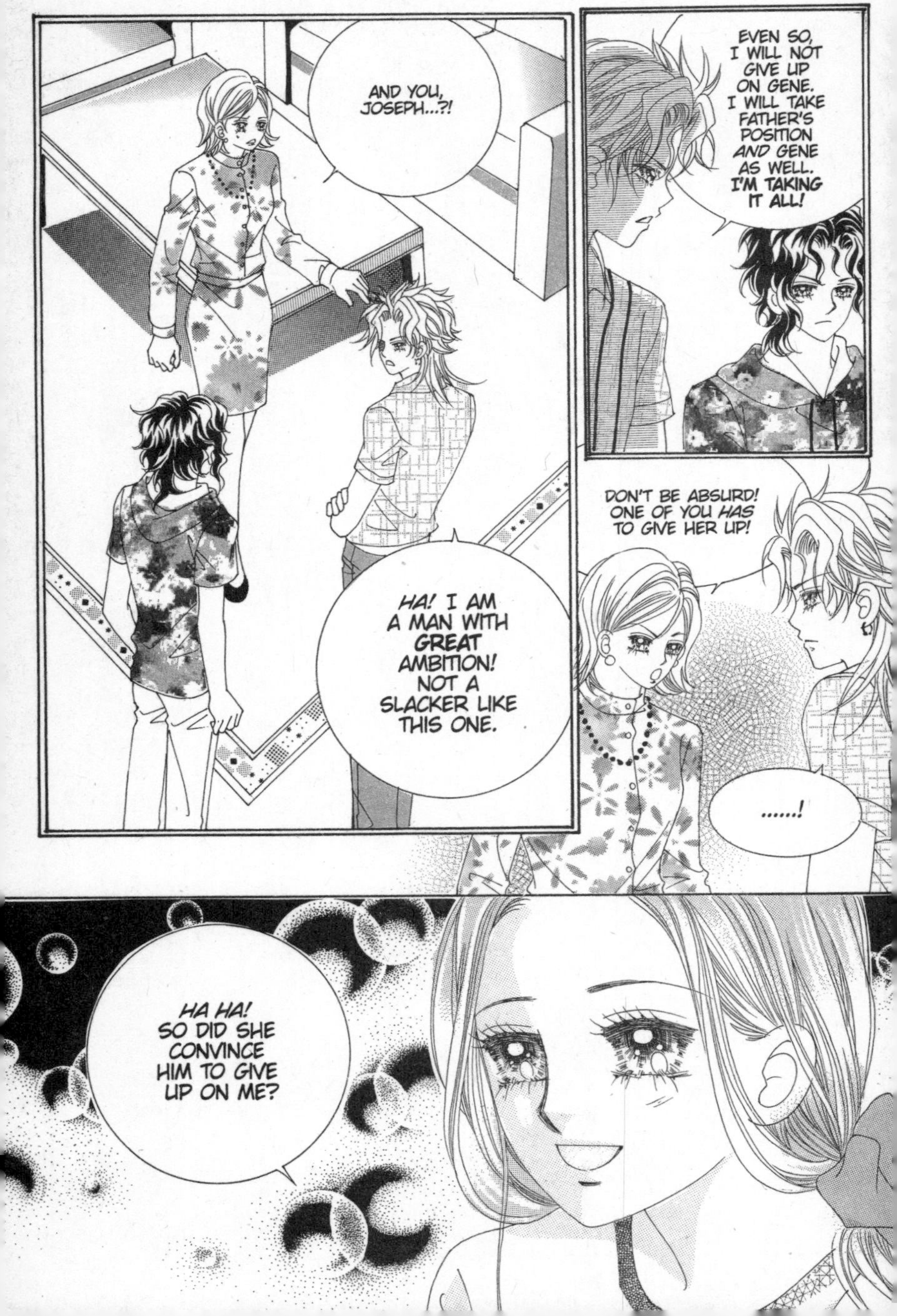
AND YOU, JOSEPH...?!
HA! I AM A MAN WITH GREAT AMBITION! NOT A SLACKER LIKE THIS ONE.
EVEN SO, I WILL NOT GIVE UP ON GENE. I WILL TAKE FATHER'S POSITION AND GENE AS WELL. I'M TAKING IT ALL!
DON'T BE ABSURD! ONE OF YOU HAS TO GIVE HER UP!
......!
HA HA! SO DID SHE CONVINCE HIM TO GIVE UP ON ME?

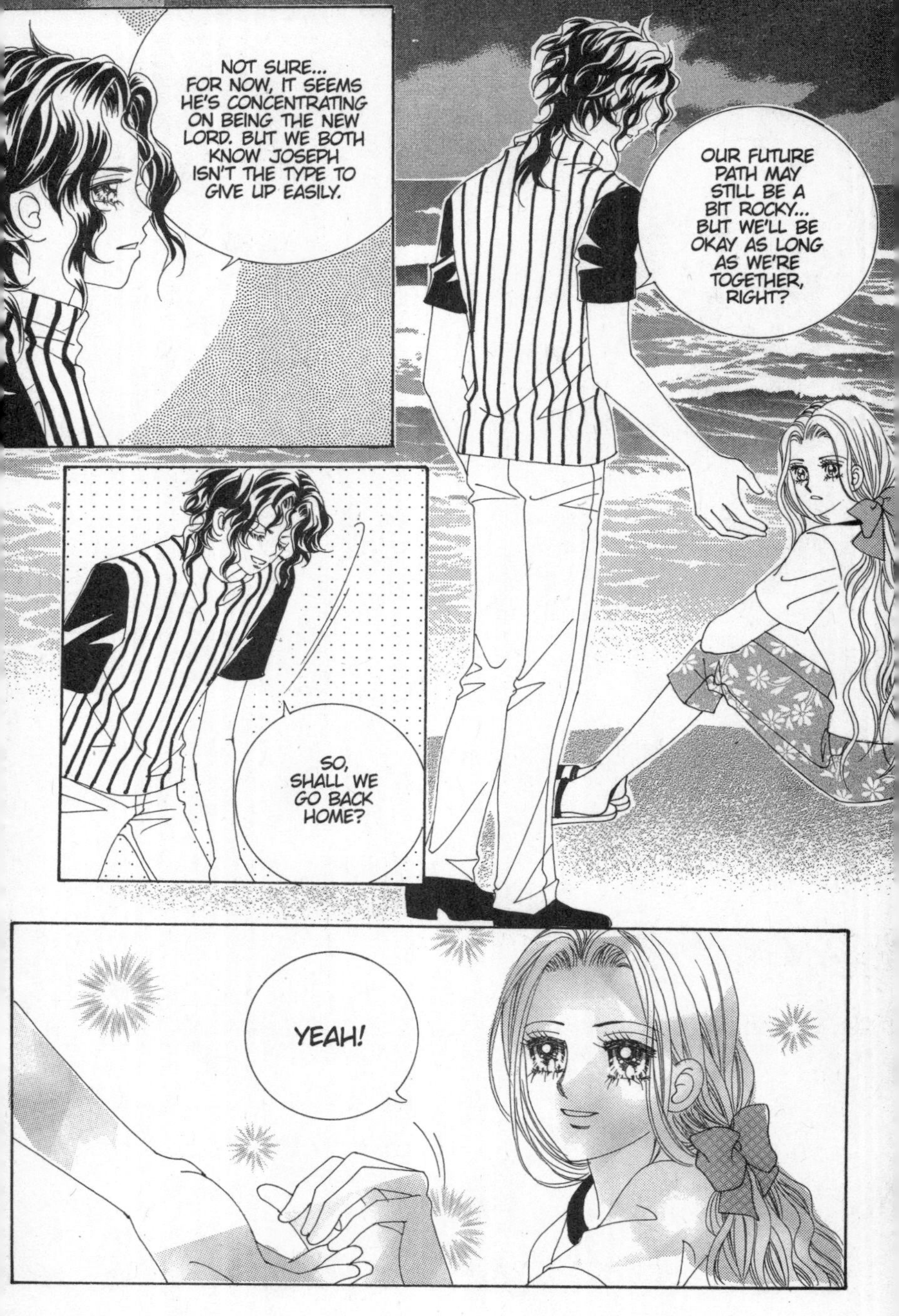
NOT SURE... FOR NOW, IT SEEMS HE'S CONCENTRATING ON BEING THE NEW LORD. BUT WE BOTH KNOW JOSEPH ISN'T THE TYPE TO GIVE UP EASILY.
OUR FUTURE PATH MAY STILL BE A BIT ROCKY... BUT WE'LL BE OKAY AS LONG AS WE'RE TOGETHER, RIGHT?
SO, SHALL WE GO BACK HOME?
YEAH!

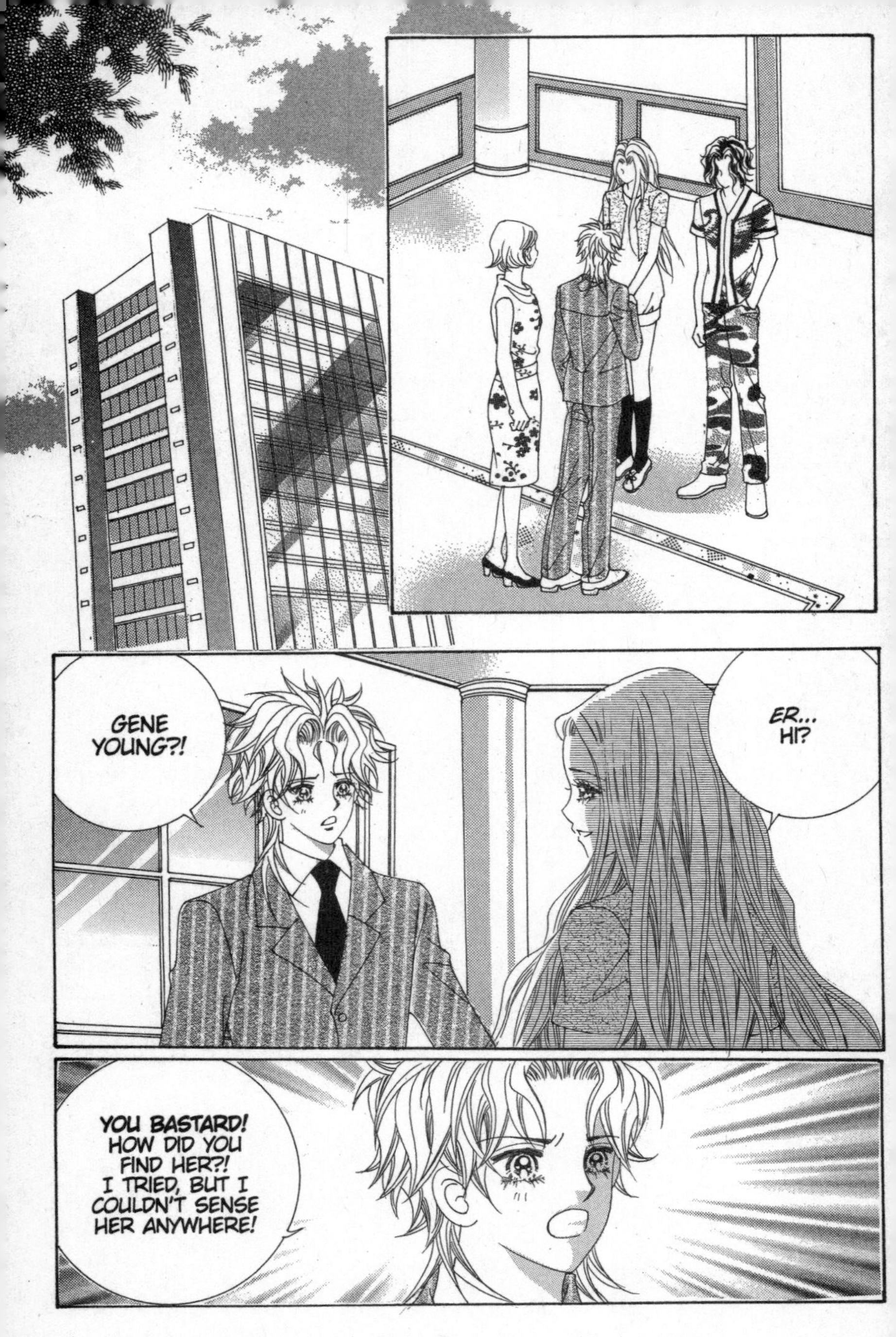
GENE YOUNG?!
ER... HI?
YOU BASTARD! HOW DID YOU FIND HER?! I TRIED, BUT I COULDN'T SENSE HER ANYWHERE!

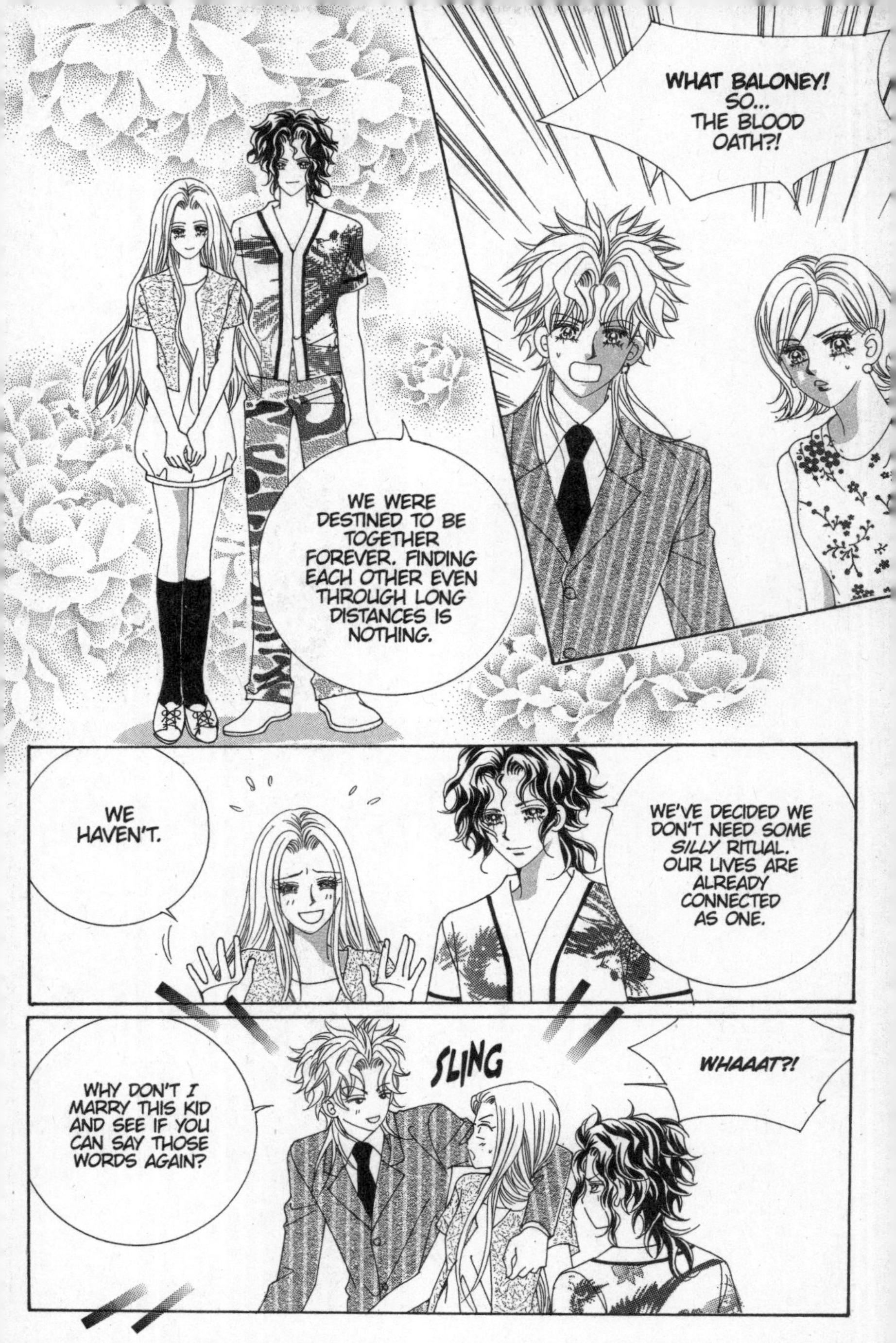
WE WERE DESTINED TO BE TOGETHER FOREVER. FINDING EACH OTHER EVEN THROUGH LONG DISTANCES IS NOTHING.
WHAT BALONEY! SO... THE BLOOD OATH?!
WE HAVEN'T.
WE'VE DECIDED WE DON'T NEED SOME *SILLY* RITUAL. OUR LIVES ARE ALREADY CONNECTED AS ONE.
WHY DON'T *I* MARRY THIS KID AND SEE IF YOU CAN SAY THOSE WORDS AGAIN?
SLING
WHAAAT?!

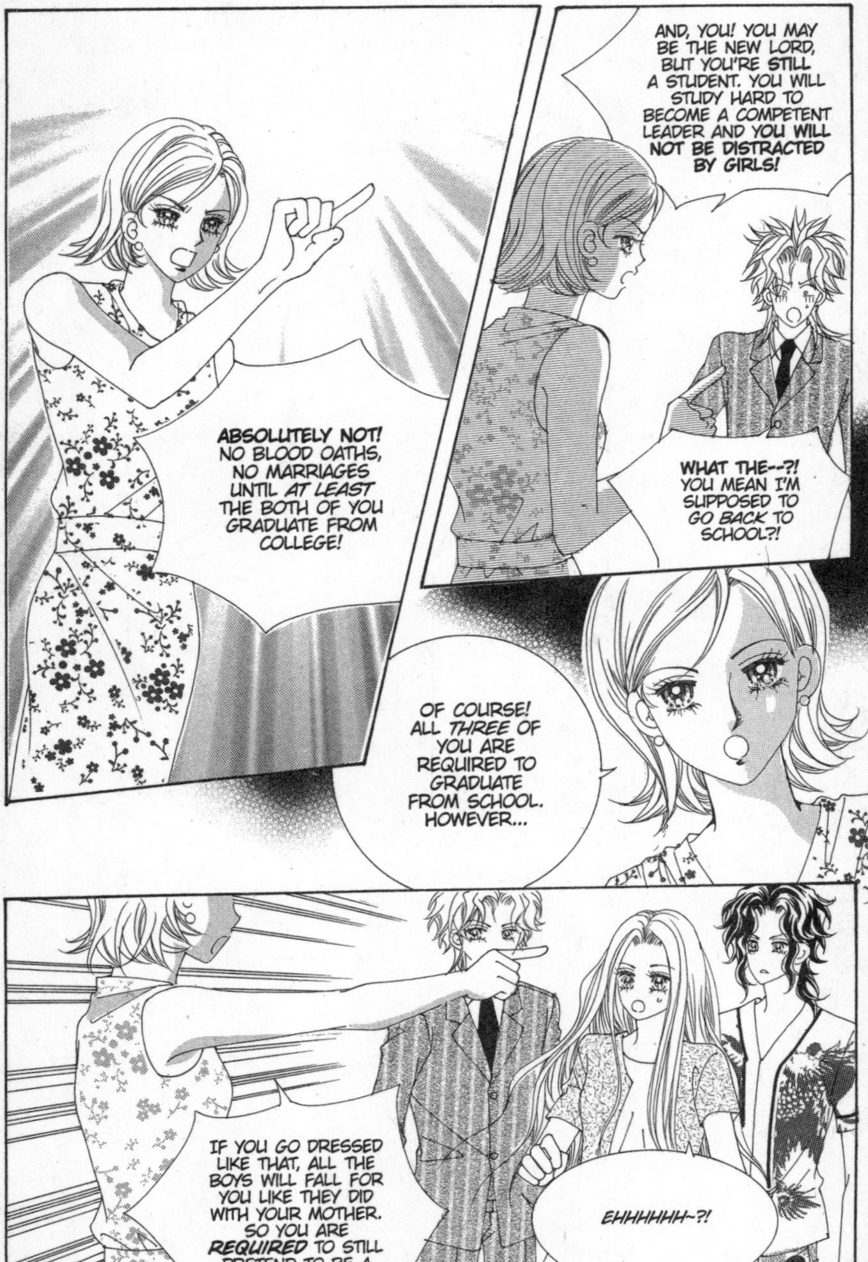
ABSOLUTELY NOT! NO BLOOD OATHS, NO MARRIAGES UNTIL AT LEAST THE BOTH OF YOU GRADUATE FROM COLLEGE!
AND, YOU! YOU MAY BE THE NEW LORD, BUT YOU'RE STILL A STUDENT. YOU WILL STUDY HARD TO BECOME A COMPETENT LEADER AND YOU WILL NOT BE DISTRACTED BY GIRLS!
WHAT THE--?! YOU MEAN I'M SUPPOSED TO GO BACK TO SCHOOL?!
OF COURSE! ALL THREE OF YOU ARE REQUIRED TO GRADUATE FROM SCHOOL. HOWEVER...
IF YOU GO DRESSED LIKE THAT, ALL THE BOYS WILL FALL FOR YOU LIKE THEY DID WITH YOUR MOTHER. SO YOU ARE REQUIRED TO STILL PRETEND TO BE A BOY IN SCHOOL!
EHHHHHH~?!

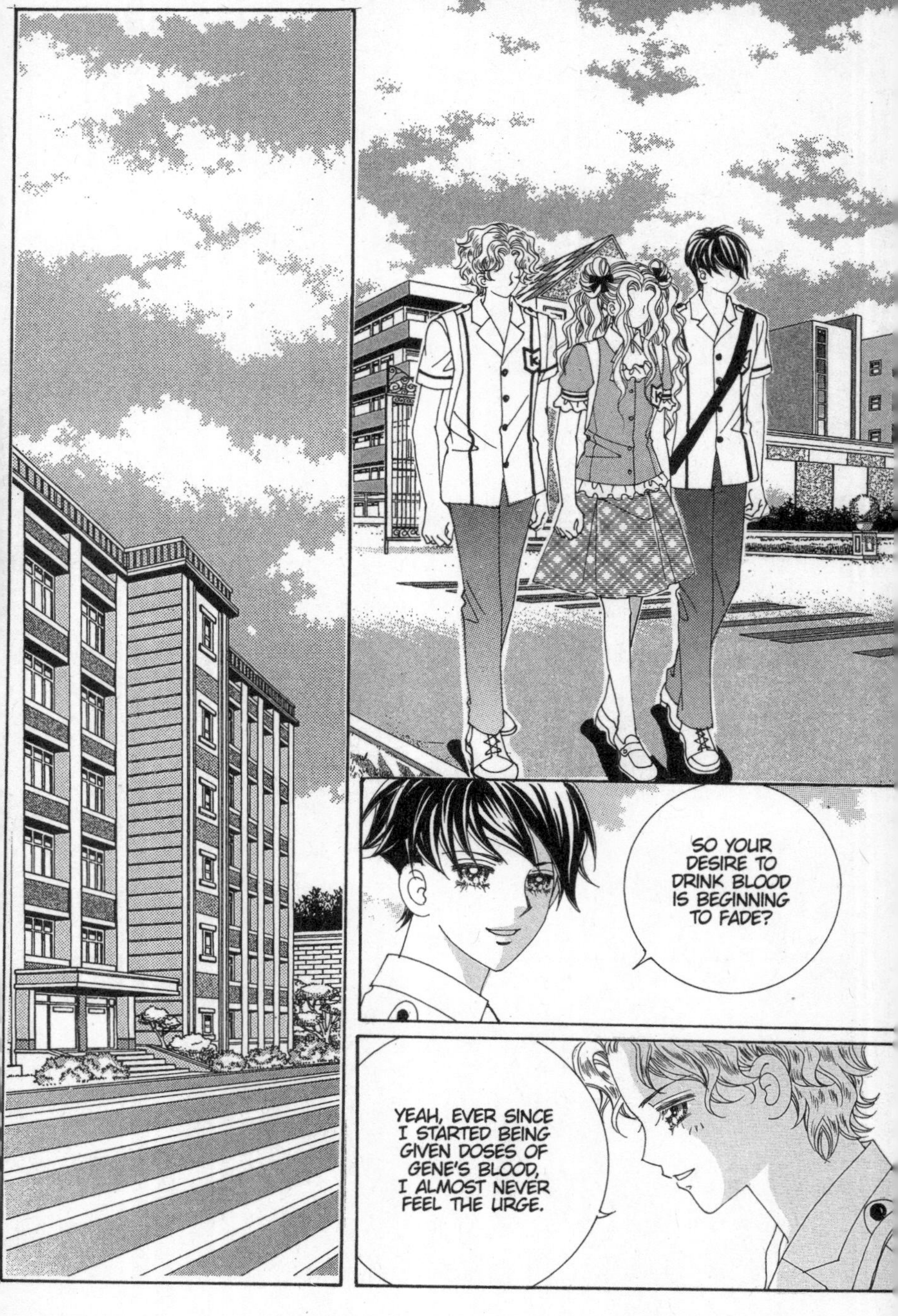
SO YOUR DESIRE TO DRINK BLOOD IS BEGINNING TO FADE?
YEAH, EVER SINCE I STARTED BEING GIVEN DOSES OF GENE'S BLOOD, I ALMOST NEVER FEEL THE URGE.

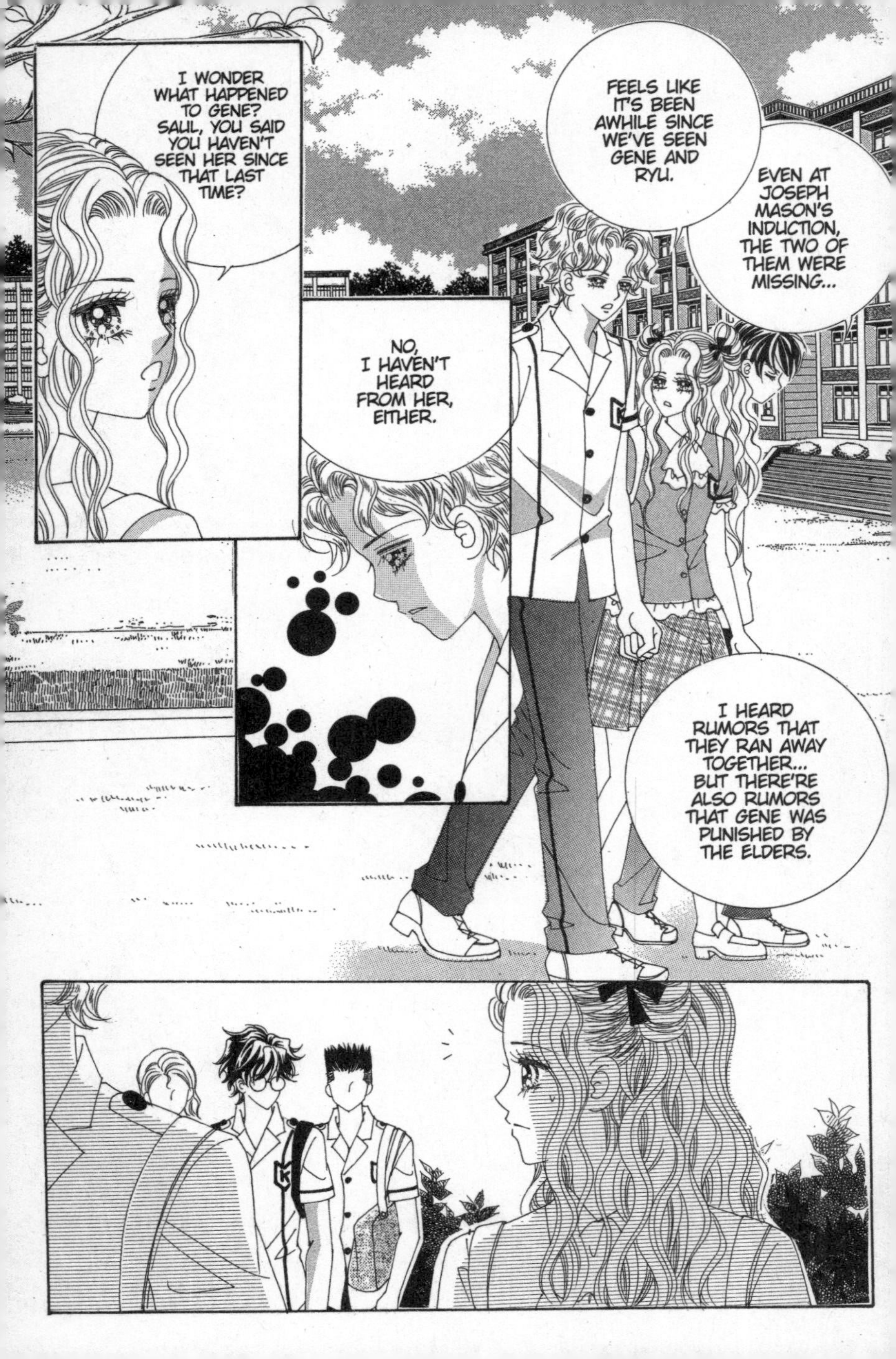

I WONDER WHAT HAPPENED TO GENE? SAUL, YOU SAID YOU HAVEN'T SEEN HER SINCE THAT LAST TIME?
NO, I HAVEN'T HEARD FROM HER, EITHER.
FEELS LIKE IT'S BEEN AWHILE SINCE WE'VE SEEN GENE AND RYU.
EVEN AT JOSEPH MASON'S INDUCTION, THE TWO OF THEM WERE MISSING...
I HEARD RUMORS THAT THEY RAN AWAY TOGETHER... BUT THERE'RE ALSO RUMORS THAT GENE WAS PUNISHED BY THE ELDERS.

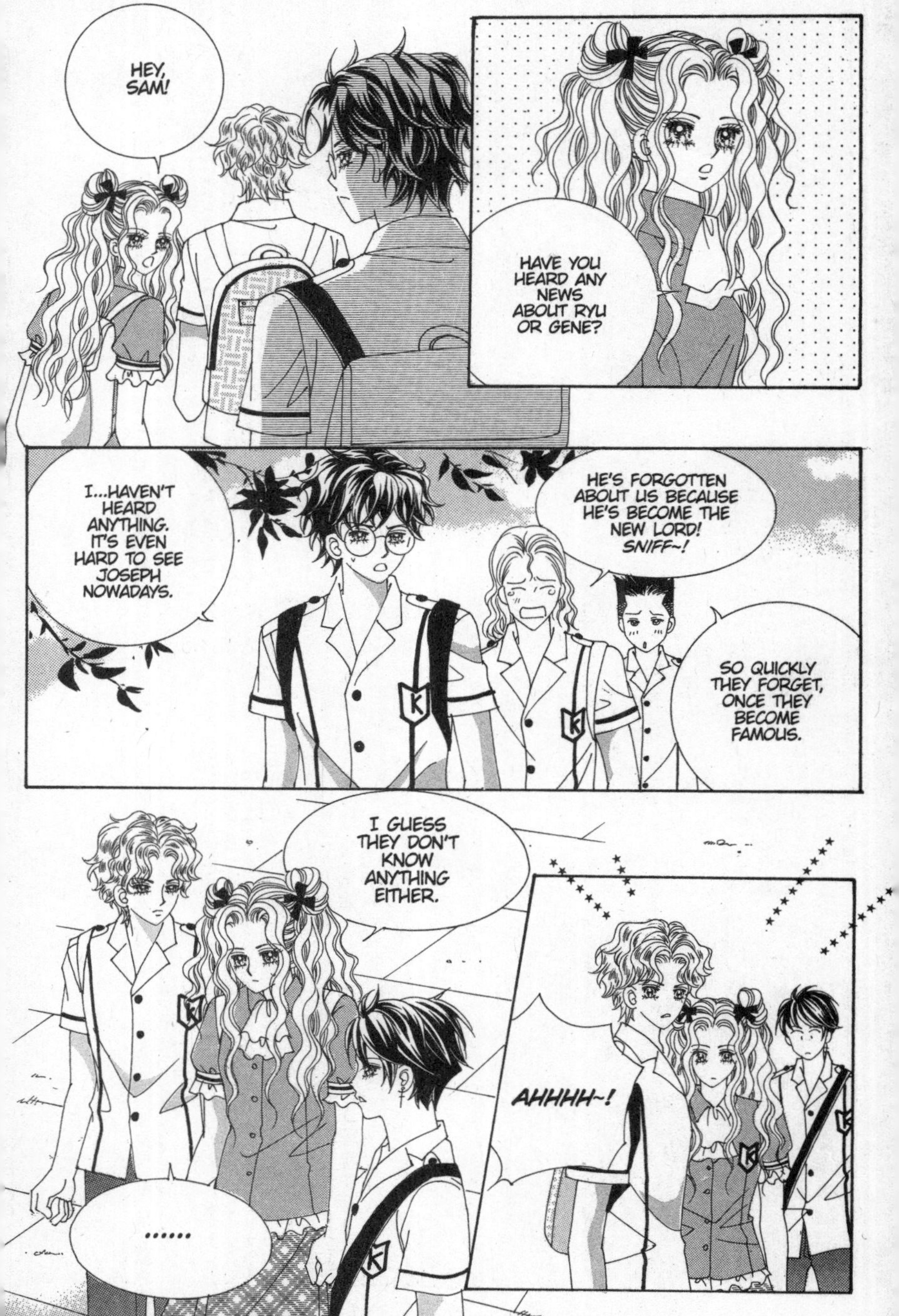

HEY, SAM!
HAVE YOU HEARD ANY NEWS ABOUT RYU OR GENE?
I...HAVEN'T HEARD ANYTHING. IT'S EVEN HARD TO SEE JOSEPH NOWADAYS.
HE'S FORGOTTEN ABOUT US BECAUSE HE'S BECOME THE NEW LORD! SNIFF~!
SO QUICKLY THEY FORGET, ONCE THEY BECOME FAMOUS.
I GUESS THEY DON'T KNOW ANYTHING EITHER.
......
AHHHH~!

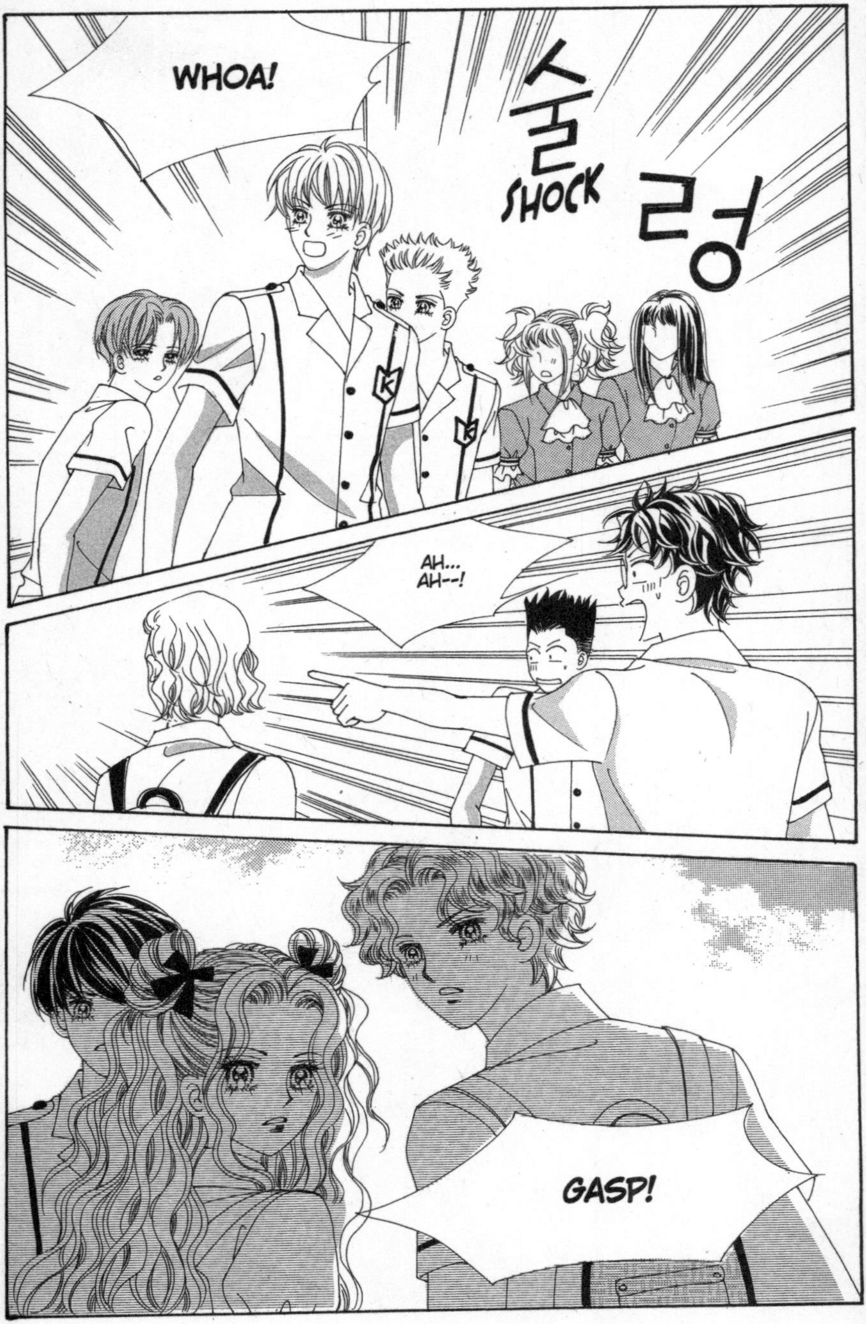
WHOA!
술렁
SHOCK
AH...
AH--!
GASP!

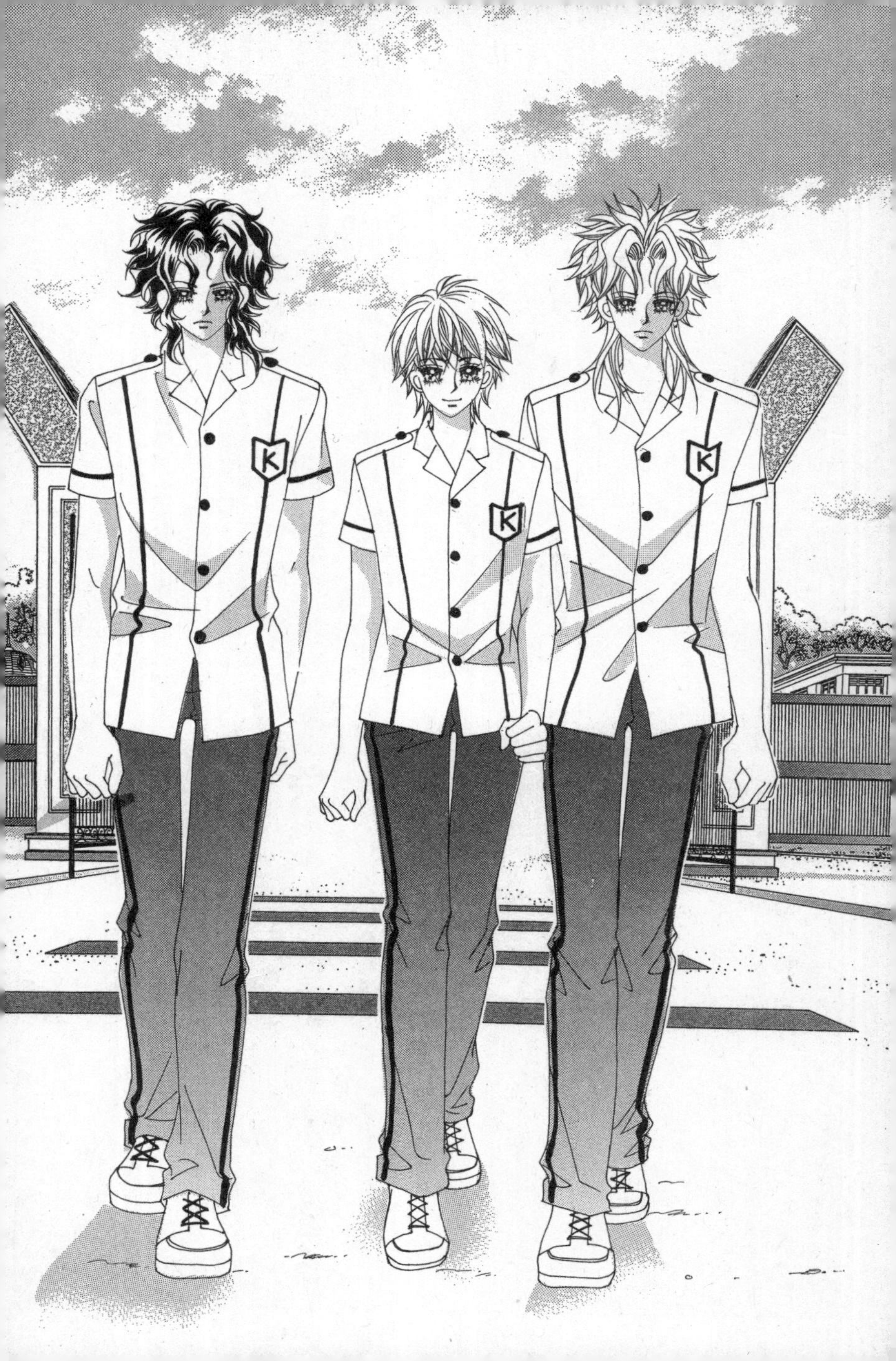

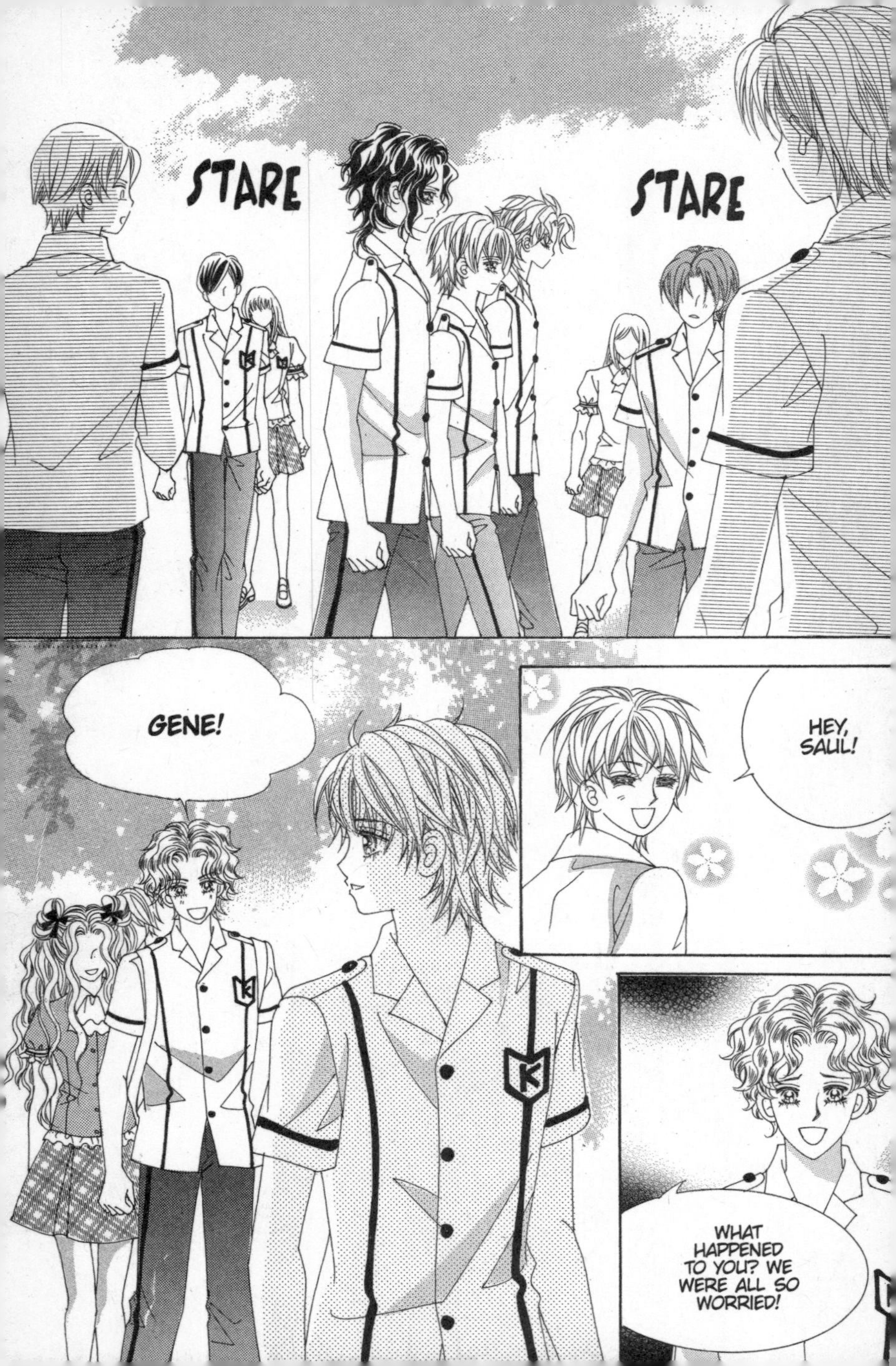
STARE
STARE
GENE!
HEY, SAUL!
WHAT HAPPENED TO YOU? WE WERE ALL SO WORRIED!

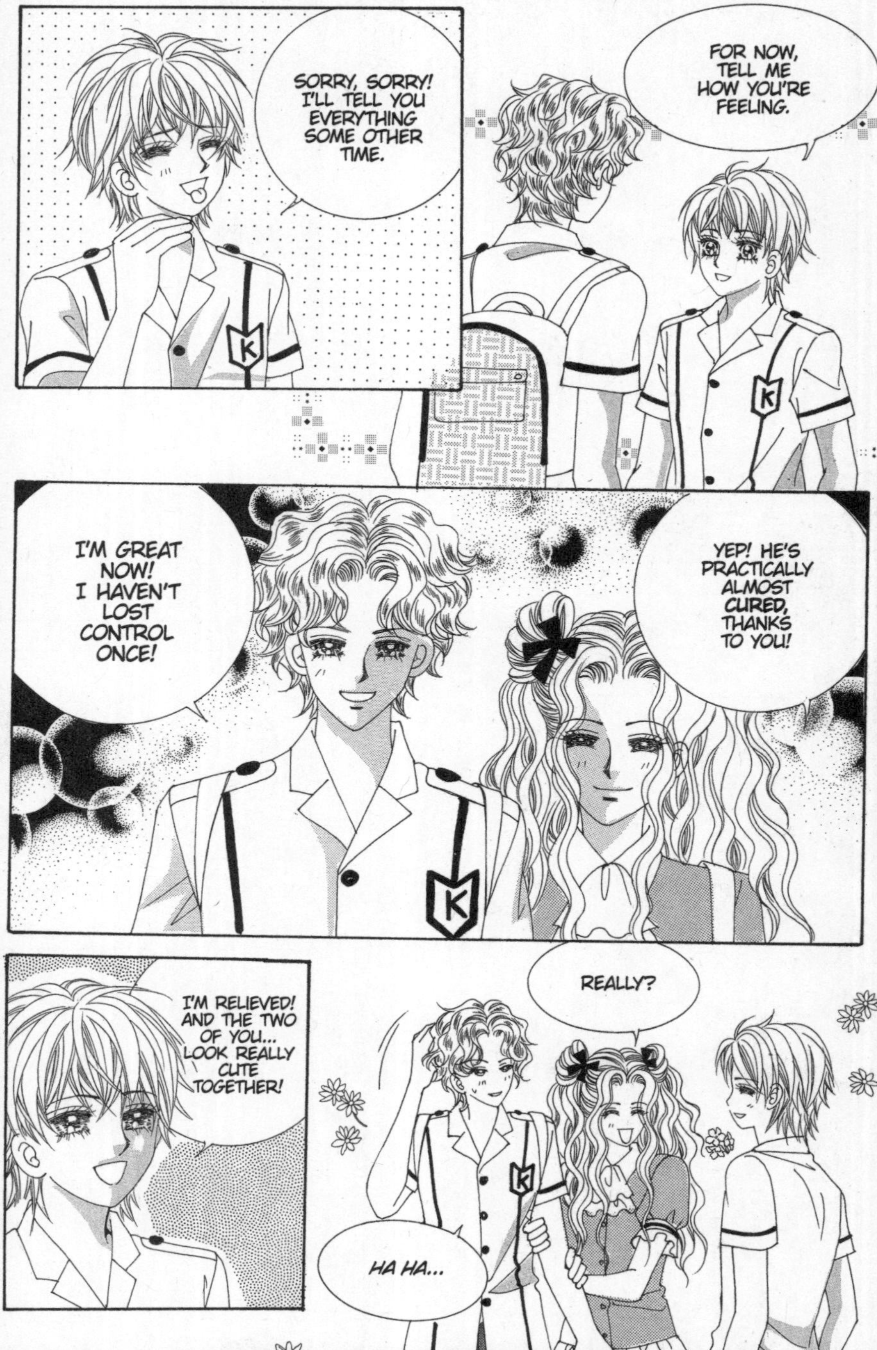
SORRY, SORRY! I'LL TELL YOU EVERYTHING SOME OTHER TIME.
FOR NOW, TELL ME HOW YOU'RE FEELING.
I'M GREAT NOW! I HAVEN'T LOST CONTROL ONCE!
YEP! HE'S PRACTICALLY ALMOST CURED, THANKS TO YOU!
I'M RELIEVED! AND THE TWO OF YOU... LOOK REALLY CUTE TOGETHER!
REALLY?
HA HA...

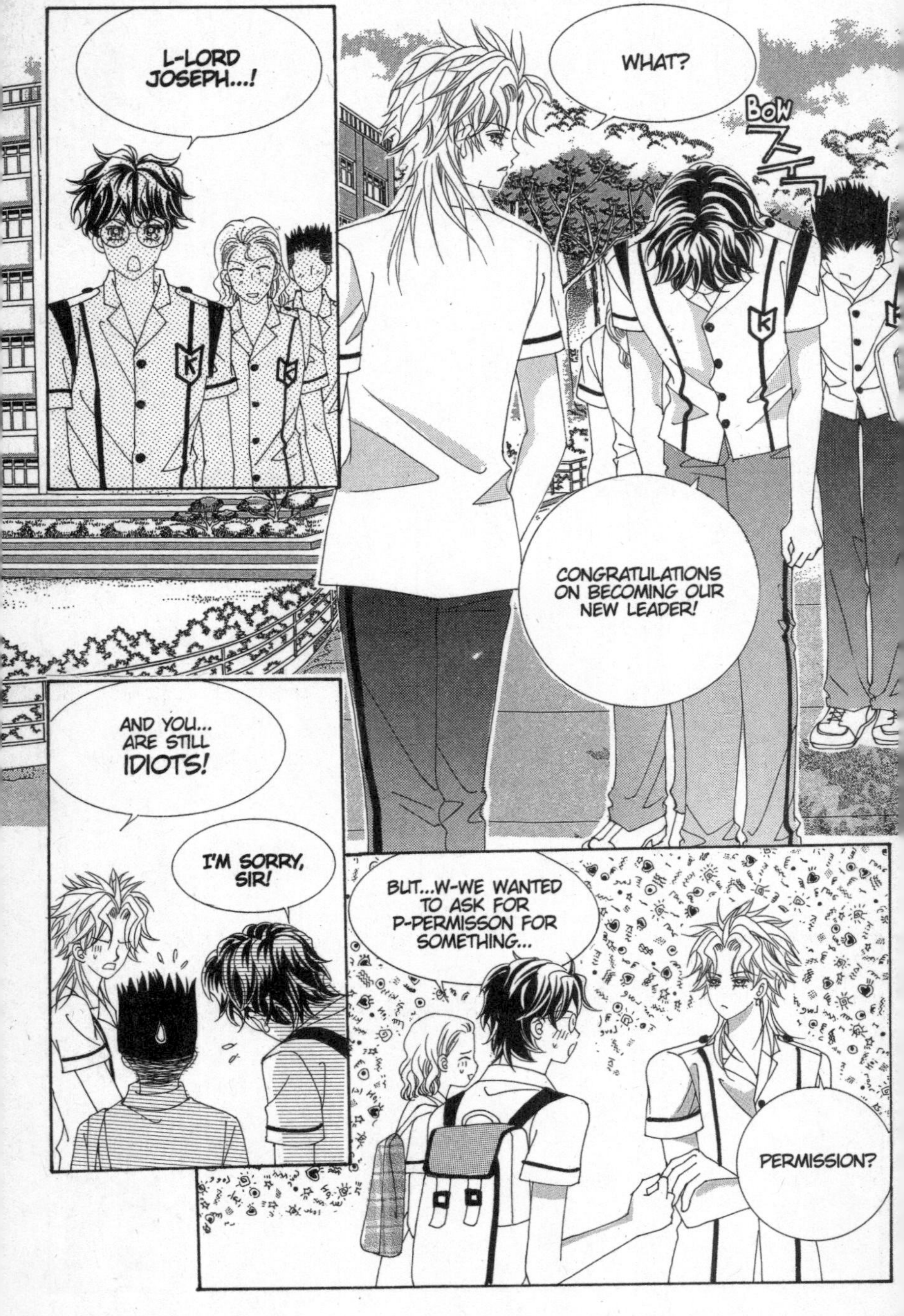
L-LORD JOSEPH...!
WHAT?
BoW
CONGRATULATIONS ON BECOMING OUR NEW LEADER!
AND YOU... ARE STILL IDIOTS!
I'M SORRY, SIR!
BUT...W-WE WANTED TO ASK FOR P-PERMISSON FOR SOMETHING...
PERMISSION?

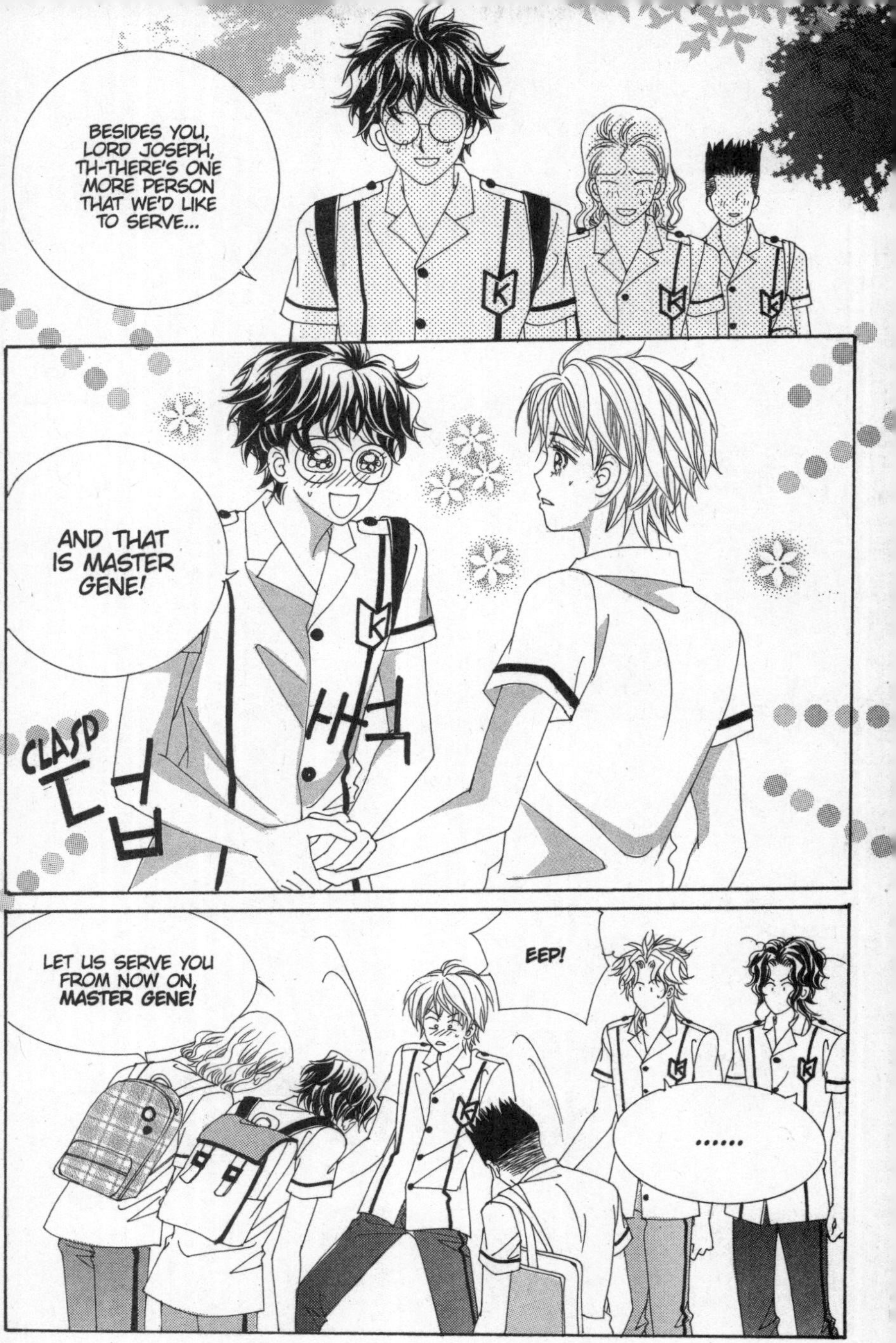
BESIDES YOU, LORD JOSEPH, TH-THERE'S ONE MORE PERSON THAT WE'D LIKE TO SERVE...
AND THAT IS MASTER GENE!
CLASP
LET US SERVE YOU FROM NOW ON, MASTER GENE!
EEP!
......

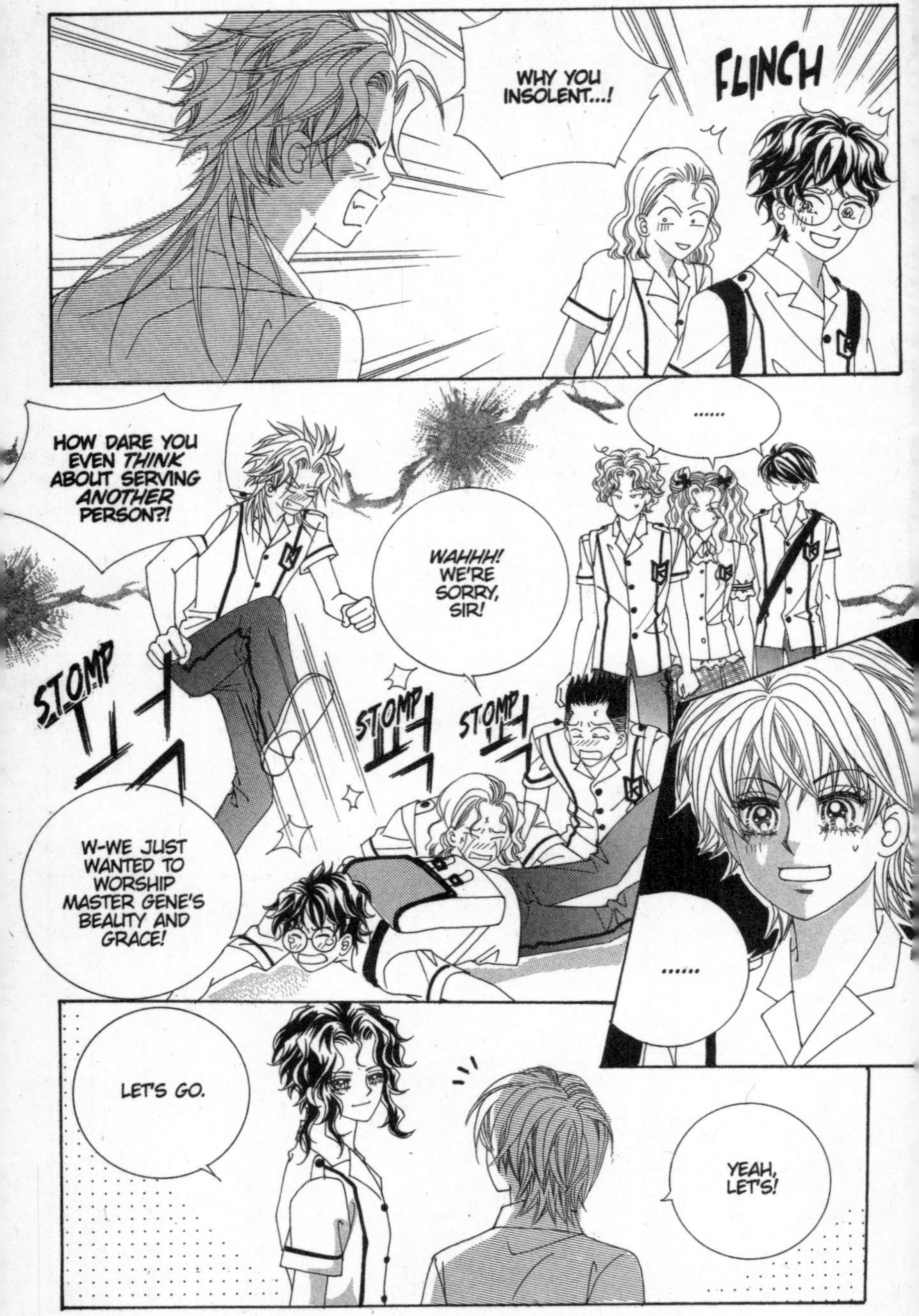
WHY YOU INSOLENT...!
FLINCH
HOW DARE YOU EVEN *THINK* ABOUT SERVING *ANOTHER* PERSON?!
......
WAHHH! WE'RE SORRY, SIR!
STOMP
STOMP
STOMP
W-WE JUST WANTED TO WORSHIP MASTER GENE'S BEAUTY AND GRACE!
......
LET'S GO.
YEAH, LET'S!

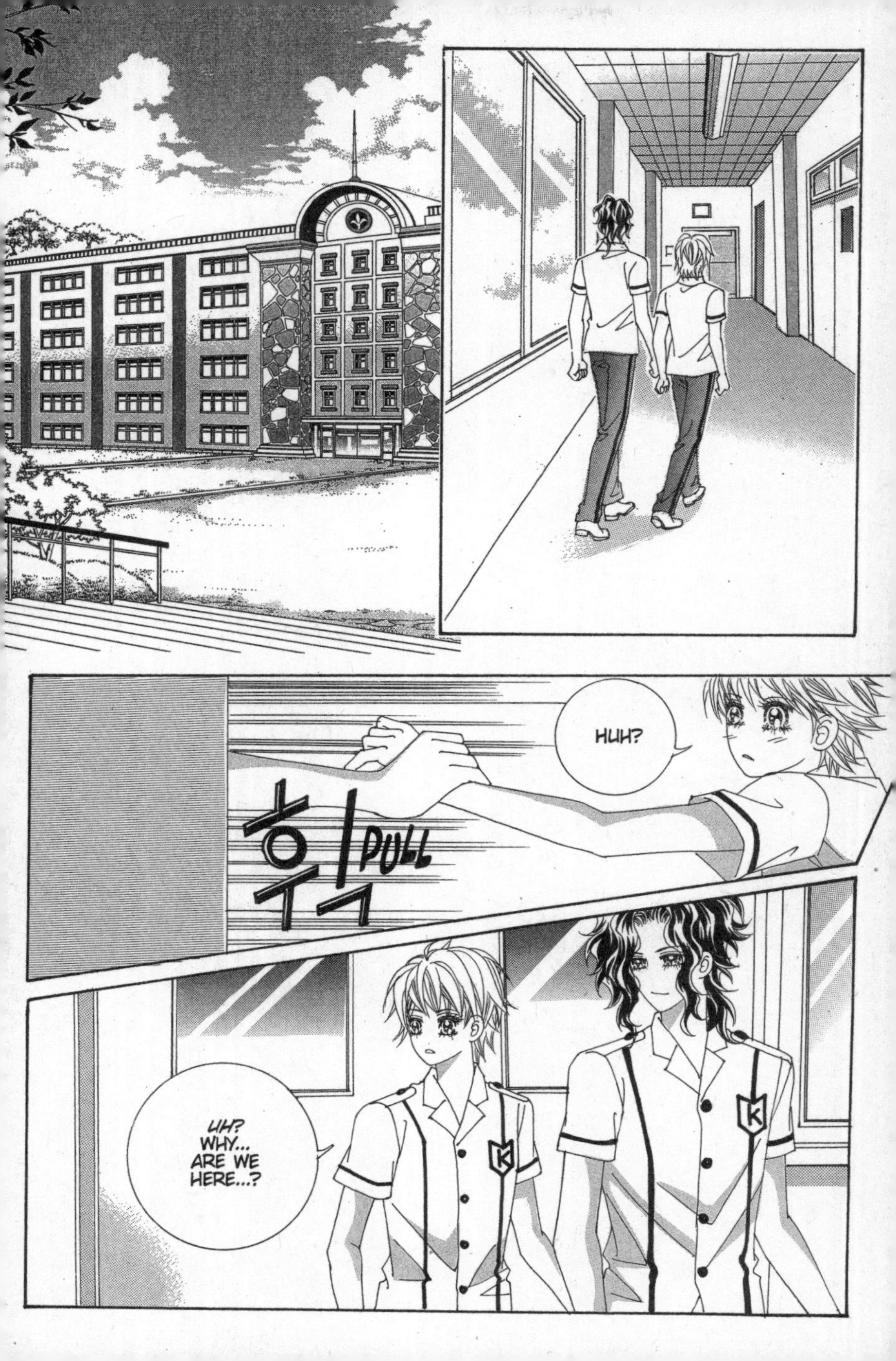
HUH?
흑
PULL
UH? WHY... ARE WE HERE...?

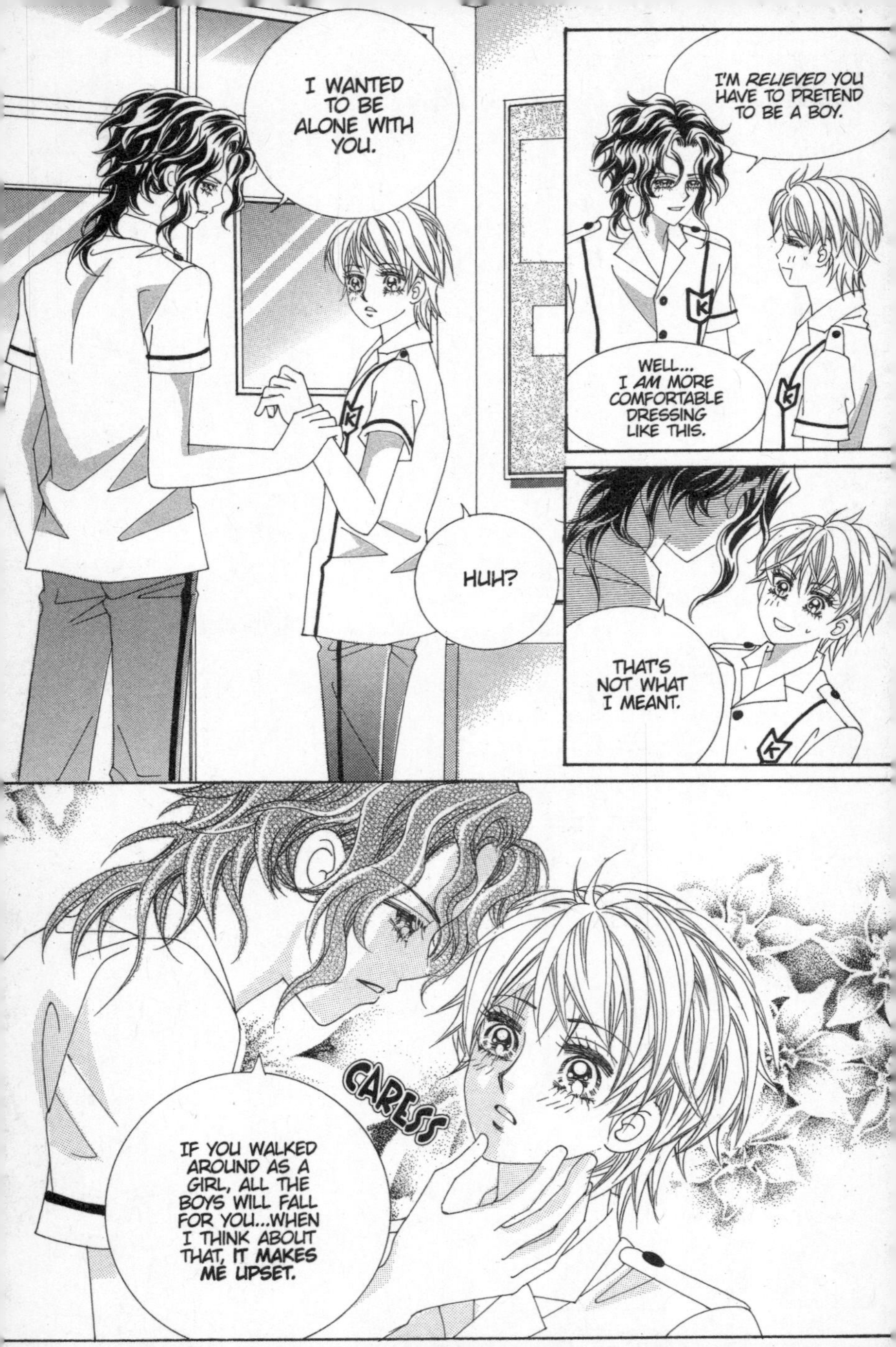
I WANTED TO BE ALONE WITH YOU.
HUH?
I'M *RELIEVED* YOU HAVE TO PRETEND TO BE A BOY.
WELL... I AM MORE COMFORTABLE DRESSING LIKE THIS.
THAT'S NOT WHAT I MEANT.
CARESS
IF YOU WALKED AROUND AS A GIRL, ALL THE BOYS WILL FALL FOR YOU...WHEN I THINK ABOUT THAT, IT MAKES ME UPSET.

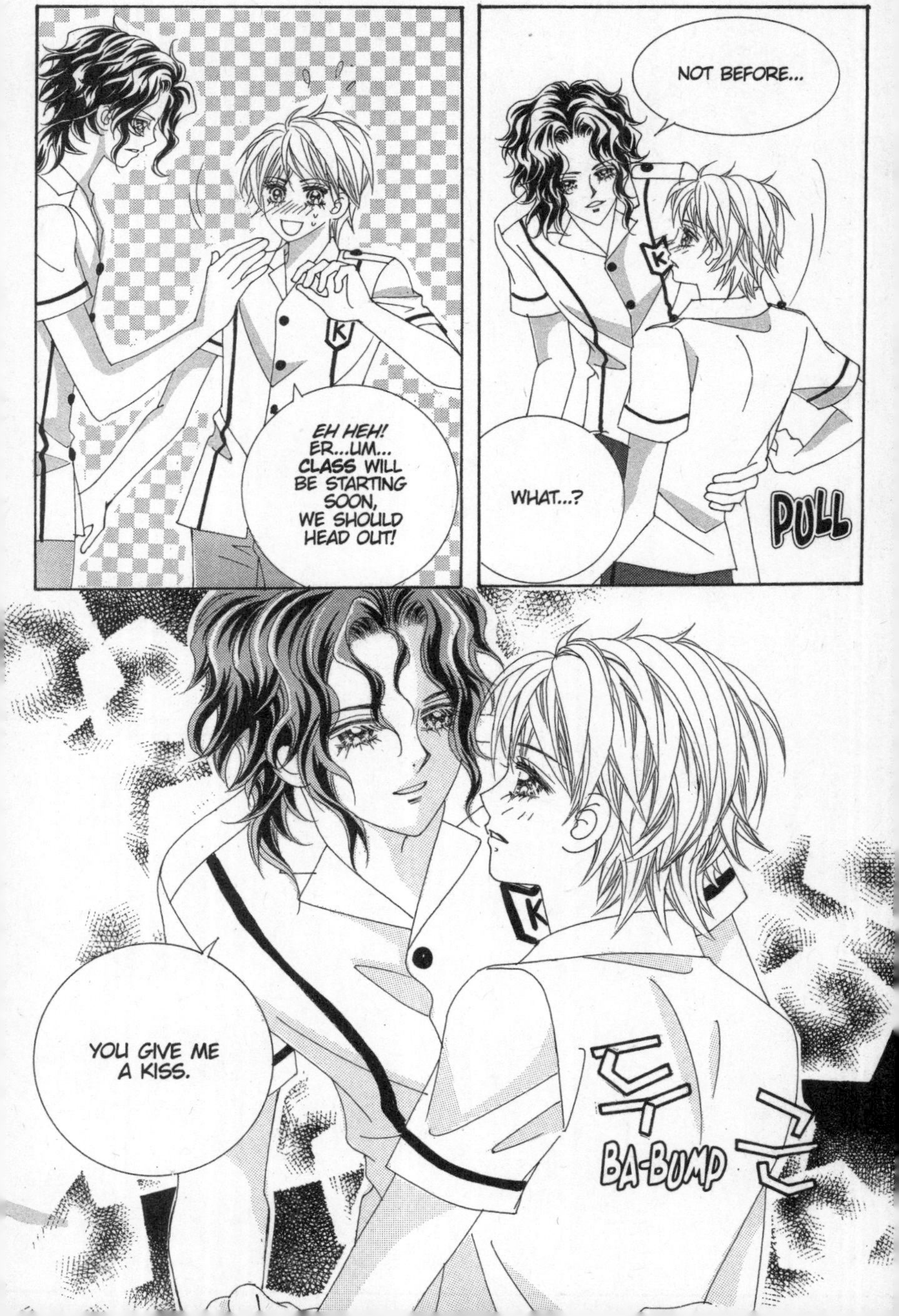
EH HEH! ER...UM... CLASS WILL BE STARTING SOON, WE SHOULD HEAD OUT!
NOT BEFORE...
WHAT...?
PULL
YOU GIVE ME A KISS.
BA-BUMP

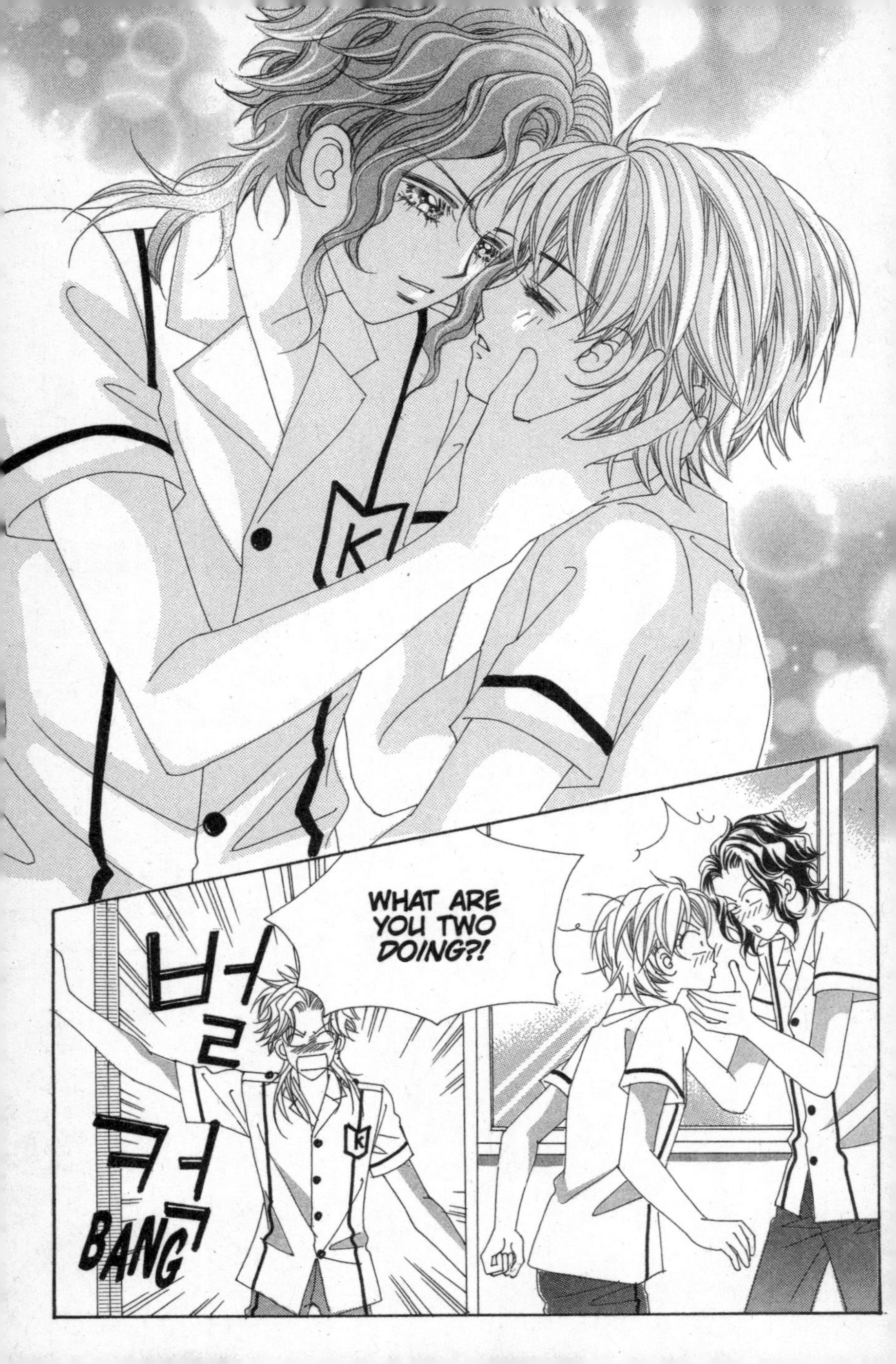
벌컥
BANG
WHAT ARE YOU TWO DOING?!

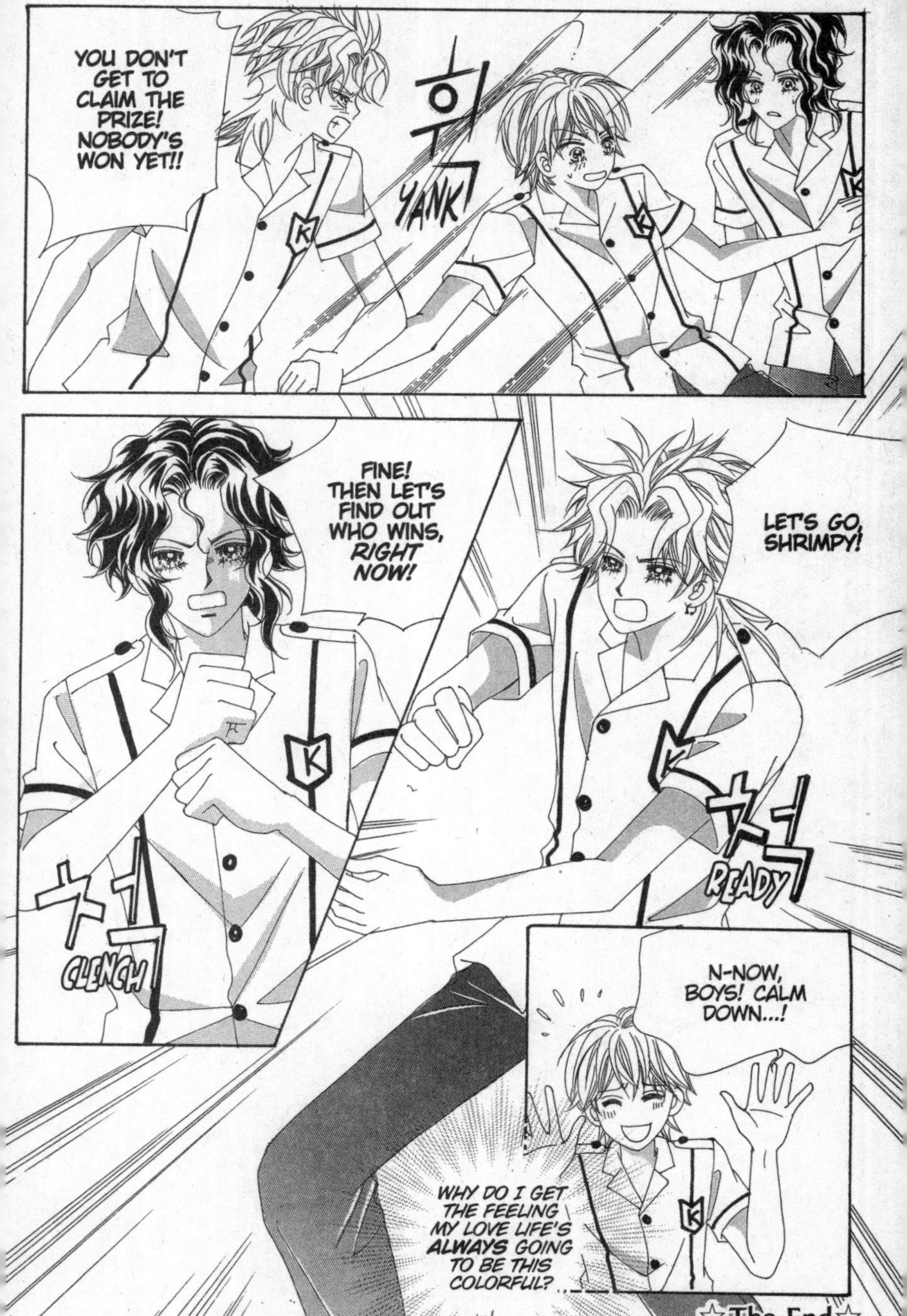
YOU DON'T GET TO CLAIM THE PRIZE! NOBODY'S WON YET!!
YANK
FINE! THEN LET'S FIND OUT WHO WINS, RIGHT NOW!
CLENCH
LET'S GO, SHRIMPY!
READY
N-NOW, BOYS! CALM DOWN...!
WHY DO I GET THE FEELING MY LOVE LIFE'S ALWAYS GOING TO BE THIS COLORFUL?

☆The End☆

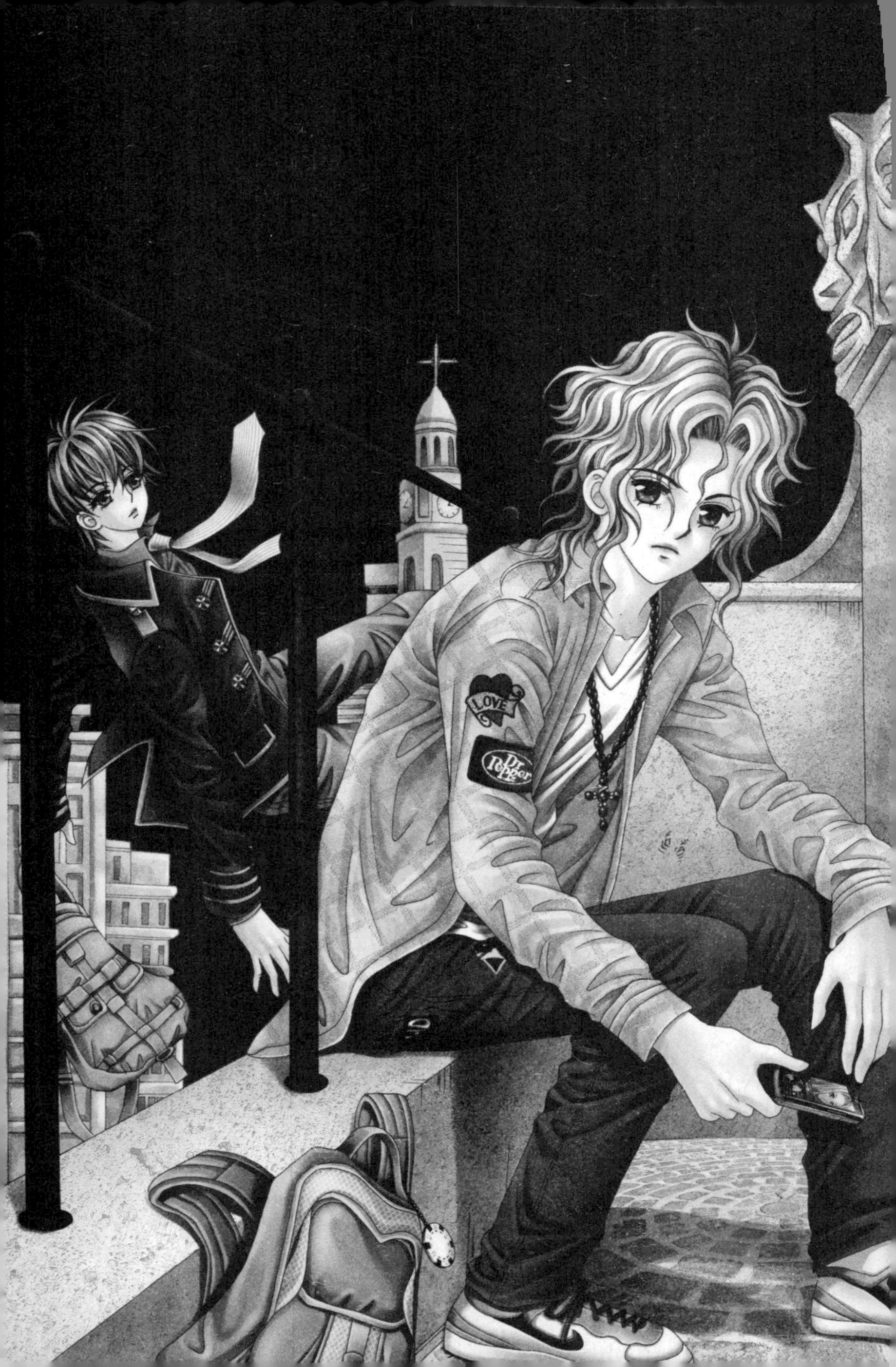
LOVE
Dr Pepper

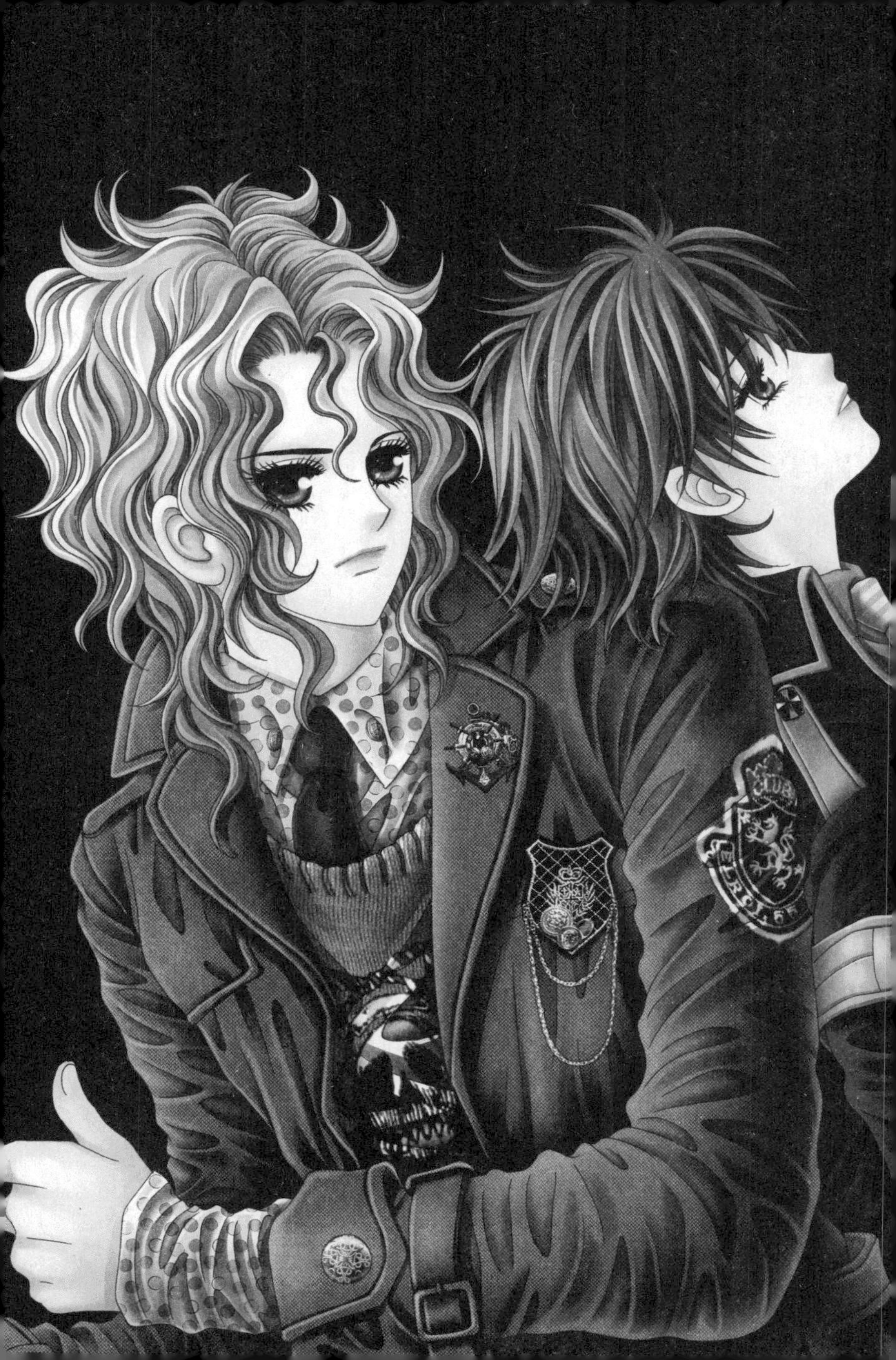
CLUB

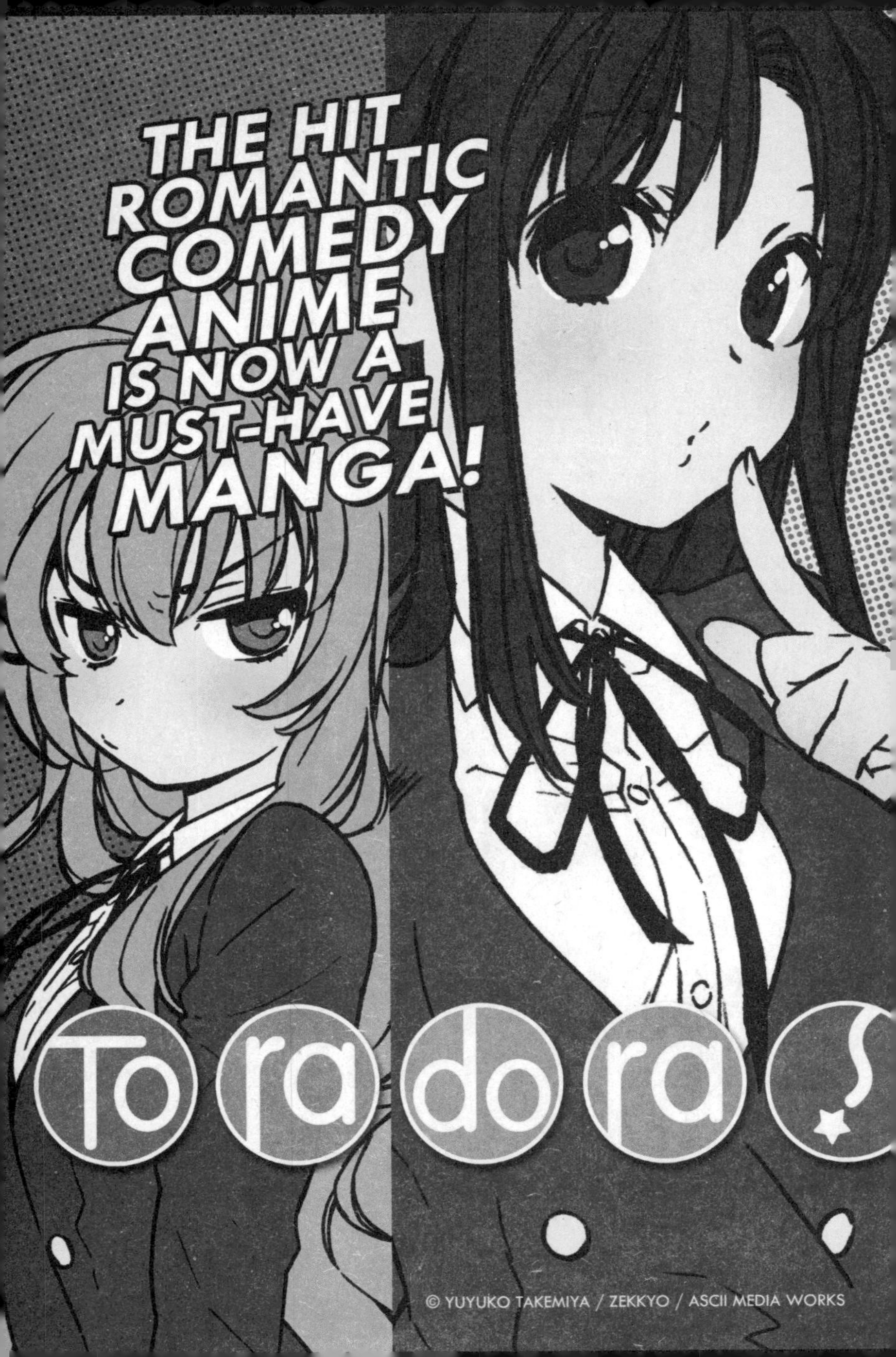
THE HIT ROMANTIC COMEDY ANIME IS NOW A MUST-HAVE MANGA!
Toradora!
© YUYUKO TAKEMIYA / ZEKKYO / ASCII MEDIA WORKS

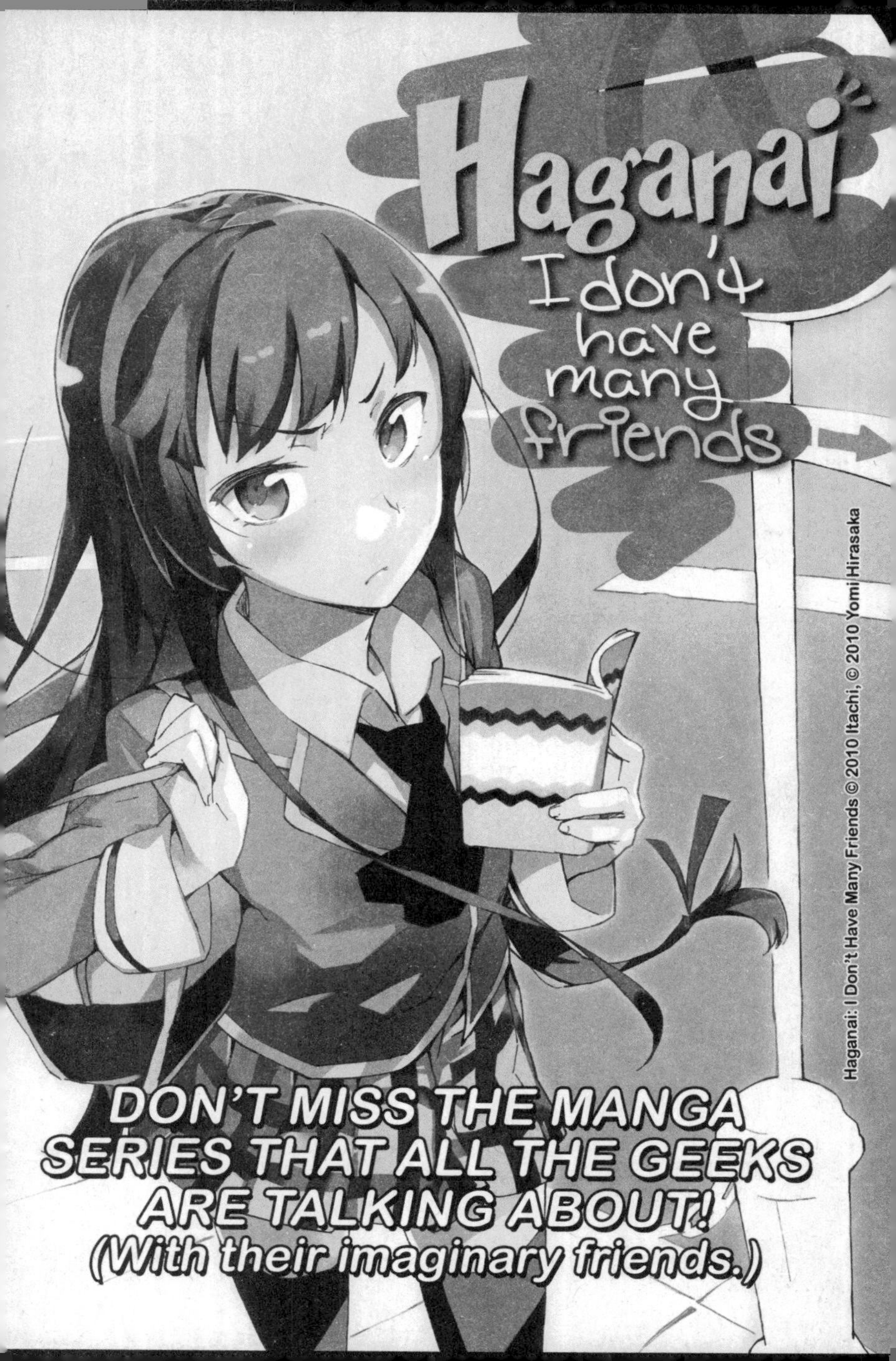
Haganai
I don't have many friends
DON'T MISS THE MANGA SERIES THAT ALL THE GEEKS ARE TALKING ABOUT!
(With their imaginary friends.)
Haganai: I Don't Have Many Friends © 2010 Itachi, © 2010 Yomi Hirasaka

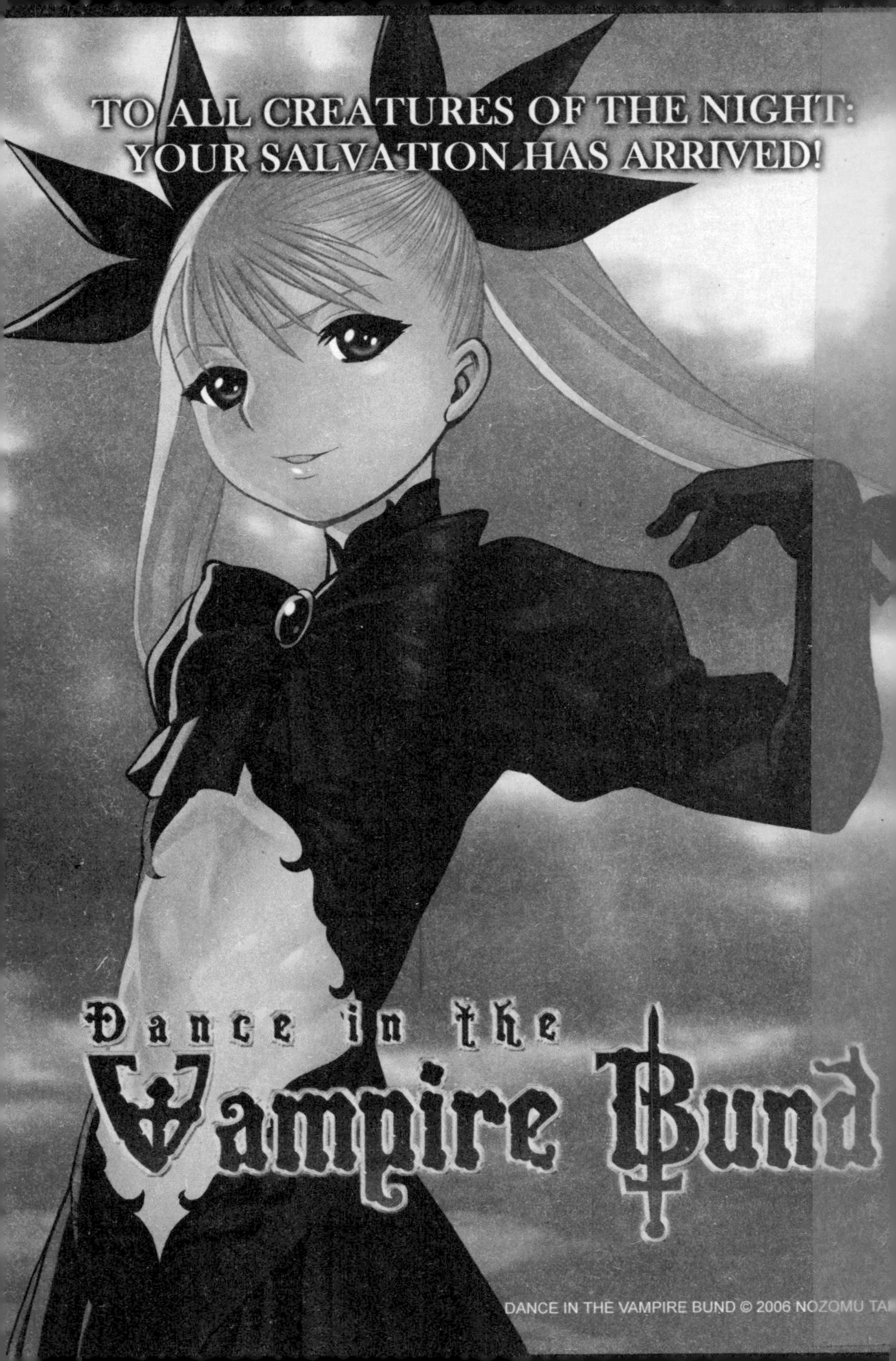
TO ALL CREATURES OF THE NIGHT:
YOUR SALVATION HAS ARRIVED!
Dance in the
Vampire Bund
DANCE IN THE VAMPIRE BUND © 2006 NOZOMU TA

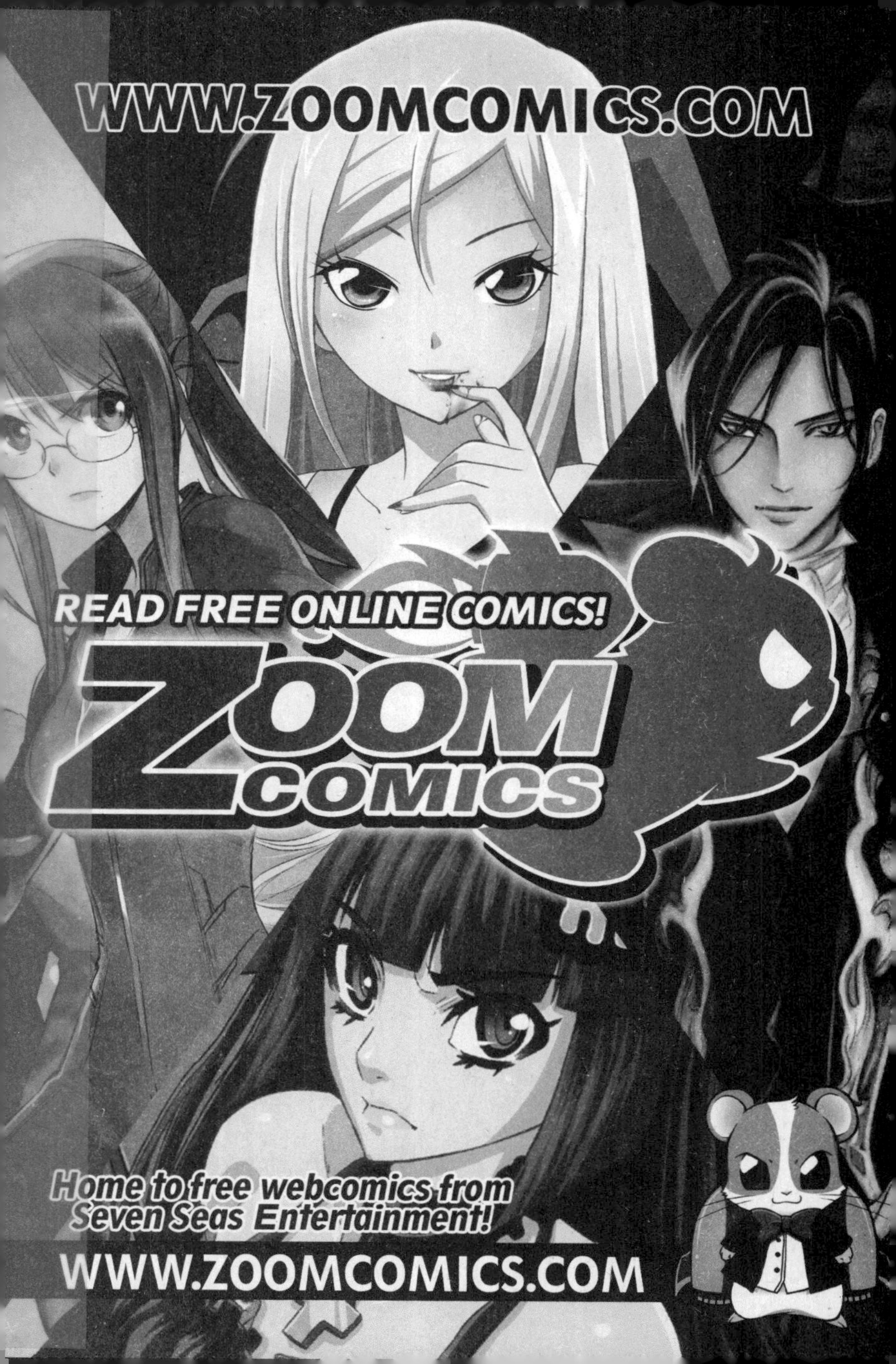
WWW.ZOOMCOMICS.COM
READ FREE ONLINE COMICS!
ZOOM COMICS
Home to free webcomics from
Seven Seas Entertainment!
WWW.ZOOMCOMICS.COM